Frommer's®
London

Our London

by Darwin Porter & Danforth Prince

LONDON IS AS OLD AS THE ELGIN MARBLES IN THE BRITISH MUSEUM, but also as cutting edge and provocative as Prince Harry's controversial 2005 Nazi party costume. Just as the handsome young prince likes to show a feisty (if misguided) independence, so does London itself. Although a member of the European Union, London still refuses to adopt the euro as its currency, clinging tenaciously to its time-honored pound sterling.

It loves tradition—the monarchy and all that jazz—but prefers to pioneer the avant-garde in Europe. It respects the old neighborhoods like Mayfair and St. James's, but every year some new section of town explodes into cultural prominence. Think Soho and Chelsea in the swinging 1960s. Think the East End of the 1990s that gave the world the ghoulish art of Damien Hirst and the "Britpack artists." In the post-millennium, head for the thumping nightlife of a recharged Brixton (yes, that was expat Madonna you saw dancing the night away at a gay club). Indeed, London has more rock groups than New York, more dance clubs than Paris, and more nude shows than Tokyo.

Only for a brief interlude—from around 1830 to 1965—did London don the tight corset of England's famous fictional prude, Mrs. Grundy. The burst of *joie de vivre* that began in the late 1960s continues today. London is its old self again—and in these pages, you'll see a few of the experiences that keep us coming back, again and again.

Britain's most famous square, **TRAFALGAR SQUARE (left)**, honors one of England's great military heroes, Horatio Viscount Nelson (1758–1805), who was killed in the Battle of Trafalgar. The lover of Lady Hamilton had a granite monument—the 44m (144 ft.) Nelson's Column, designed by E.H. Baily—erected in his honor in 1843. The figure of Nelson at the top stands 5m (16 ft.) tall—not bad for a man who was 5'4" in real life.

Covered in ellipsoid glass "pods" seemingly left behind by a flying saucer, British Airway's **LONDON EYE (above)** is the biggest observational wheel in the world. At 135m (430 ft.), it rises higher than St. Paul's Cathedral, and if it's not a foggy day in Londontown, you can see forever (well, at least for 25 miles). One of London's newest and most popular attractions—also known as "the Millennium Wheel"—it even allows you to peak into the gardens of Buckingham Palace, much to the annoyance of Her Majesty.

A celebration of splendor, the interior of **ST. PAUL'S CATHEDRAL (left)** affords a close encounter with architect Sir Christopher Wren's masterpiece. Between 1690 and 1720, Wren called upon an armada of talented designers, artisans, and artists to create "a world under the towering dome," second in size only to St. Peter's in Rome. Sir James Thronhill painted the cupola with *trompe l'oeil* frescoes depicting the life of St. Paul, and the artist nearly fell to his death while doing so.

HAMPTON COURT (above), the finest of all Tudor palaces and the greatest of England's royal abodes, is obvious testimony to why England is called "the country of gardeners." Through these gardens the lusty, pot-bellied Henry VIII chased after his teenage bride, Catherine Howard, in the 16th century. In 1838, after the first year of her reign, Queen Victoria nixed the idea of living at Hampton Court and opened both the palace and its gardens to the public.

Other than getting an invitation for a "cuppa" with the Queen at Buckingham Palace, there is no better address than the Palm Court at the **RITZ HOTEL (left)** for afternoon tea. With its marble steps, columns, and a baroque fountain, the court calls out for women to wear picture hats. Back in 1840, the Duchess of Bedford, who never could wait for dinner, launched the practice of serving afternoon tea—leading to the birth of the cucumber sandwich and a hallowed British tradition.

The lobby of **CLARIDGE'S HOTEL IN MAYFAIR (below)** with its checkerboard floor of black and white marble evokes a classical, timeless opulence. Across the floor of this lobby walked the Who's Who of the 20th century: movie stars, diplomats, kings, oil-rich sheiks, and off-the-record weekenders like Woolworth heiress Barbara Hutton and aviator Howard Hughes. The Queen often houses her overflow guests at Claridge's, complete with their own personal butlers.

© Andrea Pistolesi/Getty Images

Rotten tomatoes are no longer tossed at actors who displease theatergoers at Shakespeare's rebuilt **GLOBE THEATRE** (above) on the South Bank of the Thames. The original Globe burned down in 1613—after a 14-year run as the Bard's most preferred showcase for his comedies and dramas—but it's been reincarnated as in Shakespeare's time. Patrons select a hard, backless wooden bench in one of the three covered tiers of seating, or else stand through a performance as a "groundling."

New Yorkers may dispute this, but London's **WEST END** (right) is home to the best and most varied theatrical presentations in the English-speaking world. The Gielgud Theatre honors one of England's towering Shakespearean thespians, the late John Gielgud. Gielgud once lamented that he'd be forever remembered for "that dumb manservant part," a reference to his role as Dudley Moore's butler in the 1981 comedy, *Arthur,* which won him an Oscar.

© Peter Adams/AGE Fotostock

THREE ENDURING SYMBOLS OF LONDON are the **black taxi** in the left foreground, the clock tower **Big Ben** in the center, and a red **double-decker** bus to the right. The clock tower rises over the mock Gothic Palace of Westminster, containing both of the Houses of Parliament (Lords and Commons). Since 1858, the chimes of this clock have sounded faithfully, even during Hitler's Blitzkrieg in the early 1940s. BBC radio's daily broadcast of these deep chimes allows them to be heard throughout the city.

Central London Theaters

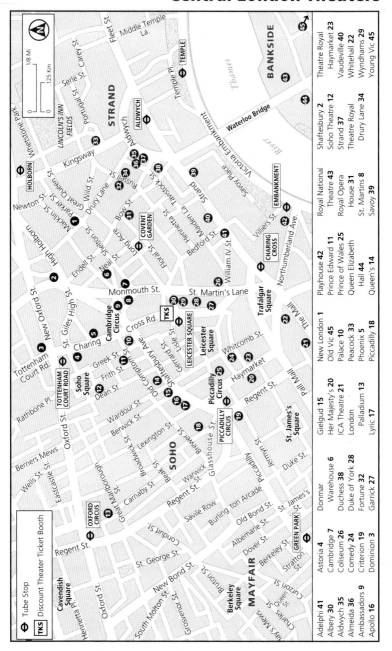

Adelphi **41**	Donmar	Gielgud **15**	New London **1**
Albery **30**	Warehouse **6**	Her Majesty's **20**	Old Vic **45**
Aldwych **35**	Duchess **38**	ICA Theatre **21**	Palace **10**
Almeida **36**	Duke of York **28**	London	Peacock **33**
Ambassadors **9**	Fortune **32**	Palladium **13**	Phoenix **5**
Apollo **16**	Garrick **27**	Lyric **17**	Piccadilly **18**

Astoria **4**	Playhouse **42**	Royal National	Shaftesbury **2**	Theatre Royal
Cambridge **7**	Prince Edward **11**	Theatre **43**	Soho Theatre **12**	Haymarket **23**
Coliseum **26**	Prince of Wales **25**	Royal Opera	Strand **37**	Vaudeville **40**
Comedy **24**	Queen Elizabeth	House **31**	Theatre Royal	Whitehall **22**
Criterion **19**	Hall **44**	St. Martin's **8**	Drury Lane **34**	Wyndhams **29**
Dominion **3**	Queen's **14**	Savoy **39**		Young Vic **45**

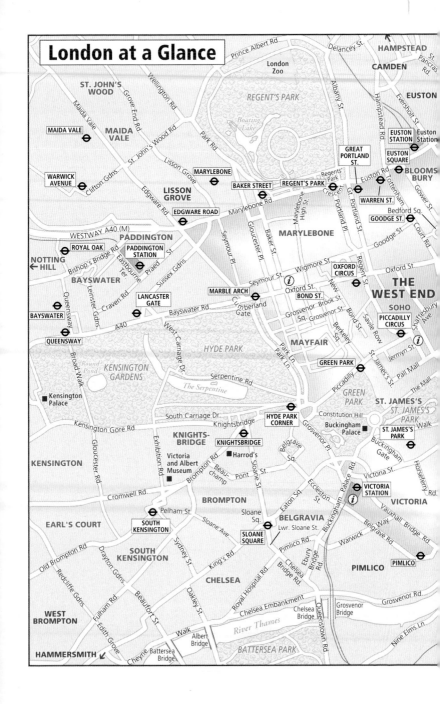

London at a Glance

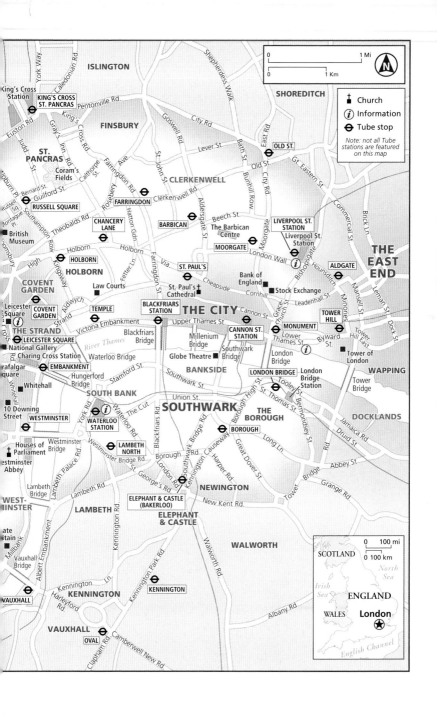

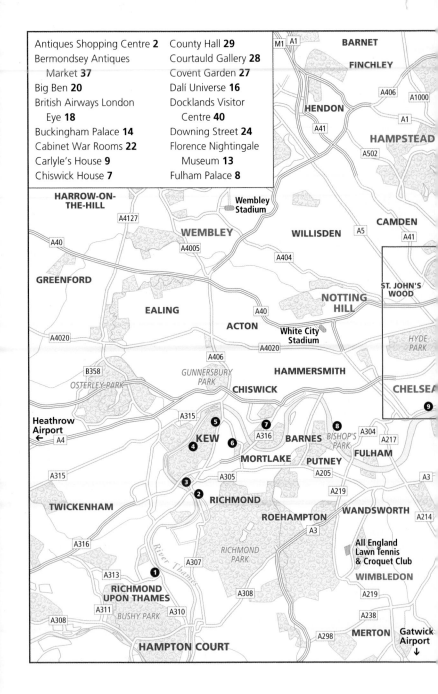

M1 A1 **BARNET**
FINCHLEY
A406 A1000
HENDON A1
A41
HAMPSTEAD
A502

HARROW-ON-THE-HILL
A4127
Wembley Stadium
WEMBLEY **WILLISDEN** A5 **CAMDEN** A41
A40 A4005
A404
GREENFORD ST. JOHN'S WOOD
EALING A40 **NOTTING HILL**
A4020 **ACTON** White City Stadium HYDE PARK
A4020
A406
GUNNERSBURY PARK **HAMMERSMITH** **CHELSEA**
OSTERLEY PARK **CHISWICK**
Heathrow Airport A315 ❺ ❼ ❽ A304
← A4 **KEW** ❹ ❻ A316 **BARNES** BISHOP'S PARK A217
A315 **MORTLAKE** **PUTNEY** **FULHAM**
❸ A305 A205 A3
❷ **RICHMOND** A219
TWICKENHAM **ROEHAMPTON** **WANDSWORTH** A214
A316 A3
River Thames RICHMOND PARK All England Lawn Tennis & Croquet Club
A313 ❶ A307 **WIMBLEDON**
RICHMOND UPON THAMES A308 A219
A311 A310 A238
A308 A298 **MERTON** Gatwick Airport ↓
BUSHY PARK
HAMPTON COURT
❾

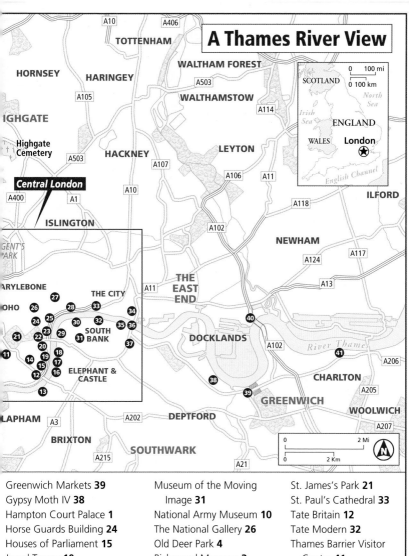

A Thames River View

Greenwich Markets **39**
Gypsy Moth IV **38**
Hampton Court Palace **1**
Horse Guards Building **24**
Houses of Parliament **15**
Jewel Tower **19**
Jubilee Gardens **30**
Kew Gardens & Palace **5**
London Transport
   Museum **27**

Museum of the Moving
   Image **31**
National Army Museum **10**
The National Gallery **26**
Old Deer Park **4**
Richmond Museum **3**
Richmond Park **6**
Saatchi Gallery **17**
Shakespeare's Globe
   Theatre **35**

St. James's Park **21**
St. Paul's Cathedral **33**
Tate Britain **12**
Tate Modern **32**
Thames Barrier Visitor
   Centre **41**
Tower Bridge **36**
Tower of London **34**
Trafalgar Square **25**
Westminster Abbey **11**
Whitehall **23**

Hyde Park and Kensington Gardens

Albert Memorial **7**

Apsley House Wellington Museum **9**

Italian Gardens **4**

Kensington Palace **2**

Marble Arch **12**

Peter Pan Statue **5**

Princess Diana Memorial Playground **1**

Round Pond **3**

The Serpentine **8**

Serpentine Gallery **6**

Speakers Corner **11**

Wellington Arch **10**

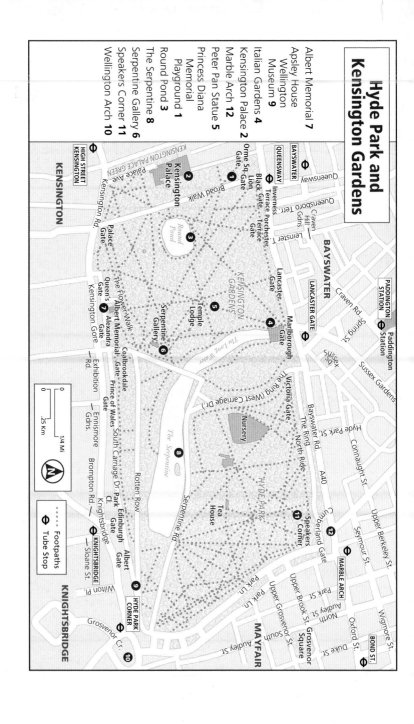

Frommer's®

London

2008

by Darwin Porter & Danforth Prince

Here's what the critics say about Frommer's:

"Amazingly easy to use. Very portable, very complete."
—*Booklist*

"Detailed, accurate, and easy-to-read information for all price ranges."
—*Glamour Magazine*

"Hotel information is close to encyclopedic."
—*Des Moines Sunday Register*

"Frommer's Guides have a way of giving you a real feel for a place."
—*Knight Ridder Newspapers*

Wiley Publishing, Inc.

Published by:

Wiley Publishing, Inc.

111 River St.
Hoboken, NJ 07030-5774

ISBN: 978-0-470-13821-2

Editor: Linda Barth
Production Editor: Katie Robinson
Cartographer: Andrew Murphy
Photo Editor: Richard Fox
Anniversary Logo Design: Richard Pacifico
Production by Wiley Indianapolis Composition Services

Front cover photo: London Horse Guards Trooping the colors
Back cover photo: Salisbury Pub exterior, near Covent Garden, with Globe Theatre beyond

For information on our other products and services or to obtain technical support, please contact our Customer Care Department within the U.S. at 800/762-2974, outside the U.S. at 317/572-3993 or fax 317/572-4002.

Wiley also publishes its books in a variety of electronic formats. Some content that appears in print may not be available in electronic formats.

Manufactured in the United States of America

5   4   3   2   1

Contents

List of Maps

About the Authors

A team of veteran travel writers, **Darwin Porter** and **Danforth Prince** have produced numerous titles for Frommer's, including best-selling guides to Italy, France, the Caribbean, England, and Germany. Porter is also a noted Hollywood biographer, and his recent releases include *Howard Hughes: Hell's Angel* and *Brando Unzipped*. He is a newspaper columnist on popular culture as well as a radio commentator, with broadcasts heard in all 50 states. Prince, formerly of the *New York Times* Paris bureau, is the president of Blood Moon Productions and other media-related firms.

An Invitation to the Reader

In researching this book, we discovered many wonderful places—hotels, restaurants, shops, and more. We're sure you'll find others. Please tell us about them, so we can share the information with your fellow travelers in upcoming editions. If you were disappointed with a recommendation, we'd love to know that, too. Please write to:

Frommer's London 2008
Wiley Publishing, Inc. • 111 River St. • Hoboken, NJ 07030-5774

An Additional Note

Please be advised that travel information is subject to change at any time—and this is especially true of prices. We therefore suggest that you write or call ahead for confirmation when making your travel plans. The authors, editors, and publisher cannot be held responsible for the experiences of readers while traveling. Your safety is important to us, however, so we encourage you to stay alert and be aware of your surroundings. Keep a close eye on cameras, purses, and wallets, all favorite targets of thieves and pickpockets.

Other Great Guides for Your Trip:

The Unofficial Guide to London
London Day by Day
London For Dummies
Frommer's Best Day Trips from London
Frommer's Memorable Walks in London
Pauline Frommer's London
Frommer's England

Frommer's Star Ratings, Icons & Abbreviations

Every hotel, restaurant, and attraction listing in this guide has been ranked for quality, value, service, amenities, and special features using a **star-rating system.** In country, state, and regional guides, we also rate towns and regions to help you narrow down your choices and budget your time accordingly. Hotels and restaurants are rated on a scale of zero (recommended) to three stars (exceptional). Attractions, shopping, nightlife, towns, and regions are rated according to the following scale: zero stars (recommended), one star (highly recommended), two stars (very highly recommended), and three stars (must-see).

In addition to the star-rating system, we also use **seven feature icons** that point you to the great deals, in-the-know advice, and unique experiences that separate travelers from tourists. Throughout the book, look for:

Finds	Special finds—those places only insiders know about
Fun Fact	Fun facts—details that make travelers more informed and their trips more fun
Kids	Best bets for kids and advice for the whole family
Moments	Special moments—those experiences that memories are made of
Overrated	Places or experiences not worth your time or money
Tips	Insider tips—great ways to save time and money
Value	Great values—where to get the best deals

The following **abbreviations** are used for credit cards:

AE	American Express	DISC	Discover	V	Visa
DC	Diners Club	MC	MasterCard		

Frommers.com

Now that you have this guidebook to help you plan a great trip, visit our website at **www. frommers.com** for additional travel information on more than 3,600 destinations. We update features regularly to give you instant access to the most current trip-planning information available. At Frommers.com, you'll find scoops on the best airfares, lodging rates, and car rental bargains. You can even book your travel online through our reliable travel booking partners. Other popular features include:

- Online updates of our most popular guidebooks
- Vacation sweepstakes and contest giveaways
- Newsletters highlighting the hottest travel trends
- Online travel message boards with featured travel discussions

What's New in London

London is the most volatile and ever-changing city in Europe—"the scene" is constantly shifting. Here are some of the latest developments.

GETTING TO KNOW LONDON

One of the best travel bargains in years, the "Oyster Card," a travel discount card, cuts pricey transportation costs in London almost in half. "Oysters" are valid on the Tube, the DLR, trams, National Rail Services, and across the entire London bus network. In a restricted zone, you never pay more than £3 ($5.70) for an entire day's travel.

WHERE TO STAY

In the financial district of London, **The Hoxton,** 81 Great Eastern St., EC2 (© 020/7550-1000), aims to cut down hotel rip-offs and does so with many innovative policies such as lowering charges on phone calls from your room. If you're really lucky, you'll book in here on a special budget rate of £1 ($1.90) a night, but that's hard to come by. The minibar, one of the greatest rip-offs in most hotels, comes here with free mineral water and milk instead of pricey liquor. See p. 93.

On a more upmarket note, **The Rockwell,** 181–183 Cromwell Rd., SW5 (© 020/7244-2000), has opened in Kensington, an independently owned bastion of deluxe comfort in a converted Georgian manse. Traditional English aesthetic meets modern design—even the power shower and bathroom fittings are by the trendy designer, Philippe Starck.

WHERE TO DINE

In the National Gallery, **The National Dining Rooms** has opened at Trafalgar Square, WC2 (© 020/7747-2525), serving traditional British cuisine at moderate prices. The dining rooms lie over the foyer of the Sainsbury Wing, opening onto a panoramic view of this landmark London square. Instead of fancy dishes from the Continent, art-loving diners get classic British cuisine with market-fresh ingredients that include the likes of mackerel pâté (reportedly a favorite dish of Queen Elizabeth herself).

In another museum-dining changeover, the **Rex Whistler** at the Tate Britain, Millbank SW1 (© 020/7887-8825), has emerged with a new name but it still offers an array of superior wines at bargain prices and continues to feature an English menu that changes every month.

Even Prince William shows up at **The Pig's Ear,** 35 Old Church St., SW1 (© 020/7352-2909), a new gastro-pub in Chelsea serving a classic British cuisine, and doing so exceedingly well. Even if you skip the chef's specialty, deep-fried pigs' ears, you might opt for the seared tuna with black olives and chicory or roast wood pigeon stuffed with mushrooms.

SIDE TRIPS FROM LONDON

Oxford In this university city, **Malmaison Oxford Castle,** 3 Oxford Castle (© 01865/2484320), is not only the quirkiest hotel in town but also one of the most intriguing. It's installed in a building where inmates were detained "at Her Majesty's Pleasure." The barred windows have been retained, but everything else in this converted Victorian prison has been brought up to date with all the modern comforts. No hotel in Oxford boasts such *luxe* bathrooms as Malmaison. The power showers, great beds, and other comforts could only be dreamed about by the former inmates.

For more on stuff to see and do in Oxford, see p. 324.

Stratford-Upon-Avon   The hometown of the Bard still lacks a truly gourmet restaurant, but the culinary scene has improved considerably. Either new chefs took over existing properties or new places opened up. **Sorrento,** 8 Ely St. (© 01789/297999), brings a taste of Italy to this family-run restaurant a 4-minute walk from the Shakespeare Theatre. A selection of well-chosen Italian wines complement the menu of Italian classics, including the fresh fish of the day. **The One Elm,** 1 Guild St. (© 01789/404919), serves modern British cuisine in its pub, ground-floor restaurant, or open-air courtyard. The charcoal grill specialties are a particular delight.

On a cultural note, the **Royal Shakespeare Theatre,** Waterside (© 07189/403444), spent much of 2007 undergoing a major restoration, with a gala reopening scheduled for 2008.

The Best of London

The British capital is alive and well and culturally more vibrant than it has been in years.

The sounds of Brit-pop and techno pour out of Victorian pubs, experimental theater is popping up on stages built for Shakespeare's plays, upstart chefs are reinventing the bland dishes British mums have made for generations, and Brits are even running the couture houses of Dior and Givenchy. In food, fashion, film, music, and just about everything else, London now stands at the cutting edge, just as it did in the 1960s.

If this sea of change worries you more than it appeals to you, rest assured that traditional London still exists, essentially intact under the veneer of hip. From high tea almost anywhere to the Changing of the Guard at Buckingham Palace, the city still abounds with the tradition and charm of days gone by.

Discovering London and making it your own can be a bit of a challenge, especially if you have limited time. Even in the 18th century, Daniel Defoe found London "stretched out in buildings, straggling, confused, out of all shape, uncompact and unequal; neither long nor broad, round nor square." The actual City of London proper is 2.6 sq. km (1 sq. mile) of very expensive real estate around the Bank of England. All of the gargantuan rest of the city is made up of separate villages, boroughs, and corporations—each with its own mayor and administration. Together, however, they add up to a mammoth metropolis.

Luckily, whether you're looking for Dickens's house or hot designer Vivienne Westwood's flagship store, only the heart of London's huge territory need concern you. The core of London is one of the most fascinating places on earth. With every step, you'll feel the tremendous influence this city exerted over global culture back when it was the capital of an empire on which the sun never set.

London is a mass of contradictions. On the one hand, it's a decidedly royal city, studded with palaces, court gardens, coats of arms, and other regal paraphernalia, yet it's also the home of the world's second-oldest parliamentary democracy (Iceland was the first).

Today London has grown less English and more international. The gent with the bowler hat is long gone; today's Londoner might have a turban, a Mohawk, or even a baseball cap. It's becoming easier to find a café au lait and a croissant than a scone and a cup of tea. The city is home to thousands of immigrants and refugees, both rich and poor, from all reaches of the world.

1 The Most Unforgettable Travel Experiences

- **Watching the Sunset at Waterloo Bridge:** This is the ideal place for watching the sun set over Westminster. You can see the last rays of light bounce off the dome of St. Paul's and the spires in the East End.

- **Enjoying a Traditional Afternoon Tea:** At The Ritz hotel, 150 Piccadilly, W1 (© **020/7493-8181;** p. 105), the tea ritual carries on as it did in Britain's heyday. You could invite the Queen of England herself here for a "cuppa." The pomp and circumstance of the British Empire live on at The Ritz—only the Empire is missing. See p. 201.

- **Cruising London's Waterways:** In addition to the Thames, London has an antique canal system, with towpath walks, bridges, and wharves. Replaced by the railroad as the prime means of transportation, the canal system was all but forgotten until it was rediscovered by a new generation. Now undergoing a process of urban renewal, the old system has been restored, with bridges painted and repaired, and paths cleaned up, for you to enjoy. See "River Cruises along the Thames," on p. 256.

- **Spending Sunday Morning at Speakers Corner:** At the northeast corner of Hyde Park, a British tradition carries on. Speakers sound off on every imaginable subject, and "in-your-face" hecklers are part of the fun. You might hear anything from denunciations of the monarchy to antigay rhetoric. Anyone can get up and speak. The only rules: You can't blaspheme, be obscene, or incite a riot. The tradition began in 1855—before the legal right to assembly was guaranteed in 1872—when a mob of 150,000 gathered to attack a proposed Sunday Trading Bill. See p. 254.

- **Studying the Turners at the Tate Britain:** When he died in 1851, J. M. W. Turner bequeathed his collection of 19,000 watercolors and some 300 paintings to the people of Britain. He wanted his finished works, about 100 paintings, displayed under one roof. Today you see not only the paintings

but also glimpses of Turner's beloved Thames through the museum's windows. The artist lived and died on the river's banks and painted its many changing moods. See p. 218.

- **Strolling through Covent Garden:** George Bernard Shaw got his inspiration for *Pygmalion* here, where the cockney lass who inspired the character of Eliza Doolittle sold violets to wealthy opera-goers. The old market, with its cauliflower peddlers and butchers in blood-soaked aprons, is long gone. What's left is London's best example of urban renewal and one of its hippest shopping districts. There's an antiques market on Monday and a crafts market Tuesday through Saturday. See p. 292 for market details. When you're parched, there are plenty of pubs to quench your thirst, including the **Nag's Head,** 10 James St., WC2 (© **020/ 7836-4678;** p. 314), an Edwardian pub that'll serve you a draft of Guinness and a plate of pork cooked in cider.

- **Rowing on the Serpentine:** When the weather's right, we head to Hyde Park's 17-hectare (42-acre) manmade lake—the name derives from its winding, snakelike shape—dating from 1730. At the Boathouse, you can rent boats by the hour. It's an idyllic way to spend a sunny afternoon. Renoir must have agreed; he depicted the custom on canvas. See p. 253.

- **Making a Brass Rubbing:** Take home some costumed ladies and knights in armor from England's age of chivalry. Make your very own brass rubbing in the crypt of St. Martin-in-the-Fields in Trafalgar Square; the staff there will be happy to show you how. See p. 230.

- **Getting to Know North London on a Sunday:** Begin by looking for some smart fashion at **Camden Market**

(p. 294), a Sunday event on Camden High Street where stallholders hawk designer jewelry and clothing. Next, walk up to Hampstead Heath off Well Walk and take the right fork, which leads to an open field with a panoramic view of London. Cap your jaunt with a visit to the **Freud Museum** (p. 260), open on Sunday until 5pm. See "Attractions on the Outskirts," on p. 258, for more information on North London.

- **Dining at Rules:** Rules, at 35 Maiden Lane, WC2 (© **020/7836-5314**), was established as an oyster bar in 1798; it may be the oldest restaurant in London. Long a venue for the theatrical elite and literary beau monde, it still serves the same dishes that delighted Edward VII and his mistress, Lillie Langtry, who began their meals with champagne and oysters upstairs. Charles Dickens had a regular table. If you're looking for an old-fashioned British dessert, finish off with the treacle sponge or apple suet pudding. See p. 160.

- **Spending an Evening at the Theater:** London is the theatrical capital of the world. The live stage offers a unique combination of variety, accessibility, and economy—and maybe a look at next season's Broadway hit. See "The Play's the Thing: London's Theater Scene," on p. 295.

- **Crawling the London Pubs:** Americans bar-hop; Londoners pub-crawl. With some 5,000 pubs within the city limits, you would certainly be crawling if you tried to have a drink in each of them! We have suggested the traditional pubs we think will make a worthwhile crawl in "The Best of London's Pubs: The World's Greatest Pub Crawl," on p. 309. While making the rounds, you can partake of that quintessentially British fare known as "pub grub," which could be anything from a ploughman's lunch (a hunk of bread, cheese, and a pickle) to shepherd's pie, to nouveau British cuisine. Today, in the right places, some of that pub grub tastes better than the fare served in many restaurants.

2 The Best Splurge Hotels

- **Covent Garden Hotel,** 10 Monmouth St., WC2 (© **800/553-6674** in the U.S. and Canada, or 020/7806-1000; www.firmdale.com):Once a hospital, this deluxe citadel of fine living is one of London's most charming boutique hotels, lying in one of the West End's hippest shopping districts. *Travel + Leisure* has pronounced it one of the 25 hottest addresses in the world. See p. 101.

- **One Aldwych,** 1 Aldwych, WC2 (© **800/745-8883** in the U.S. and Canada, or 020/7300-1000; www.onealdwych.co.uk): Once the headquarters for the London *Morning Post* at the turn of the 20th century, this luxe hotel, granted five stars by the government, attracts the fashionistas of London to its noble precincts. You're coddled in comfort here. See p. 101.

- **St. Martins Lane,** 45 St. Martin's Lane, WC2 (© **800/697-1791** in the U.S. and Canada, or 020/7300-5500; www.stmartinslane.com): This Covent Garden hotel was once a dull 1960s office building—now it's on the cutting edge, with its eccentric, irreverent design and whimsical touches. Refugees from New York or Los Angeles will feel at home in this ultra-sophisticated environment with state-of-the-art amenities. See p. 101.

- **The Sanderson,** 50 Berners St., W1 (© **800/697-1791** in the U.S. and

Canada, or 020/7300-1400; www.sandersonlondon.com): Deep in the heart of Soho, this winning choice provides a hip New York–style scene: Its owners call it an "ethereal, transparent urban spa." Everything is here, from a lush bamboo-filled roof garden to a restaurant under the general supervision of Alain Ducasse, hailed by some as the world's greatest chef. See p. 104.

• **41,** 41 Buckingham Palace Rd., SW1 (© **877/955-1515** in the U.S. and Canada, or 020/7300-0041; www.41hotel.com): Admittedly an offbeat choice in this category, this well-placed gem offers a touch of class and one of the most prestigious addresses in London (even the queen uses the road as her mailing address). Evoking the atmosphere of a private club, it offers individually designed bedrooms with luxurious touches, modern amenities, and spoil-you-rotten service. See p. 112.

• **The Milestone,** 1 Kensington Court, W8 (© **877/955-1515** in the U.S. and Canada, or 020/7917-1000; www.milestonehotel.com): In the Royal Borough of Kensington, this boutique hotel of charm and grace is installed in a converted Victorian town house across the street from Kensington Palace, where the late Princess Diana used to live. From luxurious beds to marble bathrooms, The Milestone is richly imbued with luxury. See p. 120.

3 The Best Moderately Priced Hotels

• **Windermere Hotel,** 142–144 Warwick Way, SW1 (© **020/7834-5163;** www.windermere-hotel.co.uk): Near Victoria Station, this award-winning small hotel, in a converted Victorian building from 1857, is imbued with English character and comfort. Rooms come in various sizes, some large enough to accommodate three or four overnighters, making them suitable for families. See p. 114.

• **Willett Hotel,** 32 Sloane Gardens, SW1 (© **800/270-9206** in the U.S. and Canada, or 020/7824-8415; www.eeh.co.uk): Right off Sloane Square, deep in the heart of chic Chelsea, this hotel dates from the reign of Edward VII. It has been completely modernized and brought up to date and lies only a 5-minute walk from the turned-on shopping mecca called King's Road. See p. 122.

• **The Gallery,** 8–10 Queensberry Place, SW7 (© **800/270-9206** in the U.S. and Canada, or 020/7915-0000; www.eeh.co.uk): This exclusive little town house in South Kensington is composed of two splendid former Georgian private residences that have been successfully converted to receive paying guests, who are housed in comfort. Bedrooms are romantically decorated in the Laura Ashley style, with half-canopied beds and marble-tiled bathrooms. See p. 124.

• **Hart House Hotel,** 51 Gloucester Place, Portman Square, W1 (© **020/7935-2288;** www.harthouse.co.uk): In the fashionable West End district of Marylebone, this historic building is one of a group of Georgian mansions occupied by exiled French nobles during the Revolution. Today it is one of London's better small hotels, within walking distance of many theaters and offering bedrooms of comfort and character. See p. 127.

• **Lincoln House Hotel,** 33 Gloucester Place, W1 (© **020/7486-7630;** www.lincoln-house-hotel.co.uk): Built during the reign of King George II, this successfully converted town house lies only a 5-minute walk from Marble Arch in the center of London.

Bedrooms are traditionally furnished and full of comfort and character. See p. 130.

- **St. George Hotel,** 49 Gloucester Place, W1 (© **020/7486-8586;** www. stgeorge-hotel.net): This privately owned hotel in a restored Georgian building overlooks one of London's most famous squares, Gloucester Square. A short walk from Oxford and Baker streets, the latter of Sherlock Holmes fame, it offers comfortably refurbished bedrooms that are well maintained. See p. 130.

4 The Most Unforgettable Dining Experiences

- **St. John,** 26 St. John St., EC1 (© **020/7251-0848**): In a former smokehouse north of Smithfield Market, this is London's major venue for serious carnivores. Chef Fergus Henderson is England's biggest devotee of offal cuisine—meaning "nose-to-tail cookery." This earthy food obviously will not appeal to vegetarians, but it would delight a reincarnated Henry VIII. See p. 150.
- **Fifteen,** 15 West Land Place, W1 (© **0871/330-1515;** www.fifteen restaurant.com): In Shoreditch, the author of *The Naked Chef,* James Oliver, takes "disadvantaged" young people and trains them from scratch. In just 4 months, they are tempting you with their modern British cuisine as chefs of the day. Amazingly, the food you're served is praiseworthy, even attracting some of London's Michelin-starred chefs. See p. 151.
- **Simpson's-in-the-Strand,** 100 the Strand, WC2 (© **020/7836-9112**): At least once forsake London's trendy restaurants and dine as Sir Winston did back in the post-war '50s when he was prime minister. It's partaking of "The Deadly Sins" to dine here: roast sirloin of beef; steak, kidney, and mushroom pie; and roast saddle of mutton with red currant jelly. See p. 160.
- **Gordon Ramsay at Claridge's,** Brook Street, W1 (© **020/7499-0099**): We'd cast our vote for Ramsay as the hottest and most talented chef in London today. In the city's swankiest hotel, he dazzles serious international foodies with his take on modern Continental cuisine using, for the most part, British products. Close your eyes and point to any item on the menu—chances are, you'll be delighted. See p. 172.
- **Sketch,** 9 Conduit St., W1 (© **087/ 0777-4488;** www.sketch.uk.com): Hailed by the British press as a "camp wonderland," this is a restaurant, tearoom, art gallery, bar, and patisserie. There is no more chic joint at which you could be at night. The Continental and modern British cuisine is divine as well. See p. 174.
- **Club Gascon,** 57 W. Smithfield, EC1 (© **020/7796-0600**): Chef Pascal Aussignac is all the rage, bringing a corner of southwestern France to London—and that spells Armagnac, foie gras, and duck confit. This bistro stands next to the famous meat market in Smithfield, and it's the best place in town for a foie gras pig out. See p. 148.

5 The Best Museums

- **British Museum,** Great Russell Street, WC1 (© **020/7323-8299;** www.the britishmuseum.ac.uk): When Sir Hans Sloane died in 1753, he bequeathed to England his vast collection of art and antiquities. This formed the nucleus of a huge collection that's come to include such remarkable objects as the Rosetta Stone and the Parthenon sculptures (which Greece wants back). See p. 208.

- **National Gallery,** Trafalgar Square, WC2 (© **020/7747-2885;** www. nationalgallery.org.uk): One of the world's greatest collections of Western art—from Leonardo da Vinci to Rembrandt to Picasso—dazzles the eye at this museum. The gallery is especially rich in Renaissance works. See p. 215.

- **Tate Britain,** Millbank, SW1 (© **020/7887-8888;** www.tate.org.uk): Sir Henry Tate, a sugar producer, started it all with 70 or so paintings. The collection grew considerably when artist J. M. W. Turner bequeathed some 300 paintings and 19,000 watercolors to England upon his death. Having handed International Modernism over to the Tate Modern, the Tate Britain now concentrates on British work dating back to 1500. See p. 218.

- **Victoria and Albert Museum,** Cromwell Road, SW7 (© **020/7942-2000;** www.vam.ac.uk): This is the greatest decorative arts museum in the world, boasting the largest collection of Renaissance sculpture outside Italy. It is also strong on medieval English treasures and has the greatest collection of Indian art outside India. See p. 222.

- **Gilbert Collection,** Somerset House, the Strand, WC2 (© **020/7240-9400;** www.gilbert-collection.org.uk): This is the permanent home of the Gilbert Collection of decorative arts, one of the most important bequests ever left to the state. The exhibition of some 800 objects in gold, silver, and mosaics, and gold snuffboxes—collected by Sir Arthur Gilbert—is hailed as one of the greatest in the world; its silver collection rivals that of the Victoria and Albert Museum. See p. 245.

- **Science Museum,** Exhibition Road, SW7 (© **087/0870-4868;** www. sciencemuseum.org.uk): The collection here of scientific artifacts is among the largest, most significant, and most comprehensive in the world. Everything is here, from King George III's collection of scientific instruments in the 18th century to the *Apollo 10* space module. See p. 251.

6 The Best Activities for Families

- **Sightseeing:** London is filled with attractions that appeal to young and old—take **Madame Tussaud's** wax museum (p. 249), that all-time favorite. There's more: everything from **London's Transport Museum** to the **National Army Museum** (p. 250) and, of course, the **Natural History Museum** (p. 250). A cruise along the Thames (see "River Cruises along the Thames," on p. 256) is a great way to spend an afternoon, as is a trip to the **London Zoo** (p. 269).

- **Trips Out of London:** Board a riverboat for a **cruise to Greenwich** (p. 256), with its **National Maritime Museum** and other amusements. Part of the fun is getting there. In Greenwich you'll find many attractions, including the **Old Royal Observatory.** See "Greenwich," under "Attractions on the Outskirts," on p. 262.

- **Royal London:** No kid wants to leave London without a visit to the **Tower of London** (p. 220). And, of course, children will want to see the **Changing of the Guard** (p. 212). For castles that evoke Disney, take them on a trip to **Windsor Castle** (p. 320) or **Hampton Court Palace** (p. 264).

- **Playgrounds:** London brims with parks, nicknamed "green lungs," including **Regent's Park,** with its two boating lakes, one just for children. An afternoon in sprawling **Hampstead Heath** (see "Hampstead," under "Attractions on the Outskirts," on p. 259) can fill enjoyable hours, as can a stroll through **Kensington Gardens,** with its playgrounds. **Battersea Park** has a small children's zoo and adventure playground. For more information on **Regent's Park, Kensington Gardens,** and **Battersea Park,** see "Parks & Gardens," under "More Central London Attractions," on p. 253.

- **Entertainment:** London has a number of theaters designed for children, notably **Little Angel Theatre,** which hosts regular visiting puppeteers. The minimum age is 3. See p. 268.

7 The Best Things to Do for Free (or Almost)

- **Visit Museums:** London's greatest museums are now free. The world-class treasure troves where you can now roam without charge include the British Museum, National Gallery, National Portrait Gallery, Tate Britain, Tate Modern, Natural History Museum, Science Museum, Victoria and Albert Museum, Museum of London, and Sir John Soane's Museum. And don't forget the British Library, with its marvelous collection of literary gems. See chapter 8 for listings.

- **Watch the Changing of the Guard:** This Buckingham Palace event has more pomp and circumstance than any other royal ceremony on earth. See p. 212.

- **Explore Hampstead Heath:** Take the Tube north to Hampstead for the most delightful ramble in London, following in the footsteps of Keats and other luminaries. The heath's near-wilderness feel is a delicious contrast to London's other manicured parks. Drop in later for a pint at a local pub.

- **Take in a Spectacular City View:** Take the Tube to Tower Hill or Tower Gateway, then cross Tower Bridge. Wander along the South bank of the mighty Thames at night and gaze upon London's historic landmarks and skyscrapers, floodlit in all their evening spectacle.

- **Soak Up the Scene in Regent's Park:** Once the exclusive hunting grounds of royalty, it's now used by everyone from footballers to barefoot couples in summer. Regent's Park is home to the London Zoo, the Open Air Theatre's Shakespeare in the Park, the Prince Regent's original grand terraces, and Queen Mary's rose gardens. See p. 254.

- **Go to Court at the Old Bailey Public Gallery, Warwick Passage:** Britain's Central Criminal Court, or the "Old Bailey," was built on the foundations of the infamous Newgate Gaol. These courtrooms have seen it all, from Oscar Wilde to the Yorkshire Ripper (but never Jack). Robed and bewigged barristers and judges still administer justice with much formality and theatricality. See p. 238.

2

A Traveler's Guide to London's Art & Architecture

by Reid Bramblett

No one artist, period, or museum defines London's art and architecture; rather, the city builds upon the work of artists and craftsmen from its earliest days to the thriving, sometimes shocking art scene today, which could shape the look and view of the city in the future. You can see the art of London in medieval illuminated manuscripts, Thomas Gainsborough portraits, and Damien Hirst's pickled cows and sharks; its architecture from Roman walls and Norman castles to baroque St. Paul's Cathedral and towering postmodern skyscrapers. Let us illuminate some of the art and architecture that surrounds you in this graceful, exciting city.

1 Art 101

CELTIC & MEDIEVAL (CA. 800 B.C.–16TH C.)

The Celts, mixed with Scandinavian and Dutch tribes, ruled England until the Romans established rule in A.D. 43. Celtic art survived the Roman conquest and Dark Ages Christianity mainly as carved swirls and decorations on the "Celtic Crosses" in medieval cemeteries. During the Dark and Middle Ages, colorful Celtic images and illustrations decorated "illuminated manuscripts" copied by monks. Plenty of these have ended up in London's libraries and museums.

Important examples and artists of this period include:

- **Wilton Diptych,** National Gallery. The first truly British painting was crafted in the late 1390s for Richard II by an unknown artist who mixed Italian and Northern European influences.
- **Lindisfarne Gospels,** British Library. One of Europe's greatest illuminated manuscripts from the 7th century.
- **Matthew Paris** (d. 1259). A Benedictine monk who illuminated his own writings, Paris was the St. Albans Abbey chronicler. Examples of his work, including *Chronica Majora* and *Historia Anglorum,* are now in the British Library and Cambridge's Corpus Christi College.

THE RENAISSANCE & BAROQUE (16TH–18TH C.)

While the Renaissance was more of a Southern European movement, London's museums contain the works of many important old masters from Italy and Germany. The word *Renaissance* means "rebirth"—in this case, the renewed use of classical styles and forms. Artists strove for greater naturalism, using newly developed techniques such as linear perspective to achieve new heights of realism. A few foreign Renaissance artists did come to English courts and had an influence on some local artists; however, significant Brits didn't emerge until the baroque period.

The baroque mixes a kind of super-realism based on using peasants as models and an exaggerated use of light and dark, called chiaroscuro, with compositional complexity and explosions of dynamic fury, movement, color, and figures.

Significant artists of this period include:

- **Pietro Torrigiano** (1472–1528). An Italian sculptor, Pietro fled from Florence after breaking the nose of his classmate, Michelangelo. In London, he crafted tombs in Westminster Abbey for the Tudors, including Henry VII and Elizabeth of York. The Victoria and Albert Museum has Pietro's terra-cotta bust of Henry VII.
- **Hans Holbein the Younger** (1497–1543). A German Renaissance master of penetrating portraits, Holbein the Younger cataloged many significant figures in 16th-century Europe. You'll find examples in the National Gallery, the National Portrait Gallery, and Windsor Castle.
- **Anton Van Dyck** (1599–1641). This Belgian painted royal portraits in the baroque style for Charles I and other Stuarts, setting the tone for British portraiture for the next few centuries and earning a knighthood. You'll find his works in the National Portrait Gallery, the National Gallery, the Wallace Collection, and Wilton House, with more in Oxford's Ashmolean Museum.
- **William Hogarth** (1697–1764). Influenced by Flemish masters, Hogarth painted and engraved scenes of everyday life. His serial works, such as *The Rake's Progress* (in Sir John Soane's Museum), were popular morality tales presented as a sort of early version of a comic strip. Seek out his other works in the National Gallery, the Tate Britain, and Cambridge's Fitzwilliam Museum.
- **Sir Joshua Reynolds** (1723–92). A staunch traditionalist and fussy baroque painter, Reynolds was the first president of London's Royal Academy of Arts. Reynolds spent much of his career casting his noble patrons as ancient gods in portrait compositions cribbed from old masters. Many of his works are in the National Gallery, the Tate Britain, the Wallace Collection, the Dulwich Picture Gallery, and Oxford's Cathedral Hall.
- **Thomas Gainsborough** (1727–88). Although Gainsborough was a classical/baroque portraitist like Reynolds, he could be more original. When not immortalizing noble patrons such as Jonathan Buttell (better known as "Blue Boy"), he painted quite a collection of landscapes for himself. His works grace the National Gallery and the National Portrait Gallery, Cambridge's Fitzwilliam Museum, Oxford's Cathedral Hall and Ashmolean Museum, and Gainsborough's House, a museum and gallery in his birthplace in Suffolk.

THE ROMANTICS (LATE 18TH TO 19TH C.)

The Romantics idealized the Romantic tales of chivalry; had a deep respect for nature, human rights, and the nobility of peasantry; and were suspicious of progress. Their paintings tended to be heroic, historic, dramatic, and beautiful. They were inspired by critic and art theorist **John Ruskin** (1819–1900), who was among the first to praise pre-Renaissance painting and Gothic architecture.

Significant artists of this period include:

- **William Blake** (1757–1827). A Romantic archetype, Blake snubbed the Royal Academy of Arts to do his own engraving, prints, illustrations, poetry, and painting.

He believed in divine inspiration, but it was the vengeful Old Testament God he channeled; his works were filled with melodrama, muscular figures, and sweeping lines. See his work at the Tate Britain.

- **J. M. W. Turner** (1775–1851). Turner, called by some "The First Impressionist," was a prolific artist whose mood-laden, freely brushed watercolor landscapes influenced Monet. London and the Thames River were frequent subjects. He bequeathed his collection of some 19,000 watercolors and 300 paintings to the people of Britain. The Tate Britain's Clores Gallery displays the largest number of Turner's works, and others grace the National Gallery and Cambridge's Fitzwilliam Museum.

- **John Constable** (1776–1837). A little obsessed with clouds, Constable was a great British landscapist whose scenes (especially those of happy agrarian peasants) got more idealized with each passing year—while his compositions and brushwork became freer. You'll find his best stuff in the National Gallery and the Victoria and Albert Museum.

- **Pre-Raphaelites** (1848–70). This "Brotherhood" declared art had gone all wrong with Raphael (1483–1520) and set about to emulate the 15th-century Italian painters who preceded him—though their symbolically imbued, sweetly idealized, hyperrealistic work actually looks nothing like it. They loved depicting scenes from Romantic poetry and Shakespeare as well as the Bible. There were seven founders and many followers, the most important of whom were Dante Rossetti, William Hunt, and John Millais; you can see work by all three at the Tate Britain and Oxford's Ashmolean Museum.

THE 20TH CENTURY

The only artistic movement or era the Brits can claim a major stake in is contemporary art, with many young British artists bursting onto the international gallery scene just before and after World War II. The 20th century, if anything, showed the greatest artists searching for a unique, individual expression rather than adherence to a particular school.

Important artists of this period include:

- **Ben Nicholson** (1894–1982). The most famous of Britain's abstract artists, Nicholson is known for his low-relief abstract paintings using layered cardboard and minimalist colors (his most famous are just white). His work is in the Tate Modern and Cambridge's Fitzwilliam Museum.

- **Henry Moore** (1898–1986). A sculptor, Moore saw himself as a sort of reincarnation of Michelangelo. He mined his marble from the same quarries as the Renaissance master and let the stone itself dictate the flowing, abstract, surrealistic figures carved from it. Moore did several public commissions (*Knife Edge* [1967] at Abingdon St. Gardens underground garage; *The Arch* [1979] on the east bank of the Longwater in Kensington Gardens) and started working in bronze after the 1950s. His sculptures also grace the Tate Modern and Cambridge's Fitzwilliam Museum and Clare College.

- **Francis Bacon** (1909–92). A dark, brooding expressionist, Bacon used formats, such as the triptych (usually reserved for religious subjects) to show man's foibles. Examples of his work are in the Tate Modern, including *Triptych August 1972* (1972).

- **Lucien Freud** (b. 1922). Freud's portraits and nudes inhabit a depressing world of thick paint, fluid lines, and harsh light. The grandson of psychiatrist Sigmund

Freud, this artist has pieces at the Tate Modern, including *Girl With a White Dog* (1950–51) and *Standing in Rags* (1988–89).

- **David Hockney** (b. 1937). Hockney employs a less pop-arty style than his American contemporary Andy Warhol—though Hockney does reference modern technologies and culture—and is much more playful with artistic traditions. The Tate Modern is the place to see his creations, including *Mr. and Mrs. Clark and Percy* (1970–71).
- **Damien Hirst** (b. 1965). The guy who pickles cows, Hirst is a celebrity/artist whose work aims to shock. He's a winner of Britain's Turner Prize, and his work is prominent in the collection of Charles Saatchi (whose influential Saatchi Gallery in London displays his holdings) and was featured in "Sensation," the exhibition that traveled to New York City where it prompted protest, vandalism, and the formation of a decency commission.

2 Architecture 101

While each architectural era in London has its own distinctive features, there are some elements, floor plans, and terms common to many.

From the Romanesque period on, most **churches** consist of either a single wide **aisle** or a wide central **nave** flanked by two narrow, shorter aisles. The aisles are separated from the nave by a row of **columns,** or square stacks of masonry called **piers,** connected by **arches.** Sometimes—especially in the medieval Norman and Gothic eras—there is a second level to the nave, above these arches (and hence above the low roof over the aisles) punctuated by windows, called a **clerestory.** Often between the arches and clerestory windows there is a small passageway inside the wall called the **triforium,** open on the nave side via a series of small arches.

This main nave/aisle assemblage is usually crossed by a perpendicular corridor called a **transept** near the far, east end of the church, so that the floor plan looks like a **Latin Cross.** The shorter, east arm of the nave is called the **chancel;** it often houses the stalls of the **choir** and the **altar.** Some churches use a **rood screen** (so called because it supports a *rood,* the Saxon word for crucifixion) to separate the nave from the chancel. If the far end of the chancel is rounded off, it is called an **apse.** An **ambulatory** is a corridor outside the altar and choir area, separating it from the ring of smaller chapels radiating off the chancel and apse.

Some churches, especially after the Renaissance when mathematical proportion became important, were built on a **Greek Cross** plan, each axis the same length, like a giant +.

It's worth pointing out that very few buildings (especially churches) were built in only one style. They often took centuries to complete, during which time tastes would change and plans would be altered.

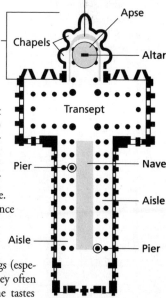

Church Floor Plan

NORMAN (1066–1200)

Aside from a smattering of ancient sites—**preclassical** stone circles at Stonehenge and Avebury, and **Roman** ruins such as the Bath spa and Hadrian's Wall—the oldest surviving architectural style in England dates to when the 1066 Norman Conquest brought the Romanesque era to Britain, where it flourished as the **Norman style.**

Churches were large, with a wide nave and aisles to fit the masses that came to hear Mass and worship at the altars of various saints. But to support the weight of all that masonry, the walls had to be thick and solid (pierced by only a few small windows) and resting on huge piers, which gives Norman churches a dark, somber, mysterious feeling.

Some of the features of this style include:

- **Rounded arches.** These load-bearing architectural devices allowed the architects to open up wide naves and spaces, channeling the weight of the stone walls and ceiling across the curve of the arch and down into the ground via the columns or pilasters.
- **Thick walls.**
- **Infrequent and small windows.**
- **Huge piers.** These are square stacks of masonry.
- **Chevrons.** These zigzagging decorations often surround a doorway or wrap around a column.

White Tower, London (Gundulf, 1078), William the Conqueror's first building in Britain, is the central keep of the Tower of London. The tower's fortress-thick walls and rounded archways provide a textbook example of a Norman-era castle. **St. John's Chapel,** located in the White Tower, is one of the few remaining Norman churches in England.

White Tower

GOTHIC (1150–1550)

The French Gothic style invaded England in the late 12th century, trading rounded arches for pointy ones—an engineering discovery that freed architects from the thick walls of Norman structures and allowed ceilings to soar, walls to thin, and windows to proliferate.

Instead of dark, somber, relatively unadorned Norman interiors that forced the eyes of the faithful toward the altar, the Gothic interior enticed the churchgoers' gazes upward to high ceilings filled with light. While the priests conducted Mass in Latin, the peasants could "read" the Bible stories in the stained-glass windows.

The squat exteriors of the Norman churches were replaced by graceful buttresses and soaring spires, which rose from town centers.

The Gothic style made comebacks in the 17th century as **Laudian Gothic** in some Oxford and Cambridge buildings, in the 18th century as **rococo** or **Strawberry Hill Gotick,** and in the 19th century as **Victorian Gothic Revival,** discussed below.

The Gothic proper in Britain can be divided into three periods or styles: **Early English** (1150–1300), **Decorated** (1250–1370), and **Perpendicular** (1350–1550). Although each has identifiable features, they all include:

- **Pointed arches.** The most significant development of the Gothic era was the discovery that pointed arches could carry far more weight than rounded ones.
- **Ribbed vaulting.** In Gothic buildings, the square patch of ceiling between four columns arches up to a point in the center, creating four sail shapes. This is called a **cross-vault.** The X separating these four sails is often reinforced with ridges called **ribbing.** As the Gothic progressed, the spaces between the structural ribbing became more decorative, often filled with **tracery** (delicate and lacelike carved stone). In the Perpendicular style, **fan vaulting** (cone-shape concave vaults springing from the same point) was often used.

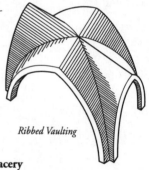

Ribbed Vaulting

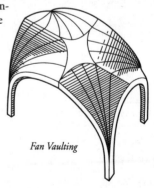

Fan Vaulting

- **Flying buttresses.** These freestanding exterior pillars connected by graceful, thin arms of stone help channel the weight of the building and its roof out and down into the ground.
- **Plate tracery.** The tip of a window, or the tips of two side-by-side windows, is often filled with a flat plate of stone pierced by a **light** (tiny window), which is either round or in a **trefoil** (three round petals, like a clover) or **quatrefoil** (four petals) shape.
- **Stained glass.** The multitude and size of Gothic windows allowed them to be filled with Bible stories and symbolism writ in the colorful patterns of stained glass. The use of stained glass was more common in the later Gothic periods.

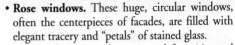

- **Rose windows.** These huge, circular windows, often the centerpieces of facades, are filled with elegant tracery and "petals" of stained glass.
- **Spires.** These pinnacles seem to defy gravity and reach toward heaven itself.
- **Gargoyles.** These are drain spouts disguised as wide-mouthed creatures or human heads.
- **Choir screen.** Serving as the inner wall of the ambulatory and the outer wall of the choir section, the choir screen is often decorated with carvings or tombs.

Among England's towering Gothic achievements, **Salisbury Cathedral** (1220–65) is almost unique for the speed with which it was built and the uniformity of its architecture. **King's College Chapel** (1446–1515) at Cambridge has England's most magnificent fan vaulting, along with some fine stained glass. At Windsor are two great examples, the **College Chapel** at Eton College (the stained glass is modern, and the fan vaulting painstakingly redone in 1957, but the 15th-century murals are original), and the **St. George's Chapel** in Windsor Castle (a gorgeous nave vault with fan vaulting in the aisles and carved choir stalls).

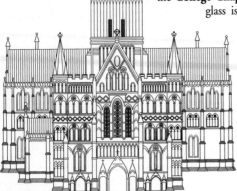

Salisbury Cathedral

RENAISSANCE (1550–1650)

While Italy and even France were experimenting with the Renaissance ideals of proportion, classical inspiration, and mathematical precision to create unified, balanced structures, England was trundling along with the late **Tudor Gothic Perpendicular** style (the Tudor use of red brick became a major feature of later Gothic revivals) in places such as Hampton Court Palace.

It wasn't until the Elizabethan era that the Brits turned to the **Renaissance** style sweeping the Continent. Architect **Inigo Jones** (1573–1652), England's greatest Renaissance architect, brought back from his travel in Italy a fevered imagination full of the exactingly classical theories of **Palladianism,** as developed by **Andrea Palladio** (1508–80). Although Jones applied what he'd learned to several English structures, most English architects at this time tempered the Renaissance style with a heavy dose of Gothic-like elements.

Little specifically identifies Renaissance buildings, except:

- **A sense of proportion.**
- **A reliance on symmetry.**

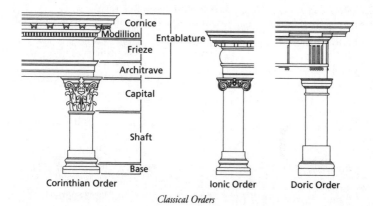

Classical Orders

- **The use of classical orders.** This idea specifies three different column types: Corinthian, Ionic, and Doric.

Noteworthy structures in this style by Inigo Jones include the **Queen's House,** Greenwich (1616–18 and 1629–35); the **Queen's Chapel,** St. James's Palace (1623–25), and the **Banqueting House,** Whitehall (1619–22), both in London; and the state rooms of Wiltshire's **Wilton House** (1603), where Shakespeare performed and D-day was planned. Recently, **Shakespeare's Globe Theatre** dusted off one of Jones's never-realized plans and used it to construct the new indoor theater.

BAROQUE (1650–1750)

England's greatest architect was **Sir Christopher Wren** (1632–1723), a scientist and member of Parliament who got the job of rebuilding London after the Great Fire of 1666. He designed 53 replacement churches alone, plus the new St. Paul's Cathedral and numerous other projects.

The identifiable features of the baroque as practiced by Wren and others include:

- **Classical architecture rewritten with curves.** The baroque is similar to the Renaissance; however, many of the right angles and ruler-straight lines are exchanged for curves of complex geometry and an interplay of concave and convex surfaces. The overall effect is to lighten the appearance of structures and to add some movement of line.
- **Complex decoration.** Unlike the sometimes severe and austere designs of Renaissance and other classically inspired styles, the baroque was often playful and apt to festoon structures with decorations to liven things up.

St. Paul's Cathedral, London (1676–1710), is the crowning achievement both of the English baroque and of Christopher Wren himself. The city's other main Wren attraction is the **Royal Naval College,** Greenwich (1696).

A student of Wren, **Nicholas Hawksmoor** practiced a baroque more fanciful than that of his teacher. Hawksmoor left London several churches, including **St. Mary Woolnoth** (1716–24); **St. George's,** Bloomsbury (1716–30); **Christ Church,** Spitalfields (1714–29); and **St. Anne's,** Limehouse (1714–30).

NEOCLASSICAL & GREEK REVIVAL (1714–1837)

Many 18th-century architects cared little for the baroque, and during the Georgian era (1714–1830), a restrained, simple neoclassicism reigned, balanced between a resurgence of the precepts of Palladianism (see "Renaissance," above) and an even more distilled vision of classical theory called Greek Revival.

Buildings in these styles may be distinguished by:

- **Mathematical proportion, symmetry, and classical orders.** These classical ideals first rediscovered during the Renaissance are the hallmark of every classically styled era.
- **Crescents and circuses.** The Georgians were famous for these seamless, curving rows of identical stone town houses with tall windows, each one simple yet elegant inside.
- **Open double-arm staircases.** This feature was a favorite of the neo-Palladians.

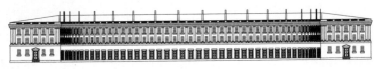

Crescent

The chapel in **Greenwich Hospital** (1779–88) is a fine example of the style, courtesy of the most textbook of Greek Revivalists, James "Athenian" Stuart. The greatest site by Greek Revivalist John Soane is his own idiosyncratic house at **No. 13 Lincoln's Inn Fields** (1812–13), now Sir John Soane's Museum (other Soane buildings include the **Dulwich Picture Gallery** and the facade of the **Bank of England** in Bartholomew Lane). Another example of this style is the **British Museum** (Robert and Sidney Smirke, 1823).

VICTORIAN GOTHIC REVIVAL (1750–1900)

While neoclassicists were reinterpreting the classical age, the Romantic movement swept up many others with rosy visions of the past. Their imaginary and fairytale version of the Middle Ages led to such creative developments as the pre-Raphaelite painters (see "The Romantics," above) and Gothic Revival architects, who really got a head of steam under their movement during the eclectic Victorian era.

Buildings in the Victorian Gothic Revival style can be distinguished by:

- **Mishmash of Gothic features.** Look at the Gothic features described earlier, and then imagine going on a shopping spree through them at random. How to tell the copycats from the original? Victorian buildings are much younger, so they tend to be in better shape. They're also often much larger than original Gothic buildings.
- **Eclecticism.** Few Victorians bothered with getting all the formal details of a particular Gothic era right (London's Houses of Parliament comes closest). They just wanted to make sure the overall effect was pointy with pinnacled turrets, busy with decorations, and medieval.
- **Grand scale.** These buildings tend to be very large. This was usually accomplished by using Gothic only on the surface, with Industrial Age engineering underneath.

Charles Barry designed the British seat of government, the **Palace of Westminster** (Houses of Parliament; 1835–52), in a Gothic idiom that sticks pretty faithfully to the

Palace of Westminster

old Perpendicular period's style. His clock tower, usually called Big Ben after its biggest bell, has become an icon of London.

The massive pinnacled and redbrick Victorian St. Pancras Chambers (formerly the Midlands Hotel; George Gilbert Scott, 1867) at **St. Pancras Station** makes for a quirky entrance to the Industrial Age phenomenon of rail travel. (And, while purely industrial and not Gothic, the station's steel-and-glass train shed, designed by William Henry Barlow, was an engineering marvel, the widest in the world at its time.) The **Albert Memorial** (George Gilbert Scott, 1863–72), a massive Gothic canopy by the same architect, was commissioned by Queen Victoria in memory of her husband. Like St. Pancras, the **Natural History Museum** (Alfred Waterhouse, 1873–81) is a delightful marriage of imposing neo-Gothic clothing hiding an Industrial Age steel-and-iron framework.

THE 20TH CENTURY

For the first half of the 20th century, London was too busy expanding into suburbs (in an architecturally uninteresting way) and fighting world wars to pay much attention to architecture. After the Blitz, much of central London had to be rebuilt, but most of the new buildings that went up in the City held to a functional school of architecture aptly named **Brutalism.** It wasn't until the late 1970s and 1980s that **postmodern** architecture gave British architects a bold new direction.

Identifiable features of postmodern architecture in London include:

- **The skyscraper motif.** Glass and steel as high as you can stack it.
- **A reliance on historic details.** Like the Victorians, postmodernists also recycled elements from architectural history, from classical to exotic.

The **Lloyd's Building** (1978–86) is *the* British postmodern masterpiece by architect Richard Rogers, who had a hand in the design of Paris's funky Centre Pompidou. Britain's tallest building, **Canary Wharf Tower** (César Pelli, 1986), is the centerpiece of the early 1990s Canary Wharf office complex and commercial development. **Charing Cross** (Terry Farrell, 1991) capped the famous old train station with an enormous postmodern office-and-shopping complex in glass and pale stone.

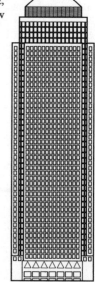

Canary Wharf Tower

3

Planning Your Trip to London

This chapter tackles the how-to's of your trip to London—tips for getting your trip together and getting on the road, whether you're a frequent traveler or a first-timer.

1 Visitor Information & Maps

Visit Britain maintains a website at **www.visitbritain.com**. You can also get information from **Visit Britain** offices. There's one in the **United States** at 551 Fifth Ave., 7th Floor, New York, NY 10176-0799 (© **800/462-2748** or 212/986-2266). In Canada call © **888/ VISITUK.** In **Australia,** Level 2, 15 Blue St., North Sydney 2060 (© **02/9021- 4400**). In **New Zealand,** go to the Fay Richwhite Building, 17th Floor, 151 Queen St., Auckland 1 (© **0800/700- 741;** fax 09/377-6965). For a full information packet on London, write to **Visit London Tourist Board,** Glen House, Stag Place, Victoria, SW1E 5LT (© **020/ 7234-5800;** www.visitlondon.co.uk). You can call the recorded-message service.

WHAT'S ON THE WEB? The most useful site was created by a very knowledgeable source, namely Visit Britain. A wealth of information is available at **www.visitbritain.com**, which lets you order brochures online, provides trip-planning hints, and even grants prompt answers to e-mail questions. This site covers all of Great Britain. Visit London, the official visitor organization for the city, offers more specific information about the city on its website, **www.visitlondon. com**. The site gives users the opportunity to organize their trip online by booking discounted rail tickets, accommodations, restaurants, and a London Pass that offers free or reduced entry to more than 50 London attractions. The Visit London website includes both comprehensive information on what's new in town and more specific sections, including Kids Love London, Gay London, and London by Night. Go to **www.baa.com** for a guide and terminal maps for Heathrow, Gatwick, Stansted, and other London-area airports, including flight arrival times, duty-free shops, airport restaurants, and info on getting from the airports to downtown London. Getting around London can be confusing, so you might want to visit **www.tfl.gov.uk** for up-to-the-minute transit info. For the latest details on London's theater scene, consult **www.officiallondontheatre.co.uk** or **www.londontheatre.co.uk**.

FINDING MAPS At **www.multimap. com**, you can access detailed street maps of the whole United Kingdom—just key in the location or even just the postal code, and a map of the area with the location circled will appear. For directions to specific places in London, consult **www. streetmap.co.uk**.

Destination: London—Pre-Departure Checklist

- Did you pack your passport or identity card? Citizens of E.U. countries can cross into Britain for as long as they wish with an identity card. Citizens of other countries must have a passport.
- If you purchased traveler's checks, have you recorded the check numbers and stored that document separately from the checks?
- Did you pack your camera and an extra set of camera batteries, and purchase enough film?
- Do you have a safe, accessible place to store money?
- Did you bring ID cards that may entitle you to discounts, such as AAA and AARP cards, student IDs, and so forth?
- Did you bring emergency drug prescriptions and extra glasses and/or contact lenses?
- Do you have your credit card PIN?
- If you have an e-ticket, do you have documentation (a printout with the confirmation number)?
- Did you leave a copy of your itinerary with someone at home?
- Did you check to see if any travel advisories have been issued by the **U.S. State Department** (http://travel.state.gov)?
- Do you have the address and phone number of your country's embassy with you?

2 Entry Requirements & Customs

PASSPORTS

For information on how to get a passport, go to "Passports" in the "Fast Facts" section of this chapter—the websites listed provide downloadable passport applications as well as the current fees for processing passport applications. For an up-to-date, country-by-country listing of passport requirements around the world, go to the "Foreign Entry Requirement" Web page of the U.S. State Department at **http://travel.state.gov**. Children do require their own passports when visiting London—see "Family Travel" (p. 44) for more information.

VISAS

Citizens of the United States, Canada, Australia, New Zealand, and South Africa require a passport to enter the United Kingdom, but not a visa. Irish citizens and citizens of European Union countries need only an identity card. The maximum stay for non–European Union visitors is 6 months. Some Customs officials request proof that you have the means to leave the country (usually a round-trip ticket) and, if you don't have a return ticket, means of support while you're in Britain (someone in the U.K. will have to vouch that they are supporting you, or you may be asked to show documents that indicate that you have an income). If you're planning to fly on from the United Kingdom to a country that requires a visa, it's wise to secure the visa before you leave home.

CUSTOMS REGULATIONS

For information on what you can bring into and take out of London, go to **"Customs"** in the **"Fast Facts"** section of chapter 5.

3 When to Go

CLIMATE

Charles Dudley Warner once said that the trouble with the weather is that everybody talks about it but nobody does anything about it. Well, Londoners talk about weather more than anyone—and they've actually done something about it: Air-pollution control has resulted in the virtual disappearance of the pea-soup fogs that once blanketed the city.

A typical London-area weather forecast for a summer day predicts "scattered clouds with sunny periods and showers, possibly heavy at times." Summer temperatures seldom rise above 78°F (25°C), nor do they often drop below 35°F (2°C) in winter. London, being in one of the mildest parts of the country, can be very pleasant in the spring and fall. Yes, it rains, but you'll rarely get a true downpour. Rains are heaviest in November, when the city averages 2½ inches.

The British consider chilliness wholesome and usually try to keep room temperatures about 10° below the American comfort level, so bring sweaters year-round if you tend to get cold.

London's Average Daytime Temperature & Rainfall

	Jan	Feb	Mar	Apr	May	June	July	Aug	Sept	Oct	Nov	Dec
Temp. (°F)	40	40	44	49	55	61	64	64	59	52	46	42
Temp. (°C)	4.4	4.4	6.7	9.4	12.8	16.1	17.8	17.8	15.0	11.1	7.8	5.6
Rainfall (in.)	2.1	1.6	1.5	1.5	1.8	1.8	2.2	2.3	1.9	2.2	2.5	1.9

CURRENT WEATHER CONDITIONS

A good way to check conditions is at the Weather Channel's website: www.weather.com. In London, you can turn to BBC One–TV for the weather.

LONDON CALENDAR OF EVENTS

For an exhaustive list of events beyond those listed here, check http://events.frommers.com, where you'll find a searchable, up-to-the-minute roster of what's happening in cities all over the world.

January

January Sales. Most shops offer good reductions at this time. Many sales start as early as late December to beat the post-Christmas slump.

London Parade. Bands, floats, and carriages contribute to the merriment as the parade wends its way from Parliament Square to Berkeley Square in Mayfair. January 1. Procession starts around noon.

London Boat Show, ExCel, Docklands, E16 XL. The largest boat show in Europe. Call ⓒ **0870/060-0246** or visit www.londonboatshow.com for details. Mid-January.

Charles I Commemoration. This is the anniversary of the execution of King Charles I "in the name of freedom and democracy." Hundreds of cavaliers march through central London in 17th-century dress, and prayers are said at the Banqueting House in Whitehall. Free. Call ⓒ **0870/751-5178** for details. Last Sunday in January.

February

Chinese New Year. The famous Lion Dancers appear in Soho. Free. Either late January or early February (based on the lunar calendar). Call ⓒ **0870/156-6366** for schedule and event details.

Great Spitalfields Pancake Race, Old Spitalfields Market, Brushfield Street, E1. Teams of four run in relays, tossing pancakes. To join in, call ☎ 020/7375-0441 or visit www.alternativearts.co.uk. At noon on Shrove Tuesday (last day before Lent).

March

St. David's Day, Chelsea Barracks. A member of the Royal Family presents the Welsh Guards with the principality's national emblem, a leek. Call ☎ 020/7234-5800 for more information. March 1 (or the nearest Sun).

Oranges and Lemons Service, at St. Clement Danes, the Strand, WC2. As a reminder of the nursery rhyme "Bells of St. Clements," children are presented with the fruits during the church service, and the church bells ring out the rhyme (part of which is "Oranges and Lemons, Say the bells of St. Clements") at 9am, noon, and 6pm; call ☎ 020/7242-8282; www.st-clement-danes.co.uk for information. Third week of March.

Westminster Abbey on Holy Week Tuesday; call ☎ 020/7654-4900; www.westminster-abbey.org for information. Free. Late March or early April.

April

Easter Parade. Floats, marching bands, and a full day of Easter Sunday activities enliven Battersea Park. Free. Easter Sunday.

Harness Horse Parade. A morning parade of heavy-working horses in superb gleaming brass harnesses and plumes, at Battersea Park. Call ☎ 017/3764-6132; www.lhhp.co.uk. Easter Monday.

Boat Race, Putney to Mortlake. Oxford and Cambridge universities' rowing teams ("eights") battle upstream with awesome power. Park yourself at one of the Thames-side pubs along the route to see the action. Early April; call ☎ 020/7780-6999; www.theboat race.org.

Flora London Marathon. Thirty thousand competitors run from Greenwich Park to Buckingham Palace. Call ☎ 020/7902-0200 or visit www.london-marathon.co.uk for more information or to register for the marathon. Mid- to late April.

The Queen's Birthday. The Queen's birthday is celebrated with 21-gun salutes in Hyde Park and by troops in parade dress on Tower Hill at noon. April 21.

National Gardens Scheme. More than 3,000 private gardens in London are open to the public on set days, and tea is sometimes served. Pick up the NGS guidebook for £8 ($15) from most bookstores, or contact the National Gardens Scheme Charitable Trust, Hatchlands Park, East Clandon, Guildford, Surrey GU4 7RT (☎ 014/8321-1535; www.ngs.org.uk). Late April to early May.

May

Covent Garden May Fayre and Puppet Festival, Covent Garden. There is a procession of puppets, puppeteers, and a brass band at 10am; a service at St. Paul's on Bedford Street at 10:30am; then Punch and Judy shows until 6pm at the site where British diarist Pepys watched them in 1662. Everything is free. Call ☎ 020/7375-0441; www.alternativearts.co.uk for details. Second Sunday in May.

The Royal Windsor Horse Show, Home Park, Windsor Castle. You might spot a royal at this multiday horse-racing and horse-showing event. Call ☎ 01753/860-633-0633 or visit www.royal-windsor-horse-show.co.uk for more details. Mid-May.

Glyndebourne Festival Opera Season, Sussex. The Glyndebourne Festival presents opera performances in a beautiful setting, with champagne picnics before and between the shows. Since the completion of the Glyndebourne opera house, one of the world's best, tickets are a bit easier to come by. Call ℂ **1273/812-321** or visit www. glyndebourne.com for a schedule and to purchase tickets. The season runs from mid-May to late August.

Chelsea Flower Show, Chelsea Royal Hospital. This show exhibits the best of British gardening, with displays of plants and flowers from all seasons. The show runs from 8am to 8pm; tickets are £18 to £40 ($34–$76). Tickets must be purchased in advance; they are available through the Royal Horticultural Society (www.rhs.org.uk). Call ℂ **0845/ 260-5000** for information. Four days in May.

June

Trooping the Colour, Horse Guards Parade, Whitehall. The official birthday of the Queen (as opposed to her actual birthday, which is Apr 21) is held on a designated date in June. Seated in a carriage, the monarch inspects her regiments and takes their salute as they parade their colors. It's a quintessentially British event, with exquisite pageantry and pomp. Tickets for the parade and for two reviews, held on preceding Saturdays, are allocated by ballot. Those interested in attending must apply for tickets between January 1 and the end of February, enclosing a stamped, self-addressed envelope or International Reply Coupon—exact dates and ticket prices are supplied later. The drawing is held in mid-March, and successful applicants *only* are informed in April. For details, and to apply for tickets, write to **HQ Household Division,** Horse Guards, Whitehall, London SW1X 6AA,

enclosing a self-addressed envelope and International Reply Coupon (available at any post office). Call ℂ **020/ 7976-0850;** www.trooping-the-colour. co.uk for more information.

Vodafone Derby Stakes, Epsom Downs Racecourse, Epsom, Surrey. These famous horse races constitute the best-known event on the British horse-racing calendar. It's also a chance for men to wear top hats and women, including the Queen, to put on silly millinery creations. Grandstand tickets range from £28 to £35 ($53–$67). Call ℂ **01372/726311** or visit www. epsomderby.co.uk for more information and to buy tickets. The "darby" (as it's pronounced) is run the first week in June.

Royal Academy's Summer Exhibition, Burlington House in Piccadilly Circus, W1. The Royal Academy, founded in 1768 with Sir Joshua Reynolds as president and Thomas Gainsborough as a member, has sponsored summer exhibitions of living painters' work for some 2 centuries. Visitors can browse and purchase art. Call ℂ **0870/848-8484** or visit www. royalacademy.org.uk for details. Early June to mid-August.

Grosvenor House Art and Antique Fair, Le Méridien Grosvenor House, 86–90 Park Lane, W1 3AA. This is a very prestigious antiques fair featuring the world's leading dealers and more than £400 million ($760 million) worth of fine art and antiques. Call ℂ **020/7399-8100** or visit www. grosvenor-antiquesfair.co.uk for more information. Second week of June.

Royal Ascot Week, Ascot, Berkshire, SL5 7JN. Ascot Racecourse is open year-round for guided tours, events, exhibitions, and conferences. There are 25 race days throughout the year, with the feature race meetings being the

Royal Meeting in June, Diamond Day in late July (p. 25), and the Festival at Ascot in late September (p. 26). For Royal Ascot week, which runs from mid- to late June, everyone (including the Queen) shows up in their finery to watch 24 races over 4 days. For further information and tickets, call © **0870/727-1234** or visit www.ascot.co.uk. Tickets should be purchased in advance. Mid- to late June.

Lawn Tennis Championships, Wimbledon, Southwest London. Ever since players in flannels and bonnets took to the grass courts at Wimbledon in 1877, this tournament has drawn a socially prominent crowd. You'll still find an excited hush at Centre Court (where the most hotly contested championship matches are held). Savoring strawberries and cream is part of the experience. Tickets for Centre and Number One courts are handed out through a lottery; write to **All England Lawn Tennis Club,** P.O. Box 98, Church Road, Wimbledon, London SW19 5AE (© **020/8944-1066**) between August and December. Include a self-addressed and stamped envelope with your letter. A number of tickets are set aside for visitors from abroad, so you may be able to purchase some in spring for this year's games; call to inquire. Outside court tickets are available daily, but *be prepared to wait in line.* Call © **020/8944-1066** or visit www.wimbledon.org. Late June to early July.

City of London Festival. This is an annual arts celebration held throughout the city. Call © **0845/120-7502** or visit www.colf.org for information about programs and venues. Late June to early July.

Shakespeare Under the Stars, Open Air Theatre, Inner Circle, Regent's Park, NW1 4NU. If you want to see *Macbeth, Hamlet,* or *Romeo and Juliet* (or any other Shakespeare play), our advice is to bring a blanket and a bottle of wine to watch the Bard's works performed at the Open Air Theatre. Performances are Monday through Saturday at 8pm, plus Wednesday, Thursday, and Saturday at 2:30pm. Call © **0845/673-2154** or visit www.openairtheatre.org.uk for more information and to buy tickets. There is an on-site box office, but it's best to purchase tickets in advance. Previews begin in late June, and the season lasts until early September.

July

Kenwood Lakeside Concerts, north side of Hampstead Heath. Fireworks and laser shows enliven the excellent performances at these annual outdoor concerts on Hampstead Heath. Classical music drifts across the lake to the fans every Saturday and Sunday in summer from early July to late August. Call © **0870/156-6366** for a schedule and information and to buy tickets. Tickets are popular, so buy yours in advance. Early July to late August.

Hampton Court Palace Flower Show, East Molesey, Surrey. This 5-day international flower show is eclipsing its sister show in Chelsea; here, you can purchase the exhibits on the last day. Call © **0845/260-5000** or visit www. rhs.org.uk for exact dates and details. Early to mid-July.

Diamond Day, Ascot, Berkshire, SL5 7JN. This is one of the most important horse races on the international racing calendar. The major event of Ascot's summer season, it is a stylish sporting and social occasion where Brits appear in all their finery. More than £1 million ($1,900,000) in prize money is at stake at this horse race, and the world's greatest thoroughbreds are on display here. Tickets must be booked early. For more information, call © **087/0727-1234** or visit www.ascot.co.uk. End of July.

The Proms, Royal Albert Hall. "The Proms"—the annual Henry Wood Promenade Concerts at Royal Albert Hall—attract music aficionados from around the world. Staged daily, the concerts were launched in 1895 and are the principal summer venue for the BBC Symphony Orchestra. Banners, balloons, and Union Jacks on parade contribute to the festive summer atmosphere. Call ℂ **020/7589-8212** or visit www.bbc.co.uk/proms for more information and for tickets. Tickets should be bought in advance. Mid-July to mid-September.

August

Notting Hill Carnival, Notting Hill. This is one of the largest street festivals in Europe, attracting more than a half-million people annually. You'll find live reggae and soul music combined with great Caribbean food. Free. Call ℂ **020/7727-0072** or visit www.portowebbo.co.uk for information. Two days in late August (usually the last Sun and Mon).

September

Chelsea Antiques Fair, Chelsea Old Town Hall, King's Road, SW3. This is a gathering of England's best antiques dealers. Call ℂ **018/2574-4074** or visit www.penman-fairs.co.uk. Mid-September.

Open House, citywide. During this 2-day event, the public has access to buildings of architectural significance that are normally closed. Visit **www.londonopenhouse.org** for a schedule and further information. Mid- to late September.

Horse of the Year Show, NEC Arena, Birmingham. This is the premier equestrian event on the English calendar. Riders fly in from all over to join in this festive event of jumping competitions, parading, and pony showing. For more information, call ℂ **0870/777-4567** or visit www.hoys.co.uk. End of September to early October.

Raising of the Thames Barrier, Unity Way, SE18. Once a year, in September, a full test is done on the flood barrier. All 10 of the massive steel gates are raised out of the river for inspection, and you can get a close look at this miracle of modern engineering. Call ℂ **020/8854-1373** for the exact date and time (usually a Sun near the end of Sept).

The Ascot Festival, Ascot, Berkshire, SL5 7JN. This is Britain's greatest horse-racing weekend, providing the grand finale to the summer season at Ascot. The 3-day "meeting" combines some of the most valuable racing of the year with other entertainment. A highlight of the festival is the £250,000 ($475,000) Watership Down Stud Sales race restricted to 2-year-old fillies. Other racing highlights include the Queen Elizabeth II Stakes, with the winning horse crowned champion miler in Europe. To book tickets, call ℂ **0870/727-1234** or visit www.ascot.co.uk. Last weekend in September.

October

Opening of Parliament, House of Lords, Westminster. The monarch opens Parliament in the House of Lords by reading an official speech written by the Prime Minister's office. The Queen rides from Buckingham Palace to the House of Lords in a royal coach accompanied by the Yeoman of the Guard and the Household Cavalry. The Strangers' Gallery at the House of Lords is open to spectators on a first-come, first-served basis. Call ℂ **020/7219-3000** or visit www.parliament.uk. Late October to mid-November.

Judges Service, Westminster Abbey. The judiciary attends a service in Westminster Abbey to mark the opening of the law term. Afterward, in full regalia—wigs and all—they form a procession and walk to the House of Lords for their "Annual Breakfast." You'll have a great view of the procession from behind the Abbey. First Monday in October at 10am.

Quit Rents Ceremony, Royal Courts of Justice, WC2. The City Solicitor pays one of the Queen's officials a token rent for properties leased from the kingdom long, long ago. Two fagots of wood, a billhook, and a hatchet pay for land in Shropshire, and 61 nails and 6 horseshoes pay for a long-gone forge in the Strand. Call © **020/7947-6000** for free tickets. Early October.

November

Guy Fawkes Night. On the anniversary of the Gunpowder Plot, an attempt to blow up King James I and his Parliament, huge bonfires are lit throughout the city and Guy Fawkes, the most famous conspirator, is burned in effigy. Free. Check *Time Out* for locations. November 5.

Lord Mayor's Procession and Show, from the Guildhall to the Royal Courts of Justice, in The City of London. This annual event marks the inauguration of the new lord mayor of The City of London. The Queen must ask permission to enter the City—a right jealously guarded by London merchants during the 17th century. You can watch the procession from the street; the show is by invitation only. Call © **020/ 7222-4345** or visit www.lordmayor show.org for more information. Second Saturday in November.

December

Caroling under the Norwegian Christmas Tree. There's caroling most evenings beneath the tree in Trafalgar Square. December.

Harrods After-Christmas Sale, Knightsbridge. Call © **020/7730-1234** or visit www.harrods.com for dates. Truly voracious shoppers camp overnight outside the store so that they have first pickings. Late December.

Watch Night, St. Paul's Cathedral. A lovely New Year's Eve service takes place at 11:30pm. Call © **020/7236-4128** or visit www.stpauls.co.uk for information. December 31.

4 Getting There

BY PLANE

Don't worry about which airport, Heathrow versus Gatwick, to fly into unless you are extremely pressed for time. Heathrow is closer to central London than Gatwick, but there is fast train service from both of the airports to the West End (see "Getting into Town from the Airport," below). **High season** on most airlines' routes to London is usually from June to the beginning of September. This is the most expensive and most crowded time to travel. **Shoulder season** is from April to May, early September to October, and December 15 to 24. **Low season** is from November 1 to December 14 and December 25 to March 31.

FROM THE UNITED STATES
American Airlines (© **800/433-7300;** www.aa.com) offers daily nonstop flights to London's Heathrow Airport from eight U.S. gateways: New York's JFK (nine times daily), Chicago's O'Hare (once a day), Boston's Logan (once daily), Miami International (twice daily), Los Angeles International (two to three times daily), Newark and LaGuardia (three times daily), and Dallas (once daily).

British Airways (© **800/247-9297;** www.britishairways.com) offers mostly nonstop flights from 19 U.S. cities to Heathrow and Gatwick. With more add-on options than any other airline, British

Airways can make a visit to Britain cheaper than you might expect. Of particular interest are the "Value Plus," "London on the Town," and "Europe Escorted" packages that include airfare and discounted accommodations throughout Britain.

Continental Airlines (© 800/231-0856; www.continental.com) flies daily to Gatwick Airport from Newark, Houston, and Cleveland.

Depending on the day and season, **Delta Air Lines** (© 800/221-1212; www.delta.com) runs either one or two daily nonstop flights between Atlanta and Gatwick. Delta also offers nonstop daily service from Cincinnati.

Although **Air India** (© 800/223-7776 or 212/407-1300; www.airindia.com) doesn't immediately come to mind when you think of flying from the U.S. to London, it's a viable option and is competitively priced. Air India offers daily flights from New York's JFK and three flights a week—Tuesday, Friday, and Sunday—from Chicago to London's Heathrow Airport.

Northwest KLM Airlines (© 800/225-2525; www.nwa.com) flies nonstop from Minneapolis and Detroit to Gatwick.

United Airlines (© 800/241-6522; www.united.com) flies nonstop from New York's JFK and Chicago's O'Hare to Heathrow two or three times a day, depending on the season. United also offers nonstop service three times a day from Dulles Airport, near Washington, D.C., to London's Gatwick, plus once-a-day service to Heathrow from Newark, Los Angeles, San Francisco, and Boston.

Virgin Atlantic Airways (© 800/821-5438; www.virgin-atlantic.com) flies daily to either Gatwick or Heathrow from Boston; Newark; New York's JFK; Los Angeles; San Francisco; Washington, D.C.'s Dulles; Miami; Orlando; and Las Vegas.

FROM CANADA   For travelers departing from Canada, **Air Canada** (© 888/

247-2262; www.aircanada.com) flies daily to London Heathrow nonstop from Vancouver, Montreal, and Toronto. There are also frequent direct flights from Calgary and Ottawa.

FROM AUSTRALIA   Qantas (© 612/13-13-13; www.qantas.com) flies from both Sydney and Melbourne daily. **British Airways** (© 1300-767-177; www.britishairways.com) has five to seven flights weekly from Sydney and Melbourne. Both airlines have a stop in Singapore.

FROM SOUTH AFRICA South African Airways (© 011/978-5313; www.flysaa.com) schedules two daily flights from Johannesburg and two daily flights from Cape Town. From Johannesburg, both **British Airways** (© 011/441-8600; www.britishairways.com) and **Virgin Atlantic Airways** (© 011/340-3400; www.virgin-atlantic.com) have daily flights to Heathrow. British Airways flies five times weekly from Cape Town.

FLYING FOR LESS: TIPS FOR GETTING THE BEST AIRFARE

- Passengers who can book their ticket either **long in advance or at the last minute,** or who **fly midweek** or **at less-trafficked hours** may pay a fraction of the full fare. If your schedule is flexible, say so, and ask if you can secure a cheaper fare by changing your flight plans.

- Search **the Internet** for cheap fares. The most popular online travel agencies are **Travelocity.com** (www.travelocity.co.uk), **Expedia.com** (www.expedia.co.uk and www.expedia.ca), and **Orbitz.com.** In the U.K., go to **Travelsupermarket** (© 0845/345-5708; www.travelsupermarket.com), a flight search engine that offers flight comparisons for the budget airlines whose seats often end up in bucket-shop sales. Other websites for booking airline tickets online include

Cheapflights.com, SmarterTravel. com, Priceline.com, and **Opodo** (www.opodo.co.uk). Meta search sites (which find and then direct you to airline and hotel websites for booking) include **Sidestep.com** and **Kayak.com**—the latter includes fares for budget carriers like jetBlue and Spirit as well as the major airlines. **Site59.com** is a great source for last-minute flights and getaways. In addition, most **airlines** offer online-only fares that even their phone agents know nothing about. British travelers should check **Flights International** (☎ **0800/018-7050;** www.flights-international.com) for deals on flights all over the world.

- Keep an eye on local newspapers for **promotional specials** or **fare wars,** when airlines lower prices on their most popular routes.
- **Consolidators,** also known as bucket shops, are wholesale brokers in the airline-ticket game. Consolidators buy deeply discounted tickets ("distressed" inventories of unsold seats) from airlines and sell them to online ticket agencies, travel agents, tour operators, corporations, and, to a lesser degree, the general public. Consolidators advertise in Sunday newspaper travel sections (often in small ads with tiny type), both in the U.S. and the U.K. They can be great sources for cheap international tickets. On the down side, bucket-shop tickets are often rigged with restrictions, such as stiff cancellation penalties (as high as 50%–75% of the ticket price). And keep in mind that most of what you see advertised is of limited availability. Several reliable consolidators are worldwide and available online. **STA Travel** (www.statravel.com) has been the world's leading consolidator for students

since purchasing Council Travel, but its fares are competitive for travelers of all ages. **Flights.com** (☎ **800/ TRAV-800;** www.flights.com) has excellent fares worldwide, particularly to Europe. It also has "local" websites in 12 countries. **FlyCheap** (☎ **800/ FLY-CHEAP;** www.1800flycheap. com) has especially good fares to sunny destinations. **Air Tickets Direct** (☎ **800/778-3447;** www.air ticketsdirect.com) is based in Montreal and leverages the currently weak Canadian dollar for low fares; it also books trips to places that U.S. travel agents won't touch, such as Cuba.

- Join **frequent-flier clubs.** Frequent-flier membership doesn't cost a cent, but it does entitle you to free tickets or upgrades when you amass the airline's required number of frequent-flier points. You don't even have to fly to earn points; **frequent-flier credit cards** can earn you thousands of miles for doing your everyday shopping. But keep in mind that award seats are limited, seats on popular routes are hard to snag, and more and more major airlines are cutting their expiration periods for mileage points—so check your airline's frequent-flier program so you don't lose your miles before you use them. *Inside tip:* Award seats are offered almost a year in advance, but seats also open up at the last minute, so if your travel plans are flexible, you may strike gold. To play the frequent-flier game to your best advantage, consult the community bulletin boards on **FlyerTalk (www.flyertalk.com)** or go to Randy Petersen's **Inside Flyer (www.insideflyer.com)**. Petersen and friends review all the programs in detail and post regular updates on changes in policies and trends.

Tips **Getting through the Airport**

- Arrive at the airport at least 1 hour before a domestic flight and 2 hours before an international flight. You can check the average wait times at your airport by going to the TSA **Security Checkpoint Wait Times** site (waittime/tsa.dhs.gov).
- Know what you can carry on and what you can't. For the latest updates on items you are prohibited to bring in carry-on luggage, go to **www. tsa.gov/travelers/airtravel**.
- Beat the ticket-counter lines by using the self-service electronic ticket kiosks at the airport or even printing out your boarding pass at home from the airline website. Using curbside check-in is also a smart way to avoid lines.
- Help speed up security before you're screened. Remove jackets, shoes, belt buckles, heavy jewelry, and watches and place them either in your carry-on luggage or the security bins provided. Place keys, coins, cellphones, and pagers in a security bin. If you have metallic body parts, carry a note from your doctor. When possible, keep packing liquids in checked baggage.
- Use a TSA-approved lock for your checked luggage. Look for Travel Sentry certified locks at luggage or travel shops and Brookstone stores (or online at www.brookstone.com).

GETTING INTO TOWN FROM THE AIRPORT

LONDON HEATHROW AIRPORT Located west of London in Hounslow ((C) 087/0000-0123 for flight information; www.heathrowairport.co.uk), Heathrow is one of the world's busiest airports. It has four terminals, each relatively self-contained. Terminal 4 handles the long-haul and transatlantic operations of British Airways. Most transatlantic flights on U.S.-based airlines arrive at Terminal 3. Terminals 1 and 2 receive the intra-European flights of several European airlines.

It takes 35 to 40 minutes by the Underground (Tube) and costs £3.50 ($6.65) to make the 24km (15-mile) trip from Heathrow to the center of London. A taxi is likely to cost from £46 to £50 ($87–$95). For more information about Tube or bus connections, call (C) 020/7222-1234.

The British Airport Authority now operates **Heathrow Express** ((C) 084/5600-1515;** www.heathrowexpress.com),

a 100mph train service running every 15 minutes daily from 5:10am until 11:40pm between Heathrow and Paddington Station in the center of London. Trips cost £7 ($13) each way. Children under 15 go for free (when accompanied by an adult). The trip takes 15 minutes each way between Paddington and Terminals 1, 2, and 3, and 23 minutes from Terminal 4. The trains have special areas for wheelchairs. From Paddington, passengers can connect to other trains and the Underground, or they can hail a taxi. You can buy tickets on the train or at self-service machines at Heathrow Airport (they're also available from travel agents).

GATWICK AIRPORT While Heathrow still dominates, more and more scheduled flights land at relatively remote **Gatwick** ((C) 087/0000-2468;** www.gatwickairport.com for flight information). It's located some 40km (25 miles) south of London in West Sussex, but it's only a 30-minute train ride away. From

Gatwick, the fastest way into London is via the **Gatwick Express trains** (© **084/ 5850-1530;** www.gatwickexpress.co.uk), which leave for Victoria Station in London every 30 minutes during the day and every hour at night. The one-way charge is £15 ($29) Express Class for adults, £23 ($44) for First Class, half-price for children 5 to 15, and free for children under 5. There are also Airbus **buses** from Gatwick to Victoria Coach Station (which is adjacent to Victoria Rail Station) operated by **National Express** (© **087/ 0580-8080;** www.nationalexpress.com), approximately every hour from 4:15am to 9:15pm; the round-trip fare is £13 ($25) per person, and the trip takes approximately 1½ hours. A **taxi** from Gatwick to central London usually costs £77 to £97 ($146–$184). However, you must negotiate a fare with the driver before you enter the cab; the meter doesn't apply because Gatwick lies outside the Metropolitan Police District. For further transportation information, call © **0800/ 747-737.**

LONDON STANSTED AIRPORT Located in Essex, some 80km (50 miles) northeast of London's West End, **Stansted** (© **087/0000-0303;** www. stanstedairport.com) mostly handles flights to and from the European continent. From Stansted, your best bet to central London is the **Stansted Express train** (© **084/5600-7245;** www.stansted express.com) to Liverpool Street Station, which runs every 15 minutes from 8am to 4:30pm, and every 30 minutes in the early mornings, evening weekdays, and weekends. It costs £16 ($30) for a standard ticket and £25 ($48) for first class, and takes 45 minutes.

LONDON CITY AIRPORT Located just 5km (3 miles) east of the bustling business community of Canary Wharf and 9.5km (6 miles) east of the City, **London City Airport** (© **020/7646-0088;** www.londoncityairport.com) is served by 14 airlines (Air Wales, British Airways, Cirrus Airlines, CityJet, Fly Be, Jet Magic, KLM, Lufthansa, Luxair, OLT, Scot Airways, Swiss International Airlines, and VLM) that fly from 18 cities in western Europe and Scandinavia. The nearest Underground station is Canning Town on the Jubilee line where you can connect directly to the London Airport by the Docklands Light Railway (trip time: 10 min.).

A shuttle bus can take you to Canary Wharf, where trains from the Dockland Line Railway make frequent 10-minute runs to the heart of London's financial district, known as "the City." Here, passengers can catch the Underground from the Bank Tube stop.

In addition, London Transport bus no. 473 goes from the City Airport to East London, where you can board any Underground at the Plaistow Tube stop.

LONG-HAUL FLIGHTS: HOW TO STAY COMFORTABLE

- Your choice of airline and airplane will definitely affect your leg room. Find more details about U.S. airlines at **www.seatguru.com**. For international airlines, the research firm Skytrax has

---

Tips Don't Stow It—Ship It

Though pricey, it's sometimes worthwhile to travel luggage-free, particularly if you're toting sports equipment, meetings materials, or baby equipment. Specialists in door-to-door luggage delivery include **Virtual Bellhop** (www.virtualbellhop. com), **SkyCap International** (www.skycapinternational.com), **Luggage Express** (www.usxpluggageexpress.com), and **Sports Express** (www.sportsexpress.com).

Tips **Getting from One London Airport to the Other**

Some visitors will need to transfer from one airport to the other. One bus company offers these transfers. **National Express** (© 020/8593-771 or 0870/574-7777; www.nationalexpress.com) buses leave from both terminals at Gatwick and Terminals 1, 3, and 4 at Heathrow. Trip time is about an hour, with a one-way fare costing £19 ($36).

---

posted a list of average seat pitches at **www.airlinequality.com**.

- Emergency exit seats and bulkhead seats typically have the most legroom. Emergency exit seats are usually left unassigned until the day of a flight (to ensure that someone able-bodied fills the seats); it's worth getting to the ticket counter early to snag one of these spots for a long flight. Many passengers find that bulkhead seating (the row facing the wall at the front of the cabin) offers more legroom, but keep in mind that bulkhead seats have no storage space on the floor in front of you.

- To have two seats for yourself in a three-seat row, try for an aisle seat in a center section toward the back of coach. If you're traveling with a companion, book an aisle and a window seat. Middle seats are usually booked last, so chances are good you'll end up with three seats to yourselves. And in the event that a third passenger is assigned the middle seat, he or she will probably be more than happy to trade for a window or an aisle.

- Ask about entertainment options. Many airlines offer seatback video systems where you get to choose your movies or play video games—but only on some of their planes. (Boeing 777s are your best bet.)

- To sleep, avoid the last row of any section or the row in front of an emergency exit, as these seats are the least likely to recline. Avoid seats near

highly trafficked toilet areas. Avoid seats in the back of many jets—these can be narrower than those in the rest of coach. Or reserve a window seat so you can rest your head and avoid being bumped in the aisle.

- Get up, walk around, and stretch every 60 to 90 minutes to keep your blood flowing. This helps avoid **deep vein thrombosis,** or "economy-class syndrome." See the box "Avoiding 'Economy-Class Syndrome,'" p. 40.

- Drink water before, during, and after your flight to combat the lack of humidity in airplane cabins. Avoid alcohol, which will dehydrate you.

- If you're flying with kids, don't forget to carry on toys, books, pacifiers, and snacks and chewing gum to help them relieve ear pressure buildup during ascent and descent.

BY CAR

If you plan to take a rented car across or under the Channel, check with the rental company about license and insurance requirements before you leave.

FERRIES FROM THE CONTINENT

There are many "drive-on, drive-off" car-ferry services across the Channel. The most popular ports in France for Channel crossings are Boulogne and Calais, where you can board Stena ferries taking you to the English ports of Dover and Folkestone. For details, see "Car & Passenger Ferries," under "By Boat," below.

EUROTUNNEL

The Chunnel accommodates not only trains, but also passenger cars, charter buses, taxis, and motorcycles. Eurotunnel, a nearly 1km-long (½-mile) train carrying motor vehicles under the English Channel (© **08705/353535;** www.eurotunnel. com), connects Calais, France, with Folkestone, England, and vice versa. It operates 24 hours a day, 365 days a year, running every 15 minutes during peak travel times and at least once an hour at night.

With Eurotunnel, gone are weather-related delays, seasickness, and a need for reservations. Before boarding Eurotunnel, you stop at a tollbooth to pay and then pass through Immigration for both countries at one time. During the ride, you travel in bright, air-conditioned carriages, remaining inside your car or stepping outside to stretch your legs. An hour later, when you reach England, you drive off toward London. The cost of Eurotunnel varies according to the season and the day of the week. Count on at least £150 ($285) per car for a round-trip ticket. **Note:** Thanks to severe traffic congestion, expensive fees for bringing a car into much of the heart of the city, and high-priced parking, we don't recommend driving into London. Stores selling duty-free goods, restaurants, and service stations are available to travelers on both sides of the Channel. A bilingual staff is on hand to assist travelers at both the British and French terminals.

BY TRAIN
VIA THE CHUNNEL FROM THE CONTINENT

Since 1994, when the Channel Tunnel opened, the **Eurostar Express** train has been operating twice-daily passenger service between London and both Paris and Brussels. The $15-billion tunnel, one of the great engineering feats of all time, is the first link between Britain and the Continent since the Ice Age.

Rail Europe (© **888/382-7245;** www. raileurope.com) sells tickets on the *Eurostar* for direct train service between Paris or Brussels and London. A one-way fare between Paris and London, for example, costs £95 to £208 ($181–$395) for

---

⌒Tips Coping with Jet Lag

Jet lag is a pitfall of traveling across time zones. If you're flying north–south and you feel sluggish when you touch down, your symptoms will be the result of dehydration and the general stress of air travel. When you travel east–west or vice versa, however, your body becomes thoroughly confused about what time it is, and everything from your digestive system to your brain is knocked for a loop. Traveling east, say from Chicago to Paris, is more difficult on your internal clock than traveling west, say from London to Atlanta, because most peoples' bodies are more inclined to stay up late than fall asleep early.

Here are some tips for combating jet lag:

- **Reset your watch** to your destination time before you board the plane.
- **Drink lots of water** before, during, and after your flight. Avoid alcohol.
- **Exercise and sleep well** for a few days before your trip.
- If you have trouble sleeping on planes, **fly eastward on morning flights.**
- **Daylight** is the key to resetting your body clock. At the website for **Outside In** (www.bodyclock.com), you can get a customized plan of when to seek and avoid light.

first class, or £50 to £140 ($95–$266) for second class. In London, make reservations for *Eurostar* at © **087/0518-6186,** or 800/EUROSTAR in the U.S. and Canada (www.eurostar.com). *Eurostar* trains arrive and depart from London's Waterloo Station, Paris's Gare du Nord, and Brussels's Central Station.

BRITRAIL TRAVEL PASSES

If you're traveling beyond London anywhere in the United Kingdom, consider purchasing a **BritRail Consecutive Pass.** These passes allow you to travel for a consecutive number of days for a flat rate. In first class, adults pay $349 for 4 days, $499 for 8 days, $748 for 15 days, $950 for 22 days, and $1,124 for 1 month. In second class, fares are $232 for 4 days, $332 for 8 days, $499 for 15 days, $631 for 22 days, and $748 for 1 month. Seniors (60 and over) qualify for discounts in first class travel and pay $296 for 4 days, $425 for 8 days, $636 for 15 days, $808 for 22 days, and $956 for 1 month of first-class travel. Passengers under 26 qualify for a **Youth Pass:** $185 for 4 days, $265 for 8 days, $400 for 15 days, $505 for 22 days, and $599 for 1 month. One child (under age 15) can travel free with each adult or senior pass by requesting the **BritRail Family Pass** when buying the adult pass. Additional children pay half the regular adult fare.

A more versatile pass is the **BritRail FlexiPass,** which allows you to travel whenever you want during a 2-month period of time. In first class, it costs $436 for 4 days, $638 for 8 days, and $960 for 15 days of travel. Second class costs $293 for 4 days, $425 for 8 days, and $644 for 15 days of travel.

BritRail Passes allow unlimited travel in England, Scotland, and Wales on any British Rail scheduled train over the whole of the network during the validity of the pass without restrictions.

A pass for travel in *England only,* the **BritRail England Consecutive Pass** is sold at a price 20% lower than regular BritRail Passes (which cover rail travel throughout the U.K.). Starting at $185 for 4 consecutive days of travel in standard class, the BritRail England Pass is also offered for 8, 15, or 22 consecutive days or 1 month or as a FlexiPass (days may be consecutive or nonconsecutive) for 4, 8, or 15 days within a 2-month period. It is also available in first class, starting at $279 and at discounted prices for seniors (60 and over) in first class and youth (under 26) in standard class. As with other BritRail Passes, one child under 15 may travel free when accompanied by an adult or senior purchasing a BritRail England Pass and requesting the Family Pass.

To call ACP International in the United States, dial © **866/BRITRAIL** or 877/477-1066. You can purchase tickets and passes on the Web at **www.britrail. com**. For hotels, trip planning, promotions, and vacation packages through BritRail, visit www.britainsecrets.com.

The **BritRail London Plus Pass** is best suited for visitors wishing to make day trips in Southern England to Oxford, Cambridge, Brighton, Canterbury, or Salisbury. For 2 days within an 8-day period adults pay $113, first class, $74 second class; 4 days in an 8-day period $187 first class, $140 second class; and 7 days within a 15-day period $249 first class, $187 second class. One child (under age 15) can travel free with each adult or senior pass by requesting the **BritRail Family Pass** when buying the adult pass. Additional children pay half the regular adult fare.

BY BUS

National Express (www.nationalexpress. com) offers several passes for the explorer who'd like to hop around Britain. These include *Hobo,* costing £79 ($150) for 7 days of bus travel. Sample itineraries are suggested but you can also plot your own—that's how flexible this pass is. There's no need to book. *Footloose* at £139 ($264) grants 2 weeks of bus travel from a choice of 1,000 destinations throughout the U.K. Finally, *Rolling Stone* at £219 ($416) lets you travel by bus coach in the U.K. for 28 days. You plan your own trip using the journey planner offered by National Express.

To the delight of the frugal traveler, a new no-frills bus service has been introduced in England. **Megabus.com** (✆ **0901/332-0031;** 10p (19¢) per minute) charges the lowest bus fares in the country—only £5 ($9.50) for a single journey on any route. From London, popular stops include Oxford, Brighton, and the old port of Plymouth. The network uses double-decker buses that once rolled through the streets of Hong Kong. Reserve at **www.megabus.com**, which levies a booking charge of less than $1.

Bus connections to Britain from the Continent, using the Eurotunnel (Chunnel) or ferry services, are generally not very comfortable, although some lines are more convenient than others. One line with a relatively good reputation is **Eurolines,** 52 Grosvenor Gardens, SW1W OAU (✆ **08705/143219;** www.eurolines. co.uk). They book passage on buses traveling two times a day between London and Paris (9 hr.); three times a day from Amsterdam (12 hr.); three times a week from Munich (24 hr.); and three times a week from Stockholm (44 hr.). On longer routes, which use alternating drivers, the bus proceeds almost without interruption, taking only occasional breaks for meals.

BY BOAT
CROSSING THE ATLANTIC
The **Cunard Line,** 6100 Blue Lagoon Dr., Suite 400, Miami, FL 33126 (✆ **800/ 7-CUNARD;** www.cunardline.com),

boasts that its newly launched flagship, *Queen Mary 2,* is the only five-star-plus luxury ocean liner providing regular transatlantic service—some 15 voyages a year between April and December. *QM2* is the largest, longest, tallest, grandest ocean liner ever; she set sail from Southampton on her maiden voyage on January 12, 2004. Carrying 2,620 passengers, the ship cost a staggering $800 million to build. Athletes find not just a good gym but also a virtual playing field, and hedonists can enjoy a world-class spa. There's even a planetarium—it's a veritable city at sea. Many passengers appreciate the cruise's graceful introduction to British mores, as well as the absolute lack of jet lag. Fares vary, based on the season and the cabin grade. Many packages are offered, which include inexpensive airfare from your home city to the point of departure, plus a return flight to your home city from London on British Airways.

CAR & PASSENGER FERRIES
P&O Ferries (✆ **087/0598-0333;** www.poferries.com) operates car and passenger ferries between Dover (England) and Calais (France) only. Trip time is 75 minutes at a cost of £50 ($90) one-way for a car and driver, or £20 ($36) for a foot passenger round-trip. Once you arrive in Dover, you can pick up a BritRail train to London (see "By Train," above). Traveling from Portsmouth (England) to Cherbourg (France), **Brittany Ferries** (✆ **087/0366-5333;** www. brittany-ferries.co.uk), can take from 2 hours and 45 minutes up to 5 hours.

Norfolk Line (✆ **0870/642-114;** www.norfolkline-ferries.com) accepts motorists only—no foot passengers—on its ferry rides between Dover in England and Dunkerque in France. There are up to 24 sailings a day, costing from £19 ($36) one way, the price based on transporting a car and five passengers. Bookings are non-refundable.

It's always advisable to bring money in a variety of forms on a vacation: a mix of cash, credit cards, and traveler's checks. You should also exchange enough petty cash to cover airport incidentals, tipping, and transportation to your hotel before you leave home, or withdraw money upon arrival at an airport ATM.

In many international destinations, ATMs offer the best exchange rates. Avoid exchanging money at commercial exchange bureaus and hotels, which often have the highest transaction fees.

POUNDS & PENCE

Britain's decimal monetary system is based on the pound (£), which is made up of 100 pence (written as "p"). Pounds are also called "quid" by Britons. There are £1 and £2 coins, as well as coins of 50p, 20p, 10p, 5p, 2p, and 1p. Banknotes come in denominations of £5, £10, £20, and £50.

As a general guideline, the price conversions in this book have been computed at the rate of £1 = $1.90 (U.S.). Bear in mind, however, that exchange rates fluctuate daily.

THE BRITISH POUND VS. THE U.S. DOLLAR, THE EURO, AND THE CANADIAN DOLLAR

Conversion rates between the world's major currencies can and do fluctuate frequently, and their relative differences at the time of your visit could affect the costs of your trip. The chart below should be accepted only for approximate values of relatively small financial transactions. If you're planning on any major expenditures, check for updated ratios at the time of your trip. The chart below was compiled just before press time of this edition with the following ratios: 1 British pound was the equal of US$1.90, or of 1.50€, or of C$3.

Foreign Currencies & the U.S. Dollar

UK£	US$	Euro €	C$	UK£	US$	Euro €	C$
1.00	1.90	1.50	2.30	75.00	142.50	112.50	172.50
2.00	3.80	3.00	4.60	100.00	190.00	150.00	230.00
3.00	5.70	4.50	6.90	125.00	237.50	187.50	287.50
4.00	7.60	6.00	9.20	150.00	285.00	225.00	345.00
5.00	9.50	7.50	11.50	175.00	332.50	262.50	402.50
6.00	11.40	9.00	13.80	200.00	380.00	300.00	460.00
7.00	13.30	10.50	16.10	225.00	427.50	337.50	517.50
8.00	15.20	12.00	18.40	250.00	475.00	375.00	575.00
9.00	17.10	13.50	20.70	275.00	522.50	412.50	632.50
10.00	19.00	15.00	23.00	300.00	570.00	450.00	690.00
15.00	28.50	22.50	34.50	350.00	665.00	525.00	805.00
20.00	38.00	30.00	46.00	400.00	760.00	600.00	920.00
25.00	47.50	37.50	57.50	500.00	950.00	750.00	1,150.00
50.00	95.00	75.00	115.00	1,000.00	1,900.00	1,500.00	2,300.00

What Things Cost in London	UK£	US$	Euro €	C$
Taxi from Heathrow to Central London	40.00–70.00	76.00–133.00	60.00–105.00	92.00–161.00
Underground from Heathrow to Central London	4.00	7.60	6.00	9.20
Double room at The Dorchester (very expensive)	405.00	769.50	607.50	931.50
Double room at the Hallam Hotel (moderate)	100.00	190.00	150.00	230.00
Double room at the Boston Court (inexpensive)	69.00	131.10	103.50	158.70
Lunch for one at Lindsay House (expensive)	20.00	38.00	30.00	46.00
Lunch for one at Ye Olde Cheshire Cheese (inexpensive)	12.00	22.80	18.00	27.60
Dinner for one, without wine, at Bibendum, the Oyster Bar (expensive)	36.00	68.40	54.00	82.80
Dinner for one, without wine, at Porter's EnglishRestaurant (moderate)	22.00	41.80	33.00	50.60
Dinner for one, without wine, at Cork & Bottle Wine Bar (inexpensive)	16.00	36.10	24.00	36.80
Pint of beer	3.00	5.70	4.50	6.90
Coca-Cola (large)	2.00	3.80	3.00	4.60
Cup of coffee	1.65	3.15	2.50	3.80
Admission to British Museum	Free	Free	Free	Free
Movie ticket	7.50	14.25	11.25	17.25
Theater ticket	20.00–80.00	38.00–152.00	30.00–120.00	46.00–184.00

ATMs

The easiest and best way to get cash away from home is from an ATM (automated-teller machine), sometimes referred to as a "cash machine," or a "cashpoint." The **Cirrus** (© **800/424-7787;** www.mastercard.com) and **PLUS** (© **800/843-7587;** www.visa.com) networks span the globe. Go to your bank card's website to find ATM locations at your destination. Be sure you know your daily withdrawal limit before you depart. *Note:* Many banks impose a fee every time you use a card at another bank's ATM, and that fee can be higher for international transactions (up to $5 or more) than for domestic ones (where they're rarely more than $2). In addition, the bank from which you withdraw cash may charge its own fee. For international withdrawal fees, ask your bank.

Note: Banks that belong to the **Global ATM Alliance** charge no transaction fees for cash withdrawals at other Alliance member ATMs; these include Bank of America, Scotiabank (Canada, Caribbean, and Mexico), Barclays (U.K. and parts of Africa), and Deutsche Bank (Germany, Poland, Spain, and Italy), and BNP Paribus (France).

CREDIT CARDS

Credit cards are another safe way to carry money. They also provide a convenient record of all your expenses, and they generally offer relatively good exchange rates. You can withdraw cash advances from your credit cards at banks or ATMs, but high fees make credit-card cash advances a pricey way to get cash. Keep in mind that you'll pay interest from the moment of your withdrawal, even if you pay your monthly bills on time. Also, note that many banks now assess a 1% to 3% "transaction fee" on **all** charges you incur abroad (whether you're using the local currency or your native currency). The Discover Card is not yet widely accepted in London, but most other major credit cards are.

TRAVELER'S CHECKS

These days, traveler's checks are less necessary because most English cities and towns, especially London, have 24-hour ATMs, allowing you to withdraw small amounts of cash as needed. But if you prefer the security of the tried and true, you might want to stick with traveler's checks—provided you don't mind showing an ID every time you want to cash a check. *Note:* Exchange rates are more favorable at your destination. Nevertheless, it's often helpful to exchange at least some money before going abroad (standing in line at the exchange bureau in the London airport could make you miss the next bus leaving for downtown after a long flight).

You can buy traveler's checks at most banks. They are offered in denominations of $20, $50, $100, $500, and sometimes $1,000. Generally, you'll pay a service charge ranging from 1% to 4%.

The most popular traveler's checks are offered by **American Express** (*C* 800/807-6233 or, for cardholders, **800/221-7282**—this number accepts collect calls, offers service in several foreign languages, and exempts Amex gold and platinum cardholders from the 1% fee); **Visa** (*C* **800/732-1322**—AAA members can obtain Visa checks for a $9.95 fee [for checks up to $1,500] at most AAA offices or by calling *C* **866/339-3378**); and **MasterCard** (*C* **800/223-9920**).

Be sure to keep a record of the traveler's checks' serial numbers separate from your checks in the event that they are stolen or lost. You'll get a refund faster if you know the numbers.

American Express, Thomas Cook, Visa, and **MasterCard** offer **foreign currency traveler's checks,** useful if you're traveling to one country or to the Euro zone; they're accepted at locations where dollar checks may not be.

Another option is the new prepaid traveler's check cards, reloadable cards that work much like debit cards but aren't linked to your checking account. The **American Express Travelers Cheque Card,** for example, requires a minimum deposit, sets a maximum balance, and has

---

Tips **Emergency Cash—the Fastest Way**

If you need emergency cash over the weekend when all the banks and American Express offices are closed, you can have money wired to you from **Western Union** (*C* **800/325-6000;** www.westernunion.com). You must present a valid ID to pick up the cash at the Western Union office.

a one-time issuance fee of $14.95. You can withdraw money from an ATM (for a fee of $2.50 per transaction, not including bank fees), and the funds can be purchased in dollars, euros, or pounds. If you lose the card, your available funds will be refunded within 24 hours.

6 Travel Insurance

The cost of travel insurance varies widely, depending on the destination, the cost and length of your trip, your age and health, and the type of trip you're taking, but expect to pay between 5% and 8% of the vacation itself. You can get estimates from various providers through **InsureMy Trip.com**. Enter your trip cost and dates, your age, and other information, for prices from more than a dozen companies.

U.K. citizens and their families who make more than one trip abroad per year may find an annual travel insurance policy works out cheaper. Check **www.money supermarket.com**, which compares prices across a wide range of providers for single- and multitrip policies.

Most big travel agents offer their own insurance and will probably try to sell you their package when you book a holiday. Think before you sign. **Britain's Consumers' Association** recommends that you insist on seeing the policy and reading the fine print before buying travel insurance. **The Association of British Insurers** (© 020/7600-3333; www.abi. org.uk) gives advice by phone and publishes *Holiday Insurance,* a free guide to policy provisions and prices. You might also shop around for better deals: Try **Columbus Direct** (© 0870/033-9988; www.columbusdirect.net).

TRIP-CANCELLATION INSURANCE

Trip-cancellation insurance will help retrieve your money if you have to back out of a trip or depart early, or if your travel supplier goes bankrupt. Trip cancellation traditionally covers such events as sickness, natural disasters, and State Department advisories. The latest news in trip-cancellation insurance is the availability of **expanded hurricane coverage** and the **"any-reason"** cancellation coverage—which costs more but covers cancellations made for any reason. You won't get back 100% of your prepaid trip cost, but you'll be refunded a substantial portion. **TravelSafe** (© **888/885-7233;** www. travelsafe.com) offers both types of coverage. Expedia also offers any-reason cancellation coverage for its air-hotel packages.

For details, contact one of the following recommended insurers: **Access America** (© 866/807-3982; www.accessamerica. com); **Travel Guard International** (© 800/826-4919; www.travelguard.com); **Travel Insured International** (© 800/ 243-3174; www.travelinsured.com); and **Travelex Insurance Services** (© 888/ 457-4602; www.travelex-insurance.com).

MEDICAL INSURANCE

For travel overseas, most U.S. health plans (including Medicare and Medicaid) do not provide coverage, and the ones that do often require you to pay for services upfront and reimburse you only after you return home.

As a safety net, you may want to buy travel medical insurance, particularly if you're traveling to a remote or high-risk area where emergency evacuation might be necessary. If you require additional medical insurance, try **MEDEX Assistance** (© 410/453-6300; www.medexassist.com) or **Travel Assistance International** (© **800/821-2828;** www.travelassistance. com; for general information on services, call the company's **Worldwide Assistance Services, Inc.,** at © 800/777-8710).

Canadians should check with their provincial health plan offices or call **Health Canada** (℗ **866/225-0709;** www.hc-sc.gc.ca) to find out the extent of their coverage and what documentation and receipts they must take home in case they are treated overseas.

LOST-LUGGAGE INSURANCE

On international flights (including U.S. portions of international trips), baggage coverage is limited to approximately $9.07 per pound, up to approximately $635 per checked bag. If you plan to check items more valuable than what's covered by the standard liability, see if your homeowner's policy covers your valuables, get baggage insurance as part of your comprehensive travel-insurance package, or buy Travel Guard's "BagTrak" product.

If your luggage is lost, immediately file a lost-luggage claim at the airport, detailing the luggage contents. Most airlines require that you report delayed, damaged, or lost baggage within 4 hours of arrival. The airlines are required to deliver luggage, once found, directly to your house or destination free of charge.

7 Health

STAYING HEALTHY

You'll encounter few health risks while traveling in England. The tap water is safe to drink, the milk is pasteurized, and health services are good. The mad cow disease crisis appears to be over, as does the epidemic of foot-and-mouth disease. Traveling to London doesn't pose any health risk.

WHAT TO DO IF YOU GET SICK AWAY FROM HOME

If you need an ambulance while in London, call ℗ **999.** If you need a doctor, your hotel can recommend one, or you can contact your embassy or consulate. Outside London, dial ℗ **100** and ask the operator for the local police, who will give you the name, address, and telephone number of a doctor in your area. Also see "Fast Facts: London," in chapter 5, p. 79.

In general, you may have to pay all medical costs upfront and be reimbursed later. Medicare and Medicaid do not provide coverage for medical costs outside the U.S. Find out what medical services your health insurance covers before leaving home. To protect yourself, consider buying

---

Avoiding "Economy-Class Syndrome"

Deep vein thrombosis, or as it's known in the world of flying, "economy-class syndrome," is a blood clot that develops in a deep vein. It's a potentially deadly condition that can be caused by sitting in cramped conditions—such as an airplane cabin—for too long. During a flight (especially a long-haul flight), get up, walk around, and stretch your legs every 60 to 90 minutes to keep your blood flowing. Other preventative measures include frequent flexing of the legs while sitting, drinking lots of water, and avoiding alcohol and sleeping pills. If you have a history of deep vein thrombosis, heart disease, or another condition that puts you at high risk, some experts recommend wearing compression stockings or taking anticoagulants when you fly; always ask your physician about the best course for you. Symptoms of deep vein thrombosis include leg pain or swelling, or even shortness of breath.

Healthy Travels to You

The following government websites offer up-to-date health-related travel advice.
- **Australia:** www.dfat.gov.au/travel
- **Canada:** www.hc-sc.gc.ca/index_e.html
- **U.K.:** www.dh.gov.uk/PolicyAndGuidance/HealthAdviceForTravellers
- **U.S.:** www.cdc.gov/travel

medical travel insurance (see "Medical Insurance," under "Travel Insurance," above). *Note:* U.S. visitors who become ill while they're in England are eligible only for free *emergency* care. For other treatment, including follow-up care, you'll be asked to pay.

If you suffer from a chronic illness, consult your doctor before your departure. For conditions like epilepsy, diabetes, or heart problems, wear a **MedicAlert Identification Tag** (© **888/ 633-4298;** www.medicalert.org), which will immediately alert doctors to your condition and give them access to your records through MedicAlert's 24-hour hot line.

Contact the **International Association for Medical Assistance to Travellers (IAMAT;** © 716/754-4883; www.iamat.org) for tips on travel and health concerns in London or England. In Canada, call © **416/652-0137.** The United States **Centers for Disease Control and Prevention** (© **800/394-1945;** www.cdc.gov) provides up-to-date information on necessary vaccines and health hazards by region or country and offers tips on food safety. The website **www. tripprep.com**, sponsored by a consortium of travel medicine practitioners, may also offer helpful advice on traveling abroad. You can find listings of reliable clinics overseas at the **International Society of Travel Medicine** (www.istm.org).

Very few health insurance plans pay for medical evacuation back to the U.S. (which can cost $10,000 and up). A number of companies offer medical evacuation services anywhere in the world. If you're ever hospitalized more than 242km (150 miles) from home, **MedjetAssist** (© **800/ 527-7478;** www.medjetassistance.com) will pick you up and fly you to the hospital of your choice virtually anywhere in the world in a medically equipped and staffed aircraft 24 hours day, 7 days a week. Annual memberships are $225 individual, $350 family; you can also purchase short-term memberships.

U.K. nationals will need a **European Health Insurance Card (EHIC)** to receive free or reduced-cost health benefits during a visit to an European Economic Area (EEA) country (European Union countries plus Iceland, Liechtenstein, and Norway) or Switzerland. The European Health Insurance Card replaces the E111 form, which is no longer valid. For advice, ask at your local post office or see **www.dh.gov.uk/travellers**.

We list **hospitals** and **emergency numbers** in chapter 5 under "Fast Facts," p. 79.

If you suffer from a chronic illness, consult your doctor before your departure. Pack **prescription medications** in your carry-on luggage, and carry them in their original containers, with pharmacy labels—otherwise they won't make it through airport security. Carry the generic name of prescription medicines, in case a local pharmacist is unfamiliar with the brand name.

8 Safety

STAYING SAFE

Like all big cities, London has its share of crime, but in general, it is one of the safer destinations in Europe. Pickpockets are the major concern. Violent crime is relatively rare, especially in the heart of London, which hasn't seen a Jack the Ripper in a long time. Even so, it is not wise to go walking in parks after dark. King's Cross at night can also be a dangerous area, frequented by prostitutes and their clients. In London, take all the precautions a prudent traveler would in going to any city, be it Los Angeles, Paris, or New York. Conceal your wallet or hold on to your purse, and don't flaunt your wealth by displaying jewelry or cash. In these uncertain times, it is always prudent to check the U.S. State Department's travel advisories at **http://travel.state.gov**.

9 Specialized Travel Resources

TRAVELERS WITH DISABILITIES

Most disabilities shouldn't stop anyone from traveling. There are more options and resources out there than ever before. Many London hotels, museums, restaurants, and sightseeing attractions have wheelchair ramps. Persons with disabilities are often granted special discounts at attractions and, in some cases, nightclubs. These discounts are called "concessions" in Britain. It always pays to ask. Free information and advice are available from **Holiday Care Service,** The Hawkins Suite, Enham Place, Andover SP11 6JS (**℡ 0845/124-9971;** fax 0845/124-9972; www.holidaycare.org).

Bookstores in London often carry *Access in London,* a publication listing hotels, restaurants, sights, shops, and more for persons with disabilities. It costs £12 ($23).

The transport system, cinemas, and theaters are still extremely hard for the disabled to negotiate, but **Transport for London** does publish a leaflet called *Access to the Underground,* which gives details on elevators and ramps at individual Underground stations; call **℡ 020/7222-5600** or visit www.tfl.gov.uk. And the **London black cab** (**℡ 0845/108-3000;** www. londonblackcab.com), is perfectly suited for those in wheelchairs; the roomy interiors have plenty of room for maneuvering.

London's most visible organization for information about access to theaters, cinemas, galleries, museums, and restaurants is **Artsline,** 54 Chalton St., London NW1 1HS (**℡ 020/7388-2227;** fax 020/7383-2653; www.artsline.org.uk). It offers free information about wheelchair access in general, easily wheelchair-accessible tourist attractions and cinemas, theaters with hearing aids, and sign language–interpreted tours and theater productions. Artsline will mail information to North America, but it's more helpful to contact them once you arrive in London; the line is staffed Monday to Friday 9:30am to 5:30pm.

Organizations that offer a vast range of resources and assistance to disabled travelers include **MossRehab** (**℡ 800/CALL-MOSS;** www.mossresourcenet.org); the **American Foundation for the Blind** (**AFB; ℡ 800/232-5463;** www.afb.org); and **SATH (Society for Accessible Travel & Hospitality; ℡ 212/447-7284;** www.sath.org). **AirAmbulanceCard.com** is now partnered with SATH and allows you to preselect top-notch hospitals in case of an emergency.

Access-Able Travel Source (**℡ 303/232-2979;** www.access-able.com) offers a comprehensive database on travel agents from around the world with experience in accessible travel, destination-specific access information, and links to such resources as service animals, equipment rentals, and access guides.

Many travel agencies offer customized tours and itineraries for travelers with disabilities. Among them are **Flying Wheels Travel** (© 507/451-5005; www.flying wheelstravel.com); and **Accessible Journeys** (© 800/846-4537 or 610/521-0339; www.disabilitytravel.com).

Flying with Disability (www.flying-with-disability.org) is a comprehensive information source on airplane travel. **Avis Rent a Car** (© 888/879-4273) has an "Avis Access" program that offers services for customers with special travel needs. These include specially outfitted vehicles with swivel seats, spinner knobs, and hand controls; mobility scooter rentals; and accessible bus service. Be sure to reserve well in advance.

Also check out the quarterly magazine *Emerging Horizons* (www.emerging horizons.com), available by subscription ($16.95 a year U.S.; $21.95 outside U.S).

The "Accessible Travel" link at **Mobility-Advisor.com** (www.mobility-advisor.com) offers a variety of travel resources to disabled persons.

British travelers should contact **Holiday Care** (© 0845/124-9971 in U.K. only; www.holidaycare.org.uk) to access a wide range of travel information and resources for disabled and elderly people.

GAY & LESBIAN TRAVELERS

London has one of the most active gay and lesbian scenes in the world; we've recommended a number of the city's best gay clubs, lounges, and bars in chapter 10, "London After Dark."

One of the best places for information on what's hot in London's gay and lesbian scene is **Gay's the Word,** 66 Marchmont St., WC1 N1AB (© 020/7278-7654; www.gaystheword.co.uk; Tube: Russell Sq.), London's best gay-oriented bookstore and the largest such store in Britain. The staff is friendly and helpful and will offer advice about the ever-changing gay scene in London. It's open Monday through Saturday from 10am to 6:30pm and Sunday from 2 to 6pm. At Gay's the Word, as well as at other gay-friendly venues, you can find a number of gay publications, many free, including the popular *Boyz* and *Pink Paper* (this one has a good section aimed at lesbian readers). Also check out *9X,* filled with data about all the new clubs and whatever else is hot on the scene.

The International Gay and Lesbian Travel Association (IGLTA; © 800/448-8550 or 954/776-2626; www.iglta.org) is the trade association for the gay and lesbian travel industry, and offers an online directory of gay- and lesbian-friendly travel businesses and tour operators.

Many agencies offer tours and travel itineraries specifically for gay and lesbian travelers. **Above and Beyond Tours** (© 800/397-2681; www.abovebeyond tours.com) are gay Australia tour specialists. San Francisco–based **Now, Voyager** (© 800/255-6951; www.nowvoyager.com) offers worldwide trips and cruises. And **Olivia** (© 800/631-6277; www.olivia.com) offers lesbian cruises and resort vacations.

Gay.com Travel (© 800/929-2268 or 415/644-8044; www.gay.com/travel or www.outandabout.com), is an excellent online successor to the popular *Out & About* print magazine. It provides regularly updated information about gay-owned, gay-oriented, and gay-friendly lodging, dining, sightseeing, nightlife, and shopping establishments in every important destination worldwide. British travelers should click on the "Travel" link at **www.uk.gay.com** for advice and gay-friendly trip ideas.

The Canadian website **GayTraveler** (gaytraveler.ca) offers ideas and advice for gay travel all over the world.

The following travel guides are available at many bookstores, or you can order them from any online bookseller: *Spartacus International Gay Guide, 35th Edition* (Bruno Gmünder Verlag; www.spartacusworld.com/gayguide) and *Odysseus: The International Gay Travel Planner, 17th Edition* (www.odyusa.com); and the *Damron* guides (www.damron.com), with separate, annual books for gay men and lesbians.

SENIOR TRAVEL

Many discounts are available to seniors in London. Be advised that in England you sometimes have to be a member of a British seniors association to get discounts. Public-transportation reductions, for example, are available only to holders of British Pension books. However, many attractions do offer discounts for seniors (Britain defines seniors as women 60 or over, and men 65 or over). Even if discounts aren't posted, ask if they're available.

If you're over 60, you're eligible for special 10% discounts on **British Airways** through its Privileged Traveler program. You also qualify for reduced restrictions on Advanced Purchases airline ticket cancellations. Discounts are also granted for British Airways' tours and for intra-Britain air tickets booked in North America. **British Rail** offers seniors discounted rates on first-class rail passes around Britain. See "By Train," under "Getting There," earlier in this chapter.

Don't be shy about asking for discounts, but carry some kind of identification that shows your date of birth. Also, mention that you're a senior when you make your hotel reservations. Many hotels offer seniors discounts.

Members of **AARP** (formerly known as the American Association of Retired Persons), 601 E St. NW, Washington, DC 20049 (℃ **888/687-2277;** www.aarp.org), get global discounts on hotels, airfares, and car rentals. AARP offers members a wide range of benefits, including *AARP: The Magazine* and a monthly newsletter. Anyone over 50 can join.

Many reliable agencies and organizations target the 50-plus market. **Elderhostel** (℃ **800/454-5768;** www.elderhostel.org) arranges study programs for those aged 55 and over (and a spouse or companion of any age) in the U.S. and in more than 80 countries around the world. Most courses last 5 to 7 days in the U.S. (2–4 weeks abroad), and many include airfare, accommodations in university dormitories or modest inns, meals, and tuition.

Recommended publications offering travel resources and discounts for seniors include the quarterly magazine *Travel 50 & Beyond* (www.travel50andbeyond.com); *Travel Unlimited: Uncommon Adventures for the Mature Traveler* (Avalon); *101 Tips for Mature Travelers,* available from Grand Circle Travel (℃ **800/959-0405;** www.gct.com); and *Unbelievably Good Deals and Great Adventures That You Absolutely Can't Get Unless You're Over 50* (McGraw-Hill), by Joann Rattner Heilman.

FAMILY TRAVEL

For the best places to stay and eat, see "Family-Friendly Hotels," p. 100, and "Family-Friendly Restaurants," p. 156. For details on sightseeing, check out the section called "Especially for Kids" on p. 265. To locate accommodations, restaurants, and attractions that are particularly kid-friendly, refer to the "Kids" icon throughout this guide.

On airlines, you must request a special menu for children at least 24 hours in advance. Bring your own baby food; you can ask a flight attendant to warm it.

Arrange ahead of time with your hotel for such necessities as a crib, bottle warmer, and car seat (in England, small children aren't allowed to ride in the front seat). You can also rent baby equipment from **Chelsea Baby Hire,** 31 Osborne House, SW19 6PW (© 020/8789-9673; www.chelseababyhire.com). The **London black cab** (© 0845/108-3000; www.londonblackcab.com) is a lifesaver for families; the roomy interior allows a stroller to be lifted right into the cab without unstrapping baby.

Babysitters can also be found for you at most hotels. Just ask at the front desk.

Before you go, help your kids to check out London Tourist Board's **Kids Love London** at **www.kidslovelondon.com**, a site created to give kids the lowdown on kid-friendly attractions, events, restaurants, and more.

Recommended family travel websites include **Family Travel Forum** (www.familytravelforum.com), a comprehensive site that offers customized trip planning; **Family Travel Network** (www.familytravelnetwork.com), an online magazine providing travel tips; **Travel WithYourKids.com** (www.travelwithyourkids.com), a comprehensive site written by parents for parents offering sound advice for long-distance and international travel with children.

STUDENT TRAVEL

The **International Student Travel Confederation** (ISTC; www.istc.org) was formed in 1949 to make travel around the world more affordable for students. Check out its website for comprehensive travel services information and details on how to get an **International Student Identity Card (ISIC),** which qualifies students for substantial savings on rail passes, plane tickets, entrance fees, and more. It also provides students with basic health and life insurance and a 24-hour helpline. The card is valid for a maximum of 18 months. You can apply for the card online or in person at **STA Travel** (© 800/781-4040 in North America; www.statravel.com), the biggest student travel agency in the world; check out the website to locate STA Travel offices worldwide. If you're no longer a student but are still under 26, you can get an **International Youth Travel Card (IYTC)** from the same people, which entitles you to some discounts. **Travel CUTS** (© 800/592-2887; www.travelcuts.com) offers similar services for both Canadians and U.S. residents. Irish students may prefer to turn to **USIT** (© 01/602-1904; www.usit.ie), an Ireland-based specialist in student, youth, and independent travel.

The **International Students House,** 229 Great Portland St., W1W 5PN (© 020/7631-8310; www.ish.org.uk), lies at the foot of Regent's Park across from the Tube stop for Great Portland Street. It's a beehive of activity, offering discos and film showings. See p. 97 for information on renting rooms here.

University of London Student Union, Malet Street, WC1E 7HY (© 020/7631-0101; www.ulu.co.uk; Tube: Goodge St.

(Tips **Traveling with Minors**

All children must have their own passport when traveling to London. To obtain a passport, the child **must** be present—that is, in person—at the center issuing the passport. Both parents must be present as well. If not, then a notarized statement from the parents is required. Any questions parents or guardians might have can be answered by calling the **National Passport Information Center** at © 877/487-2778 Monday to Friday 8am to 8pm Eastern Standard Time, or log onto the U.S. State Department website at http://travel.state.gov and do a search for "Foreign Entry Requirements."

or Russell Sq.), is the best place to go to learn about student activities in the Greater London area. The Union has a swimming pool, a fitness center, a gymnasium, a general store, a sports shop, a ticket agency, banks, bars, inexpensive restaurants, venues for live events, an office of STA Travel (see above), and many other facilities. It's open Monday to Thursday 8:30am to 11pm, Friday 8:30am to 1pm, Saturday 9am to 2pm, and Sunday from 9:30am to 10:30pm. Bulletin boards at the Union provide a rundown on events, some of which you will be able to attend, although others might be "closed door."

SINGLE TRAVELERS

Many people prefer traveling alone, and for independent travelers, solo journeys offer infinite opportunities to make friends and meet locals. Unfortunately, the travel industry is geared toward couples, so singles often wind up paying the penalties of traveling alone (like supplemental room fees) if they don't know how to avoid them. Single travelers can avoid these supplements, of course, by agreeing to room with other single travelers on the trip. An even better idea is to find a compatible roommate before you go from one of the many roommate-locator agencies.

Travel Buddies Singles Travel Club (© 800/998-9099; www.travelbuddies worldwide.com), based in Canada, runs small, intimate, single-friendly group trips and will match you with a roommate free of charge. TravelChums (© 212/787-2621; www.travelchums.com) is an Internet-only travel-companion matching service with elements of an online personals–type site, hosted by the respected New York–based Shaw Guides travel service.

Many reputable tour companies offer singles-only trips. Singles Travel International (© 877/765-6874; www.singles travelintl.com) offers singles-only escorted tours to places like London, Alaska, Fiji, and the Greek Islands. Backroads (© 800/462-2848; www.backroads.com) offers "Singles + Solos" active-travel trips to destinations worldwide.

For more information, check out Eleanor Berman's classic *Traveling Solo: Advice and Ideas for More Than 250 Great Vacations, 5th Edition* (Globe Pequot), updated in 2005.

VEGETARIAN TRAVEL

Happy Cow's Vegetarian Guide to Restaurants & Health Food Stores (www.happycow.net) has a restaurant guide with more than 6,000 restaurants in 100 countries. **VegDining.com** also lists vegetarian restaurants (with profiles) around the world **Vegetarian Vacations** (www.vegetarian-vacations.com) offers vegetarian tours and itineraries.

10 Sustainable Tourism/Ecotourism

Each time you take a flight or drive a car CO_2 is released into the atmosphere. You can help neutralize this danger to our planet through "carbon offsetting"—paying someone to reduce your CO_2 emissions by the same amount you've added. Carbon offsets can be purchased in the U.S. from companies such as **Carbonfund.org** (www.carbonfund.org) and **TerraPass** (www.terrapass.org), and from **Climate Care** (www.climatecare.org) in the U.K.

Although one could argue that any vacation that includes an airplane flight can't be truly "green," you can go on holiday and still contribute positively to the environment. You can offset carbon emissions from your flight in other ways. Choose forward-looking companies that embrace responsible development practices, helping

Frommers.com: The Complete Travel Resource

It should go without saying, but we highly recommend **Frommers.com**, voted Best Travel Site by *PC Magazine*. We think you'll find our expert advice and tips; independent reviews of hotels, restaurants, attractions, and preferred shopping and nightlife venues; vacation giveaways; and an online booking tool indispensable before, during, and after your travels. We publish the complete contents of over 128 travel guides in our **Destinations** section covering nearly 3,800 places worldwide to help you plan your trip. Each weekday, we publish original articles reporting on **Deals and News** via our free **Frommers.com Newsletter** to help you save time and money and travel smarter. We're betting you'll find our new **Events** listings (http://events.frommers.com) an invaluable resource; it's an up-to-the-minute roster of what's happening in cities everywhere—including concerts, festivals, lectures, and more. We've also added weekly **Podcasts, interactive maps,** and hundreds of new images across the site. Check out our **Travel Talk** area featuring **Message Boards** where you can join in conversations with thousands of fellow Frommer's travelers and post your trip report once you return.

preserve destinations for the future by working alongside local people. An increasing number of sustainable tourism initiatives can help you plan a family trip and leave as small a "footprint" as possible on the places you visit.

Responsible Travel (www.responsibletravel.com) contains a great source of sustainable travel ideas and is run by a spokesperson for responsible tourism in the travel industry. **Sustainable Travel International** (www.sustainabletravelinternational.org) promotes responsible tourism practices and issues an annual Green Gear & Gift Guide.

You can find eco-friendly travel tips, statistics, and touring companies and associations—listed by destination under "Travel Choice"—at the TIES website, www.ecotourism.org. Also check out **Conservation International** (www.conservation.org)—which, with *National Geographic Traveler,* annually presents **World Legacy Awards** (www.wlaward.org) to those travel tour operators, businesses, organizations,

and places that have made a significant contribution to sustainable tourism. **Ecotravel.com** is part online magazine and part ecodirectory that lets you search for touring companies in several categories (water-based, land-based, spiritually oriented, and so on).

In the U.K., **Tourism Concern** (www.tourismconcern.org.uk) works to reduce social and environmental problems connected to tourism and find ways of improving tourism so that local benefits are increased.

The **Association of British Travel Agents (ABTA;** www.abtamembers.org/responsibletourism) acts as a focal point for the U.K. travel industry and is one of the leading groups spearheading responsible tourism.

The **Association of Independent Tour Operators (AITO;** www.aito.co.uk) is a group of interesting specialist operators leading the field in making holidays sustainable.

11 Staying Connected

TELEPHONES

To call London: If you're calling London from the United States:

1. Dial the international access code, 011.
2. Dial the country code, 44.
3. Dial the city code, 20, and then the number. (London's official city code is 020, but you will dial 20 because you always have to omit the zero from the area code when calling London from outside England.) So the whole number you'd dial would be 011-44-20-0000-0000.

To make international calls: To make international calls from London, first dial 00 and then the country code (U.S. or Canada, 1; Ireland, 353; Australia, 61; New Zealand, 64). Next, dial the area code and number. For example, if you wanted to call the British Embassy in Washington, D.C., you would dial 00-1-202-588-7800.

Or call through one of the following long-distance access codes: **AT&T USA Direct** (✆ **0800/890-011**), **Canada Direct** (✆ **0800/890-016**), **Australia** (✆ **0800/890-061**), or **New Zealand** (✆ **0800/890-064**). Common country codes are **U.S. and Canada,** 1; **Australia,** 61; **New Zealand,** 64; and **South Africa,** 27.

For directory assistance: Dial ✆ **118212** for a full range of services; for the rest of Britain, dial ✆ **118118.** See also "Area Codes" in the "Fast Facts: London" box in chapter 5.

For operator assistance: If you need operator assistance in making a call, dial ✆ **100.**

Toll-free numbers: Numbers beginning with 0800 within London are toll-free, but calling a 1-800 number in the U.S. from England is not toll-free. In fact, it costs the same as an overseas call.

To call within London: Dial the local seven- or eight-digit number.

To call within Britain (outside London): Phone numbers outside the major cities consist of an exchange code plus telephone number. To dial the number, you need to dial the exchange code first. Information sheets on call-box walls give the codes in most instances. If your code isn't there, call the operator by dialing ✆ **100.**

There are three types of public pay phones: those taking only coins, those accepting only phone cards (called Cardphones), and those taking both phone cards and credit cards. At coin-operated phones, insert your coins before dialing. The minimum charge is 40p (75¢).

CELLPHONES

The three letters that define much of the world's **wireless capabilities** are GSM (Global System for Mobiles), a big, seamless network that makes for easy cross-border cellphone use throughout Great Britain and the rest of Europe and dozens of other countries worldwide. In the U.S., T-Mobile, AT&T Wireless, and Cingular use this quasi-universal system; in Canada, Microcell and some Rogers customers are GSM, and all Europeans and most Australians use GSM.

If your cellphone is on a GSM system, and you have a world-capable multiband phone such as many Sony Ericsson, Motorola, or Samsung models, you can make and receive calls across civilized areas around much of the globe. Just call your wireless operator and ask for "international roaming" to be activated on your account. Unfortunately, per-minute charges can be high, usually $1 to $1.50 in Britain.

That's why it's important to buy an "unlocked" world phone from the get-go. Many cellphone operators sell "locked" phones that restrict you from using any other removable computer memory phone chip (called a **SIM card**) cards than the ones they supply. Having an unlocked phone allows you to install a cheap, prepaid SIM card (found at a local retailer) in your destination country. (Show your phone to the salesperson; not all phones work on all networks.) You'll get a local phone number and much, much lower calling rates. Unlocking an already locked phone can be complicated, but it can be done; just call your cellular operator and say you'll be going abroad for several months and want to use the phone with a local provider.

For many, **renting** a phone is a good idea. While you can rent a phone from any number of overseas sites, including kiosks at airports and at car-rental agencies, we suggest renting the phone before you leave home. That way you can give loved ones and business associates your new number, make sure the phone works, and take the phone wherever you go—especially helpful for overseas trips through several countries, where local phone-rental agencies often bill in local currency and may not let you take the phone to another country.

Phone rental isn't cheap. You'll usually pay $40 to $50 per week, plus airtime fees of at least a dollar a minute. If you're traveling to London, though, local rental companies often offer free incoming calls within their home country, which can save you big bucks. The bottom line: Shop around.

Two good wireless rental companies are **InTouch USA** (✆ 800/872-7626; www.intouchglobal.com) and **Roadpost** (✆ 888/290-1616 or 905/272-5665; www.roadpost.com). Give them your itinerary, and they'll tell you what wireless products you need. InTouch will also, for free, advise you on whether your existing phone will work overseas.

If you have not arranged to rent a cellphone before you depart, your best deal in London is through **Rent-A-Mobile** (✆ 01704/544-015; www.rent-a-mobile. co.uk), which, among other locations, will deliver your phone to you at Heathrow Airport Terminal 2, Gatwick South Terminal, or your hotel in London. If you're renting a car, perhaps to tour England after a visit to London, you can also arrange cellphone rental through your car-rental company. The phone rentals from **Auto Europe** (✆ 888/223-5555 in the U.S., or 0800/358-1229 in Britain; www.autoeurope.com) are especially recommended.

For trips of more than a few weeks spent in one country, **buying a phone** becomes economically attractive, as many nations have cheap, no-questions-asked prepaid phone systems. Stop by a local cellphone shop and get the cheapest package; you'll probably pay less than $100 for a phone and a starter calling card. Local calls may be as low as 10¢ per minute, and in many countries incoming calls are free.

VOICE-OVER INTERNET PROTOCOL (VoIP)

If you have Web access while traveling, you might consider a broadband-based telephone service (in technical terms, **Voice-over-Internet Protocol,** or **VoIP**) such as Skype (www.skype.com) or Vonage (www.vonage.com), which allows you to make free international calls if you use its services from your laptop or in a cybercafe. The people you're calling must also use the service for it to work; check the sites for details.

INTERNET/E-MAIL
WITHOUT YOUR OWN COMPUTER

There are cybercafes throughout the heart of commercial London, with fees averaging about £2 ($3.80) per hour. For an **Internet Exchange,** there are some 22 locations at libraries all over London—call ✆ 020/8742-4000 for the location nearest you. You can also use **www.cyber captive.com** and **www.cybercafe.com** to find cybercafes in London.

Aside from formal cybercafes, most **youth hostels** nowadays have at least one

Online Traveler's Toolbox

Veteran travelers usually carry some essential items to make their trips easier. Following is a selection of handy online tools to bookmark and use.

- **Airplane Food** (www.airlinemeals.net)
- **Airplane Seating** (www.seatguru.com and www.airlinequality.com)
- **Foreign Languages for Travelers** (www.travlang.com)
- **Maps** (www.mapquest.com)
- **Subway Navigator** (www.subwaynavigator.com)
- **Time and Date** (www.timeanddate.com)
- **Travel Warnings** (http://travel.state.gov, www.fco.gov.uk/travel, www. voyage.gc.ca, or www.dfat.gov.au/consular/advice)
- **Universal Currency Converter** (www.xe.com/ucc)
- **Visa ATM Locator** (www.visa.com), **MasterCard ATM Locator** (www. mastercard.com)
- **Weather** (www.intellicast.com and www.weather.com)

computer on which you can access the Internet. And most **public libraries** across the world offer Internet access free or for a small charge. Avoid **hotel business centers,** unless you're willing to pay exorbitant rates.

Most major airports have **Internet kiosks** that provide basic Web access for a per-minute fee that's usually higher than cybercafe prices. Check out copy shops like **Kinko's** (FedEx Kinko's), which offers computer stations with fully loaded software (as well as Wi-Fi).

To retrieve your e-mail, ask your **Internet service provider (ISP)** if it has a Web-based interface tied to your existing e-mail account. If your ISP doesn't have such an interface, you can use the free **mail2web** service (www.mail2web.com) to view (but not reply to) your home e-mail. For more flexibility, you may want to open a free Web-based e-mail account with **Yahoo! Mail** (http://mail.yahoo.com). (Microsoft's Hotmail is another popular option, but Hotmail has severe spam problems.) Your home ISP may be able to forward your e-mail to the Web-based account automatically.

If you need to access files on your office computer, look into a service called **GoToMyPC** (www.gotomypc.com). The service provides a Web-based interface for you to access and manipulate a distant PC from anywhere—even a cybercafe—provided your "target" PC is on and has an always-on connection to the Internet (such as with high-speed cable). The service offers top-quality security, but if you're worried about hackers, use your own laptop rather than a cybercafe to access the GoToMyPC system.

WITH YOUR OWN COMPUTER

More and more hotels, resorts, airports, cafes, and retailers are going **Wi-Fi** (wireless fidelity), becoming "hotspots" that offer free high-speed Wi-Fi access or charge a small fee for usage. Most laptops sold today have built-in wireless capability. To find public Wi-Fi hotspots at your destination, go to **www.jiwire.com**; its Hotspot Finder holds the world's largest directory of public wireless hotspots.

For dial-up access, most business-class hotels throughout the world offer dataports for laptop modems, and a few thousand hotels in Europe now offer free high-speed Internet access.

Wherever you go, bring a **connection kit** of the right power and phone adapters, a spare phone cord, and a spare Ethernet network cable—or find out whether your hotel supplies them to guests. British current is 240 volts, AC, so you'll need a converter or transformer for U.S.-made electrical appliances, as well as an adapter that allows the plug to match British outlets. Some (but not all) hotels supply them for guests. If you've forgotten one, you can buy a transformer/adapter at most branches of **Boots the Chemist.**

12 Packages for the Independent Traveler

Package tours are simply a way to buy the airfare, accommodations, and other elements of your trip (such as car rentals, airport transfers, and sometimes even activities) at the same time and often at discounted prices.

One good source of package deals is the airlines themselves. Most major airlines offer air/land packages, including **American Airlines Vacations** (© 800/321-2121; www.aavacations.com), **Delta Vacations** (© 800/654-6559; www.deltavacations.com), **Continental Airlines Vacations** (© 800/301-3800; www.covacations.com), and **United Vacations** (© 888/854-3899; www.unitedvacations.com). Several big **online travel agencies**—Expedia, Travelocity, Orbitz, Site59, and Lastminute.com—also do a brisk business in packages.

British Airways Holidays (© 877/4-A-VACATION; www.baholidays.com) offers the most diversified packages in all price ranges. BA books not only the government-rated four-star hotels, but also the more moderate two-star hotels (the latter charging moderate tariffs). BA is also a pioneer in student/youth specials.

If you're seeking cut-rate package deals, try **Liberty Travel** (© **888/271-1584;** www.libertytravel.com) and **British Travel International** (© **727/643-5710;** www.britishtravel.com).

Travel packages are also listed in the travel section of your local Sunday newspaper. Or check ads in the national travel magazines such as *Arthur Frommer's Budget Travel Magazine, Travel & Leisure, National Geographic Traveler,* and *Condé Nast Traveler.*

(*Tips*) **Ask Before You Go**

Before you invest in a package deal or an escorted tour:

- Always ask about the **cancellation policy.** Can you get your money back? Is there a deposit required?
- Ask about the **accommodations choices and prices** for each. Then look up the hotels' reviews in a Frommer's guide and check their rates online for your specific dates of travel. Also find out what types of rooms are offered.
- Request a complete **schedule.** (Escorted tours only)
- Ask about the **size** and demographics of the group. (Escorted tours only)
- Discuss what is included in the **price** (transportation, meals, tips, airport transfers, and so on). (Escorted tours only)
- Finally, look for **hidden expenses.** Ask whether airport departure fees and taxes, for example, are included in the total cost—they rarely are.

13 Escorted General-Interest Tours

Escorted tours are structured group tours, with a group leader. The price usually includes everything from airfare to hotels, meals, tours, admission costs, and local transportation.

The two largest tour operators conducting escorted tours of Europe are **Globus/Cosmos** (© 866/755-8581; www.globusandcosmos.com) and **Trafalgar** (© 800/854-0103; www.trafalgartours.com). Both of these companies offer first-class tours of London that include seeing the major sites, shopping, dining, and even day trips to places like Stratford-upon-Avon. There's little difference in the companies' services (though Globus/Cosmos is slightly more of a budget choice than the upmarket Trafalgar), so choose your tour based on the itinerary and preferred date of departure. Brochures are available at travel agencies, and all tours must be booked through travel agents.

Despite the fact that escorted tours require big deposits and predetermine hotels, restaurants, and itineraries, many people derive security and peace of mind from the structure they offer. Escorted tours—whether they're navigated by bus, motor coach, train, or boat—let travelers sit back and enjoy the trip without having to drive or worry about details. They take you to the maximum number of sights in the minimum amount of time with the least amount of hassle. They're particularly convenient for people with limited mobility and they can be a great way to make new friends.

On the downside, you'll have little opportunity for serendipitous interactions with locals. The tours can be jam-packed with activities, leaving little room for individual sightseeing, whim, or adventure—plus they often focus on the heavily touristed sites, so you miss out on many a lesser-known gem.

Before you invest in an escorted tour, ask about the **cancellation policy:** Is a deposit required? Can they cancel the trip if they don't get enough people? Do you get a refund if they cancel? If *you* cancel? How late can you cancel if you are unable to go? When do you pay in full? *Note:* If you choose an escorted tour, think strongly about purchasing trip-cancellation insurance, especially if the tour operator asks you to pay upfront. See the section on "Travel Insurance," earlier in this chapter.

4

Suggested London Itineraries

The Queen would perhaps scoff at the idea of tackling her beloved city in just 1 day—or even 2 or 3 days. But what does she know, really?

If that's all the time you have, we want to help you make the most of it by providing a ready-made itinerary that will allow you to have a complete, unforgettable trip. Of course, there is always a hidden London that awaits discovery as you seek out its secret treasures on your own, but that can wait for another day and another trip.

You can make the most of your short time by fortifying yourself with an old-fashioned English breakfast—order "the works," perhaps skipping the blood pudding or sautéed kidneys if you're faint of heart. That way, if you sleep late (or have a "real tuck-in" as the Brits say), you might even skip lunch, so as not to lose precious daylight hours in your rushed schedule.

1 The Best of London in 1 Day

Touring London in a day seems ridiculous at first, considering that it's a sprawling metropolis filled with treasures, but it can be done if you get an early start and have a certain discipline, plus a lot of stamina. Since Britain is the world's most famous kingdom, this "greatest hits" itinerary focuses on royal London, monumental London, and political London, with some great art thrown in to satisfy the inner soul. After an early morning trip to Westminster Abbey, you'll want to see London's greatest plaza, Trafalgar Square, take a grand "royal stroll," visit the National Gallery, and perhaps poke into Whitehall, seeing 10 Downing St. (home of the prime minister). A pint of lager in a Victorian pub and a night in a West End theater will cap your day very nicely. **Start:** *Tube to Westminster.*

❶ Westminster Abbey ✸✸✸
This early English Gothic abbey is the shrine of the nation, and most of England's kings and queens have been crowned here—and many are buried here as well. We always like to get here when it opens at 9:30am before the crowds descend. Architecturally, its two highlights are the fan-vaulted Henry VII's Chapel (one of the loveliest in all of Europe) and the shrine to Edward Confessor, containing the tombs of five kings and three queens. For a final look, walk over to the Poets' Corner, where everybody from Chaucer to Shelley and Keats are buried. See p. 223.

As you emerge from Westminster Abbey, you confront the virtual symbol of London itself:

❷ The Houses of Parliament and "Big Ben" ✸✸
Guarded over by "Big Ben" (the world's most famous timepiece), the former royal Palace of Westminster shelters both the

House of Lords and the House of Commons and has done so since the 11th century. Gaining admission to the debating chambers requires a long wait and a lot of red tape that the "Day 1 Visitor" will have to forego, but at least you can admire the massive architectural pile from the outside before passing on your way.

If you feel you've missed something, duck into the Jewel Tower across the street (p. 214), one of only two surviving buildings from the medieval Palace of Westminster. Here you can see an exhibition of the history of Parliament and even use a touch-screen computer that takes you on a virtual tour of both Houses of Parliament. See p. 213.

Continue walking north along Whitehall until you reach:

❸ No. 10 Downing St.

Hang a left and look down Downing Street to number 10, flanked by policemen. Because of security concerns, it is no longer possible to walk down the street—you can only look down it through the gates on Whitehall. The official residence of the prime minister isn't much of a sight and is rather modest, but it's been the home of everybody from Sir Winston Churchill to Margaret Thatcher. Today Gordon Brown and his family call it home. Although the building is hardly palatial, it's the most famous address in Britain, other than Buckingham Palace, and all visitors seem to want to take a peek.

After that look, continue north to:

❹ Trafalgar Square ★★

The hub of London, this is Britain's most famous square and the scene of many a demonstration. A 44m (144-ft.) granite statue of Horatio Viscount Nelson (1758–1805) dominates the square. As you walk around this square, noting the ferocious pigeons "dive-bombing," you'll know that you're in the very heart of London

where thousands amass on New Year's Eve to ring in another year. See p. 215.

Right on this square, you can enter the:

❺ National Gallery ★★★

On the north side of Trafalgar Square looms this massive gallery. All the big names, from Leonardo da Vinci to Rembrandt, from van Gogh to Cézanne, strut their stuff here. Displaying some of the most important art ever created, the panoramic galleries cover eight centuries. This is one of the greatest art museums on the planet. On even the most rushed of schedules, you'll want to devote at least 1½ hours to its galleries. Since everybody's taste in art differs, check out our Insider's Tip under the National Gallery preview (p. 216). A computer makes it easy and convenient for you. Select 10 paintings you'd most like to see, and a computer will design your own map and print it out for you.

Directly north of Trafalgar Square, you enter the precincts of:

❻ Covent Garden ★

The old fruit-and-vegetable market of Eliza Doolittle fame is long gone, and the market has been recycled into one of the most bustling and exciting sections of London today. Begin with a walk around **The Piazza ★★**, the center of Covent Garden. When architect Inigo Jones designed it in 1633, it became London's first square. To its south you'll see **St. Paul's Church ★**, which Jones called "the handsomest barn in England." Immediately to the southeast of St. Paul's you can enter the **Jubilee Market** and to its immediate east the **London Transport Museum.** After wandering around the gardens and after a heavy morning of sightseeing, even with a full English breakfast, you may be ready for lunch. For our pounds sterling, there is no better place for lunch in all of London than Covent Garden.

7 **PORTERS ENGLISH RESTAURANT** 🍴🍴
We suggest a visit to our dear old friend, the Earl of Bradford, who owns and runs this venerable Covent Garden favorite. Try one of Lady Bradford's old English pies (ever had lamb and apricot?), and finish off with her fabled steamed pudding, made with ginger and banana. 17 Henrietta St., WC2. ✆ 020/7836-6466. Tube: Covent Garden or Leicester Sq. See p. 162.

The day is marching on, and you should too if you want to take in more that London has to offer.

At Covent Garden, take the Tube (subway, to Americans) to Charing Cross Station to the south of Covent Garden. After disembarking here, prepare yourself for one of the grandest strolls in all of Britain, walking west along:

8 **The Mall** 🍴🍴 **& Buckingham Palace** 🍴🍴

A stroll along the Mall all the way west to Buckingham Palace is the most aristocratic walk in Britain. Passing King George's IV's glorious Carlton House terrace on your right, you can enjoy the same view Elizabeth II sees when she rides in her gilded "fairy-tale" coach to open Parliament every year.

Whether you can actually go inside Buckingham Palace itself depends on the time of year. For possible visits, see the information on p. 209. We've deliberately skipped the Changing of the Guard ceremony, which isn't held every day and is often difficult to schedule. It's an overrated attraction anyway.

After viewing Buckingham Palace, at least from the outside, walk along Constitution Hill to the Tube stop at Hyde Park Corner. Once there, head east for one big final attraction for the afternoon.

9 **The Tower of London** 🍴🍴🍴

We prefer to visit this attraction later in the afternoon, when some of the hordes pouring out of tour buses have departed. A first-time visitor to London wouldn't dare miss this old symbol of blood and gore standing on the Thames for 900 years. Many famous Englishmen have lost their heads at the Tower. It's been a palace, a prison, and a royal mint, but mostly it's a living museum of British history. Since you don't have a lot of time, take one of the hour-long guided tours conducted by the much-photographed Beefeaters. They make the history of the Tower come alive with their often humorous and irreverent commentary.

After viewing the Tower, we suggest you head back to your hotel and take a much-needed break before descending on London by night.

We like to begin our evening with a pint in an evocative London pub. Try one of the best and also one of the most famous:

10 **THE SALISBURY**
This Art Nouveau pub is in the heart of the theater district. You can enjoy a drink and a quick pub dinner of home-cooked pies or freshly made salads before heading out to see the show of your choice. 90 St. Martin's Lane, WC2. ✆ 020/7836-5863. Tube: Leicester Sq. See p. 315.

11 **A Night at a London Theater**
Before purchasing your ticket, read our box on "Ticket Bargains" (p. 296), and you might save a lot of money. Unless you've got your heart set on seeing a big London hit, perhaps a musical, we suggest your one-and-only night in London be spent at **Shakespeare's Globe Theatre** (p. 298). This is a replica of the Elizabethan original where the Bard premiered many of his plays. The productions, often performed in Elizabethan costume as in Shakespeare's days, are of the highest

quality, often showcasing the talents of many of Britain's greatest thespians, both young and old.

Head back to your hotel for a well-earned night of rest and promise yourself you'll come back to London soon.

2 The Best of London in 2 Days

If you've already made your way through "The Best in 1 Day," you'll find your second full-day tour takes in a different part of London. You've seen Royal London. Now visit what might be called "Academic London" by heading to the history-rich district of Bloomsbury, following in the footsteps of Charles Dickens and Virginia Woolf. After lunch, head for "the City," London's financial district, and wander around St. Paul's Cathedral, masterpiece of Sir Christopher Wren. Then have a thrilling afternoon riding the British Airways London Eye and visiting the Tate Modern. *Start: Russell Square.*

❶ The British Museum ★★★

This is the mammoth home of one of the world's greatest treasure troves—much of it plundered from other parts of the globe when Britannia ruled the waves. The most exciting of these treasures are the Elgin Marbles, stolen from Greece, and the Rosetta Stone, stolen from Egypt. You'll need at least 2 hours for even the most cursory of visits. An easy-to-follow map at the entrance will help you hit all the highlights, including the legendary Black Obelisk, dating from around 860 B.C. and exhibited in the Nimrud Gallery. You can't see everything, so don't even try. But you'll see enough to convince yourself you need to make another visit some time in the future. End your quickie tour in the modern Great Court covering the celebrated Reading Room where Karl Marx wrote *Das Kapital.* See p. 208 for more information.

The museum doesn't open until 10am, but early birds can arrive before and take a brisk morning walk, getting the feel of this famous district. Our favorite square for wandering is **Russell Square** (you can take the Tube straight there), followed by **Bedford Square** to the east and **Bloomsbury Square** to the southeast.

After the British Museum, it's time for lunch. You've already dined in Covent Garden (see Day 1), so it's time to head for "the City," the financial district of London in the East End.

❷ BOW WINE VAULTS

No place in the City is more evocative and atmospheric than this venerated choice for lunch. Here you can mingle with the movers and shakers of the City's financial district, enjoying well-prepared, affordable food and a drink in the bar or in the more formal street-level dining room. We always go for the Dover sole or the mixed grill (no one does this dish better than the English). 10 Bow Churchyard, EC4. ☏ 020/7248-1121. Tube: St. Paul's. See p. 312.

Fortified for the afternoon, you can begin your descent on yet another monument:

❸ St. Paul's Cathedral ★★★

Wren's Cathedral, the fifth to be built on this spot, is not filled with great art and treasures. But it's an adventure nonetheless. The thrill comes in climbing to the dome and taking in the Whispering Gallery (259 steps), the Stone Gallery (530 steps), and especially the panoramic sweep ★★★ from the Inner Golden Gallery on top of the dome. See p. 217.

❹ Tate Modern ✦✦✦

On the south side of the Thames, the relatively new Tate Modern (p. 219), shelters the greatest collection of international 20th-century art in Britain, ranking with the Pompidou in Paris but not the equal of New York's Museum of Modern Art. You'll see all the Warhols, Picassos, and Pollocks an art devotee could ever dream of. Allow at least 1½ hours for the most cursory of visits.

Head for Westminster Bridge (Tube: Westminster), the embarkation point for the:

❺ British Airways London Eye ✦

The world's largest observation wheel is the fourth-tallest structure in London, with panoramic views that extend on a clear day for 40km (25 miles). Each of the 32 futuristic-looking "pods" carries visitors to a bird's-eye view of London, making a complete rotation every 30 minutes. Currently, it's the most popular ride in London. See p. 257.

❻ Royal National Theatre

For your final night in London (assuming you're skipping Day 3), we'd recommend a night at the Royal National Theatre. On the South Bank of the Thames, this is one of the world's great stage companies—not just one theater, but a trio of modern auditoriums, each with the latest equipment and great acoustics. Even the Queen attends for one of the new plays, comedies, musicals, or whatever. There is always a major event being presented here, often with the greatest thespians or musicians in the world. You can arrive early for a pretheater meal in one of the cultural complex's dining facilities, such as the main restaurant, the Mezzanine. See p. 297.

3 The Best of London in 3 Days

Having sampled the charms of London in just 2 days, make your third and final day a little different by skipping out of town and heading for nearby Windsor Castle, which the Queen prefers as a royal residence to Buckingham Palace itself. She's got a point there—it's rather splendid. Return to London in time for a final afternoon of sightseeing in Hyde Park and elegant Mayfair, home to some of the world's most expensive real estate. *Start: Waterloo Station or Paddington Station (depending on your hotel location).*

❶ Windsor Castle ✦✦✦

In just half an hour, a train from London will deliver you to the royal town of Windsor (p. 318), site of England's most legendary castle. The first castle here was ordered built by William the Conqueror, and much of English history has unfolded within its walls. If you skipped the Changing of the Guard ceremony in London, you can see an even more exciting pageant here, though it takes place only from April to July Monday to Saturday at 11am (winter hours differ slightly—see p. 321 for more details). On a first visit to the castle, don't miss its greatest attraction, **St. George's Chapel** ✦✦✦, where British monarchs are entombed, and try to budget enough time to see the state apartments, including George IV's elegant chambers. No, you can't go into the Queen's present bedchamber. Before leaving the castle precincts, wander the beautifully landscaped Jubilee Garden spread over 8 hectares (2 acres).

Since you'll need 2 hours to explore Windsor Castle, this will put you in the little town for lunch, which, incidentally, is not a gourmet citadel.

2 HOUSE ON THE BRIDGE

This charming restaurant lies adjacent to the bridge that links Windsor with the exclusive prep school of Eton. The school itself has turned out some of England's greatest men, including the Duke of Wellington and the poet known as "mad Shelley" to his fellow pupils. In atmospheric surroundings, you can enjoy the restaurant's fixed-price lunch of English and international dishes. In summer, opt for one of the outdoor tables in a garden leading down to the Thames. We'd recommend both the oak-smoked salmon and the grilled Dover sole, rushed here fresh every day from the southern coast. Windsor Bridge ℂ **01753/860914.** See p. 324.

After lunch, with your precious time fading, we suggest an immediate return to London, arriving at Waterloo or Paddington Station, where you can hook up with the Tube leading to:

3 Hyde Park ⟨⟨⟨⟩⟩

Adjoining Kensington Gardens, Hyde Park (p. 253; Tube: Marble Arch) was the former deer-hunting ground of Henry VIII. Allow at least 30 minutes for a stroll through the scenic grandeur of London's "green lung." Our favorite oasis in the park is a miniature lake known as the **Serpentine,** where you can row, sail model boats, or even swim. In the northeast corner of the park, at **Speakers Corner,** you can hear everything from protesters calling for the overthrow of the monarchy to sex advocates demanding legalization of child prostitution in Britain. Any point of view goes here. You can even make a speech of your own. After taking in the landmark Marble Arch (a gate originally designed as the entrance to Buckingham Palace), stroll east along Upper Brook Street to:

4 Grosvenor Square

In the heart of Mayfair, and one of the world's most famous squares, this was the grandest of all London addresses for two centuries. In modern times, its former allure has been diminished by Eero Saarinen's outsized and grandiose **U.S. Embassy** (1956), which led to the demolition of the west side of the square. As you cross the square through the garden, take in William Reid Dick's bronze statue of Franklin D. Roosevelt, who honeymooned with Eleanor at Brown's Hotel in Mayfair.

Time out for some ritzy shopping (or at least window shopping) along:

5 Oxford Street

From Grosvenor Square (northeast corner), cut north up Duke Street until you reach the junction of Oxford Street (p. 273), at which point you can head east, moving deeper into the heart of commercial and theatrical London. A shopping mecca since 1908 when the American retail magnate, Gordon Selfridge, opened Selfridge's Department Store, this is the most popular street in London for out-of-town shoppers. It is no longer a "lurking place for cutthroats," as an early-18th-century writer called Oxford Street, although with the present pound-to-dollar ratio, you might indeed consider some of today's merchants highway robbers. Many of the fruit-and-flower vendors you encounter along Oxford Street are the great-grandchildren of former traders, their style of making a living passed on from one generation to the next. When you come to New Bond Street, cut southeast along:

6 New & Old Bond Streets

London's most luxurious shopping street, consisting of both Old and New Bond streets (p. 273; Tube: Bond St.), links Piccadilly with Oxford Street. "The Bonds" have both traditional old English shops and outlets for the latest and hottest international designers. In the Georgian era, the beau monde of London promenaded here, window shopping. Young rakes hung out here "looking for virgins." Later, the fun-loving set ranging from the Prince of Wales to the celebrated photographer Cecil Beaton and others, could be seen parading up and down the tiny Old Bond Street, with its deluxe art galleries. Today this dazzling thoroughfare of shops is celebrated for haute everything, from couture to jewelry.

Once you reach the intersection with Piccadilly, continue east, passing on your left the:

⑦ Burlington Arcade

The Burlington Arcade (p. 274; Tube: Piccadilly Circus) closes at 5:30pm, so, of course, try to get there before then. The blueprint for all London arcades, the Burlington Arcade opened back in 1815, and it's been going strong ever since. The glass-roofed, Regency-style passage is lined with exclusive shops and boutiques and lit by wrought-iron lamps. Luxury items such as jewelry and designer cashmeres are sold here. Look for the Beadles, London's representative of Britain's oldest police force.

On the opposite side of Piccadilly, you enter the precincts of the world's most famous food department store:

☕ FORTNUM & MASON ★★★

Founded in 1707, this deluxe purveyor of fancy foodstuffs is still grocer to the Queen. "Mr. Fortnum" and "Mr. Mason" still present a footman's show on the outside clock every hour. See p. 276. You can enjoy an elegant tea in St. James Restaurant, 181 Piccadilly. ℂ 020/7734-8040.

After tea, continue walking east into:

⑨ Piccadilly Circus ★

What Times Square is to New York, Piccadilly Circus is to London. Dating from 1819, the circus (or square) centers on a statue of Eros from 1893. That symbol of love is about the only thing that occasionally brings together the diverse group of people who converge on the circus. This is the traffic hub of London, and you're at the doorway to "theaterland" if you'd like to cap your visit to the West End with a final show.

At the end of 3 days, realize that the time was ridiculously short to take in the allure of London—and promise yourself some future visit, when you can discover such London neighborhoods as trendy Chelsea or aristocratic Belgravia and take a day trip on a boat sailing down the river to Hampton Court.

5

Getting to Know London

England's largest city is like a great wheel, with Piccadilly Circus at its hub and dozens of communities branching out from it. Since London is such a large conglomeration of neighborhoods and areas, each with its own personality, first-time visitors are sometimes intimidated until they get the hang of it. Many visitors spend all their time in the West End, where most of the attractions are, with a visit to the City (London's financial district) to see the Tower of London.

This chapter provides a brief orientation to the city's neighborhoods and tells you how to get around London by public transport or on foot. In addition, the "Fast Facts" section helps you find everything from babysitters to camera-repair shops.

1 Orientation

ARRIVING

For information on getting into London from the various airports, see "Getting into Town from the Airport," on p. 30.

BY TRAIN

Each of London's train stations is connected to the city's vast bus and Underground network, and each has phones, restaurants, pubs, luggage storage areas, and London Regional Transport Information Centres.

BY CAR

Once you arrive on the English side of the Channel, the M20 takes you directly into London. *Remember to drive on the left.* Two roadways encircle London: The A406 and A205 form the inner beltway; the M25 rings the city farther out. Determine which part of the city you want to enter and follow signposts.

We suggest you keep driving in London to the bare minimum. Because of parking problems and heavy traffic, getting around London by car is not a viable option. If you're arriving in London by car, plan to leave it in a garage and rely on public transportation or taxis. Call ahead and see if your hotel has parking (and what the charges are), or ask the staff to give you the name and address of a garage nearby.

VISITOR INFORMATION

The London Tourist Board's **London Visitor Centre,** 1 Regent St., London SW1Y 4XT (© 020/7234-5800; www.visitlondon.com; Tube: Piccadilly Circus), can help you with almost anything, from the most superficial to the most serious. Located within a 10-minute walk from Piccadilly Circus, it deals chiefly with procuring accommodations in all price categories through an on-site travel agency (www.LastMinute.com), which can also book transit on British Rail or with bus carriers throughout the U.K. There's a kiosk for procuring theater or group tour tickets, a book shop loaded with titles dealing with travel in the British Isles, a souvenir shop, and a staff that's pleasant, helpful, and friendly.

It's open year-round Monday 9:30am to 6:30pm, Tuesday to Friday 9am to 6:30pm, and Sunday 10am to 4pm. Between October and May, Saturday hours are 10am to 4pm, and between June and September, Saturday hours are 9am to 5pm.

A roughly equivalent organization conceived to help foreign visitors with their inquiries and confusion about London is the **London Information Centre,** at Leicester Square W1 (© **020/7292-2333;** www.londoninformationcentre.com; Tube: Leicester Sq.). Be aware that the London Information Centre is a privately owned, commercially driven organization that may have a vested interest in steering you toward a particular venue.

For additional help in navigating your way through the logistics of one of the world's biggest cities, call © **0800/LONDON** for city information and to book sometimes discounted rates for London hotels, theaters, sightseeing tours, and airport transfers. A sales staff is available daily from 8am to midnight.

CITY LAYOUT

AN OVERVIEW OF LONDON

While **Central London** doesn't formally define itself, most Londoners today would probably accept the Underground's Circle Line as a fair boundary.

"The City" (the financial district) is where London began; it's the original square mile that the Romans called *Londinium,* and it still exists as its own self-governing

---

Tips London Fights Gridlock with Hits to Motorists' Wallets

In a much-debated but desperately-needed attempt to ease traffic congestion in central London, the city's authorities began charging motorists a supplemental fee of £8 ($15) per vehicle per day if they entered some of the city's most densely populated neighborhoods. Known locally as the "Congestion Charge," it's levied every Monday to Friday between 7am and 6:30pm. A network of at least 700 cameras records license plate numbers, which are checked against a database; if you haven't paid by midnight the day after you enter the zone, you face steep penalties. These traffic fees, at least according to the mayor (who rides the Tube), have cut car usage by 10% to 15%. Neighborhoods affected include Bloomsbury, Soho, Covent Garden, parts of Southwark, Westminster, Mayfair, Green Park (with the notable exception of Park Lane, traffic on which is not affected), the streets around St. James's Park, and virtually everywhere in the City (that is, the financial district) of London. In February 2007 the zone was extended to the west of London, covering Kensington, Notting Hill Gate, Bayswater, Chelsea, Knightsbridge, Belgravia, and Pimlico.

How can a visitor, say, in a rental car, pay the required fee? Most Londoners log onto **www.CCLondon.com** and pay with a credit card or bank transfer online. Barring that, certificates showing proof of payment are widely available at key underground and railway stations (including Victoria); coin-operated machines, newspaper kiosks and shops, petrol (gasoline) stations, and supermarkets. Before renting a car to drive into central London (which isn't a good idea in the first place), check with your rental company about how the charges will apply to you. You can also pay by telephone by calling © **0845/900-1234.** To find the nearest shop (mainly newsagents) at which you can pay log on to **www.paypoint.co.uk.** Many car parks have coin-operated machines where you can pay.

entity. Rich in historical, architectural, and social interest, the City is one of the world's great financial areas. Even though the City is jeweled with historic sights, it empties out in the evenings and on weekends, and there are lots of better places to stay if you are looking for a hopping nightlife scene.

The **West End,** where most of London's main attractions are found, is unofficially bounded by the Thames to the south, Farringdon Road/Street to the east, Marylebone Road/Euston Road to the north, and Hyde Park and Victoria Station to the west. Most visitors will spend their time in the West End, whether at Buckingham Palace, the British Museum, or the shops and theaters of Soho. You'll find the greatest concentration of hotels and restaurants in the West End. Despite attempts to extend central London's nocturnal life to the south side of the Thames(notably the ambitious South Bank Arts Centre—London's energy fades when it crosses the river. Still, the new urban development of Docklands, the tourist attraction of the new Globe Theatre, and some up-and-coming residential neighborhoods are infusing energy into the area across the river.

Farther west are the upscale neighborhoods of Belgravia, Kensington, Knightsbridge, Chelsea, Paddington and Bayswater, Earl's Court, and Notting Hill. This is also prime hotel and restaurant territory. To the east of the City is the **East End,** which forms the eastern boundary of **Inner London** (Notting Hill and Earl's Court roughly form the western boundary). Inner London is surrounded, like a doughnut, by the sprawling hinterland of **Outer London.**

FINDING YOUR WAY AROUND

It's not easy to find an address in London, as the city's streets—both names and house numbers—follow no pattern whatsoever. London is checkered with innumerable squares, mews, closes, and terraces that jut into, overlap, or otherwise interrupt whatever street you're trying to follow. And house numbers run in odds and evens, clockwise and counterclockwise—when they exist at all. Many establishments, such as the Four Seasons Hotel and Langan's Brasserie, don't have numbers, even though the building right next door is numbered. Just ask if you're having trouble finding something. Throughout this book, street addresses are followed by designations like SW1 and EC1, which are postal areas. The original post office was at St. Martin-le-Grand in the City, so the postal districts are related to where they lie geographically from there. Victoria is SW1 since it's the first area southwest of St. Martin-le-Grand; Covent Garden is west (west central), so its postal area is WC1 or WC2; Liverpool Street is east central of St. Martin-le-Grand, so its postal area is EC1.

If you plan to explore London in any depth, you'll need a detailed street map with an index. No Londoner is ever without a *London A to Z,* the ultimate street-by-street reference guide, available at bookstores and newsstands. There's even a *Mini A to Z,* which is easier to carry around and ideal for all but the most myopic.

LONDON'S NEIGHBORHOODS IN BRIEF

The City & Environs

The City When Londoners speak of "the City" (EC2, EC3), they mean the original square mile that's now the British version of Wall Street. The buildings of this district are known all over the world: the Bank of England, the London Stock Exchange, and famed insurance company Lloyd's of London. The City was the original site of *Londinium,* the first settlement of the Roman conquerors. Despite its age, the City doesn't easily reveal its past. Although it retains some of its medieval character, much of the City has been swept away by the Great Fire of 1666, the bombs of 1940, the IRA bombs of the 1990s, and the zeal of modern developers. Landmarks include Sir Christopher Wren's masterpiece, **St. Paul's Cathedral,** which stood virtually alone in the surrounding rubble after the Blitz. Some 2,000 years of history unfold at the City's **Museum of London** and at the **Barbican Centre,** opened by Queen Elizabeth in 1982.

Following the Strand eastward from Trafalgar Square, you'll come to Fleet Street. In the 19th century, this corner of London became the most concentrated newspaper district in the world. William Caxton printed the first book in English here, and the *Daily Consort,* the first daily newspaper printed in England, was launched at Ludgate Circus in 1702. In recent times, however, most London tabloids have abandoned Fleet Street for the Docklands across the river. Where the Strand becomes Fleet Street stands Temple Bar, where the actual City of London begins. The Tower of London looms at the eastern fringe of the City, shrouded in legend, blood, and history, and permanently besieged by battalions of visitors.

The average visitor will venture into the City during the day to sample its attractions or to lunch at pubs such as **Ye Olde Cheshire Cheese,** then return to the West End for evening amusement. As a hotel district, the City wasn't even on the map until recent times. The opening of the **Great Eastern Hotel** has brought a lot of business clients who prefer to stay here to avoid the traffic jams involved in getting into and out of the City. Stay in the City if you would prefer a hotel in a place like New York's Wall Street instead of a midtown address. If you can't afford the Great Eastern, consider the cheaper

Rookery in newly fashionable Smithfield. The City lures hotel guests who prefer its quirky, quiet, offbeat flavor at night, when it's part ghost town, part movie set. There is some nightlife here, including pubs and restaurants. It's fun to wander the area when all the crowds are gone, pondering the thought that you're walking the same streets Samuel Johnson trod so long ago.

The City of London still prefers to function on its own, separate from the rest of London. It maintains its own **Information Centre** at St. Paul's Churchyard, EC4 (© **020/7332-1456**), which is open daily from 10am to 5:50pm.

The East End Traditionally, this was one of London's poorest districts, nearly bombed out of existence during World War II. In the words of one commentator, Hitler created "instant urban renewal" here. The East End extends east from the City Walls, encompassing Stepney, Bow, Poplar, West Ham, Canning Town, and other districts. The East End is the home of the cockney. To be a true cockney, it's said that you must be born within the sound of the Bow Bells of **St. Mary-le-Bow** church, an old church rebuilt by Sir Christopher Wren in 1670.

These days, many immigrants to London make their homes in the East End. London is pushing eastward, and the East End may even become fashionable someday soon. Today you'll find lots of trendy bars, clubs, restaurants, and boutiques or vintage clothing outlets. Much of the fashionable life is found around Hoxton Square and its peripheries, such as Shoreditch and the northern half of Brick Lane and mostly attracts the under-30 set. There is an array of contemporary galleries in the area. Brick Lane, incidentally, is a great place for some curry dishes if you can deal with all those

Central London Neighborhoods

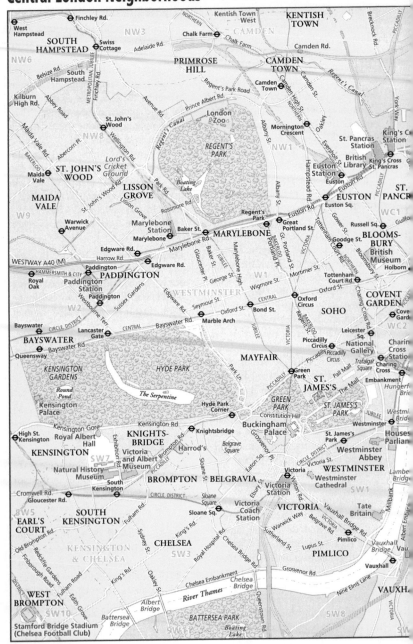

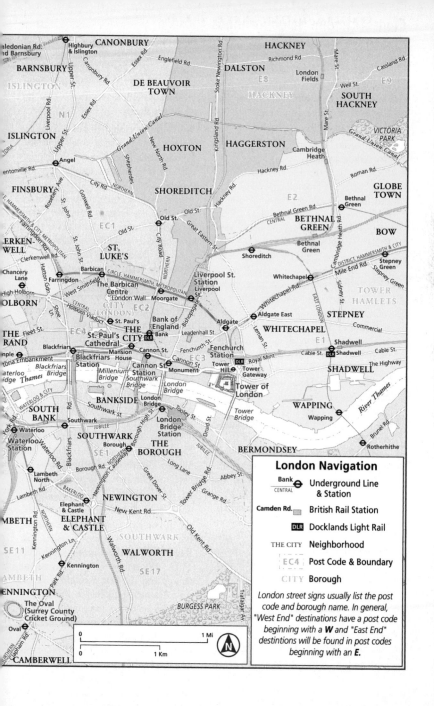

London Navigation

Bank ━━━━ CENTRAL	Underground Line & Station
Camden Rd.	British Rail Station
DLR	Docklands Light Rail
THE CITY	Neighborhood
EC4	Post Code & Boundary
CITY	Borough

London street signs usually list the post code and borough name. In general, "West End" destinations have a post code beginning with a W and "East End" destinations will be found in post codes beginning with an E.

waiters on the street trying to hustle you into their restaurant. Attractions you may want to visit if you're in the area include St. Clement Danes church, the Temple of Mithras, and Sir Christopher Wren's Monument to the Great Fire of 1666.

Docklands In 1981, the London Docklands Development Corporation (LDDC) was formed to redevelop Wapping, the Isle of Dogs, the Royal Docks, and Surrey Docks, in the most ambitious scheme of its kind in Europe. The area is bordered roughly by Tower Bridge to the west and London City Airport and the Royal Docks to the east. Many businesses have moved here; Thames-side warehouses have been converted to Manhattan-style lofts and museums, entertainment complexes, shops, and an ever-growing list of restaurants have popped up at this 21st-century river city in the making.

Canary Wharf, on the Isle of Dogs, is the heart of Docklands. This 28-hectare (69-acre) site is dominated by a 240m-high (787-ft.) tower, which is the tallest building in the United Kingdom, and was designed by César Pelli. The Piazza of the tower is lined with shops and restaurants. On the south side of the river at Surrey Docks, Sir Terence Conran has converted the Victorian warehouses of Butler's Wharf into offices, workshops, houses, shops, and restaurants. Butler's Wharf is also home to the **Design Museum.** Chances are, you'll venture here for sights and restaurants, not for lodging, unless you've got business in the area. The area is fun during the day and home to some of London's finest restaurants, offering good food and a change of pace from the West End—this is post-millennium London, whereas the West End is the essence of tradition. See our recommendations in chapter 7, "Where to Dine." To get to Docklands,

take the Underground to Tower Hill and pick up the **Docklands Light Railway** (© **020/7222-1234**), which operates Monday to Saturday from 5:30am to 12:30am, from 7am to 11:30pm Sunday.

South Bank Although not officially a district, this is where you'll find the **South Bank Arts Centre,** the largest arts center in Western Europe and still growing. Reached by Waterloo Bridge (or on foot by Hungerford Bridge), it lies across the Thames from the Victoria Embankment. Culture buffs flock to its galleries and halls, which encompass the **National Theatre, Queen Elizabeth Hall, Royal Festival Hall,** and the **Hayward Gallery.**

Although its day as a top hotel district in London may come in a decade or so (since there's no room left in the West End), that hasn't happened yet. The South Bank is a destination for daytime adventures and for evening cultural attractions. You may want to dine here during a day's or evening's exploration of the area. See our recommendations in chapter 7, "Where to Dine."

Nearby are such neighborhoods as Elephant and Castle, and Southwark, home to **Southwark Cathedral.** To get here, take the Tube to Waterloo Station.

Clerkenwell This neighborhood, north and a bit west of the City, was the site of London's first hospital and is the home of several early churches. **St. Bartholomew-the-Great,** built in 1123, still stands as London's oldest church and the best example of large-scale Norman building in the city. In the 18th century, Clerkenwell declined into a muck-filled cattle yard, home to cheap gin distilleries. During a 19th-century revival, John Stuart Mill's London Patriotic Club moved here in 1872, and William Morris's socialist press called Clerkenwell home in the 1890s—Lenin worked here editing

Iskra. The neighborhood again fell into disrepair but has recently been reinvented by the moneyed and groovy. A handful of hot restaurants and clubs have sprung up, and art galleries line St. John's Square and the border of Clerkenwell Green. Lest you think the whole area has become trendy, know that trucks still rumble into **Smithfield Market** throughout the night, unloading thousands of beef carcasses. Farringdon is Clerkenwell's central Tube stop.

No one ever accused Clerkenwell of being a hotel district. But it is increasingly known for having some of London's better restaurants, which have been pushed out of the West End by high rents. See our recommendations in chapter 7, "Where to Dine."

West End Neighborhoods

Bloomsbury This district, a world within itself, is bound roughly by Euston Road to the north, Gower Street to the west, and Clerkenwell to the east. It is, among other things, the academic heart of London. There are three colleges in Bloomsbury, including **University College** London, the grandest and the oldest. A branch of the **University of London** is also here. Writers like Virginia Woolf, who lived in the area (it figured in her novel *Jacob's Room*), have fanned the neighborhood's reputation as a place devoted to liberal thinking, arts, and "sexual frankness." The novelist and her husband, Leonard, were unofficial leaders of a group of artists and writers known as the Bloomsbury Group. However, despite its student population, Bloomsbury is a fairly staid neighborhood. The heart of Bloomsbury is **Russell Square,** whose outlying streets are lined with moderately priced to expensive hotels and B&Bs. It's a noisy but central place to stay. Most visitors come to see the **British Museum,** one of the world's greatest repositories of treasures from

around the globe. The **British Telecom Tower** (1964) on Cleveland Street is a familiar landmark.

Of all the areas described so far, this is the only one that could be called a hotel district. Hotel prices have risen dramatically in the past decade but are nowhere near the levels of those in Mayfair and St. James's. Bloomsbury's hotels are comparable in price to what you'll find in Marylebone to the west. But Bloomsbury is more convenient—at its southern doorstep lie the restaurants and nightclubs of Soho, the theater district, and the markets of Covent Garden. If you stay here, it's a 5-minute Tube ride to the heart of the action of the West End.

At the western edge of Bloomsbury you'll find **Fitzrovia,** bounded by Great Portland, Oxford, and Gower streets, and reached by the Goodge Street Tube. Goodge Street, with its many shops and pubs, forms the heart of the village. Fitzrovia was once the stamping ground for writers and artists like Ezra Pound, Wyndham Lewis, and George Orwell, among others. The bottom end of Fitzrovia is a virtual extension of Soho, with a cluster of Greek restaurants.

Holborn The old borough of Holborn (*Ho*-burn), which abuts the City southeast of Bloomsbury, encompasses the heart of legal London—this is where you'll find the city's barristers, solicitors, and law clerks. Still Dickensian in spirit, the area preserves the Victorian author's literary footsteps in the two Inns of Court (where law students perform their apprenticeships and where barristers' chambers are located), featured in *David Copperfield,* and as the Bleeding Heart Yard of *Little Dorrit* fame. **The Old Bailey** courthouse, where judges and lawyers still wear old-fashioned wigs, has stood for English justice through the years—Fagin went to the gallows from this site in *Oliver*

Twist. Everything in Holborn is steeped in history. For example, as you're downing a half-pint of bitter at the **Viaduct Tavern,** 126 Newgate St. (Tube: St. Paul's), you can reflect on the fact that the pub was built over the notorious Newgate Prison. You might come here for some sightseeing, perhaps quenching your thirst in a historic pub.

Covent Garden & the Strand The flower, fruit, and "veg" market is long gone (since 1970), but memories of Professor Higgins and his "squashed cabbage leaf," Eliza Doolittle, linger on. **Covent Garden** contains the city's liveliest group of restaurants, pubs, and cafes outside Soho, as well as some of the city's hippest shops. The restored marketplace here, with its glass and iron roofs, has been called a magnificent example of urban recycling. London's **theater district** begins in Covent Garden and spills over into Leicester Square and Soho. Inigo Jones's **St. Paul's Covent Garden** is known as the actors' church; over the years, it has attracted everybody from Ellen Terry to Vivien Leigh. The **Theatre Royal Drury Lane** was where Charles II's mistress, Nell Gwynne, made her debut in 1665 and was also where Irish actress Dorothea Jordan caught the eye of the Duke of Clarence, later William IV. The **Strand** forms the southern border of Covent Garden. It's packed with theaters, shops, first-class hotels, and restaurants. Old pubs, **Dr. Johnson's House,** and tearooms fragrant with brewing Twinings English tea evoke memories of the rich heyday of this district as the center of London's activity. The Strand runs parallel to the Thames River, and to walk it is to follow in the footsteps of Charles Lamb, Mark Twain, Henry Fielding, James Boswell, William Thackeray, and Sir Walter Raleigh, among others. The Strand's **Savoy Theatre** helped make Gilbert and Sullivan household names.

You'll probably come here for theater or dining rather than for a hotel room. Covent Garden has few hotels (although those few are very nice). We recommend the best ones (beginning on p. 101). Expect to spend a lot for the privilege of staying in such a central zone. The Strand, of course, has always been known for its swank Savoy Hotel.

Piccadilly Circus & Leicester Square Piccadilly Circus, with its statue of Eros, is the heart and soul of London. Its traffic, neon, and jostling crowds make *circus* an apt word to describe this place. Piccadilly, which was the western road out of London, was named for the "picadil," a ruffled collar created by Robert Baker, a 17th-century tailor. If you want grandeur, retreat to the Regency promenade of exclusive shops, the **Burlington Arcade,** designed in 1819. The English gentry—tired of being mud-splashed by horses and carriages along Piccadilly—came here to do their shopping. Some 35 shops, offering a treasure trove of expensive goodies, await you. A bit more tawdry is **Leicester Square,** a hub of theaters, restaurants, movie palaces, and nightlife—it's London's equivalent of New York's Times Square. Leicester Square changed forever in the Victorian era, when four towering entertainment halls were opened. Over time, the old entertainment palaces changed from stage to screen; today three of them still show films. In another sign of the times, the old Café de Paris is no longer a chic cabaret—now it's a disco.

There are a few hotels here, although they're invariably expensive. Stay here if you'd want a hotel in Times Square in New York. It's convenient for those who want to be at the center of the action. The downside is the noise, congestion, and pollution.

Soho A nightclubber's paradise, Soho is a confusing grid of streets crammed with restaurants. It's a great place to visit, but you probably won't want to stay here (there aren't many hotels, anyway). These densely packed streets in the heart of the West End are famous for their cosmopolitan mix of people and trades. A decade ago, much was heard about the decline of Soho with the influx of sex shops; even the pub where Dylan Thomas used to drink himself into oblivion became a sex cinema. Since then, non-sex-oriented businesses have returned, and fashionable restaurants and shops prosper. Soho is now the heart of London's expanding gay scene.

Soho starts at Piccadilly Circus and spreads out, more or less bordered by Regent Street to the west, Oxford Street to the north, Charing Cross Road to the east, and the **theaters along Shaftesbury Avenue** to the south. Carnaby Street, a block from Regent Street, was the center of the universe in the Swinging '60s but is now a schlocky tourist trap, though a few quality stores have opened recently. Across Shaftesbury Avenue is London's **Chinatown,** centered on Gerrard Street. It's small, authentic, and packed with good restaurants. **Soho's** heart—featuring great delicatessens, butchers, fish stores, and wine merchants—is farther north, on Brewer, Old Compton, and Berwick streets (Berwick St. features a wonderful open-air fresh-food market). To the north of Old Compton Street, Dean, Frith, and Greek streets have fine restaurants, pubs, and clubs. The British movie industry is centered on Wardour Street. The average visitor comes to Soho to dine because many of its restaurants are convenient to the theater district. Most travelers don't stay in Soho, but a certain action-oriented visitor prefers the *joie de vivre* of the neighborhood as compared to staid Bloomsbury or swank Mayfair. Does

this sound like you? Check out Soho's accommodations, starting on p. 103.

Marylebone West of Bloomsbury and Fitzrovia, Marylebone extends north from Marble Arch, at the eastern edge of Hyde Park. Most first-time visitors head here to explore **Madame Tussaud's** waxworks or walk along **Baker Street** in the footsteps of Sherlock Holmes. The streets form a near-perfect grid, with the major ones running north-south between Regent's Park and Oxford Street. Architect Robert Adam laid out **Portland Place,** one of the most characteristic squares in London, from 1776 to 1780. At **Cavendish Square,** Mrs. Horatio Nelson waited for the return of Admiral Nelson. Marylebone Lane and High Street retain a bit of small-town atmosphere, but this is otherwise a rather anonymous area. Dickens wrote nearly a dozen books while he resided here. At **Regent's Park,** you can visit Queen Mary's Gardens or, in summer, see Shakespeare performed in an open-air theater. **Marylebone** has emerged as a major "bedroom" district for London, competing with Bloomsbury to its east. It's not as convenient as Bloomsbury, but the hub of the West End's action is virtually at your doorstep if you lodge here, northwest of Piccadilly Circus and facing Mayfair to the south. Once known only for its town houses turned into B&Bs, the district now offers accommodations in all price ranges, catering to everyone from rock stars to frugal family travelers.

Mayfair Bounded by Piccadilly, Hyde Park, and Oxford and Regent streets, this is the most elegant, fashionable section of London, filled with luxury hotels, Georgian town houses, and swank shops. The area is sandwiched between Piccadilly Circus and Hyde Park. It's convenient to London's best shopping and close to the West End theaters yet (a bit snobbily) removed from the peddlers and commerce of Covent Garden and Soho.

Grosvenor Square (pronounced *Grov*-nor) is nicknamed "Little America" because it's home to the American Embassy and a statue of Franklin D. Roosevelt. **Berkeley Square** (*Bark*-ley) was made famous by the song "A Nightingale Sang in Berkeley Square." You'll want to dip into this exclusive section at least once. One of the curiosities of Mayfair is **Shepherd Market,** a village of pubs, two-story inns, restaurants, and book and food stalls, nestled within Mayfair's grandness. The hotels of Mayfair, especially those along Park Lane, are the most expensive and grand in London. This is the place if you're seeking sophisticated, albeit expensive, accommodations close to the **Bond Street** shops, boutiques, and art galleries. If "address" is important to you, and you're willing to pay for a good one, Mayfair has a bed waiting for you.

St. James's Often called "Royal London," St. James's basks in its associations with everybody from the "merrie monarch" Charles II to Elizabeth II, who lives at its most famous address, **Buckingham Palace.** The neighborhood begins at **Piccadilly Circus** and moves southwest, incorporating **Pall Mall, The Mall, St. James's Park,** and **Green Park.** It's "frightfully convenient," as the English say; within its confines are American Express and many of London's leading department stores. This is the neighborhood where English gentlemen seek haven at that male-only bastion of English tradition, the gentlemen's club, where poker is played, drinks are consumed, and pipes are smoked (St. James's Club is one of the most prestigious of these institutions). Be sure to stop in at **Fortnum & Mason,** 181 Piccadilly, the world's most

luxurious grocery store. Launched in 1788, the store sent hams to the Duke of Wellington's army and baskets of tinned goodies to Florence Nightingale in the Crimea. Hotels in this neighborhood tend to be expensive, but if the Queen should summon you to Buckingham Palace, you won't have far to go.

Westminster Westminster has been the seat of the British government since the days of Edward the Confessor (1042–66). Dominated by the **Houses of Parliament** and **Westminster Abbey,** the area runs along the Thames to the east of St. James's Park. **Trafalgar Square,** one of the city's major landmarks, is located at the area's northern end and remains a testament to England's victory over Napoleon in 1805. The square is home to the landmark National Gallery, which is filled with glorious paintings. Whitehall is the main thoroughfare, linking Trafalgar Square with **Parliament Square.** You can visit Churchill's Cabinet War Rooms and walk by **Downing Street** to see **Number 10,** home to Britain's prime minister (though the street itself is fenced in and guarded these days). No visit is complete without a call at **Westminster Abbey,** one of the greatest Gothic churches in the world. It has witnessed a parade of English history, beginning with William the Conqueror's coronation here on Christmas Day 1066.

Westminster also encompasses **Victoria,** an area that takes its name from bustling Victoria Station, "the gateway to the Continent." Many B&Bs and hotels have sprouted up here because of the neighborhood's proximity to the rail station. Victoria is cheap and convenient if you don't mind the noise and crowds.

Welfare recipients occupy many hotels along Belgrave Road. If you've arrived without a hotel reservation, you'll find the pickings better on the streets off Belgrave Road. Your best bet is to walk along Ebury Street, east of Victoria Station and Buckingham Palace Road. Here you'll find some of the best moderately priced lodgings in central London. Since you're near Victoria Station, the area is convenient for day trips to Oxford, Windsor, or Canterbury.

Beyond the West End

Knightsbridge One of London's most fashionable neighborhoods, Knightsbridge is a top residential, hotel, and shopping district just south of Hyde Park. **Harrods** on Brompton Road is its chief attraction. Founded in 1901, Harrods has been called "the Notre Dame of department stores." Right nearby, **Beauchamp Place** (*Bee*-cham) is one of London's most fashionable shopping streets, a Regency-era, boutique-lined street with a scattering of restaurants. Most hotels here are deluxe or first class.

Knightsbridge is one of the most convenient areas of London, ideally located if you want to head east to the theater district or the Mayfair shops, or west to Chelsea or Kensington's restaurants and attractions. Knightsbridge is also a swank address, with many fine hotels, although none are at the level of the palaces of Mayfair.

Belgravia South of Knightsbridge, this area has long been an aristocratic quarter of London, rivaling Mayfair in grandeur. Although it reached its pinnacle of prestige during the reign of Queen Victoria, the Duke and Duchess of Westminster still live at **Eaton Square,** and Belgravia remains a hot area for chic hotels. The neighborhood's centerpiece is **Belgrave Square.** When town houses were built from 1825 to 1835, aristocrats followed—the Duke of Connaught, the Earl of Essex, and even Queen Victoria's mother.

Belgravia is a tranquil district. If you lodge here, no one will ever accuse you of staying on the "wrong side of the tracks." The neighborhood is convenient to the little restaurants and pubs of Chelsea, which is located to Belgravia's immediate west. Victoria Station is located to its immediate east, so Belgravia is convenient if you're planning to take day trips from London.

Chelsea This stylish Thames-side district lies south and to the west of Belgravia. It begins at **Sloane Square,** with **Gilbert Ledward's Venus fountain** playing watery music. The area has always been a favorite of writers and artists, including Oscar Wilde (who was arrested here), George Eliot, James Whistler, J. M. W. Turner, Henry James, and Thomas Carlyle (whose former home can be visited). Mick Jagger and Margaret Thatcher (not together) have been more recent residents, and the late Princess Diana and her "Sloane Rangers" (a term used to describe posh women, derived from Chelsea's Sloane Square) of the 1980s gave the area even more recognition. There are some swank hotels here and a scattering of modestly priced ones. The main drawback to Chelsea is inaccessibility. Except for Sloane Square, there's a dearth of Tube stops, and unless you like to take a lot of buses or expensive taxis, you may find getting around a chore.

Chelsea's major boulevard is **King's Road,** where Mary Quant launched the miniskirt in the 1960s and where the English punk look began. King's Road runs the length of Chelsea; it's at its liveliest on Saturday. The outrageous fashions of the King's Road boutiques aren't typical of otherwise upmarket Chelsea, an elegant village filled with town houses and little mews dwellings that only successful stockbrokers and solicitors can afford to occupy. On the Chelsea/Fulham border is **Chelsea Harbour,** a luxury development of apartments and restaurants with a marina. You can spot its tall tower from far away; the golden ball on top moves up and down to indicate the tide level.

Kensington This Royal Borough (W8) lies west of Kensington Gardens and Hyde Park and is traversed by two of London's major shopping streets, **Kensington High Street** and **Kensington Church Street.** Since 1689, when asthmatic William III fled Whitehall Palace for Nottingham House (where the air was fresher), the district has enjoyed royal associations. In time, Nottingham House became Kensington Palace, and the royals grabbed a chunk of Hyde Park to plant their roses. Queen Victoria was born here. Kensington Palace, or "KP," as the royals say, was home to the late Princess Margaret (who had 20 rooms with a view) and is still home to Prince and Princess Michael of Kent, and the Duke and Duchess of Gloucester. Kensington Gardens is now open to the public, ever since George II decreed that "respectably dressed" people would be permitted in on Saturday—provided that no servants, soldiers, or sailors came (as you might imagine, that rule is long gone). During the reign of William III, Kensington Square developed, attracting artists and writers. Thackeray wrote *Vanity Fair* while living here. With all those royal associations, Kensington is a fashionable neighborhood. If you're a frugal traveler, head for South Kensington (see below) for moderately priced hotels and B&Bs. Southeast of Kensington Gardens and Earl's Court, primarily residential **South Kensington** is often called "museumland" because it's dominated by a complex of museums and colleges, including the **Natural History Museum,** the **Victoria and Albert Museum,** and the **Science Museum;** nearby is **Royal Albert Hall.**

South Kensington boasts some fashionable restaurants and town-house hotels. One of the neighborhood's curiosities is the **Albert Memorial,** completed in 1872 by Sir George Gilbert Scott; for sheer excess, this Victorian monument is unequaled in the world.

A hotel room in Kensington is a prestigious address. But as Princess Margaret may have told you, you're at the far stretch of the West End, lying some 20 minutes by Tube from the heart of the theater district. As for South Kensington, it was once considered the "boondocks," although with the boundaries of the West End expanding, the neighborhood is much closer to the action than it has ever been before.

Earl's Court Earl's Court lies below Kensington, bordering the western half of Chelsea. For decades a staid residential district, drawing genteel ladies wearing pince-nez glasses, Earl's Court now attracts a younger crowd (often gay), particularly at night, to its pubs, wine bars, and coffeehouses. It's a popular base for budget travelers, thanks to its wealth of B&Bs and budget hotels and its convenient access to central London: A 15-minute Tube ride takes you into the heart of Piccadilly.

West Brompton Once regarded as a hinterland, this neighborhood is seen today as an extension of central London. It lies directly south of Earl's Court (take the Tube to West Brompton) and southeast of West Kensington. Its focal point is the sprawling **Brompton Cemetery,** a flower-filled "green lung" (park) and burial place of such famous names as Frederick Leyland, the pre-Raphaelite patron, who died in 1892. It has many good restaurants, pubs, and taverns, as well as some budget hotels.

Paddington & Bayswater Paddington radiates out from Paddington

Station, north of Hyde Park and Kensington Gardens. It's one of the major B&B centers in London, attracting budget travelers who fill the lodgings in Sussex Gardens and Norfolk Square. After the first railway was introduced in London in 1836, a circle of sprawling railway terminals, including Paddington Station (which was built in 1838), spurred the growth of this middle-class area. Just south of Paddington, north of Hyde Park, and abutting more fashionable Notting Hill to the west is **Bayswater,** also filled with a large number of B&Bs that attract budget travelers. Inspired by Marylebone and elegant Mayfair, a relatively prosperous set of Victorian merchants built terrace houses around spacious squares in this area.

Paddington and Bayswater are sort of "in between" areas of London. If you've come to London to see the attractions in the east, including the British Museum, the Tower of London, and the theater district, you'll find yourself commuting a lot. Stay here for moderately priced lodgings (there are expensive hotels, too) and for convenience to transportation. Rapidly gentrifying, this area ranges from seedy to swank.

On the other (north) side of Westway/Marylebone Road are **Maida Vale** and **St. John's Wood,** two villages that have been absorbed by central London. Maida Vale lies west of **Regent's Park,** north of Paddington, and next to the more prestigious St. John's Wood (home to the Beatles' Abbey Road Studios). The area is very sports-oriented; if you take the Tube to Maida Vale, you'll find Paddington Recreation Ground, plus a smaller "green lung" called Paddington Bowling and Sports Club. The area is also home to some of the BBC studios.

Notting Hill Increasingly fashionable Notting Hill is bounded on the east by

Bayswater and on the south by Kensington. Hemmed in on the north by Westway and on the west by the Shepherd's Bush ramp leading to the M40, it has many turn-of-the-century mansions and small houses sitting on quiet, leafy streets, plus a growing number of hot restaurants and clubs. Gentrified in recent years, it's becoming an extension of central London. Hotels are few, but increasingly chic.

Even more remote than Paddington and Bayswater, Notting Hill lies at least another 10 minutes west of those districts. In spite of that, many young professional visitors to London wouldn't stay anywhere else.

In the northern half of Notting Hill is the hip neighborhood known as **Notting Hill Gate,** home to Portobello Road, which boasts one of London's most famous street markets. The area Tube stops are Notting Hill Gate, Holland Park, and Ladbroke Grove.

Nearby **Holland Park,** an expensive residential neighborhood, promotes itself as "10 minutes by Tube from practically anywhere," a bit of an exaggeration.

Shepherd's Bush To the immediate west of Notting Hill Gate, this increasingly fashionable area is attracting a slew of artists and photographers, and in their wake a number of trendy new hangouts. Old milk-bottling factories are being turned into chic dives, and so on. The area is close to more upscale districts such as Holland Park and Notting Hill Gate. The main BBC national office is in Shepherd's Bush, and, yes, that is Kate Moss rushing along Goldhawk Road.

Farther Afield

Greenwich To the southeast of London, this suburb, which contains the prime meridian—"zero" for the reckoning of terrestrial longitudes—enjoyed

Greater London Area

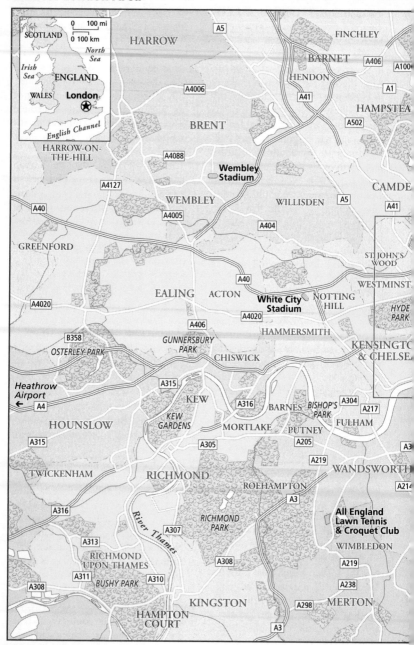

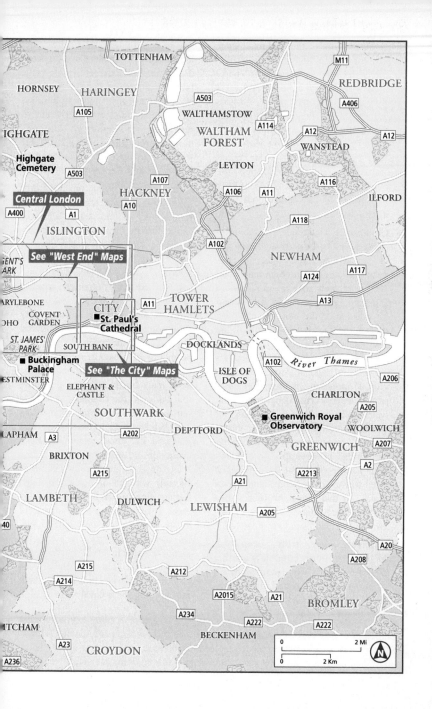

its heyday under the Tudors. Henry VIII and both of his daughters, Mary I and Elizabeth I, were born here. Greenwich Palace, Henry's favorite, is long gone, though. Today's visitors come to this lovely port village for nautical sights along the Thames, including visits to the tiny *Gipsy Moth IV,* a 16m (52-ft.) ketch in which Sir Francis Chichester sailed solo around the world from 1966 to 1967. Other attractions include the **National Maritime Museum.**

Hampstead This residential suburb of north London, beloved by Keats and Hogarth, is a favorite excursion for Londoners. Everyone from Sigmund Freud and D. H. Lawrence to Anna Pavlova and John Le Carré has lived here, and it's still one of the most desirable districts in the Greater London area. It has few hotels and, of course, is quite far from central London. Nonetheless, it's an attractive residential area, and many visitors appreciate its charms. Hampstead's centerpiece is Hampstead Heath, nearly 320 hectares (790 acres) of meadows and woodland; it maintains its rural atmosphere even though it's surrounded by cityscapes on all sides. The hilltop village of Hampstead is filled with cafes, tearooms, and restaurants, and there are pubs galore, some with historic pedigrees. Take the Northern Line to Hampstead Heath station.

Highgate Along with Hampstead, Highgate in north London is another choice residential area, particularly on or near **Pond Square** and along Highgate High Street. Once celebrated for its "sweet salutarie airs," Highgate has long been a desirable place for Londoners to live; locals still flock to its taverns and pubs for "exercise and harmless merriment" as they did in the old days. Today most visitors come to see **Highgate Cemetery,** London's most famous burial ground. It's the final resting place of such figures as Karl Marx and George Eliot.

Hammersmith Sitting on the north bank of the Thames, just to the west of Kensington, Hammersmith will fool you at first into thinking it's an industrial park, thanks to the stretch of factories between Putney and Hammersmith bridges. Actually, the area is predominantly residential. Its most attractive feature is its waterfront, filled with boathouses, small businesses, some very good restaurants, and artists' studios. Beyond Hammersmith Bridge, the neighborhood blossoms with 18th-century homes behind lime and catalpa trees, more boathouses, and pubs that spill out onto the riverbank as soon as warm weather hits. Some of London's best chefs have fled the heart of the West End and its ridiculous rents to open quality dining rooms here. See p. 199.

Nearby is the delightful old village of **Barnes,** with its ironwork-decorated Barnes Terrace. **Hammersmith Terrace,** a favorite stamping ground of artists, adds color to the neighborhood. Another stretch of gracious homes lies along **Chiswick Mall,** curling into Church Street. This area imitates an English village before thrusting you back into London along Great West Road.

2 Getting Around

Remember that cars drive on the left and vehicles have the right of way over pedestrians. Wherever you walk, always look both ways before stepping off a curb.

BY PUBLIC TRANSPORTATION

The London Underground and the city's buses operate on the same system of six fare zones. The fare zones radiate in rings from the central zone 1, which is where most visitors spend the majority of their time. Zone 1 covers the area from Liverpool Street in the east to Notting Hill in the west, and from Waterloo in the south to Baker Street, Euston, and King's Cross in the north. To travel beyond zone 1, you need a multizone ticket. Note that all single one-way, round-trip, and 1-day pass tickets are valid only on the day of purchase. Tube and bus maps should be available at any Underground station. You can download them before your trip from the excellent **London Transport (LT)** website: www.tfl.gov.uk/tfl. There are also **LT Information Centres** at several major Tube stations: Euston, King's Cross, Oxford Circus, St. James's Park, Liverpool Street Station, and Piccadilly Circus, as well as in the British Rail stations at Euston and Victoria and in each of the terminals at Heathrow Airport. Most of them are open daily (some close Sun) from at least 9am to 5pm. A 24-hour public-transportation information service is also available at © **020/7222-1234.**

DISCOUNT PASSES   If you plan to use public transportation a lot, there are a range of fare discounts available. **Travelcard**s offer unlimited use of buses, Underground, Docklands Light Railway, and National Rail services in Greater London for any period ranging from a day to a year. Travelcards are available from Underground ticket offices, LT Information Centres, main post offices in the London area, many newsagents, and some newsstands. Children under age 11 generally travel free on the Tube and buses.

The **1-Day Travelcard** allows you to go anywhere throughout Greater London. For travel anywhere within zones 1 and 2, the cost is £6.60 ($13) for adults or £3.30 ($6.25) for children 5 to 15. The **Off-Peak 1-Day Travelcard,** which is valid after 9:30am on weekdays is even cheaper. For two zones, the cost is £5.10 ($9.70) for adults and £2 ($3.80) for children 5 to 15.

The system now features a **3-Day Travel Card,** allowing adults to travel within zones 1 and 2 for £16–£20 ($30–$38) depending on the time (peak or off-peak), and allowing children to go for £6–£8.20 ($11–$16).

1-Week Travelcards cost adults £23 ($44) and children £12 ($23) for travel in zones 1 and 2.

Consider purchasing the **Oyster Card,** a travel discount card that's all the rage. You can prepay for single fares which cost considerably less than a paper ticket—usually about half the price. Oysters are valid on the Tube, DLR, tram, and National Rail services within your chosen zones and across the entire London bus network. For 24-hour information, call the Oyster hotline at © **0870/849-9999.** The card has a daily price cap which is frozen, meaning you never pay more than £3 ($5.70) regardless of how many trips you make in 1 day. You can buy an Oyster Card at any ticket office for £3 ($5.70).

THE UNDERGROUND

The Underground, or Tube, is the fastest and easiest way to get around. All Tube stations are clearly marked with a red circle and blue crossbar. Routes are conveniently color-coded.

If you have British coins, you can get your ticket at a vending machine. Otherwise, buy it at the ticket office. You can transfer as many times as you like as long as you stay in the Underground. Children 4 and under travel free if accompanied by an adult.

Slide your ticket into the slot at the gate and pick it up as it comes through on the other side and hold on to it—it must be presented when you exit the station at your destination. If you're caught without a valid ticket, you'll be fined £20 ($38) on the spot. If you owe extra money, you'll be asked to pay the difference by the attendant at the exit. The Tube runs roughly from 5am to 12:30am (7:30am–10:30pm on Sun). After that, you must take a taxi or night bus to your destination. For information on the London Tube system, call the **London Underground** at © **020/7222-1234,** but expect to stay on hold for a good while before a live person comes on the line. Information is also available on **www.tfl.gov.uk**.

The Jubilee Line Extension has been extended eastward to serve the growing suburbs of the southeast and the Docklands area. This east–west axis helps ease traffic on some of London's most hard-pressed underground lines. The line also makes it much easier to reach Greenwich.

BY BUS

The comparably priced bus system is almost as good as the Underground and gives you better views of the city. To find out about current routes, pick up a free bus map at one of London Transport's Travel Information Centres, listed above. The map is available in person only, not by mail. You can also obtain a map at **www.tfl.gov.uk**.

As with the Underground, fares vary according to distance traveled. Generally, bus fares are £2/$3.80 (£1/$1.90 with an oyster card), slightly less than Tube fares. If you want your stop called out, simply ask the conductor or driver. To speed up bus travel, passengers have to purchase tickets before boarding. Drivers no longer collect fares on board. Some 300 roadside ticket machines serve stops in central London—in other words, it's "pay as you board." You'll need the exact fare, however, as ticket machines don't make change.

Buses generally run 24 hours a day. A few night buses have special routes, running once an hour or so; most pass through Trafalgar Square. Keep in mind that night buses are often so crowded (especially on weekends) that they are unable to pick up passengers after a few stops. You may find yourself waiting a long time. Consider taking a taxi. Call the 24-hour **hot line** (© **020/7222-1234**) for schedule and fare information.

BY TAXI

London cabs are among the most comfortable and best-designed in the world. You can pick one up either by heading for a cab rank or by hailing one in the street (the taxi is available if the yellow taxi sign on the roof is lit); once it has stopped for you, a taxi is obliged to take you anywhere you want to go within 9.5km (6 miles) of the pickup point, provided it's within the metropolitan area. To **call a cab,** phone © **020/7272-0272.**

The meter starts at £2.20 ($4.20), with increments of £2 ($3.80) per mile thereafter, based on distance or time. Surcharges are imposed after 8pm and on weekends and public holidays. All these tariffs include VAT. Fares usually increase annually. It's recommended that you tip 10% to 15% of the fare.

If you call for a cab, the meter starts running when the taxi receives instructions from the dispatcher, so you could find that the meter already reads a few pounds more than the initial drop of £2.20 ($4.20) when you step inside.

Minicabs are also available, and they're often useful when regular taxis are scarce or when the Tube stops running. These cabs are meterless, so you must negotiate the fare in advance. Unlike regular cabs, minicabs are forbidden by law to cruise for fares. They operate from sidewalk kiosks, such as those around Leicester Square. If you need to call one, try **Brunswick Chauffeurs/Abbey Cars** (✆ **020/8969-2555**) in west London, **London Cabs, Ltd.** (✆ **020/8778-3000**) in south London, or **Newham Minicars** (✆ **020/8472-1400**) in south London. Minicab kiosks can be found near many Tube or BritRail stops, especially in outlying areas.

If you have a complaint about taxi service or if you leave something in a cab, contact the **Public Carriage Office,** 15 Penton St., N1 9PU (Tube: Angel Station). If it's a complaint, you must have the cab number, which is displayed in the passenger compartment. Call ✆ **0845/602-7000** or 020/7222-1234 with complaints.

BY CAR

Don't drive in congested London. It is easy to get around without a car, traffic and parking are nightmares, and—to top it off—you'd have to drive from what you normally consider the passenger seat on the wrong side of the road. It all adds up to a big headache. Another reason not to drive is that you will have to pay a "Congestion Charge" of £8 ($15) between 7am and 6pm Monday to Friday, covering most of Central London.

BY BICYCLE

One of the most popular bike-rental shops is **On Your Bike,** 52–54 Tooley St., London Bridge, SE1 (✆ **020/7378-6669;** www.onyourbike.com; Tube: London Bridge), open Monday through Friday from 8am to 7pm, Saturday from 10am to 6pm, and Sunday 11am to 5pm. The first-class mountain bikes, with high seats and low-slung handlebars, cost £12 ($23) for the first day and £8 ($15) for each day thereafter, or £36 ($68) per week, and require a £110 ($209) deposit on a credit card.

FAST FACTS: London

American Express The main office is at 30–31 Haymarket, SW1 (✆ 020/7484-9600; Tube: Piccadilly Circus). Full services are available Monday through Saturday from 9am to 6pm. On Sunday from 10am to 5pm, only the foreign-exchange bureau is open.

Area Codes London now has only one area code: **020.** Within the city limits, you don't need to dial it; use only the eight-digit number. If you're calling London from home before your trip, the country code for England is **44.** It must precede the London area code. When you're calling London from outside Britain, drop the "0" in front of the local area code.

ATM Networks See "Money" p. 36

Babysitters If your hotel can't recommend a sitter, call **Sitters** (© **0800/ 389-0038** or 020/7935-3000; www.babysitter.co.uk). The rates are Sunday to Friday £7 ($13) per hour, Saturday £7.50 ($14) per hour with a 4-hour minimum. Guest membership costs £10 ($19) and is valid for 1 month. You must also pay a booking fee at a cost of £6 ($11) per day booking or £5 ($9.50) per evening booking.

Business Hours Banks are usually open Monday to Friday 9:30am to 3:30pm. Business offices are open Monday to Friday 9am to 5pm; the lunch break lasts an hour, but most places stay open during that time. Pubs and bars stay open from 11am to 11pm Monday to Saturday and from noon to 10:30pm on Sunday. Stores generally open at 10am and close at 5pm, staying open until 7pm on Thursday. Some stores are now open on Sunday, usually 11am to 5pm.

Camera Repair **Sendean,** Shop 2, 9–12 St. Anne's Court, W1F (© **0871/ 750-2463;** www.sendeancameras.co.uk), gives free estimates and does quick work. It's open weekdays from 10:30am to 6pm and accepts American Express, MasterCard, and Visa.

Car Rentals See "Getting Around," p. 76.

Climate See "When to Go," in chapter 3.

Customs
What You Can Bring into London
Non-E.U. Nationals 18 and Older: You can bring in, duty-free, 200 cigarettes, or 100 cigarillos, or 50 cigars, or 250 grams of smoking tobacco. The amount allowed for each of these goods is doubled if you live outside Europe.

You can also bring in 2 liters of wine and either 1 liter of alcohol over 22% or 2 liters of wine under 22%. In addition, you can bring in 2 ounces of perfume and a quarter liter of eau de toilette. Visitors 15 and over may also bring in other goods totaling £145 ($276); the allowance for those 14 and under is £73 ($139). (Customs officials tend to be lenient about general merchandise, realizing the limits are unrealistically low.)

You can't bring your pet straight to England. Six months' quarantine is required before it is allowed in. An illegally imported animal may be destroyed.

E.U. Citizens: Visitors from fellow European Union countries can bring into Britain any amount of goods, as long as the goods are intended for their personal use—not for resale.

The current policy for bringing pets into the U.K. from the E.U. is under review. Right now, animals or pets of any kind are forbidden from entering without a long quarantine period.

What You Can Bring Home from London
U.S. Citizens: For specifics on what you can bring back and the corresponding fees, download the invaluable free pamphlet *Know Before You Go* online at **www.cbp.gov.** (Click on "Travel," and then click on "Know Before You Go.")

Or contact **U.S. Customs & Border Protection (CBP)**, 1300 Pennsylvania Ave., NW, Washington, DC 20229 (© **877/287-8667**) and request the pamphlet.

Canadian Citizens: For a clear summary of Canadian rules, write for the booklet *I Declare,* issued by the **Canada Border Services Agency** (© **800/461-9999** in Canada, or 204/983-3500; **www.cbsa-asfc.gc.ca**).

U.K. Citizens: For information, contact **HM Customs & Excise** at © **0845/010-9000** (from outside the U.K., 020/8929-0152), or consult their website at **www.hmce.gov.uk**.

Australian Citizens: A helpful brochure available from Australian consulates or Customs offices is *Know Before You Go.* For more information, call the **Australian Customs Service** at © **1300/363-263,** or log on to **www.customs.gov.au**.

New Zealand Citizens: Most questions are answered in a free pamphlet available at New Zealand consulates and Customs offices: *New Zealand Customs Guide for Travellers, Notice no. 4.* For more information, contact **New Zealand Customs,** The Customhouse, 17–21 Whitmore St., Box 2218, Wellington (© **04/473-6099** or 0800/428-786; **www.customs.govt.nz**).

Dentists For dental emergencies, call **Eastman Dental Hospital** (© **020/7915-1000**; Tube: King's Cross or Chancery Lane).

Doctors Call © **999** in a medical emergency. Some hotels have physicians on call for emergencies. For nonemergencies, try **Medical Express,** 117A Harley St., W1 (© **020/7499-1991**; www.medicalexpressclinic.com; Tube: Regent's Park). A private British clinic, it's not part of the free British medical establishment. The clinic is open Monday to Friday 9am to 6pm and Saturday 10am to 2pm.

Documents See "Entry Requirements & Customs," in chapter 3.

Driving Rules See "Getting Around," p. 76.

Drugstores In Britain they're called chemists. Every police station has a list of emergency chemists. One of the most centrally located is **Bliss the Chemist,** 5–6 Marble Arch, W1 (© **020/7723-6116**; Tube: Marble Arch), open daily from 9am to midnight. Every London neighborhood has a branch of **Boots the Chemist,** Britain's leading pharmacy.

Electricity British current is 240 volts, AC, so you'll need a converter or transformer for U.S.-made electrical appliances, as well as an adapter that allows the plug to match British outlets. Some (but not all) hotels supply them for guests. If you've forgotten one, you can buy a transformer/adapter at most branches of **Boots the Chemist.**

Embassies & High Commissions The **U.S. Embassy** is at 24 Grosvenor Sq., W1 (© **020/7499-9000**; www.usembassy.org.uk; Tube: Bond St.). Hours are Monday through Friday from 8:30am to 5:30pm. However, for passport and visa information, go to the **U.S. Passport and Citizenship Unit,** 55–56 Upper Brook St., London, W1 (© **020/7499-9000**, ext. 2563; Tube: Marble Arch or Bond St.). Passport and Citizenship Unit hours are Monday to Friday 8:30 to 12:30pm.

The **Canadian High Commission,** MacDonald House, 38 Grosvenor St., W1 (© **020/7258-6600;** www.canada.org.uk; Tube: Bond St.), handles visas for Canada. Hours are Monday to Friday 8:30am to 5pm; 8 to 11am for immigration services.

The **Australian High Commission** is at Australia House, the Strand, WC2 (© **020/7379-4334;** www.australia.org.uk; Tube: Charing Cross or Aldwych). Hours are Monday to Friday 9am to 5pm; 9 to 11am for immigration services; passports 9:30am to 3:30pm.

The **New Zealand High Commission** is at New Zealand House, 80 Haymarket at Pall Mall, SW1 (© **020/7930-8422;** www.nzembassy.com; Tube: Charing Cross or Piccadilly Circus). Hours are Monday to Friday 10am to 4pm.

The **Irish Embassy** is at 17 Grosvenor Place, SW1 (© **020/7235-2171;** http:// ireland.embassyhomepage.com; Tube: Hyde Park Corner). Hours are Monday to Friday 9:30am to 1pm and 2 to 5pm.

Emergencies In London, for police, fire, or an ambulance, dial © **999.**

Eyeglass Repair **David Clulow** has 10 offices in Central London; the one in Soho, 70 Old Compton St., W1 (© **020/7287-1128),** can handle most repairs and fills eyeglass prescriptions. Open Monday to Friday 10am to 6:30pm, Saturday 10am to 7pm.

Holidays In England, public holidays include New Year's Day, Good Friday, Easter Monday, May Day (first Mon in May), spring and summer bank holidays (last Mon in May and Aug, respectively), Christmas Day, and Boxing Day (Dec 26).

Hospitals The following offer emergency care in London, 24 hours a day, with the first treatment free under the National Health Service: **Royal Free Hospital,** Pond Street (© **020/7794-0500;** Tube: Belsize Park), and **University College Hospital,** 25 Grafton Way (© **0845/155-5000;** Tube: Warren St.). Many other London hospitals also have accident and emergency departments.

Hot Lines If you're in some sort of substance abuse or legal emergency, call **Release** (© **020/7729-9904),** open from Monday to Friday from 11am to 1pm. **The Rape and Sexual Abuse Hotline** (© **0845/122-1331)** is open daily Monday to Friday noon to 2:30pm and 7 to 9:30pm, and on weekends and bank holidays from 2:30pm to 5pm. **Alcoholics Anonymous** (© **020/7833-0022)** answers its help line daily from 10am to 10pm. For issues related to sexual health and sexually transmitted diseases, call the **Sexual Health Information Line** at © **0800/567-123.**

Information See "Visitor Information," earlier in this chapter.

Internet Access See "Staying Connected," p. 48.

Legal Aid In every case where legal aid is required by a foreign national within Britain, the British Tourist Authority advises visitors to contact their embassy.

Liquor Laws The legal drinking age for hard liquor is 18. However, persons aged 16 and up can drink beer, cider, or wine in a restaurant if accompanied by a person who is 18 years of age (or older) and if that person actually purchases the drink. Children under 14 aren't allowed in pubs, except in certain rooms, and then only when accompanied by a parent or guardian. Don't drink and drive—penalties are stiff. Breaking decades of tradition, England in 2005 abandoned its strict, often draconian, liquor laws, and began allowing 24-hour alcohol sales in England and Wales. Many pubs no longer close at 11pm, which used to be "last call." Of course, it's up to the publican, but many, if they elect to do so, could stay open day and night. That is true at least in theory. But most publicans have applied for or been granted only a 1- or 2-hour extension at this point. It's not total Nirvana for the pub owners, however. Some counties are stationing undercover officers in pubs to fine staff members who serve liquor to visibly drunk customers, and the problems of drunk drivers on the highway, policemen fear, will only increase.

Lost & Found Be sure to tell all of your credit card companies the minute you discover your wallet has been lost or stolen, and file a report at the nearest police precinct. Your credit card company or insurer may require a police report number or record of the loss. Most credit card companies have an emergency toll-free number to call if your card is lost or stolen; they may be able to wire you a cash advance immediately or deliver an emergency credit card in a day or two. American cardholders can call the toll-free numbers below in case of an emergency—Visa at 0800/891-725, American Express at 0800/587-6023, and MasterCard at 020/7557-5000 (the latter is not a toll-free number).

If you need emergency cash over the weekend when all banks and American Express offices are closed, you can have money wired to you via **Western Union** (© **800/325-6000;** www.westernunion.com).

Mail An airmail letter to North America costs 50p (95¢) for 10 grams; postcards also require a 50p (95¢) stamp; letters generally take 7 to 10 days to arrive from the United States. See "Post Offices," below, for locations.

Maps See "Finding Your Way Around," under "Orientation," earlier in this chapter.

Measurements See the chart on the inside front cover of this book for details on converting metric measurements to nonmetric equivalents.

Money See "Money," in chapter 3.

Newspapers & Magazines The Times, Daily Telegraph, Daily Mail, and *Guardian* are dailies carrying the latest news. The *International Herald Tribune,* published in Paris, and an international edition of *USA Today,* beamed via satellite, are available daily (*USA Today* will be printed as a newsletter). Copies of *Time* and *Newsweek* are sold at most newsstands. Magazines such as *Time Out, City Limits,* and *Where* contain useful information about the latest happenings in London.

Passports Allow plenty of time before your trip to apply for a passport; processing normally takes 3 weeks but can take longer during busy periods (especially spring). And keep in mind that if you need a passport in a hurry, you'll pay a higher processing fee.

For Residents of Australia: You can pick up an application from your local post office or any branch of Passports Australia, but you must schedule an interview at the passport office to present your application materials. Call the **Australian Passport Information Service** at ℂ **131-232**, or visit the government website at www.passports.gov.au.

For Residents of Canada: Passport applications are available at travel agencies throughout Canada or from the central **Passport Office**, Department of Foreign Affairs and International Trade, Ottawa, ON K1A 0G3 (ℂ **800/567-6868**; www.ppt.gc.ca).

For Residents of Ireland: You can apply for a 10-year passport at the **Passport Office**, Setanta Centre, Molesworth Street, Dublin 2 (ℂ **01/671-1633**; www.irl-gov.ie/iveagh). Those under age 18 and over 65 must apply for a 3-year passport. You can also apply at 1A South Mall, Cork (ℂ **021/272-525**) or at most main post offices.

For Residents of New Zealand: You can pick up a passport application at any New Zealand Passports Office or download it from their website. Contact the **Passports Office** at ℂ **0800/225-050** in New Zealand or 04/474-8100, or log on to www.passports.govt.nz.

For Residents of the United States: Whether you're applying in person or by mail, you can download passport applications from the U.S. State Department website at **http://travel.state.gov**. To find your regional passport office, either check the U.S. State Department website or call the **National Passport Information Center** toll-free number (ℂ **877/487-2778**) for automated information.

Police In an emergency, dial ℂ **999** (no coins are needed).

Post Offices The **main post office** is at 24–28 William IV St., WC2 (ℂ **020/7484-9307**; Tube: Charing Cross). It operates as three separate businesses: inland and international postal service and banking (Mon–Fri 8:30am–6:30pm and Sat 9am–5:30pm); philatelic postage-stamp sales (Mon–Fri 8:30am–6:30pm and Sat 9am–5:30pm) for collectors; and the postal shop, selling greeting cards and stationery (Mon–Sat 8:30am–6:30pm). Other post offices and post-office branches are open Monday to Friday from 9am to 5:30pm and Saturday from 9am to 12:30pm. Many post office branches and some main post offices close for an hour at lunchtime.

Restrooms They're marked by PUBLIC TOILETS signs in streets, parks, and Tube stations; many are automatically sterilized after each use. The English often call toilets "loos." You'll also find well-maintained lavatories in all larger public buildings, such as museums and art galleries, large department stores, and railway stations. It's not really acceptable to use the lavatories in hotels, restaurants, and pubs if you're not a customer, but we can't say that we always stick to this rule. Public lavatories are usually free, but you may need a small coin to get in or to use a proper washroom.

Safety See "Health & Safety," in chapter 3.

Smoking As of July 1, 2007 a smoking ban went into effect in England. Smoking is now banned in all indoor public places such as pubs, restaurants, and clubs.

Taxes To encourage energy conservation, the British government levies a tax on gasoline (petrol). With VAT included, the actual tax comes out to be an astonishing 70%. There is also a 17.5% national value-added tax (VAT) that is added to all hotel and restaurant bills and is included in the price of many items you purchase. This can be refunded if you shop at stores that participate in the Retail Export Scheme (signs are posted in the window). See the "How to Get Your VAT Refund" box on p. 272.

In October 1994, Britain imposed a departure tax. Currently it is £40 ($76), but it is included in the price of your ticket. For business or first-class travel, the tax is £80 ($152).

Time Zone England follows Greenwich Mean Time ([GMT]; 5 hr. ahead of Eastern Standard Time [EST]). Most of the year, Britain is 5 hours ahead of the time observed on the East Coast of the United States. When it's noon in New York, it's 5pm in London. Because the U.S. and Britain observe daylight saving time at slightly different times of the year, there's a brief period (about a week) in the spring when London is 6 hours ahead of New York.

Tipping For cab drivers, add about 10% to 15% to the fare on the meter. However, if the driver loads or unloads your luggage, add something extra.

In hotels, porters receive £1 ($1.90) per bag, even if you have only one small suitcase. Hall porters are tipped only for special services. Maids receive £1.50 ($2.85) per day. In top-ranking hotels, the concierge will often submit a separate bill showing charges for newspapers and other items; if he or she has been particularly helpful, tip extra.

Hotels often add a service charge of 10% to 15% to most bills. In smaller bed-and-breakfasts, the tip is not likely to be included. Therefore, tip people for special services, such as the waiter who serves you breakfast. If several people have served you in a bed-and-breakfast, you may ask that 10% to 15% be added to the bill and divided among the staff.

Restaurants rarely add more than 12.5% onto the bill, but often they do not, leaving the tip to your discretion. In a nightclub with table service, the tip may be added to the bill but not if you're only ordering drinks at the bar. The same is true of a wine bar. Waiters in deluxe restaurants and nightclubs are accustomed to the extra 5%. Sommeliers (wine stewards) get about £1 ($1.90) per bottle of wine served. Tipping in pubs isn't common, but in wine bars, the server usually gets about £1 ($1.90) per round of drinks if it's table service.

Barbers and hairdressers expect 10% to 15%. Tour guides expect £2 ($3.80), though it's not mandatory. Gas station attendants are rarely tipped, and theater ushers don't expect tips.

Transit Information See "Getting Around," earlier in this chapter. For more information on travel on London's Tube and bus system, call © **020/7222-1234** 24 hours a day, but expect to stay on hold for a good while before a live person comes on the line.

Water London's water is safe to drink. Tap water is free in restaurants, so be sure to ask for it if you don't want to pay for bottled water.

Weather Call © **020/7939-9946** for current weather information, but chances are, the line will be busy. You can also tune into 1152 AM (LBC News) for weather reports.

6

Where to Stay

The good news is that more than 10,000 hotel rooms have opened in London post-millennium, relieving the overcrowding that existed during peak travel months. The downside? Most of these hotels are in districts far from the city center and are of the no-frills budget-chain variety.

Post millennium, some hoteliers have decided to adapt former public or institutional buildings rather than start from scratch. For example, the imposing County Hall building in the S1 district now boasts two chains: a luxurious Marriott and a leaner, meaner Travel Inn. Another trend is a shift away from the West End to such respectable sections as Greenwich (now a virtual suburb of London), Docklands, and even the City (London's financial district). With all the vast improvements and upgrades made at the turn of the 21st century, chances are, you'll like your room. What you won't like is the price. Even if a hotel remains scruffy, London hoteliers have little embarrassment about jacking up prices. Hotels in all categories remain overpriced.

London boasts some of the most famous hotels in the world—temples of luxury like Claridge's and The Dorchester, and more recent rivals like the Four Seasons. The problem is that there are too many of these high-priced hotels (and now there are many budget options) and not enough moderately priced options.

Even at the luxury level, you may be surprised at what you don't get. Many of the stately Victorian and Edwardian gems are so steeped in tradition that they lack modern conveniences standard in other luxury hotels around the world. A few have modernized with a vengeance, but others retain amenities from the Boer War era. London does have some cutting-edge, chintz-free hotels that seem to have been flown in straight from Los Angeles—complete with high-end sound systems and gadget-filled marble bathrooms. But these hotels are not necessarily superior; though they're streamlined and convenient, they frequently lack the personal service and spaciousness that characterize the grand old hotels.

Since the late 1990s and post-millennium, new boutique hotels have been generating lots of excitement. With their charm, intimacy, and attention to detail, they're an attractive alternative to larger, stuffier establishments. The "boutiquing" of the hotel scene continues—the city offers more personally run and privately operated hotels than ever. We've surveyed the best of them, concentrating on reasonably priced choices.

If you're looking for budget options, don't despair. London has some good-value places in the lower price ranges, and we've included the best of these. An affordable option is a bed-and-breakfast. The following reliable services will recommend and arrange a B&B room for you: **The London Bed and Breakfast Agency Limited** (© **020/7586-2768;** fax 020/7586-6567; www.londonbb.com) is a reputable agency that can provide inexpensive accommodations in selected private homes for £30 to £50 ($57–$95) per person per night, based on double occupancy (although some accommodations will cost a lot more). **London B&B** (© **800/872-2632** in the U.S.; fax 619/531-1686; www.londonbandb.com) offers B&B accommodations in private family residences or unhosted apartments. Homes are inspected for quality and comfort, amenities, and convenience.

Instead of B&Bs, some savvy visitors prefer long-term options, including self-catering accommodations or else vacation or apartment rentals. One of the best establishments for arranging this type of rental is **Coach House London Rentals** ★★, 2 Tunly Rd., London SW17 7QJ (© **020/8772-1939;** fax 020/8181-6152; www.rentals.chslondon.com). The agency represents more than 75 properties, ranging from modest studio flats for friendly couples to spacious homes that can sleep up to 12. The minimum length of a stay is 5 nights, and a car can be sent to the airport to pick you up.

For the upmarket traveler, the aptly named **Uptown Reservations,** 8 Kelso Place, London W8 5QD (© **020/7937-2001;** fax 020/7937-6660; www.uptownres.co.uk), features attractive, comfortably furnished accommodations in elegant private homes in swanky districts of the city. You share your digs with the hosts themselves, many of whom are artists, diplomats, or, in some rare cases, lords of the realm who need extra money for living expenses. A substantial breakfast is included in the price.

Amazing discounts, seemingly unavailable elsewhere, are offered by **Visit Hotels.com,** 37B New Cavendish St., London W1G 8JR (© **08704/352-422;** fax 08704/325-423; www.visithotels.com). Sometimes discounts on a room can range up to 70%.

You can also look for deals on online travel booking sites like **Travelocity, Expedia, Orbitz, Priceline,** and **Hotwire,** or you can book hotels through **Hotels.com, Quikbook** (www.quikbook.com), and **Travelaxe** (www.travelaxe.net).

HotelChatter.com is a daily webzine offering smart coverage and critiques of hotels worldwide. Go to **TripAdvisor.com** or **HotelShark.com** for helpful independent consumer reviews of hotels and resort properties. It's a good idea to **get a confirmation number** and **make a printout** of any online booking transaction.

It's true that you can almost always get a room at a deluxe hotel if you're willing to pay the price. But during certain peak periods, including the high season (roughly April to October) and during trade shows, seasonal events, and royal occasions, rooms in all kinds of hotels may be snatched up early. Book ahead. If you arrive without a reservation, begin your search for a room as early in the day as possible. If you arrive late at night, you may have to take what you can get, often at a much higher price than you'd like.

The vast majority of the hotels and B&Bs listed below offer nonsmoking rooms—just ask for one when you book.

RATE REGULATIONS All hotels, motels, inns, and guesthouses in Britain with four bedrooms or more (including self-catering accommodations) must display notices listing minimum and maximum overnight charges in a prominent place in the reception area or at the entrance. The prices must include any service charge and may include VAT. If VAT isn't included, then it must be shown separately. And if meals are included, this must be stated.

SAVING ON YOUR HOTEL ROOM
The **rack rate** is the maximum rate a hotel charges for a room. Hardly anybody pays this price, however, except in high season or on holidays. To lower the cost of your room:

- **Ask about special rates or other discounts.** You may qualify for corporate, student, military, senior, frequent flier, trade union, or other discounts.
- **Dial direct.** When booking a room in a chain hotel, you'll often get a

better deal by calling the individual hotel's reservation desk rather than the chain's main number.

- **Book online.** Many hotels offer Internet-only discounts or supply rooms to Priceline, Hotwire, or Expedia at rates much lower than the ones you can get through the hotel itself.

- **Remember the law of supply and demand.** You can save big on hotel rooms by traveling in a destination's off-season or shoulder seasons, when rates typically drop, even at luxury properties.

- **Look into group or long-stay discounts.** If you come as part of a large group, you should be able to negotiate a bargain rate. Likewise, if you're planning a long stay (at least 5 days), you might qualify for a discount. As a general rule, expect 1 night free after a 7-night stay.

- **Sidestep excess surcharges and hidden costs.** Many hotels have adopted the unpleasant practice of nickel-and-diming guests with opaque surcharges. When you book a room, ask what is included in the room rate, and what is extra. Avoid dialing direct from hotel phones, which can have exorbitant rates. And don't be tempted by the room's minibar offerings: Most hotels charge through the nose for water, soda, and snacks. Finally, ask about local taxes and service charges, which can increase the cost of a room by 15% or more.

- **Book an efficiency.** A room with a kitchenette allows you to shop for groceries and cook your own meals. This is a big money saver, especially for families on long stays.

- **Consider enrolling in hotel chains' "frequent-stay" programs,** which are upping the ante lately to win the loyalty of repeat customers. Frequent guests can now accumulate points or credits to earn free hotel nights, airline miles, in-room amenities, merchandise, tickets to concerts and events, discounts on sporting facilities—and even credit toward stock in the participating hotel, in the case of the Jameson Inn hotel group. Perks are awarded not only by many chain hotels and motels (Hilton HHonors, Marriott Rewards, Wyndham ByRequest, to name a few) but individual inns and B&Bs. Many chain hotels partner with other hotel chains, car-rental firms, airlines, and credit-card companies to give consumers additional incentive to do repeat business.

LANDING THE BEST ROOM

Somebody has to get the best room in the house. It might as well be you. You can start by joining the hotel's frequent-guest program, which may make you eligible for upgrades. A hotel-branded credit card usually gives its owner "silver" or "gold" status in frequent-guest programs for free. Always ask about a corner room. They're often larger and quieter, with more windows and light, and they often cost the

---

Tips **Upstairs, Downstairs**

Elevators are called "lifts." Some of them are just as Victorian as the edifices in which they operate. They are, however, regularly inspected and completely safe. Many hotels (and especially B&Bs) lack even these rudimentary elevators, making them inaccessible for individuals with disabilities. If you have mobility issues, call ahead and make sure there isn't a steep, narrow staircase between the lobby and your guest room.

same as standard rooms. When you make your reservation, ask if the hotel is renovating; if it is, request a room away from the construction. Ask about nonsmoking rooms and rooms with views. Be sure to request your choice of twin, queen- or king-size beds. If you're a light sleeper, ask for a quiet room away from vending or ice machines, elevators, restaurants, bars, and discos. Ask for a room that has been recently renovated or refurbished.

If you aren't happy with your room when you arrive, ask for another one. Most lodgings will be willing to accommodate you.

1 Best Hotel Bets

- **Best in the East End:** The first luxury hotel to be built in Holborn, **Renaissance London Chancery Court,** 252 High Holborn, WC1 (© 800/468-3571 or 020/7829-9888), opened in 2001 and became an instant hit. A 1914 landmark building has been stunningly transformed into this citadel of luxury and plush comfort. See p. 97.

- **Best for a Romantic Getaway:** Hip couples check into the **Covent Garden Hotel,** 10 Monmouth St., WC2 (© 800/553-6674 or 020/7806-1000), which has been hailed as 1 of the 25 hottest places to stay in the world. The former hospital is now the epitome of chic comfort, with rooms so elegant and stylish that romance is inevitable. See p. 101.

- **Best Historic Hotel:** Founded by the former manservant to Lord Byron, the stylish **Brown's Hotel,** 30 Albemarle St., W1 (© 020/7493-6020), dates back to Victorian times. It's one of London's most genteel hotels, with its legendary afternoon tea and paneled bar. See p. 105.

- **Best for Business Travelers:** Wheelers and dealers head to **The Langham,** 1C Portland Place, W1 (© 800/223-6800 or 020/7636-1000), which boasts sleek styling and grand public rooms. At times, it seems all the world's business is conducted from this nerve center. See p. 126.

- **Best Trendy Hotel: St. Martins Lane,** 45 St. Martin's Lane (© 800/697-1791 or 020/7300-5500), is almost without challenge in this category. Ian Schrager has brought New York cutting-edge style to a 1960s building in Covent Garden. It's his first hotel outside the U.S., and it's eccentric, irreverent, and whimsical. Would Nicole Kidman go anywhere else? See p. 101.

- **Best for Thoroughly British Ambience:** In a gaslit courtyard in back of St. James's Palace, **Dukes Hotel,** 35 St. James's Place, SW1 (© 800/381-4702 or 020/7491-4840), has an unsurpassed dignity. From the bread-and-butter pudding served in the clubby dining room to the impeccable service, at Dukes there will always be an England. See p. 109.

- **Best Modern Design: The Hempel,** 31–35 Craven Hill Garden Sq., W2 (© 020/7298-9000), might be housed in a trio of 1800s row houses, but the renovations by designer Anouska Hempel are purely modern. A grand Italian sense of proportion is balanced with Asian simplicity, and soothing monochromatic tones prevail. See p. 131.

- **Best Service: 22 Jermyn Street,** 22 Jermyn St., SW1 (© 800/682-7808 or 020/7734-2353), does more for its guests than any other hotel in London. The owner has outfitted a room on the sixth floor with a superbly equipped computer center, which guests are free to use. He'll also inform you of the hottest and newest restaurants (along with old favorites), the best shopping, and even what's hot in theater. The staff won't deny any reasonable request—they even grant some unreasonable ones. See p. 110.

- **Best Location:** Creaky, quirky, **The Fielding Hotel,** 4 Broad Court, Bow Street, WC2 (© **020/7836-8305**), is hardly London's finest, but oh, the location! It's in an alleyway in the center of Covent Garden—the heart of London excitement— almost opposite the Royal Opera House, with pubs, shops, markets, restaurants, even street entertainment, right outside your door. Stay here, and London is at your fingertips. See p. 102.

- **Best Health Club & Pool: The Savoy,** the Strand, WC2 (© **020/7836-4343**), has a health club and large swimming pool atop the historic Savoy Theatre, overlooking the heart of London. It's the best gym in central London; the views make it extra special. There's a massage room, plus state-of-the-art health and beauty treatments. See p. 102.

- **Best Boutique Hotel: The Beaufort,** 33 Beaufort Gardens, SW3 (© **020/ 7584-5252**), is a gem that's sure to charm. Personal service and tranquility combine for a winning choice, a private but not snobbish place 183m (200 yd.) from the famed Harrods Department Store. Even longtime patrons of Claridge's and The Dorchester have deserted those bastions of luxury to check into The Beaufort. See p. 115.

- **Best Inexpensive Hotel:** In this price category, it's hard to be chic, but **The Pavilion,** 34–36 Sussex Gardens, W2 (© **020/7262-0905**), manages to do it. Known for its bedrooms' wacky themes, this theatrical and slightly outrageous hotel attracts models and music-industry folks. Rooms range in decor from Asian bordello ("Enter the Dragon") to 1970s kitsch ("Honky-Tonk Afro"). See p. 133.

- **Best for Families Who Don't Want to Break the Bank: The Colonnade Town House,** 2 Warrington Crescent, W9 (© **020/7286-1052**), stands in the canal-laced Little Venice section. This family-friendly hotel lets children under 12 stay free in their parent's room and the staff can also arrange babysitting. This residential area of London is safe at night, with tree-lined avenues leading down to a canal. It's got a real neighborhood feel to it. See p. 136.

- **Best B&B:** Year after year, **Aster House,** 3 Sumner Place, SW7 (© **020/7581-5888**), keeps its standards high and remains one of London's best B&Bs. A friendly, inviting, welcoming place, it's safely tucked away on a tree-lined street in the heart of South Kensington. See p. 118.

- **Best for Value:** In historic Bloomsbury, site of the British Museum, **The Jenkins Hotel,** 45 Cartwright Gardens, WC1 (© **020/7387-2067**), has been hailed by London's *Mail on Sunday* as one of the city's "10 best hotel values"—and we heartily concur. This homey, Georgian-style hotel is straight out of an Agatha Christie TV show (indeed, it was featured on *Poirot*). See p. 98.

2 In & Around the City

There are precious few hotels within the confines of the City (the financial district). If you plan to do a lot of business or sightseeing in the City and you're not very interested in shopping, theater, and nightlife, then the location might be perfect for you. (For a map showing the location of the following hotels as well as restaurants in the City, see "Where to Stay & Dine in & Around 'The City,'" on p. 147.)

VERY EXPENSIVE

Great Eastern Hotel 🏨🏨 Terrence Conran's monolithic hotel is one of only three hotels in London's financial district. One London writer claimed it was "nosebleed territory" for visitors to London, saying: "Just try meeting someone for a drink who lives in fashionable Chelsea." Still, back in 1884 the Great Eastern sprouted up next to Liverpool Street Station. The hotel lies at the doorstep of two increasingly trendy London "villages," Shoreditch and Hoxton, with their explosive arts scenes. The building was the creation of Charles Barry, better known for his Houses of Parliament. The hotel was once a tired and dreary relic, but today it's exterior is abloom in all its Victorian glory, with a stained-glass dome and roof towers. Inside it is sleek and modern, with Jacob Jacobsen's chrome-plated architect's lamps (the goose-necked type you find in offices) lighting up the interior. In the bedrooms, the upholstery comes in traditional fabrics such as houndstooth and herringbone. Full bathrooms are state-of-the-art, and the beds offer grand comfort.

Liverpool St., London EC2M 7QN. ⓒ 020/7618-5000. Fax 020/7618-5001. www.great-eastern-hotel.co.uk. 267 units. £295–£345 ($561–$656) double; from £445 ($846) suite. AE, DC, MC, V. Tube: Liverpool St. Station. **Amenities:** 4 restaurants; 3 bars; health club; massage; tour desk; business center; room service; laundry service; dry cleaning; nonsmoking rooms; rooms for those w/limited mobility. *In room:* A/C, TV, Wi-Fi, hair dryer, minibar, safe, iron.

Threadneedles 🏨🏨 *(finds)* This was the first luxury hotel built in the City, home to many of London's major financial institutions. The building, on Threadneedle Street (hence the name), was constructed in 1856 and was originally designed to be a bank, complete with solid oak doors and marble columns. The conversion to its latest role is successful. Contemporary comforts are found in the midsize to spacious bedrooms and suites. The limestone bathrooms contain tub/shower combinations, and there are such elegant touches as Egyptian-cotton and duck-down duvets on the beds. This luxury boutique hotel lies near the Bank of England, which is also known as "The Old Lady of Threadneedle Street."

5 Threadneedle St., London EC2R 8AY. ⓒ 020/7657-8080. Fax 020/7657-8100. www.theetongroup.com. 70 units. £125–£275 ($238–$523) double; £305–£440 ($580–$836) suite. AE, DC, MC, V. Tube: Bank. **Amenities:** Restaurant; bar; room service; babysitting; laundry service; same-day dry cleaning; nonsmoking rooms; rooms for those w/limited mobility. *In room:* A/C, TV, Wi-Fi, coffeemaker, minibar, hair dryer, safe, trouser press.

EXPENSIVE

Malmaison London 🏨🏨 Who could imagine that this used to be a dreary nursing home? Talk about recycling. The Victorian mansion block overlooks a green cobbled square and is the first London showcase for the U.K.-only hotel chain, known for its highly polished European staff, clever contemporary designs, state-of-the-art facilities, and chic little brasseries serving French classics. On the southern rim of once dreary, now trendy, Clerkenwell in East London, Malmaison is awash in dark teakwood, with tall, glowing floor lamps, tasteful fabrics in neutral shades, and a portrait and bust in the lobby of Napoléon and Josephine who spent many a "wanton night" at the original Château Malmaison outside Paris. Guest rooms are individually designed and larger than average for central London. They are adorned with dark wood, along with luxurious bathrooms with a tub and separate power-shower cubicle. We love the limestone-look tiles, the mammoth hospital white towels, the shiny black marble, and the hotel's own jasmine and geranium toiletries.

18–21 Charterhouse Sq., London EC1M 6AH. ⓒ 020/7012-3700. Fax 020/7012-3702. www.malmaison.com. 97 units. £195–£215 ($371–$409) double; £395 ($751) suite. Tube: Barbican or Farringdon. **Amenities:** Restaurant; bar;

health club; room service; laundry service; dry cleaning; nonsmoking rooms. *In room:* A/C, TV, minibar, beverage maker, iron, trouser press.

The Zetter ✸✸✸   Heaven will be a letdown after this. Imagine hallway vending machines dispensing champagne and espresso makers providing complimentary *café* on every floor. This converted Victorian warehouse, located between the financial district and the West End, also features seven rooftop studios with patios and panoramic views of the London skyline and a sky-lit atrium flooding the building's core with natural light. Many of the features and "scars" of the original structure were retained, as tradition was blended with chic, urban modern design. The small-to-midsize, elegantly furnished guest rooms are located over the five upper floors of the property, off balconies circling the atrium. Unplastered brick walls reach up to "floating" ceilings and customized wallpaper panels. Secondhand furnishings are set beside classic modern pieces. The designers certainly achieved their stated goal of "a great bed, a great shower, and state-of-the-art in-room technology." Bathrooms live up to their reputation as a "sensory experience," with "Raindance" shower and natural health toiletries. Consider the Zetter restaurant even if you don't stay here. The fashionistas of London flock here for both traditional and modern interpretations of Italian regional cuisine.

St John's Square, 86–88 Clerkenwell Rd., London EC1M 5RJ. © **020/7324-4444.** Fax 020/7324-4445. www.thezetter.com. 59 units. Mon–Thurs £150–£330 ($285–$627) double; Fri–Sun £130–£330 ($247–$627) double. AE, DC, MC, V. Tube: Farringdon. **Amenities:** Restaurant; bar; room service; in-room spa treatments; nonsmoking rooms; rooms for those w/limited mobility. *In room:* A/C, TV, safe.

INEXPENSIVE

The Hoxton *Value*   Opened near London's financial district in 2006, The Hoxton's stated aim is helping travelers avoid hotel rip-offs. It has many innovative policies—for example, instead of getting gouged for in-room phone calls, you're charged only 10¢ a minute here for calls to the United States. The hotelier, Sinclair Beecham, bases his price structure on budget airlines, including an occasional £1 ($1.90) promotional rate—but don't get your hopes up. Everything is simplified here: The "Light Pret" breakfast—freshly squeezed orange juice, a granola yogurt, and a banana—is hung on your doorknob. The small bedrooms are functionally but tastefully furnished, each with either queen size or 2 single beds. Instead of a high-priced minibar in your room, there's a fridge filled with mineral water and milk.

81 Great Eastern St., London EC2A 3HU. © **020/75550-1000.** Fax 020/7550-1090. www.hoxtonhotels.com. 205 units. £79–£149 ($150–$283) double. AE, DC, MC, V. Tube: Old Street. **Amenities:** Grill; bar. *In room:* TV, Wi-Fi, hair dryer.

3 The West End

BLOOMSBURY

EXPENSIVE

The Academy Hotel ✸   The Academy is in the heart of London's publishing district. If you look out your window, you'll see where Virginia Woolf and other literary members of the Bloomsbury Group passed by every day. Many original architectural details were preserved when these three 1776 Georgian row houses were joined, and the hotel was substantially upgraded in the 1990s, with bathrooms added to each bedroom (whether there was space or not). Fourteen have a tub/shower combination; the rest have showers only. The beds, so they say, were built to "American specifications." True or not, they promise you a restful night's sleep. Grace notes include glass panels,

Where to Stay in the West End

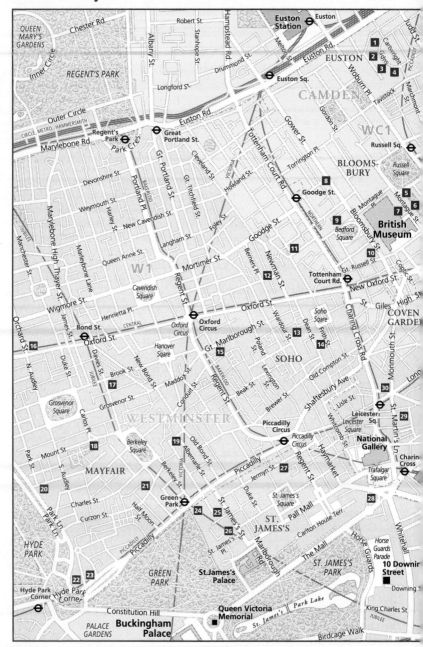

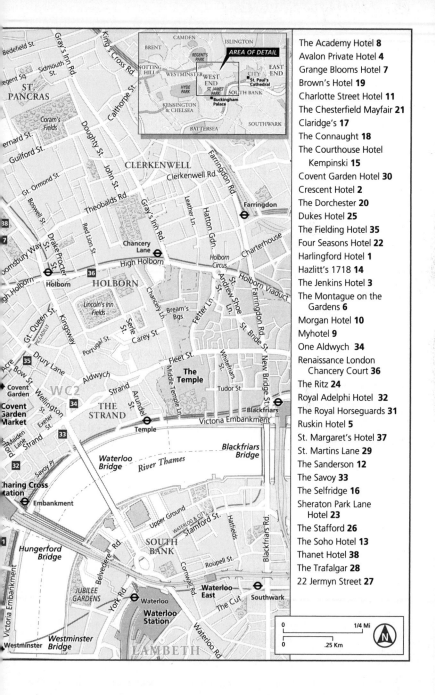

The Academy Hotel **8**
Avalon Private Hotel **4**
Grange Blooms Hotel **7**
Brown's Hotel **19**
Charlotte Street Hotel **11**
The Chesterfield Mayfair **21**
Claridge's **17**
The Connaught **18**
The Courthouse Hotel
  Kempinski **15**
Covent Garden Hotel **30**
Crescent Hotel **2**
The Dorchester **20**
Dukes Hotel **25**
The Fielding Hotel **35**
Four Seasons Hotel **22**
Harlingford Hotel **1**
Hazlitt's 1718 **14**
The Jenkins Hotel **3**
The Montague on the
  Gardens **6**
Morgan Hotel **10**
Myhotel **9**
One Aldwych **34**
Renaissance London
  Chancery Court **36**
The Ritz **24**
Royal Adelphi Hotel **32**
The Royal Horseguards **31**
Ruskin Hotel **5**
St. Margaret's Hotel **37**
St. Martins Lane **29**
The Sanderson **12**
The Savoy **33**
The Selfridge **16**
Sheraton Park Lane
  Hotel **23**
The Stafford **26**
The Soho Hotel **13**
Thanet Hotel **38**
The Trafalgar **28**
22 Jermyn Street **27**

colonnades, and intricate plasterwork on the facade. With overstuffed armchairs and half-canopied beds, rooms sometimes evoke English country-house living—but that of the poorer relations. Guests in the know always request rooms opening on the garden in back and not those in front with ducted fresh air, though the front units do have double-glazing to cut down on noise. The theater district and Covent Garden are within walking distance.

21 Gower St., London WC1E 6HG. (℗ 020/7631-4115. Fax 020/7636-3442. www.theetoncollection.com. 49 units. £140–£165 ($266–$314) double; £180 ($342) suite. AE, DC, MC, V. Tube: Tottenham Court Rd., Goodge St., or Russell Sq. **Amenities:** Bar; room service; laundry service; same-day dry cleaning; nonsmoking rooms. *In room:* A/C, TV, minibar, beverage maker, hair dryer, iron, safe, trouser press.

Grange Blooms Hotel ✦   This restored 18th-century town house has quite a pedigree: It stands in what were formerly the grounds of Montague House (now the British Museum). It has had a distinguished, if eccentric, list of former occupants: everybody from Richard Penn (the Whig member of Parliament from Liverpool) to Dr. John Cumming, who firmly believed he'd witness the end of the world (on long winter nights, his ghostly presence has supposedly been spotted). Even though it's in the heart of London, the house has a country-home atmosphere, complete with fireplace, period art, and copies of *Country Life* in the magazine rack. Guests take morning coffee in a walled garden overlooking the British Museum. In summer, light meals are served. The small- to medium-size bedrooms are individually designed with traditional elegance, in beautifully muted tones, and the tub/shower combination bathrooms are well maintained.

7 Montague St., London WC1B 5BP. (℗ 020/7323-1717. Fax 020/7636-6498. www.grangehotels.com. 26 units. £110–£139 ($209–$264) double. AE, DC, MC, V. Tube: Russell Sq. **Amenities:** Restaurant; bar; courtesy car; room service; laundry service; dry cleaning; nonsmoking rooms. *In room:* TV, minibar, coffeemaker, hair dryer, trouser press.

The Montague on the Gardens ✦✦   This member of the deluxe Red Carnation Hotel Group—others include The Rubens at the Palace (p. 113) and The Milestone (p. 120)—offers a winning combination of plush accommodations and exceptional service. The location is right across the street from the British Museum and a short walk from the West End and the shopping on Oxford and Bond streets. One staff member aptly describes the Montague as a "country house hotel in the heart of London." The public rooms are meticulously (if not minimally) decorated in various woods, light fabrics, and antiques, conjuring the atmosphere of an expensive manor home.

Guest rooms are individually sized and decorated; most aren't huge, but all are cozy and spotless. The beds are most comfortable; some are four-posters and most sport half-canopies. Bi-level deluxe king rooms feature pullout couches and would be classified as suites in many other hotels. Rooms overlooking the garden offer the best views and are quiet, although guaranteeing one for your stay will cost you a bit more. Forty-two of the rooms have been restored and decorated with hand-carved furniture, showing influences of the famous Bloomsbury literary set. They are all front-facing, and many contain private balconies.

15 Montague St., London WC1B 5BJ. (℗ 877/955-1515 in the U.S. and Canada, or 020/7637-1001. Fax 020/7312-0407. www.redcarnationhotels.com. 99 units. £245–£355 ($466–$675) double; £395–£405 ($751–$770) suite. AE, DC, MC, V. Tube: Russell Sq. **Amenities:** 2 restaurants; 4 lounges; bar; health club; steam room; sauna; massage; business center; room service; laundry service; dry cleaning; nonsmoking rooms; rooms for those w/limited mobility. *In room:* A/C, TV, fax (in some rooms), tea/coffeemaker, hair dryer, iron, safe.

Myhotel ✦ *Finds*   Creating shock waves among staid Bloomsbury hoteliers, Myhotel is a London row house on the outside with an Asian *moderne*-style interior. It is designed according to feng shui principles—the ancient Chinese art of placement that utilizes the flow of energy in a space. The rooms have mirrors, but they're positioned so you don't see yourself when you first wake up—feng shui rule no. 1 (probably a good rule, feng shui or no feng shui). Rooms are havens of comfort, taste, and tranquillity. Excellent sleep-inducing beds are found in all rooms, along with a small bathroom with a tub. Each guest is assigned a personal assistant responsible for that guest's happiness, and tipping is discouraged. Aimed at today's young, hip traveler, Myhotel lies within a short walk of Covent Garden and the British Museum.

11–13 Bayley St., Bedford Sq., London WC1B 3HD. ℂ 020/7667-6000. Fax 020/7667-6044. www.myhotels.co.uk. 78 units. £189–£265 ($359–$504) double; from £319 ($606) suite. AE, DC, MC, V. Tube: Tottenham Court Rd. or Goodge St. **Amenities:** Restaurant; bar; exercise room; car at discounted rate; room service; babysitting; laundry service; same-day dry cleaning; nonsmoking rooms. *In room:* A/C, TV, beverage maker, hair dryer, safe, trouser press (in some).

Renaissance London Chancery Court 𝄞𝄞𝄞   This landmark 1914 building in the financial district opened as a hotel in 2003, and it's retained some of the best architectural features of its Edwardian heyday while becoming cutting edge in its modern comforts. The building has been used as a backdrop for such films as *Howard's End* and *The Saint* because filmmakers were drawn to its soaring archways and classical central courtyard. The glamorous and exceedingly comfortable rooms are all furnished with fine linens and decorated in hues of cream, red, and blue. The bathrooms are about the most spacious in London, clad in Italian marble with lavish tub/shower combinations. The best accommodations are on the sixth floor, opening onto a cozy interior courtyard hidden from the busy world outside.

252 High Holborn, WC1V 7EN. ℂ 800/468-3571 in the U.S. and Canada, or 020/7829-9888. Fax 020/7829-9889. www.renaissancehotels.com. 357 units. £255–£345 ($485–$656) double; £380–£480 ($722–$912) suite. AE, DC, MC, V. Tube: Holborn. Parking £35 ($67). **Amenities:** Restaurant; 2 bars; cocktail lounge; gym; luxurious spa; sauna; courtesy car; business center; room service; massage; babysitting; laundry service; dry cleaning; nonsmoking rooms; rooms for those w/limited mobility. *In room:* A/C, TV, minibar, coffeemaker, hair dryer, iron, safe.

MODERATE

Harlingford Hotel *Value*   This hotel is comprised of three town houses built in the 1820s and joined together around 1900 by a bewildering array of staircases and meandering hallways. Set in the heart of Bloomsbury, it's run by a management that seems genuinely concerned about the welfare of its guests, unlike the management at many of its neighboring hotel rivals. (They even distribute little mincemeat pies to their guests during the Christmas holidays.) Double-glazed windows cut down on street noise, and all the bedrooms are comfortable and inviting. The shower-only bathrooms are small, however, since the house wasn't originally designed for them. The most comfortable rooms are on the second and third levels, but expect to climb some steep

---

Value Cheap Lodging for Students

The International Students House, 229 Great Portland St., W1W 5PN (ℂ 020/7631-8310; www.ish.org.uk), offers blandly furnished, institutional rooms, but it's hard to beat the price: £26 ($49) per person for a double, and £19 ($36) per person in a four-person mixed room. A £10 ($19) key deposit is charged but refunded at the end of your stay. Facilities include laundry machines, a bar, an Internet cafe, a fitness center, and sunbeds. Reserve way in advance because these rooms go very quickly.

English stairs (there's no elevator). Avoid the rooms on ground level, as they are darker and have less security. As an added bonus, you'll have use of the tennis courts in Cartwright Gardens.

61–63 Cartwright Gardens, London WC1H 9EL. ⓒ 020/7387-1551. Fax 020/7387-4616. www.harlingfordhotel. com. 43 units. £99 ($188) double; £110 ($209) triple; £115 ($219) quad. Rates include English breakfast. AE, MC, V. Tube: Russell Sq., King's Cross, or Euston. **Amenities:** Use of tennis courts in Cartwright Gardens. *In room:* TV, coffeemaker, hair dryer.

INEXPENSIVE

Avalon Private Hotel   A bit of a comedown after the Harlingford (see above), this hotel is easier on the purse. One guidebook from Queen Victoria's day claimed the Bloomsbury neighborhood attracted "medical and other students of both sexes and several nationalities, American folk passing through London, literary persons 'up' for a week or two's reading in the British Museum, and Bohemians pure and simple." The same might be said for today's patrons of this hotel, which was built in 1807 as two Georgian houses in residential Cartwright Gardens. Guests have use of a semiprivate garden across the street with tennis courts. Top-floor rooms, often filled with students, are reached via steep stairs, but bedrooms on the lower levels have easier access. A professional decorator recently added many Victorian-inspired touches to the hotel, in addition to new carpeting, making it more inviting. The bedrooms were also recently renewed with new linens and fresh curtains. Private bathrooms with showers are extremely small. Most guests in rooms without bathrooms have to use the corridor bathrooms (four bedrooms to a bathroom), which are generally adequate and well maintained.

46–47 Cartwright Gardens, London WC1H 9EL. ⓒ 020/7387-2366. Fax 020/7387-5810. www.avalonhotel.co.uk. 27 units (5 with shower). £63 ($120) double without shower; £82 ($156) double with shower; £74 ($141) triple without shower, £95 ($181) triple with shower; £84 ($160) quad without shower, £104 ($198) quad with shower. Rates include English breakfast. AE, DC, MC, V. Tube: Russell Sq., King's Cross, or Euston. **Amenities:** Use of tennis courts in Cartwright Gardens; coin-op washers and dryers; same-day dry cleaning; nonsmoking rooms. *In room:* TV, coffeemaker, safe.

Crescent Hotel   Although Ruskin and Shelley no longer pass by, the Crescent still stands in the heart of academic London. The private square is owned by the City Guild of Skinners (who are furriers, as you might have guessed) and guarded by the University of London, whose student residential halls are across the street. You have access to the gardens and private tennis courts belonging to the City Guild of Skinners. The hotel owners view Crescent as an extension of their home and welcome you to its comfortably elegant Georgian surroundings, which date from 1810. Some guests have been returning for 4 decades. Bedrooms range from small singles with shared bathrooms to more spacious twin and double rooms with private showers. All have extras such as alarm clocks. Twins and doubles have private plumbing, with tiny bathrooms. Many rooms are singles, ranging in price from £49 to £79 ($93–$150) depending on the plumbing.

49–50 Cartwright Gardens, London WC1H 9EL. ⓒ 020/7387-1515. Fax 020/7383-2054. www.crescenthotelof london.com. 27 units, 18 with bathroom (some with shower only, some with tub and shower). £95 ($181) double with bathroom; £118 ($224) family room. Rates include English breakfast. MC, V. Tube: Russell Sq., King's Cross, or Euston. **Amenities:** Use of tennis courts in Cartwright Gardens; babysitting. *In room:* TV, coffeemaker.

The Jenkins Hotel ⓐ *Value*   Followers of the Agatha Christie TV series *Poirot* will recognize this Cartwright Gardens residence—it was featured in the series. The antiques are gone and the rooms are small, but some of the original charm of the Georgian house remains. All the rooms have been redecorated in traditional Georgian style, and many have been completely refurbished with new beds and upholstery. The location is great, near the British Museum, theaters, and antiquarian bookshops.

There are some drawbacks: no lift and no reception or sitting room. But this is a place where you can settle in and feel at home.

45 Cartwright Gardens, London WC1H 9EH. ℂ **020/7387-2067.** Fax 020/7383-3139. www.jenkinshotel. demon.co.uk. 13 units. £85 ($162) double; £105 ($200) triple. Rates include English breakfast. MC, V. Tube: Russell Sq., King's Cross, or Euston. **Amenities:** Use of washer/dryer; use of tennis courts in Cartwright Gardens; all non-smoking rooms. *In room:* TV, fridge with soft drinks, coffeemaker, hair dryer, safe.

Morgan Hotel   Located in a row of Georgian houses, each built in the 1790s, this hotel is easily recognizable by its gold-tipped iron/board fence railings. The flower boxes outside preview the warmth and hospitality inside. The family management does all the work themselves, and they have such a devoted following that it's hard to get a reservation in summer. Several rooms, each individually designed, overlook the British Museum. Even if things are a bit cramped and the stairs are rather steep, the rooms are pleasant and the atmosphere congenial. The carpeted bedrooms have big beds (by British standards), dressing tables with mirrors, ample wardrobe space, and batik bedspreads. Eleven of the rooms have air-conditioning. The suites are worth the extra money if you can afford it. They all have kitchenettes and spacious bathrooms equipped with showers. The suites are furnished tastefully with polished dark English pieces, framed English prints, and decorator fabrics, and they also have irons and ironing boards.

24 Bloomsbury St., London WC1B 3QJ. ℂ **020/7636-3735.** Fax 020/7636-3045. www.morganhotel.co.uk. 21 units. £100 ($190) double; £130 ($247) triple; £135–£190 ($257–$361) suite. Rates include English breakfast. MC, V. Tube: Russell Sq. or Tottenham Court Rd. **Amenities:** Breakfast room, all nonsmoking rooms. *In room:* A/C, TV, kitchenette in suites, hair dryer, iron in suites, safe.

Ruskin Hotel   Although the hotel is named for author John Ruskin, the ghosts of other literary legends who lived nearby haunt you: Mary Shelley plotting her novel, *Frankenstein,* and James Barrie fantasizing about *Peter Pan.* This hotel has been managed for 2 decades by a hard-working family and enjoys a repeat clientele. Management keeps the place spic-and-span, though you shouldn't expect a decorator's flair. The furnishings, though well polished, are a bit worn. Double-glazing in the front blots out the noise, but we prefer the cozily old-fashioned chambers in the rear, as they open onto a park. Sorry, no elevator. The greenery in the cellar-level breakfast room provides a nice touch, and the breakfast is big enough to fortify you for a full day at the British Museum next door. *Insider's Tip:* Although the private bathrooms are ridiculously small, the shared bathrooms in the hall are generous and well maintained; all have shower units.

23–24 Montague St., London WC1B 5BH. ℂ **020/7636-7388.** Fax 020/7323-1662. www.ruskinhotellondon.com. 33 units, 6 with bathroom. £67 ($127) double without bathroom, £84 ($160) double with bathroom; £84 ($160) triple without bathroom, £98 ($186) triple with bathroom. Rates include English breakfast and tax. AE, DC, MC, V. Tube: Russell Sq. or Tottenham Court Rd. *In room:* Coffeemaker, hair dryer.

St. Margaret's Hotel   As you trudge along Bedford Place in the footsteps of Hogarth, Yeats, and Dickens, you'll come across this hotel, composed of four interconnected Georgian town houses. Furnishings are a mismatched medley, a bit tattered here and there, but endurable and fine nevertheless. All is forgiven on a spring day when you look out back onto the Duke of Bedford's private gardens in full bloom. Rooms are fairly large, except for a cramped single here or there. Many still retain their original fireplaces, which is how the rooms were once heated. Families should ask for no. 53, which features a glassed-in garden along the back. A single guest who doesn't mind sharing a shower-only bathroom will find ample space in no. 24. Guests have use of two lounges, one with a TV.

26 Bedford Place, London WC1B 5JH. ℂ 020/7636-4277 or 020/7580-2352. Fax 020/7323-3066. www.stmargarets hotel.co.uk. 64 units, 16 with bathroom (5 with shower). £69 ($130) double without shower, £84 ($160) double with shower; £97 ($184) double with shower and bathroom. Rates include English breakfast. MC, V. Tube: Holborn or Russell Sq. **Amenities:** Breakfast room; 2 lounges; laundry service; same-day dry cleaning; all nonsmoking rooms; rooms for those w/limited mobility. *In room:* TV.

Thanet Hotel   Most of the myriad hotels around Russell Square become almost indistinguishable at some point, but the Thanet stands out. It no longer charges the same rates it did when it appeared in *England on $5 a Day,* but it's still a winning choice and an affordable option close to the British Museum, the theater district, and Covent Garden. It's a landmark-status building on a quiet Georgian terrace between Russell and Bloomsbury squares. Although it has been repeatedly restored, many original features remain. For the most part, the Orchard family (third-generation hoteliers) offers small, adequately furnished rooms. However, scattered throughout the hotel are some unacceptable bedrooms. One guest reported that the foot of her lumpy bed was higher than the head. Ask to see the room before accepting it. This place is always full, so it must be doing something right, and indeed many of the bedrooms are fine. It depends largely on which rooms were most recently renovated—ask for those. All units are equipped with shower-only bathrooms that are very small but neatly maintained. Washbasins in the bathrooms must have been designed for Tiny Tim.

8 Bedford Place, London WC1B 5JA. ℂ **020/7636-2869.** Fax 020/7323-6676. www.thanethotel.co.uk. 16 units. £100 ($190) double; £112 ($213) triple; £120 ($228) quad. Rates include English breakfast. AE, MC, V. Tube: Holborn or Russell Sq. **Amenities:** Breakfast room; all nonsmoking rooms. *In room:* TV, coffeemaker, hair dryer.

⟨Kids⟩ Family-Friendly Hotels

Although the bulk of their clients are business travelers, the major hotel chains are also geared to family fun. Look for special summer packages at most hotel chains between June and August. Some of the most generous offers come from the **Travelodge** (ℂ **800/578-7878** in the U.S.) and **Hilton International** (ℂ **800/445-8667** in the U.S.) chains. For best results, call the 800-number and ask about family packages. Here are some other family-friendly spots:

The Colonnade Town House (p. 136)   Located in the canal-laced Little Venice section of London, this hotel lets children under 12 stay free in their parent's room and the staff can arrange babysitting. This residential area is safe, with tree-lined avenues leading down to a canal. With its shops, cafes, and restaurants, Little Venice has a real neighborhood feel to it.

Hart House Hotel (p. 127)   This small, family-run B&B is right in the center of the West End, near Hyde Park. Many of its rooms are triples. If you need even more space, special family suites, with connecting rooms, can be arranged.

The Vicarage Hotel (p. 125)   This is one of the most family-friendly hotels in the general area of Kensington and Notting Hill Gate. A Victorian town house, it offers many bedrooms that are large enough to accommodate four, all at an affordable price.

COVENT GARDEN & THE STRAND
VERY EXPENSIVE

Covent Garden Hotel ✦✦✦ This former hospital building lay neglected for years until it was reconfigured in 1996 by hot hoteliers Tim and Kit Kemp—whose flair for interior design is legendary—into one of London's most charming boutique hotels in one of the West End's hippest shopping neighborhoods. *Travel + Leisure* called this hotel 1 of the 25 hottest places to stay in the *world*. It remains so. Behind a bottle-green facade reminiscent of a 19th-century storefront, the hotel has a welcoming lobby outfitted with elaborate inlaid furniture and elegant draperies, plus a charming restaurant. Upstairs, accessible via a dramatic stone staircase, soundproof bedrooms are furnished in English style with Asian fabrics, many adorned with hand-embroidered designs. The hotel has a decorative trademark—each room has a clothier's mannequin, a female form draped in the fabric that decorates that particular room. And each room comes with luxurious amenities including full granite-and-mahogany bathrooms with double vanities and deep soaking tubs. Some guests prefer the attic rooms with their sloping ceilings and small arched windows.

10 Monmouth St., London WC2H 9HB. ✆ **800/553-6674** in the U.S. or 020/7806-1000. Fax 020/7806-1100. www.firmdale.com. 58 units. £220–£310 ($418–$589) double; £350–£950 ($665–$1,805) suite. AE, DC, MC, V. Tube: Covent Garden or Leicester Sq. **Amenities:** Restaurant; bar; small exercise room; tour desk; business services; salon; room service; massage; babysitting; laundry service; same-day dry cleaning; nonsmoking rooms; video library. *In room:* A/C, TV, minibar, hair dryer, safe.

One Aldwych ✦✦ Just east of Covent Garden, this government-rated five-star hotel occupies the classic-looking 1907 building that served as headquarters for the now-defunct *Morning Post*. Before its conversion in 1998, all but a fraction of its interior was gutted and replaced with an artfully simple layout. Although a first-rate hostelry in every way, it lacks the cutting-edge chic of the Covent Garden Hotel (see above). The bedrooms are sumptuous, decorated with elegant linens and rich colors, and accessorized with raw-silk curtains, deluxe furnishings, and electrical outlets that can handle both North American and European electrical currents. Bathrooms boast full tubs and showers, plus luxurious toiletries. There are original works of art and bespoke furniture in every room along with fresh fruit and flowers supplied daily. On Friday, Saturday, and Sunday movies are shown in the screening room. Guests can purchase a package that includes a meal in the restaurant, a glass of champagne, and the movie.

1 Aldwych, London WC2B 4RH. ✆ **800/745-8883** or 020/7300-1000. Fax 020/7300-1001. www.onealdwych.co.uk. 105 units. £360–£435 ($684–$827) double; £575–£1,450 ($1,093–$2,755) suite. AE, DC, MC, V. Parking £36 ($68). Tube: Temple. **Amenities:** 2 restaurants; 3 bars; indoor heated pool; health club; spa; sauna; screening room; concierge; room service; massage; babysitting; laundry service; same-day dry cleaning; nonsmoking rooms; rooms for those w/limited mobility. *In room:* A/C, TV, Wi-Fi, minibar, hair dryer, safe.

St. Martins Lane ✦✦✦ "Eccentric and irreverent, with a sense of humor," is how Ian Schrager describes his cutting-edge Covent Garden hotel, which he transformed from a 1960s office building into a chic enclave. This was the first hotel Schrager designed outside the United States, after a string of successes from New York to West Hollywood. The mix of hip design and a sense of cool have been imported across the pond. Whimsical touches abound. For example, a string of daisies replaces DO NOT DISTURB signs. Rooms are all white, but you can use the full-spectrum lighting to make them any color. Floor-to-ceiling glass windows in every room offer a panoramic view of London, and down comforters and soft pillows ensure a good night's sleep. Bathrooms are spacious and state-of-the-art, with deluxe toiletries.

45 St. Martins Lane, London WC2N 4HX. © 800/697-1791 in the U.S. or 020/7300-5500. Fax 020/7300-5501. www.stmartinslane.com. 204 units. £220–£375 ($418–$713) double; from £375 ($713) suite. AE, DC, MC, V. Tube: Covent Garden or Leicester Sq. **Amenities:** Restaurant; 2 bars; gym; spa services from nearby spa on request; courtesy car; business center; room service; babysitting; laundry service; same-day dry cleaning; nonsmoking rooms; rooms for those w/limited mobility; video library. *In room:* A/C, TV, minibar, hair dryer, safe.

The Savoy 🏨🏨🏨   Although not as swank as The Dorchester, this London landmark is the premier hotel in the Strand/Covent Garden area. Richard D'Oyly Carte built it in 1889 as an annex to his nearby Savoy Theatre, where many Gilbert and Sullivan operettas were originally staged. Each room is individually decorated with color-coordinated accessories, solid and comfortable furniture, large closets, and an eclectic blend of antiques, such as gilt mirrors, Queen Anne chairs, and Victorian sofas. Forty-eight units have their own sitting rooms. The handmade beds—real luxury models—have top-of-the-line crisp linen fabrics and other lavish appointments. Some bathrooms have tubs, but most have a tub/shower combination. Bathrooms are spacious, with deluxe toiletries. The suites overlooking the river are the most sought after, and for good reason—the vistas are the best in London. *Tip:* Ask for one of the newer rooms (in what was formerly a storage space)—they're among the best in the hotel, with views of the Thames and Parliament.

The Strand, London WC2R 0EU. © 020/7836-4343. Fax 020/7240-6040. www.fairmont.com/savoy. 263 units. £249–£359 ($473–$682) double; from £479 ($910) suite. AE, DC, MC, V. Parking £37 ($70). Tube: Charing Cross or Covent Garden. **Amenities:** 5 restaurants (including Savoy Grill and the River Restaurant, which overlooks the Thames); 2 bars; health club; spa; sauna; indoor swimming pool; business services; room service; babysitting; laundry service; dry cleaning; nonsmoking rooms; rooms for those w/limited mobility. *In room:* A/C, TV, minibar, hair dryer, safe.

MODERATE

The Fielding Hotel 🏨 *Finds*   One of London's more eccentric hotels, the Fielding is cramped, quirky, and quaint, and an enduring favorite. The hotel is named after novelist Henry Fielding of *Tom Jones* fame, who lived in Broad Court. It lies on a pedestrian street still lined with 19th-century gas lamps. The Royal Opera House is across the street, and the pubs, shops, and restaurants of lively Covent Garden are just beyond the front door. Rooms are small but charmingly old-fashioned and traditional. Some units are redecorated or at least "touched up" every year, though floors dip and sway, and the furnishings and fabrics, while clean, have known better times. The bathrooms, some with antiquated plumbing, are equipped with showers. But many love the hotel's rickety charm and with a location like this, in the heart of London, the Fielding keeps guests coming back. Children under 13 are not welcome.

4 Broad Court, Bow St., London WC2B 5QZ. © 020/7836-8305. Fax 020/7497-0064. www.the-fielding-hotel.co.uk. 24 units. £100–£120 ($190–$228) double; £140 ($266) suite. AE, DC, MC, V. Tube: Covent Garden. **Amenities:** All nonsmoking rooms. *In room:* TV, coffeemaker.

INEXPENSIVE

Royal Adelphi Hotel   If you care most about being in a central location, consider the Royal Adelphi. Close to Covent Garden, the theater district, and Trafalgar Square, it's an unorthodox choice away from the typical B&B stomping grounds. London has far better B&Bs, but not in this part of town. Although the bedrooms call to mind London's swinging 1960s heyday, accommodations are decently maintained and comfortable, with good beds. Plumbing, however, is a bit creaky, and the lack of air-conditioning can make London feel like summer in the Australian outback during the city's few hot days.

21 Villiers St., London WC2N 6ND. ⓒ 020/7930-8764. Fax 020/7930-8735. www.royaladelphihotel.co.uk. 47 units, 34 with bathroom. £70 ($133) double without bathroom, £92 ($175) with bathroom; £120 ($228) triple with bathroom. Rates include continental breakfast and tax. AE, DC, MC, V. Tube: Charing Cross or Embankment. **Amenities:** Bar. *In room:* TV, coffeemaker, hair dryer.

TRAFALGAR SQUARE
EXPENSIVE

The Royal Horseguards ⓕ   The London flagship of Thistle, a popular hotel chain in Great Britain, the Royal Horseguards is close to Parliament, Charing Cross, and Horse Guards, with rooms opening onto the Thames River near Trafalgar Square. This bustling area of London becomes relatively quiet at night. The hotel maintains some of the atmosphere it once knew during its years as a men's club: MPs still frequent the place, especially the bar, where a light signals them to finish their liquor and get back to vote in Parliament. Rooms have been refurbished, and for the most part they are comfortable, although we've found that many of them are too small, especially if you've arrived in London with a lot of luggage. Those accommodations with a river view are the best and the largest. The hotel is geared mainly to business travelers but could be ideal for sightseers as well. Most doubles are at the low end of the price scale.

2 Whitehall Court, London SW1A 2EJ. ⓒ 0870/333-9122. Fax 0870/333-9222. www.thistlehotels.com/royal horseguards. 280 units. £150–£245 ($285–$466) double; from £235 ($447) suite. AE, DC, MC, V. Parking £40 ($76). Tube: Embankment. **Amenities:** Restaurant; bar; exercise room; business center; room service; laundry service; same-day dry cleaning; nonsmoking rooms. *In room:* A/C (in some), TV, minibar, coffeemaker, hair dryer, iron, safe.

The Trafalgar ⓕⓕ   In the heart of landmark Trafalgar Square, this is Hilton's first boutique hotel in London. The facade of this 19th-century structure was preserved, while the guest rooms inside were refitted to modern standards. Because of the original architecture, many of the rooms are uniquely shaped and sometimes offer split-level layouts. Large windows open onto panoramic views of Trafalgar Square. The decor in the rooms is minimalist, and comfort is combined with simple luxury, including the deluxe tiled bathrooms with tub/shower combinations. The greatest view of London's cityscape is from the hotel's rooftop garden.

Unusual for London, the bar, Rockwell, specializes in bourbon, with more than 100 brands. Jago is the hotel's organic-produce restaurant, serving comfort food.

2 Spring Gardens, Trafalgar Sq., London SW1A 2TS. ⓒ 800/774-1500 in the U.S. or 020/7870-2900. Fax 020/7870-2911. www.thetrafalgar.com. 129 units. £175–£330 ($333–$627) double; from £439 ($834) suite. AE, DC, MC, V. Parking £30 ($57). Tube: Charing Cross. **Amenities:** Restaurant; bar; gym; spa; courtesy car; business services; room service; laundry service; same-day dry cleaning; nonsmoking rooms; rooms for those w/limited mobility. *In room:* A/C, TV, minibar, beverage maker, hair dryer, safe.

SOHO
VERY EXPENSIVE

The Courthouse Hotel Kempinski ⓕⓕ   Everybody from Oscar Wilde to Mick Jagger has passed through the doors of this historic courthouse. But today, under the German hotel chain, Kempinski, the hospitality is better than ever. In a spectacular reclamation of an existing structure, the hotel retains many aspects of its landmark building, including original Robert Adams fireplaces. A bar occupies three of the original prison cells. The judges' bench, witness stand, and dock still take center stage in Silk, the hotel's deluxe dining room. The location is among the best in London, opposite the department store Liberty's and Carnaby Street, just off Regent Street.

Bedrooms are midsize to spacious, each comfortably and tastefully decorated, with 13 suites located in the former judges' robing rooms. The best rooms are in the new wing, which was built on the site of a former police station. Each comes with a marble-clad bathroom with tub and shower. Our favorite retreat here is the roof terrace where light meals and cocktails are served. A fully equipped spa features a large indoor pool. We love the use of colors in this hotel, especially aubergine (eggplant to Americans) and apple green.

19–21 Great Marlborough St., London W1F 7HL. (*C*) **800/426-3135** in the U.S. or 020/7297-5555. Fax 020/7297-5566. www.courthouse-hotel.com. 116 units. £290–£390 ($551–$741) double; from £550 ($1045) suite. AE, DC, MC, V. Tube: Oxford Circus. **Amenities:** 2 restaurants; bar; roof terrace; gym; indoor pool; spa; room service; laundry service; same-day dry cleaning; nonsmoking rooms. *In room:* A/C, TV, minibar, safe.

The Sanderson (*Finds*) Ian Schrager, the king of New York hip, has brought Tenth Avenue in Manhattan to London. For his latest London hotel, Schrager secured the help of talented partners, Philippe Starck and Andra Andrei, to create an "ethereal, transparent urban spa," in which walls are replaced by glass and sheer layers of curtains. The hotel is located in a former corporate building near Oxford Street, north of Soho, and the dreary grid facade of aluminum squares and glass remains. But the transformation of the rest of the building has been remarkable, and the hotel features a lush bamboo-filled roof garden, a large courtyard, and spa. That's not all—Alain Ducasse, arguably the world's greatest chef, directs its restaurant. The accommodations are cutting edge—your bed is likely to be an Italian silver-leaf sleigh attended by spidery polished stainless-steel night tables and draped with a fringed pashmina shawl the color of dried lemon verbena.

50 Berners St., London W1T 3NG. (*C*) **800/697-1791** or 020/7300-1400. Fax 020/7300-1401. www.sanderson london.com. 150 units. £250–£460 ($475–$874) double; from £615 ($1,169) suite. Ask about weekend specials. AE, DC, MC, V. Tube: Oxford Circus or Tottenham Court Rd. **Amenities:** Restaurant; 2 bars; health club; spa; business services; room service; in-room massage; babysitting; laundry service; same-day dry cleaning; nonsmoking rooms; rooms for those w/limited mobility. *In room:* A/C, TV, minibar, hair dryer, safe.

The Soho Hotel (*Finds*) A former parking garage in the heart of bustling Soho just became our favorite nest in London. British hoteliers Kit and Tim Kemp have come up with a stunner here—when it's time to check out, we never want to leave this luxury lair in a cul-de-sac off Dean Street. The theaters of Shaftesbury are only a block or two away, as is the Ivy Restaurant.

All the extremely spacious bedrooms are individually designed in granite and oak, with walk-in showers, double basins, and bath products by London perfumer Miller Harris. There are four penthouses on the fifth floor with tree-lined terraces opening onto panoramic sweeps of London. All the famous Kemp touches can be found, from boldly striped furnishings to deep bathtubs for a late-night soak. The glitterati, mostly actors and filmmakers, can be seen hanging out at the bar or dining in the trendy onsite restaurant.

4 Richmond Mews, London W1D 3DH. (*C*) **020/7559-3000.** Fax 020/7559-3003. www.firmdalehotels.com. 85 units. £240–£295 ($456–$561) double; from £350 ($665) suite. AE, MC, V. Tube: Oxford Circus or Piccadilly Circus. **Amenities:** Restaurant; bar; exercise room; gym; on-site personal trainer; 2 private cinemas; beauty salon; room service. *In room:* A/C, TV, minibar, hair dryer, safe.

EXPENSIVE

Charlotte Street Hotel (*Finds*) In North Soho, a short walk from the heartbeat of Soho Square, this town house has been luxuriously converted into a high-end hotel that is London chic at its finest, possessing everything from a Los Angeles–style juice bar to a private screening room. The latter has made the hotel a hit with the movie, fashion, and media crowd, many of whom had never ventured to North Soho before. One local told us, "Charlotte Street is for those who'd like to imagine themselves in California." Midsize to spacious bedrooms have fresh, modern, English interiors and everything from two-line phones with voice mail to dataports and fax outlets. Bathrooms are state-of-the-art, designed in solid granite and oak with twin basins, walk-in showers, and even color TVs. Guests can relax in the elegant drawing room and library with a log-burning fireplace. The decor evokes memories of Virginia Woolf's Bloomsbury set, including works of art by Roger Fry, Duncan Grant, and by her sister, Vanessa Bell.

15–17 Charlotte St., London W1T 1RJ. © 800/553-6674 in the U.S. or 020/7806-2000. Fax 020/7806-2002. www.firmdale.com. 52 units. £210–£295 ($399–$561) double; £350–£950 ($665–$1,805) suite. AE, MC, V. Tube: Tottenham Court Rd. **Amenities:** Restaurant; bar; exercise room; room service; laundry service; same-day dry cleaning; nonsmoking rooms; rooms for those w/limited mobility. *In room:* A/C, TV, fax, Wi-Fi, minibar, hair dryer, safe.

Hazlitt's 1718 *Finds* This gem, housed in three historic homes on Soho Square, is one of London's best small hotels. Built in 1718, the hotel is named for William Hazlitt, who founded the Unitarian Church in Boston and wrote four volumes on the life of his hero, Napoleon.

Hazlitt's is a favorite with artists, actors, and models. It's eclectic and filled with odds and ends picked up around the country at estate auctions. Some find its Georgian decor a bit spartan, but the 2,000 original prints hanging on the walls brighten it considerably. Many bedrooms have four-poster beds, and some bathrooms have their original claw-foot tubs (only two units have a shower, while the rest are hand-held). Some of the floors dip and sway, and there's no elevator, but it's all part of the charm. It has just as much character as the Fielding Hotel (see above) but is a lot more comfortable. Some rooms are a bit small, but most are spacious, all with state-of-the-art appointments. Most bathrooms have 19th-century styling but up-to-date plumbing, with oversize tubs and old brass fittings. Accommodations in the back are quieter but perhaps too dark, and only those on the top floor have air-conditioning. Swinging Soho is at your doorstep; the young, hip staff will be happy to direct you to the local hot spots.

6 Frith St., London W1D 3JA. © 020/7434-1771. Fax 020/7439-1524. www.hazlittshotel.com. 23 units. £205–£255 ($390–$485) double; £300 ($570) suite. AE, DC, MC, V. Tube: Leicester Sq. or Tottenham Court Rd. **Amenities:** Room service; babysitting; laundry service; same-day dry cleaning; nonsmoking rooms. *In room:* A/C, TV, minibar, hair dryer, safe.

MAYFAIR
VERY EXPENSIVE

Brown's Hotel Almost every year a hotel sprouts up trying to evoke an English country-house ambience with Chippendale and chintz; this quintessential townhouse hotel watches these competitors come and go, and it always comes out on top. Brown's was founded by James Brown, a former manservant to Lord Byron, who knew the tastes of well-bred gentlemen and wanted to create a dignified, clublike place for them. He opened its doors in 1837, the same year Queen Victoria took the throne.

Brown's occupies 14 historic houses just off Berkeley Square. Its guest rooms, completely renovated, vary considerably in decor, but all show restrained taste in decoration and appointments; even the wash basins are antiques. Accommodations range in size from small to extra spacious; some suites have four-poster beds. Bathrooms come in a variety of sizes, but they are beautifully equipped with robes, luxurious cosmetics, tubs, and showers.

30 Albemarle St., London W1S 4BP. © 020/7493-6020. Fax 020/7493-9381. www.brownshotel.com. 117 units. £245–£545 ($466–$1,036) double; from £800 ($1,520) suite. AE, DC, MC, V. Off-site parking £53 ($101). Tube: Green

Park. **Amenities:** Restaurant; bar; health club; spa; business center; room service; laundry service; same-day dry cleaning; nonsmoking rooms. *In room:* A/C, TV, minibar, hair dryer, safe.

Claridge's ✦✦✦ That once-fading 1812 beauty has experienced a $75-million rebirth, and its staid image has changed. *Dynasty* diva Joan Collins may have staged her latest marriage here, but now Kate Moss is spotted in the hip bar, Elizabeth Hurley strolls through the lobby, and Gordon Ramsay—Britain's most talked-about and controversial chef (and also its best)—is loud-mouthing it in the kitchen and swinging sharp knives for the benefit of the cameras. What would Queen Victoria have said about his foul tongue and fiery temper? She might also have been amazed at the Arab influence: sheiks from the Middle East send their wives to stay here when on shopping expeditions in London.

If you want to live in the total lap of luxury, at an even tonier address than The Connaught and The Dorchester, make it Claridge's. Though renovations have been extensive, much of the Art Deco style of the 1930s remains, and you'll expect Fred Astaire and Ginger Rogers to emerge, dancing, at any minute. There are other distinctive styles here as well, ranging from modern to neoclassical, and the hotel's strong sense of tradition and old-fashioned "Britishness" are intact, in spite of the gloss and the hip clientele. Stand anywhere in any of the halls, and you'll find it easy to imagine the Duke of Windsor striding through the halls, trailed by his two-timing wife. Afternoon tea at Claridge's remains a quintessentially English tradition. The accommodations here are the most diverse in London, ranging from the costly and stunning Brook Penthouse—complete with a personal butler—to the less-expensive so-called superior queen rooms with queen-size beds. You'll find sumptuous fabrics, exceedingly comfortable beds, elegant linens, chandeliers, and all sorts of modern amenities in the bedrooms. The bathrooms are the most elegant in Britain, with enormous tubs and showerheads the size of frying pans.

Brook St., London W1A 2JQ. ✆ 020/7629-8860. Fax 020/7499-2210. www.claridges.co.uk. 203 units. £189–£539 ($359–$1,024) double; from £459 ($872) suite. AE, DC, MC, V. Parking £50 ($95). Tube: Bond St. **Amenities:** 3 restaurants; 2 bars; health club; spa; business services; salon; room service; massage; babysitting; laundry service; same-day dry cleaning; nonsmoking rooms; rooms for those w/limited mobility. *In room:* A/C, TV, fax, minibar, beverage maker, hair dryer, safe.

The Connaught ✦✦✦ This elegant hotel in the heart of Mayfair is one of Europe's most prestigious. It is not the most glamorous, nor even the most fashionable in London, but it nonetheless coddles you in comfort and luxury, with a hospitality that's legendary. It has the atmosphere of an English country house—a world of fresh flowers, crystal chandeliers, Wedgwood, and antiques. The hotel guarantees privacy even if you're a film-star sex symbol or Barbara Bush (the former president's wife is a fan of The Connaught). Situated near Grosvenor Square, this brick house is like a club, with many repeat guests demanding their favorite rooms. There is something of an aura of aristocratic decay at The Connaught, just as the country gentry like it, whereas The Dorchester (see below) has more flash.

Rooms range from medium to large and are filled with antiques, chintz, and tasteful details such as gilt-trimmed white paneling. Sumptuous beds are dressed in the finest Irish linens. Marble fireplaces, ornate plasterwork, and oak paneling add to the stately allure of the rooms. The large, old-fashioned bathrooms are still intact and are outfitted with robes and deep tubs.

Carlos Place, London W1K 2AL. ✆ 800/63-SAVOY in the U.S. or 020/7499-7070. Fax 020/7495-3262. www.the-savoy-group.com/connaught. 92 units. £229–£299 ($435–$568) double; £329–£1,089 ($625–$2,069) suite. AE,

DC, MC, V. Parking £41 ($78). Tube: Green Park. **Amenities:** 2 restaurants; 2 bars; health club; spa services arranged in advance; courtesy car; business services; room service; babysitting; laundry service; same-day dry cleaning; non-smoking rooms; rooms for those w/limited mobility. *In room:* A/C, TV, fax, minibar, hair dryer, iron, safe.

The Dorchester 🏨🏨🏨   One of London's best hotels, it has all the elegance of The Connaught, but without the upper-crust attitude that can verge on snobbery. Few hotels have the time-honored experience of "The Dorch," which has maintained a tradition of fine comfort and cuisine since it opened in 1931.

Breaking from the neoclassical tradition, the most ambitious architects of the era designed a building of reinforced concrete clothed in terrazzo slabs. The Dorchester boasts guest rooms outfitted with Irish linen sheets on comfortable beds, plus all the electronic gadgetry you'd expect, and double- and triple-glazed windows to keep out noise, along with plump armchairs, cherry-wood furnishings, and, in many cases, four-poster beds piled high with pillows. The large bathrooms are equally stylish, with mottled Carrara marble and Lalique-style sconces, makeup mirrors and posh toiletries, and deep tubs. The best rooms offer views of Hyde Park.

53 Park Lane, London W1A 2HJ. 📞 800/727-9820 in the U.S. or 020/7629-8888. Fax 020/7409-0114. www.the dorchester.com. 250 units. £405–£525 ($770–$998) double; from £695 ($1,321) suite. AE, DC, MC, V. Parking £40 ($76). Tube: Hyde Park Corner or Marble Arch. **Amenities:** 3 restaurants; bar; health club; spa; hairdresser; tour desk; car-rental desk; courtesy car; business services and center; small shopping arcade; 2 salons; room service; babysitting; laundry service; same-day dry cleaning; nonsmoking rooms; rooms for those w/limited mobility. *In room:* A/C, TV, minibar, hair dryer, safe.

Four Seasons Hotel 🏨🏨   This deluxe hostelry has captured the imagination of glamour-mongers the world over ever since it was inaugurated by Princess Alexandra in 1970. Its clientele includes heads of state, superstars, and top business execs. Sitting tastefully behind a modern facade in one of the most exclusive neighborhoods in the world, it's located opposite its major competitors, the London Hilton and the Inter-Continental, but has better food, better rooms, and more style and refinement than either of its rivals. Even so, it falls just a little bit short of the platinum credentials of The Dorchester and The Connaught (see above), both longer established. Inside, acres of superbly crafted paneling and opulent but conservative decor create the impression that the hotel is far older than it is.

The guest rooms are large and beautifully outfitted with well-chosen chintz, reproductions, plush upholstery, and dozens of well-concealed electronic extras. Most rooms are medium size, although some are quite large, and all are maintained in perfect condition. There is plenty of desk space, and in many instances tall windows open onto stand-up balconies. Mattresses are of the finest quality, as are bed linens. Bathrooms are ample, with thoughtful extras such as deep tubs, robes, and deluxe toiletries.

Hamilton Place, Park Lane, London W1A 1AZ. 📞 800/819-5053 or 020/7499-0888. Fax 020/7493-1895. www.four seasons.com. 219 units. £405–£420 ($770–$798) double; £595 ($1,131) conservatory double; from £750 ($1,425) suite. AE, DC, MC, V. Parking £25 ($48). Tube: Hyde Park Corner. **Amenities:** Restaurant; bar; access to nearby indoor tennis courts; health club; tour desk; business services; room service; massage; babysitting; laundry service; same-day dry cleaning; nonsmoking rooms; rooms for those w/limited mobility. *In room:* A/C, TV, fax, minibar, hair dryer, safe.

Sheraton Park Lane Hotel 🏨🏨   Since 1924, this has been the most traditional of the Park Lane mansions, even more so than The Dorchester. The hotel was sold in 1996 to the Sheraton Corporation, which continues to upgrade it but maintains its quintessential British style. Its Silver Entrance remains an Art Deco marvel that has been used as a backdrop in many films, including the classic BBC miniseries *Brideshead Revisited.*

Overlooking Green Park, the hotel offers luxurious accommodations that are a good deal—well, at least for pricey Park Lane, where anything under $500 a night is a bargain. Many suites have marble fireplaces and original marble bathrooms. The rooms have all benefited from impressive refurbishment. All have double-glazed windows to block out noise. The most tranquil rooms open onto a street in the rear. Rooms opening onto the court are dark. In the more deluxe rooms, you get trouser presses and better views. Bathrooms are generally spacious and well equipped with tub/shower combos; many also have robes.

Piccadilly, London W1J 7BX. © 800/325-3535 in the U.S. or 020/7499-6321. Fax 020/7499-1965. www.starwood.com/sheraton. 305 units. £199–£340 ($378–$646) double; from £289 ($549) suite. AE, DC, MC, V. Parking £35 ($67). Tube: Hyde Park Corner or Green Park. **Amenities:** 2 restaurants; bar; health club; 1920s palm court; business center; room service; laundry service; same-day dry cleaning; nonsmoking rooms; rooms for those w/limited mobility. *In room:* A/C (in most rooms), TV, minibar, hair dryer, iron, safe (in most).

EXPENSIVE

The Chesterfield Mayfair 🐀🐀   Just a short distance from Berkeley Square, the elegant Chesterfield serves up a traditional English atmosphere and offers a lot more bang for your buck than most hotels in pricey Mayfair. The hotel, once home to the Earl of Chesterfield, still sports venerable features that evoke an air of nobility, including richly decorated public rooms featuring woods, antiques, fabrics, and marble. The secluded Library Lounge is a great place to relax, and the glassed-in conservatory is a good spot for tea. The sumptuously decorated restaurant is well regarded, as is the bar, where a pianist plays on most nights.

The guest rooms are generally not huge, but they are dramatically decorated and make excellent use of space—there's a ton of closet and counter space. The spotless marble bathrooms are similarly compact but are well equipped with bathrobes and heated floors. For a more memorable experience, book one of the themed junior or executive suites, which offer excellent value for Mayfair. You'll get larger amounts of space, upgraded amenities (DVD players and umbrellas, for example), complimentary canapés, and theatrical decorating schemes. Most executive rooms have Jacuzzi tubs or separate tubs and power showers, and some have wholly separate sitting rooms.

35 Charles St., London W1J 5EB. © 877/955-1515 in the U.S. and Canada, or 020/7491-2622. Fax 020/7491-4793. www.chesterfieldmayfair.com. 110 units. £295–£325 ($561–$618) double; £395–£525 ($751–$998) suite. Special packages available. AE, DC, MC, V. Tube: Green Park. **Amenities:** 2 restaurants; bar; use of nearby health club; business services; room service; babysitting; laundry service; same-day dry cleaning; nonsmoking rooms. *In room:* A/C, TV, minibar (in suite), coffeemaker, hair dryer, iron, safe.

The Selfridge 🐀   The location, right next door to Selfridge's food hall off Oxford Street, is wonderful, especially for shoppers. In fact, the hotel's seven floors look as if they are part of Selfridge's itself. This mammoth hotel is a member of the Thistle hotel chain and caters to an even mix of business and leisure travelers. Ignore the drab entrance; the hotel brightens considerably in the second-floor reception room, with its wingback chairs, antique art, pine-paneled walls, and a rustic bar whose half-timbered decor was brought and installed piece by piece from an English barn that stood in the Middle Ages. The rooms are hardly the finest in this part of town, but they are usually affordable, especially if you snag one of the promotional. Accommodations are well maintained, nicely decorated, tranquil, and generally spacious, with small bathrooms. Double-glazing on the windows cuts back on noise. *Tip:* Try for a room facing Orchard Street, as these are larger. Also, the best rooms are the premium units on floors three to five.

Orchard St., London W1H 6JS. ℭ **0870/333-9117.** Fax 0870/333-9217. www.thistle.co.uk. 294 units. £115–£280 ($219–$532) double; £195–£350 ($371–$665) suite. AE, DC, MC, V. Parking £35 ($67). Tube: Bond St. **Amenities:** 2 restaurants; bar; room service; babysitting; laundry service; same-day dry cleaning. *In room:* A/C, TV, coffeemaker, hair dryer, safe (in some).

ST. JAMES'S
VERY EXPENSIVE

The Ritz 🌟🌟🌟   Built in French Renaissance style and opened by César Ritz in 1906, this hotel overlooking Green Park is synonymous with luxury. Gold-leafed molding, marble columns, and potted palms abound, and a gold-leafed statue, *La Source,* adorns the fountain of the oval-shaped Palm Court. After a major restoration, the hotel is better than ever: New carpeting and air-conditioning have been installed in the guest rooms, and an overall polishing has recaptured much of The Ritz's original splendor. Still, this Ritz lags far behind the much grander one in Paris (with which it is not affiliated). The Belle Epoque guest rooms, each with its own character, are spacious and comfortable. Many have marble fireplaces, elaborate gilded plasterwork, and a decor of soft pastel hues, and a few have their original brass beds. Bathrooms are elegantly appointed in either tile or marble and filled with deep tubs with showers, robes, phones, and deluxe toiletries. Corner rooms are grander and more spacious.

150 Piccadilly, London W1J 9BR. ℭ **877/748-9536** in the U.S. or 020/7493-8181. Fax 020/7493-2687. www.theritz london.com. 133 units. £260–£520 ($494–$988) double; from £500 ($950) suite. Children under 16 stay free in parent's room. AE, DC, MC, V. Parking £53 ($101). Tube: Green Park. **Amenities:** 2 restaurants (including the Palm Court); bar; exercise room; spa; business services; room service; massage; babysitting; laundry service; same-day dry cleaning; nonsmoking rooms; rooms for those w/limited mobility. *In room:* A/C, TV, fax, minibar, hair dryer, safe.

EXPENSIVE

Dukes Hotel 🌟🌟🌟   Dukes provides elegance without ostentation in what was presumably someone's "Upstairs, Downstairs" town house. Along with its nearest competitors, The Stafford and 22 Jermyn Street, it caters to those looking for charm, style, and tradition in a hotel. It stands in a quiet courtyard off St. James's Street; turn-of-the-20th-century gas lamps help put you into the proper mood before entering the front door. Each well-furnished guest room is decorated in the style of a particular English period, ranging from Regency to Edwardian. All rooms are equipped with marble bathrooms containing tub/shower combinations. It's a lot cozier, more intimate, and even more clubbish than The Stafford, and Dukes is more tranquil since it's set in its own gaslit alley.

35 St. James's Place, London SW1A 1NY. ℭ **800/381-4702** in the U.S. or 020/7491-4840. Fax 020/7493-1264. www.dukeshotel.co.uk. 90 units. £300–£420 ($570–$798) double; from £625 ($1,188) suite. AE, DC, MC, V. Parking £55 ($105). Tube: Green Park. **Amenities:** Restaurant; bar; health club; spa; tour desk; business services; room service; babysitting; laundry service; same-day dry cleaning; nonsmoking rooms; rooms for those w/limited mobility. *In room:* A/C, TV, minibar, hair dryer, safe.

The Stafford Hotel 🌟🌟🌟   Famous for its American Bar, its St. James's address, and the warmth of its Edwardian decor, The Stafford is in a cul-de-sac off one of London's most centrally located and busiest neighborhoods. The Stafford competes well with Dukes for a tasteful, discerning clientele.

   All the guest rooms are individually decorated, reflecting the hotel's origins as a private home. Many singles contain queen-size beds. Some of the deluxe units offer four-posters that will make you feel like Henry VIII. Nearly all the bathrooms are clad in marble with tubs and stall showers, toiletries, and chrome fixtures. A few of the hotel's more modern accommodations, boasting king-size beds, are located in the restored

---

Tips How to Avoid Getting "Knocked Up"

If you don't want a rude awakening, remember to hang the DO NOT DISTURB sign on your doorknob (or bolt the door, if that's an option). English hotel service personnel have a disconcerting habit of bursting in simultaneously with their knock.

---

stable mews across the yard. Much has been done to preserve the original style of these rooms, including preservation of the original A-beams on the upper floors. You can bet that no 18th-century horse ever slept with the electronic safes, stereo systems, and quality furnishings (mostly antique reproductions) these rooms feature. Units on the top floor are small. In 2007, 26 luxury junior and master suites were added in The Stafford Mews, each filled with antiques and luxury facilities.

16–18 St. James's Place, London SW1A 1NJ. ⓒ 800/525-4800 in the U.S. or 020/7493-0111. Fax 020/7493-7121. www.thestaffordhotel.co.uk. 107 units. £355–£470 ($675–$893) double; from £495 ($941) suite. AE, DC, MC, V. Tube: Green Park. **Amenities:** Restaurant; American bar; health club privileges nearby; business services; room service; babysitting; laundry service; same-day dry cleaning; all nonsmoking rooms. *In room:* A/C, TV, fax, hair dryer, safe.

22 Jermyn Street ⍟⍟⍟   This is London's premier town-house hotel, a bastion of elegance and discretion. Set behind a facade of gray stone with neoclassical details, this structure, only 45m (148 ft.) from Piccadilly Circus, was built in 1870 for English gentlemen doing business in London. The Togna family has been in charge since 1915. The place was radically renovated in 1990, and 22 Jermyn has reveled in its role as a chic, upscale boutique hotel ever since. It offers an interior filled with greenery and the kind of art you might find in an elegant private home. The sixth floor features one of the best-equipped computer centers in London, which guests may use for free. This hotel doesn't have the bar or restaurant facilities of The Stafford or Dukes, but its recently refurbished rooms are more richly appointed, done in traditional English style with fresh flowers and chintz. Beds are luxurious and bathrooms are clad in granite and contain deep tubs and showers, luxurious toiletries, and phones. If you like space, ask for one of the studios in the rear.

22 Jermyn St., London SW1Y 6HL. ⓒ 800/682-7808 in the U.S. or 020/7734-2353. Fax 020/7734-0750. www.22jermyn.com. 18 units. £220 ($418) double; £310–£350 ($589–$665) suite. AE, DC, MC, V. Parking £40 ($76). Tube: Piccadilly Circus. **Amenities:** Access to nearby health club and spa; business services; room service; massage; babysitting; laundry service; same-day dry cleaning; nonsmoking rooms. *In room:* TV, Wi-Fi, minibar, hair dryer, safe.

4 Westminster & Victoria
VERY EXPENSIVE

The Goring ⍟⍟⍟   For tradition and location, the Goring is our first choice in Westminster. Just behind Buckingham Palace, it lies within easy reach of the royal parks, Victoria Station, Westminster Abbey, and the Houses of Parliament. It also offers the finest personal service of all its nearby competitors.

Built in 1910 by O. R. Goring, this was the first hotel in the world to have central heating and a private bathroom in every room. Today's guest rooms still offer all the comforts, including luxurious refurbished bathrooms with extra-long tubs, red marble walls, dual pedestal basins, bidets, deluxe toiletries, and power showerheads. There is an ongoing refurbishment of the bedrooms, including frequent replacement of

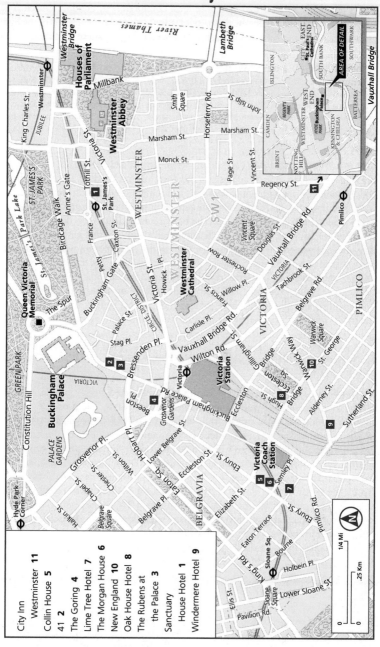

City Inn
  Westminster **11**
Collin House **5**
41 **2**
The Goring **4**
Lime Tree Hotel **7**
The Morgan House **6**
New England **10**
Oak House Hotel **8**
The Rubens at
  the Palace **3**
Sanctuary
  House Hotel **1**
Windermere Hotel **9**

linens. The beds, in fact, are among the most comfortable in London. Queen Anne and Chippendale are usually the decor styles, and the maintenance level is of the highest order. The rooms overlooking the garden are best. The charm of a traditional English country hotel is conjured in the paneled drawing room, where fires crackle in the ornate fireplaces on nippy evenings.

15 Beeston Place, Grosvenor Gardens, London SW1W OJW. ⓒ 020/7396-9000. Fax 020/7834-4393. www.goring hotel.co.uk. 71 units. £320–£490 ($608–$931) double; £490–£650 ($931–$1,235). AE, DC, MC, V. Parking £30 ($57). Tube: Victoria. **Amenities:** Grand afternoon tea in the drawing room (a London highlight); classic restaurant; bar; free use of nearby health club; room service; babysitting; laundry service; same-day dry cleaning; nonsmoking rooms; rooms for those w/limited mobility. *In room:* A/C, TV, hair dryer, safe.

EXPENSIVE

City Inn Westminster ⓡ   Next door to Tate Britain and Parliament, this purpose-built inn with a vast array of rooms is at the nexus of elite London. The River Thames and London Eye are within a short walk. The lobby is graced with stone floors, oak walls, and leather chairs, and the on-site restaurant specializes in game and salmon, as befits the hotel's Scottish ownership. The best accommodations are the 67 City Club rooms or the 16 suites, but all units are comfortable with a fresh, light, and contemporary design. Business clients predominate during the week, but on weekends rates are often slashed to bargain prices. Ask about this when booking. Try, if possible, for a guest room opening onto the Thames or else views of Parliament. Rooms are soundproof with 18 inches of concrete between each unit. Bathrooms are small but with power showers. You can drink and dine in the City Café restaurant and bar with its al fresco terrace, and the stylish Millbank Lounge bar is a popular rendezvous point at night.

30 John Islip St., London SW1P 4DD. ⓒ 020/7630-1000. Fax 020/7233-7575. www.cityinn.com. 460 units. £225 ($428) double; £265 ($504) city club room; £550 ($1,045) suite. AE, DC, MC, V. Tube: Pimlico or Westminster. **Amenities:** Restaurant; 2 bars; room service; gym; rooms for those w/limited mobility. *In room:* A/C, TV, minibar, beverage maker, hair dryer, iron.

41 ⓡⓡⓡ *Finds*   This relatively unknown but well-placed gem is a treasure worth seeking out, especially if you're looking for a touch of class. The property offers the intimate atmosphere of a private club along with a level of personal service that's impossible to achieve at larger hotels. It's best suited to couples or those traveling alone—especially women, who will be made to feel comfortable, thanks to excellent security. The cordial staff goes the extra mile to fulfill a guest's every wish, and they pay special attention to making sure their women guests feel safe. The surroundings match the stellar service. Public areas feature an abundance of mahogany, antiques, fresh flowers, and rich fabrics. Read, relax, or watch TV in the library-style lounge, where a complimentary continental breakfast, afternoon snacks, and evening canapés (all included in the room rate) are served each day.

Guest rooms are individually sized, but all feature elegant black-and-white color schemes, magnificent beds with Egyptian-cotton linens, and "AV centers" that offer free Internet access and DVD/CD players. Most rooms have working fireplaces. The spotless marble bathrooms sport separate tubs and power showers (only one room has a tub/shower combo) and feature Penhaligon toiletries. The bi-level junior suites toss in a separate seating area (good for families looking for extra space) and Jacuzzi tubs.

41 Buckingham Palace Rd., London SW1W OPS. ⓒ 877/955-1515 in the U.S. or Canada, or 020/7300-0041. Fax 020/7300-0141. www.41hotel.com. 28 units. £295–£315 ($561–$599) double; £495–£695 ($941–$1,321) suite. Rates include continental breakfast, afternoon snacks, and evening canapés. Special Internet packages and discounts available. AE, DC, MC, V. Tube: Victoria. **Amenities:** Lounge; bar; access to nearby health club; massage; business

center; room service; babysitting; laundry service; dry cleaning; nonsmoking rooms; 1 room for those w/limited mobility. *In room:* A/C, TV, minibar, beverage maker, hair dryer, iron, safe.

The Rubens at the Palace *ᏪᏪ* *Value*   The very British Rubens is popular with Americans and Europeans seeking traditional English hospitality while enjoying the latest in creature comforts. And its location is one of the best in town—directly across the street from Buckingham Palace, only a 2-minute walk from Victoria Station. The public rooms are lavishly decorated with antiques, fabric wallcoverings, and fresh flowers. A pianist plays in the military-style Cavalry Bar, the ideal place for a nightcap, on most evenings.

The size and decor of the guest rooms vary, but all feature grand comfort. Bathrooms range in size, but most have deep tubs. Housed in a private wing, each of the eight "Royal Rooms" is named for an English monarch and is decorated in the style of that ruler's period but also features modern luxuries like flat-screen TVs and heated bathroom floors. Some Royal Rooms aren't particularly big, but if it's available and your budget allows, we suggest the Henry the Eighth room, a relatively large Tudor fantasy done up in red and gold, with a half-canopy bed fit for a king, and a spacious marble bathroom. *Note:* Check the hotel's website for specials; the hotel often runs promotions that can make it an attractive value option.

39 Buckingham Palace Rd., London SW1W OPS. ℂ **877/955-1515** in the U.S. or Canada, or 020/7834-6600. Fax 020/7828-5401. www.redcarnationhotels.com. 172 units. £195–£275 ($371–$523) double; £265–£295 ($504–$561) Royal Room; £395–£495 ($751–$941) suite. AE, DC, MC, V. Tube: Victoria. **Amenities:** 2 restaurants; lounge; bar; access to nearby health club; tour desk; room service; babysitting; laundry service; same-day dry cleaning; nonsmoking rooms. *In room:* A/C, TV, minibar (in suites), coffeemaker, hair dryer, iron, safe.

MODERATE

Lime Tree Hotel   The Wales-born Davies family, longtime veterans of London's B&B business, have transformed a run-down guesthouse into a cost-conscious, cozy hotel for budget travelers. The simply furnished bedrooms are scattered over four floors of a brick town house; each has been recently refitted with new curtains and cupboards. The front rooms have small balconies overlooking Ebury Street; units in the back don't have balconies but are quieter and feature views over the hotel's small rose garden. The Lime Tree's rooms tend to be larger than other hotel rooms offered at similar prices, and breakfasts are generous. Six rooms come with a tub/shower combination, the rest with shower only. Buckingham Palace, Westminster Abbey, and the Houses of Parliament are within easy reach, as is Harrods. The popular Ebury Wine Bar is nearby.

135–137 Ebury St., London SW1W 9RA. ℂ **020/7730-8191.** Fax 020/7730-7865. www.limetreehotel.co.uk. 25 units. £110–£140 ($209–$266) double; £145–£170 ($276–$323) triple; £165–£185 ($314–$352) quad. Rates include English breakfast. AE, DC, MC, V. No children under 5. Tube: Victoria. **Amenities:** Breakfast room; all nonsmoking rooms. *In room:* TV, coffeemaker, hair dryer, safe.

New England   A family-run business for nearly a quarter of a century, this hotel shut down at the millennium for a complete overhaul. Today it's better than ever and charges an affordable price. Its elegant 19th-century exterior conceals a completely bright and modern interior. On a corner in the Pimlico area, which forms part of the City of Westminster, the hotel is neat and clean and one of the most welcoming in the area—it justly prides itself on its clientele of "repeats." It's also one of the few hotels in the area with an elevator. All the bathrooms have power showers.

20 Saint George's Dr., London SW1V 4BN. ℂ **020/7834-1595.** Fax 020/7834-9000. www.newenglandhotel.com. 25 units. £95–£109 ($181–$207) double; £129–£139 ($245–$264) triple; £139–£145 ($264–$276) quad. Rates include breakfast. MC, V. Tube: Victoria. **Amenities:** All nonsmoking rooms. *In room:* TV, hair dryer.

Sanctuary House Hotel 🐾 Only in the new London, where hotels are bursting into bloom like daffodils, would you find a hotel so close to a national treasure like Westminster Abbey. And a pub hotel, no less, with rooms on the upper floors above the tavern—the place was opened by Fuller Smith and Turner, a traditional British brewery. Accommodations have a rustic feel, but they have first-rate beds, along with restored bathrooms with tub/shower combinations. Downstairs, the Sanctuary's pub/restaurant offers old-style British meals, ignoring changing culinary fashions. "We like tradition," one of the perky staff members told us. "Why must everything be trendy? Some people come to England nostalgic for the old. Let others be trendy." And actually, the food is excellent if you appreciate the roast beef, Welsh lamb, and Dover sole that pleased the palates of Churchill and his contemporaries. Naturally, there's always plenty of brew on tap.

33 Tothill St., London SW1H 9LA. ℂ **020/7799-4044.** Fax 020/7799-3657. www.fullershotels.com. 34 units. £99–£175 ($188–$333) double. AE, DC, MC, V. Tube: St. James's Park. **Amenities:** Restaurant; pub; room service; laundry service; dry cleaning; nonsmoking rooms; rooms for those w/limited mobility. *In room:* A/C, TV, coffeemaker, hair dryer, trouser press.

Windermere Hotel 🐾 *Value* This award-winning small hotel is an excellent choice near Victoria Station. The Windermere was built in 1857 as a pair of private dwellings on the site of the old Abbot's Lane. The lane linked Westminster Abbey to its abbot's residence—so all the kings of medieval England trod here. A fine example of early Victorian classical design, the hotel has lots of English character. All the accommodations contain a private bathroom—some with shower, others with tub baths. Rooms come in a wide range of sizes, some accommodating three or four lodgers. The cheaper ones are somewhat cramped. The ground-floor rooms facing the street tend to be noisy at night, so avoid them if you're a light sleeper.

142–144 Warwick Way, London SW1V 4JE. ℂ **020/7834-5163.** Fax 020/7630-8831. www.windermere-hotel.co.uk. 22 units. £114–£139 ($217–$264) double; £149 ($283) family room. Rates include English breakfast. AE, MC, V. Tube: Victoria. **Amenities:** Restaurant; bar; room service; all nonsmoking rooms. *In room:* TV, coffeemaker, hair dryer, safe.

INEXPENSIVE

Collin House 🐾 This B&B emerges as a winner on a street lined with the finest Victoria Station–area B&Bs. William IV had just begun his reign when this house was constructed in 1830. Private, shower-only bathrooms have been discreetly installed, and everything works efficiently. For rooms without bathrooms, there are adequate hallway facilities, some of which are shared by only two rooms. Traffic in this area of London is heavy, and the front windows are not soundproof, so be warned if you're a light sleeper. Year after year, the owners make improvements in the furnishings and carpets. All guest rooms, which vary in size, are comfortably furnished and well maintained. Two rooms are large enough for families. A generous breakfast awaits you each morning in the basement of this nonsmoking facility.

104 Ebury St., London SW1W 9QD. ℂ **888/465-1123** in the U.S. or ℂ/fax 020/7730-8031. www.collinhouse.co.uk. 12 units, 8 with bathroom (shower only). From £60 ($114) double without bathroom, from £76 ($144) double with bathroom; from £75 ($143) triple without bathroom. Rates include English breakfast. AE, MC, V. Tube: Victoria. *In room:* TV, safe, coffeemaker, no phone.

The Morgan House This Georgian house has a convenient address, but its rooms are often fully booked in summer. Morgan's finest feature is a small courtyard open to guests. Many rooms are small to midsize, while others are large enough to house up to four people in reasonable comfort. Guest rooms are individually decorated and

---

 **Hot & Cold**

Hotel rooms in London aren't kept as warm as in other parts of the world. Bring a sweater if you find yourself chilly at a lower-than-usual room temperature. In summer, rooms without air-conditioning can get quite hot. Don't assume your hotel, even at the luxury level, has central air; many have only partial air-conditioning or none at all. Call ahead and ask if this is a concern for you.

---

have orthopedic mattresses. Hallway bathrooms are well maintained and adequate for guests who don't have their own private facilities. A hearty English breakfast is served in a bright, cheerful room.

120 Ebury St., London SW1W 9QQ. ✆ 020/7730-2384. Fax 020/7730-8442. www.morganhouse.co.uk. 11 units, 4 with private bathroom. £72 ($137) double without bathroom; £92 ($175) double with bathroom; £92 ($175) triple without bathroom, £112 ($213) triple with bathroom; £132 ($251) family room with bathroom. Rates include English breakfast. MC, V. Tube: Victoria. **Amenities:** Breakfast room. *In room:* TV, coffeemaker, hair dryer, phone only for receiving calls.

Oak House Hotel 🎯 *Finds*   This little jewel of a hotel, perhaps the smallest in the area, is a real find, with lots of homespun charm. The Symingtons, who own the place and also live here, bring their Scottish hospitality to their home in the Victoria Station area. When Mr. Symington isn't putting on his kilt to do the Scottish war dance, he's out driving a London taxi. Mrs. Symington is here to welcome you to her tidily maintained bedrooms, which are small yet handsomely furnished and appointed. Half of the rooms have double beds; the others contain twins. The closets are small, so you'll have to hang your garments on hooks and store other items on shelves. Shower-only bathrooms are adequate and spotlessly maintained.

29 Hugh St., London SW1V 1QJ. ✆ 020/7834-7151. 6 units. £50 ($95) single or double. No credit cards. Tube: Victoria. *In room:* TV, coffeemaker, hair dryer.

5 Hotels from Knightsbridge to South Kensington

KNIGHTSBRIDGE
VERY EXPENSIVE

The Beaufort 🎯🎯   If you'd like to stay at one of London's finest boutique hotels, offering personal service in an elegant, tranquil town-house atmosphere, head here. The Beaufort, only 180m (590 ft.) from Harrods, sits in a cul-de-sac behind two Victorian porticoes and an iron/board fence. Owner Diana Wallis, a television producer, combined a pair of adjacent houses from the 1870s, ripped out the old decor, and created a graceful and stylish hotel that has the feeling of a private house. You register at a small desk extending off a bay-windowed parlor, and then climb a stairway to your room, just as the Queen of Sweden did during her stay. Each guest room is tasteful and bright, individually decorated in a modern color scheme and adorned with well-chosen paintings by London artists. Rooms come with earphone radios, flowers, and a selection of books—the junior suites off use of a mobile phone in addition to a personal fax/answering machine. Most bedrooms are exceedingly small, but they're efficiently organized. The most deluxe and spacious rooms are in the front. Those in the back are smaller and darker. Included in the rates are a 24-hour free bar, continental breakfast, and light meals from room service, plus English cream teas each afternoon, and chocolates in each room. Bathrooms are adequate and tidily maintained, with tub/shower combinations.

Where to Stay from Knightsbridge to South Kensington

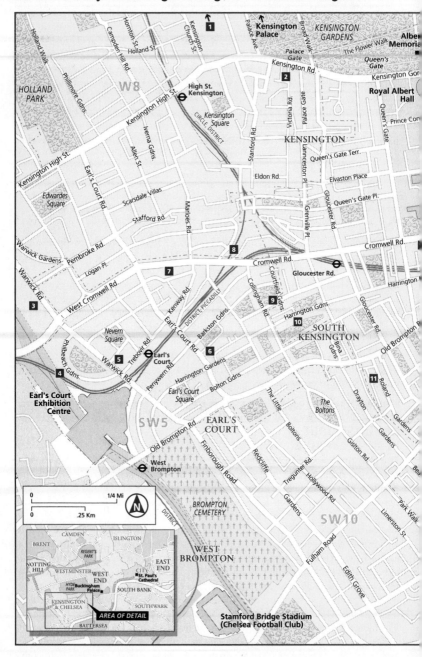

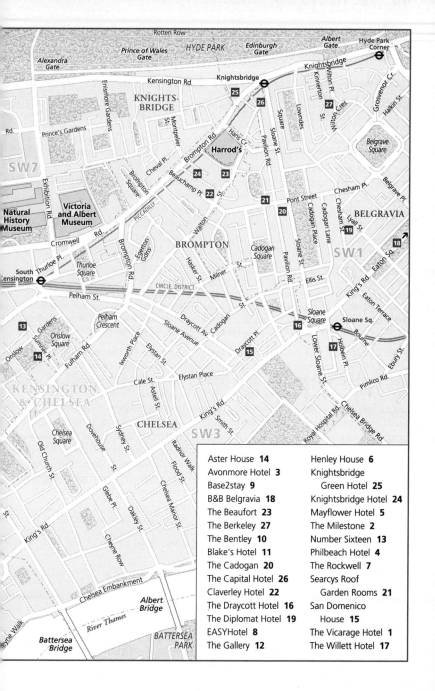

Aster House **14**
Avonmore Hotel **3**
Base2stay **9**
B&B Belgravia **18**
The Beaufort **23**
The Berkeley **27**
The Bentley **10**
Blake's Hotel **11**
The Cadogan **20**
The Capital Hotel **26**
Claverley Hotel **22**
The Draycott Hotel **16**
The Diplomat Hotel **19**
EASYHotel **8**
The Gallery **12**
Henley House **6**
Knightsbridge
   Green Hotel **25**
Knightsbridge Hotel **24**
Mayflower Hotel **5**
The Milestone **2**
Number Sixteen **13**
Philbeach Hotel **4**
The Rockwell **7**
Searcys Roof
   Garden Rooms **21**
San Domenico
   House **15**
The Vicarage Hotel **1**
The Willett Hotel **17**

33 Beaufort Gardens, London SW3 1PP. ⓒ 020/7584-5252. Fax 020/7589-2834. www.thebeaufort.co.uk. 29 units. £205–£270 ($390–$513) double; from £325 ($618) junior suite. AE, DC, MC, V. Tube: Knightsbridge. **Amenities:** Bar; access to nearby health club; junior suites include complimentary limo to or from the airport; room service; babysitting; laundry service; same-day dry cleaning; nonsmoking rooms. In room: A/C, TV, Wi-Fi, hair dryer, iron.

The Berkeley ⭒⭒⭒　One of London's most appealing hotels, The Berkeley is housed in a travertine-faced French Regency–inspired building in Knightsbridge near Hyde Park. The building, completed in 1972, replaced the original Berkeley hotel, which was built in the late 19th century and was frequently visited and widely praised by Noel Coward. During the new construction, some of original architectural embellishments were salvaged, including what is now the popular Blue Bar. Inside you'll find an understated environment inspired by Art Deco and French classical design but with a contemporary edge. Adjacent to the small lobby is the Caramel Room where tea, drinks, informal dining, and even a doughnut menu are served. Each of the accommodations offers high-end style, but most elegant of all are the suites, many of which have elegant paneling and luxurious, marble-and-tile-trimmed baths. The Berkeley offers two world-class restaurants, both established by celebrity chefs (Gordon Ramsay and Marcus Wareing). The Roman arches that surround the rooftop swimming pool are one of many highlights within this extraordinary hotel.

Wilton Place, London SW1X 7RL. ⓒ 800/63-SAVOY (72869) or 020/7235-6000. Fax 020/7235-4330. www.savoy group.com or www.the-berkeley.com. 157 units. £229–£529 ($435–$1,005) double; £399–£3,300 ($758–$6,270) suite. AE, DC, MC, V. Tube: Knightsbridge or Hyde Park Corner. **Amenities:** 2 restaurants; 2 bars; rooftop swimming pool; health club w/sauna; spa; room service; babysitting; laundry service; dry cleaning; nonsmoking rooms; rooms for those w/limited mobility. In room: A/C, TV, minibar, beverage maker, hair dryer, safe, trouser press.

The Capital Hotel ⭒⭒⭒　We'd be delighted to check in here for the season. Only 45m (148 ft.) from Harrods department store, this family-run town-house hotel is also at the doorstep of the shops of Knightsbridge and the "green lung" of Hyde Park. There are 49 bedrooms here, and while you get many of the luxuries and services of a mammoth hotel, warmth, intimacy, and an attention to detail are the hallmarks of this oasis. Famed designer Nina Campbell created the spacious bedrooms, furnishing them with sumptuous fabrics, art, and antiques. David Linley, nephew of Her Majesty, also assisted in the design. Bathrooms with tubs and showers are luxurious. The liveried doorman standing outside has welcomed royalty, heads of state, and international celebrities to this hotel. For dining, you don't have far to go: The restaurant, directed by chef Eric Chavot, has already achieved the distinction of two Michelin stars.

22 Basil St., London SW3 1AT. ⓒ 020/7589-5171. Fax 020/7225-0011. www.capitalhotel.co.uk. 49 units. £240–£365 ($456–$694) double; £400–£850 ($760–$1,615) suite. AE, DC, MC, V. Tube: Knightsbridge. Parking £30 ($57) per night. **Amenities:** Restaurant; bar; access to nearby health club; 24-hr. room service; babysitting; laundry service; same-day dry cleaning; nonsmoking rooms. In room: A/C, TV, Wi-Fi, minibar, hair dryer, safe, trouser press (in some).

EXPENSIVE

Aster House ⭒⭒⭒ (Value)　This is the winner of the 2004 London Tourism Award for best B&B in London and it's just as good now as it was then. Within an easy walk of Kensington Palace, the late Princess Diana's home, and the museums of South Kensington, it's a friendly, inviting, and well-decorated lodging on a tree-lined street. The area surrounding the hotel, Sumner Place, looks like a Hollywood set depicting Victorian London. Aster House guests eat breakfast in a sunlit conservatory and can feed the ducks in the pond outside. Since the B&B is a Victorian building spread across five floors, each unit is unique in size and shape. Rooms range from spacious,

— I don't speak sign language.

A hotel can close for all kinds of reasons.

Our Guarantee ensures that if your hotel's undergoing construction, we'll let you know in advance. In fact, we cover your entire travel experience. See www.travelocity.com/guarantee for details.

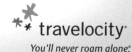
travelocity*
You'll never roam alone.

So many places, so little time?

TOKYO 7766 miles
LONDON 3818 miles
4682 miles
TORONTO 5087 miles
SYDNEY 4947 miles
NEW YORK 2556 miles
LOS ANGELES
HONG KONG 5638 miles

with a four-poster bed, to a Lilliputian special with a single bed. Some beds are draped with fabric tents for extra drama, and each room is individually decorated in the style of an English manor-house bedroom. The small bathrooms are beautifully kept, with showers ("the best in Europe," wrote one guest) or tubs and showers.

3 Sumner Place, London SW7 3EE. © 020/7581-5888. Fax 020/7584-4925. www.asterhouse.com. 14 units. £165–£225 ($314–$428) double. Rates include buffet breakfast. MC, V. Tube: South Kensington. **Amenities:** Breakfast room; lounge; laundry service; same-day dry cleaning; all nonsmoking rooms. *In room:* A/C, TV, coffeemaker, hair dryer, safe.

Claverley Hotel ♠

Located on a quiet cul-de-sac, this tasteful hotel, one of the neighborhood's very best, is just a few blocks from Harrods. It's a small, cozy place accented with Georgian-era accessories. The lounge has the atmosphere of a country house, and complimentary tea, coffee, and biscuits are served all day in the Reading Room. Most bedrooms have wall-to-wall carpeting and comfortably upholstered armchairs, and each has a tidy bathroom with a shower stall. The rooms have a marble bathroom and power shower, and are individually decorated, some with four-poster beds.

13–14 Beaufort Gardens, London SW3 1PS. © 800/747-0398 in the U.S. or 020/7589-8541. Fax 020/7584-3410. www.claverleyhotel.co.uk. 33 units. £149–£199 ($283–$378) double; £219 ($416) junior suite. Rates include English breakfast. AE, DC, MC, V. Parking £27 ($51) nearby. Tube: Knightsbridge. **Amenities:** Lounge; laundry service; all nonsmoking rooms. *In room:* TV, Wi-Fi, hair dryer, safe.

Knightsbridge Green Hotel ♠

Repeat guests from around the world view this dignified 1890s structure as their home away from home. In 1966, when it was converted into a hotel, the developers kept its wide baseboards, cove moldings, high ceilings, and spacious proportions. Even without kitchens, the well-furnished suites come close to apartment-style. The well-appointed marble bathrooms are deluxe, most with tubs and power showers. Most rooms are spacious, with adequate storage space. Bedrooms are decorated with custom-blended colors and are often individualized—one has a romantic sleigh bed. This is a solid choice for lodging, just around the corner from Harrods.

159 Knightsbridge, London SW1X 7PD. © 020/7584-6274. Fax 020/7225-1635. www.theKGHotel.co.uk. 28 units. £140–£160 ($266–$304) double; from £160 ($304) suite. AE, DC, MC, V. Tube: Knightsbridge. **Amenities:** Room service; laundry service; same-day dry cleaning; all nonsmoking rooms. *In room:* A/C, TV, beverage maker, hair dryer, safe, trouser press.

Knightsbridge Hotel ♠♠ (Value)

The Knightsbridge Hotel attracts visitors from all over the world seeking a small, comfortable hotel in a high-rent district. It's fabulously located, sandwiched between fashionable Beauchamp Place and Harrods, with many of the city's top theaters and museums close at hand. Built in the early 1800s as a private town house, the Knightsbridge sits on a tranquil, tree-lined—and traffic free—square. Kit and Tim Kemp, who have been celebrated for their upmarket boutique London hotels, have gone more affordable with a revamp of this hotel in the heart of the shopping district. All the Kemp "cult classics" are found here, including such *luxe* touches as granite-and-oak bathrooms, their famed honor bar, and Frette linens. Not surprisingly, the hotel was an instant hit. The beautifully furnished rooms have shower-only private bathrooms clad in marble or tile. Most bedrooms are spacious and furnished with traditional English fabrics. The best rooms are nos. 311 and 312 at the rear, each with a pitched ceiling and a small sitting area.

10 Beaufort Gardens, London SW3 1PT. © 020/7584-6300. Fax 020/7584-6355. www.firmdalehotels.com. 44 units. £180–£260 ($342–$494) double; from £295 ($561) suite. AE, DC, MC, V. Tube: Knightsbridge. **Amenities:** Self-service bar; room service; babysitting; laundry service; same-day dry cleaning. *In room:* TV, minibar, hair dryer, safe.

Searcys Roof Garden Rooms ⭐ *Finds*   Searcy's, one of London's best catering firms, operates this recycled surprise: an old pumping station that has been turned into a hotel that's only a hop, skip, and a jump from Harrods and the boutiques of Sloane Street. At this Knightsbridge oasis, you press a buzzer and are admitted to a freight elevator that carries you to the third floor. Upstairs, you'll encounter handsomely furnished rooms with antiques, tasteful fabrics, comfortable beds (some with canopies), and often a sitting alcove. Some of the bathtubs are right in the room instead of in a separate unit. Check out the rooftop garden.

30 Pavilion Rd., London SW1X 0HJ. © 020/7584-4921. Fax 020/7823-8694. www.30pavilionroad.co.uk. 10 units. £160 ($304) double. Rates include continental breakfast. AE, DC, MC, V. Tube: Knightsbridge. **Amenities:** Room service; laundry service; dry cleaning; nonsmoking rooms. *In room:* A/C, TV, Wi-Fi.

KENSINGTON
VERY EXPENSIVE

The Bentley ⭐⭐⭐   Following an 8-year renovation, this hotel is the epitome of charm, for those who prefer opulence to minimalism. Located in the heart of Kensington, The Bentley is the Rolls-Royce (or at least the Bentley) of London hotels. Six hundred tons of marble were imported from Turkey, Africa, and Italy to adorn the place. Gorgeous silk fabrics adorn its spacious rooms and suites, each with a *luxe* marble-lined bathroom with walk-in showers and Jacuzzis. The fixtures are gold plate, and in the bedrooms are deep pile carpets and Louis XIV accessories. The Imperial Suite even boasts a grand piano. Le Kalon Spa is one of the most luxurious of any hotel in London.

27–31 Harrington Gardens, London SW7 4JX. © 020/7244-5555. Fax 020/7244-5566. www.thebentley-hotel.com. 64 units. MC, V. £450 ($855) double; from £600 ($1,140) suite. Tube: South Kensington. **Amenities:** 2 restaurants; bar; gym; spa; sauna; room service; babysitting; laundry service; dry cleaning; rooms for those w/limited mobility. *In room:* A/C, TV, minibar, hair dryer, safe.

The Milestone ⭐⭐⭐   This outstanding boutique hotel, conveniently located in a Victorian town house across the street from Kensington Palace, offers modern luxury in an intimate, traditional setting. The Milestone's beautiful public rooms are awash with fresh flowers, dark woods, antique furnishings, and fabric wallcoverings, creating the cozy atmosphere of a private manor house.

Guest rooms and suites are spread over six floors and vary in size and shape (a few rooms are a bit small). They feature a full range of amenities, luxurious beds, and marble bathrooms, some of which have Jacuzzis. All accommodations are individually and creatively decorated, though some are more theme-intensive than others. The masculine Savile Row Room is "papered" in pinstriped material and sports a tailor's dummy and books on men's fashion; the serene Royal Studio has a small balcony and a sleigh bed; and the bilevel Club Suite offers an English library–style lounge, complete with an antique billiards table. You can request a room overlooking the palace and Kensington Gardens, but be advised that these have original leaded windows, which look wonderful but can't be double-glazed, so traffic noise does leak through.

1 Kensington Court, London W8 5DL. © 877/955-1515 in the U.S. and Canada, or 020/7917-1000. Fax 020/7917-1010. www.milestonehotel.com. 63 units. £310–£490 ($589–$931) double; £610–£910 ($1,159–$1,729) suite. AE, DC, MC, V. Tube: High St. Kensington. **Amenities:** 2 restaurants; lounge; bar; indoor heated pool; health club; Jacuzzi; sauna; concierge; room service; babysitting; laundry service; same-day dry cleaning; nonsmoking rooms. *In room:* A/C, TV, fax, Wi-Fi, minibar, coffeemaker, hair dryer, iron, safe.

EXPENSIVE
The Diplomat Hotel ⭐ *Finds*   Part of the Diplomat's charm is that it's a small and reasonably priced hotel located in an otherwise prohibitively expensive neighborhood.

Only minutes from Harrods department store, it was built in 1882 as a private residence by noted architect Thomas Cubbitt. The registration desk is framed by the sweep of a partially gilded circular staircase; above it, cherubs gaze down from a Regency-era chandelier. The staff is helpful, well mannered, and discreet. The high-ceilinged guest rooms are tastefully done in Victorian style. You get good—not grand—comfort here. Rooms are a bit small and usually furnished with twin beds. Bathrooms, with shower stalls, are also small but well maintained.

2 Chesham St., London SW1X 8DT. ℂ 020/7235-1544. Fax 020/7259-6153. www.thediplomathotel.co.uk. 26 units. £125–£170 ($238–$323) double. Rates include English buffet breakfast. AE, DC, MC, V. Tube: Sloane Sq. or Knightsbridge. **Amenities:** Snack bar; business services; babysitting; laundry service; same-day dry cleaning. *In room:* TV, coffeemaker, hair dryer, trouser press.

The Rockwell 𝒜𝒜𝒜 *Finds*   One of London's latest hotels proves that high style doesn't always come at a high price tag in London. This independently owned bastion of deluxe comfort occupies a converted Georgian manse in South Kensington. Its bedrooms are tricked out with oak furnishings and Neisha Crosland wallpaper, each crafted to combine traditional English aesthetics with modern design. The bedrooms themselves are large and inviting and dressed with the finest of Egyptian cotton, feather pillows, and Merino wool blankets. Each room has a bespoke solid-oak cupboard and desk. All the accommodations contain such extras as a glazed power shower and bathroom fittings by Philippe Starck. Rooms are bright and airy with large windows and simple lines. Preferred are the garden units with their own private patios. On site is the trendy One-Eight-One bistro whose menu is based on British fare given a contemporary twist. Yes, it's a place that serves lavender ice cream.

181–183 Cromwell Rd., London SW5 0SF. ℂ 020/7244-2000. Fax 020/7244-2001. www.therockwellhotellondon. co.uk. 40 units. £150–£180 ($285–$342) double. AE, DC, MC, V. Tube: Earl's Court or Gloucester Rd. **Amenities:** Restaurant; bar; room service; laundry service; gym membership. *In room:* A/C, TV, Wi-Fi, safe, minibar.

INEXPENSIVE

B + B Belgravia 𝒜𝒜   In its first year of operation (2005), this elegant town house won a top Gold Award as "the best B&B in London." It richly deserves it. Design, service, quality, and comfort paid off. The prices are also reasonable, the atmosphere in this massively renovated building is stylish, and the location grand: just a 5-minute walk from Victoria Station. The good-sized bedrooms are luxuriously furnished, each with a private bathroom with all the latest modern plumbing. In the guest lounge with its comfy sofas, an open fire burns on chilly nights. There is also a DVD library, and tea and coffee are served 24 hours a day. The full English breakfast is one of the finest in the area.

64–66 Ebury St., Belgravia, London SW1W 9QD. ℂ 020/7259-8570. Fax 020/7259-8591. www.bb-belgravia.com. 17 units. £99 ($188) double; £125 ($238) family room. Rates include a full English breakfast. AE, MC, V. Tube: Victoria Station. **Amenities:** Communal lounge; breakfast room. *In room:* TV, dataport.

CHELSEA
EXPENSIVE

The Cadogan 𝒜𝒜   Perhaps best known as the spot Oscar Wilde was arrested for so-called indecent acts, this late Victorian terra-cotta brick hotel had grown a bit stale before design doyenne Grace Leo-Andrieu, known for her work on the Lancaster and the Montalembert in Paris, transformed it in 2003. In the late 1890s, the halls rang with the laughter of Lillie Langtry, mistress of Edward VII. Today you get "stardust" wallpaper in the Drawing Room, Chanel-style tweeds on the upholstery, ostrich feathers strewn across pillows, and cheeky silver wallpaper in the very room (no. 118) where Wilde himself met his fate. The spacious and individually decorated bedrooms come in many styles and arrangements, even studios, some with two bathrooms. Rooms and suites are either contemporary with smooth lines and bold splashes of color or Edwardian style with period details and country-house furnishings. The various bathrooms are luxurious, with tubs and showers. Innovative cuisine is served in the comfortable yet stately dining room, though you can still order a traditional Victorian breakfast of finnan haddock with a poached egg.

75 Sloane Street, London SWIX 9SG. ⓒ 020/7235-7141. Fax 020/7245-0994. www.cadogan.com. 50 units. £265–£355 ($504–$675) double; from £375 ($713) suite. AE, DC, MC, V. Tube: Sloane Sq. or Knightsbridge. **Amenities:** Restaurant; bar; lounge; fitness room; use of tennis courts in private gardens; room service; laundry service; dry cleaning; nonsmoking rooms; rooms for those w/limited mobility. *In room:* A/C, TV, fridge, hair dryer.

The Draycott Hotel 𝕣𝕣𝕣 Everything about this place, radically upgraded into a government five-star rating, reeks of British gentility, style, and charm. So attentive is the staff, who manage to be both hip and cordial, that past clients, including John Malkovich, Pierce Brosnan, and Gerard Depardieu, are greeted when they enter. The hotel took its present-day form when a third brick-fronted town house was added to a pair of interconnected town houses that had been functioning as a five-star hotel since the 1980s. That, coupled with tons of money spent on English antiques, rich draperies, and an upgrade of those expensive infrastructures you'll never see, including security, have transformed this place into a gem. The location, close to Sloane Square, Harrods, and the bustling thoroughfares of Knightsbridge, is one of this hotel's best assets. Bedrooms are each outfitted differently, each with *haute* English style and plenty of fashion chic.

26 Cadogan Gardens, London SW3 2RP. ⓒ 800/747-4942 or 020/7730-6466. Fax 020/7730-0236. www.draycott hotel.com. 35 units. £230–£290 ($437–$551) double; £370 ($703) suite. AE, DC, MC, V. Tube: Sloane Sq. **Amenities:** Complimentary tea daily at 4pm; complimentary champagne daily at 6pm; complimentary hot chocolate daily at 9:30pm; bar; bar snacks; room service; laundry service/dry cleaning; access to nearby spa and fitness club; Internet station. *In room:* A/C, TV, minibar.

San Domenico House 𝕣𝕣 This "toff" (dandy) address, a red-brick Victorian-era town house that has been tastefully renovated in recent years, is located in Chelsea near Sloane Square. It combines valuable 19th-century antiques with modern comforts. Our favorite spot here is the rooftop terrace; with views opening onto Chelsea, it's ideal for a relaxing breakfast or drink. Bedrooms come in varying sizes, ranging from small to spacious, but all are opulently furnished with flouncy draperies, tasteful fabrics, and sumptuous beds. Many rooms have draped four-poster or canopied beds and, of course, antiques. The deluxe bathrooms have tub/shower combinations, with chrome power showers, wall-width mirrors (in most rooms), and luxurious toiletries.

29 Draycott Place, London SW3 2SH. ⓒ 800/324-9960 in the U.S. or 020/7581-5757. Fax 020/7584-1348. www. sandomenicohouse.com. 16 units. £225–£255 ($428–$485) double; £285 ($542) suite. AE, DC, MC, V. Tube: Sloane Sq. **Amenities:** Airport transportation (with prior arrangement); business services; limited room service; babysitting; laundry service; same-day dry cleaning. *In room:* A/C, TV, minibar, hair dryer.

MODERATE
The Willett Hotel 𝕣 *Value* On a tree-lined street leading off Sloane Square, this dignified Victorian town house lies in the heart of Chelsea. Named for the famous London architect William Willett, its stained glass and chandeliers reflect the opulence of the days when Prince Edward was on the throne. Under a mansard roof with bay windows, the hotel is a 5-minute walk from the shopping mecca of King's Road and close

to such stores as Peter Jones, Harrods, and Harvey Nichols. The hotel shut down for most of 2007 for a complete overhaul. Individually decorated bedrooms come in a wide range of sizes. All rooms have well-kept bathrooms, equipped with tub/shower combos.

32 Sloane Gardens, London SW1W 8DJ. ℂ 800/270-9206 or 020/7824-8415. Fax 020/7730-4830. www.eeh.co.uk. 19 units. £110–£200 ($209–$380) double; £200 ($380) triple. Rates include English breakfast. AE, DC, MC, V. Tube: Sloane Sq. **Amenities:** Room service; laundry service; same-day dry cleaning; nonsmoking rooms. *In room:* A/C (in most rooms), TV, fridge (in some), coffeemaker, hair dryer, iron, safe.

SOUTH KENSINGTON
VERY EXPENSIVE
Blake's Hotel *⟨★★★⟩*   Actress Anouska Hempel's opulent and highly individual creation is one of London's best small hotels. No expense was spared in converting this former row of Victorian town houses into one of the city's most original places to stay. It offers an Arabian Nights atmosphere down in old Kensington: The richly appointed lobby boasts British Raj–era furniture from India, and individually decorated, elaborately appointed rooms contain such treasures and touches as Venetian glassware, cloth-covered walls, swagged draperies, and even Empress Josephine's daybed. Live out your fantasy: Choose an ancient Egyptian funeral barge or a 16th-century Venetian boudoir. Rooms in the older section have the least space and aren't air-conditioned but are chic nevertheless. Beds are deluxe, and the marble bathrooms are richly outfitted with a tub/shower combination and robes.

33 Roland Gardens, London SW7 3PF. ℂ 800/926-3173 in the U.S. or 020/7370-6701. Fax 020/7373-2144. www.blakeshotels.com. 48 units. £265–£375 ($504–$713) double; from £645 ($1,226) suite. AE, MC, V. Parking £2 ($3.80) per hr. Tube: Gloucester Rd. **Amenities:** Restaurant; fitness room; tour desk; secretarial services; room service; massage; babysitting; laundry service; same-day dry cleaning; nonsmoking rooms. *In room:* TV, Wi-Fi, minibar, hair dryer, safe.

EXPENSIVE
Number Sixteen *⟨★⟩*   This luxurious pension is composed of four early Victorian town houses linked together. The scrupulously maintained front and rear gardens make this one of the most idyllic spots on the street. The rooms are decorated with an eclectic mix of English antiques and modern paintings, although some of the decor looks a little faded. Accommodations range from small to spacious and have themes such as tartan and maritime. The beds are comfortable, and bathrooms are tiled and outfitted with vanity mirrors, heated towel racks, and hand-held showers over small tubs. There's an honor-system bar in the library. On chilly days, a fire roars in the fireplace of the flowery drawing room, although some prefer the more masculine library. Breakfast can be served in your bedroom, in the conservatory, or if the weather's good, in the garden, with its bubbling fountain and fishpond.

16 Sumner Place, London SW7 3EG. ℂ 800/592-5387 in the U.S. or 020/7589-5232. Fax 020/7584-8615. www.numbersixteenhotel.co.uk. 42 units. £150–£265 ($285–$504) double. AE, DC, MC, V. Parking £36 ($68). Tube: South Kensington. **Amenities:** Honor bar; lounge; access to nearby health club; room service; babysitting; laundry service; same-day dry cleaning; nonsmoking rooms. *In room:* TV, minibar, hair dryer, safe.

MODERATE
Avonmore Hotel *⟨★⟩ (Finds)*   The refurbished Avonmore is easily accessible to West End theaters and shops, yet it's in a quiet neighborhood, only 2 minutes from the West Kensington stop on the District Line. This privately owned place—a former National Award winner as the best private hotel in London—boasts wall-to-wall carpeting in each tastefully decorated room. Bathrooms are well maintained, coming either with a tub bath or shower. The owner, Margaret McKenzie, provides lots of personal service.

An English breakfast is served in a cheerful room, and a wide range of drinks is available in the cozy bar.

66 Avonmore Rd., London W14 8RS. ℂ 020/7603-4296. Fax 020/7603-4035. www.avonmorehotel.co.uk. 9 units. £80–£110 ($152–$209) double; £90–£130 ($171–$247) triple. Rates include English breakfast. AE, MC, V. Tube: West Kensington. **Amenities:** Bar; room service; nonsmoking rooms. *In room:* TV, minibar, coffeemaker, hair dryer.

Base2stay *(Value)*   Down in Kensington a new concept in hotels has emerged, offering great value by providing "a synthesis" of what guests really need and use—minus the frills. The fluff has been edited, but what you get is a stylish, comfortably furnished accommodation with a small kitchenette. The cheapest rooms contain bunk beds for 2, and accommodations are rather flexible here, including suites that can be made by interconnecting rooms. Living may be stripped to the basics, but this is no hostel, as there is a 24-hour reception service as well as daily maid service.

25 Courtfield Gardens, London SW5 OPG. ℂ 800/511-9821 in the U.S. or 020/7491-2948. www.base2stay.com. 67 units. £90 ($171) bunk beds for two; £99–£110 ($188–$209) double; £175 ($333) deluxe units for 4 guests. AE, MC, V. Tube: Earl's Court. **Amenities:** Nonsmoking rooms. *In room:* A/C, TV, kitchenette.

EASYHotel *(Value)*   This hotel runs on the principle that guests would rather have smaller hotel rooms and pay less. If you're claustrophobic, it is definitely not for you—some of the rooms don't even have windows (if you can get a room that does, it makes a big difference). The rooms are 6 to 7 sq. m. (65–75 sq. ft.), with most of the space taken up by standard double beds. Just off Cromwell Road between South Kensington and Earl's Court, EASY offers all doubles with cramped bathrooms containing a shower. There are flatscreen TVs in every unit, but a £5 ($9.50) fee is assessed to use the set. As management jokingly says, "Our rooms come in three sizes: small, very small, and tiny." One staff member is permanently on-site, but no services are offered, and other than the reception desk, there is no common area. Food and entertainment can be found in the immediate area. Instead of phoning the hotel, all EASYHotel bookings are taken by credit card through its website.

14 Lexham Gardens, Kensington, London W8 5JE. www.easyhotel.com. 34 units. £30–£50 ($57–$95) double. MC, V. Tube: South Kensington or Earl's Court. **Amenities:** Reception desk; all nonsmoking rooms; rooms for those w/limited mobility. *In room:* A/C, TV.

The Gallery *(Finds)*   This is the place to go if you want to stay in an exclusive little town-house hotel but don't want to pay £300 ($570) a night for the privilege. Two splendid Georgian residences have been restored and converted into this remarkable hotel, which remains relatively unknown. The location is ideal, near the Victoria and Albert Museum, Royal Albert Hall, Harrods, Knightsbridge, and King's Road. Bedrooms are individually designed and decorated in Laura Ashley style, with half-canopied beds and marble-tiled bathrooms with brass fittings and tub/shower combinations. The junior suites have private roof terraces, minibars, Jacuzzis, and air-conditioning. A team of butlers takes care of everything. The lounge, with its mahogany paneling, moldings, and deep colors, has the ambience of a private club. The drawing room beckons you to relax and read in a quiet corner. The Gallery Room displays works by known and unknown artists for sale.

8–10 Queensberry Place, London SW7 2EA. ℂ 800/270-9206 in the U.S. or 020/7915-0000. Fax 020/7915-4400. www.eeh.co.uk. 36 units. £145–£180 ($276–$342) double; £200 ($380) triple; £275 ($523) junior suite. Rates include buffet English breakfast. AE, DC, MC, V. Tube: South Kensington. **Amenities:** Bar; access to nearby health club; courtesy car; business center; room service; babysitting; laundry service; same-day dry cleaning; nonsmoking rooms; 24-hr. butler service. *In room:* A/C (in most rooms), TV, coffeemaker, hair dryer, safe.

INEXPENSIVE

The Vicarage Hotel 🐾 (Kids) Owners Eileen and Martin Diviney enjoy a host of admirers on all continents. Their much-improved hotel is tops for old-fashioned English charm, affordable prices, and hospitality. On a residential garden square close to Kensington High Street, not far from Portobello Road Market, this Victorian town house retains many original features. Individually furnished in country-house style, the guest rooms can accommodate up to four, making it a great place for families. If you want a little nest to hide away in, opt for the very private top-floor aerie (no. 19). Guests find the corridor shower-only bathrooms adequate and well maintained. Guests meet in a cozy sitting room for conversation and to watch the "telly." As a thoughtful extra, hot drinks are available 24 hours a day. In the morning, a hearty English breakfast awaits.

10 Vicarage Gate, London W8 4AG. ⊙ 020/7229-4030. Fax 020/7792-5989. www.londonvicaragehotel.com. 17 units, 9 with bathroom. £46 ($87) single without bathroom; £78 ($148) double without bathroom, £102 ($194) double with bathroom; £95 ($181) triple without bathroom; £102 ($194) family room for 4 without bathroom. Rates include English breakfast. AE, MC, V. Tube: High St. Kensington or Notting Hill Gate. *In room:* Beverage maker, hair dryer, no phone.

EARL'S COURT
MODERATE

Henley House (Value) This B&B stands out from the pack around Earl's Court—and it's a better value than most. The red-brick Victorian row house is on a communal fenced-in garden that you can enter by borrowing a key from the reception desk. The staff takes a keen interest in the welfare of its guests and is happy to take bewildered newcomers under their wing, so this is an ideal place for London first-timers. A ground-floor sitting room overlooks a rear courtyard. The decor is bright and contemporary; a typical room has warmly patterned Anna French wallpaper, chintz fabrics, and solid-brass lighting fixtures. Each room is fitted with a well-maintained shower-only bathroom. Breakfast is a cheerful event, served in a room decorated with terracotta accents and pots of dried flowers. For those who prefer to stay in rather than hit the area's hot spots (mostly gay bars), there's a shelf of books you're welcome to borrow.

30 Barkston Gardens, London SW5 0EN. ⊙ 020/7370-4111. Fax 020/7370-0026. www.henleyhousehotel.com. 21 units. £59 ($112) double; £69 ($131) triple. Rates include continental breakfast. AE, DC, MC, V. Tube: Earl's Court. **Amenities:** Breakfast room; lounge; nonsmoking rooms. *In room:* TV, coffeemaker, hair dryer.

Mayflower Hotel Originally a private Victorian town house, this family-run hotel extends a warm welcome. It stands out among the many B&B disasters along this street by offering clean, comfortable, and inviting accommodations. The Queen of England doesn't send overflow guests here, but frugal travelers delight in the prices. The area is young and vibrant and is experiencing gentrification. The renovated hotel is looking better than ever and is a lot more luxurious than before. Rooms are Eastern influenced (the owner is Anglo-Indian) with carved dark wooden beds and wardrobes, plus Egyptian cotton sheets. The marbled bathrooms have also been restored. An elevator carries guests to every floor, and there are luggage-storage facilities if you want to venture into the countryside with a lighter load than you brought to (or acquired in) London. Added features include a juice bar and lounge furnished in dark walnut with leather sofas. There is also a "tropical" garden outside.

26–28 Trebovir Rd., London SW5 9NJ. ⊙ **020/7370-0991.** Fax 020/7370-0994. www.mayflower-group.co.uk. 48 units. £89–£155 ($169–$295) double; £110–£165 ($209–$314) triple; £135–£195 ($257–$371) family room; £129–£279 ($245–$530) suite. Rates include continental breakfast. AE, MC, V. Parking £20 ($38). Tube: Earl's Court. **Amenities:** Breakfast room, juice bar, lounge, business services; laundry service; same-day dry cleaning; all nonsmoking rooms. *In room:* TV, Wi-Fi, coffeemaker, hair dryer, safe, trouser press.

Philbeach Hotel One of Europe's largest gay hotels, the Philbeach is a Victorian row house on a wide crescent behind the Earl's Court Exhibition Centre. Open to both men and women, it offers standard budget-hotel rooms. The showers are tiny, but the private and shared baths are clean. Room no. 8A, a double with bathroom, has a balcony overlooking the small back garden.

30–31 Philbeach Gardens, London SW5 9EB. ⓒ 020/7373-1244. Fax 020/7244-0149. www.philbeachhotel.co.uk. 40 units, 16 with bathroom. £50 ($95) single without bathroom; £59 ($112) single with bathroom; £63 ($120) double without bathroom; £81 ($154) double with bathroom. Rates include continental breakfast. AE, MC, V. Tube: Earl's Court. **Amenities:** Restaurant (Thai cuisine); gay bar (Jimmies); laundry service; same-day dry cleaning. *In room:* TV, coffeemaker.

6 Hotels from Marylebone to Holland Park

MARLEBONE
VERY EXPENSIVE

The Langham 🕸🕸 After it was bombed during World War II, this well-located hotel languished as dusty office space for the BBC until the early 1990s, when it was painstakingly restored. The Langham's public rooms reflect the power and majesty of the British Empire at its apex. Guest rooms are somewhat less opulent but are still attractively furnished and comfortable, featuring French Provincial furniture and red-oak trim. All bathrooms are well kept and contain full tub/shower combinations. The hotel is within easy reach of Mayfair and Soho restaurants and theaters, and Oxford and Regent streets shopping. Plus, Regent's Park is just blocks away.

1C Portland Place, London W1B 1JA. ⓒ 800/223-6800 or 020/7636-1000. Fax 020/7323-2340. www.langham hotels.com. 427 units. £199–£350 ($378–$665) double; £349–£490 ($663–$931) club room; £289–£749 ($549–$1,423) suite. AE, DC, MC, V. Tube: Oxford Circus. **Amenities:** 2 restaurants; bar; Edwardian-style palm court; indoor heated pool; health club; spa; sauna; tour desk; courtesy car; business center; room service; massage; babysitting; laundry service; same-day dry cleaning; nonsmoking rooms; rooms for those w/limited mobility. *In room:* A/C, TV, minibar, beverage maker, hair dryer, safe.

EXPENSIVE

Dorset Square Hotel 🕸🕸🕸 Just steps from Regent's Park, this is one of London's best and most stylish "house hotels"—it even overlooks Thomas Lord's (the man who set up London's first private cricket club) first cricket pitch. Hot hoteliers Tim and Kit Kemp have furnished the interior of these two Georgian town houses with a comfy mix of antiques, reproductions, and chintz that makes you feel as if you're in an elegant private home. The Kemps are interior decorators known for their bold and daring taste, and the impressive bedrooms are decorated in a distinctly personal (and beautiful) style. Eight rooms feature crown-canopied beds, and all appointments are of a very high standard. The full marble bathrooms are exquisite, with robes, deluxe toiletries, and tub/shower combinations.

39–40 Dorset Sq., London NW1 6QN. ⓒ 020/7723-7874. Fax 020/7724-3328. www.dorsetsquare.co.uk. 37 units. £230–£270 ($437–$513) double; from £350 ($665) suite. AE, MC, V. Parking £33 ($63) daily, free on weekends. Tube: Baker St. or Marylebone. **Amenities:** Restaurant; bar; room service; massage; babysitting; laundry service; same-day dry cleaning; nonsmoking rooms. *In room:* A/C, TV, Wi-Fi, minibar, hair dryer, iron, safe.

Durrants Hotel 🕸 This historic hotel (established in 1789) off Manchester Square with its Georgian-detailed facade is snug, cozy, and traditional—almost like a poor man's Brown's (p. 105). We find it to be one of the most quintessentially English of all London hotels. You could invite the Queen to Durrants for tea. Over the 100 years they have owned the hotel, the Miller family has incorporated several neighboring houses into the original structure. A walk through the pine-and-mahogany-paneled public rooms is like stepping back in time: You'll even find an 18th-century letter-writing room. The bedrooms are rather bland except for elaborate cove moldings and comfortable furnishings, including good beds. Some are air-conditioned, and some are, alas, small. Bathrooms are tiny, with tub/shower combinations but little room to maneuver.

26–32 George St., London W1H 5BJ. (C) 020/7935-8131. Fax 020/7487-3510. www.durrantshotel.co.uk. 92 units. £185 ($352) double; £199 ($378) family room for 3; from £325 ($618) suite. AE, MC, V. Tube: Bond St. or Baker St. **Amenities:** Restaurant; bar; room service; babysitting; laundry service; same-day dry cleaning; rooms for those w/limited mobility. *In room:* A/C (in most), TV, hair dryer, safe (in most).

The Mandeville Hotel *&&*   Call it refurbished London. In trendy Marylebone Village, just a short stroll from Selfridges and Bond Street shops, The Mandeville has been totally restored, its former 166 bedrooms restructured into 142 units. This once-staid property is now a hot address—one of London's leading decorators, Stephen Ryan, was brought in to restyle the lobby, restaurant, and bar. In the de Ville Restaurant, a modern British cuisine is served against a backdrop of floral wallpaper punctuated by theatrical clear Perspex-framed paintings and Venetian-mask wall lights. The de Vigne Bar is a favorite rendezvous point—try the Honey Suckle cocktail—champagne, honey vodka, rose-petal liquor, elderflower, and fresh raspberries.

Mandeville Place, London W1U 2BE. (C) 020/7935-5599. Fax 020/7935-9588. www.mandeville.co.uk. 142 units. £275–£300 ($523–$570) double; from £400 ($760) suite. AE, DC, MC, V. Tube: Bond St. **Amenities:** Restaurant; bar; gym; room service; laundry service/dry cleaning; all nonsmoking rooms; rooms for those w/limited mobility. *In room:* A/C, TV, minibar (in some), beverage maker, hair dryer, iron, safe.

MODERATE

Hallam Hotel   This heavily ornamented stone-and-brick Victorian—one of the few on the street to escape the Blitz—is just a 5-minute stroll from Oxford Circus. It's the property of brothers Grant and David Baker, who maintain it well. The hotel is warm and friendly, and the central location that you get for these prices can't be beat. The guest rooms are comfortably furnished with good beds. Some of the singles are so small they're called "cabinettes." Several of the twin-bedded rooms are quite spacious and have adequate closet space. Bathrooms, which have shower stalls, are a bit cramped.

12 Hallam St., Portland Place, London W1N 5LF. (C) 020/7580-1166. Fax 020/7323-4527. www.hallamhotel.com. 25 units. £90 ($171) single; £100 ($190) double. Rates include English breakfast. AE, DC, MC, V. Tube: Oxford Circus. **Amenities:** Bar. *In room:* TV, coffeemaker, hair dryer.

Hart House Hotel *& Kids*   Hart House is a long-enduring favorite with Frommer's readers. In the heart of the West End, this well-preserved historic building (one of a group of Georgian mansions occupied by exiled French nobles during the French Revolution) lies within easy walking distance of many theaters. The rooms—done in a combination of furnishings, ranging from Portobello antique to modern—are spic-and-span, each one with a different character. Favorites include no. 7, a triple with a big bathroom and shower. Ask for no. 11, on the top floor, if you'd like a brightly lit aerie. Housekeeping rates high marks here, and each bedroom is comfortably appointed with chairs, an armoire, a desk, and a large chest of drawers. The shower-only bathrooms, although small, are efficiently organized. Hart House has long been known as a good, safe place for traveling families. Many of its rooms are triples. Larger families can avail themselves of special family accommodations with connecting rooms.

51 Gloucester Place, Portman Sq., London W1U 8JF. (C) 020/7935-2288. Fax 020/7935-8516. www.harthouse.co.uk. 15 units. £110 ($209) double; £135 ($257) triple; £155 ($295) quad. Rates include English breakfast. MC, V. Tube: Marble Arch or Baker St. **Amenities:** Babysitting; all nonsmoking rooms. *In room:* TV, coffeemaker, hair dryer.

Where to Stay from Marylebone to Holland Park

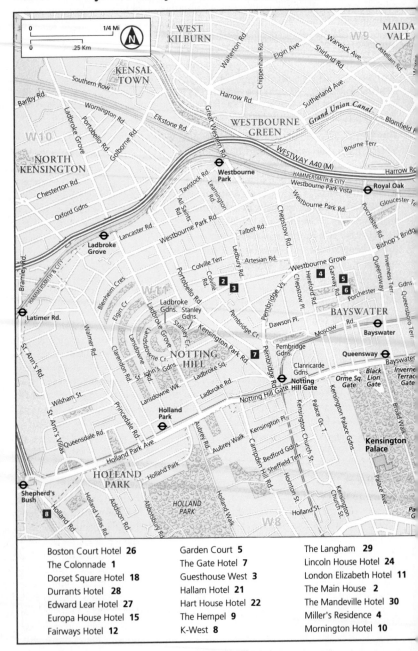

Boston Court Hotel **26**	Garden Court **5**	The Langham **29**
The Colonnade **1**	The Gate Hotel **7**	Lincoln House Hotel **24**
Dorset Square Hotel **18**	Guesthouse West **3**	London Elizabeth Hotel **11**
Durrants Hotel **28**	Hallam Hotel **21**	The Main House **2**
Edward Lear Hotel **27**	Hart House Hotel **22**	The Mandeville Hotel **30**
Europa House Hotel **15**	The Hempel **9**	Miller's Residence **4**
Fairways Hotel **12**	K-West **8**	Mornington Hotel **10**

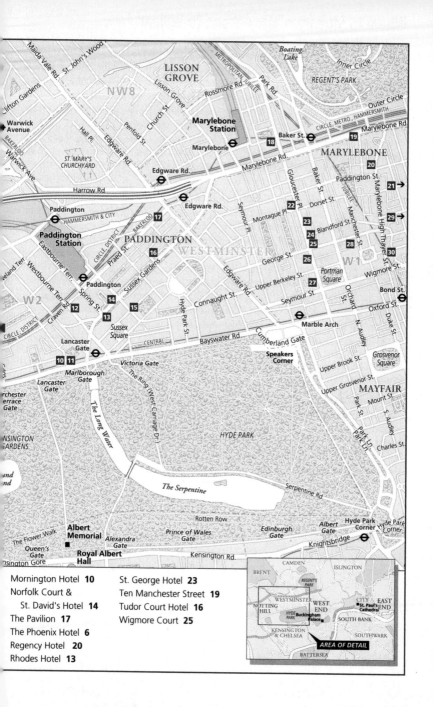

Mornington Hotel **10**

Norfolk Court &
   St. David's Hotel **14**

The Pavilion **17**

The Phoenix Hotel **6**

Regency Hotel **20**

Rhodes Hotel **13**

St. George Hotel **23**

Ten Manchester Street **19**

Tudor Court Hotel **16**

Wigmore Court **25**

Lincoln House Hotel   Built in the late 18th century, under the reign of King George III, this refurbished and tastefully decorated hotel is a converted town house with lots of character. Only a 5-minute walk from Marble Arch tube, it occupies one of the most central locations in London, near Oxford Street northeast of Hyde Park. Midsize bedrooms are completely modernized but decorated in a traditional fashion, each with a small bathroom shower. You have a choice of enjoying an English breakfast downstairs or a continental breakfast served in your room.

33 Gloucester Place, London W1U 8HY. ℂ 020/7486-7630. Fax 020/7486-0166. www.lincoln-house-hotel.co.uk. 24 units. £89–£115 ($169–$219) double; £129 ($245) triple; £139 ($264) family room. Rates include breakfast. AE, DC, MC, V. Tube: Marble Arch. **Amenities:** Breakfast in room. *In room:* TV, Wi-Fi, fridge (in some), beverage maker, hair dryer, trouser press.

St. George Hotel 🅐 *Value*   A short walk from Oxford and Baker streets, this privately owned hotel in a restored Georgian building overlooks landmark Gloucester Square. Its midsize bedrooms are attractively and comfortably refurbished in red-and-white tones, with such modern amenities as key-card doors and electronic built-in room safes. Bathrooms are well appointed, each with a tub and a shower. Two accommodations have bathrooms that are outside the room but for the sole use of occupants of a particular unit. These bathrooms have showers, as do most of the standard doubles. A few superior units have bathtubs and showers. A wide range of rooms is available, from single to quad, the latter ideal for families. The hotel also offers a variety of services, from airport pickup to side-trip bookings (which must be planned in advance).

49 Gloucester Place, London W1U 8JE. ℂ 020/7486-8586. Fax 020/7486-6567. www.stgeorge-hotel.net. 19 units. £75–£150 ($143–$285) double; £175 ($333) triple; £200 ($380) quad. Rates include English breakfast. AE, MC, V. Tube: Marylebone Rd. **Amenities:** Airport pickup; breakfast room. *In room:* A/C (in some), TV, fridge (in some), beverage maker, hair dryer, safe.

Ten Manchester Street 🅐 *Value*   Constructed in 1919 as a residence hall for nurses, this terraced red-brick building is now a smart town-house hotel. We like its location in Marylebone, close to those top shopping destinations, Bond and Regent streets, and near chic boutiques and numerous cafes and restaurants. The guest rooms are small but well designed and are furnished with comfort in mind, and each has a well-organized bathroom with tub and shower. The hotel has the aura of a private home, thanks to the inviting atmosphere and helpful staff.

10 Manchester St., London W1M 5PG. ℂ 020/7486-6669. Fax 020/7224-0348. 46 units. £75–£100 ($143–$190) double; £100–£125 ($190–$238) triple. Rates include continental breakfast. AE, DC, MC, V. Tube: Baker St. or Bond St. **Amenities:** Lounge, same-day dry cleaning; nonsmoking rooms. *In room:* TV, fridge, coffeemaker, hair dryer, trouser press.

INEXPENSIVE

Boston Court Hotel   Upper Berkeley is a classic street of B&Bs; in days of yore, it was home to Elizabeth Montagu (1720–1800), "queen of the bluestockings," who defended Shakespeare against attacks by Voltaire. Today, it's a good, safe, respectable retreat at an affordable price. This unfrilly hotel offers accommodations in a centrally located Victorian-era building within walking distance of Oxford Street shopping and Hyde Park. The small, basic rooms have been refurbished and redecorated with a no-nonsense decor and have well-kept bathrooms with private showers.

26 Upper Berkeley St., Marble Arch, London W1H 7QL. ℂ 020/7723-1445. Fax 020/7262-8823. www.boston courthotel.co.uk. 15 units (4 with shower only). £69 ($131) double with shower only; £75–£79 ($143–$150) double with bathroom; £85–£89 ($162–$169) triple with bathroom. Rates include continental breakfast. MC, V. Tube: Marble Arch. **Amenities:** Laundry service; nonsmoking rooms. *In room:* TV, coffeemaker, hair dryer.

Edward Lear Hotel   This popular hotel, situated 1 block from Marble Arch, is made all the more desirable by the bouquets of fresh flowers in its public rooms. It occupies a pair of brick town houses dating from 1780. The western house was the London home of 19th-century artist and poet Edward Lear, famous for his nonsense verse, and his illustrated limericks adorn the walls of one of the sitting rooms. Steep stairs lead up to cozy rooms which range from spacious to broom-closet size. Bedrooms are looking better than ever following a wholesale renovation in 2007. If you're looking for classiness, know that the bacon on your plate comes from the same butcher used by the Queen. One major drawback to the hotel: This is a very noisy part of town. Rear rooms are quieter. Bathrooms are well maintained, most with a shower and tub.

28–30 Seymour St., London W1H 7JB. ☎ 020/7402-5401. Fax 020/7706-3766. www.edlear.com. 31 units, 4 with bathroom; 8 with shower only. £67 ($127) double without bathroom, £74 ($141) double with shower only; £89 ($169) double with bathroom; £79 ($150) triple without bathroom, £89 ($169) triple with shower only; £99 ($188) triple with bathroom. Rates include English breakfast and tax. AE, MC, V. Tube: Marble Arch. *In room:* TV, coffeemaker.

Regency Hotel   The building is from the 1800s, and there has been a hotel of some kind here since the Blitz. In 1991, the place was gutted and renovated into its present form. One of the better hotels on the street, it offers simple, conservatively decorated modern bedrooms scattered over four floors and a breakfast room set in what used to be the cellar. Bathrooms, though small, are well kept and come mostly with tub/shower combinations. The neighborhood is protected as a historic district, and Marble Arch, Regent's Park, and Baker Street all lie within a 15-minute walk.

19 Nottingham Place, London W1U 5LQ. ☎ 020/7486-5347. Fax 020/7224-6057. www.regencyhotelwestend.co.uk. 20 units. £89 ($169) double; £110–£125 ($209–$238) family room. Rates include English breakfast. AE, DC, MC, V. Parking £23 ($44) nearby. Tube: Baker St. or Regent's Park. *In room:* TV, minibar on request, coffeemaker, hair dryer, trouser press or iron.

Wigmore Court *(Value*   A convenient family hotel, this inn lies near the street made famous as the fictional address of Sherlock Holmes—Baker Street. It's also close to Marble Arch, Oxford Street, and Madame Tussaud's. A somber Georgian structure, it has been converted into a fine B&B suitable only for serious stair climbers, as there is no elevator. There's traffic noise outside, so request a room in the rear. Bedrooms, many quite spacious, are comfortably furnished. Most units contain double or twin beds, plus a small bathroom. About half of the bathrooms have tub/shower combos.

23 Gloucester Place, London W1U 8HS. ☎ 020/7935-0928. Fax 020/7487-4254. www.wigmore-court-hotel.co.uk. 19 units. £70–£99 ($133–$188) double; £120–£145 ($228–$276) triple. MC, V. Tube: Marble Arch. **Amenities:** Coin-op washers and dryers; guest kitchen. *In room:* TV, coffeemaker.

PADDINGTON & BAYSWATER
VERY EXPENSIVE

The Hempel ✪✪✪   Set in a trio of nearly identical 19th-century row houses, this hotel is the statement of flamboyant interior designer and actress Anouska Hempel. Don't expect the swags, tassels, and elegance of her better-established hotel, Blake's (p. 123)—the atmosphere here is radically different. The Hempel manages to combine a grand Italian sense of proportion with Asian Zen-like simplicity. Soothing monochromatic tones prevail. Symmetrical fireplaces flank the deliberately sparse lobby, and carefully positioned mementos from Asia show up throughout the hotel, including Thai bullock carts that double as coffeetables.

Bedrooms continue the minimalist theme, except for their carefully concealed battery of electronic accessories, which includes a VCR, satellite TV, CD player, DVD player, twin phone lines, and a modem hookup. Bathrooms have cut-stone walls, countertops, and bathtubs. The hotel mostly caters to business travelers from around the world, who appreciate its tactful service and undeniably snobbish overtones.

31–35 Craven Hill Garden Sq., London W2 3EA. © 020/7298-9000. Fax 020/7402-4666. www.the-hempel.co.uk. 46 units. £295–£315 ($561–$599) double; from £480 ($912) suite. AE, DC, MC, V. Tube: Lancaster Gate or Queensway. **Amenities:** Restaurant; bar; lounge; access to health club; tour desk; business services; room service; massage; babysitting; laundry service; same-day dry cleaning; nonsmoking rooms; rooms for those w/limited mobility. *In room:* A/C, TV, Wi-Fi, minibar, coffeemaker, hair dryer, safe.

EXPENSIVE

London Elizabeth Hotel ⭐   This elegant Victorian town house is ideally situated, overlooking Hyde Park. Amid the buzz and excitement of central London, the hotel's atmosphere is an oasis of charm and refinement. Even before the hotel's recent £3-million ($5.7-million) restoration, it oozed character. Individually decorated rooms range from executive to deluxe and remind us of an English country house. Deluxe rooms are fully air-conditioned, and some contain four-poster beds. Executive units usually contain one double or twin bed. Some rooms have special features such as Victorian antique fireplaces, and all contain first-rate bathrooms with showers and tubs. Suites are pictures of grand comfort and luxury—the Conservatory Suite boasts its own veranda, part of the house's original 1850 conservatory.

Lancaster Terrace, Hyde Park, London W2 3PF. © 800/721-5566 in the U.S. or 020/7402-6641. Fax 020/7224-8900. www.londonelizabethhotel.co.uk. 49 units. £140–£180 ($266–$342) double; £200–£270 ($380–$513) suite. Rates include buffet breakfast. AE, DC, MC, V. Parking £10 ($19). Tube: Lancaster Gate or Paddington. **Amenities:** Restaurant; bar; room service; laundry service; same-day dry cleaning; nonsmoking rooms. *In room:* A/C (in some), TV, hair dryer.

Miller's Residence ⭐⭐ *Finds*   Staying here is like spending a night in Charles Dickens's Old Curiosity Shop. Others say the little hotel looks like the set of *La Traviata*. Miller's calls itself an 18th-century rooming house, and there's nothing quite like it in London. A roaring log fire blazes in the large book-lined drawing room in winter. The individually designed rooms are named after romantic poets. They vary in shape and size, but all are luxuriously furnished with antiques, prints, and tasteful curios. Each room contains a small bathroom with a shower and tub. In addition to its double rooms, Miller's offers two sumptuous suites with multiple bedrooms, a drawing room, and a fully equipped kitchen.

111A Westbourne Grove, London W2 4UW. © 020/7243-1024. Fax 020/7243-1064. www.millersuk.com. 9 units. £150–£185 ($285–$352) double; £230 ($437) suite. Rates include continental breakfast. AE, DC, MC, V. Tube: Bayswater or Notting Hill Gate. **Amenities:** Limited business services; babysitting; laundry service; same-day dry cleaning. *In room:* TV, kitchen in suites.

MODERATE

Mornington Hotel ⭐   Affiliated with Best Western, the Mornington brings a touch of northern European hospitality to the center of London. Just north of Hyde Park and Kensington Gardens, the hotel has a Victorian exterior and a Scandinavian-inspired decor. The area isn't London's most fashionable, but it's close to Hyde Park and convenient to Marble Arch, Oxford Street shopping, and the ethnic restaurants of Queensway. Renovated guest rooms are tasteful and comfortable, all with pay movies. Bathrooms are small but tidy, with showers and tubs. Every year we get a Christmas card from "the gang," as we refer to the hotel staff—and what a helpful crew they are.

12 Lancaster Gate, London W2 3LG. © 800/633-6548 in the U.S. or 020/7262-7361. Fax 020/7706-1028. www. bw-morningtonhotel.co.uk. 66 units. £144–£156 ($274–$296) double. Rates include Scandinavian and English breakfast. AE, DC, MC, V. Tube: Lancaster Gate. **Amenities:** Bar; courtesy car; business center; laundry service; same-day dry cleaning; nonsmoking rooms. *In room:* TV, coffeemaker.

The Pavilion ⚓ (Finds)   Until the early 1990s, this was a rather ordinary-looking B&B. Then a team of entrepreneurs with ties to the fashion industry took over and redecorated the rooms with sometimes wacky themes, turning it into an idiosyncratic little hotel. The result is a theatrical and often outrageous decor that's appreciated by the many fashion models and music-industry folks who regularly make this their temporary home in London. Rooms are, regrettably, rather small, but each has a distinctive style. Examples include a kitschy 1970s room ("Honky-Tonk Afro"), an Asian bordello–themed room ("Enter the Dragon"), and even rooms with 19th-century ancestral themes. One Edwardian-style room, a gem of emerald brocade and velvet, is called "Green with Envy." Each contains tea-making facilities and small bathrooms with excellent showers.

34–36 Sussex Gardens, London W2 1UL. ℂ 020/7262-0905. Fax 020/7262-1324. www.pavilionhoteluk.com. 30 units. £100 ($190) double; £120 ($228) triple. Rates include continental breakfast. AE, MC, V. Parking £10 ($19). Tube: Edgeware Rd. In room: TV, beverage maker.

The Phoenix Hotel   This hotel, a member of the Best Western chain, occupies the entire south side of Kensington Gardens Square, one of the most famous garden squares in Europe. Well situated in an ethnically mixed neighborhood, The Phoenix is composed of a series of 1854 town houses. The atmosphere is welcoming. Well-furnished bedrooms keep to a smart international standard, with a palette of muted tones. Everything is designed for comfort and ease, including the luggage racks. Bathrooms, most of which contain tub/shower combinations, are a bit small but well kept. The bar is a good place to unwind, and moderately priced meals are served in the downstairs cafe. Our biggest complaint? The public areas are too small for a hotel of this size.

1–8 Kensington Gardens Sq., London W2 4BH. ℂ 800/528-1234 in the U.S. or 020/7229-2494. Fax 020/7727-1419. www.phoenixhotel.co.uk. 130 units. £155 ($295) double; £215 ($409) triple; £240 ($456) family room. Rates include buffet breakfast. AE, DC, MC, V. Tube: Bayswater Station. **Amenities:** Cafe; bar; limited business services; room service; laundry services; same-day dry cleaning; nonsmoking rooms. In room: TV, hair dryer.

INEXPENSIVE

Europa House Hotel   This family-run hotel attracts visitors who want a room with a private bathroom but at shared-bathroom prices. Like most hotels along Sussex Gardens, the bedrooms are a bit cramped, but they're well maintained. Each room has color-coordinated decor, and most have been recently refurbished. Some units are custom built for groups, with three, four, or five beds per unit. Some of the multiple rooms have rather thin mattresses, but most are firm and comfortable. A hearty English breakfast awaits you in the bright dining room every morning.

151 Sussex Gardens, London W2 2RY. ℂ 020/7723-7343. Fax 020/7224-9331. www.europahousehotel.org.uk. 20 units. £60–£70 ($114–$133) double; from £90 ($171) family room. Rates include English breakfast. AE, DC, MC, V. Free parking. Tube: Paddington. **Amenities:** Breakfast room; nonsmoking rooms. In room: TV, coffeemaker, hair dryer.

Fairways Hotel   A small hotel near Hyde Park, and a favorite of bargain hunters, this welcoming, well-run B&B is the domain of Jenny and Steve Adams. The black-and-white town house is easily recognizable: Just look for its colonnaded front entrance with a wrought-iron/board balustrade stretching across the second floor. Scorning the modern, the Adamses opt for traditional charm and character. They call their breakfast room "homely" (Americans might say "homey")—it's decorated with photos of the family and a collection of china. Bedrooms are attractive and comfortably furnished, with hot and cold running water and intercoms. Bathrooms are small but tidy, and some have showers and tubs. Those who share the corridor bathrooms will find them clean and well maintained. The home-cooked breakfast is plenty of fortification for a full day of sightseeing.

186 Sussex Gardens, London W2 1TU. ℂ/fax 020/7723-4871. www.fairways-hotel.co.uk. 17 units, 10 with bathroom. £60 ($114) double without bathroom; £70 ($133) double with bathroom; £80 ($152) triple with bathroom; £90 ($171) family room with bathroom. MC, V. Tube: Paddington or Lancaster Gate. *In room:* TV, coffeemaker, hair dryer (on request), safe.

Garden Court

You'll find this hotel on a tranquil Victorian garden square in the heart of the city. Two private houses (dating from 1870) were combined to form one efficiently run hotel, located near such attractions as Kensington Palace, Hyde Park, and the Portobello Antiques Market. Each year, rooms are redecorated and refurbished, although an overall renovation plan seems to be lacking. Most accommodations are spacious, with good lighting, generous shelf and closet space, and comfortable furnishings. If you're in a room without a bathroom, you'll generally have to share with the occupants of only one other room. There are many homelike touches throughout the hotel, including ancestral portraits and silk flowers. Each room is individually decorated and "comfy"; it's like visiting your great-aunt. Rooms open onto the square in front or the gardens in the rear. Shower-and-tub bathrooms are installed in areas never intended for plumbing, so they tend to be very cramped.

30–31 Kensington Gardens Sq., London W2 4BG. ℂ 020/7229-2553. Fax 020/7727-2749. www.gardencourt hotel.co.uk. 34 units, 16 with bathroom. £68 ($129) double without bathroom, £99 ($188) double with bathroom; £140 ($266) triple with bathroom; £160 ($304) family room. Rates include English breakfast. MC, V. Tube: Bayswater. **Amenities:** Lounge; coin-op washers and dryers. *In room:* TV, hair dryer.

Norfolk Court & St. David's Hotel

George and Foula Neokledos, two of the most welcoming hosts in this highly concentrated B&B area, run these two properties with a certain friendly, personalized style. Only a 2-minute walk from Paddington Station, these small, friendly hotels were built when Norfolk Square knew a grander age. The bluebloods are long gone, but the area is still safe and recommendable. The refurbished bedrooms are well maintained and furnished comfortably, and you can't beat the price. In the rooms that do have showers, a cubicle shower does the job, though it's not the best spot for lingering. We are big fans of the large breakfast.

14–20 Norfolk Sq., London W2 1RS. ℂ 020/7723-4963. Fax 020/7402-9061. www.stdavidshotels.com. 75 units (70 with bathroom). £59 ($112) double without bathroom; £69 ($131) double with bathroom or shower; £80 ($152) triple with shower; £100 ($190) quad with shower; £120 ($228) family room. Rates include English breakfast. AE, MC, V. Tube: Paddington. **Amenities:** Laundry service; same-day dry cleaning. *In room:* TV.

Rhodes Hotel

This elegant late-Georgian house, just a short stroll from Hyde Park, is decorated with a certain theatrical flair. The owners, Chris and Maria Crias, have poured many pounds into their hotel to give it a cozy charm, with a Victorian curtained lounge, Greek murals, lacquered walls, and trompe l'oeil bambini on puffy clouds. Creature comforts weren't ignored, either. You'll find air-conditioning—a bit of a rarity in the neighborhood, especially at these prices—plus new rugs and clean bathrooms with tub/shower combos in all of the bedrooms. The best room, no. 220, has access to a little roof terrace, where you can sit out and enjoy a drink if you BYOB. The superior accommodations have Jacuzzi baths and private terraces. There's an excellent bunkroom for families. Good coffee and lively conversations make breakfast here an event.

195 Sussex Gardens, London W2 2RJ. ℂ 0870/870-7577. Fax 0870/870-7677. www.rhodeshotel.co.uk. 36 units. £60–£90 ($114–$171) double; £75–£95 ($143–$181) triple. Rates include continental buffet breakfast. MC, V. Tube: Paddington or Lancaster Gate. **Amenities:** Breakfast room; nonsmoking rooms. *In room:* A/C, TV, fridge, coffeemaker, hair dryer.

Tudor Court Hotel   Originally built in the 1850s and much restored and altered, this Victorian structure is now a boutique hotel of tranquillity and comfort, only a 3-minute walk from Paddington Station. It is a standout in a section of less desirable hotels. Bedrooms are midsize, completely restored, and comfortably furnished, with a choice of single, double (or twin), triple, and family rooms available. Most come with a private bathroom with shower. The bathless rooms have a wash basin, with facilities right outside the door. The hotel's maintenance and affordable price make this one a winner—that, plus a helpful staff.

Tudor Court Hotel, 10–12 Norfolk Sq., London W2 1RS. ℂ **020/7723-6553**. Fax 020/7723-0727. www.tudorc.demon.co.uk. 36 units, 19 with bathroom. £69 ($131) double without bathroom, £89 ($169) double with bathroom; £79 ($150) triple without bathroom, £99 ($188) triple with bathroom. Rates include English breakfast. AE, DC, MC, V. Tube: Paddington. **Amenities:** Breakfast room; luggage room. *In room:* TV.

NOTTING HILL GATE
EXPENSIVE

Guesthouse West ⭐ ⓥⓐⓛⓤⓔ   In the heart of Notting Hill, this hip, upmarket B&B lies in a stucco-fronted Edwardian house in the fashionable part of Westbourne Grove. Much of the family atmosphere of the original private home has been retained, and midsize bedrooms are comfortable, with understated style. But this is not your typical B&B: Private bathrooms have toiletries supplied by the chic nearby shop, Space NK; room service is provided by Alastair Little's acclaimed Italian deli, Tavola; and MyChocolate chocolatiers offer a "chocolate-making" workshop to parties that book all 20 rooms. Even if you're not a guest, drop in to the ground-floor 1950s-styled bar, created by the savvy entrepreneurs of Woody's and the Bush Bar and Grill.

163–165 Westbourne Grove, London WII 2RS. ℂ **020/7792-9800**. Fax 020/7792-9797. www.guesthousewest.com. 20 units. £150–£180 ($285–$342). Rates include breakfast. AE, MC, V. Tube: Notting Hill. **Amenities:** Bar; room service; babysitting; nonsmoking rooms. *In room:* A/C, TV, Wi-Fi.

MODERATE

The Gate Hotel   This antiques-hunters' favorite is the only hotel along the length of Portobello Road—and because of rigid zoning restrictions, it will probably remain the only one for years to come. It was built in the 1820s as housing for farmhands at the now-defunct Portobello Farms and has functioned as a hotel since 1932. It has two cramped but cozy bedrooms on each of its three floors. Be prepared for some *very* steep English stairs. Rooms are color-coordinated, with a bit of style, and have such extras as full-length mirrors and built-in wardrobes. Bathrooms are small, with tiled shower stalls (there is a tub/shower combo in one room). Housekeeping is excellent. Especially intriguing are the wall paintings that show the original Portobello Market: Every character looks straight from a Dickens novel. The on-site manager can direct you to the attractions of Notting Hill Gate and nearby Kensington Gardens, both within a 5-minute walk.

6 Portobello Rd., London W11 3DG. ℂ **020/7221-0707**. Fax 020/7221-9128. www.gatehotel.com. 7 units. £75–£99 ($143–$188) double; £90–£110 ($171–$209) triple. Rates include continental breakfast (served in room). AE, MC, V. Tube: Notting Hill Gate or Holland Park. **Amenities:** Room service. *In room:* TV, minibar, beverage maker, hair dryer, iron.

The Main House ⭐⭐ ⒻⒾⓝⒹⓈ   Each beautifully appointed room takes up a whole floor of this Victorian town house in Notting Hill, close to Portobello Road, the antiques markets, art galleries, and designer shops. Such attractions as Kensington Palace and Albert Hall are within walking distance. Russian princesses, Japanese pop stars, and Los Angeles film producers have already discovered this spot. Owner and creator Caroline

Main is a former African explorer, Mayfair nightclub owner, and DJ. To furnish the house, she shopped "quirky" on Portobello Road, picking up gilded mirrors, watercolors of elegantly dressed 1930s women, and similar antiques. The ceilings are dramatically high, and the gleaming wood floors are swathed in animal skins. All rooms have freshly renewed private bathrooms with showers.

6 Colville Rd., London W11 2BP. ⓒ 020/7221-9691. www.themainhouse.co.uk. 4 suites. £130 ($247) suite. MC, V. Parking £2 ($3.80) per hour. Tube: Notting Hill Gate. Bus: 23, 27, 52, 94, or 328. **Amenities:** Reduced rate at nearby health club and spa; bike rental; courtesy car to and from point of arrival; room service; laundry service; same-day dry cleaning. *In room:* TV, Wi-Fi, hair dryer, safe.

IN NEARBY MAIDA VALE
MODERATE
The Colonnade ⭐ *Kids*   Tired of large chain hotels? Head for this boutique charmer in the canal-laced "Little Venice" (an appellation bestowed by Lord Byron) area of London. A handsome Victorian edifice, the hotel was built in 1886 as two different structures, one of which was a hospital. An unusually shaped elevator, which was used to transport stretchers, still remains. Before he purchased his own place in Hampstead, Sigmund Freud stayed here in 1938. Each midsize bedroom is individually decorated, and many feature four-poster beds and small terraces. Tasteful fabrics and antiques evoke town-house living. The least desirable units are two small basement bedrooms. They are impeccably furnished but subject to rumblings from the Underground. Families might want to opt for the spacious two-level JFK suite. All units have well-maintained bathrooms with tub/shower combinations, and half of the rooms are for nonsmokers. Thoughtful extras abound, including Penhaligon's toilet articles, Frette Egyptian-cotton bed linens, complimentary fresh fruit, and dual-line phones with voice mail.

2 Warrington Crescent, London W9 1ER. ⓒ 020/7286-1052. Fax 020/7286-1057. www.theetongroup.com. 43 units. £110–£155 ($209–$295) double; £150–£195 ($285–$371) suite. AE, DC, MC, V. Tube: Warwick Ave. **Amenities:** Room service; massage; laundry service; same-day dry cleaning. *In room:* A/C, TV, minibar, coffeemaker, hair dryer, iron, safe, trouser press.

SHEPHERD'S BUSH
EXPENSIVE
K-West ⭐⭐ *Finds*   This cutting-edge hotel is where South Beach (Miami, that is) meets New York's East Village. A hotel as modern as tomorrow has been fashioned out of the former home of the BBC administration center. In spite of its off-center Shepherd's Bush location, it attracts cool guests, especially media mavens and touring musicians. The latter can be seen rocking all night long in the chic K Lounge and recovering the next day with an Asian head massage in the spa. Swanky suites and elegant bedrooms in an avant-garde neutral style await this cosmopolitan crowd of guests. Room decor uses soft taupes, creams, and browns with stainless steel and sandblasted glass. Creative modern dishes are served at the stylish Kanteen (which is anything but) with its luxurious leather seating and rich blues and reds. Everything from Philippe Starck designs to state-of-the-art plumbing is found in this bastion of chic. The young, good-looking staff scurries around catering to your needs (at least some of your needs).

Richmond Way, London W14 0AX. ⓒ **0870/027-4343.** Fax 0870/811-2612. www.k-west.co.uk. 220 units. £129–£159 ($245–$302) double; from £215 ($409) suite. AE, DC, MC, V. Parking £5 ($9.50) for 3 hrs., £1.50 ($2.85) per extra hour after that. Tube: Shepherd's Bush. **Amenities:** Restaurant; bar; gym; spa; sauna; room service; laundry service; dry cleaning; nonsmoking rooms; rooms for those w/limited mobility. *In room:* A/C, TV, Wi-Fi, beverage maker, hair dryer, iron, safe.

7 The South Bank

NEAR LONDON BRIDGE

EXPENSIVE

London Bridge Hotel *✦*   Many guests to London today prefer to stay in a hotel on the emerging South Bank, near many sightseeing and cultural attractions. If you're among them, you can't do much better than lodging at this independently owned, government-rated four-star hotel. A former telephone exchange building, this 1915 structure was successfully recycled into a bastion of comfort and charm. Bedrooms are completely up-to-date and offer homelike comfort and plenty of amenities. Rooms in the front have double glazing on windows to cut down on noise. The best luxuries are found on the executive floor, in the deluxe rooms, and in the executive kings and suites. Dining and drinking facilities are first class, including a new restaurant, Georgetown, which evokes colonial days with a mixture of Malaysian, Chinese, and Indian flavors. A state-of-the-art gymnasium is in an adjacent building with direct access from the hotel.

8–18 London Bridge St., London SE1 9SG. ℂ 020/7855-2200. Fax 020/7855-2233. www.londonbridgehotel.co.uk. 138 units. £100–£210 ($190–$399) double; from £210 ($399) suite. Children under 12 stay free when sharing parent's room. AE, DC, MC, V. Tube: London Bridge. **Amenities:** 3 restaurants; bar; free access to nearby health club; room service; babysitting; laundry service; dry cleaning; nonsmoking rooms; rooms for those w/limited mobility. *In room:* A/C, TV, minibar, coffeemaker, hair dryer, iron, safe, trouser press.

8 Near the Airports

NEAR HEATHROW

The reason for staying at one of the hotels below is obvious: you either want to catch an early plane or are arriving too late to search for a hotel in central London. Unless you like plane-spotting, there isn't much reason to hang out. The hotels below provide transportation to and from the airport.

VERY EXPENSIVE

Radisson Edwardian Heathrow *✦*   The poshest digs at Heathrow, this deluxe hotel lies just south of the M4 about 5 minutes east of the long tunnel that leads to terminals 1, 2, and 3. Since 1991, it has housed tired air travelers from all over the world. The grand spa has a swimming pool and two whirlpools. You'll enter the hotel through a courtyard with potted trees. Persian rugs, brass-railed staircases, and chandeliers live up to the "Edwardian" in the hotel's name. Rooms are medium in size but adorned with hand-painted hardwood furnishings. The bathrooms are in tile and marble, with robes, a shower, and a tub. All in-room televisions have a channel reserved to broadcast flight information. Car hire is also available.

140 Bath Rd., Hayes, Middlesex UB3 5AW. ℂ 800/333-3333 in the U.S. or 020/8759-6311. Fax 020/8759-4559. www.radissonedwardian.com. 459 units. £109–£163 ($207–$310) double; £260–£360 ($494–$684) suite. AE, DC, MC, V. Parking £8 ($15). Hotel Hoppa bus service. **Amenities:** 2 restaurants; bar; health club; sauna; salon; room service; massage; laundry service; same-day dry cleaning; nonsmoking rooms; rooms for those w/limited mobility. *In room:* A/C, TV, Wi-Fi, minibar, hair dryer, safe, iron, trouser press.

EXPENSIVE

Hilton London Heathrow Airport *✦*   This first-class hotel, with a five-story atrium that evokes a hangar, is linked to Heathrow's Terminal 4 by a covered walkway. A glass wall faces the runways, so you can see planes land and take off. You can take buses to terminal 1, 2, or 3. Medium-size bedrooms are standard, decorated with built-in wood furniture and comfortable sofas. Bathrooms are tiled and trimmed in marble, and each contains a phone, tub, and shower. The best accommodations are on the fifth floor because they offer better extras (bathrobes, and so forth) as well as a private lounge with airport vistas. All rooms are soundproofed.

Terminal 4, Hounslow TW6 3AF. (C) **800/774-1500** in the U.S. or 020/8759-7755. Fax 020/8759-7579. www.hilton.co.uk/heathrow. 395 units. £100–£290 ($190–$551) double; from £545 ($1,036) suite. AE, DC, MC, V. Parking £12 ($23). Tube: Heathrow Terminal 4. **Amenities:** 3 restaurants; 2 bars; indoor heated pool; health club; sauna; tour desk; car rental desk; business services and center; room service; babysitting; laundry service; same-day dry cleaning; non-smoking rooms; rooms for those w/limited mobility; TV w/flight information. *In room:* A/C, TV, minibar, coffeemaker, hair dryer, trouser press.

MODERATE

Holiday Inn London—Heathrow   This is your best bet in the moderate range at London's major airport. The decor is bland but not unpleasant. Rooms are midsize, with immaculate bathrooms containing shower stalls.

Sipson Way, Bath Rd., Hayes, Middlesex UB7 0DP. (C) **800/897-1121** in the U.S., or 020/8990-0000 in the U.K. Fax 020/8564-7744. www.london-heathrow.holiday-inn.com. 230 units. Mon–Thurs £90–£170 ($171–$323) double; Fri–Sun £50–£97 ($95–$184) double. Children 18 and under stay free in parent's room. AE, DC, MC, V. Parking £9 ($17). Tube: Heathrow Terminals 1, 2, 3. **Amenities:** Restaurant; bar; exercise room; business center; room service; babysitting; laundry service; same-day dry cleaning; nonsmoking rooms; rooms for those w/limited mobility. *In room:* A/C, TV, minibar (in executive rooms), coffeemaker, hair dryer, iron.

INEXPENSIVE

The Swan   Dating from the days of diarist Samuel Pepys, the Swan is on the south bank of the Thames, beside Staines Bridge and within a 15-minute drive of Heathrow. The shower-only bathrooms are small, but the corridor bathroom is adequate. The attractive inn has a reputation for good food ranging from bar snacks to traditional English fare. Food is served in a gazebo-style dining room. Staines was an important Roman settlement, and many buildings in the area date from the 17th century.

The Hythe, Staines, Middlesex TW18 3JB. (C) **01784/452494.** Fax 01784/461593. 11 units. £86–£100 ($163–$190) double; £112 ($213) family room. Rates include English breakfast. AE, DC, MC, V. Tube: Heathrow (you must take a taxi from there). **Amenities:** Restaurant; bar; laundry; dry cleaning; nonsmoking rooms. *In room:* TV, coffeemaker, hair dryer, iron.

NEAR GATWICK

EXPENSIVE

Hilton London Gatwick Airport ⭐   This deluxe five-floor hotel—Gatwick's most convenient—is linked to the airport terminal by a covered walkway; an electric buggy service transports people between the hotel and the airport. The most impressive part of the hotel is the first-floor lobby. Its glass-covered portico rises four floors and contains a scale replica of the de Havilland Gypsy Moth airplane *Jason*, used by Amy Johnson on her solo flight from England to Australia in 1930. The reception area has a lobby bar and lots of greenery. The well-furnished, soundproof rooms have triple-glazed windows and tidily kept bathrooms equipped with a tub and shower. Rooms were recently refurbished, including the executive floor and all the junior suites.

South Terminal, Gatwick Airport, West Sussex RH6 0LL. (C) **800/774-1500** in the U.S. or 01293/518080. Fax 01293/528980. www.hilton.co.uk/gatwick. 791 units. £115–£300 ($219–$570) double; from £350 ($665) suite. AE, DC, MC, V. Parking £16 ($30). **Amenities:** 2 restaurants; 2 bars; fitness center; tour desk; car-rental desk; business center; salon; room service; babysitting; laundry service; same-day dry cleaning; nonsmoking rooms; rooms for those w/limited mobility. *In room:* A/C, TV, coffeemaker, hair dryer, trouser press.

INEXPENSIVE

The Manor House   Owners Steve and Jo Jeffries include transportation from Gatwick as part of the price. There is a courtesy pick-up from the airport operating in the morning between 6 and 10. Their home is a sprawling neo-Tudor affair on .8 hectares (2 acres) of land, surrounded by fields on all sides. It was built in 1894 as a supplemental home for the lord of Ifield, who occupied a larger house nearby and never actually moved in. Two of the rooms share a bathroom; the others have bathrooms with showers. Each accommodation has flowered wallpaper and simple, traditional accessories. Breakfast is the only meal served.

Bonnetts Lane, Ifield, Crawley, Sussex RH11 0NY. © **01293/512298.** Fax 01293/518046. www.manorhousegatwick. co.uk. 6 units, 4 (doubles) with private bathroom. £50 ($95) double; from £55 ($105) family unit; £55 ($105) triple. Rates include English breakfast. MC, V. Parking £2 ($3.80). **Amenities:** All nonsmoking rooms. *In room:* TV, coffeemaker, no phone.

7

Where to Dine

In 1946, George Mikes, Britain's famous Hungarian-born humorist, wrote about the cuisine of his adopted country: "The Continentals have good food. The English have good table manners."

Quite a lot has happened since.

London has emerged as one of the great food capitals of the world. Both its veteran and upstart chefs have fanned out around the globe for culinary inspiration and returned with innovative dishes, flavors, and ideas that London diners have never seen before. These chefs are pioneering a style called "Modern British," which is forever changing and innovative, yet familiar in many ways.

Traditional British cooking has made a comeback, too. The dishes that British mums have been forever feeding their families are fashionable again. Yes, we're talking British soul food: bangers and mash, Norfolk dumplings, nursery puddings, cottage pie. This may be a rebellion against the minimalism of the nouvelle cuisine of the 1980s, but maybe it's just plain nostalgia. Pig's nose with parsley-and-onion sauce may not be your idea of cutting-edge cuisine, but Simpson's-in-the-Strand is serving it for breakfast.

These days, many famous chefs spend more time writing cookbooks and appearing on TV than in their own kitchens. That chef you've read about in *Condé Nast Traveler* or *Travel & Leisure* may not be in the kitchen when you get here. But don't worry: The cuisine isn't suffering. An up-and-coming new chef, perhaps even better than the one you heard about, has probably taken over the kitchen.

If you want a lavish meal, London is the place: Gourmet havens such as Le Gavroche and a half-dozen others are reviewed in the following pages. We've also included many affordable restaurants where you can dine well and still pay off your mortgage. You'll find that London's food revolution has infiltrated every level of the dining scene—even the lowly pub has entered the culinary sweepstakes. Believe the unthinkable: At certain pubs, you can now dine better than in many restaurants. In some, standard pub grub has given way to Modern British and Mediterranean-style fare; in others, oyster bars have taken hold.

1 Some Dining Notes

HOURS   Restaurants in London keep varied hours, but in general, lunch is offered from noon to 2pm and dinner from 7:30 to 9:30pm, although more restaurants are staying open later. Sunday is the usual closing day for restaurants, but there are exceptions. (Many also close for a few days around Christmas, so call ahead during the holidays.) We've listed serving hours in the descriptions below.

RESERVATIONS   Nearly all places, except pubs, cafeterias, and fast-food joints, prefer or require reservations. Almost invariably, you get a better table if you book in advance. For a few of the famous places, you might need to reserve weeks in advance, even before leaving home. (Reservations should always be confirmed when you get to London.) However, if you haven't made reservations, even at a "reservations required" restaurant, it's worth trying to walk into the restaurant if you are in the area. If they do have room, you won't be turned down.

TAXES & TIPPING   All restaurants and cafes are required to display the prices of their food and drink in a place visible from outside. Charges for service, as well as any minimums or cover charges, must also be made clear. The prices shown must include 17.5% VAT. Most restaurants add a 10% to 15% service charge to your bill, but check to make sure. If nothing has been added, leave a 10% to 15% tip. It is not considered rude to tip, so feel free to leave something extra if service was good.

A NOTE ABOUT PRICES   When restaurants are classified as Moderate or Inexpensive, most main courses are at the lower end of the price scale. That doesn't mean the chefs don't prepare some expensive dishes. Often they do, especially if they offer shellfish. But if you avoid the highest-priced dishes, you can dine moderately or inexpensively at our selections.

2 Best Dining Bets

- **Best Spot for a Celebration:** There's no spot in all of London that's more fun than **Quaglino's,** 16 Bury St., SW1 (℅ **020/7930-6767**), which serves Continental cuisine. On some nights, as many as 800 diners show up at Sir Terence Conran's gargantuan Mayfair eatery. It's the best place in London to celebrate almost any occasion—and the food's good, too. There's live jazz every evening and on Sunday at lunch. See p. 179.
- **Best for Value:** Called the market leader in cafe salons, **Veronica's,** 3 Hereford Rd., W2 (℅ **020/7229-5079**), serves not only some of the best traditional British fare, but also some of the most affordable. Many of the chef's recipes are based on medieval or Tudor culinary secrets, and some even go back to the days of the conquering Romans. See p. 198.
- **Best Modern British Cuisine:** In a former smokehouse just north of Smithfield Market, **St. John,** 26 St. John St., EC1 (℅ **020/7251-0848**), serves a modern interpretation of British cuisine like none other in town. The chefs here believe in using offal (those parts of the animal that are usually discarded)—after all, why use just parts of the animal when you can use it all? Although some diners are a bit squeamish at first, they're usually hooked once they get past the first bite. Book ahead of time. See p. 150.
- **Best Traditional British Cuisine:** There is no restaurant in London quite as British as **Simpson's-in-the-Strand,** 100 the Strand, WC2 (℅ **020/7836-9112**), which has been serving the finest English roast beef since 1828. Henry VIII, were he to return, would surely pause for a feast here. This place is such a British institution that you'll think they invented roast saddle of mutton. See p. 160.
- **Best for Kids:** The owner, the Earl of Bradford, feeds you well and affordably at **Porters English Restaurant,** 17 Henrietta St., WC2 (℅ **020/7836-6466**). Kids of all ages dig Lady Bradford's once secretly guarded recipe for banana-and-ginger pudding, along with the most classic English pies served in Central London, including such old-fashioned favorites as lamb and apricot; and ham, leek, and cheese. See p. 162.

- **Best Continental Cuisine: Le Gavroche,** 43 Upper Brook St., W1 (**© 020/ 7408-0881**), was one of the first London restaurants to serve the modern French approach to cuisine, and it's lost none of its appeal. If you want to know why, order *pigeonneau de Bresse en vessie aux deux celeris:* The whole bird is presented at your table, enclosed in a pig's bladder; the pigeon is removed, and then carved and served on a bed of braised fennel and celery. Trust us—it's fabulous. See p. 172.

- **Best Indian Cuisine:** London's finest Indian food is served at **Café Spice Namaste,** in a landmark Victorian hall near Tower Bridge, 16 Prescot St., E1 (**© 020/7488-9242**). You'll be tantalized by an array of spicy southern and northern Indian dishes. We like the cuisine's Portuguese influence; the chef, Cyrus Todiwala, is from Goa (a Portuguese territory absorbed by India), where he learned many of his culinary secrets. See p. 148.

- **Best Italian Cuisine:** At **Zafferano,** 15 Lowndes St., SW1 (**© 020/7235-5800**), master chefs prepare delectable meals with ingredients that conjure up the Mediterranean shores. The most refined palates of Knightsbridge come to this chic, rustic trattoria for dishes like pheasant and black-truffle ravioli with rosemary. See p. 182.

- **Best Innovative Cuisine:** Irish chef Richard Corrigan brings sophisticated modern British cuisine to **Lindsay House,** 21 Romilly St., W1 (**© 020/7439-0450**). The menu is dependent on what looks good at the daily market combined with the chef's inspiration. After you sample his breast of wood pigeon with foie gras and pumpkin chutney, you'll want to kidnap him for your kitchen. See p. 166.

- **Best for Spotting Celebrities: Archipelago,** 110 Whitfield St., W1 (**© 020/ 7383-3346**), is small and intimate, a cozy retreat for Hugh Hefner and the other celebs in London. Media headliner Michael Von Hruschka runs this Thai and French restaurant with whimsy and many precious touches, such as a drink list that's delivered to the table inside an ostrich eggshell. But the cuisine doesn't depend on gimmicks—it's first-rate in both ingredients and preparation. See p. 156.

- **Best Seafood: Back to Basics,** 21A Foley St., W1 (**© 020/7436-2181**), is no fish-and-chips joint. Stefan Plaumer's Fitzrovia bistro serves some of the freshest seafood in town. You name it: broiled, grilled, baked, or poached; anything except fried—and the chefs will cook the fish to your specifications. An array of delicacies from the sea awaits you here, from plump, tasty mussels to sea bass given an extra zing with chili oil. See p. 156.

- **Best Wine-Bar Food: Cork & Bottle Wine Bar,** 44–46 Cranbourn St., WC2 (**© 020/7734-7807**), serves the best wine-bar food in London. The raised ham-and-cheese pie alone is worth the trek across town—it's hardly your typical quiche. Also try the Mediterranean prawns with garlic and asparagus, or the lamb in ale. The wine selection is superb, with a strong emphasis on selections from Australia. See p. 165.

- **Best Cantonese Cuisine: Fung Shing,** 15 Lisle St., WC2 (**© 020/7437-1539**), is a culinary landmark, serving the finest Cantonese cuisine in London, both traditional and innovative. The seasonal specials are the way to go. Stewed duck with yams, tender ostrich in yellow-bean sauce, and a delectable whole sea bass are some of the delicious treats. See p. 163.

- **Best Late-Night Dining:** Evoking a high-end Chicago or New York steakhouse, the *Titanic*-sized **Astor Bar and Grill,** 20 Glasshouse St., W1 (**© 020/7734-4888**), is installed in a former Art Deco ballroom off Piccadilly Circus. American and Continental cuisine is served in a cosmopolitan atmosphere until 3am Monday to Saturday.

• **Best Japanese Cuisine:** Robert De Niro and his gang have generated much excitement about **Nobu,** in the Metropolitan Hotel, 19 Old Park Lane, W1 (*©* **020/ 7447-4747**). The sushi chefs create gastronomic pyrotechnics with their raw dishes. See p. 173.

3 Restaurants by Cuisine

AFTERNOON TEA
The Blue Room, Soho (p. 204, $)
Claridge's, Mayfair *©* (p. 201, $$$)
The Georgian Restaurant, Knightsbridge (p. 202, $$$)
The Lanesborough, Knightsbridge (p. 202, $$$)
The Orangery, Kensington *©* (p. 204, $)
The Palm Court, Mayfair (p. 202, $$$)
Richoux, Knightsbridge (p. 203, $$)
Ritz Palm Court, St. James's *©©©* (p. 202, $$$)
St. James Restaurant & The Fountain Restaurant, St. James's (p. 202, $$$)
The Tearoom at the Chelsea Physic Garden, Chelsea (p. 204, $)

AMERICAN
Ed's Easy Diner, Soho (p. 170, $)
Hard Rock Cafe, Mayfair (p. 176, $$)
Spoon, Soho *©* (p. 165, $$$$)

ASIAN
(See also Cantonese, Chinese, Japanese, Szechuan, and Thai)
E&O, Ladbroke Grove (p. 199, $$)
Imperial City, the City *©* (p. 148, $$)
Oxo Tower Restaurant, South Bank *©* (p. 155, $$$)
Yauatcha, Soho *©* (p. 170, $)

BELGIAN
Belgo Centraal, Covent Garden & the Strand (p. 161, $$)

BRITISH—MODERN
Admiral Codrington, Kensington & South Kensington *©* (p. 189, $$)
Alastair Little, Soho *©* (p. 166, $$$)

Balans, Soho (p. 169, $)
Bush Bar & Grill, Marylebone *©* (p. 195, $$)
Circus, St. James's (p. 178, $$)
Clarke's, Kensington & South Kensington *©* (p. 189, $$$)
The Collection, Knightsbridge *©* (p. 183, $$)
The Cow, Notting Hill Gate *©* (p. 198, $$)
The Criterion Brasserie, Soho *©* (p. 167, $$)
Fifteen, Shoreditch *©©* (p. 151, $$$)
The Gun, Docklands *©* (p. 154, $$)
The Ivy, Piccadilly Circus & Leicester Square *©©* (p. 163, $$$)
Launceston Place, Kensington & South Kensington *©* (p. 189, $$$)
Lindsay House, Soho *©©* (p. 166, $$$)
Marcus Wareing at the Savoy Grill, Covent Garden & the Strand *©©* (p. 157, $$$$)
Menu, Mayfair *©©©* (p. 173, $$$$)
The Portrait Restaurant, Trafalgar Square *©* (p. 171, $$)
Prism, the City *©©* (p. 146, $$$)
Rex Whistler, Westminster & Victoria *©©* (p. 180, $$)
St. John, Clerkenwell *©©* (p. 150, $$)
Simpson's-in-the-Strand, Covent Garden & the Strand *©©* (p. 160, $$$)
Sketch, Mayfair *©©* (p. 174, $$$$)

BRITISH—TRADITIONAL
Brown's, Piccadilly Circus & Leicester Square (p. 164, $)

Key to Abbreviations: $$$$ = Very Expensive $$$ = Expensive $$ = Moderate $ = Inexpensive

Butler's Wharf Chop House, Docklands ⍟ (p. 152, $$$)

The Enterprise, Kensington & South Kensington (p. 190, $$)

Fox and Anchor, the City ⍟ (p. 149, $)

The George, Covent Garden & the Strand (p. 162, $)

The George & Vulture, the City (p. 149, $)

Greens Restaurant & Oyster Bar, St. James's (p. 178, $$)

Langan's Bistro, Marylebone (p. 196, $$)

Langan's Brasserie, Mayfair (p. 176, $$)

The National Dining Rooms, Trafalgar Square (p. 171, $$)

The Pig's Ear, Chelsea ⍟ (p. 188, $)

Porters English Restaurant, Covent Garden & the Strand ⍟⍟ (p. 162, $$)

Rules, Covent Garden & the Strand ⍟ (p. 160, $$$)

Shepherd's, Westminster & Victoria (p. 180, $$$)

Simpson's-in-the-Strand, Covent Garden & the Strand ⍟⍟ (p. 160, $$$)

The Stockpot, Piccadilly Circus & Leicester Square (p. 165, $)

Veronica's, Paddington & Bayswater ⍟⍟ (p. 198, $$)

Ye Olde Cheshire Cheese, the City (p. 150, $)

CANTONESE

Fung Shing, Piccadilly Circus & Leicester Square ⍟⍟ (p. 163, $$$)

Jenny Lo's Teahouse, Westminster & Victoria (p. 180, $)

Royal China, Paddington & Bayswater ⍟ (p. 197, $$$)

Zen Central, Mayfair (p. 177, $$)

CHINESE

(See also Cantonese and Szechuan)

Chuen Cheng Ku, Soho ⍟ (p. 167, $$)

Hakkasan, Soho ⍟ (p. 168, $$)

CONTINENTAL

Admiral Codrington, Kensington & South Kensington ⍟ (p. 189, $$)

Alastair Little, Soho ⍟ (p. 166, $$$)

Brown's, Piccadilly Circus & Leicester Square (p. 164, $)

Cantina Vinopolis, South Bank ⍟ (p. 155, $$)

The Court Restaurant, Bloomsbury (p. 157, $)

Drones, Knightsbridge ⍟ (p. 183, $$)

"hush", Mayfair (p. 176, $$)

Mash, Marylebone ⍟ (p. 196, $$)

Quaglino's, St. James's ⍟ (p. 179, $$)

Shampers, Soho (p. 169, $$)

Sketch, Mayfair ⍟⍟ (p. 174, $$$$)

The Stockpot, Piccadilly Circus & Leicester Square (p. 165, $)

Tom Aikens, Kensington & South Kensington ⍟⍟⍟ (p. 188, $$$$)

Union Cafe, Marylebone (p. 196, $$)

Vertigo 42, the City ⍟ (p. 149, $)

Villandry, Marylebone ⍟ (p. 197, $$)

The Wolseley, St. James's ⍟⍟ (p. 179, $$)

CYPRIOT

Halepi, Paddington & Bayswater ⍟ (p. 197, $$)

Sarastro, Covent Garden & the Strand ⍟ (p. 162, $)

EUROPEAN

The Engineer, Camden Town ⍟ (p. 200, $$)

The Enterprise, Kensington & South Kensington (p. 190, $$)

Gordon Ramsay at Claridge's, Mayfair ⍟⍟⍟ (p. 172, $$$$)

Greenhouse, Mayfair (p. 175, $$$)

Kensington Place, Kensington & South Kensington (p. 190, $$)

FRENCH

Archipelago, Bloomsbury ⍟⍟ (p. 156, $$$)

Aubergine, Chelsea ⍟⍟ (p. 186, $$$$)

Bibendum/The Oyster Bar,
Kensington & South Kensington ✸
(p. 188, $$$)

Bush Bar & Grill, Marylebone ✸
(p. 195, $$)

Café des Amis, Covent Garden &
the Strand (p. 161, $$)

Club Gascon, the City ✸✸ (p. 148,
$$)

The Criterion Brasserie, Soho ✸
(p. 167, $$)

Gordon Ramsay, Chelsea ✸✸✸
(p. 186, $$$$)

Langan's Bistro, Marylebone
(p. 196, $$)

Langan's Brasserie, Mayfair (p. 176, $$)

Le Cercle, Chelsea ✸✸ (p. 187, $$$)

Le Gavroche, Mayfair ✸✸✸ (p. 172,
$$$$)

Les Trois Garçons, Shoreditch ✸✸
(p. 151, $$$)

Mirabelle, Mayfair ✸ (p. 173, $$$$)

Mon Plaisir, Covent Garden & the
Strand (p. 161, $$)

Oriel, Chelsea (p. 187, $)

Orrery, Marylebone ✸✸ (p. 194, $$$)

Petrus, Knightsbridge ✸✸ (p. 182,
$$$$)

Plateau, Canary Wharf (p. 154, $$$)

The Square, Mayfair ✸✸✸ (p. 174,
$$$$)

GREEK

Halepi, Paddington & Bayswater ✸
(p. 197, $$)

HUNGARIAN

The Gay Hussar, Soho ✸ (p. 167, $$)

INDIAN

Amaya, Knightsbridge ✸ (p. 182,
$$$)

The Bengal Clipper, Docklands ✸
(p. 153, $$)

Café Spice Namaste, the City ✸✸
(p. 148, $$)

Deya, Marylebone ✸✸ (p. 195, $$)

Mela, Soho ✸ (p. 168, $$)

Rasa Samudra, Soho ✸ (p. 168, $$)

Soho Spice, Soho (p. 169, $$)

Tamarind, Mayfair ✸ (p. 176, $$$)

Veeraswamy, Soho (p. 170, $)

Zaika, Kensington & South Kensing-
ton ✸✸ (p. 191, $$)

Zen Central, Mayfair (p. 177, $$)

INTERNATIONAL

Circus, St. James's (p. 178, $$)

The Collection, Knightsbridge ✸
(p. 183, $$)

Cork & Bottle Wine Bar, Piccadilly
Circus & Leicester Square ✸✸
(p. 165, $)

Greens Restaurant & Oyster Bar, St.
James's (p. 178, $$)

The Ivy, Piccadilly Circus & Leicester
Square ✸✸ (p. 163, $$$)

Le Metro, Knightsbridge (p. 183, $)

Le Pont de la Tour, Docklands ✸
(p. 153, $$$)

Maze, Mayfair ✸✸ (p. 175, $$$)

Odin's, Marylebone ✸ (p. 194, $$$)

Orrery, Marylebone ✸✸ (p. 194, $$$)

Oxo Tower Restaurant, South Bank ✸
(p. 155, $$$)

Prince Bonaparte, Notting Hill Gate
(p. 198, $)

Villandry, Marylebone ✸ (p. 197, $$)

ITALIAN

Assaggi, Marylebone ✸✸ (p. 191,
$$$)

Caldesi, Marylebone (p. 195, $$)

Joe's Café, South Kensington ✸
(p. 190, $$)

Locanda Locatelli, Marylebone ✸✸
(p. 194, $$$)

Quo Vadis, Soho ✸ (p. 166, $$$)

The River Café, Hammersmith ✸✸
(p. 200, $$$$)

Zafferano, Knightsbridge ✸✸
(p. 182, $$$$)

JAPANESE

Nobu, Mayfair ✸✸ (p. 173, $$$$)

Satsuma, Soho (p. 168, $$)

Wagamama, Bloomsbury (p. 157, $)

MEDITERRANEAN

Bibendum/The Oyster Bar, Kensington & South Kensington ⭐ (p. 188, $$$)

Bluebird, Chelsea ⭐ (p. 186, $$$)

Leon, Mayfair ⭐ (p. 177, $)

Menu, Mayfair ⭐⭐⭐ (p. 173, $$$$)

MOROCCAN

Momo, Mayfair (p. 177, $$)

Pasha, Kensington & South Kensington (p. 191, $$)

NORTH AFRICAN

Momo, Mayfair (p. 177, $$)

Moro, Clerkenwell ⭐⭐ (p. 150, $$)

PACIFIC RIM

Suze, Mayfair (p. 178, $)

PORTUGUESE

Eyre Brothers, Shoreditch ⭐ (p. 152, $$)

SEAFOOD

Back to Basics, Bloomsbury ⭐⭐ (p. 156, $$)

Greens Restaurant & Oyster Bar, St. James's (p. 178, $$)

J. Sheekey, Piccadilly Circus & Leicester Square ⭐ (p. 163, $$$)

Livebait's Café Fish, Piccadilly Circus & Leicester Square ⭐ (p. 164, $$)

Randall & Aubin, Piccadilly Circus & Leicester Square ⭐ (p. 164, $$)

Vertigo 42, the City ⭐ (p. 149, $)

SPANISH

Moro, Clerkenwell ⭐⭐ (p. 150, $$)

STEAK

Black & Blue, Knightsbridge ⭐ (p. 183, $$)

Notting Grill, Ladbroke Grove ⭐ (p. 199, $$)

SZECHUAN

Jenny Lo's Teahouse, Westminster & Victoria (p. 180, $)

Royal China, Paddington & Bayswater ⭐ (p. 197, $$$)

Zen Central, Mayfair (p. 177, $$)

THAI

Archipelago, Bloomsbury ⭐⭐ (p. 156, $$$)

Blue Elephant, Kensington & South Kensington ⭐ (p. 190, $$)

The Engineer, Camden Town ⭐ (p. 200, $$)

Nahm, Mayfair ⭐⭐ (p. 175, $$$)

Sri Nam, Canary Wharf ⭐ (p. 154, $$$)

TURKISH

Sarastro, Covent Garden & the Strand ⭐ (p. 162, $)

VEGETARIAN

Mildreds, Soho ⭐ (p. 170, $)

<hr>

4 In & Around the City

THE CITY

EXPENSIVE

Prism ⭐⭐ MODERN BRITISH   In the financial district, called the City, this restaurant attracts London's movers and shakers, at least those with demanding palates. Harvey Nichols—known for his chic department store in Knightsbridge—took this 1920s neo-Grecian hall, in the former Bank of New York, and installed Mies van der Rohe chairs in chrome and lipstick-red leather. In this setting, traditional English dishes from the north are given a light touch—try the tempura of Whitby cod, or cream of Jerusalem artichoke soup with roasted scallops and truffle oil. For a first course, you may opt for a small, seared calf's liver with a mushroom risotto, or try a savoy cabbage salad with Parma ham, seasoned with flecks of Parmesan. The menu

Where to Stay & Dine In & around "the city"

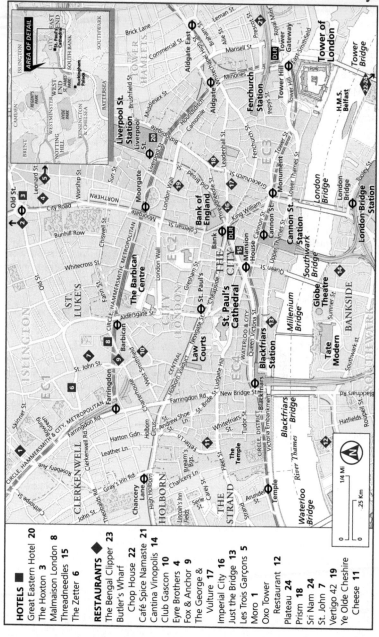

HOTELS ■
Great Eastern Hotel **20**
The Hoxton **3**
Malmaison London **8**
Threadneedles **15**
The Zetter **6**

RESTAURANTS ◆
The Bengal Clipper **23**
Butler's Wharf
  Chop House **22**
Café Spice Namaste **21**
Cantina Vinopolis **14**
Club Gascon **10**
Eyre Brothers **4**
Fox & Anchor **9**
The George &
  Vulture **17**
Imperial City **16**
Just the Bridge **13**
Les Trois Garçons **5**
Moro **1**
Oxo Tower
  Restaurant **12**
Plateau **24**
Prism **18**
Sri Nam **24**
St. John **7**
Vertigo 42 **19**
Ye Olde Cheshire
  Cheese **11**

reveals the chef has traveled a bit—note such dishes as Moroccan spiced chicken livers, lemon-and-parsley couscous, and a zesty chile sauce.

147 Leadenhall St., EC3. ✆ 020/7256-3875. Reservations required. Main courses £18–£24 ($34–$46). AE, DC, DISC, MC, V. Mon–Fri 11:30am–3pm and 6–10pm. Tube: Bank or Monument.

MODERATE

Café Spice Namaste *✿✿* INDIAN   This is our favorite Indian restaurant in London, where the competition is stiff. It's cheerfully housed in a landmark Victorian hall near Tower Bridge, just east of the Tower of London. The Parsi chef, Cyrus Todiwala, is a former resident of Goa (a Portuguese territory absorbed by India long ago), where he learned many of his culinary secrets. He concentrates on southern and northern Indian dishes, with a strong Portuguese influence. Chicken and lamb are prepared a number of ways, from mild to spicy-hot. As a novelty, Todiwala occasionally even offers a menu of emu dishes; when marinated, the meat is rich and spicy and evocative of lamb. Emu is not the only dining oddity here. Ever have ostrich gizzard kebab, alligator *tikka,* or minced moose, bison, or blue boar? Many patrons journey here just for the complex chicken curry known as *xacutti.* Lambs' livers and kidneys are also cooked in the tandoor. A weekly specialty menu complements the long list of regional dishes. The homemade chutneys alone are worth the trip; our favorite is made with kiwi. All dishes come with fresh vegetables and Indian bread. With its exotic ingredients, often time-consuming preparation, impeccable service, warm hospitality, and spicy but subtle flavors, this is no Indian dive.

16 Prescot St., E1. ✆ 020/7488-9242. Reservations required. Main courses £12–£19 ($23–$36). AE, DC, MC, V. Mon–Fri noon–3pm and 6:15–10:30pm; Sat 6:30–10:30pm. Tube: Tower Hill.

Club Gascon *✿✿* *Finds* FRENCH   This slice of southwestern France serves such tasty treats as foie gras, Armagnac, and duck confit. Chef Pascal Aussignac has been all the rage in London ever since he opened this bistro next to the meat market in Smithfield. He dedicates the place to his favorite ingredient: foie gras. Foie gras appears in at least nine different incarnations on the menu, and most of the first-class ingredients are imported from France. His menu is uniquely divided into these categories: "The Salt Route," "Ocean," and "Kitchen Garden." The best way to dine here is to arrive in a party of four or five and share the small dishes, each harmoniously balanced and full of flavor. Dishes are accompanied by a carefully selected glass of wine. After a foie gras pig-out, proceed to such main courses as a heavenly quail served with pear and rosemary honey. A cassoulet of morels and truffles transforms a plain but perfectly cooked steak. To finish an absolutely elegant repast—dare we call it too rich?—there is a selection of "puds," as the British say, ranging from strawberries with basil sorbet to a confit of rhubarb and sherry vinegar. If those don't interest you, opt for a moist almond tart with a biting shot of Granny Smith apple juice.

57 West Smithfield, EC1. ✆ 020/7796-0600. Reservations required. Main courses £15–£20 ($29–$38); 5-course fixed-price menu £39 ($74). AE, MC, V. Mon–Fri noon–2pm and 7–10pm; Sat 7–10:30pm. Tube: Barbican.

Imperial City *✿* ASIAN   In the undercroft of the Royal Exchange Building, this restaurant, with its sleek modern interior and exotic fish tanks, serves authentic Southeast Asian cuisine. High-quality food and a first-rate presentation keep a stream of diners flowing in. There are familiar starters such as Mandarin spareribs or razor clams with chile-laced black beans, but also unusual ones, such as crispy seaweed with walnuts. A whole or half Peking duck is served, as is a braised mixed seafood pot for two. Chilean sea bass with sea cucumber and star anise is a delight, as is wok-fried duck breast with cherries and wild ginger. Vegetarians will be delighted here, but so will meat eaters. Ever had crocodile with cashew nuts? The wok-fried venison with black pepper and snow peas is a winner, as is the beef with lemon grass. The typical rice and noodles dishes are also served, topped off by such desserts as a mango-and-toffee cheesecake.

Royal Exchange, Cornhill EC3. © 020/7256-3437. Reservations recommended. Main courses £8.95–£28 ($17–$53). Fixed-price menu £25 ($48). AE, DC, MC, V. Mon–Fri noon–3pm and 5–11pm. Tube: Bank or Monument.

INEXPENSIVE

Fox and Anchor ★ *Finds* TRADITIONAL BRITISH   For British breakfast at its best, try this place, which has been serving traders from the nearby Smithfield meat market since 1898. Breakfasts are gargantuan, especially if you order the "Full House"—a plate with at least eight items, including sausage, bacon, kidneys, eggs, beans, black pudding, and fried bread, along with unlimited tea or coffee, toast, and jam. Add a Black Velvet (champagne with Guinness), or the more fashionable Bucks Fizz (orange juice and champagne, known in the U.S. as a mimosa). The staff serves an even bigger breakfast called "The Full Monty" including a Guinness. Of course, those with more delicate stomachs might settle for some smoked salmon and scrambled eggs. The Fox and Anchor is noted for its fine English ales, which are all available at breakfast. Butchers from the market, spotted with blood, still appear, as do nurses getting off their shifts, and clerks and City tycoons who've been making millions all night. For lunch and dinner the food is standard pub fare, including fish and chips, steak-and-kidney pie, and a choice of steaks, followed by such classic British desserts as sticky toffee pudding or chocolate fudge cake.

115 Charterhouse St., EC1. © 020/7253-4838. Reservations recommended. "Full house" breakfast £6 ($11); Full Monty breakfast £9.95 ($19); main courses £6.50–£12 ($12–$23). AE, MC, V. Mon–Fri from 7am, closing time varies from 9–11pm. Tube: Barbican or Farringdon.

The George & Vulture TRADITIONAL BRITISH   Dickens enthusiasts seek out this Pickwickian place. Founded in 1660, it claims that it's "probably" the world's oldest tavern, referring to an inn that operated on this spot in 1175. While they no longer put up overnight guests here, The George & Vulture does serve English lunches (but no dinners) in a warren of small dining rooms scattered over the tavern's three floors. Besides the daily specials, the menu includes a mixed grill, a loin chop, a lamb-based hot pot, and a grilled Dover-sole filet with tartar sauce. Potatoes and buttered cabbage are the standard vegetables, and the apple tart is always reliable. The system is to arrive and give your name, then retire to any of the three different pubs (Simpson's Bar, the Cross Key's Pub, or the Jamaican pub across the way) on the same narrow street for a drink; you're "fetched" when your table is ready. Afterward, be sure to explore the mazes of pubs, shops, wine houses, and other old buildings near the tavern. The Pickwick Club, a private literary group, meets here four times a year for reunion dinners.

3 Castle Court, Cornhill, EC3. © 020/7626-9710. Reservations accepted before 12:45pm. Main courses £7–£12 ($13–$23). AE, MC, V. Mon–Fri noon–2:30pm. Tube: Bank or Monument.

Vertigo 42 ★ *Finds* CONTINENTAL/SEAFOOD   This is a relatively unknown little spot, on the 42nd floor of Tower 42 in the heart of the City, that offers one of London's most spectacular views. After securing a special security pass downstairs, you're taken to Vertigo 42 in a high-speed elevator. Dining here is like being on top of the world—you take in a bird's-eye view of London, from the Canada Tower to the Law Courts. We prefer to come here as the sun sets and the city lights begin to twinkle. Blue binoculars are provided if you want a more intimate view of the cityscape. Seven champagnes are served by the glass, and there's an array of well-presented, very tasty food. Appetizers feature the likes of layered smoked salmon with herb butter and a mustard dressing, followed by seared scallops or a filet steak with Roquefort butter and caramelized onions. The food is more of a bar menu, and there isn't a large choice of mains. You must be 18 or older to patronize this restaurant.

Tower 42, Old Broad St., EC2. ⓒ 020/7877-7842. www.vertigo42.co.uk. Reservations required. Main courses £13–£19 ($25–$36); fixed-price lunch menu £15 ($29). AE, DC, MC, V. Mon–Fri noon–3pm and 5–11pm. Closed weekends. Tube: Liverpool St.

Ye Olde Cheshire Cheese *Kids* TRADITIONAL BRITISH   The foundation of this carefully preserved building was laid in the 13th century, and it holds the most famous of the old City chophouses and pubs. Established in 1667, it claims to be the spot where Dr. Samuel Johnson (who lived nearby) entertained admirers with his acerbic wit. Charles Dickens and other literary lions also patronized the place. Later, many of the ink-stained journalists and scandalmongers of 19th- and early-20th-century Fleet Street made it their watering hole. You'll find five bars and two dining rooms here. The house specialties include "Ye Famous Pudding" (steak, kidney, mushrooms, and game) and Scottish roast beef with Yorkshire pudding and horseradish sauce. Sandwiches, salads, and standby favorites such as steak-and-kidney pie are also available, as are dishes such as Dover sole. The Cheshire is the best and safest venue to introduce your children to a British pub.

Wine Office Court, 145 Fleet St., EC4. ⓒ 020/7353-6170. Main courses £8–£10 ($15–$19). AE, DC, MC, V. Meals: Mon–Sat noon–9:30pm; Sun noon–5pm. Drinks and bar snacks: Mon–Sat 11am–11pm; Sun noon–6pm. Tube: St. Paul's or Blackfriars.

CLERKENWELL
MODERATE

Moro 𝒢𝒢 NORTH AFRICAN/SPANISH   If you've been hearing about all the trendy restaurants in Clerkenwell and want to try one, make it Moro. With its streamlined interior and its kitchen in open view, it lures in the chic and fashionable. The aroma of delicious meats on the charcoal grill will attract carnivores, but vegetarian meals are also available. At the long zinc bar, you can fill up on some of the city's best tapas, or a Maghreb-inspired dinner of impeccable quality. The restaurant's recipes were inspired by the epoch when Arab culture met European culture in southern Spain (8th–15th c.). Starters include fried stuffed sardines flavored with coriander and cumin or else charcoal-grilled small filets of pork with ham and sweet peppers. For a tantalizing main, dig into the charcoal-grilled lamb chops with grilled peppers or the wood-roasted bream with a Seville orange sauce, lentils, and fresh spinach. Desserts are always tempting and made fresh daily, including Málaga raisin ice cream with sherry or a yogurt cake with pistachios and pomegranates. Extra-fresh products go into the creation of these dishes, and no seasoning or flavor overpowers. Tapas are available at the bar Monday to Saturday 12:30 to 10:30pm, including quail eggs, Manchego cheese, and octopus salad.

34–36 Exmouth Market, EC1. ⓒ 020/7833-8336. www.moro.co.uk. Reservations recommended. Main courses £15–£18 ($29–$34). Tapas £2.50–£3 ($4.75–$5.70). AE, DC, MC, V. Mon–Sat 12:30–2:30pm and 7–10:30pm. Tube: Farringdon.

St. John 𝒢𝒢 MODERN BRITISH   Located in a former smokehouse just north of Smithfield Market, this air-conditioned, canteenlike dining room is the restaurant of choice for carnivores. It is a showcase for the talents of owner/chef Fergus Henderson, a leader in the offal movement, which advocates the use of all animal parts in cuisine. In true British tradition, he uses the entire animal—we're talking neck, trotters, tail, liver, heart, the works. It's called nose-to-tail cookery.

Don't think you'll be served warmed-over haggis: The food is excellent and flavor-packed. There's an earthiness and simplicity to this cuisine that's unequaled in London. The grilled lamb chops, garnished with sliced pig's tongue, bacon, salsify, and dandelion, are matchless. Roast bone marrow appears with a parsley salad, and pork chops are called pig chops. It's hard these days to find an eel, bacon, and clam stew, but you'll discover one here. French wines wash it all down. Desserts run to puddings such as vanilla-rice or dates and walnuts with butterscotch. Dessert oddity? Where else can you get a good goat curd, marc (the product of grapes and their seeds after pressing), and rhubarb concoction these days? The breads served here can also be purchased in an on-site bakery.

26 St. John St., EC1. ℂ 020/7251-0848. Reservations required. Main courses £14–£23 ($27–$44). AE, DC, MC, V. Mon–Fri noon–3pm; Mon–Sat 6pm–11pm. Tube: Farringdon.

SHOREDITCH
EXPENSIVE

Fifteen 𝒢𝒢 MODERN BRITISH   When Jamie Oliver, author of *The Naked Chef,* opened this restaurant, it created a media blitz—he even chronicled his trials and tribulations on a six-part TV show on the Food Network called "Jamie's Kitchen." Oliver takes "disadvantaged" young people and trains them from scratch in just 4 months before turning them loose as your chef for the day, with all the profits going to charity. In a red-brick Victorian building, convenient for touring the trendy Hoxton Square art galleries, the decor is contemporary and clean cut, not unduly gussied up.

What to expect in the way of food? Although a bit hyped in the media, it's quite sumptuous and has won the praise of London's battle-toughened food critics such as Fay Maschler of *The Evening Standard,* who felt that Jamie should be "knighted" for his efforts. She claimed that Fifteen serves some of the best dishes she's sampled in a long time. Even Michelin-starred chefs have shown up here raving about the dishes, especially the succulent pastas. There are two dining venues here—a ground-floor trattoria and a downstairs restaurant, the latter the only place to order the set menus quoted below. Dishes we've sampled and enjoyed here include a light fish-laced gnocchi and a braised shoulder of lamb ravioli with a light rosemary butter sauce. Among some of the more delectable main dishes you are likely to be served are chargrilled halibut in a lemon crème fraîche or loin of pork pot roasted with balsamic vinegar flavoring and bay leaves. Desserts are always a surprise, including such treats as a lemon tart with lime syrup and a limoncello mascarpone. It's easier to get a reservation at the trattoria, as the staff keeps some tables free every night for walk-ins. The trick is to turn up immediately when the place opens.

15 Westland Pl. ℂ 0871/330-1515. www.fifteenrestaurant.com. Reservations required as far in advance as possible. Main courses £8–£18 ($15–$34); breakfast £2–£8.50 ($3.80–$16); fixed-price lunch Mon–Fri £22–£25 ($42–$48); fixed-price 6-course dinner £50–£60 ($95–$114). Mon–Sat 7:30–11am; Sun 9–11am. Daily noon–3pm and 6–10pm. AE, MC, V. Tube: Old St.

Les Trois Garçons 𝒢𝒢 *Finds* FRENCH   As trendy London moves east, and once-seedy districts like Shoreditch (north of the City) become cutting edge, eye-popping restaurants like Les Trois Garçons are bound to follow. The three "garçons" of the restaurant's name are Hassan Abdullah, Michel Lassere, and Stefan Karlson. They took this pub, which opened early in Victoria's reign, and turned it into one of the hottest reservations for London's young, fashionable set. This fun, campy restaurant lies among a row of garages and secondhand shops. You can't miss the flaming torches guarding the entrance. Inside, stuffed animals, including a British bulldog, are adorned with glittering tiaras. That's Quentin the crocodile balanced on top of the baby grand. In such a setting, the cuisine could be second to the entertainment. But, happily, the restaurant serves an excellent and modern French menu, beautifully prepared and making full use of first-rate ingredients. Making an excellent starter is the parsnip veloute with Roquefort-filled tortellini or a carpaccio of Scottish beef with a Cabernet Sauvignon vinaigrette and poached quail eggs. For main courses, we've enjoyed both the wild Scottish turbot and langoustines with a Jerusalem artichoke purée and sautéed chanterelles and the seared lamb filet with lamb kidneys and braised endives. For dessert, try a tarte tatin with vanilla-bean ice cream or a chocolate fondant with passion fruit and banana sorbet.

1 Club Row, E1. ✆ 020/7613-1924. www.loungelover.co.uk. Reservations essential. Main courses £18–£27 ($34–$51). Fixed price menu £24 ($46) 2 courses, £28 ($53) 3 courses. AE, MC, V. Mon–Sat 7pm–midnight. Tube: Liverpool St.

MODERATE

Eyre Brothers ⭐ *Finds* PORTUGUESE   At night, more and more of trendy London flocks to Shoreditch. Their goal is often this restaurant, inaugurated by David Eyre (his brother Robert is the host), who virtually revolutionized pub grub in London at the dawn of the millennium, but in another location. This setting in Shoreditch is more elegant and refined than his old quarters, featuring mahogany paneling and elegantly appointed tables. The chef is often inspired by Portuguese cuisine—and by the cuisine of former Portuguese colonies like Mozambique. A typical example: tiger prawns piripiri (in a hot chili marinade). Succulent T-bones are grilled on the open fire here as in the style of Lisbon. The fresh catch of the day, perhaps yellowfin tuna, is also grilled to one's request. The house specialty is a marvelous banquet of roast suckling pig flavored to perfection. For starters, try the Spanish garlic and ham soup with smoked paprika and sherry, or octopus with green peppers, coriander, and sherry vinegar. Other tempting mains include salt cod filet cooked with tomatoes, peppers, and onions or slow-cooked lamb shank with dried Choricero peppers and garbanzos. Always count on temptations for dessert, including a burnt orange tart made with fresh blood oranges or braised apples with hazelnuts and cinnamon flavoring with baked rhubarb in syrup.

70 Leonard St., EC2. ✆ 020/7613-5346. www.eyrebrothers.co.uk. Reservations required. Main courses £12–£24 ($23–$46). AE, DC, MC, V. Mon–Fri noon–3pm; Mon–Sat 6:30–10:45pm. Tube: Old St.

DOCKLANDS
EXPENSIVE

Butler's Wharf Chop House ⭐ TRADITIONAL BRITISH   At the edge of the Thames near Tower Bridge, the Butler's Wharf complex holds condos, rental apartments, offices, and an assortment of food and wine shops collectively known as the Gastrodome. Built in the mid–19th century as a warehouse, it's now another Terence Conran playland. From its windows, diners and shoppers enjoy sweeping views of some of the densest river traffic in Europe. Of the four restaurants housed here (others are listed in this chapter), this one is closest to Tower Bridge. It maintains its commitment to moderate prices. The Chop House was modeled after a large boathouse, with banquettes, lots of exposed wood, flowers, candles, and windows overlooking Tower Bridge and the Thames. Lunchtime crowds include workers from the city's financial district; evening crowds are made up of friends enjoying a leisurely meal.

Dishes are largely adaptations of British recipes such as fish and chips with mushy peas or steak-and-kidney-pudding with oysters, even roast pork loin with applesauce. The bar features several English wines, among other offerings, plus a half-dozen French clarets by the jug.

36E Shad Thames, SE1. ✆ 020/7403-3403. Reservations recommended. Main courses £14–£26 ($27–$49); 2-course fixed-price lunch £22 ($42); 3-course fixed-price lunch £26 ($49). AE, DC, MC, V. Mon–Sun noon–3pm; Mon–Sat 6–11pm (6–10pm May–Oct). Tube: Tower Hill or London Bridge.

Le Pont de la Tour ✶ INTERNATIONAL   Located in Butler's Wharf, the **Bar and Grill's** live piano music (on evenings and weekends) and wide choice of wines and cocktails creates one of the most convivial atmospheres in the area. Although such dishes as ham and foie gras terrine, and langoustines mayonnaise are featured, the culinary star is a heaping platter of fresh shellfish—perfect when shared with a friend, accompanied by a bottle of wine.

In bold contrast is the large, more formal room known simply as the **Restaurant.** Filled with burr oak furniture and decorated with framed lithographs of early-20th-century Parisian cafe society, it offers excellent food and a polite but undeniable English reserve. The menu may list such temptations as roast rabbit wrapped in herbs with pancetta and a mustard vinaigrette, or whole roast-buttered lobster with herbs. One especially winning selection is best end of lamb, with a black olive and herb crust in a red-pepper sauce. All the fish is excellent, but none better than the Dover sole, which can be ordered grilled or meunière.

36D Shad Thames, Butler's Wharf, SE1. ✆ 020/7403-8403. Reservations highly recommended in the Bar and Grill; recommended in the Restaurant. Bar and Grill main courses £12–£22 ($23–$42); fixed-price lunch menu £13–£15 ($25–$29). The Restaurant main courses £18–£35 ($34–$67); 3-course fixed-price lunch menu £30 ($57). AE, DC, MC, V. The Restaurant Sun–Fri noon–3pm, Mon–Sun 6–11pm. Bar and Grill daily noon–3pm and 6–11pm. Tube: Tower Hill or London Bridge.

MODERATE

The Bengal Clipper ✶ INDIAN   This former spice warehouse by the Thames serves what it calls "India's most remarkable dishes." The likable and often animated restaurant is outfitted with cream-colored walls, tall columns, and modern artwork inspired by Moghul Dynasty–era depictions of royal figures, soaring trees, and well-trained elephants. Seven windows afford sweeping views over the industrialized Thames-side neighborhood, and live piano music plays in the background. The cuisine includes many vegetarian choices derived from the former Portuguese colony of Goa and the once-English colony of Bengal. There is a zestiness and spice to the food, but it's never overpowering. The chefs keep the menu fairly short so that all ingredients can be purchased fresh every day.

A tasty specialty is stuffed *murgh masala,* a tender breast of chicken with potatoes, onions, apricots, and almonds, cooked with yogurt and served with a delectable curry sauce. The perfectly cooked duckling (off the bone) comes in a tangy sauce with a citrus bite. One of the finest dishes we tasted in North India is served here and has lost nothing in the transfer: marinated lamb simmered in cream with cashew nuts, seasoned with fresh ginger. One of the best offerings from the Goan repertoire is the *karkra chop,* a spicy patty of minced crab blended with mashed potatoes and peppered with Goan spices.

Shad Thames, Butler's Wharf, SE1. ✆ 020/7357-9001. Reservations recommended. Main courses £8–£15 ($15–$29); set menu £10 ($19) (available July–Apr); Sunday buffet £7.75 ($15). AE, DC, MC, V. Mon–Sat noon–2:30pm and 6–11:30pm; Sun noon–4pm and 6–11pm. Tube: Tower Hill.

The Gun ☆ MODERN BRITISH   This public house dates back 250 years and is steeped in maritime history. Admiral Lord Nelson is said to have made love to Lady Hamilton in a secluded secret bedchamber above this pub. Much remains from its past, including a gorgeous oak bar and walls decorated with nautical memorabilia. There's also a terrace for alfresco drinking. With the recent improvement in cuisine, it has emerged as one of London's leading gastro-pubs, attracting visitors from the West End. Now lovingly restored, it is no longer the down-market Docklands dive of yore, attracting seedy sailors.

White linen-covered tables, open wood fires, and the smell of such luxury ingredients as truffles greet today's serious foodie. From some of the tables there is a view across the Thames of the Millennium Dome. Lord Nelson would be astonished at such "conceits" as an "amuse" of fennel froth served in espresso cups. Start perhaps with the spicy, chilled gazpacho or else the potted duck with apricots, moving on to such mains as grilled Aberdeen rib-eye steaks with snails and a homemade wild mushroom brioche. The fish pie is usually a good bet, as the seafood is bought daily from nearby Billingsgate Market. Most fish is served whole: tell your waiter if you want the head or tail chopped off. For dessert, try the basket of rosewater ice cream with honey and strawberries.

27 Coldharbour, Docklands, E14. ☎ 020/7515-5222. Reservations recommended. Main courses £13–£16 ($25–$30). AE, MC, V. Food served Mon–Fri noon–3pm and 6–10:30pm; Sat 10:30am–4pm and 6–10:30pm; Sun 10:30am–4pm and 6–9:30pm. Tube: South Quay.

CANARY WHARF
EXPENSIVE

Plateau FRENCH   Entrepreneur Terence Conran has succeeded again with the opening of this trend-setting restaurant at Canary Wharf, serving a modern French cuisine. The chef proudly boasts that he appeals to both high- and lowbrow palates— and so he does, succeeding admirably. The atmosphere is retro chic, with Harry Bertoia chrome chairs and Eero Saarinen tables. The location is on the fourth floor at the top of the Canada Place building, with panoramic views of London. There are two different dining sections divided by a semi-open-to-view kitchen. One is a chic bar and grill, the other a more formal restaurant, each with its own terrace. There are also bars and a cigar room.

In the bar and grill, partake of food enjoyed in the 20s and 30s, notably Colchester native oysters followed by Billingsgate fish pie. The upgraded cuisine in the main restaurant is quite sumptuous—a foie gras terrine with champagne jelly followed by such main courses as venison stew with spaetzle and savoy cabbage. For dessert, we'd suggest roasted figs with honey and port with a side of cumin-flavored ice cream.

Canada Place, Canary Wharf, E14. ☎ 020/7715-7100. Reservations recommended. Bar and grill main courses £10–£20 ($19–$38). Fixed-price menus £17–£21 ($32–$40). Restaurant main courses £20–£30 ($38–$57). Fixed-price menus (only dinner) £25–£30 ($48–$57). AE, DC, MC, V. Restaurant Mon–Fri noon–3pm; Mon–Sat 6–10:30pm; Sun noon–4pm. Bar and grill Mon–Sat noon–11pm; Sun noon–4pm. Tube: Canary Wharf.

Sri Nam ☆ *Finds* THAI   Celebrity chef Ken Hom is the chief exponent of Thai cookery in London, and even the Thai community agrees he's the best. Some of his culinary secrets are revealed in his book, *Foolproof Thai Cookery.* At Canary Wharf, Sri Nam brings an authentic and very spicy (read: hot) cuisine to foodies who like to dine on the Thames. There's a buzz-filled cafe-bar on the ground floor and a more formal restaurant upstairs. The Thai cuisine served here is a fusion of modern and traditional, the latter in theory the type served to the "King of Siam." The Asian bar on the ground floor serves drinks from the Far East, plus beers and wines. The ground-floor bar also caters to those seeking speedy lunches or an early supper.

Climb the sweeping staircase for more serious dishes served against a backdrop of rich, dark woods; lush silks; and bright lanterns. The classic star of the menu is *pad thai,* a delightful stir-fry of noodles with eggs, vegetables, and bean sprouts, garnished with ground peanuts and fresh coriander. Also served here (and rarely seen on other London menus) is lamb masaman, a curry from south Thailand, featuring lamb flavored with peanuts and potatoes. The signature dish—and is it ever good—is the Thai green chicken curry with chiles, coconut milk, bamboo shoots, baby eggplant, and lime leaves.

N. Colonnade, 10 Cabot Sq., Canary Wharf, E14. ℂ 020/7715-9515. Reservations required. Main courses £6–£14 ($11–$27). Fixed-price menus £22–£28 ($42–$53). AE, DC, MC, V. Mon–Fri noon–3pm and 5–11pm. Tube: Canary Wharf.

SOUTH BANK
EXPENSIVE
Oxo Tower Restaurant ⍟ INTERNATIONAL   In the South Bank complex, on the eighth floor of the Art Deco Oxo Tower Wharf, you'll find this dining sensation operated by the department store Harvey Nichols. Down the street from the rebuilt Globe Theatre, the 140-seat restaurant could be visited for its view alone (of St. Paul's Cathedral and the City, all the way to the Houses of Parliament), but the cuisine is also stellar. The decor is chic 1930s style.

The cuisine, under chef David Sharland, is rich and prepared with finesse. Menu items change based on the season and the market. Count on a modern interpretation of British cookery, as well as English classics. The fish is incredibly fresh here. The whole sea bass for two is delectable, as is the roast rump of lamb with split pea, mint purée, and balsamic vinegar sauce. We were impressed with the roast filet of plaice with olive oil and truffle cabbage cream, and the roast squab with buttered cabbage and a foie-gras sauce.

Barge House St., South Bank, SE1. ℂ 020/7803-3888. Main courses £17–£25 ($32–$48); 3-course fixed-price lunch £30 ($57). AE, DC, MC, V. Mon–Sat noon–2:30pm and 6–11pm; Sun noon–3pm and 6:30–10pm. Tube: Blackfriars or Waterloo.

MODERATE
Cantina Vinopolis ⍟ *Finds* CONTINENTAL   Not far from the re-created Globe Theatre of Shakespeare's heyday, this place has been called a "Walk-Through Wine Atlas." In the revitalized Bankside area, south of the Thames near Southwark Cathedral, this bricked, walled, and high-vaulted brasserie was converted from long-abandoned Victorian railway arches. Inside you can visit both the Vinopolis Wine Gallery and the Cantina Restaurant. Although many come here just to drink the wine, the food is prepared with quality ingredients (very fresh), and the menu is sensibly priced. Start with a bit of heaven like the pea-and-ham soup. Dishes are full of flavor and never overcooked. Pan-fried snapper, with crushed new potatoes and *salsa verde,* won us over. A rump of lamb was tender and perfectly flavored and served with a polenta cake. Many of the dishes have the good country taste you'd find in a trattoria in the countryside of southern Italy. Naturally, the wine list is the biggest in the U.K.

1 Bank End, London Bridge, SE1. ℂ 020/7940-8333. Reservations required. Main courses £10–£20 ($19–$38); 3-course fixed-price menu £38 ($72). AE, DC, MC, V. Mon–Sat noon–3pm and 6–10:30pm; Sun noon–4pm. Tube: London Bridge.

(Kids) Family-Friendly Restaurants

Hard Rock Cafe (Mayfair; p. 176)   This is a great place for kids old enough to busy themselves with rock-and-roll memorabilia as they wait for their familiar burgers, fries, and salads with Thousand Island dressing.

Porters English Restaurant (Covent Garden & the Strand; p. 162)   This restaurant serves traditional English meals that most kids love—especially the pies, stews, and steamed "spuds." They'll get a kick out of ordering the wonderfully named bubble-and-squeak (that's cabbage and potatoes) and mushy peas.

Royal China (Paddington & Bayswater; p. 197)   If there's a dim sum lover in your family, head for this eatery. We saw a young brother and sister devouring a dish of seafood golden cups—stir-fried scallops, prawns, water chestnuts, and mushrooms in crispy puff pastry.

Simpson's-in-the-Strand (Covent Garden & the Strand; p. 160)   If your offspring is an aspiring Henry VIII, take him here for the best roasts in London, including tender roast sirloin of beef. For dessert, he might be introduced to such English favorites as treacle rolls.

Ye Olde Cheshire Cheese (the City; p. 150)   Fleet Street's famous chophouse, established in 1667, is an eternal favorite. If "ye famous pudding" turns your kids off, sandwiches and roasts will tempt them.

5 The West End

BLOOMSBURY

EXPENSIVE

Archipelago 🐦🐦 FRENCH/THAI   This cozy restaurant is a celebrity favorite, attracting the likes of Madonna and Hugh Hefner. Archipelago is definitely on the see-and-be-seen circuit. Media darling Michael Von Hruschka has decorated the restaurant in a whimsical style, with everything from birdcages to a Buddha serving as props. There are precious touches, such as the drink list written on delicate paper and inserted in an ostrich eggshell. Everything is presented in exquisite boxes, and even the bill comes in a "book." Amazingly, with all the attention paid to the environment, the cuisine does not suffer in ingredients or preparation. Begin with a coconut-and-lemon-grass soup or the most delectable small-carrot spring rolls. Vegetable couscous and fish-and-banana risotto are delectable, and tiramisu is given an original touch with the addition of ginger wine. Crocodile, peacock, and kangaroo appear on the menu along with chicken, fish, lamb, and even vegetarian options.

110 Whitfield St., W1. ℂ 020/7383-3346. Reservations required as far in advance as possible. Main courses £13–£20 ($25–$38). Fixed-price lunch menu £12 ($23). AE, DC, MC, V. Mon–Fri noon–2:30pm; Mon–Sat 6–10:30pm. Tube: Goodge St.

MODERATE

Back to Basics 🐦🐦 SEAFOOD   Ursula Higgs's bistro draws discerning palates seeking some of the freshest seafood in London. When the weather's fair, you can dine outside. Otherwise, retreat indoors to a vaguely Parisian setting with a blackboard menu and checked tablecloths. The fish is served in large portions, and you can safely forgo an appetizer unless you're ravenous. More than a dozen seafood dishes are offered; the fish can be broiled, grilled, baked, or poached, but frying is not permitted. In other words, this is no fish and chippie. Start with a bowl of tasty, plump mussels or sea bass flavored with fresh basil and chili oil. Brill appears with green peppercorn butter, and plaice is jazzed up with fresh ginger and soy sauce. For the meat eater, there is a T-bone steak or roast chicken. Also try the pastas and the vegetarian dishes. Freshly made salads accompany most meals, and an excellent fish soup is offered daily. For dessert, try the bread pudding or the freshly made apple pie.

21A Foley St., W1. ℂ 020/7436-2181. Reservations recommended. Main courses £11–£17 ($21–$32). AE, DC, MC, V. Mon–Sat noon–3pm and 6–10:30pm. Tube: Oxford Circus or Goodge St.

INEXPENSIVE

The Court Restaurant CONTINENTAL   Nothing in London brings culture and cuisine together quite like this restaurant on the sixth floor of the British Museum, with views opening onto Norman Foster's millennium development, the Great Court. The restaurant overlooks the famous round Reading Room and nestles close to the spectacular glass-and-steel roof. For museum buffs, it's the perfect venue for morning coffee, hot or cold lunches, afternoon tea, or dinner.

The chef turns out a menu of familiar favorites. You can watch the cooks as they prepare the market-fresh dishes for the day. The food has drawn mixed reviews from our readers, although many dishes we've sampled had real flavor, including the radicchio risotto with prosciutto served with grilled foie gras or the filet of beef with red peppers and a red-pepper marmalade. Scottish salmon with beurre blanc and spiced lentils is another generally reliable dish. Come here for the dramatic setting, knowing that the cuisine is secondary. On the plus side, the museum serves its own beer, and it can compete with the product of any brewery.

The British Museum, Great Russell St., WC1. ℂ 020/7323-8990. Reservations required. Main courses £13–£16 ($25–$30). AE, MC, V. Mon–Wed 11am–5:30pm; Thurs–Fri 11am–10:30pm; Sat–Sun 11am–5:30pm. Tube: Holborn, Tottenham Court Rd., or Russell Sq.

Wagamama JAPANESE   This noodle joint, in a basement just off New Oxford Street, is noisy and overcrowded, and you'll have to wait in line for a table. It calls itself a "non-destination food station" and caters to some 1,200 customers a day. Many dishes are built around ramen noodles with your choice of chicken, beef, or salmon. Try the tasty *gyoza,* light dumplings filled with vegetables or chicken. Vegetarian dishes are available, but skip the so-called Korean-style dishes.

4 Streatham St., WC1. ℂ 020/7323-9223. Reservations not accepted. Main courses £6–£10 ($11–$19). AE, MC, V. Mon–Sat noon–11pm; Sun noon–10pm. Tube: Tottenham Court Rd.

COVENT GARDEN & THE STRAND

The restaurants in and around Covent Garden and the Strand are the most convenient choices when you're attending theaters in the West End.

VERY EXPENSIVE

Marcus Wareing at the Savoy Grill ★★ MODERN BRITISH   Dinner at the Savoy Grill has long been a London tradition, attracting celebrities visiting the West End, but the room had gone stale. Now, under one of the country's premier chefs, Marcus Wareing, the old glory of the Grill has come back. Wareing has brought the fabled Savoy Grill back to its former glory, and in 2007 the Michelin Guide honored

Where to Dine in the West End & Theatre District

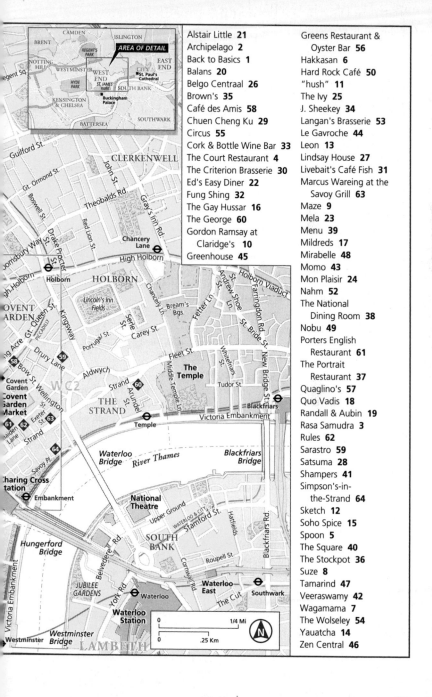

him with a star. The old carving trolley of English roasts has been done away with and an updated menu now rests in your hand. Even the decor has been brightened. Intensity of flavor and market-fresh ingredients characterize the new menu. For starters, go daring by ordering the caramelized calves' sweetbreads on pancetta with onion marmalade, or else the roasted hand-dived scallops with a fresh pea purée and a tomato confit. Gourmets along the Strand praise—and we concur—the crispy pavé of salmon with crushed new potatoes and lobster, or the pan-fried filet of John Dory with sautéed romaine lettuce and a parsnip purée. Meat and poultry dishes are still a strong point with the chefs, especially the braised Wiltshire pork belly with sautéed Jerusalem artichokes and the rump of Cornish lamb with cherry tomatoes and black olives.

The Strand, WC2. ✆ **020/7592-1600.** Reservations required. Set lunch £30 ($57); prestige tasting menu £65 ($124); a la carte, a selection of 3 courses £55 ($105). AE, MC, V. Mon–Fri noon–2:45pm and 5:45–11pm; Sat noon–4pm and 5:45–11pm; Sun noon–10pm. Tube: Charing Cross or Covent Garden.

EXPENSIVE

Rules ⊛ TRADITIONAL BRITISH   If you're looking for London's most quintessentially British restaurant, eat here. London's oldest restaurant was established in 1798 as an oyster bar; today, the antler-filled Edwardian dining rooms exude nostalgia. You can order such classic dishes as Irish or Scottish oysters, jugged hare, and mussels. Game and fish dishes are offered from mid-August to February or March, including wild Scottish salmon; wild sea trout; wild Highland red deer; and game birds like grouse, snipe, partridge, pheasant, and woodcock. As a finale, the "great puddings" continue to impress.

35 Maiden Lane, WC2. ✆ **020/7836-5314.** Reservations recommended. Main courses £17–£28 ($32–$53). AE, DC, MC, V. Mon–Sat noon–11:30pm; Sun noon–10:30pm. Tube: Covent Garden.

Simpson's-in-the-Strand ⊛⊛ *Kids* TRADITIONAL and MODERN BRITISH Simpson's is more of an institution than a restaurant. Long a family favorite with lots of large tables, it has been in business since 1828, and as a result of a recent £2-million ($3.8-million) renovation, it's now better than ever with its Adam paneling, crystal, and an army of grandly formal waiters (to whom nouvelle cuisine means anything after Henry VIII) serving traditional British fare. The owners object to the word "menu" here—"too French." It's called "bill of fare." At least men and women can now dine together—before 1904 such an "outrage" was forbidden. Over the years the dress code has become more relaxed—in other words, Elizabeth Taylor in trousers would no longer be forbidden to enter. Famous diners of yesterday include everyone from Charles Dickens to Charles Chaplin, and the restaurant is often used as a setting for films, including for Alfred Hitchcock's *Sabotage.*

Most diners agree that Simpson's serves the best roasts in London, an array that includes roast sirloin of beef; roast saddle of mutton with red-currant jelly; roast Aylesbury duckling; and steak, kidney, and mushroom pie. For a pudding, you might order the treacle roll and custard or Stilton with vintage port. Simpson's also serves traditional breakfasts. The most popular one is "The Ten Deadly Sins": a plate of sausage; fried egg; streaky and back bacon; black pudding; lambs' kidneys; bubble-and-squeak; baked beans; lambs' liver; and fried bread, mushrooms, and tomatoes. That will certainly fortify you for the day.

100 the Strand (next to the Savoy Hotel), WC2. ✆ **020/7836-9112.** Reservations required. Main courses £16–£25 ($30–$48); 2-course fixed-price pre-theater dinner £23 ($44); 3-course fixed-price pre-theater dinner £28 ($53); breakfast from £16 ($30). AE, DC, MC, V. Mon–Fri 7:15–10:30am; Mon–Sat 12:15–2:30pm and 5:45–10:45pm; Sun noon–3pm and 6–9pm. Tube: Charing Cross or Embankment.

MODERATE

Belgo Centraal BELGIAN   Chaos reigns supreme in this cavernous basement, where mussels *marinières* with frites, plus 100 Belgian beers, are the raison d'être. Take a freight elevator past the busy kitchen and into a converted cellar, divided into two large eating areas. One section is a beer hall seating about 250; the menu here is the same as in the restaurant, but you don't need reservations. The restaurant side has three nightly seatings: 5:30, 7:30, and 10pm. Between 5:30 and 8pm you can choose one of three fixed-price menus. Although heaps of fresh mussels are the big attraction, you can opt for fresh Scottish salmon, roast chicken, a perfectly done steak, or one of the vegetarian specialties. Gargantuan plates of wild boar sausages arrive with *stoemp*—Belgian mashed spuds and cabbage. Belgian stews, called *waterzooï*, are also served. With waiters in maroon monk's habits and black aprons barking orders into headset microphones, it's all a bit bizarre.

50 Earlham St., WC2. ℂ 020/7813-2233. Reservations required for the restaurant. Main courses £9–£18 ($17–$34); fixed-price menus £21–£26 ($40–$49). AE, DC, MC, V. Mon–Thurs noon–11pm; Fri–Sat noon–11:30pm; Sun noon–10:30pm. Closed Christmas. Tube: Covent Garden.

Café des Amis FRENCH   For more than half a century, Café des Amis has been entertaining theater-goers with the two-fisted drinks at its bar and the fine Gallic cuisine in its restaurant. With its service by French waiters and its sophisticated Continental decor, it brings a touch of Paris to the heart of London. Dishes are both traditional and modern, but with reduced calories since the days of Escoffier. The wine list from France, including champagne, is one of the best in Covent Garden. The cafe is a good choice for a pre- or post-theater meal, or a romantic dinner even if you're not attending a play or musical.

The menu is not completely conventional (although there are plenty of French classics). There are modern touches as well, none more so than the soupe au chocolat with black-pepper ice cream. You might begin with French onion soup or shellfish bisque, perhaps seared scallops with chorizo and roasted hazelnuts. Among the mains we've savored are roasted line-caught sea bass in a vinaigrette with palourd clams, and pot-roasted lamb flavored with cinnamon and cloves. Desserts are often more English than French, as evoked by poached Yorkshire rhubarb flavored with ginger and served with a cream custard.

11–14 Hanover Place (off Long Acre), WC2. ℂ 020/7379-3444. Reservations recommended. Main courses £15–£19 ($29–$36). Fixed-price menus £15 ($29) for 2 courses, £17 ($32) for 3 courses. AE, DC, MC, V. Daily 11:30am–1am. Tube: Covent Garden.

Mon Plaisir *Value* FRENCH   Serving fine French cuisine for more than half a century, Mon Plaisir is London's oldest French restaurant. It's so authentic that its pewter-topped bar once graced the lounge of a Lyonnais bordello. Your table (with white cloths, no longer paper) will be in one of four different rooms. The menu wanders into nostalgia with its *classiques* but has been modernized as well. Its pre-theater fixed-price menu is one of the best deals in the West End. It's not to everyone's taste but gourmets delight in the pigs' trotter stuffed with foie gras and langoustines, a dish evoking the old markets of Les Halles in Paris. Of course, there are snails with garlic and a traditional French onion soup. The fish dishes are fresh and tantalizing, including coquilles Saint-Jacques (scallops). A delicious coq au vin, another classic, is cooked in burgundy. For dessert, why not the pan-fried brioche with poached pear and—get this—beer ice cream?

21 Monmouth St., WC2. ℂ 020/7836-7243. Reservations recommended. Main courses £15–£19 ($29–$37); £15 ($29) pre-theater menu. AE, DC, MC, V. Mon–Fri noon–2:15pm; Mon–Sat 5:50–11:15pm. Tube: Covent Garden.

Porters English Restaurant 🌟🌟 *(Kids)* TRADITIONAL BRITISH   The seventh earl of Bradford serves "real English food at affordable prices." He succeeds notably— and not just because Lady Bradford turned over her carefully guarded recipe for banana-and-ginger steamed pudding. This comfortable, two-storied restaurant is family-friendly, informal, and lively. Porters specializes in classic English pies, including Old English fish pie, lamb and apricot, and, of course, bangers and mash. The overwhelming favorite is steak, Guinness, and mushroom pie. Main courses are so generous—and accompanied by vegetables and side dishes—that you hardly need appetizers. They have also added grilled English fare to the menu, with sirloin and lamb steaks and marinated chicken. Porters is famous for its mouthwatering puddings. Where can you find a good spotted dick these days? It's a steamed syrup sponge with sultanas. Another favorite is a dark chocolate chip pudding made with steamed chocolate sponge, chocolate chips, and chocolate custard. Even the ice cream is homemade. The bar does quite a few exotic cocktails, as well as beers, wine, and English mead. A traditional English tea is served from 2:30 to 5:30pm. Who knows? You may even bump into His Lordship.

17 Henrietta St., WC2. 📞 **020/7836-6466**. Reservations recommended. Main courses £10–£17 ($19–$32); fixed-price lunch and pre-theatre menu £12 ($23); fixed-price menu £22 ($42). AE, MC, V. Mon–Sat noon–11:30pm; Sun noon–10:30pm. Tube: Covent Garden or Leicester Sq.

INEXPENSIVE

The George TRADITIONAL BRITISH   Go here for the atmosphere of old England. Although its half-timbered facade would make you believe it's older than it is, this pub has been around *only* since 1723, when it was built as a coffeehouse. Set on the Strand, at the lower end of Fleet Street opposite the Royal Courts of Justice, The George is a favorite of barristers, their clients, and the handful of journalists who haven't moved to other parts of London. The pub's illustrious history saw Samuel Johnson having his mail delivered here and Oliver Goldsmith enjoying many tankards of what eventually became draught Bass. Today the setting seems only slightly changed, as much of the original architecture is still intact. Hot and cold platters, including bangers and mash, fish and chips, steak-and-kidney pie, and lasagna, are served from a food counter at the back of the pub. Other main dishes include 3 Cumberland sausages with mashed potatoes and red onion gravy or chicken Parmagiana. Additional seating is available in the basement, where a headless cavalier is said to haunt the same premises where he enjoyed his liquor in an earlier (and less headless) day. Although the place has long hours (see below), the actual food service is Monday to Thursday 11am to 3pm, Friday and Saturday noon to 9pm, and Sunday noon to 6:30pm.

213 the Strand, WC2. 📞 **020/7353-9638**. Main courses £7–£10 ($13–$19). AE, MC, V. Mon–Thurs 11am–11:30pm; Fri–Sat noon–midnight; Sun noon–7pm. Tube: Temple.

Sarastro 🌟 CYPRIOT/TURKISH   The setting here makes you feel like you're in the prop room of an opera house. As the manager says, "We're the show after the show." The decor is sort of neo-Ottoman, and the cuisine celebrates the bounty of the Mediterranean, especially Turkey and Cyprus. In a Victorian building behind the Theatre Royal, the restaurant is decorated with battered urns, old lamps, fading lampshades, and knickknacks—it looks like an old Turkish curiosity shop. Ten opera boxes adorn three sides of the restaurant; the royal box is the most desired. The restaurant takes its name from a character in Mozart's *The Magic Flute*. Live opera performances are staged from time to time. You can begin your meal with such starters as grilled

Mediterranean prawns with garlic mushrooms, or else stuffed vine leaves and hummus. Some of the best mains include a filet or sirloin steak with a red wine sauce or else lamb meatballs, or perhaps fettuccine with cream, mushrooms and Parma ham. The fish dishes are fresh, including grilled lemon sole and monkfish with tomatoes and onions. The dessert specialty is a pastry, Sekerprare, cooked in honey and topped with pistachio nuts.

126 Drury Lane, WC2. © 020/7836-0101. www.sarastro-restaurant.com. Reservations required. Main courses £7.50–£15 ($14–$29). Fixed-price menu £24 ($46); pre-theater menu £13 ($25). AE, DC, MC, V. Daily noon–11:45pm. Tube: Covent Garden.

PICCADILLY CIRCUS & LEICESTER SQUARE

Piccadilly Circus and Leicester Square lie at the doorstep of the West End theaters. All the choices below (along with those in the "Covent Garden & the Strand" and "Soho" sections) are good candidates for dining before or after a show.

EXPENSIVE

Fung Shing 🟆🟆 CANTONESE   In a city where the competition is stiff, Fung Shing emerges as London's finest Cantonese restaurant. Firmly established as a culinary landmark, it dazzles with classic and nouvelle Cantonese dishes. Look for the seasonal specials. Some of the dishes may be a bit experimental—notably stir-fried fresh milk with scrambled egg white—but you'll feel right at home with the soft-shell crab sautéed in a light batter and served with tiny rings of red-hot chile and deep-fried garlic. Chinese gourmets come here for the fried intestines; you may prefer the hot pot of stewed duck with yam. The spicy sea bass and the stir-fried crispy chicken are worthy choices. There are more than 150 dishes from which to choose and most are moderate in price.

15 Lisle St., WC2. © 020/7437-1539. Reservations required. Main courses £8–£23 ($15–$44). AE, DC, MC, V. Daily noon–11:30pm. Tube: Leicester Sq.

The Ivy 🟆🟆 MODERN BRITISH/INTERNATIONAL   Effervescent and sophisticated, The Ivy is the dining choice of visiting theatrical luminaries and has been intimately associated with the theater district ever since it opened in 1911. With its ersatz 1930s look and tiny bar near the entrance, this place is fun and hums with the energy of London's glamour scene. The kitchen has a solid appreciation for fresh ingredients and a talent for preparation. Some appetizers may be a bit much for you, including wild rabbit salad with black pudding, whereas others are more readily appealing, including Bang Bang chicken (chicken with a glossy peanut glaze). The crispy duck and watercress salad is another favorite starter. For years, a 14-ounce Dover sole has been enjoyed by celebrities and wannabees alike. Mains feature a chargrilled fish of the day, and carnivores take to the sautéed veal kidneys or the escalope of veal Holstein. The Ivy hamburger continues to appear on the menu. Desserts are familiar, including chocolate pudding soufflé or steamed rhubarb sponge pudding with custard.

1–5 West St., WC2. © 020/7836-4751. Reservations required. Sat–Sun fixed-price lunch £24 ($46). Main courses £8–£27 ($15–$51). AE, DC, MC, V. Mon–Sat noon–3pm; daily 5:30pm–midnight (last order); Sun noon–3:30pm. Tube: Leicester Sq.

J. Sheekey 🟆 SEAFOOD   British culinary tradition lives on at this fish joint, long a favorite of West End actors. The jellied eels that delighted Laurence Olivier and Vivien Leigh are still on the menu, along with an array of fresh oysters from the coasts of Ireland and Brittany and that Victorian favorite, fried whitebait. Sheekey's fish pie is still featured, as is Dover sole. The old "mushy" peas are here, but the chefs also offer the likes of steamed organic sea beet. Opt for the traditional dishes or specials based on the fresh catch of the day. The double chocolate pudding soufflé is a delight, and many favorite puddings remain.

28–32 St. Martin's Court, WC2. © 020/7240-2565. Reservations recommended. Main courses £7–£35 ($13–$67). AE, DC, MC, V. Mon–Sat noon–3pm and 5:30pm–midnight; Sun noon–3:30pm and 6pm–midnight. Tube: Leicester Sq.

MODERATE

Livebait's Café Fish ℛ SEAFOOD   Don't you love the name? The catch of the day can be chargrilled or pan-fried as you desire. We know of no better place in London to sample seafood favorites enjoyed by Brits back in the days of Sir Winston Churchill—we're talking smoked haddock kedgeree (a mixture of fish, rice, and hard-boiled eggs), cockles, steamed mussels, smoky grilled sardines, and the like. We like to go when Dover sole is on the menu, but it's dependent on the catch, so call ahead. This eclectic menu includes fish flown all the way from the U.S. Unlike some of the soggy chips (fries) at nearby dives, the ones here are crisp and fluffy. Our moist-fleshed sea bream, served with a crisp skin, made us want to "hasten ye back" to the restaurant the next night. From Grandma's pantry comes Bailey's cheesecake or sticky toffee pudding to finish off the meal.

36–40 Rupert St., W1. © 020/7287-8989. Reservations recommended. Main courses £12–£40 ($23–$76); fixed-price menu (available all day) £13–£15 ($25–$29). AE, MC, V. Mon–Sat noon–11pm; Sun 2–9pm. Tube: Piccadilly Circus.

Randall & Aubin ℛ *Finds* SEAFOOD   Past the sex boutiques of Soho you stumble upon this real discovery, whose consultant is TV chef Ed Baines, an ex-Armani model who turned this butcher shop into a cool, hip champagne-and-oyster bar. It's an ideal place to take a lover for a *Sex and the City* type of meal and some champagne or a bottle of wine. You're never rushed here. The impressive shellfish display of the night's goodies is the "bait" used to lure you inside. Chances are you won't be disappointed. Loch Fyne oysters, lobster with chips, pan-fried fresh scallops—the parade of seafood we've sampled here has in each case been genuinely excellent. The *soupe de poisson* (fish soup) is the best in Soho, or else you might try one of the hors d'oeuvres such as delightful Japanese-style fish cakes or fresh Cornish crab. Yes, they still have Sevruga caviar for lotto winners. For the rare meat-only eater, there is a limited array of dishes such as a perfectly roasted chicken on the spit that has been flavored with fresh herbs. The lemon tart with crème fraîche rounds off a perfect meal.

16 Brewer St., W1. © 020/7287-4447. Reservations not accepted. Main courses £8–£26 ($15–$49). AE, DC, MC, V. Mon–Sat noon–11pm; Sun 4–10pm. Tube: Piccadilly Circus or Leicester Sq.

INEXPENSIVE

Brown's CONTINENTAL/TRADITIONAL BRITISH   The decor of this popular restaurant is reminiscent of an Edwardian brasserie, with mirrors, dark-wood trim, and cream-colored walls. The staff is attentive, hysterically busy, and high spirited. The most amazing thing about the restaurant is its size. It's a cavernous labyrinth of tables complemented by a bar where (often single) patrons tend to be good-looking, happy-go-lucky, and usually up for a chat. Expect well-prepared cuisine here, hauled out through the stand-up crowds to battered tables and bentwood chairs by an army of well-intentioned European staff. Without ever rising to greatness, mains are well prepared and rather tasty, especially the chargrilled chicken with air-dried ham, melted Taleggio cheese, and a hollandaise sauce, and the salmon with an herby mustard crust. The braised lamb shank is another good dish, served in a beer sauce, and you can order whole lemon sole in a burnt butter sauce. The site of the restaurant was originally conceived in 1787 as a magistrate's court. Today the somber overtones of the court are gone, as the restaurant is usually awash with bubbly theatergoers either headed to or coming from a West End play.

82–84 St. Martins Lane, WC2. © 020/7497-5050. Reservations recommended for groups. 2-course fixed-price pre-theater menu £11 ($21), available 4–6:30pm Mon–Sat; main courses £8.50–£17 ($16–$32). AE, DC, MC, V. Sun–Mon noon–10:30pm; Tues noon–11pm; Wed–Sat noon–11:30pm. Tube: Leicester Sq. or Covent Garden.

Cork & Bottle Wine Bar ★★ (Value INTERNATIONAL Don Hewitson, a connoisseur of fine wines for more than 30 years, presides over this trove of blissful fermentation. The ever-changing wine list features an excellent selection of Beaujolais Crus from Alsace, 30 selections from Australia, 30 champagnes, and a good selection of California labels. If you want something to wash down, the most successful dish is a raised cheese-and-ham pie, with a cream cheese–like filling and crisp well-buttered pastry—not your typical quiche. There's also chicken and apple salad, black pudding, Mediterranean prawns with garlic and asparagus, lamb in ale, and a Thai chicken wings platter.

44–46 Cranbourn St., WC2. © 020/7734-7807. Reservations not accepted after 6:30pm. Fixed-price menu £11–£14 ($21–$27); main courses £8–£13 ($15–$25); glass of wine from £3.50 ($6.65). AE, DC, MC, V. Mon–Sat 11am–midnight; Sun noon–11pm. Tube: Leicester Sq.

The Stockpot (Value CONTINENTAL/TRADITIONAL BRITISH Pound for pound (British pounds, that is), we'd hazard a guess that this cozy little restaurant offers one of the best dining bargains in London. Mains include such familiar favorites as beef Stroganoff or penne with ham and broccoli. You might also opt for the fish cakes with chips and salad or else a vegetable moussaka. Desserts include Jello and ice cream (remember childhood?) or else a rhubarb crumble with vanilla custard. At these prices, the food is hardly refined, but it's filling and satisfying nonetheless. During peak hours, The Stockpot has a share-the-table policy in its two-level dining room.

38 Panton St. (off Haymarket, opposite the Comedy Theatre), SW1. © 020/7839-5142. Reservations accepted for groups for dinner. Main courses £3.40–£5.50 ($6.45–$10); fixed-price 2-course meal £6.50 ($12). No credit cards. Mon–Tues 11:30am–11:30pm; Wed–Sat 11:30am–midnight; Sun noon–11:30pm. Tube: Piccadilly Circus or Leicester Sq.

SOHO

The restaurants of Soho are conveniently located for those rushing to have dinner before an evening at one of the West End theaters.

VERY EXPENSIVE

Spoon ★ AMERICAN Located in the Sanderson Hotel, this is a branch of the Spoon to which master chef Alain Ducasse lures *tout Paris*. Like its Parisian namesake, it features Monsieur Ducasse's "American fusion" cuisine. This is the only place you can go in London to eat a Frenchman's take on that American favorite—macaroni and cheese. Although some menu items seem designed more to shock, much of what is offered here is really good, especially the crab ceviche (crab marinated in lime juice) or the iced tomato soup (great choice) offered at the beginning. Spoon's chefs allow you to compose your own meal or at least pair up ingredients—perhaps a beautiful sole with a crushed lemon confit, or do you prefer it with satay sauce? You decide. You choose from a trio of columns: main course, sauce, and accompanying side dish. We generally find the restaurant ridiculously overpriced but on one visit we reconsidered when the entertainment of the evening arrived. Our fellow diners turned out to be none other than Madonna and her husband, Guy Ritchie.

50 Berners St., W1. © 020/7300-1444. Reservations required. Fixed-price lunch £29 ($55). Main courses £20–£50 ($38–$95). AE, DC, MC, V. Daily noon–3pm; Mon–Sat 6–11pm; Sun noon–2pm and 6–10:30pm. Tube: Oxford Circus.

EXPENSIVE

Alastair Little ⍟ CONTINENTAL/MODERN BRITISH   In an 1830 brick-fronted town house (which supposedly housed John Constable's art studio for a brief period), this informal, cozy restaurant is a pleasant place to enjoy a well-prepared lunch or dinner. Some critics claim that Alastair Little is the best chef in London, but lately he's been buried under the avalanche of new talent. Actually, Little is not often here; he spends a good deal of time at other enterprises. The talented Sue Lewis is usually in charge. Style is modern European with a slant toward Italian. The menu changes daily. Starters are always tantalizing, including the roast pear and Pecorino cheese salad or Tuscan chestnut soup with Capezzena oil. Main dishes show skill and a wise use of market-fresh ingredients, as evoked by such dishes as roast breast and braised leg of pheasant with beet root and roast celeriac or the rump of lamb with artichokes and French beans. Roasted cod comes in a mussel sauce and is quite delightful. For dessert, you can select an array of British cheeses or order such classics as a chocolate and apricot tart with crème fraîche. Ever have olive-oil cake? It's served here with a winter-fruit compote.

49 Frith St., W1. ⍟ **020/7734-5183**. Reservations recommended. Fixed-price 3-course dinner £45 ($86); fixed-price 3-course lunch £35 ($67). AE, DC, MC, V. Mon–Fri noon–3pm; Mon–Sat 6–11:30pm. Tube: Leicester Sq. or Tottenham Court Rd.

Lindsay House ⍟⍟ MODERN BRITISH   Irish-born chef Richard Corrigan is one of our all-time favorites in London. As in an old-fashioned speakeasy, you ring the doorbell for admittance to a Regency town house deep in Soho. Unfolding before you are gilded mirrors and bare wooden floors. The staircase delivers you to one of two floors. Corrigan is one of the most inventive chefs in London, with creative offerings changing daily based on market availability. What inspires Corrigan at the market is what will end up on your plate at night. You might start with smoked eel and foie gras terrine or else crispy frog's legs and watercress. For your main course, expect such delights as loin of rabbit roasted and stuffed with chorizo or else stuffed pigs' trotters with sweetbreads and morels. Desserts are also a pleasant surprise, including Irish apple tart with single malt cream or a lime soufflé with Mascarpone sorbet.

21 Romilly St., W1. ⍟ **020/7439-0450**. Reservations recommended. Lunch main courses £9–£22 ($17–$42); pre-theatre fixed-price menu £27 ($51); 3-course fixed-price dinner £56 ($106). AE, DC, MC, V. Mon–Fri noon–2:30pm; Mon–Sat 6–11pm. Tube: Leicester Sq.

Quo Vadis ⍟ ITALIAN   This hypertrendy restaurant occupies the former apartment house of Communist patriarch Karl Marx, who would never recognize it. It was an Italian restaurant (also called Quo Vadis) from 1926 until the mid-1990s, when its interior was ripped apart and reconfigured into the stylish, postmodern place you'll find today. The stark street-level dining room is a museum-style showcase for dozens of modern paintings by the controversial Damien Hirst and other contemporary artists. But many bypass the restaurant altogether for the upstairs bar, where Hirst has put a severed cow's head and a severed bull's head on display in separate aquariums. Why? They're catalysts to conversation and satirical odes to the destructive effects of Mad Cow Disease.

Quo Vadis is associated with Marco Pierre White, but don't expect to see the temperamental culinary superstar; as executive chef, he functions as only a consultant. Also, don't expect that the harassed and overburdened staff will have the time to pamper you. As for the food? It's appealingly presented and very good, but not nearly as artful or innovative as the setting might lead you to believe. Starters include such lusty fare as eggplant and zucchini fritters or baked potatoes with caviar and sour cream. Authentically flavorful mains feature spaghettini with lobster or grilled sea bass with fresh oranges and olive oil. The grilled Aberdeen Angus steak appears unexpectedly with grilled oysters. For dessert, who else tops vine-ripened white peaches with champagne? Enticing new additions are always cropping up in the chef's repertoire, depending on what's good and fresh in any season.

26–29 Dean St., W1. ✆ 020/7437-9585. Reservations required. Main courses £13–£20 ($25–$38). AE, DC, MC, V. Mon–Fri noon–3pm; Mon–Sat 5:30–11:30pm. Tube: Leicester Sq. or Tottenham Court Rd.

MODERATE

Chuen Cheng Ku ✖ CHINESE   This is one of the finest places in Soho's New China. Taking up several floors, Chuen Cheng Ku has the longest Cantonese menu in town. Specialties of the house are paper-wrapped prawns, rice in lotus leaves, steamed spareribs in black-bean sauce, and shredded pork with cashew nuts—all served in generous portions. Other featured dishes include lobster with ginger and spring onion, sliced duck in chile and black-bean sauce, and Singapore noodles (thin, rich noodles, sometimes mixed with curry and pork, and sometimes with shrimp and red and green pepper). Dim sum is served from 11am to 6pm. We note, however, that the standard of service has slipped over the years.

17 Wardour St., W1. ✆ 020/7734-3281. www.chuenchengku.co.uk. Reservations recommended on weekend afternoons. Main courses £7–£16 ($13–$30); fixed-price menus £9.80–£23 ($19–$44). AE, DC, MC, V. Mon–Sat 11am–11:45pm; Sun 11am–11:15pm. Closed Dec 24–25. Tube: Piccadilly Circus or Leicester Sq.

The Criterion Brasserie ✖ FRENCH/MODERN BRITISH   Designed by Thomas Verity in the 1870s, this palatial neo-Byzantine mirrored marble hall is a glamorous backdrop for a superb cuisine, served under a golden ceiling, with theatrical peacock-blue draperies. The menu is wide ranging, offering everything from Paris brasserie food to "nouvelle-classical," a combination of classic French cooking techniques with some of the lighter, more experimental leanings of modern French cuisine. The food is excellent but falls short of sublime. Start with beef carpaccio in a mustard dressing or else spaghetti with clams and chile, to be followed by such fish as wild sea bass with a shellfish fondue or else roast suckling pig in applesauce.

224 Piccadilly, W1. ✆ 020/7930-0488. Main courses £15–£30 ($29–$57). 2-course fixed-price lunch £15 ($29); 3-course fixed-price lunch £18 ($34). AE, MC, V. Mon–Sat noon–2:30pm, 5:30–11:30pm; Sun noon–3:30pm and 5:30–10:30pm. Tube: Piccadilly Circus.

The Gay Hussar ✖ HUNGARIAN   Is it still the best Hungarian restaurant in the world? That's what some say. We can't agree until we've sampled every Hungarian restaurant in the world, but we're certain Gay Hussar would be near the top. Since 1953, it's been an intimate place with authentic cuisine, a loyal clientele of politicians, and a large international following, especially among visiting Hungarians. You can begin with a chilled wild-cherry soup or mixed Hungarian salami. Gutsy main courses include cabbage stuffed with minced veal and rice, half a perfectly done chicken in mild paprika sauce with cucumber salad and noodles, roast duck with red cabbage and Hungarian-style caraway potatoes, and, of course, veal goulash with egg dumplings. Expect gigantic portions. For dessert, go with either the poppy-seed strudel or the walnut pancakes.

2 Greek St., W1. ✆ 020/7437-0973. www.gayhussar.co.uk. Reservations recommended. Main courses £9.50–£17 ($18–$32); fixed-price 2-course lunch £17 ($32); fixed-price 3-course lunch £19 ($36). AE, DC, MC, V. Mon–Sat 12:15–2:30pm and 5:30–10:45pm. Tube: Tottenham Court Rd.

Hakkasan (Finds) CHINESE   Asian mystique and pastiche are found in this offbeat restaurant in a seedy alley off Tottenham Court Road. This is another London venture created by Alan Yau, who became a city-wide dining legend because of his Wagamama noodle bars. Designer Christian Liaigre created a dining room encapsulated in a lattice wood "cage" evocative of antique Chinese doors. The leather sofas are emblazoned with dragons, and a bar runs the length of the restaurant. Come here for great dim sum and tantalizing cocktails. Feast on such dishes as *har gau* (steamed prawn dumplings) and strips of tender barbecued pork. The spring roll is refreshing with the addition of fried mango and a delicate prawn-and-scallop filling. Steamed scallop *shumai* (dumplings) with *tobiko* caviar are fresh and meltingly soft. Desserts in most of London's Chinese restaurants are hardly memorable, but the offerings here are an exception to that rule, especially the layered banana sponge cake with chocolate cream.

8 Hanway Place. (C) 020/7907-1888. Reservations recommended. Main courses £10–£40 ($19–$76). AE, MC, V. Mon–Fri noon–2:45pm; Mon–Wed and Sun 6–11pm; Sat noon–4pm; Thurs–Sat 6–11:45pm. Tube: Tottenham Court Rd.

Mela (Value) INDIAN   Serious foodies know you'll likely be served some of London's finest Indian cuisine at this address. The *London Evening Standard* named this the best Indian restaurant in Britain in 2004, and it is as good now as it was back then. Expect robust aromas and earthy flavors. Our spiced duck flavored with spring onions, ginger, and coriander evoked some of the best country dining in India. Eggplant came stuffed with a spicy lamb mince and was superb, as was the whole fresh fish of the day in a spicy marinade flavored with saffron and cooked whole in a charcoal oven. Some of the best curries in the city are served here. Tawa cookery (which in India is street food, cooked on a hot plate) is a specialty. At Mela, the fresh meats and other ingredients are cooked straight on a hot plate. Look for the chef's special Tawa dish of the day, perhaps queen prawns cooked with onions and fresh tomatoes. Save room for one of their special desserts.

152–156 Shaftesbury Ave., WC2. (C) 020/7836-8635. www.melarestaurant.co.uk. Reservations required. Main courses £6–£22 ($11–$42); 3-course dinner £37 ($70); 3-course fixed-price meal available before 7pm £11 ($21). AE, MC, V. Mon–Thurs noon–11:30pm; Fri noon–11:45pm; Sat 1–11:45pm; Sun noon–10:30pm. Tube: Tottenham Court Rd. or Leicester Sq.

Rasa Samudra (Value) INDIAN   This outpost offers the best southern Indian cuisine in town, and all the dishes are fish or vegetable based—no meat. While most of London's Indian restaurants specialize in the cuisine of the north, Rasa Samundra features cookery of the southern state of Kerala, focusing on specialties from the sea. Owner Das Sreedharan's mother has trained all the chefs, and the results are delectable. Try *malslam pattichathu* (kingfish cooked in fresh spices, with green chile and coconut paste), *para konju nirachathu* (lobster cooked with black pepper, garlic, and Indian shallots, and served with whole-lemon and beet-root curry), *masala dosa* (paper-thin rice and black-grain pancakes filled with potato and ginger masala), and *moru kachlathu* (green bananas and mangoes cooked in a yogurt sauce with turmeric and onions). Rasa also offers a range of appetizers, side orders, breads, rice, and desserts. Most dishes are at the lower end of the price scale.

5 Charlotte St., W1. (C) 020/7637-0222. www.rasarestaurants.com. Reservations required. Main courses £6.25–£13 ($12–$25); fixed-price dinner £23–£30 ($44–$57). AE, DC, MC, V. Mon–Sat noon–3pm and 6–11pm; Sun 6–11pm. Tube: Tottenham Court Rd.

Satsuma JAPANESE   This funky Japanese canteen is all the rage in London. The clean lines, stark white walls, and long wooden tables suggest an upmarket youth hostel. But patrons come for good food at reasonable prices, and the restaurant is ideal for a pre-theater visit. Your meal comes in a lacquered bento box on a matching tray. Try the chicken teriyaki or fresh chunks of tuna and salmon. The dumplings are excellent, as is the *miso* soup. A specialty is the large bowl of seafood ramen, with noodles swimming in a well-seasoned broth studded with mussels, scallops, and prawns. Tofu steaks are a delight, as are *udon* noodles with wok-fried chicken and fresh vegetables. You can finish with deep-fried tempura ice cream.

56 Wardour St., W1. ℂ 020/7437-8338. Reservations not accepted. Main courses £5–£15 ($9.50–$29). AE, DC, MC, V. Mon–Tues noon–11pm; Wed–Thurs noon–11:30pm; Fri–Sat noon–midnight; Sun noon–10:30pm. Tube: Piccadilly Circus or Leicester Sq.

Shampers CONTINENTAL   This is a favorite of West End wine-bar aficionados. In addition to the street-level wine bar serving snacks, there's a more formal basement-level restaurant. In either venue, you can order such main dishes as grilled calf's liver with bacon, chips, and salad; pan-fried large prawns with ginger, garlic, and chili; and platters of cheeses. Salads are popular, including grilled eggplant salad with tomato, avocado, buffalo mozzarella, and pesto; and spicy chicken salad. The platter of Irish mussels cooked in a cream-and-tarragon sauce is everybody's favorite. The restaurant is no longer closed in the evening, and the wine bar also serves an extensive menu, offering fresh squid, tuna steak, pan-fried tiger prawns, free-range chicken, and other tasty specialties. There is also a special daily menu.

4 Kingly St. (between Carnaby and Regent sts.), W1. ℂ 020/7437-1692. Reservations recommended. Main courses £9–£15 ($17–$29). AE, DC, MC, V. Restaurant Mon–Sat noon–11pm. Wine bar Mon–Sat 11am–11pm. Closed Dec 24–Jan 2. Tube: Oxford Circus or Piccadilly Circus.

Soho Spice INDIAN   This is one of central London's most stylish Indian restaurants, combining a hip atmosphere with the flavors and scents of southern India. You might opt for a drink at the cellar bar before heading to the street-level dining room, decorated in saffron, cardamom, bay, and pepper hues. A staff member dressed in similarly vivid apparel will propose a wide array of choices, including slow-cooked Indian tandoori specials that feature lamb, chicken, fish, or vegetables with combinations of spices. The a la carte menu offers a variety of courses, including *jhinga hara pyaz,* spicy queen prawns with fresh spring onions; and *paneer pasanda,* cottage cheese slices stuffed with spinach and served with almond sauce. The cuisine will satisfy traditionalists but also has a modern flair.

124–126 Wardour St., W1. ℂ 020/7434-0808. Reservations required. Main courses £9–£12 ($17–$23). AE, V. Mon–Tues noon–midnight; Wed–Sat noon–3am; Sun noon–10:30pm. Tube: Tottenham Court Rd.

INEXPENSIVE

Balans MODERN BRITISH   Located on one of London's most gay-friendly streets, Old Compton Street, Balans is the city's best-known gay restaurant and has been since its inauguration in 1993. Some diehard fans take all their meals here. Its extensive hours of service are almost without equal in London. Although the food is deemed "British," it is an eclectic cuisine, borrowing freely from whatever kitchen the chef chooses, from the Far East to America. Daily specials are posted on a large board. For starters, try the smoked duck salad with quail eggs or pan-seared scallops with a cauliflower cheese gratin. Main dish temptations include pumpkin ravioli in a shallot and truffle sauce or swordfish steak with black bean rice and a lime and coriander salsa. Rump of lamb is an especially tasty dish flavored with garlic and rosemary. Balans has a party pub atmosphere and is a good place to meet people.

60 Old Compton St., W1. ⓒ 020/7439-2183. www.balans.co.uk. Reservations recommended. Main courses £9–£18 ($17–$34). AE, MC, V. Mon–Thurs 8am–5am; Fri–Sat 8am–6am; Sun 8am–2am. Tube: Piccadilly Circus or Leicester Sq.

Ed's Easy Diner AMERICAN   This is one of four branches of this popular retro American diner. It's the kind of place Michael J. Fox might have walked into in *Back to the Future*. Featuring 1950s and 1960s rock 'n' roll on the jukebox, a horseshoe-shape counter with the kitchen in the middle, and a staff that fits the theme, the restaurant offers not only good diner staples such as burgers, onion rings, waffles, corned-beef hash, and cheesecake, but also good people-watching, with a broad cross-section of fashion trends on parade around the counter. The milkshakes and malts are popular items, as are the bowls of chili and 5 different types of fries with 5 sauces on the side. Other locations include Piccadilly and Leicester Square.

12 Moor St., W1. ⓒ 020/7434-4439. www.edseasydiner.co.uk. Reservations not accepted. Main courses £5–£10 ($9.50–$19). Sun–Thurs 10am–11pm; Fri–Sat 10am–midnight. Closed Christmas. Tube: Leicester Sq. or Tottenham Court Rd.

Mildreds 🐝 *Finds* VEGETARIAN   Mildreds may sound like a 1940s Joan Crawford movie, but it's one of London's most enduring vegetarian and vegan dining spots. It was vegetarian long before such restaurants became trendy. Jane Muir and Diane Thomas worked in various restaurants together before opening their own place. Today they run a busy, bustling diner with casual, friendly service. Sometimes it's a bit crowded and tables are shared. They do a mean series of delectable stir-fries. The ingredients in their dishes are naturally grown, and they strongly emphasize the best seasonal produce. The menu changes daily but always features an array of homemade soups, casseroles, and salads. Organic wines are served, and portions are very large. Save room for the desserts, especially the tofu cheesecake.

45 Lexington St., W1. ⓒ 020/7494-1634. www.mildreds.co.uk. Reservations not accepted. Main courses £6–£8.25 ($11–$16). No credit cards. Mon–Sat noon–11pm. Tube: Tottenham Court Rd.

Veeraswamy *Value* INDIAN   The oldest Indian restaurant in England, originally established in the 1920s, Veeraswamy has been restyled and rejuvenated and is looking better than ever. Its menu has been redone, and today it serves some of the most affordable fixed-price menus in Central London, the heart of the city. Shunning the standard fare offered in most London-based Indian restaurants, Veeraswamy features authentic, freshly prepared dishes—the kind that would be served in a private Indian home. Try almost anything: spicy oysters, brochette of monkfish, chicken curry with almonds, succulent tandoori chicken, or tender and flavorful lamb curry. One of our favorite dishes is lamb with turnips from Kashmir, flavored with large black cardamoms, powdered fennel, and a red chile powder, giving the dish a savory flavor and a vivid red color.

Victory House, 99 Regent St., W1. ⓒ 020/7734-1401. www.veeraswamy.com. Reservations recommended. Lunch and pre-/post-theater menu Mon–Sat £17 ($32); Sun 3-course menu £20 ($38); lunch and dinner main courses £11–£24 ($21–$46). AE, DC, MC, V. Mon–Fri 12:30–2:15pm and 5:30–10:30pm; Sat 12:30–2:30pm and 5:30–10:30pm; Sun 12:30–2:30pm and 6–10pm. Tube: Piccadilly Circus.

Yauatcha ⭐ ASIAN   This Asian eatery is a showcase for Alan Yau, who won Britain's first Michelin star for his Chinese cooking at London's Hakkasan. This is a more informal dim sum outlet where service, at best, is most casual, and it's so popular you're practically rushed through your meal on a 90-minute time frame to make way for newly arriving patrons. But the food is worth it if you don't mind a slight hassle.

Tips **Après-Theater Dining**

For years, lower-priced menus and a lack of late-night eateries convinced most theatergoers to dine before the show. But the city now accommodates those who prefer dining after the theater. **Quaglino's** (p. 179) is a vast establishment that stays open until 11:30pm or midnight. If a hamburger or steak will do, head for the **Hard Rock Cafe** (p. 176).

Near Piccadilly Circus, you can make it to **Circus** (p. 178) before the last orders go in at midnight, or order from the bar menu until 1:30am. **Balans** (p. 169), which caters to a gay crowd, serves until the wee hours.

The ground floor is a chic teahouse and patisserie, and the restaurant is in the basement. Dim sum, among the finest in London, is served for both lunch and dinner. The roast venison dim sum is spectacular, with a flaky pastry and all butter. The prawn and date dumplings literally melt in your mouth. Visitors from China like to order the sharks' fin consommé. Other notable specialties include har gau—scallops and prawns with fish eggs or a pan-fried bean curd roll with prawns and yellow chives. The Chinese chive dumplings are among the best we've ever tasted. The uniforms of the waiters are by Tim Yip, who won an Oscar for art direction in *Crouching Tiger, Hidden Dragon*.

15 Broadwick St., W1. ℂ 020/7494-8888. Main courses £3–£24 ($5.70–$46). AE, MC, V. Mon–Sat noon–midnight; Sat noon–11pm; Sun noon–10:30pm. Tube: Oxford Circus.

TRAFALGAR SQUARE
MODERATE

The National Dining Rooms TRADITIONAL BRITISH In the National Gallery, this dining choice lies over the foyer of the Sainsbury Wing, providing a panoramic view of fabled Trafalgar Square. The view is more memorable than the cuisine—the location and setting are the chief lures. Classic dishes using market-fresh ingredients go into the starters such as warm watercress mousse with braised pearl onions or smoked mackerel pâté with apple and chicory. Savor such main dishes as monkfish, mullet, and mussel stew or else baked lemon chicken with savoy cabbage and creamed potatoes. The cheese selection from Great Britain is amazing in its variety, everything from traditionally aged Stilton to soft goat's cheese from the Cotswolds. Finish off with one of the freshly baked cakes such as layered chocolate or walnut and banana. There is a cafe offshoot in the basement of the main building, which is a good choice for sandwiches, pastas, soups, and pastries.

In the National Gallery, Trafalgar Sq., WC2. ℂ 020/7747-2525. Reservations not required. Main courses £11–£23 ($21–$44). AE, MC, V. Daily 10am–5:30pm; Wed 10am–8:45pm. Tube: Charing Cross.

The Portrait Restaurant ℛ MODERN BRITISH This rooftop restaurant on the fifth floor of the National Portrait Gallery's Ondaatje Wing is a sought-after dining ticket. Along with the view (Nelson's Column, the London Eye, Big Ben, and the like), you get superb meals. Patrons usually go for lunch, not knowing that dinner is also served on Thursday and Friday nights. All the main courses are filled with flavor. In spring, there's nothing finer than the green English asparagus, and the high quality of the produce really shines through in such dishes as roast breast of guinea fowl with truffles and wild mushrooms or pan-fried filet of Scotch salmon with bacon-and-onion potato cakes. For your pudding, nothing is finer than steamed chestnut and honey pudding with toffee and pecan sauce. Chefs aren't afraid of simple preparations mainly because they are assured of the excellence of their products. The wine list features some organic choices.

In the National Portrait Gallery, Trafalgar Sq., WC2. © 020/7312-2490. Reservations recommended. Main courses £12–£29 ($23–$55). AE, MC, V. Daily 11:45am–2:45pm. Thurs–Fri 5:30pm–8:30pm. Tube: Leicester Sq. or Charing Cross.

MAYFAIR
VERY EXPENSIVE
Gordon Ramsay at Claridge's 𝄞𝄞𝄞 EUROPEAN   Gordon Ramsay is the hottest chef in London today. In addition to his Chelsea restaurant, called Gordon Ramsay (p. 186), he now rules the eatery at staid, traditional Claridge's hotel, legendary since 1860, when Queen Victoria stopped in for tea with the Empress Eugenie. The famed dining room, with its Art Deco decor, still retains many of its original Victorian architectural features, but the cuisine is hardly the same. Victoria most definitely wasn't served an *amuse-bouche* of pumpkin soup dribbled with truffle oil and studded with truffles.

Although the menu changes frequently, a memorable culinary highlight began with such starters as crispy Gloucester pork belly with sautéed langoustines, purée of Savoy cabbage, and quail's eggs. Whoever thought celeriac risotto with toasted pine nuts and Reggiano parmesan could taste so good? Dishes are always inventive, including steamed line-caught sea bass with roasted salsify and vanilla *jus* and braised Cornish turbot with Oscietra caviar and coriander sauce. A rich, meaty dish—perhaps to be appreciated by a budding Henry VIII—is West Country pork cheeks cooked in honey and cloves and served with braising juices. Desserts are always a surprise and always a bit different perhaps from what you've had before—peanut butter parfait with milk mousse and cherry sauce or assiette of pineapple three ways (ravioli, bavarois, and Tatin).

Brook St., W1. © 020/7499-0099. Reservations required as far in advance as possible. Fixed-price lunch £30 ($57); a la carte menu £65 ($124); 6-course fixed-price dinner £75 ($143); early-bird fixed-price menu (5:45–6:30pm) £30 ($57). AE, DC, MC, V. Mon–Fri noon–2:45pm and 5:45–11pm; Sat–Sun noon–3pm; Sat 5:45–11pm; Sun 6–10:30pm. Tube: Bond St.

Le Gavroche 𝄞𝄞𝄞 FRENCH   Although challengers come and go, this luxurious "gastro-temple" remains the number-one choice in London for classical French cuisine. It may have fallen off briefly in the early 1990s, but it's fighting its way back to stellar ranks. There's always something special coming out of the kitchen of Michel Roux, Jr., the son of the chef who founded the restaurant in 1966. The service is faultless, and the ambience formally chic without being stuffy. The menu changes constantly, depending on the fresh produce that's available and the current inspiration of the chef. But it remains classically French, though not of the "essentially old-fashioned bourgeois repertoire" that some critics suggest. Signature dishes honed over years of unswerving practice include the town's grandest cheese soufflé (souffle Suissesse); warm foie gras with crispy, cinnamon-flavored crepes; and Scottish filet of beef with port wine sauce and truffled macaroni. Depending on availability, game is often served as well. A truly Gallic dish is the cassoulet of snails with frog thighs or the mousseline of lobster in a champagne sauce.

43 Upper Brook St., W1. © 020/7408-0881. Fax 020/7491-4387. Reservations required as far in advance as possible. Main courses £27–£40 ($51–$76); fixed-price lunch £48 ($91); *menu exceptional* £95 ($181) without wine, £150 ($285) with wine. AE, MC, V. Mon–Fri noon–2pm and 6:30–11pm; Sat 6:30–11pm. Tube: Marble Arch.

(Finds **The Best Charcuterie in Mayfair**

Born-to-shop aficionados who spend hours trawling Oxford Street, Bond Street, and South Moulton often retreat to **Truc Vert,** 42 North Audley St., W1 (© **020/7491-9988;** www.trucvert.co.uk), for a refreshing respite. This is a combination grocery store and dining room, with rush-seated chairs and tables draped in paper. In an elegantly casual atmosphere, it offers an array of some of the finest charcuterie products in Mayfair, along with cheese, wines, tasty sandwiches, homemade salads, and daily quiches and soups. You can also secure the makings of a picnic here. Make sure to try the chocolate-orange mousse tart. Open Monday to Saturday 7:30am to 9:30pm, Sunday 9:30am to 3pm. Tube: Bond Street.

Menu ✺✺✺ MEDITERRANEAN/MODERN BRITISH   The dining room at the regal Connaught used to be stodgily traditional with sumptuous roasts hauled out on their shiny carving trolley. A bevy of old-school waiters served old-school boys, and British tradition seemed eternal. Well, out with the old and in with the new in the form of Angela Hartnett, who learned her way around the pots and pans as a protégé to Gordon Ramsay, arguably London's most outstanding chef. Hartnett has breathed new life into this grand bastion of cuisine. Even the decor, under designer Nina Campbell, has been lightened and brightened with plush colors, contemporary art, and soft lighting, with crisp white tablecloths placed over black tulip-and-olive skirts.

The starters are ever changing and always memorable, as evoked by the pumpkin tortellini or the roasted Orkney scallops with cauliflower purée and a truffle vinaigrette. Your palate may also be charmed by mains such as leg, saddle, and braised neck of lamb or Anjou pigeon with golden raisins and a caper berry purée. Try also the Cornish Dover sole with sevruga caviar.

The Connaught, 16 Carlos Place, W1. © 020/7592-1222. Reservations essential. 3-course fixed-price lunch and pre-theatre menu £30 ($57); 3-course fixed-price dinner menu £60 ($114); prestige menu £70 ($133). AE, DC, MC, V. Mon–Fri 7–10:30am, Sat–Sun 7–11am; daily noon–2:45pm; Mon–Sat 5:45–11pm; Sun 6–10:30pm. Tube: Green Park.

Mirabelle ✺ FRENCH   From Marlene Dietrich and Noel Coward to Princess Margaret and Aristotle Onassis, to Johnny Depp and the tabloid stars of today, Mirabelle, located in the heart of Mayfair, attracts the rich and famous and the paparazzi who follow them. The interior is Art Deco, with a sexy red-leather floor and a little English garden. On the menu, the chefs remain French classicists. For a starter, try tarte tatin of endive with scallops served with orange butter or else a parfait of foie gras with truffles. The chef takes justifiable pride in such mains as roast venison or grilled sea bass with eggplant caviar. The pastry chef shines with such desserts as prune and Armagnac soufflé or vanilla cream with champagne-poached strawberries.

56 Curzon St., W1. © 020/7499-4636. www.whitestarline.org.uk. Reservations required. Main courses £18–£25 ($34–$48); set lunch £18–£21 ($34–$40). AE, MC, V. Mon–Fri noon–2:30pm; Mon–Sat 6–11:30pm; Sat–Sun noon–3pm; Sun 6–10:30pm. Tube: Green Park.

Nobu ✺✺ JAPANESE/SOUTH AMERICAN   This innovative restaurant, a celebrity haunt, owes much to its founders, actor Robert de Niro and chef Nobu Matsuhisa. The kitchen staff is brilliant and as finely tuned as their New York counterparts. The sushi chefs create gastronomic pyrotechnics. Those on the see-and-be-seen circuit don't seem to mind the high prices that go with these incredibly fresh dishes. Elaborate preparations lead to perfectly balanced flavors. Where else can you find an excellent sea urchin tempura? Salmon tartare with caviar is a brilliant appetizer. Follow with a perfectly done filet of sea bass in a sour bean paste or soft-shell crab rolls. The squid pasta is sublime, as is sukiyaki; the latter dish is incredibly popular and with good reason. Cold sake arrives in a green bamboo pitcher.

In the Metropolitan Hotel, 19 Old Park Lane, W1. ℂ 020/7447-4747. Reservations required one month to the day in advance. Main courses £10–£30 ($19–$57); sushi and sashimi £5–£10 ($9.50–$19) per piece; fixed-price lunch menu £50 ($95); fixed-price dinner menu £70 ($133). AE, DC, MC, V. Mon–Fri noon–2:15pm; Mon–Thurs 6–10:15pm; Fri–Sat 6–11pm; Sat 12:30–2:30pm; Sun 12:30–2:30pm and 6–9:30pm. Tube: Hyde Park Corner.

Sketch CONTINENTAL/MODERN BRITISH   Inaugurated in 2003, this restaurant, tearoom, art gallery, bar, and patisserie became an overnight sensation. Food, art, and music are artfully harmonized. In a converted 18th-century building in Mayfair, Mourad ("Momo") Mazouz, along with a team of chefs and designers, masterminded this fashionable creation. The British press hailed Sketch as a "camp wonderland."

You can come here to dine elegantly but also to bar-hop, as there are a number of venues that, to confuse matters, change their agendas as the day progresses. For example, one section is an art gallery by day and "gastro-brasserie" by night. Whimsical and informal, the Parlour is for light lunches and delectable teas. In the Lecture Room and Library, each dish represents different sensations. The Art Gallery becomes a restaurant and bar at night. The East Bar is a popular late-night rendezvous and The Glade is open for lunches and light snacks.

The menu showcases a cuisine that is both bold and imaginative—and also delicious. For starters, you get not only fresh Tsarskaya oysters, but they come with lemon, shallots, vinegar, and warm rye bread pudding. The fresh pumpkin soup is always invigorating. Well-flavored, tender lamb is served with a beet-root cake, white cabbage, and dried fruits, and the roasted and caramelized baby tuna comes with steamed zucchini, red pepper, celery leaves, and toasted sesame seeds.

9 Conduit St., W1. ℂ 087/0777-4488. www.sketch.uk.com. Reservations essential for dining. Main courses £15–£30 ($29–$57). Snacks and small meals £8–£24 ($15–$46). Lecture Room and Library 3-course fixed-price dinner £35 ($67); 7-course vegetarian fixed-price dinner £65 ($124). Art Gallery Mon–Sat 7pm–2am (last food order 11pm Mon–Wed and 1am Thurs–Sat); Lecture Room and Library Tues–Fri noon–2:30pm and Tues–Sat 6:30–10:30pm. Parlour Mon–Fri 8am–9pm, Sat 10am–9pm; The Glade Mon–Sat noon–3pm; East Bar daily 6:30pm–2am. AE, MC, V. Tube: Oxford Circus.

The Square FRENCH   Hip, chic, casual, sleek, and modern, The Square still doesn't scare Le Gavroche as a competitor for first place on London's dining circuit, but it is certainly a restaurant to visit on a serious gastronomic tour of London. Chef Philip Howard delivers the goods at this excellent restaurant. You get creative, personalized cuisine in a cosseting atmosphere with abstract modern art on the walls. The chef has a magic touch, with such concoctions as a starter of terrine of partridge with smoked foie gras and pear with cider jelly or else a lasagna of Cornish crab with a champagne foam. For a main course we urge you to try the peppered aged rib-eye of Ayrshire beef with smoked shallots, Tuscan snails, and a red wine sauce, or else the roast saddle of hare with port-glazed endive. The fish dishes such as steamed turbot with buttered langoustine claws and poached oysters is always fresh, and Bresse pigeon is as good as it is in its hometown in France. Desserts are exceedingly rich, especially the raisin-and-Guinness soufflé with black velvet ice cream, and the Brillat-Savarin cheesecake with orange and cardamon.

6–10 Bruton St., W1. ℂ 020/7495-7100. Reservations required. Fixed-price lunch £25–£30 ($48–$57); dinner £65 ($124). AE, DC, MC, V. Mon–Fri noon–3pm; Mon–Sat 6:30–10:45pm; Sun 6:30–10pm. Tube: Bond St. or Green Park.

EXPENSIVE

Greenhouse EUROPEAN   Head chef Antonin Bonnet is inspired, producing first-class dishes without destroying the natural flavor of his ingredients. Regrettably, all this good food comes at a price, and the Greenhouse is no longer the moderate restaurant it used to be but rather an expensive one.

Peerless technique goes into such starters as Cornish crab with coconut dressing, or shellfish flavored with kaffair lime leaves. Fine ingredients are also reflected in the main dishes such as Limousin filet of beef flavored with mustard and served with fondant potatoes. The Shetland organic cod appears with hummus, and a Bresse mallard duckling comes with spicy endives and an orange marmalade. For many diners, cheese is their dessert specialty; it's one of the largest selections in London. You can order yummy confections as well. The menu is backed up by a very large wine list with some 500 selections.

27A Hays Mews, W1. ℂ 020/7499-3331. www.greenhouserestaurant.co.uk. Reservations required. 3-course fixed-price dinner £60 ($114); fixed-price lunch £32 ($61). AE, DC, MC, V. Mon–Fri noon–2:30pm; Mon–Sat 6:45–11pm. Closed Christmas and bank holidays. Tube: Green Park.

Maze 🐸🐸 INTERNATIONAL   Gordon Ramsay is London's leading chef. Our nomination for most promising chef is Jason Atherton, a one-time Ramsay protégé. Atherton learned his master's secrets and has plenty of creative culinary imagination of his own. One reviewer claimed Atherton combined "Spain's progressive technique with Gallic voluptuousness and a dash of British wit." And so he does. His combinations may sound a bit bizarre, but the resulting flavors and ingredients taste sublime.

He's a chef who appeals to "grazers" (that is, those diners who enjoy a series of small plates or tapas). The changing seasons are reflected by what rests on your plate. In a New York–inspired interior by the American architect David Rockwell, Atherton enthralls with dish after dish. Take his starters. Go for the Orkney scallops roasted with spices and served with a peppered golden raisin purée or else the foie gras marinated in Pinot Noir. For a main, we'd recommend the roasted partridge with plum preserves or the roast Scottish filet of beef with Landes foie gras and an ox cheek cottage pie.

We kid you not about one of the desserts: a peanut butter and cherry jam sandwich. One of our party found it "to die for," a favorable reaction. You might opt instead for the mango parfait with orange and anise jelly along with coriander shoots.

10–13 Grosvenor Sq., W1. ℂ 020/7107-0000. Reservations required. Fixed-price lunch £29–£43 ($55–$82); main dishes (small platters) £8–£30 ($15–$57). AE, DC, MC, V. Daily noon–2:30pm and 6–10:30pm. Tube: Bond St.

Nahm 🐸🐸 THAI   The cookery here is extraordinary, and we like the fact that the chef makes few, if any, concessions to Western palates. David Thompson even purchases rare books on Thai cookery and re-creates dishes that may have been lost for centuries. Take, for example, the salmon roe and fresh seafood mixed with spices and served in a fresh betel leaf, all of it garnished with watermelon. It sounds off-putting but is actually a taste sensation. The chef is against the "fusion fad," even though he's a Westerner himself (Australian), and is instead dedicated to the tenets of Thai cuisine. He's considered such an expert that even some of the citadels of haute Thai cuisine in Thailand seek his advice. Try the aromatic curry of beef with cucumber relish. For dessert, sample the addictive white sticky rice with mango topped with a coconut cream sauce.

In the Halkin Hotel, Halkin St., SW1. ℭ **020/7333-1234.** Reservations recommended. Main courses £12–£23 ($23–$44); fixed-price lunch £20–£26 ($38–$49); 3-course fixed-price dinner £50 ($95). AE, DC, MC, V. Mon–Fri noon–2:30pm and 7–11pm; Sat 7–11pm; Sun 7–10pm. Tube: Hyde Park Corner.

Tamarind ⍟ INDIAN   In favor with critics as well as the lunchtime business crowd, Tamarind is the most popular Indian restaurant in Mayfair. The basement dining room has gold pillars and a tandoor window so you can watch the chefs pull their flavorful dishes from the ovens. Chef Alfred Prasad leads a culinary brigade from Delhi that maintains the style of cooking they knew at home. The team selects the best, freshest ingredients in the markets each day. The kitchen prides itself on nouvelle dishes but also excels at traditional Indian fare. The monkfish marinated in saffron and yogurt is delectable, and the mixed kebab platter, all cooked in a charcoal-fired tandoor, is extraordinary—these chefs are the kings of kebabs. Your best bet for a curry? Opt for the prawns in a five-spice mixture. Vegetarians will find delicious refuge here, especially if they go for the *dal Bukhari*, a black-lentil specialty of northwest India.

20 Queen St., W1. ℭ **020/7629-3561.** Reservations required. Main courses £13–£28 ($25–$53); fixed-price dinner menu £45–£65 ($86–$124); 3-course fixed-price lunch £20 ($38); pre-theater menu £19 ($36). AE, DC, DISC, MC, V. Sun–Fri noon–2:45pm; Mon–Sat 6–11:30pm; Sun 6:30–10:30pm. Tube: Green Park.

MODERATE

Hard Rock Cafe ⍟*Kids* AMERICAN   This is the original Hard Rock, and it's served more than 12 million people since it opened in 1971. Just like every other Hard Rock Cafe, there's usually a line (or, in this case, a queue) of people waiting to get in, plus an equally long line of people buying T-shirts. You'll find better-than-average burgers and a good selection of beers here. The collection of rock memorabilia at the original is a far sight better than the collections at later facsimiles. The restaurant also accepts U.S. dollars.

150 Old Park Lane, W1. ℭ **020/7514-1700.** www.hardrock.com. Reservations not accepted. Main courses £6–£15 ($11–$29). AE, DC, MC, V. Sun–Thurs 11:30am–12:30am; Fri–Sat 11:30am–1am. Closed Dec 25–26. Tube: Green Park or Hyde Park Corner.

"hush" CONTINENTAL   This is a charming, trendy oasis for attractive locals— and the food isn't bad, either. Located next to a number of outdoor restaurants in a cul-de-sac, "hush" is the hippest of the lot. And it offers some of London's best al fresco dining. On the ground floor expect a chic decor with a combination of light-wood tables and limestone floors, with touches of warm "spice" colors. The well-chosen menu features traditional brasserie food—in this case, such items as smoked haddock fish cakes, lobster and chips with garlic butter, and most definitely the "hush" hamburger which some critics have hailed as "the best in London." Start with Andalusian gazpacho or a meze platter (a selection of Greek hors d'oeuvres), and then try the sautéed calf's liver or Toulouse sausages with creamed potatoes and a mustard sauce. The desserts are hard to resist, especially the champagne jelly with mixed berries or the lemon cheesecake with raspberries.

8 Lancaster Court, Brook St., W1. ℭ **020/7659-1511.** Reservations recommended. Main courses £11–£24 ($21–$46); fixed-price menus £35–£40 ($67–$76). AE, DC, MC, V. Bar daily 11am–11pm; brasserie daily 7am–11pm; restaurant noon–2pm and 6:30pm–midnight. Tube: Bond St.

Langan's Brasserie FRENCH/TRADITIONAL BRITISH   In its heyday in the early 1980s, this was one of the hippest restaurants in London, and the upscale brasserie still welcomes an average of 700 diners a day. The 1976 brainchild of actor Michael Caine and chef Richard Shepherd, Langan's sprawls over two noisy floors filled with potted plants and ceiling fans that create a 1930s feel. The menu is "mostly English with a French influence," and includes spinach soufflé with anchovy sauce, quail eggs in a pastry case served with a sautéed hash of mushrooms and hollandaise sauce, and prawn salad with Marie-Rose sauce. There's also a selection of English pub fare, including bangers and mash, and fish and chips. The dessert menu is a journey into nostalgia: bread-and-butter pudding, treacle tart with custard, apple pie with clotted cream . . . wait, how did mango sorbet slip in here?

Stratton St., W1. ℂ 020/7491-8822. www.langansrestaurants.co.uk. Reservations recommended. Main courses £14–£21 ($27–$40). AE, DC, MC, V. Mon–Fri 12:15–11:45pm; Sat 7pm–midnight. Tube: Green Park.

Momo MOROCCAN/NORTH AFRICAN   You'll be greeted here by a friendly, casual staff member, and the setting is like Marrakesh, with stucco walls, a wood-and-stone floor, patterned wood window shades, burning candles, and banquettes. You can fill up on the freshly baked bread, along with appetizers such as garlicky marinated olives and pickled carrots spiced with pepper and cumin—all gifts from the chef. Other appetizers are also tantalizing, especially the *briouat:* paper-thin and very crisp triangular packets of puffed pastry filled with saffron-flavored chicken and other treats. One of the chef's specialties is *pastilla au pigeon,* a traditional poultry pie with almonds. Many diners visit for the *couscous maison,* among the best in London. Served in a decorative pot, this aromatic dish of raisins, meats (including merguez sausage), chicken, lamb, and chickpeas is given added flavor with *marissa,* a powerful hot sauce from the Middle East. There is also a tearoom and a bazaar based on a Moroccan souk, plus a terrace in summer. The on-site Kemia Bar serves Arabic tapas—called Kemia—for £4 to £6 ($7.60–$11) per dish.

25 Heddon St., W1. ℂ 020/7434-4040. www.momoresto.com. Reservations required. Main courses £15–£20 ($29–$38); fixed-price lunch £11–£16 ($21–$30). AE, DC, MC, V. Mon–Sat noon–2:30pm and 6:30–11:30pm; Sun 6:30–11pm. Tube: Piccadilly Circus or Oxford Circus.

Zen Central CANTONESE/INDIAN/SZECHUAN   Somehow, movie stars always seem to know the best places to dine in a foreign city. So when we heard that Eddie Murphy and Tom Cruise were heading here, we followed. We didn't spot any stars, but we found a designer-chic Mayfair restaurant with a cool, dignified black-and-white decor. Mirrors cover much of the interior—maybe that's why movie stars like it?

Though there is little catering to conventional Western palates, the cuisine is first-rate and served by a competent staff. Start with the soft-shell crabs cooked in a crust of salt. The steamed sea bass is perfectly cooked and served with a black bean sauce. Pork chops with lemon grass have a Thai flavor, and the baked lobster with crushed roast garlic and slivers of tangerine peel is worth a trip from anywhere. The chef's braised fish cheeks, sharks' fins, and bird's nest soup serve up flavors enjoyed in China. Vegetarian meals are also available, and most dishes are at the lower end of the price scale.

20 Queen St., W1. ℂ 020/7629-8103. Reservations recommended. Fixed-price menus £28–£42 ($53–$80); main courses £11–£17 ($21–$32). Daily 12:15–11:15pm.

INEXPENSIVE

Leon 🌟 *Value* MEDITERRANEAN   Its biggest fans call it "gourmet fast food." While gourmet it is not, this is a great place to eat without being rushed during a day of shopping on Oxford Street. Plus, it does what its nearby competitors don't do: It produces fresh, wholesome food at affordable prices. Everything is freshly cooked, so certain dishes may be variable, but we find ourselves returning in spite of a flaw here and there. Everything on the menu is fresh, often organic. The freshly made salads, chicken nuggets (made with succulent breast meat and doused in a creamy yogurt and garlic sauce), and hearty stews are good. Even the chili con carne is different. It's a bowl of spicy, tender minced beef with black kidney beans and is served with a fluffy organic brown rice speckled with pumpkin, sunflower, and sesame seeds, and accompanied by a tasty cabbage and beet root slaw. Your drink of choice might be a ginger and carrot juice. Save room for the chocolate brownie, just like mama used to make. The brownie is "zinged" up with orange zest and swaddled in sinful scoops of ice cream made from Jersey cream. Leon is also the best place in the area for breakfast—try the organic porridge.

35 Great Marlborough St., W1. ℂ 020/7437-5280. Reservations not required. Breakfast from £4.50 ($8.55). Main courses £4.30–£6.50 ($8.15–$12). AE, MC, V. Mon–Fri 8am–10:30pm; Sat 9:30am–10:30pm; Sun 10:30am–6:30pm. Tube: Oxford Circus.

Suze PACIFIC RIM   This wine bar lies between Upper Brook Street and Oxford Street. The owners attach equal importance to their food and to their impressive wine list (some wines are sold by the glass). On the ground floor, you can enjoy fine wines along with a well-chosen selection of bar food—the mezzanine features more formal dining and a full menu. Upon arrival, a basket of homemade bread, along with olives, goat cheese, salami, and roasted peppers, is placed before you. The menu has been upgraded and made more sophisticated and appealing. Begin perhaps with the timbale of plum tomato and peppercorn mousse with an avocado salad or else New Zealand green shell mussels with lime leaf, coriander, and ginger broth. For a main we'd suggest fresh Australian fish with chips and a salad or New Zealand lamb filet with a vegetable medley. Dessert delights include a rhubarb pannacotta with Australian rosella plum syrup.

41 N. Audley St., W1. ℂ 020/7491-3237. Reservations recommended. Main courses £10–£18 ($19–$34). AE, MC, V. Mon–Sat noon–11pm. Tube: Bond St.

ST. JAMES'S
MODERATE

Circus *(Value)* INTERNATIONAL/MODERN BRITISH   During pre- and post-theater hours this place buzzes with London foodies anxious to sample the wares of chef Richard Lee. A minimalist haven for power design and eating in the very heart of London, this restaurant took over the ground floor and basement of what used to be the Granada Television building at the corner of Golden Square and Beak Street. The place evokes a London version of a Left Bank Parisian brasserie. Appetizers include such classics as French onion soup with Gruyère, and mussels marinière with french fries. One of our all-time favorite dishes here is a red onion tart with Roquefort and walnuts. Chicken is marinated and roasted with rosemary and lemon, and the grilled onglet steak with pan-fried shallots is one of the tastiest cuts of beef you are likely to sample. The rum baba with poached apricot will make your day.

1 Upper James St., W1. ℂ 020/7534-4000. Reservations required. Main courses £10–£20 ($19–$38); fixed-price menus £22 ($42). AE, DC, MC, V. Daily noon–3pm, Mon–Sat 6pm–midnight; bar menu daily 5.30pm–3am. Tube: Piccadilly Circus.

Greens Restaurant & Oyster Bar INTERNATIONAL/SEAFOOD/TRADITIONAL BRITISH   Critics say it's a triumph of tradition over taste, but as far as seafood in London goes, this is a tried-and-true favorite, thanks to an excellent menu with moderately priced dishes, a central location, and a charming staff. This place has a cluttered entrance leading to a crowded bar where you can sip fine wines and, from September to April, enjoy oysters. The oyster bar is run by Simon Parker-Bowles, Camilla's ex-brother-in-law. In the faux-Dickensian dining room, you can choose from a long menu of fresh seafood dishes, which changes monthly depending on what is in season. Starters are vibrant, yet earthy fare, including Dorset crab salad, potted shrimp with wholemeal toast, and pan-fried foie gras with apple purée. The chefs are at the top of their form in turning out such mains as seafood platters, filet of halibut with a mussel veloute, or grilled Dover sole with hollandaise sauce. Meat dishes are also superb, including rump of lamb with roast garlic polenta or steak tartare. To finish, opt for the gingerbread and butter pudding or a rich chocolate and cherry trifle.

36 Duke St., St. James's, SW1. © 020/7930-4566. www.greens.org.uk. Reservations required. Main courses £13–£43 ($25–$82); most dishes are moderately priced. AE, DC, MC, V. Mon–Sat 11:30am–3pm and 5:30–11pm, Sun noon–3pm and 5:30–9pm (closed Sun May–Aug). Tube: Green Park.

Quaglino's ⓡ CONTINENTAL   Come here for fun, not culinary subtlety and finesse. In 1993, noted restaurateur and designer Sir Terence Conran brought this restaurant—first established in 1929 by Giovanni Quaglino—into the postmodern age with a vital new decor. Menu items have been criticized for their quick preparation and standard format, but considering that on some nights up to 800 people show up, the marvel is that this place functions as well as it does. That's not to say there isn't an occasional delay. The menu changes often, but your choice of an appetizer might include wild mushroom and truffle soup or else goat's cheese tart with caramelized onions. You can settle for an old favorite for a main dish—haddock and chips—or else go for the whole roasted sea bass with braised fennel. Their oyster selection is one of the best in Central London. Although some diners shy away from organ meats these days, not the English who still order calf's liver with bacon. Desserts are mostly old favorites such as apple and blackberry crumble or sticky toffee pudding with walnut ice cream. *Note:* A mezzanine with bar features live jazz every night and Sunday at lunch.

16 Bury St., SW1. © 020/7930-6767. Reservations recommended. Main courses £11–£32 ($21–$61); fixed-price menu (available only for lunch and pre-dinner theater from 5:30–6:30pm) 2 courses £17 ($32), 3 courses £19 ($36). AE, DC, MC, V. Daily noon–3pm; Mon–Thurs 5:30–midnight; Fri–Sat 5:30pm–1am; Sun 5:30–11pm. Tube: Green Park.

The Wolseley ⓡⓡ CONTINENTAL   Two of London's top restaurateurs, Jeremy King and Chris Corbin, formerly of The Ivy, offer one of the finest and most serviceable restaurants in London. With its vaulted ceilings and pillars, polished marble, wrought-iron chandeliers, and Art Deco interior, The Wolseley recalls a Viennese cafe, but for much of the past century it was a bank and later an automobile showroom. Now it's the idyllic spot for afternoon tea (second only to the Palm Court of the Ritz Hotel). We often duck out of our hotel for breakfast here (served from 7am), ordering such old favorites as fried duck eggs with Ayrshire bacon or smoked fish cakes with poached eggs. There is an all-day menu offering light fare. For dinner, the menu grows more elaborate, including such dishes as Weiner Holstein with fried egg and anchovies, grilled lobster with butter, and even roast Landaise chicken with Lyonnaise potatoes. A specialty is the spit-roasted suckling pig with apple sauce. Desserts range from a baked vanilla cheesecake to *coupes*.

160 Piccadilly, St. James's, W1. © 020/7499-6996. www.thewolseley.com. Reservations required. Main courses £9–£22 ($17–$42); afternoon tea £7.75–£19 ($15–$36); breakfast £2.50–£12 ($4.75–$23). AE, DC, MC, V. Mon–Fri 7am–midnight; Sat 8am–midnight; Sun 8am–11pm. Tube: Green Park.

6 Westminster & Victoria

EXPENSIVE

Shepherd's TRADITIONAL BRITISH   Some observers claim that many of the inner workings of the British government operate from the precincts of this conservative, likable restaurant. Set in the shadow of Big Ben, it enjoys a regular clientele of barristers, members of Parliament, and their constituents from far-flung districts. Don't imagine that the intrigue occurs only at lunchtime; evenings seem just as ripe an hour for negotiations, particularly over the restaurant's roast rib of Scottish beef served with (what else?) Yorkshire pudding. So synchronized is this place to the goings-on at Parliament that a Division Bell rings in the dining room, calling MPs back to the House of Commons when it's time to vote. Even the decor is designed to make them feel at home, with leather banquettes, sober 19th-century accessories, and a worthy collection of European portraits and landscapes.

The menu reflects years of British culinary tradition, and dishes are prepared intelligently, with fresh ingredients. In addition to the classic roast, dishes include a cream-based mussel stew, hot salmon and potato salad with dill dressing, salmon and prawn fish cakes in spinach sauce, roast leg of lamb with mint sauce, wild rabbit, marinated venison with braised red cabbage in juniper sauce, and the English version of crème brûlée, known as "burnt Cambridge cream."

Marsham Court, Marsham St. (at the corner of Page St.), SW1. © 020/7834-9552. Reservations recommended. Fixed-price menu 2 courses £29 ($55), 3 courses £33 ($63). AE, DC, MC, V. Mon–Fri 12:15pm–2:45pm and 6:30–11pm (last order at 11pm). Tube: Pimlico or St. James.

MODERATE

Rex Whistler ★★ *Value* MODERN BRITISH   This restaurant, located in the Tate Britain art museum, is particularly attractive to wine fanciers. It offers what may be the best bargains for superior wines anywhere in Britain. Bordeaux and burgundies are in abundance, and the management keeps the markup between 40% and 65%, rather than the 100% to 200% added in most restaurants. In fact, the prices here are lower than they are in most wine shops. Wine begins at £15 ($29) per bottle, or £4 ($7.60) per glass. Oenophiles frequently come for lunch. The restaurant offers an English menu that changes about every month. Dishes might include pheasant casserole, pan-fried skate with black butter and capers, and vegetarian selections. One critic found the staff and diners as traditional "as a Gainsborough landscape." Access to the restaurant is through the museum's main entrance on Millbank.

Millbank, SW1. © 020/7887-8825. Reservations recommended. Main courses £15 ($29), breakfast from £4.75 ($9.05), afternoon tea £6.95 ($13). AE, DC, MC, V. Sat–Sun 10–11:30am; daily 11:30am–3pm; daily 3:30–5pm for afternoon tea. Tube: Pimlico. Bus: 77 or 88.

INEXPENSIVE

Jenny Lo's Teahouse CANTONESE/SZECHUAN   London's noodle dives don't get much better than this. The late Ken Lo, whose Memories of China once offered the best Chinese dining in London and whose grandfather was the Chinese ambassador to the Court of St. James, made his reputation as a cookbook author. He passed many of his culinary secrets on to his daughter Jenny. Belgravia matrons and young professionals come here for perfectly prepared, reasonably priced fare. Ken Lo cookbooks contribute to the dining room decor of black refectory tables set with paper napkins and chopsticks. Opt for such fare as a vermicelli rice noodle dish (a large plate

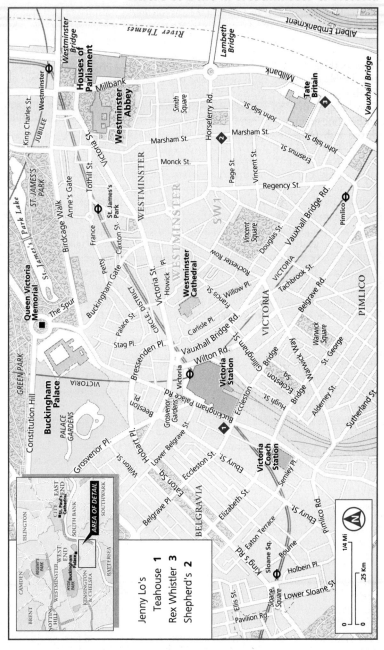

Jenny Lo's
Teahouse **1**
Rex Whistler **3**
Shepherd's **2**

of noodles topped with grilled chicken breast and Chinese mushrooms) or white noodles with minced pork. Rounding out the menu are stuffed Peking dumplings, chile-garnished spicy prawns, and wonton soup with slithery dumplings. The black-bean-seafood noodle dish is a delight, as is the chile beef soup.

14 Eccleston St., SW1 9LT. ℂ 020/7259-0399. Reservations not accepted. Main courses £6.50–£8 ($12–$15). No credit cards. Mon–Fri noon–3pm; Mon–Sat 6–10pm. Tube: Victoria Station.

7 Knightsbridge to South Kensington

KNIGHTSBRIDGE
VERY EXPENSIVE

Petrus ✺✺ FRENCH   Clubby and not at all stuffy, this is the domain of chef Marcus Wareing, a former boxer from Lancashire. The restaurant serves nouvelle French food in the grand tradition of Wareing's mentor (and London's hottest chef), Gordon Ramsay. You'll find excellent food prepared with technical precision and a touch of whimsy, served in a sleek, opulent setting. The chef's six-course tasting menu is the best way to appreciate Wareing's culinary ambitiousness. You'll be dazzled by such starters as Scottish scallops with orange-flavored carrots or roasted quail with an onion fondant. We've been delighted with the mains, including slow-poached wild sea bass with chanterelles, and roasted loin of lamb flavored with saffron and cumin. Desserts are sublime, especially the white chocolate mousse with mango salad and a passion-fruit sorbet or the peanut parfait with a Valrhona chocolate mousse.

The Berkeley Hotel, Wilton Place, SW1. ℂ 020/7235-1200. Reservations required. Fixed-price 3-course lunch menu £30 ($57), fixed-price 3-course dinner menu £60 ($114), 8-course tasting menu £80 ($152). AE, MC, V. Mon–Fri noon–2:30pm; Mon–Sat 6–11pm. Tube: Hyde Park Corner or Knightsbridge.

Zafferano ✺✺ ITALIAN   There's something honest and satisfying about this restaurant, where decor consists of little more than ochre-colored walls, immaculate linens, and a bevy of diligent staff members. A quick review of past clients includes Margaret Thatcher, Richard Gere, Princess Margaret, and Eric Clapton. The modernized interpretation of Italian cuisine features such dishes as ravioli of pheasant with black truffles, wild pigeon with garlic purée, sea bream with spinach and balsamic vinegar, and monkfish with almonds. Other choice dishes include linguine with lobster and fresh tomatoes or a crayfish risotto. The owners pride themselves on one of the most esoteric and well-rounded collections of Italian wine in London: You'll find as many as 20 different vintages each of Brunello and Barolo and about a dozen vintages of Sassecaia.

15 Lowndes St., SW1. ℂ 020/7235-5800. www.zafferanorestaurant.com. Reservations required. Main courses £15–£40 ($27–$72). Set-price lunch menu £26–£35 ($49–$67), set-price dinner menu £30–£50 ($57–$95). AE, MC, V. Mon–Fri noon–2:30pm; Sat–Sun 12:30–3pm; daily 7–11pm (until 10:30pm on Sun). Tube: Knightsbridge.

EXPENSIVE

Amaya ✺ INDIAN   This chic restaurant, a hot dining ticket, is said to have introduced the "grazing" concept to Indian food. Dishes are shared, hopefully with a party of friends, so that you can pick and choose at random. This is no mere curry house but an ambitious restaurant with skilled chefs standing over grills and tandoor ovens in the eye-catching open kitchen. After devouring the rock oysters in a ginger-studded coconut sauce, we knew we were in for a special meal—and we were right. Our table shared grilled baby eggplant sprinkled with mango powder. Chicken Tikka is one of the signature dishes, the lamb chops are fork tender, and the lobster beautifully spiced.

Vegetarians delight in the tandoor-cooked broccoli in a yogurt sauce. One of our favorites was the artichoke biryani baked in a pastry-sealed pot. For dessert, try the fresh pomegranate granite which is sugar-free.

Halkin Arcade, Motcomb St., SW1. ℂ 020/7823-1166. Reservations required. Main courses £9.50–£28 ($18–$53). AE, DC, MC, V. Mon–Fri 12:30–2:15pm; Sat 12:30–2:30pm; Sun 12:45–2:45pm; Mon–Sat 6:30–11pm; Sun 6:30–10:15pm. Tube: Knightsbridge.

MODERATE

Black & Blue Ⓖ STEAK The atmosphere is marvelously informal, the prices affordable, and the steaks of high quality, each from a traditionally reared, grass-fed Scottish cow. Take your pick—Scottish sirloin, rib-eye, T-bone. We especially like the *côte de boeuf,* a hefty rib of beef for two to share. The sauces served with the steaks are divine. There are also burgers, chargrilled chicken, and fish dishes on the changing menu, even freshly made salads and platters for the vegetarian.

215–217 Kensington Church St., W8. Reservations required. Main courses £7.50–£15 ($14–$29). MC, V. Mon–Thurs noon–11pm; Fri–Sat noon–11:30pm. Tube: Notting Hill Gate.

The Collection Ⓖ INTERNATIONAL/MODERN BRITISH   This is a temple to voyeurism and the vanities, catering to the aesthetics and preoccupations of the fashion industry. It occupies an echoing warehouse; the only access is by a 9m (30-ft.) catwalk that feels like it should have couture models striding along it. Yummy menu items include appetizers like Thai spiced chicken and coconut soup, and artichoke hearts salad with fresh fennel and Pecorino cheese, followed by such mains as grilled tiger prawns in coriander oil with couscous, and honey-roasted duck with Asian pear and bok choi. You might also order the grilled swordfish with pickled Asian vegetables, followed by such desserts as banana tarte tatin, and English strawberries with mascarpone. Don't overlook this place as a stop on your after-dark bar-hop.

264 Brompton Rd., SW3. ℂ 020/7225-1212. www.the-collection.co.uk. Reservations recommended. Main courses £11–£25 ($21–$48), early-dinner 3-course menu Mon–Fri 6–7:15pm £18 ($34). AE, MC, V. Mon–Sat 6–11:30pm. Tube: South Kensington.

Drones Ⓖ CONTINENTAL   Britain's wonder chef, Marco Pierre White, took this once-famous but stale restaurant and has turned it once again into a chic dining venue, decorated with black-and-white photographs of celebrities lining the wall. Redesigned by David Collins, it is now referred to as "the Ivy of Belgravia." The food and Art Deco ambience are delightful, as is the staff. Food is fresh and delicately prepared, including such favorites as cauliflower cream soup with truffles and sea scallops, and smoked haddock and rice pudding. All the delectable meat and fish dishes are prepared with consummate care and served with a certain finesse. Always expect some unusual flavor combination, such as oxtail *en daube* with a rutabaga purée and a bourguignon garnish. For dessert, a summer specialty is gelée of red fruits with a raspberry syrup drizzle.

1 Pont St., SW1. ℂ 020/7235-9555. Reservations required. Main courses £14–£22 ($27–$42), 2-course fixed-price menu £15 ($29), 3-course fixed-price menu £18 ($34). Mon–Sat noon–2:30pm; Sun noon–4pm; Mon–Sat 6–11pm. Tube: Knightsbridge.

INEXPENSIVE

Le Metro INTERNATIONAL   Located just around the corner from Harrods, Le Metro draws a fashionable crowd to its basement precincts. The place serves good, solid, reliable food prepared with flair. The menu changes frequently. You might begin with the homemade soup of the day with freshly baked bread or the twice-baked cheese

Where to Dine from Knightsbridge to South Kensington

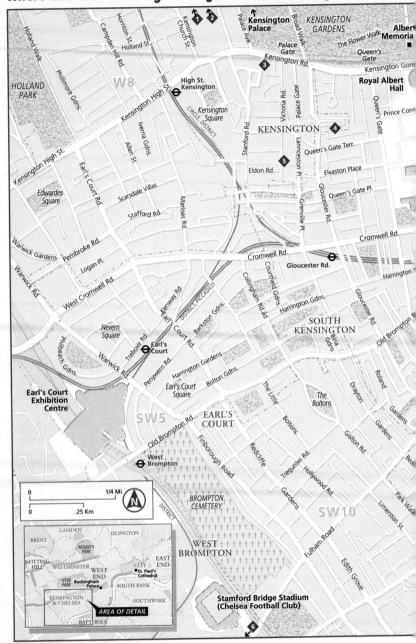

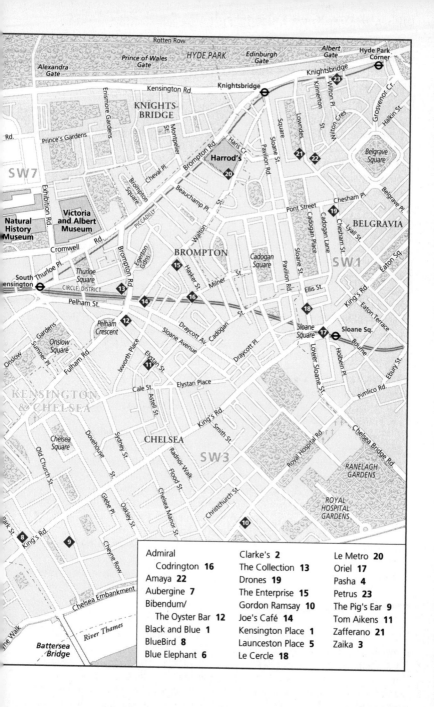

Admiral Codrington **16**	Clarke's **2**	Le Metro **20**
Amaya **22**	The Collection **13**	Oriel **17**
Aubergine **7**	Drones **19**	Pasha **4**
Bibendum/ The Oyster Bar **12**	The Enterprise **15**	Petrus **23**
	Gordon Ramsay **10**	The Pig's Ear **9**
Black and Blue **1**	Joe's Café **14**	Tom Aikens **11**
BlueBird **8**	Kensington Place **1**	Zafferano **21**
Blue Elephant **6**	Launceston Place **5**	Zaika **3**
	Le Cercle **18**	

soufflé with an arugula salad. For a main, opt for such dishes as salmon fish cakes with horseradish mayonnaise or pork, leek, and herb sausages with red onion gravy.

28 Basil St., SW3. ℂ 020/7589-6286. Main courses £7.50–£10 ($14–$19). AE, DC, MC, V. Mon–Sat 7am–11pm; Sun 8am–4pm. Tube: Knightsbridge.

CHELSEA
VERY EXPENSIVE

Aubergine ⭐⭐ FRENCH Aubergine (French for eggplant) is luring savvy diners down to the lower reaches of Chelsea, where chef William Drabble took over from the renowned Gordon Ramsay. Although popular with celebrities, the restaurant remains unpretentious and refuses to pander to the whims of the rich and famous. (Madonna was once refused a late-night booking!)

Every dish is satisfyingly flavorsome, from warm salad of truffled vegetables with asparagus purée to roasted monkfish served with crushed new potatoes, roasted leeks, and red-wine sauce. Starters charm and delight palates, ranging from ravioli of crab with mussels, chile, ginger, and coriander *nage* to terrine of foie gras with confit of duck and pears poached in port. Also resting on your Villeroy & Boch aubergine plate might be mallard with a celeriac fondant, or *assiette* of lamb with a thyme-scented *jus*. Another stunning main course is a tranche of sea bass with bouillabaisse potatoes. A new dish likely to catch your eye is roasted veal sweetbreads with caramelized onion purée and a casserole of flap mushrooms. There are only 14 tables, so bookings are imperative.

11 Park Walk, SW10. ℂ 020/7352-3449. Reservations required and accepted up to 4–8 weeks in advance. 3-course fixed-price lunch £34 ($65), 3-course fixed-price dinner £64 ($122), menu gourmand £130 ($247). AE, DC, MC, V. Mon–Fri noon–2:15pm; Mon–Sat 7–11pm. Tube: South Kensington.

Gordon Ramsay ⭐⭐⭐ (Finds) FRENCH One of the city's most innovative and talented chefs is Gordon Ramsay. It seems all of London is rushing to sample his wares, and he has had to turn away some big names. The Queen hasn't been denied a table yet, but that's only because she hasn't called.

Every dish from this kitchen is gratifying, reflecting subtlety and delicacy without any sacrifice of the food's natural essence. Try, for example, Ramsay's celebrated cappuccino of white beans with grated truffles. His appetizers are likely to dazzle: salad of crispy pigs' trotters with calf's sweetbreads, fried quail eggs and a cream vinaigrette, or foie gras three ways—sautéed with quince, *mi-cuit* with an Earl Grey consommé, or pressed with truffle peelings. From here, you can grandly proceed to the main courses, including oven-roasted pigeon from Anjou wrapped in Parma ham with foie gras or else pan-fried filets of John Dory with crab and caviar. Desserts are equally stunning, including marinated pineapple ravioli with mango and fresh raspberries, and a caramelized tarte tatin of apples with vanilla ice cream.

68 Royal Hospital Rd., SW3. ℂ 020/7352-4441. Reservations essential (1 month in advance). Fixed-price lunch 3 courses £40 ($76), dinner 3 courses £85 ($162), 7 courses £110 ($209). AE, DC, MC, V. Mon–Fri noon–2:30pm and 6:30–11pm. Tube: Sloane Sq.

EXPENSIVE

Bluebird ⭐ MEDITERRANEAN This enormous space resounds with clinking silverware and peals of laughter from a loyal clientele. Locals and staff alike refer to it as a *restaurant de gare*—a railway-station restaurant. Downstairs are a cafe, upscale deli, and housewares store under separate management. But most of the business occurs upstairs at this restaurant, which can hold 220 diners at a time. You'll find a color scheme of red-and-blue canvas cutouts in the shape of birds in flight. Tables are close together, but the scale of the place makes dining private and intimate. The massive menu emphasizes savory, precisely cooked cuisine, some emerging from a wood-burning stove used to roast everything from lobster to game. An immense shellfish bar stocks every crustacean you can think of, and the liquor bar does a thriving business with the Sloane Square subculture. Starter temptations include Serrano ham with fresh tomato tostados or chopped steak tartare, perhaps wild mushrooms on brioche. We're fond of the venison shank in a bitter chocolate sauce (don't knock it until you've tried it). You might also try the lamb with lentils and cepe mushrooms. Dessert treats include an iced chestnut parfait with vanilla butterscotch or a Valrhona chocolate fondant with ice cream.

Oh, the name: Before it was a restaurant, the site was a garage that repaired the legendary Bluebird, an English sports car that is, alas, no longer produced.

350 King's Rd., SW3. ℂ 020/7559-1000. www.conran-restaurants.co.uk. Reservations recommended. Main courses £8–£43 ($15–$82), fixed-price lunch menu £13–£16 ($25–$30). AE, DC, MC, V. Mon–Fri 12:30–3:30pm and 6–11pm; Sat noon–3:30pm and 6–11pm; Sun noon–3:30pm and 7–10pm. Tube: Sloane Sq.

Le Cercle 🌟🌟 FRENCH   The owners of Club Gascon have come up with another winner in this chic subterranean dining room, a sort of Chelsea speak-easy. At last Sloane Street has a restaurant that is to food what the boulevard has long been to fashion. Service may not be the most efficient, and the noise level is at times deafening, but the food is absolutely amazing. Plus, you make your menu selection among an occasional famous face and a lot of lesser mortals.

For us, the best dish was tuna carpaccio with crispy pork cubes. The French-styled dishes are served as tapas-sized portions—eating a series of small plates is known as "grazing" on both sides of the Atlantic. Le Cercle introduced the concept of tapas-style dining to London. The menu is divided into seven sections according to principal ingredients. The waitstaff suggests three portions of these small plates before choosing one of the delectable desserts. The milk-fed Pyrenean lamb is meltingly tender. The chefs turn out one of the most succulent cuts of beef in London—it appears as *onglet* on the menu. Particularly memorable was the duck and fig combo and the chestnut risotto. For dessert, the chocolate fondant may arguably be the best in London. It's served with vanilla and pepper (you heard right) ice cream. Or you can opt for the divine sugar tart with a white peach sorbet. As for the cheese selection, one habitué described it to us as "top dog."

1 Wilbraham Place, SW1. ℂ 020/7901-9999. Reservations required. Set lunch (noon–3pm Mon–Sat) £15 ($29) for 3 dishes, £18 ($34) for 4 dishes; set dinner (6–6:45pm Tues–Sat) £18 ($34) 3 dishes, £22 ($42) 4 dishes; French tapas £5–£12 ($9.50–$23). AE, MC, V. Tues–Sat noon–10:45pm (snacks only 3–6pm). Tube: Sloane Sq.

INEXPENSIVE

Oriel FRENCH   Right on the corner of Sloane Square, in the heart of Chelsea, this brasserie has long been a favorite of shoppers checking out the boutiques along King's Road. The upstairs is done up in French brasserie style, rather classic with large mirrors and high ceilings. The atmosphere downstairs is more informal, and there are a few sidewalk tables for those who want to check out the Chelsea scene. If you arrive early for coffee and newspaper reading, you'll think you're at a Parisian cafe.

The food is fine but not excellent, including such brasserie standards as tuna Niçoise and steak and *pommes frites*. Other dishes include steak au poivre with a very peppery sauce, mussels marinara, and salads, which are always freshly tossed. There are also dishes for vegetarians.

50–51 Sloane Sq., SW1. ℂ 020/7730-2804. Reservations not required. Main courses £10–£15 ($19–$29). AE, DC, MC, V. Mon–Sat 8:30am–10:45pm; Sun 9am–10pm. Tube: Sloane Square.

The Pig's Ear ✸ *Finds* TRADITIONAL BRITISH   The staff is still talking about the surprise visit of Prince William. He may be heir to one of the world's most fabled fortunes, but at the end of the evening here he split the bill with his friends, paying only his fair share. This is one of the best of the gastro-pubs of Chelsea. It might be called the Pig's Ear but it's really a silk purse when it comes to food. The atmosphere is friendly and unpretentious in both the ground-floor pub area and in the wood-paneled restaurant upstairs.

Start with such dishes as Jerusalem artichoke soup with truffle oil, and chicken livers flavored with sherry vinegar. You can also try the seared tuna with black olives and chicory or the foie gras ballantine with an onion marmalade. In honor of its namesake, the chefs cook deep-fried pigs' ears. Filet of sea bass appears with beet root and baby leeks, and a roast wood pigeon is stuffed with garlic-laced portobello mushrooms.

35 Old Church St., SW3 5BS. ℂ 020/7352-2908. Reservations required in restaurant. Main courses £7.25–£17 ($14–$33). AE, DC, MC, V. Mon–Sat 7–11pm; Sun noon–3pm and 7–10:30pm. Tube: Sloane Square.

KENSINGTON & SOUTH KENSINGTON
VERY EXPENSIVE

Tom Aikens ✸✸✸ CONTINENTAL   The amazingly skilled Tom Aikens is one of the truly top-flight Gallic chefs of London. Aikens certainly was trained well, working in Paris under Joel Robuchon during the time he was proclaimed France's greatest chef. Aikens also ran the prestigious Pied-à-Terre in London. In elegant surroundings in chic Knightsbridge, the food is basically a modern interpretation of high French cuisine, with a great deal of flourish and some very elaborately worked dishes. Appetizers offer a fine preview of the chef's culinary skills, especially roasted pigeon with a foie gras parfait, and the chilled coco bean soup with poached chicken in sauterne.

Regardless of the contrast in ingredients, main courses show harmony and cohesion, as exemplified by the poached sea bass with saffron risotto and a bouillabaisse sauce. Everything sounds like an unlikely combination, but the end result is most satisfying. The menu's most voluptuous side is evoked by braised suckling pig with roasted fresh almonds, apple purée, and a pork lasagna. Desserts are a strong point, both flavorful and delicate, as suggested by the poached strawberries with both a strawberry mousse and a strawberry sorbet, and the delectable coffee and hazelnut cake with coffee mousse.

43 Elystan St., SW3. ℂ 020/7584-2003. Reservations required. Fixed-price lunch £29 ($55), fixed-price dinner £65 ($124), tasting menu £80 ($152). AE, DC, MC, V. Mon–Fri noon–2:30pm and 6:45–11pm. Tube: S. Kensington.

EXPENSIVE
Bibendum/The Oyster Bar ✸ FRENCH/MEDITERRANEAN   In trendy Brompton Cross, this still-fashionable restaurant occupies two floors of a garage that's now an Art Deco masterpiece. Though its heyday came in the early 1990s, the white-tiled room with stained-glass windows, lots of sunlight, and a chic clientele, is still an extremely pleasant place. The eclectic cuisine, known for its freshness and simplicity, is based on what's available seasonally. Dishes might include roast pigeon with celeriac purée and apple sauté, rabbit with artichoke and parsley sauce, or grilled lamb cutlets with a delicate sauce. Some of the best dishes are for splitting between two people, including Bresse chicken flavored with fresh tarragon and grilled veal chops with truffle butter.

Simpler meals and cocktails are available in **The Oyster Bar** on the building's street level. The bar-style menu stresses fresh shellfish presented in the traditional French style, on ice-covered platters adorned with strands of seaweed. It's a crustacean-lover's dream.

81 Fulham Rd., SW3. ℭ 020/7581-5817. Reservations required in Bibendum, not accepted in The Oyster Bar. Main courses £18–£25 ($34–$48), 2-course fixed-price lunch £24 ($46), 3-course fixed-price lunch £29 ($55), cold seafood platter in The Oyster Bar £57 ($108) for 2. AE, DC, MC, V. Bibendum Mon–Fri noon–2:30pm and 6:30–11pm; Sat–Sun 12:30–3pm; Sat 7–11:30pm; Sun 7–10:30pm. The Oyster Bar Mon–Sat noon–10:30pm, Sun noon–10pm. Tube: South Kensington.

Clarke's ℛ MODERN BRITISH   Sally Clarke is one of the finest chefs in London, and this is one of the hottest restaurants around. *Still*. She opened it in the Thatcher era, and it's still going strong. In this excellent restaurant, everything is bright and modern, with wood floors, discreet lighting, and additional space in the basement, where tables are more spacious and private. Some people are put off by the fact that there is only a fixed-price menu, but the food is so well prepared that diners rarely object to what ends up in front of them. The menu, which changes daily, emphasizes chargrilled foods with herbs and seasonal veggies. You might begin with an appetizer salad of blood orange with red onions, watercress, and black olive–anchovy toast; then follow that with roasted breast of chicken with black truffle, crisp polenta, and arugula. Desserts are likely to include a warm pear-and-raisin puff pastry with maple syrup ice cream. Just put yourself in Clarke's hands—you'll be glad you did.

124 Kensington Church St., W8. ℭ 020/7221-9225. Reservations recommended. Main course lunch £16 ($30), 3-course dinner £42 ($80), Sat brunch £10–£14 ($19–$27). AE, DC, MC, V. Mon–Fri 12:30–2pm and 7–10pm; Sat brunch 11am–2pm and dinner 7–10pm. Tube: High St. Kensington or Notting Hill Gate.

Launceston Place ℛ MODERN BRITISH   Launceston Place is in an almost villagelike neighborhood where many Londoners would like to live, if only they could afford it. This stylish restaurant lies within a series of uncluttered Victorian parlors, the largest of which is illuminated by a skylight. Each room contains a collection of Victorian-era oils and watercolors, as well as contemporary paintings. The restaurant has been known for its new British cuisine since 1986. The menu changes every 6 weeks, but you're likely to be served such appetizers as langoustines and herb gnocchi with roast cauliflower or a Jerusalem artichoke soup. For a tempting main course, try the grilled rump of veal with mushrooms and sweet potato or mackerel with a sauté of artichokes and salsify. Another specialty is herb-crusted plaice with shellfish linguine. For dessert, sample the likes of chocolate mousse with balsamic roasted figs or else lemon cheesecake with a blueberry compote.

1A Launceston Place, W8. ℭ 020/7937-6912. www.egami.co.uk. Reservations required. Main courses £14–£21 ($27–$40), fixed-price 2-course lunch menu £16 ($30); fixed-price 3-course lunch menu £19 ($36). AE, DC, MC, V. Daily 12:30–2:30pm; Mon–Sat 6–11:30pm; Sun 7–10pm. Tube: Gloucester Rd. or High St. Kensington.

MODERATE

Admiral Codrington ℛ *Finds* CONTINENTAL/MODERN BRITISH   Once a lowly pub, this stylish bar and restaurant is now a hotspot. The exterior has been maintained, but the old "Cod," as it is affectionately known, has emerged to offer plush dining with a revitalized decor by Nina Campbell and a glass roof that rolls back on sunny days. The bartenders still offer a traditional pint, but the sophisticated menu features such delectable fare as grilled calf's liver and crispy bacon, and pan-fried rib-eye with a truffled horseradish cream. Opt for the charbroiled tuna with eggplant caviar and a red-pepper vinaigrette.

17 Mossop St., SW3. ℂ 020/7581-0005. Reservations recommended. Main courses £9–£15 ($17–$29). AE, MC, V. Daily 11am–11pm. Tube: South Kensington.

Blue Elephant ☆ THAI   This is the counterpart of the famous L'Eléphant Bleu restaurant in Brussels. In a converted factory building in West Brompton, the Blue Elephant has been wildly popular since 1986. It remains the leading Thai restaurant in London, where the competition seems to grow daily. In an almost magical garden setting of tropical foliage, diners are treated to an array of MSG-free Thai dishes. You can begin with a "Floating Market" (shellfish in clear broth, flavored with chile paste and lemon grass), then go on to a splendid selection of main courses, for which many of the ingredients have been flown in from Thailand. We recommend the roasted-duck curry served in a clay cooking pot. You might also try a spicy fish stew with mussels, prawns, crab, and scallops or else a rich chicken curry with coconut milk and sweet basil.

3–6 Fulham Broadway, SW6. ℂ 020/7385-6595. www.blueelephant.com. Reservations required. Main courses £12–£28 ($23–$53), Royal Thai banquet £35–£39 ($67–$74), fixed-price lunch menu Mon–Fri £10–£15 ($19–$29), Sun buffet £22 ($42). AE, DC, MC, V. Mon–Sat noon–2:30pm; Sun noon–3pm; Mon–Thurs 7pm–midnight; Sat 6:30pm–midnight; Sun 7–10:30pm. Tube: Fulham Broadway.

The Enterprise EUROPEAN/TRADITIONAL BRITISH   The Enterprise's proximity to Harrods attracts both regulars and out-of-town shoppers. Although the joint swarms with singles at night, during the day it attracts the ladies-who-lunch. With banquettes, white linen, and fresh flowers, you won't mistake it for a lowly boozer. The kitchen serves respectable traditional English fare as well as European favorites, all prepared with fresh ingredients. Featured dishes include fried salmon cakes with butter spinach, golden calamari, and grilled steak with fries and salad. The juicy, properly aged, flavorful, and thin entrecôte slice of beef is about the best you can find in London.

35 Walton St., SW3. ℂ 020/7584-3148. Reservations accepted for lunch only Mon–Fri. Main courses £7–£15 ($13–$29). AE, MC, V. Daily noon–3pm and 6–10:30pm. Tube: South Kensington or Knightsbridge.

Joe's Café ☆ *Finds* ITALIAN   One of three London restaurants established by fashion designer Joseph Ettedgui, it's often filled at breakfast and lunch with well-known names from the British fashion, music, and entertainment industries, thanks to its sense of glamour and fun. No one will mind if your meal is composed exclusively of appetizers. There's a bar near the entrance, a cluster of tables for quick meals near the door, and more leisurely (and gossipy) dining available in an area a few steps up. The atmosphere remains laid-back and unstuffy, just as trendsetters in South Ken prefer it. With a name like Joe's, what else could it be? You can sample such starters as fresh crab ricotta pancake with orange dressing and baby spinach or a goat terrine with cherry tomato marmalade. Main dish allures include homemade pappardelle with a wild rabbit ragout and Pecorino cheese, and a lamb shank in a red wine sauce. A specialty is chargrilled lobster with king prawns, squid, and langoustines with a tomato concasse.

126 Draycott Ave., SW3. ℂ 020/7225-2217. www.joseph.co.uk/joes. Reservations required on weekdays, not accepted on weekends. Main courses £9–£24 ($17–$46). AE, MC, V. Mon–Sat 10am–6pm and 7–10:30pm; Sun 10:30am–5:30pm. Tube: South Kensington.

Kensington Place EUROPEAN   Rowley Leigh, the chef here, has attracted a devoted following of regulars. But word of his delicious cuisine is spreading, and now more and more visitors are rushing here to sample some of his signature dishes. For starters, try the risotto verde with mozzarella and roast peppers or the pickled herring salad with boiled eggs and potatoes. Grilled wild boar chops with polenta and herbs is another specialty. Also look for Leigh's innovative seasonal dishes. The chef has a marvelous way with grouse, venison, roast partridge, and sea bass. He grills scallops to golden perfection, and goat-cheese mousse and olives enhance even the simplest chicken dish. For dessert, you can take delight in the grilled pineapple with chili syrup (you heard that right) and coconut ice cream or the hot, bitter chocolate mousse with coffee ice cream. Everybody from pop stars to Kensington dowagers flocks to this animated, noisy bistro. The set lunch is one of the best values in the area. Save room for the steamed chocolate pudding with custard.

201 Kensington Church St., W8. © 020/7727-3184. www.egami.co.uk. Reservations required. Main courses £14–£32 ($27–$61), fixed-price dinner £25 ($48), fixed-price lunch £17 ($32). AE, DC, MC, V. Daily noon–3:30pm; Mon–Sat 6:30–11:45pm; Sun 6:30–10:15pm. Tube: Notting Hill Gate.

Pasha MOROCCAN   You'll find virtually every kind of ethnic restaurant within London, but few boast the zest and stylishness of this re-creation of a palace within the medina at Marrakech. Each of the two dining rooms is outfitted with Bedouin colors, rich upholsteries, flickering candles, and belly-dancing music. You'll enjoy regional specialties that were once sampled only by cherished royal-family guests. If you wish, you can begin your meal with Moroccan tapas, including pigeon with spices and roasted almonds in a cinnamon-flavored pastry or baked baby eggplant with cumin-flavored shallots, even chargrilled king prawns. Main dish specialties include a slow-cooked whole lamb shoulder with apricots, figs, dates, and prunes served with a cinnamon-flavored couscous and sultanas. A tagine Djaj is chicken with preserved lemon, onion confit, saffron potatoes, and green olives. The chargrilled swordfish is a very special dish flavored with pomegranates, fresh mint, and cinnamon.

1 Gloucester Rd., SW7. © 020/7589-7969. www.pasha-restaurant.co.uk. Reservations recommended. Tapas £4.50–£7.50 ($8.55–$14). Main courses £13–£20 ($25–$38). AE, DC, MC, V. Daily noon–midnight. Tube: Gloucester Rd.

Zaika ✶✶ INDIAN   Although a dish might miss here and there, this place nonetheless continues to receive accolades as one of the most accomplished of its type in Britain. In a former bank building in Kensington, the restaurant serves one innovative dish after another in flavors and combinations that may be new to you. Zaika lives up to its name, which, translated, means "sophisticated flavors." Of course, you can also order traditional dishes such as lamb and lentil patties stuffed with egg and onion. For starters, launch your repast with such delights as a platter of minced duck rolls or else morsels of tandoori chicken breast in green herbs. Main courses feature some sublime harmonies of flavor such as pan-fried and spicy sea bass with Indian couscous, raw mango, and a turmeric sauce, and—one of our favorites—"butter chicken," a classic tandoori chicken breast, with a buttery tomato sauce flavored with fenugreek, with saffron rice and stir-fried spinach. For a true feast, order the tasting menu, *Jugalbandi*.

1 High St. Kensington, W8. © 020/7795-6533. www.zaika-restaurant.co.uk. Reservations required. Main courses £13–£22 ($25–$42), 4-course lunch menu £20 ($38), 6-course *Jugalbandi* menu £38 ($72), excluding wine. AE, MC, V. Daily noon–2:45pm; Mon–Sat 6–10:45pm; Sun 6–9:45pm. Tube: High St. Kensington.

8 Marylebone to Notting Hill Gate

MARYLEBONE
EXPENSIVE

Assaggi ✶✶ *Finds* ITALIAN   Some of London's finest Italian cuisine is served in this room above a pub. This place is a real discovery and completely unpretentious.

Where to Dine from Marylebone to Notting Hill Gate

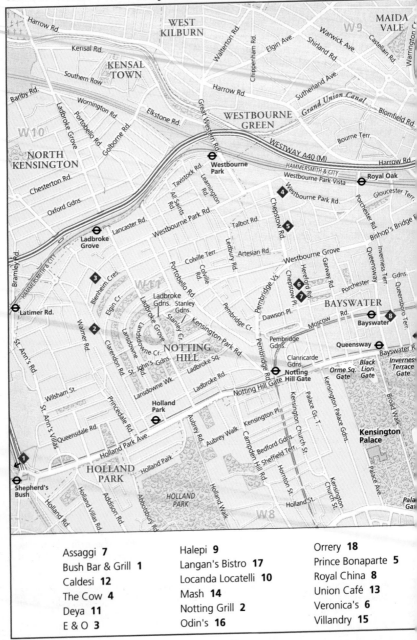

Assaggi **7**
Bush Bar & Grill **1**
Caldesi **12**
The Cow **4**
Deya **11**
E & O **3**

Halepi **9**
Langan's Bistro **17**
Locanda Locatelli **10**
Mash **14**
Notting Grill **2**
Odin's **16**

Orrery **18**
Prince Bonaparte **5**
Royal China **8**
Union Café **13**
Veronica's **6**
Villandry **15**

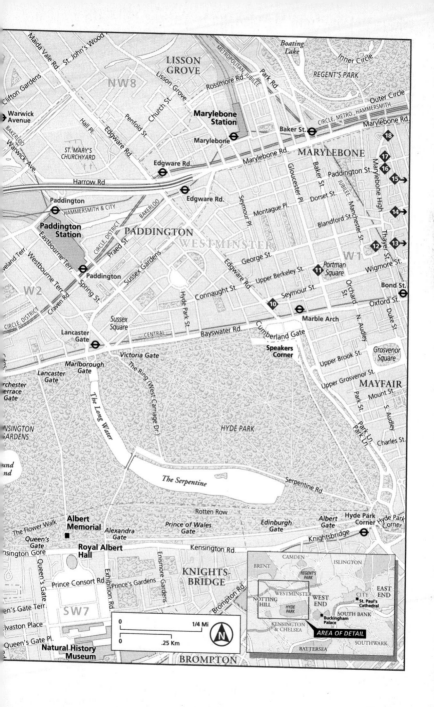

The relatively simple menu highlights the creative, outstanding cookery. All the ingredients are fresh and deftly handled by a skilled kitchen staff. Simplicity and flavor reign throughout. The appetizers, such as smoked swordfish salad and beef carpaccio, are so truly sublime that you'll want to make a meal entirely of them. At least three freshly made pastas are featured nightly. The tortellini with pork and a zesty tomato sauce is especially delicious. For a main course, opt for such delights as the thick, juicy, tender grilled veal, flavored with fresh rosemary or the grilled sea bass with braised fennel. Another savory choice is a plate of lamb cutlets (without any fat) with eggplant and a raisin salad. The flourless chocolate cake is the finest you'll find this side of northern Italy.

39 Chepstow Place, W2. ℂ **020/7792-5501**. Reservations required (as far in advance as possible). Main courses £16–£20 ($30–$38). DC, MC, V. Mon–Fri 12:30–2:30pm and 7:30–11pm; Sat 1–2:30pm and 7:30–11pm. Closed 2 weeks at Christmas. Tube: Notting Hill Gate.

Locanda Locatelli ✪✪ ITALIAN   Inside InterContinental's Churchill Hotel, this Italian restaurant is the success of the moment. Its charismatic owner, Giorgio Locatelli, is something of a celebrity himself these days. In a sleek, modern dining room with etched-glass panels and leather banquettes, you are served some of London's finest Italian fare. Beginning with the appetizers, dishes burst with flavor. We are especially fond of the artichoke and ham hock salad, and the pan-fried scallops with saffron, both served as starters. The food is superbly cooked and beautifully presented, especially the succulent homemade pastas, such as homemade chestnut tagliatelle with wild mushrooms and another homemade pasta stuffed with pheasant and served with a rosemary *jus*. We give high praise to such mains as steamed filet of hake with a garlic and parsley sauce or roast leg of rabbit with parma ham and polenta. "Heaven sent" is the best way to describe such desserts as Sicilian ricotta cake with pistachio ice cream, and chestnut mousse with a warm chocolate foam.

8 Seymour St., W1. ℂ **020/7935-9088**. www.locandalocatelli.com. Reservations required. Main courses £8–£30 ($15–$57). AE, DC, MC, V. Mon–Sat noon–3pm and 7–11pm; Sun noon–3:30pm and 7–10pm. Tube: Marble Arch.

Odin's ✪ INTERNATIONAL   Set adjacent to its slightly less expensive twin, Langan's Bistro, it features ample space between tables and an eclectic decor that includes evocative paintings and Art Deco accessories. As other restaurants nearby have come and gone, the cookery here remains solid and reliable. The standard of fresh ingredients and well-prepared dishes is always maintained. The menu changes with the seasons: Typical fare may include forest mushrooms in brioche, braised leeks glazed with mustard and tomato sauce, roast duck with applesauce and sage and onion stuffing, or roast filet of sea bass with a juniper cream sauce.

27 Devonshire St., W1. ℂ **020/7935-7296**. Reservations required. 2-course fixed-price lunch or dinner £29 ($55), 3-course fixed-price lunch or dinner £33 ($63). AE, DC, MC, V. Mon–Fri 12:30–2:30pm and 6:30–11pm. Tube: Regent's Park.

Orrery ✪✪ FRENCH/INTERNATIONAL   With ingredients imported from France, this is one of London's classic French restaurants. Sea bass from the shores of Montpellier, olive oil from Maussane-les-Alpilles, mushrooms from the fields of Calais, and poultry from Bresse—they all turn up on a highly refined menu, the creation of chef Andre Garret. On the second floor of the Conran Shop in Marylebone, Orrery changes its menu seasonally to take advantage of the best produce. Garret is a purist in terms of ingredients. Our favorites among his first-rate dishes are Bresse pigeon with savoy cabbage and mushroom ravioli, or duckling with an endive *tatin* and *cepe* (flap mushrooms) sauce. Everything has a brilliant often-whimsical touch, as evoked by the sautéed leeks in pumpkin oil. Skipping the blueberry soufflé, we ended with a cheese plate featuring a Banton goat cheese from Provence so fresh that it oozed onto the plate. Enjoy lazy summer evenings on a fourth-floor terrace while drinking and ordering light fare from the bar menu.

55 Marylebone High St., W1. © 020/7616-8000. Reservations required. Main courses £19–£25 ($36–$48), 3-course fixed-price lunch £24 ($46), 6-course fixed-price dinner £50–£58 ($95–$110). AE, DC, MC, V. Daily noon–3pm; Sun–Wed 6:30–10:30pm; Thurs–Sat 6:30–11pm. Tube: Baker St.

MODERATE

Bush Bar & Grill ⭐ *Finds* FRENCH/MODERN BRITISH   Hip, lighthearted, and sought after by the quasi-celebrities of London's world of media and entertainment, this bar and brasserie was established in 2000 by the owners of the city's most exclusive private clubs, Woody's and The Groucho Club. Both of these are membership-only venues in other parts of town. At the tables near you at this spin-off restaurant (not a members-only spot), you're likely to see members of those clubs plus celebs like Jerry Hall, Kate Moss, cookbook author Nigella Lawson, pop singer Kylie Minogue, and writers from such publications as *British Vogue* and *Tatler*. The setting was originally conceived as a milk-bottling plant, but since a team of decorators revamped it, it evokes an arts-conscious Manhattan bistro with a neoindustrial decor, exposed air ducts, and a busy kitchen that's open to view. Chefs here place an emphasis on organic produce, preparing dishes that include starters like wild boar and foie gras terrine with apple chutney, and stuffed baby squid with anchovies. For a main dish, try the roast rack of lamb with Rösti potatoes or braised mussels in cider with smoked bacon and thyme. You can finish with such desserts as lemon drizzle cake with custard or sherry cheesecake.

45a Goldhawk Rd., W12 8QP, © 020/8746-2111. www.bushbar.co.uk. Reservations required. Main courses £10–£16 ($19–$30), fixed-price menus served at lunch (daily) and dinner (Mon–Sat) until 7:30pm £23–£28 ($44–$53). AE, MC, V. Mon–Wed noon–11pm; Thurs noon–midnight; Fri–Sat noon–1am; Sun noon–6pm. Tube: Goldhawk Rd.

Caldesi ITALIAN   Good food, reasonable prices, fresh ingredients, and authentic Tuscan family recipes attract a never-ending stream of patrons to this eatery founded by owner and head chef Giancarlo Caldesi. The extensive menu includes a wide array of pasta, fish, and meat dishes. Start with the excellent *insalata Caldesi*, made with tomatoes slow-roasted in garlic and rosemary oil, and served with mozzarella flown in from Tuscany. Pasta dishes include an especially flavor-filled homemade tortellini stuffed with salmon. Monkfish and prawns are flavored with wild fennel and fresh basil, or you might sample the tender duck breast *à l'orange*, steeped in white wine, honey, thyme, and rosemary.

15–17 Marylebone Lane, W1. © 020/7935-9226. Reservations required. Main courses £13–£20 ($25–$38). AE, MC, V. Mon–Fri noon–2:30pm; Mon–Sat 6–11pm. Tube: Bond St.

Deya INDIAN   Two-time Oscar winner Sir Michael Caine returned to the restaurant business (he opened his first place in the 1960s) with this Indian restaurant in a historic building on Portman Square. The setting is incongruously Regency, with crystal chandeliers, but, for that touch of India, you get jaunty oversized prints of sacred Brahmins. Drop in first at the sleek international-style cocktail bar for one of those mojitos that surely would have won Papa Hemingway's approval. The menu of chef Sanjay Dwivedi is a blend of contemporary and traditional dishes and is strongly influenced by the former Portuguese colony of Goa (now under India's control). The

Goan prawn curry served with cashew coconut brown rice is one of the finest such dishes we've ever tasted. The seafood byrijana is superb, as are the buttery prawns marinated with curry leaf and mustard seed that emerge from the tandoori oven. The vegetarian menu is the most creative of any Indian restaurant in London, and service is smooth and unobtrusive.

34 Portman Sq., W1. © 020/7224-0028. Reservations recommended. Main courses £12–£16 ($23–$30), 2-course fixed-price lunch menu £15 ($29), fixed-price dinner menus £31–£42 ($59–$80). AE, DC, MC, V. Mon–Fri noon–2:45pm; Mon–Sat 6–11pm (bar opens 5pm). Tube: Marble Arch.

Langan's Bistro FRENCH/TRADITIONAL BRITISH   This unpretentious bistro is still around—although perhaps it's not quite the happening scene it was when actor Sir Michael Caine founded it back in the 1960s. Of the restaurants in this chain (see Langan's Brasserie, p. 176), it's the least expensive but the most visually appealing. Set behind a brightly colored storefront, the dining room is decorated with clusters of Japanese parasols, mirrors, surrealistic paintings, and old photographs. The menu is "mostly English with a French influence." Dishes change with the seasons but might include such starters as roast figs and goat cheese tart with walnut salad or sardines in sauce. Main courses include salmon with a cucumber and chile salsa, a confit of duck with stir-fry vegetables, and Italian beef tartare with new potatoes. Longtime brasserie favorites like mussels marinara, barbecued spareribs, and baked salmon in pastry are reassuringly familiar and as good as they ever were. Check out the dish of the day. Chocoholics should finish off with the extravaganza known as "Mrs. Langan's Chocolate Pudding." Only fixed-price menus are served here.

26 Devonshire St., W1. © 020/7935-4531. www.langansrestaurants.co.uk. Reservations recommended. Fixed-price 2-course lunch or dinner £20 ($38), 3 courses £22 ($42). AE, DC, MC, V. Mon–Fri 12:30–2:30pm; Mon–Sat 6:30–11pm. Tube: Regent's Park or Baker St.

Mash *Finds* CONTINENTAL   What is it, you ask? A bar? A deli? A microbrewery? Actually, it's all of the above, plus a restaurant. Breakfast and weekend brunch are the highlights, but don't ignore dinner. The owners of the hot Atlantic Bar & Grill have opened this "sunken chill-out zone" created by leading designer John Currin. The atmosphere is trendy, hip, breezy, and arty. The novelty decor includes curvy sci-fi lines that might remind you of a *Star Trek* set, and lizard-eye lighting fixtures, but ultimately the food is the attraction.

We were won over by such mains as a range of burgers, including one made with lamb and served with goat cheese. You might also be happily surprised by the risotto Parmigiana or the ragout of veal shank. A pan-fried halibut steak is served with wild mushrooms, beans, and truffle oil. Many diners finish off with the apple and blackberry crumble.

19–21 Great Portland St., W1. © 020/7637-5555. Reservations required. Main courses £12–£18 ($23–$34), set-price lunch or dinner £24–£28 ($46–$53). AE, DC, MC, V. Mon–Fri 8–11:30am, noon–3pm, and 6–11pm; Sat 6–11pm. Tube: Oxford Circus.

Union Cafe CONTINENTAL   After shopping along Oxford Street, restore your spirits with the exceptional food served at this sleek spot. The mainly female chefs use the finest-quality ingredients in every season. Everything from farmhouse English cheeses to free-range meat will tempt you. Rarely is any item oversauced, so natural, fresh flavors come to the fore. In most cases, the fresh fish and meat are chargrilled just right. Some of the best starters include stuffed peppers with feta cheese or fish soup with rouille. Especially good mains include roast cod filet with chives and grain mustard, and homemade crab cakes with chili jam. Linguine is flavorful with tiger prawns, mussels, and chili flavoring.

96 Marylebone Lane, W1. © 020/7486-4860. www.brinkleys.com/union. Reservations recommended. Main courses £12–£23 ($23–$44). AE, MC, V. Mon–Sat noon–3:30pm and 6:30–10:30pm; Sun 11am–4pm. Tube: Bond St.

Villandry 🐾 CONTINENTAL/INTERNATIONAL   Food lovers and gourmands flock to this food store, delicatessen, and restaurant, where racks of the finest meats, cheeses, and produce in the world are displayed and changed virtually every hour. The best of the merchandise is whimsically transformed into the restaurant's menu choices. The setting is an oversize Edwardian-style storefront north of Oxford Circus. The inside is a kind of minimalist temple dedicated to the glories of fresh produce and esoteric foodstuffs. Ingredients here change so frequently that the menu is rewritten twice a day—during our latest visit, it proposed such perfectly crafted dishes as breast of duck with fresh spinach and a gratin of baby onions, and pan-fried turbot with deep-fried celery, artichoke hearts, and hollandaise sauce.

170 Great Portland St., W1. © 020/7631-3131. Reservations recommended. Main courses £12–£22 ($23–$42). AE, MC, V. Restaurant Mon–Sat noon–3pm and 6–10:30pm; Sun 11:30am–4pm. Food store Mon–Sat 8am–10pm; Sun 10am–6pm. Tube: Great Portland St.

PADDINGTON & BAYSWATER
EXPENSIVE

Royal China 🐾 *Kids* CANTONESE/SZECHUAN   Unexpectedly delightful Szechuan and Cantonese specialties are available at this popular eatery, a family favorite. Come here for the best dim sum in London. Forget the garish decor and concentrate on what's on your plate—you'd probably have to go to Hong Kong to find Chinese cooking as authentic as this. The eight-page menu is overwhelming in its choices, and many of the classic dishes are known only to true students of Chinese cuisine. We were delighted by the Shanghai dumplings, steamed on one side and sautéed on the other. Various whole ducks and chickens are prepared with skill passed down through centuries. We noticed a table of London Chinese raving about the jellyfish with sesame oil, although we opted for the sautéed prawns with fresh mango.

13 Queensway, W2. © 020/7221-2535. www.royalchinagroup.co.uk. Reservations recommended. Main courses £7.50–£24 ($14–$46), fixed-price dinner £30–£38 ($57–$72). AE, DC, MC, V. Mon–Thurs noon–11pm; Fri–Sat noon–11:30pm; Sun 11am–10pm. Tube: Bayswater or Queensway.

MODERATE

Halepi 🐾 *Finds* CYPRIOT/GREEK   Run by the Kazolides family since 1966, this establishment is hailed by the *Automobile Association of America Guide* as the best Greek restaurant in the world. Despite its reputation, the atmosphere is informal, with rows of brightly clothed tables, *bouzouki* background music, and a large native Greek clientele.

Portions are generous. Menu items rely heavily on lamb and include kabobs, *klefticon* (baby lamb prepared with aromatic spices), moussaka (minced lamb and eggplant with béchamel sauce), and *dolmades* (vine leaves stuffed with lamb and rice). Other main courses include scallops; sea bass; Scottish halibut; huge Indonesian shrimp with lemon juice, olive oil, garlic, and spring-onion sauce; and *afelia* (filet of pork cooked with wine and spices, served with potatoes and rice). The homemade baklava is recommended for dessert. The wine list features numerous selections from Greece and Cyprus. Most dishes are moderate in price.

18 Leinster Terrace, W2. ℘ 020/7262-1070. www.halepi.co.uk. Reservations required. Main courses £10–£18 ($19–$34), set-price menu £19–£29 ($36–$55). AE, DC, MC, V. Daily noon–12:15am. Closed Dec 25–26. Tube: Queensway.

Veronica's ★★ (Finds) TRADITIONAL BRITISH   Called the "market leader in cafe salons," Veronica's offers traditional—and historical—fare at prices you won't mind paying. It's a celebration of British cuisine over a 2,000-year period, with dishes based on medieval, Tudor, and even Roman-era recipes. The chef gives these traditional dishes imaginative, modern twists. One month she'll focus on Scotland, while the next she'll concentrate on Victorian foods, dishes from Wales, or an all-Irish menu, and so on. You might start with a carrot tart perfumed with orange-flavored water and served with a minted pea purée based on an Irish recipe from 1746. Or else try the deviled whitebait with a tartare dip (deviling became popular in the 19th century and, of course, whitebait has been eaten since Medieval times, when it was caught in the Thames). Main dishes might include lamb marinated in milk and honey and roasted in red wine (based on an ancient Roman recipe). You might also order "hindle-wakes"—breast of chicken stuffed with black prunes and almonds and based on a recipe Flemish spinners brought to England in the 12th century. For dessert, you might opt for an 18th-century recipe for crème brûlée. The restaurant offers a mod-erated menu to help keep cholesterol down. The interior is brightly and attractively decorated, and the service is warm and ingratiating.

3 Hereford Rd., W2. ℘ 020/7229-5079. www.veronicasrestaurant.co.uk. Reservations required. Main courses £13–£18 ($25–$34). AE, MC, V. Mon–Sat 6–10:30pm; Sun 6–10pm. Tube: Bayswater.

NOTTING HILL GATE
MODERATE
The Cow (Finds) MODERN BRITISH   You don't have to be a young fashion vic-tim to enjoy the superb cuisine served here (although many of the diners are). Tom Conran (son of entrepreneur Sir Terence Conran) holds forth in this increasingly hip Notting Hill watering hole. It looks like an Irish pub, but the accents you'll hear are "trustafarian" rather than street-smart Dublin. Order a pint of Fuller's or London Pride and linger over the modern European menu, which changes daily but is likely to include ox tongue poached in milk; mussels in curry and cream; or a mixed grill of lamb chops, calf's liver, and sweetbreads. The seafood selections are delectable. "The Cow Special"—a half-dozen Irish rock oysters with a pint of Guinness or a glass of wine for £10 ($19)—is the star of the show. A raw bar downstairs serves other fresh seafood choices. To finish, skip the filtered coffee served upstairs (it's wretched) and opt for an espresso downstairs.

89 Westbourne Park Rd., W2. ℘ 020/7221-0021. Reservations required. Main courses £13–£19 ($25–$36). MC, V. Mon–Sat 6:30–11pm; Sun 12:30–3pm (brunch) and 7–10:30pm. Bar Mon–Wed noon–11pm, Thurs–Sat noon–mid-night, Sun noon–10:30pm; food served 12:30–3:30pm and 6:30–10:30pm. Tube: Westbourne Grove.

INEXPENSIVE
Prince Bonaparte INTERNATIONAL   This offbeat restaurant serves great pub grub in what used to be a grungy boozer before Notting Hill Gate became fashion-able. Now pretty young things show up, spilling onto the sidewalk when the evenings are warm. The pub is filled with mismatched furniture from schools and churches, and CDs of jazz and lazy blues fill the air, competing with the babble. At first it may seem that the staff doesn't have its act together, but once the food arrives, you won't care—the dishes served here are very good. The menu roams the world for inspiration:

Moroccan chicken with couscous is as good or better than any you'll find in Marrakech, and the seafood risotto is delicious. Roast lamb, tender and juicy, appears on the traditional Sunday menu. We recommend the London Pride or Grolsch to wash it all down.

80 Chepstow Rd., W2. ℂ 020/7313-9491. Reservations not required. Main courses £7–£15 ($13–$29. AE, MC, V. Mon–Sat noon–11pm; Sun noon–10:30pm. Tube: Notting Hill Gate or Westbourne Park.

LADBROKE GROVE
MODERATE

E&O ASIAN   Nicole Kidman comes here to nibble on the succulent pumpkin and litchi curry, Kate Moss to devour prawn-and-chive dumplings without fear of weight gain, and Richard Branson to feast on the barbecue roasts. In an offbeat, out-of-the-way location, E&O is hailed as the "new Ivy," a reference to the most famous restaurant in the West End theater district, also a celeb favorite (after all these years). Melburnian restaurant guru Will Ricker is known for having created several hot east London dining spots. With its tiny windows, this restaurant reminds some patrons of a dance club.

We sampled the crispy fried fish and pronounce it a winner, as is the crispy-skin chicken and the *char siu* pork—baby pork spareribs crusted with sesame seeds and served with a garlic-and-ginger sauce. Succulent sushi and sashimi appear on the menu. One London reviewer found the patrons "comically trendy," although we'd call them more fashionable instead. At least they were insiderish enough to book a table at this place.

14 Blenheim Crescent, W11. ℂ 020/7229-5454. www.eando.nu. Reservations required. Main courses £10–£32 ($19–$61). AE, DC, MC, V. Mon–Fri 12:15–3pm and 6:15–11pm; Sat 12:15–4pm and 6:15–11pm; Sun 12:30–4pm and 6:15–10:30pm. Tube: Ladbroke Grove or Notting Hill Gate.

Notting Grill ⭐ *Finds* STEAK   Notting Grill owner Anthony Worrall-Thompson looks for well-bred, well-fed animals in his search for "the Holy Grail of British meats." His dream of creating the best grill house in London, using the *crème de la crème* of beef and fish, is more or less coming true in this out-of-the-way, offbeat rendezvous for serious foodies. Since Britain is known for its great breeds of beef cattle, Worrall-Thompson features a different purebred steak each month, ranging from Welsh Black to Aberdeen Angus, from Hereford to Ruby Red. He also searches Britain for the best of lamb and pork, and regardless of food scares, he serves only British-raised meat. With little fuss or bother, he also offers succulent scallops, "Big Daddy" prawns, organic sausages, and calf's liver. He has even brought back Sir Winston's favorite, the mixed grill. Celebs, media types, and the arty crowd show up here. If they're not chowing down on the steaks, they're likely to be seen dining on the rare-breed Middle White pork or organic chicken with hand-cut chips. Middle White suckling pig and the 24-ounce T-bone steak are the chef's specialties.

123A Clarendon Rd., W11. ℂ 020/7229-1500. www.awtrestaurants.com. Reservations required. Main courses £11–£33 ($21–$63). AE, MC, V. Mon 6:30–10:30pm; Tues–Thurs noon–3pm and 6:30–10:30pm; Fri noon–3pm and 6:30–11:30pm; Sat noon–4pm and 6:30–11:30pm; Sun noon–10pm. Tube: Ladbroke Grove (a bit of a hike from the station).

9 A Bit Farther Afield
HAMMERSMITH

To see where Hammersmith lies in relation to central London, refer to the map "Greater London Area" (p. 74).

Finds The Brew House

Unknown to most visitors, there's a charming little place in North London for breakfast, afternoon tea, and lunches at one of Hampstead Heath's most alluring attractions. It's **The Brew House,** in Kenwood House (p. 261), Hampstead Lane, NW3 (*℃* **020/8341-5384**), open in summer daily from 9am to 6pm (until 4pm in winter). There is always a freshly made soup of the day and at least one vegetarian dish. Main courses are likely to include free-range sausages or else fresh Scottish salmon, and even free-range chicken. You can partake of the breakfast buffet for between £4 and £7 ($7.60–$13); at lunch main courses cost £5 to £10 ($9.50–$19). Tube: Northern line to Archway Station, then bus no. 210.

VERY EXPENSIVE

The River Café ✦✦ ITALIAN   For the best Italian cuisine in London, head to this Thames-side bistro operated by Ruth Rogers and Rose Gray. The charmingly contemporary establishment, with a polished steel bar, was designed by Ruth's husband, Richard, who also designed the Pompidou Centre in Paris. The cafe attracts a trendy crowd that comes to eat fabulous food and to see and be seen. The menu changes regularly. The owners' goal was to re-create the kind of cuisine they'd enjoyed in private homes in the Italian countryside, and they've succeeded. Some of London's chefs can be seen shopping in local markets—but not The River Café's chefs. The market comes to them: first-spring asparagus harvested in Andalusia and arriving in London within the day, live scallops and langoustines taken by divers in the icy North Sea, and a daily shipment of the finest harvest of Italy, ranging from radicchio to artichokes. Even tiny bulbs of fennel are zipped across the Channel from France. Britain's own rich bounty appears on the menu as well—in the form of pheasant and wild salmon. The best dishes are either slowly roasted or quickly seared.

Thames Wharf, Rainville Rd., W6. *℃* 020/7386-4200. www.rivercafe.co.uk. Reservations required. Main courses £26–£28 ($47–$50). AE, DC, MC, V. Mon–Thurs 12:30–3:30pm and 7–11pm; Fri–Sat 12:30–3:30pm and 7–11:30pm; Sun 12:30–3:30pm. Tube: Hammersmith.

CAMDEN TOWN

MODERATE

The Engineer ✦ *Finds* EUROPEAN/THAI   This temple to north London chic is another one of our favorites. The stylishly converted pub is owned by Abigail Osborne and Tamsin Olivier, daughter of Sir Laurence Olivier (or "Larry's Daughter," as she's called locally), and is named for Victorian bridge, tunnel, and railway builder Isambard Kingdom Brunel. It sits beside Regent's Canal, one of Brunel's creations. The pub is divided into a bar, a dining room, and a garden area for warm days. The decor is light and modern. The cuisine is modern European with a Thai influence and relies on seasonal produce and organic meat and eggs. For an appetizer, try a crispy potato and onion tart with truffle oil or the Tequila-cured salmon. For mains, we'd recommend the baked salmon filet wrapped in Parma ham and served with a saffron and anchovy sauce, or the Moroccan spiced lamb flavored with coriander and served with dates and couscous. For dessert, nothing is richer than the baked banana and toffee cheesecake, although you might opt for the pear and almond tart with pistachio crème fraîche.

65 Gloucester Ave., NW1. ℭ **020/7722-0950.** www.the-engineer.com. Reservations recommended. Main courses £13–£17 ($25–$32). MC, V. Mon–Fri noon–3pm and 7–11pm; Sat 12:30–3:30pm and 7–11pm; Sun 12:30–3:30pm and 7–10pm. Tube: Chalk Farm or Camden Town.

10 Teatime

Everyone should indulge in a formal afternoon tea at least once while in London. It's a relaxing, drawn-out, civilized affair that usually consists of three courses, all elegantly served on delicate china: first, dainty finger sandwiches (with the crusts cut off, of course), then fresh-baked scones served with jam and deliciously decadent clotted cream (Devonshire cream), and then an array of bite-size sweets. All the while, an indulgent server keeps the pot of tea of your choice fresh at hand. Sometimes ports and aperitifs are on offer to accompany your final course. High tea, popular with the before-theater crowd, includes an extra serving or two, including a sandwich, making it, in essence, a light supper. Having tea is a quintessentially British experience, and we've listed our favorite tea venues below. Note that for the most popular hotels (especially The Ritz), you should make reservations as far in advance as possible. If you go to a place that doesn't take reservations, show up at least half an hour early, especially between April and October. Jacket and tie are often required for gentlemen, and jeans and sneakers are usually frowned upon.

The British Empire no longer comes to a grinding halt at 4pm with all of England rushing for their cuppa. The English still like a cup of tea in the afternoon, but in workaday London it's often consumed at desks piled high with papers. A proper sit-down tea is reserved mainly for those ladies-who-lunch who like to indulge in fattening but delectable pastries in the late afternoon. Visitors are also fond of participating in this ritual.

London is now awash in coffee-bar chains, and many Londoners have abandoned the time-honored custom of afternoon tea altogether. But not all—some are returning to this quaint custom, and the city is experiencing a tea-drinking revival.

There are variations in tea drinking, as today's London is a rainbow-hued city. Take **Mô,** at 23 Heddon St., W1B 4BH, (ℭ **020/7434-4040**). At this offshoot of a North African restaurant, you'll think you're in Morocco as you're served mint tea in gold-encrusted glasses against a backdrop of hanging lanterns and embroidered cushions. Quite different from the traditional afternoon tea Queen Victoria enjoyed!

If drinking tea with your pinky extended just isn't your style, we've also included a handful of less formal (and less expensive) alternatives. A full high tea costs more than £24 ($46) at the finest hotels.

Be careful when you make reservations that you are booking at the right "Palm Court," as there are several of them.

HIGH TEA
MAYFAIR

Claridge's ✮ Claridge's teatime rituals have managed to persevere through the years with as much pomp and circumstance as the British Empire itself. The experience is never stuffy, though; you'll feel very welcome. Tea is served in the Reading Room. A portrait of Lady Claridge gazes from above as your choice of over 30 kinds of tea is served ever so politely. The courses, served consecutively, include finger sandwiches with cheese savories, apple-and-raisin scones, and yummy pastries.

55 Brook St., W1. ✆ 020/7409-6307. Reservations essential. Jacket and tie required for men after 6pm. High tea £31 ($59), £39 ($74) including champagne. AE, DC, MC, V. Daily 3–5:30pm. Tube: Bond St.

The Palm Court This is one of the great London favorites for tea. Restored to its former charm, the lounge has an atmosphere straight from 1927, with a domed yellow-and-white glass ceiling, *torchères*, and palms in Compton stoneware *jardinières*. A delightful afternoon repast that includes a long list of teas is served daily against the background of live harp music.

In the Sheraton Park Lane Hotel, Piccadilly, W1. ✆ 020/7499-6321. Reservations recommended. Afternoon tea £25 ($48), with a glass of Park Lane champagne £32 ($61). AE, DC, MC, V. Daily 3–6pm. Tube: Hyde Park Corner or Green Park.

ST. JAMES'S
Ritz Palm Court ✪✪✪ This is the most fashionable place in London to order afternoon tea—and the hardest to get into without reserving way in advance. The spectacular setting is straight out of *The Great Gatsby*, complete with marble steps and columns, and a baroque fountain. You can choose from a wide range of teas served with delectable sandwiches and luscious pastries.

In the Ritz Hotel, Piccadilly, W1. ✆ 020/7493-8181. Reservations required at least 8 weeks in advance. Jeans and sneakers not accepted. Jacket and tie required for men. Afternoon tea £36 ($68). Champagne afternoon tea with 2 complimentary glasses of champagne is offered at 7:30pm sitting. AE, DC, MC, V. 5 seatings daily at 11:30am, 1:30, 3:30, 5:30 and 7:30pm. Tube: Green Park.

St. James Restaurant & The Fountain Restaurant This pair of tea salons functions as a culinary showplace for London's most prestigious grocery store, Fortnum & Mason. The more formal of the two, the St. James, on the store's fourth floor, is a pale green-and-beige homage to formal Edwardian taste. More hurried and less formal is The Fountain Restaurant, on the street level, where a sense of tradition and manners is very much a part of the dining experience, but in a less opulent setting. There is no longer an "official" afternoon tea at The Fountain, but you can order pots of tea plus food from an a la carte menu that includes sandwiches, scones, and the like.

In Fortnum & Mason, 181 Piccadilly, W1. The Fountain ✆ 020/7973-4140; St. James 020/7734-8040, ext. 2241. St. James afternoon tea £24–£27 ($46–$51), champagne afternoon tea £29–£32 ($55–$61), high tea £26–£29 ($49–$55), champagne high tea £31–£34 ($59–$65). The Fountain a la carte menu £3–£20 ($5.70–$38). AE, DC, MC, V. St. James Mon–Sat 3:30–5pm. The Fountain Mon–Sat 8:30am–8pm. Tube: Piccadilly Circus.

KNIGHTSBRIDGE
The Georgian Restaurant For as long as anyone can remember, tea at Harrods has been a distinctive feature of Europe's most famous department store. A flood of visitors is gracefully herded into a high-volume but elegant room. Many come here for the ritual of the tea service, as staff members haul silver pots and trolleys laden with pastries and sandwiches through the cavernous dining hall. Most exotic is Betigala tea, a rare blend from China, similar to Lapsang souchong.

On the 4th floor of Harrods, 87–135 Brompton Rd., SW1. ✆ 020/7225-6800. Reservations recommended. High tea £20 ($38) or £30 ($57) with Harrods champagne, per person. AE, DC, MC, V. Daily 3:45–5:30pm (last order). Tube: Knightsbridge.

The Lanesborough You'll suspect that many of the folks sipping exotic teas here have dropped in to inspect the public areas of one of London's most expensive hotels. The staff offers a selection of seven teas that include the Lanesborough special blend, and herbal esoterica like Rose Congou. The focal point for this ritual is the Conservatory, a glass-roofed Edwardian fantasy filled with potted plants and a sense of the long-gone

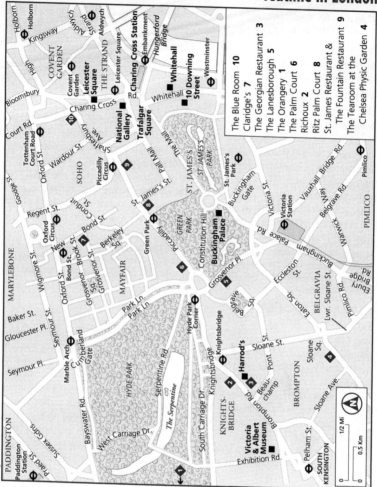

The Blue Room **10**
Claridge's **7**
The Georgian Restaurant **3**
The Lanesborough **5**
The Orangery **1**
The Palm Court **6**
Richoux **2**
Ritz Palm Court **8**
St. James Restaurant & The Fountain Restaurant **9**
The Tearoom at the Chelsea Physic Garden **4**

majesty of the Empire. The finger sandwiches, scones, and sweets are all appropriately lavish and endlessly correct. Live piano music is played during afternoon tea.

Hyde Park Corner, SW1 (in the Lanesborough Hotel). ✆ **020/7259-5599**. Reservations required. High tea £28 ($53), high tea with strawberries and champagne £37 ($70). Min. charge £9.50 ($18) per person. AE, DC, MC, V. Mon–Sat 3:30–6pm; Sun 4–6pm. Tube: Hyde Park Corner.

Richoux   There's an old-fashioned atmosphere at Richoux, established in the 1920s. You can order four hot scones with strawberry jam and whipped cream or choose from a selection of pastries. Of course, tea is obligatory; always specify lemon or cream, one lump or two. A full menu, with fresh salads, sandwiches, and burgers, is served all day. There are three other locations, open Monday through Saturday from 8am to 11pm, Sunday from 9am to 10:30pm. There's a branch at the bottom of Bond Street, 172

Piccadilly (© **020/7493-2204;** Tube: Piccadilly Circus or Green Park); one at 41A S. Audley St. (© **020/7629-5228;** Tube: Green Park or Hyde Park Corner); and one at 3 Circus Rd. (© **020/7483-4001;** Tube: St. John's Wood).

86 Brompton Rd. (opposite Harrods), Knightsbridge, SW3. © **020/7584-8300.** Full tea £17 ($32). AE, MC, V. Mon–Sat 8am–9pm; Sun 10am–9pm. Tube: Knightsbridge.

KENSINGTON

The Orangery (★ *Finds*)   In its way, The Orangery is the most amazing place for afternoon tea in the world. Set 45.7m (150 ft.) north of Kensington Palace, it occupies a long narrow garden pavilion built in 1704 by Queen Anne. In homage to her original intentions, rows of potted orange trees bask in sunlight from soaring windows, and tea is served amid Corinthian columns, ruddy-colored bricks, and a pair of Grinling Gibbons woodcarvings. There are even some urns and statuary that the royal family imported from Windsor Castle. The menu includes soups and sandwiches, with a salad and a portion of upscale potato chips known as kettle chips. The array of different teas is served with high style, accompanied by fresh scones with clotted cream and jam, and Belgian chocolate cake.

In the gardens of Kensington Palace, W8. © **020/7376-0239.** Reservations not accepted. Pot of tea only £1.95–£2.25 ($3.70–$4.30), cakes and puddings £2.50–£4.50 ($4.75–$8.55), afternoon tea £7.95–£9.95 ($15–$19), champagne tea £17 ($33). MC, V. Mar–Oct daily 10am–6pm; Nov–Feb daily 10am–5pm. Tea 3–5pm. Tube: High St. Kensington or Queensway.

CASUAL TEAROOMS
SOHO

The Blue Room   Nothing about this place will remind you of the grand tearooms above, where tea drinking is an intricate and elaborate social ritual. What you'll find here is a cozy, eccentric enclave lined with the artwork of some of the regular patrons, battered sofas that might have come out of a college dormitory, and a gathering of likeable urban hipsters to whom very little is sacred. You can enjoy dozens of varieties of tea, including herbals, served in steaming mugs. Lots of arty types gather here during the late afternoon, emulating some of the rituals of old-fashioned tea service with absolutely none of the hauteur.

3 Bateman St., W1. © **020/7437-4827.** Reservations recommended. Cup of tea £1.50 ($2.85); cakes and pastries £2–£4 ($3.80–$7.60); sandwiches £3–£6 ($5.70–$11). No credit cards. Mon–Fri 8am–10:30pm; Sat 10am–10:30pm; Sun noon–10pm. Tube: Leicester Sq.

CHELSEA

The Tearoom at the Chelsea Physic Garden   The garden encompasses a small area, crisscrossed with gravel paths and ringed with a high brick wall that shuts out the roaring traffic of Royal Hospital Road. These few spectacular acres honor the memory of industries that were spawned from seeds developed and tested within the garden's walls. Founded in 1673 as a botanical education center, the Chelsea Physic Garden's list of successes includes the exportation of rubber from South America to Malaysia and tea from China to India.

On the 4 days a week that it's open, the tearoom is likely to be filled with botanical enthusiasts sipping cups of tea as fortification for their garden treks. The setting is a banal-looking Edwardian building. Since the tearoom is secondary to the garden itself, don't expect the lavish pomp of some other teatime venues. But you can carry your cakes and cups of tea out into a garden that, despite meticulous care, always looks a bit unkempt. (Herbaceous plants within its hallowed precincts are left untrimmed to encourage bird life and seed production.) Botanists and flower lovers in general find the place fascinating.

66 Royal Hospital Rd., SW3. © 020/7352-5646. Tea with cake £5 ($9.50). MC, V (in shop only). Wed–Fri 12:30–5pm; Sun noon–6pm. Closed Nov–Mar. Tube: Sloane Sq.

8

Exploring London

Dr. Samuel Johnson said, "When a man is tired of London, he is tired of life, for there is in London all that life can afford." It would take a lifetime to explore every alley, court, street, and square in this city, and volumes to discuss them. Since you don't have a lifetime to spend, we've chosen the best London has to offer.

For the first-time visitor, the question is never what to do, but what to do first. The suggested itineraries in chapter 4 and "The Top Attractions," below, should help.

A note about admission and open hours: In the listings below, children's prices generally apply to those 16 and under. To qualify for a senior discount, you must be 60 or older (for women; men must be 65 or older). Students must present a student ID to get discounts, where available. In addition to closing on bank holidays, many attractions close around Christmas and New Year's (and, in some cases, early in May), so always call ahead if you're visiting in those seasons. All museums are closed Good Friday, December 24 through 26, and New Year's Day.

1 Sights & Attractions by Neighborhood

COVENT GARDEN & THE STRAND

Courtauld Gallery (p. 243)
Gilbert Collection ✹✹✹ (p. 245)
Hermitage Rooms at Somerset House ✹✹✹ (p. 246)
St. Paul's Church (the Actors' Church) ✹ (p. 231)

DOCKLANDS

Butler's Wharf (p. 258)
Canary Wharf (p. 258)
Design Museum (p. 244)
Exhibition Centre (p. 258)
St. Katharine's Dock (p. 257)

DULWICH

Dulwich Picture Gallery ✹ (p. 244)

EAST END

Bethnal Green Museum of Childhood (p. 265)
Geffrye Museum ✹ (p. 245)

FOREST HILLS

Horniman Museum (p. 265)

GREENWICH

National Maritime Museum ✹✹ (p. 262)
Old Royal Observatory ✹ (p. 262)
Queen's House ✹✹ (p. 262)
Ranger's House ✹✹ (p. 262)
Royal Naval College ✹✹ (p. 263)

HAMPSTEAD

Burgh House (p. 260)
Fenton House (p. 260)
Freud Museum (p. 260)
Hampstead Heath (p. 258)
Keats House ✹✹ (p. 260)
Kenwood House ✹✹ (p. 261)

HAMPTON COURT

Hampton Court Palace ✹✹✹ (p. 264)

HIGHGATE

Highgate Cemetery (p. 261)

HOLBORN

Gray's Inn ✹ (p. 237)
Lincoln's Inn ✹✹ (p. 238)
Sir John Soane's Museum ✹ (p. 253)

ISLINGTON

Estorick Collection of Modern Italian Art (p. 224)
Little Angel Theatre (p. 268)

KENSINGTON & SOUTH KENSINGTON

Hyde Park ✹✹ (p. 253)
Kensington Gardens (p. 214)
Kensington Palace ✹ (p. 214)
Linley Sambourne House ✹ (p. 248)
Natural History Museum ✹✹ (p. 250)
Science Museum ✹✹✹ (p. 251)
Victoria and Albert Museum ✹✹✹ (p. 222)

KEW

Kew Palace ✹✹ (p. 263)
Royal Botanic Gardens, Kew ✹✹✹ (p. 263)

MARYLEBONE

London Zoo ✹ (p. 269)
Madame Tussaud's (p. 249)
Regent's Park ✹✹✹ (p. 254)
Sherlock Holmes Museum (p. 252)
Wallace Collection ✹✹ (p. 253)

MAYFAIR

Handel Museum (p. 240)
Royal Academy of Arts (p. 251)

ST. JAMES'S

Buckingham Palace ✹✹ (p. 209)
Clarence House ✹✹ (p. 212)
Green Park ✹ (p. 254)
Institute of Contemporary Arts (p. 247)
The Queen's Gallery ✹✹ (p. 251)
Royal Mews ✹✹ (p. 251)
Spencer House ✹✹ (p. 239)
St. James's Church ✹ (p. 230)
St. James's Park ✹ (p. 254)

2 The Top Attractions

British Museum ✦✦✦   Set in scholarly Bloomsbury, this immense museum grew out of a private collection of manuscripts purchased in 1753 with the proceeds of a lottery. It grew and grew, fed by legacies, discoveries, and purchases, until it became one of the most comprehensive collections of art and artifacts in the world. It's impossible to take in this museum in a day.

The overall storehouse splits basically into the national collections of antiquities; prints and drawings; coins, medals, and banknotes; and ethnography. Even on a cursory first visit, be sure to see the Asian collections (the finest assembly of Islamic pottery outside the Islamic world), the Chinese porcelain, the Indian sculpture, and the prehistoric and Romano-British collections. Special treasures you might want to seek out on your first visit include the **Rosetta Stone,** in the Egyptian Room, the discovery of which led to the deciphering of hieroglyphics; the **Elgin Marbles,** a series of pediments, metopes, and friezes from the Parthenon in Athens, in the Duveen Gallery; and the legendary **Black Obelisk,** dating from around 860 B.C., in the Nimrud Gallery. Other treasures include the contents of Egyptian royal tombs (including mummies); fabulous arrays of 2,000-year-old jewelry, cosmetics, weapons, furniture, and tools; Babylonian astronomical instruments; and winged lion statues (in the Assyrian Transept) that guarded Ashurnasirpal's palace at Nimrud. The exhibits change throughout the year, so if your heart is set on seeing a specific treasure, call to make sure it's on display.

Insider's Tip: If you're a first-time visitor, you will, of course, want to concentrate on some of the fabled treasures previewed above. But what we do is duck into the British Museum several times on our visits to London, even if we have only an hour or two, to see the less heralded but equally fascinating exhibits. We recommend wandering rooms 33 and 34, and 91 to 94, to take in the glory of the Orient, covering Taoism, Confucianism, and Buddhism. The Chinese collection is particularly strong. Sculpture from India is as fine as anything at the Victoria and Albert. The ethnography collection is increasingly beefed up, especially the Mexican Gallery in room 33C, which traces that country's art from the 2nd millennium B.C. to the 16th century A.D.

Tips Timesaver

With 4km (2½ miles) of galleries, the **British Museum** is overwhelming. To get a handle on it, we recommend taking a 1½-hour overview tour for £8 ($15), £5 ($9.50) for students and children under 11. Daily at 10:30am, 1pm, or 3pm. Afterward, you can return to the galleries that most interest you. If you have limited time to spend on the museum, concentrate on the Greek and Roman rooms (nos. 11–23, 69–73, and 77–85), which hold the golden hoard of booty both bought and stolen from the Empire's once far-flung colonies. For information on the British Library, see p. 242.

A gallery for the North American collection is also nearby. Another section of the museum is devoted to the **Sainsbury African Galleries** ⟨⟩, one of the finest collections of African art and artifacts in the world, featuring changing displays selected from more than 200,000 objects. Finally, the museum has opened a new Money Gallery in room 68, tracing the story of (what else?) money. You'll learn that around 2000 B.C. in Mesopotamia, grain was used as currency, and that printed money came into being in the 10th century in China.

The museum's inner courtyard is now canopied by a lightweight, transparent roof, transforming the area into a covered square that houses a Centre for Education, exhibition space, bookshops, and restaurants. The center of the Great Court features the Round Reading Room, which is famous as the place where Karl Marx hung out while writing *Das Kapital.*

Finally, a *warning:* Watch your wallets when you're standing in crowds, particularly in front of the Rosetta Stone. The museum is free and tends to attract a few grab-happy drifters.

For information on the British Library, see p. 242.

Great Russell St., WC1. ℂ **020/7323-8299** or 020/7636-1555 for recorded information. www.thebritishmuseum. ac.uk. Free admission. Sat–Wed 10am–5:30pm; Thurs–Fri 10am–8:30pm. Tube: Holborn, Tottenham Court Rd., Goodge St., or Russell Sq.

Buckingham Palace ⟨⟩⟨⟩ *Kids*

This massive, graceful building is the official residence of the Queen. The red-brick palace was built as a country house for the notoriously rakish Duke of Buckingham. In 1762, King George III, who needed room for his 15 children, bought it. It didn't become the official royal residence, though, until Queen Victoria took the throne; she preferred it to St. James's Palace. From George III's time, the building was continuously expanded and remodeled, faced with Portland stone, and twice bombed (during the Blitz). Located in a 16-hectare (40-acre) garden, it's 108m (354 ft.) long and contains 600 rooms. You can tell whether the Queen is at home by checking to see if the Royal Standard is flying from the mast outside. For most of the year, you can't visit the palace without an official invitation. Since 1993, though, much of it has been open for tours during an 8-week period in August and September, when the royal family is usually vacationing outside London. Elizabeth II agreed to allow visitors to tour the State Room, the Grand Staircase, the Throne Room, and other areas designed by John Nash for George IV, as well as the Picture Gallery, which displays masterpieces by Van Dyck, Rembrandt, Rubens, and others. You have to buy a timed-entrance ticket the same day you plan to tour the

The Top Attractions

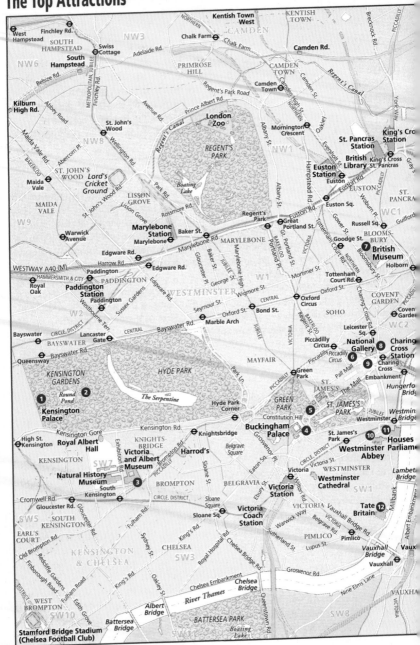

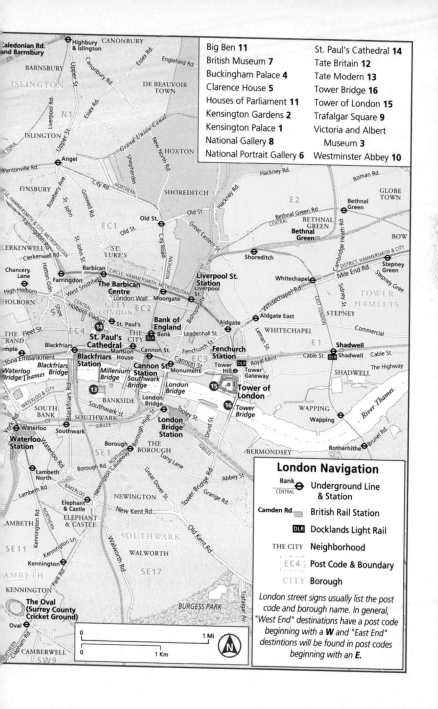

Big Ben **11**
British Museum **7**
Buckingham Palace **4**
Clarence House **5**
Houses of Parliament **11**
Kensington Gardens **2**
Kensington Palace **1**
National Gallery **8**
National Portrait Gallery **6**

St. Paul's Cathedral **14**
Tate Britain **12**
Tate Modern **13**
Tower Bridge **16**
Tower of London **15**
Trafalgar Square **9**
Victoria and Albert
Museum **3**
Westminster Abbey **10**

London Navigation

Bank / CENTRAL — Underground Line & Station

Camden Rd. — British Rail Station

DLR — Docklands Light Rail

THE CITY — Neighborhood

EC4 — Post Code & Boundary

CITY — Borough

*London street signs usually list the post code and borough name. In general, "West End" destinations have a post code beginning with a **W** and "East End" destinations will be found in post codes beginning with an **E**.*

0 ___ 1 Mi
0 ___ 1 Km

Tips The Guard Doesn't Change Every Day

The schedule for the Changing of the Guard ceremony is variable, at best. In theory, at least, the guard is changed daily from May to mid-July, at which time it goes on its "winter" schedule—that is, alternating days. Always check locally with the tourist office to see if it's likely to be staged at the time of your visit. The ceremony has sometimes been cut at the last minute, leaving thousands of visitors feeling they have missed out on a London must-see (though we say it's overrated anyway).

palace. Tickets go on sale at 9am, but rather than lining up at sunrise with all the other tourists—this is one of London's most popular attractions—book by phone with a credit card and give yourself a few more hours of sleep.

During the 8 weeks of summer, visitors are also allowed to stroll through the royal family's garden, along a 4.5km (2.75 miles) walk on the south side of the grounds, with views of a lake and the usually off-limits west side of the palace. The garden is home to 30 types of birds, including the great crested grebe, plus 350 varieties of wildflowers.

Buckingham Palace's most famous spectacle is the vastly overrated **Changing of the Guard** (daily Apr–July and on alternating days for the rest of the year). The new guard, marching behind a band, comes from either the Wellington or Chelsea barracks and takes over from the old guard in the forecourt of the palace. The ceremony begins at 11:30am, although it's frequently canceled because of bad weather, state events, and other, harder-to-fathom reasons. We like the changing of the guard at Horse Guards better (p. 237) because you can actually see the men marching and you don't have to battle such tourist hordes. However, few first-time visitors will resist the lure of the Buckingham Palace Changing of the Guard. If that includes you, arrive as early as 10:30am and claim territorial rights to a space in front of the palace. If you're not firmly anchored here, you'll miss much of the ceremony.

At end of The Mall (on the road running from Trafalgar Sq.). ✆ 020/7766-7300. www.royalcollection.org.uk. Palace tours £15 ($29) adults, £14 ($27) over 60 and students, £8.50 ($16) under 17, free ages 4 and under. Family ticket £39 ($74). Changing of the Guard free. July 26–Sept 24 (dates can vary), and additional dates may be added. Daily 9:45am–6pm. Changing of the guard daily from Apr–July at 11:30am and alternating days for the rest of the year at 11am. Tube: St. James's Park, Green Park, or Victoria.

Clarence House *★★* From 1953 until her death in 2002, the Queen Mother lived at Clarence House in a wing of St. James's Palace. It was constructed between 1825 and 1927 to the designs of John Nash. Today it is the official residence of the Prince of Wales, and is open to the public only during a specified period of the year (see below). The present Queen Elizabeth and the Duke of Edinburgh lived here following their marriage in 1947.

After the death of the Queen Mother, the house was refurbished and redecorated, with antiques and art from the royal collection. Visitors are taken on a guided tour of five of the staterooms, where much of the Queen's collection of art and furniture is on display, along with pieces added by Prince Charles. The Queen Mother had an impressive collection of 20th-century British art, including works by John Piper, Augustus John, and Graham Sutherland. She also was known for her superb collection of Fabergé and English porcelain and silver, especially pieces from her family collection (the Bowes-Lyon family).

Stable Yard Gate, SW1. © 020/7766-7303. www.royal.collection.org.uk. Admission £7.50 ($14) adults, £4 ($7.60) ages 5–16, free for children 4 and under. Aug 1–Sept 30 (dates subject to change—call first) daily 10am–5:30pm. Tube: Green Park or St. James's Park.

Houses of Parliament & Big Ben ⭑⭑

The Houses of Parliament, along with their trademark clock tower, Big Ben, are the ultimate symbols of London. They're the strongholds of Britain's democracy, the assemblies that effectively trimmed the sails of royal power. Both the House of Commons and the House of Lords are in the former royal Palace of Westminster, which was the king's residence until Henry VIII moved to Whitehall. The current Gothic Revival buildings date from 1840 and were designed by Charles Barry. (The earlier buildings were destroyed by fire in 1834.) Assisting Barry was Augustus Welby Pugin, who designed the paneled ceilings, tiled floors, stained glass, clocks, fireplaces, umbrella stands, and even inkwells. There are more than 1,000 rooms and 3km (1¾ miles) of corridors. The clock tower at the eastern end houses the world's most famous timepiece. **"Big Ben"** refers not to the clock tower itself, but to the largest bell in the chime, which weighs close to 14 tons and is named for the first commissioner of works, Sir Benjamin Hall.

You may observe debates for free from the **Stranger's Galleries** in both houses. Sessions usually begin in mid-October and run to the end of July, with recesses at Christmas and Easter. The chances of getting into the House of Lords when it's in session are generally better than for the more popular House of Commons. Although we can't promise you the oratory of a Charles James Fox or a William Pitt the Elder, the debates in the House of Commons are often lively and controversial (seats are at a premium during crises).

For years, London tabloids have portrayed members of the House of Lords as a bunch of "Monty Pythonesque upper-class twits," with one foreign secretary calling the House of Lords "medieval lumber." Today, under Labour government, the House of Lords is being shaken up as lords lose their inherited posts. Panels are studying what to do with this largely useless house, its members often descendants of royal mistresses and ancient landowners.

Those who'd like to book a tour can do so, but it takes a bit of work. Both houses are open to the general public for guided tours only for a limited season in July and August. The palace is open Monday, Tuesday, Friday, and Saturday from 9:15am to 4:30pm during those times. All tour tickets cost £7 ($13) adult; £5 ($9.50) for seniors, students, and children under 16; £22 ($42) family ticket. Children under 4 years old may enter free. For advance tickets call © 020/7219-4272.

If you arrive just to attend a session, these are free. You line up at Stephen's Gate, heading to your left for the entrance into the Commons or to the right for the Lords. The London daily newspapers announce sessions of Parliament.

Insider's Tip: The hottest ticket and the most exciting time to visit is during "Prime Minister's Question Time" on Wednesdays, which is only from noon to 12:30pm, but which must seem like hours to the prime minister, who is on the hot seat, exchanging barbs with the MPs (members of Parliament).

Foreign and Commonwealth visitors should apply to their embassy or High Commission in the U.K. for a card of introduction, which will normally permit entry during the early afternoon. Embassies and High Commissions may issue no more than four cards on any day, so visitors from certain countries may find cards are booked for several weeks ahead. Please note that such cards do not guarantee entry. Quite often, it will not be possible to admit their bearers until *after* Question Time. British embassies abroad do not issue such cards.

Across the street is the **Jewel Tower** ⍟, Abingdon Street (© **020/7222-2219**), one of only two surviving buildings from the medieval Palace of Westminster. It was constructed in 1365 as a place where Edward III could stash his treasure trove. The tower hosts an exhibition on the history of Parliament and makes for a great introduction to the inner workings of the British government. The video presentation on the top floor is especially informative. A touch-screen computer allows visitors to take a virtual tour of both houses of Parliament. The tower is open daily from 10am to 5pm April to October and 10am to 4pm November to March. Admission is £2.70 ($5.15) for adults, £2 ($3.80) for students and seniors, and £1.40 ($2.65) for children.

Westminster Palace, Old Palace Yard, SW1. House of Commons © 020/7219-4272. House of Lords © 020/7219-3107. www.parliament.uk. Free admission. House of Lords open mid-Oct to Aug Mon–Wed from 2:30pm, Thurs from 11am, and sometimes Fri (check by phone). House of Commons mid-Oct to Aug Mon 2:30–10:30pm, Tues–Wed 11:30am–7:30pm, Thurs 11:30am–6pm, Fri not always open—call ahead. Both houses are open for tours (see above). Join line at St. Stephen's entrance. Tube: Westminster.

Kensington Palace ⍟ (Kids)   Once the residence of British monarchs, Kensington Palace hasn't been the official home of reigning kings since George II, who died in 1760. William III and Mary II acquired it in 1689 as an escape from the damp royal rooms along the Thames. Since the end of the 18th century, the palace has housed various members of the royal family, and the State Apartments are open for tours.

It was here in 1837 that a young Victoria was awakened with the news that her uncle, William IV, had died and she was now the Queen of England. You can view a collection of Victoriana here, including some of her memorabilia. In the apartments of Queen Mary II is a striking 17th-century writing cabinet inlaid with tortoiseshell. Paintings from the Royal Collection line the walls. A rare 1750 lady's court dress and splendid examples of male court dress from the 18th century are on display in rooms adjacent to the State Apartments, as part of the Royal Ceremonial Dress Collection, which features royal costumes dating as far back as 200 years.

Kensington Palace was the London home of the late Princess Margaret, and is the current home of the Duke and Duchess of Kent. The palace was also the home of Diana, Princess of Wales, and her two sons. (William and Harry now live with their father at St. James's Palace.) The palace is probably best known for the millions of flowers placed in front of it during the days following Diana's death. The former apartment of the late Princess Margaret has opened to the public as an education center and an exhibition space for royal ceremonial dress.

Warning: You don't get to see the apartments where Princess Di lived or where both Di and Charles lived until they separated. Many visitors think they'll get to peek at these rooms and are disappointed. Charles and Di lived on the west side of the palace, still occupied today by minor royals.

The **Kensington Gardens** are open to the public for leisurely strolls through the manicured grounds and around the Round Pond. One of the most famous sights is the controversial Albert Memorial, a lasting tribute not only to Victoria's consort, but also to the questionable artistic taste of the Victorian era. There's a wonderful afternoon tea offered in The Orangery (p. 204).

The Broad Walk, Kensington Gardens, W8. © 0870/7515-170. Admission £12 ($23) adults, £9 ($17) seniors and students, £7.50 ($14) children, £34 ($65) family ticket. Mar–Oct daily 10am–6pm; Nov–Feb daily 10am–5pm. Tube: Queensway or Notting Hill Gate; High St. Kensington on south side.

Fun Fact Trafalgar: London's Most Famous Square

London is a city full of landmark squares. Without a doubt, the best-known is **Trafalgar Square** ✸✸; www.london.gov.uk/mayor/Trafalgar_square/index.jsp (Tube: Charing Cross), which honors one of England's great military heroes, Horatio Viscount Nelson (1758–1805). Although he suffered from seasickness, he went to sea at the age of 12 and was an admiral by age 39. Nelson was a hero of the Battle of Calvi in 1794, where he lost an eye; the Battle of Santa Cruz in 1797, where he lost an arm; and the Battle of Trafalgar in 1805, where he lost his life. He is also famous for his affair with Lady Hamilton, the subject of books and films (including *That Hamilton Woman,* with Laurence Olivier and Vivien Leigh).

The square is dominated by the 44m (144-ft.) granite *Nelson's Column,* built by E. H. Baily in 1843. The column I"wn Whitehall toward the Old Admiralty, where Lord Nelson's body lay in state. The figure of the naval hero towers 5m (16 ft.) high—not bad for a man who stood 5'4" in real life. The capital is of bronze, cast from cannons recovered from the wreck of the *Royal George,* which sank in 1782. Queen Victoria's favorite animal painter, Sir Edward Landseer, added the four lions at the base of the column in 1868. The pools and fountains weren't added until 1939; they were the last work of Sir Edwin Lutyens.

Political demonstrations take place in the square and around the column, which has the most aggressive pigeons in London. Much of the world focuses on the square via TV cameras on New Year's Eve, watching revelers jump into the chilly waters of the fountains. The Christmas tree that's installed here every December is a gift from Norway to the British people, in appreciation of Britain's sheltering the Norwegian royal family during World War II. The tree is surrounded by carolers most December evenings. Year-round, street performers (now officially licensed) will entertain you in hopes of receiving a token of appreciation for their efforts.

To the southeast of the square, at 36 Craven St., stands a house that was occupied by Benjamin Franklin from 1757 to 1774. On the north side of the square rises the National Gallery, constructed in the 1830s. In front of the building is a copy of a statue of George Washington by J. A. Houdon.

To the left of St. Martin's Place is the National Portrait Gallery, a collection of portraits of famous Brits—from Chaucer and Shakespeare to Nell Gwynne, Margaret Thatcher, and Lady Diana. Also on the square is the steeple of St. Martin-in-the-Fields, the final resting place of Sir Joshua Reynolds, William Hogarth, and Thomas Chippendale.

National Gallery ✸✸✸   This stately neoclassical building contains an unrivaled collection of Western art spanning 7 centuries—from the late 13th to the early 20th—and covering every great European school. For sheer skill of display and arrangement, it surpasses its counterparts in Paris, New York, Madrid, and Amsterdam.

The largest part of the collection is devoted to the Italians, including the Sienese, Venetian, and Florentine masters. They're now housed in the Sainsbury Wing, which was designed by noted Philadelphia architects Robert Venturi and Denise Scott Brown, and opened by Queen Elizabeth II in 1991. On display are such works as Leonardo's *Virgin of the Rocks;* Titian's *Bacchus and Ariadne;* Giorgione's *Adoration of the Magi;* and unforgettable canvases by Bellini, Veronese, Botticelli, and Tintoretto. Botticelli's *Venus and Mars* is eternally enchanting. The Sainsbury Wing is also used for large temporary exhibits.

Of the early Gothic works, the Wilton Diptych (French or English school, late 14th c.) is the rarest treasure; it depicts Richard II being introduced to the Madonna and Child by John the Baptist and the Saxon kings, Edmund and Edward the Confessor. Then there are the Spanish giants: El Greco's *Agony in the Garden* and portraits by Goya and Velázquez. The Flemish-Dutch school is represented by Brueghel, Jan van Eyck, Vermeer, Rubens, and de Hooch; the Rembrandts include two of his immortal self-portraits. None of van Eyck's art creates quite the stir that the **Arnolfini Portrait** does. You probably studied this painting from 1434 in your Art History 101 class. The stunning work depicts Giovanni di Nicolao Arnolfini and his wife (who is not pregnant, as is often thought; she is merely holding up her full-skirted dress in the contemporary fashion). There's also an immense French Impressionist and post-Impressionist collection that includes works by Manet, Monet, Degas, Renoir, and Cézanne. Particularly charming is the peep-show cabinet by Hoogstraten in one of the Dutch rooms: It's like spying through a keyhole.

British and modern art are the specialties of the Tate Gallery (see listings below), but the National Gallery does have some fine 18th-century British masterpieces, including works by Hogarth, Gainsborough, Reynolds, Constable, and Turner.

Guided tours of the National Gallery are offered twice daily, with an extra tour on Wednesday. A Gallery Guide Soundtrack is also available. A portable CD player provides audio information on paintings of your choice with the mere push of a button. Although this service is free, contributions are appreciated.

Insider's Tip: The National Gallery has a computer information center where you can design your own personal tour map for free. The computer room, located in the Micro Gallery, includes a dozen hands-on workstations. The online system lists 2,200 paintings and has background notes for each work. Using a touch-screen computer, you can design your own personalized tour by selecting a maximum of 10 paintings you would like to view. Once you have made your choices, you print a personal tour map with your selections.

N. side of Trafalgar Sq., WC2. © 020/7747-2885. www.nationalgallery.org.uk. Free admission. Thurs–Tues 10am–6pm; Wed 10am–9pm. Tube: Charing Cross or Leicester Sq.

National Portrait Gallery 𝘎𝘎   In a gallery of both remarkable and unremarkable portraits (they're collected for their subjects rather than their artistic quality), a few paintings tower over the rest, including Sir Joshua Reynolds's first portrait of Samuel Johnson ("a man of most dreadful appearance"), Nicholas Hilliard's miniature of handsome Sir Walter Raleigh, a full-length of Elizabeth I, and a Holbein cartoon of Henry VIII. There's also a portrait of William Shakespeare (with a gold earring) by an unknown artist that bears the claim of being the "most authentic contemporary likeness" of its subject. One of the most famous pictures in the gallery is the group portrait of the Brontë sisters (Charlotte, Emily, and Anne) by their brother, Bramwell. An idealized portrait of Lord Byron by Thomas Phillips is also on display.

The galleries of Victorian and early-20th-century portraits were radically redesigned. The later 20th-century portraiture includes major works by such artists as

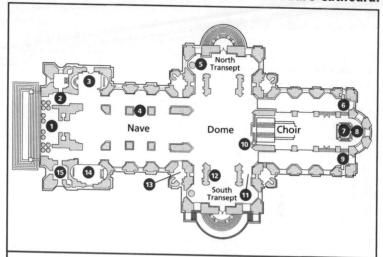

All Souls' Chapel **2**
American Memorial Chapter **8**
Anglican Martyr's Chapel **6**
Chapel of St. Michael
  & St. George **14**
Dean's Staircase **15**
Entrance to Crypt
  (Wren's grave) **11**
Font **5**

High Altar **7**
Lady Chapel **9**
Nelson Monument **12**
Pulpit **10**
St. Dunstan's Chapel **3**
Staircase to Library,
  Whispering Gallery & Dome **13**
Wellington Monument **4**
West Doorway **1**

Warhol and Hambling. Some of the more flamboyant personalities of the past 2 centuries are on show: T. S. Eliot; Disraeli; Macmillan; Sir Richard Burton (the explorer, not the actor); Elizabeth Taylor; and our two favorites, G. F. Watts's famous portrait of his great actress wife, Ellen Terry, and Vanessa Bell's portrait of her sister, Virginia Woolf. Perhaps not surprisingly, a portrait of the late Princess Diana on the Royal Landing seems to attract the most viewers.

In 2000, Queen Elizabeth opened the Ondaatje Wing of the gallery, increasing the gallery's exhibition space by over 50%. The most intriguing new space is the splendid Tudor Gallery, featuring portraits of Richard III and Henry VII. There's also a portrait of Shakespeare that the gallery acquired in 1856. Rooms lead through centuries of English monarchs, with literary and artistic figures thrown in. A Balcony Gallery taps into the cult of celebrity, displaying more recent figures whose fame has lasted longer than Warhol's 15 minutes. These include everybody from Mick Jagger to Joan Collins, and, of course, the Baroness Thatcher.

The Gallery operates a cafe and art bookshop.

St. Martin's Place, WC2. ✆ 020/7306-0055. www.npg.org.uk. Free admission; fee charged for certain temporary exhibitions. Sat–Wed 10am–6pm; Thurs–Fri 10am–9pm. Tube: Charing Cross or Leicester Sq.

St. Paul's Cathedral ✸✸✸ During World War II, newsreel footage reaching America showed St. Paul's Cathedral standing virtually alone among the rubble of the

Moments **Roses Are Red**

One of the most enjoyable activities of a spring visit to London is a stroll through the gardens of St. Paul's when the roses are in bloom.

City, its dome lit by fires caused by bombings all around it. That the cathedral survived at all is a miracle, since it was badly hit twice during the early years of the bombardment of London. But St. Paul's is accustomed to calamity, having been burned down three times and destroyed by invading Norsemen. The old St. Paul's was razed during the Great Fire of 1666, making way for a new structure designed by Sir Christopher Wren and built between 1675 and 1710. The cathedral is architectural genius Wren's ultimate masterpiece.

The classical dome of St. Paul's dominates the City's square mile. The golden cross surmounting it is 110m (361 ft.) above the ground; the golden ball on which the cross rests measures 2m (6½ ft.) in diameter, though it looks like a marble from below. In the interior of the dome is the **Whispering Gallery,** an acoustic marvel in which the faintest whisper can be heard clearly on the opposite side. Sit on one side, have your traveling companions sit on the other, and whisper away. You can climb to the top of the dome for a 360-degree view of London. A second steep climb leads from the Whispering Gallery to the **Stone Gallery,** which opens onto a panoramic view of London. Another 153 steps take you to the **Inner Golden Gallery,** situated at the top of the inner dome. Here an even more panoramic view of London unfolds.

St. Paul's Churchyard, EC4. ✆ 020/8340-9591. www.stpauls.co.uk. Cathedral and galleries £9 ($17) adults, £8 ($15) seniors and students, £3.50 ($6.65) children 6–16, £21 ($40) family ticket. Guided tours £3 ($5.70) adults, £2.50 ($4.75) students and seniors, £1 ($1.90) children 6–16; recorded tours £3.50 ($6.65), free for children 5 and under. Cathedral (excluding galleries) Mon–Sat 8:30am–4pm; galleries Mon–Sat 9:30am–4pm. No sightseeing Sun (services only). Tube: St. Paul's, Mansion House, Cannon St., and Blackfriars.

Tate Britain ✦✦✦   Fronting the Thames near Vauxhall Bridge in Pimlico, the Tate looks like a smaller and more graceful relation of the British Museum. The most prestigious gallery in Britain, it houses the national collections, covering British art from the 16th century to the present day, as well as an array of international works. In the spring of 2000, the Tate moved its collection of 20th- and 21st-century art to the **Tate Modern** (see below). This split helped to open more display space at the Tate Britain, but the collection here is still much too large to be displayed all at once, so the works on view change from time to time.

The older works include some of the best of Gainsborough, Reynolds, Stubbs, Blake, and Constable. William Hogarth is well represented, particularly by his satirical *O the Roast Beef of Old England* (known as *The Gate of Calais*). You'll find the illustrations of William Blake, the incomparable mystical poet, including such works as *The Book of Job, The Divine Comedy,* and *Paradise Lost.* The collection of works by J. M. W. Turner is the Tate's largest by a single artist—Turner himself willed most of his paintings and watercolors to the nation.

Also on display are pieces by many major 19th- and 20th-century painters, including Paul Nash, Matisse, Dalí, Modigliani, Munch, Bonnard, and Picasso. Truly remarkable are the several enormous abstract canvases by Mark Rothko, the group of paintings and sculptures by Giacometti, and the paintings by one of England's best-known modern artists, Francis Bacon. Sculptures by Henry Moore and Barbara Hepworth are also occasionally displayed.

Insider's Tip: After you've seen the grand art, don't hasten away. Drop in to the Tate Gallery Shop for some of the best art books and postcards in London. The gallery sells whimsical T-shirts with art masterpieces on them. Those ubiquitous Tate Gallery canvas bags seen all over London are sold here, as are the town's best art posters (all make great souvenirs). Invite your friends for tea at the Coffee Shop, with its excellent cakes and pastries, or lunch at Rex Whistler (p. 180). You'll get to enjoy good food, Rex Whistler art, and the best and most reasonably priced wine list in London.

Millbank, SW1. ② 020/7887-8888. www.tate.org.uk. Free admission; special exhibitions sometimes incur a charge of £6–£10 ($11–$19). Daily 10:30am–5:50pm. Tube: Pimlico.

Tate Modern ⭐⭐⭐

In the transformed Bankside Power Station in Southwark, this museum, which opened in 2000, draws some 2 million visitors a year to see the greatest collection of international 20th-century art in Britain. How would we rate the collection? At the same level of the Pompidou in Paris, with a slight edge over New York's Guggenheim. Of course, New York's Museum of Modern Art remains in a class of its own. Tate Modern is viewer-friendly, with eye-level hangings. All the big painting stars are here—a whole galaxy ranging from Dalí to Duchamp, from Giacometti to Matisse and Mondrian, from Picasso and Pollock to Rothko and Warhol. The Modern is also a gallery of 21st-century art, displaying new and exciting works.

The Tate Modern makes extensive use of glass for both its exterior and interior, offering panoramic views. Galleries are arranged over three levels and provide a variety of spaces for display. Instead of exhibiting art chronologically and by school, the Tate Modern, in a radical break from tradition, takes a thematic approach. This allows displays to cut across movements.

You can cross the Millennium Bridge, a pedestrian-only walk from the steps of St. Paul's, over the Thames to the gallery. Or else you can take the **Tate to Tate** boat (② 020/7887-8888), which takes art lovers on an 18-minute journey across the Thames from the Tate Britain to the Tate Modern, with a stop at the London Eye and the Saatchi Gallery. A day pass costs £5 ($9.50); £20 ($38) for a family pass. Leaving from Millbank Pier, this catamaran is decorated by the trademark colorful dots of that *enfant terrible* artist, Damien Hirst.

Bankside, SE1. ② 020/7887-8888. www.tate.org.uk. Free admission. Sun–Thurs 10am–6pm; Fri–Sat 10am–10pm. Tube: Southwark or Blackfriars.

Tower Bridge ⭐⭐

This is one of the world's most celebrated landmarks, and possibly the most photographed and painted bridge on earth. (Presumably, this is the one the Arizona businessman thought he was getting when he bought the London Bridge.) Despite its medieval appearance, Tower Bridge was built in 1894.

In 1993, an exhibition opened inside the bridge to commemorate its century-old history; it takes you up the north tower to high-level walkways between the two towers with spectacular views of St. Paul's, the Tower of London, and the Houses of Parliament. You're then led down the south tower and into the bridge's original engine room, containing the Victorian boilers and steam engines that used to raise and lower the bridge for ships to pass. Exhibits in the towers use animatronic characters, video, and computers to illustrate the history of the bridge.

At Tower Bridge, SE1. ② 020/7403-3761. www.towerbridge.org.uk. Tower Bridge Experience £5.50 ($10) adults, £4.25 ($8.10) students and seniors, £3 ($5.70) children 5–15, £14 ($27) family ticket, free for children 4 and under.

Tower Bridge Experience open Apr–Sept daily 10am–6:30pm; off season daily 9:30am–6pm. Closed Christmas Eve and Christmas Day. Tube: Tower Hill, London Bridge, or Fenchurch St.

Tower of London ★★★ *(Kids)*   This ancient fortress continues to pack in the crowds with its macabre associations with the legendary figures imprisoned and/or executed here. There are more spooks here per square foot than in any other building in the whole of haunted Britain. Headless bodies, bodiless heads, phantom soldiers, icy blasts, clanking chains—you name them, the Tower's got them. Centuries after the last head rolled on Tower Hill, a shivery atmosphere of impending doom still lingers over the Tower's mighty walls. Plan on spending a lot of time here.

The Tower is actually an intricately patterned compound of structures built through the ages for varying purposes, mostly as expressions of royal power. The oldest is the **White Tower,** begun by William the Conqueror in 1078 to keep London's native Saxon population in check. Later rulers added other towers, more walls, and fortified gates, until the buildings became like a small town within a city. Until the reign of James I (beginning in 1603), the Tower was also one of the royal residences. But above all, it was a prison for distinguished captives.

Every stone of the Tower tells a story—usually a gory one. In the **Bloody Tower,** according to Shakespeare, Richard III's henchmen murdered the two little princes (the young sons of his brother, Edward IV). Richard knew his position as king could not be secure as long as his nephews were alive, and there seems no reasonable doubt that the princes were killed on his orders. Attempts have been made by some historians to clear his name, but Richard remains the chief suspect, and his deed caused him to lose the "hearts of the people," according to the *Chronicles of London* at the time.

Sir Walter Raleigh spent 13 years in the Bloody Tower before his date with the executioner. On the walls of the **Beauchamp Tower,** you can still read the last messages scratched by despairing prisoners. Through **Traitors' Gate** passed such ill-fated, romantic figures as Robert Devereux, the second Earl of Essex and a favorite of Elizabeth I. A plaque marks the eerie place at **Tower Green** where two wives of Henry VIII, Anne Boleyn and Catherine Howard, plus Sir Thomas More, and the 9-day queen, Lady Jane Grey, all lost their lives.

The Tower, besides being a royal palace, a fortress, and a prison, was also an armory, a treasury, a menagerie, and, in 1675, an astronomical observatory. Reopened in 1999, the White Tower holds the **Armouries,** which date from the reign of Henry VIII, as well as a display of instruments of torture and execution that recall some of the most ghastly moments in the Tower's history. In the Jewel House, you'll find the Tower's greatest attraction, the **Crown Jewels**—some of the world's most precious stones set into robes, swords, scepters, and crowns. The Imperial State Crown is the most famous crown on earth; made for Victoria in 1837, it's worn today by Queen Elizabeth II when she opens Parliament. Studded with some 3,000 jewels (principally diamonds), it includes the Black Prince's Ruby, worn by Henry V at Agincourt. The 530-carat Star of Africa, a cut diamond on the Royal Sceptre with Cross, would make Harry Winston turn over in his grave. You'll have to stand in long lines to catch just a glimpse of the jewels as you and hundreds of others scroll by on moving sidewalks, but the wait is worth it.

The presumed prison cell of Sir Thomas More is open to the public. More left this cell in 1535 to face his executioner after he'd fallen out with King Henry VIII over the monarch's desire to divorce Catherine of Aragon, the first of his six wives. More is believed to have lived in the lower part of the Bell Tower, here in this whitewashed cell, during the last 14 months of his life, although some historians doubt this claim.

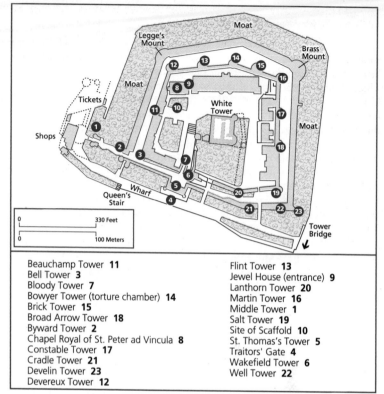

Moat

Legge's
Mount

Brass
Mount

Moat

Tickets

White
Tower

Shops

Moat

Wharf

Queen's
Stair

| 0 | 330 Feet |
| 0 | 100 Meters |

Tower
Bridge

Beauchamp Tower **11**
Bell Tower **3**
Bloody Tower **7**
Bowyer Tower (torture chamber) **14**
Brick Tower **15**
Broad Arrow Tower **18**
Byward Tower **2**
Chapel Royal of St. Peter ad Vincula **8**
Constable Tower **17**
Cradle Tower **21**
Develin Tower **23**
Devereux Tower **12**

Flint Tower **13**
Jewel House (entrance) **9**
Lanthorn Tower **20**
Martin Tower **16**
Middle Tower **1**
Salt Tower **19**
Site of Scaffold **10**
St. Thomas's Tower **5**
Traitors' Gate **4**
Wakefield Tower **6**
Well Tower **22**

A **palace** inhabited by King Edward I in the late 1200s stands above Traitors' Gate. It's the only surviving medieval palace in Britain. Guides at the palace are dressed in period costumes, and reproductions of furniture and fittings, including Edward's throne, evoke the era, along with burning incense and candles.

In 2004 several improvements were made, including the opening of a Visitors Center and the restoration of a 13th-century wharf. To the west of the Tower is the newly created Tower Hill Square, designed by Stanton Williams, with a series of pavilions housing ticketing facilities, a gift shop, and a cafeteria.

Oh, yes—don't forget to look for the ravens. Six of them (plus two spares) are all registered as official Tower residents. According to a legend, the Tower of London will stand as long as those black, ominous birds remain, so to be on the safe side, one of the wings of each raven is clipped.

One-hour guided tours of the entire compound are given by the Yeoman Warders (also known as "Beefeaters") every half-hour, starting at 9:30am, from the Middle Tower near the main entrance. The last guided walk starts about 3:30pm in summer, 2:30pm in winter—weather permitting, of course.

You can attend the nightly **Ceremony of the Keys,** the ceremonial locking-up of the Tower by the Yeoman Warders. For free tickets, write to the Ceremony of the Keys, Waterloo Block, Tower of London, London EC3N 4AB, and request a specific date,

---

Tips Tower Tips

You can spend the shortest time possible in the Tower's long lines if you buy your ticket at the kiosk at Tower Hill Tube station before emerging above ground. Even so, choose a day other than Sunday—crowds are at their worst then—and arrive as early as you can in the morning.

---

but also list alternate dates. At least 6 weeks' notice is required. Accompany all requests with a stamped, self-addressed envelope (British stamps only) or two International Reply Coupons. With ticket in hand, a Yeoman Warder will admit you at 9:35pm. Frankly, we think it's not worth the trouble you go through to see this rather cheesy ceremony, but we know some who disagree with us.

Tower Hill, EC3. ℂ 0870/756-7070. www.tower-of-london.org.uk. Admission £15 ($29) adults, £12 ($23) students and seniors, £9.50 ($18) children, £43 ($82) family ticket for 5 (but no more than 2 adults), free for children under 5. Mar–Oct Tues–Sat 9am–6pm, Sun and Mon 10am–6pm; Nov–Feb Tues–Sat 9am–5pm, Sun and Mon 10am–5pm. Tube: Tower Hill.

Victoria and Albert Museum ⭒⭒⭒   The Victoria and Albert is the greatest decorative-arts museum in the world. It's also one of the liveliest and most imaginative museums in London—where else would you find the quintessential "little black dress" in the permanent collection?

The medieval holdings include such treasures as the early-English Gloucester Candlestick; the Byzantine Veroli Casket, with its ivory panels based on Greek plays; and the Syon Cope, a unique embroidery made in England in the early 14th century. An area devoted to Islamic art houses the Ardabil Carpet from 16th-century Persia.

The V&A boasts the largest collection of Renaissance sculpture outside Italy. A highlight of the 16th-century collection is the marble group *Neptune with Triton,* by Bernini. The cartoons by Raphael, which were conceived as designs for tapestries for the Sistine Chapel, are owned by the Queen and are on display here. A most unusual, huge, and impressive exhibit is the Cast Courts, life-size plaster models of ancient and medieval statuary and architecture.

The museum has the greatest collection of Indian art outside India, plus Chinese and Japanese galleries. In complete contrast are suites of English furniture, metalwork, and ceramics, and a superb collection of portrait miniatures, including the one Hans Holbein the Younger made of Anne of Cleves for the benefit of Henry VIII, who was again casting around for a suitable wife. The Dress Collection includes a collection of corsets through the ages that's sure to make you wince. There's also a remarkable collection of musical instruments.

The V&A has opened 15 modern galleries—the **British Galleries** ⭒⭒⭒—telling the story of British design from 1500 to 1900. No other museum in the world houses such a diverse collection of British design and decorative art. From Chippendale to Morris, all of the top British designers are featured in some 3,000 items, ranging from the 5m-high (16-ft.) Melville Bed (1697) with its luxurious wild-silk damask and red-velvet hangings, to 19th-century classics such as furniture by Charles Rennie Mackintosh. One of the most prized possessions is the "Great Bed of Ware," mentioned in Shakespeare's *Twelfth Night.* Also on exhibit is the wedding suite of James II. The interactive displays hold special interest. Learning about heraldry is far more interesting when you're designing your own coat of arms. And don't miss the V&A's most

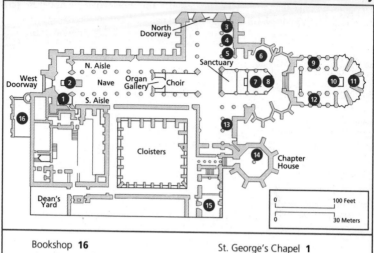

Bookshop **16**

Chapel of St. John the Baptist **6**

Chapel of St. John the Evangelist **5**

Chapter House **14**

Henry V's Chantry **8**

Poets' Corner **13**

Royal Air Force Chapel **11**

St. Andrew's Chapel **3**

St. Edward's Chapel
  (Coronation Chair) **7**

St. George's Chapel **1**

St. Michael's Chapel **4**

Tomb of Mary I &
  Elizabeth I **9**

Tomb of Henry VII **10**

Tomb of Mary,
  Queen of Scots **12**

Tomb of the Unknown Warrior/
  Memorial to Churchill **2**

Undercroft Museum **15**

bizarre gallery, Fakes and Forgeries. The impostors here are amazingly authentic—in fact, we'd judge some of them as better than the old masters themselves.

Insider's Tip: In the winter of 2004, V&A opened a suite of five renovated painting galleries that were originally built in 1850. A trio of these galleries focuses on British landscapes as seen through the eyes of Turner, Constable, and others. Constable's oil sketches were donated by his daughter, Isabel, in 1888. Another gallery showcases the bequest of Constantine Ionides, a Victorian collector, with masters such as Botticelli, Delacroix, Degas, Tintoretto, and Ingres. There's even a piano here designed by the famous Edward Burne-Jones, which once belonged to Ionides's brother.

Cromwell Rd., SW7. ② 020/7942-2000. www.vam.ac.uk. Free admission. Temporary exhibitions often £10 ($19). Daily 10am–5:45pm (Wed until 10pm); until 10pm the last Fri of each month. Tube: South Kensington.

Westminster Abbey ✸✸✸　With its identical square towers and superb archways, this early-English Gothic abbey is one of the greatest examples of ecclesiastical architecture on earth. But it's far more than that: It's the shrine of a nation, the symbol of everything Britain has stood for and stands for, and the place in which most of its rulers were crowned and where many lie buried.

Nearly every figure in English history has left his or her mark on Westminster Abbey. Edward the Confessor founded the Benedictine abbey in 1065 on this spot overlooking Parliament Square. The first English king crowned in the Abbey may have been Harold, in January 1066. The man who defeated him at the Battle of Hastings later that year, William the Conqueror, had the first recorded coronation in the Abbey on Christmas Day that same year. The coronation tradition has continued to the present day. The essentially early-English Gothic structure existing today owes more to Henry III's plans than to those of any other sovereign, although many architects, including Wren, have contributed to the Abbey.

Built on the site of the ancient Lady Chapel in the early 16th century, the **Henry VII Chapel** is one of the loveliest in Europe, with its fan vaulting, Knights of Bath banners, and Torrigiani-designed tomb for the king himself, near which hangs a 15th-century Vivarini painting, *Madonna and Child*. Also here, ironically buried in the same tomb, are Catholic Mary I and Protestant Elizabeth I (whose archrival, Mary Queen of Scots, is entombed on the other side of the Henry VII Chapel). In one end of the chapel, you can stand on Cromwell's memorial stone and view the **Royal Air Force Chapel** and its Battle of Britain memorial window, unveiled in 1947 to honor the Royal Air Force.

You can also visit the most hallowed spot in the abbey, the **shrine of Edward the Confessor** (canonized in the 12th c.). Near the tomb of Henry V is the Coronation Chair, made at the command of Edward I in 1300 to display the mystical Stone of Scone (which some think is the sacred stone mentioned in Genesis and known as Jacob's Pillar). Scottish kings were once crowned on the stone (it has since been returned to Scotland).

When you see a statue of the Bard, with one arm resting on a stack of books, you've arrived at **Poets' Corner.** Shakespeare himself is buried at Stratford-upon-Avon, but resting here are Chaucer, Samuel Johnson, Tennyson, Browning, and Dickens. There's even an American, Henry Wadsworth Longfellow, as well as monuments to just about everybody: Milton, Keats, Shelley, Henry James, T. S. Eliot, George Eliot, and others. The most stylized monument is Sir Jacob Epstein's sculptured bust of William Blake. More-recent tablets commemorate poet Dylan Thomas and Sir Laurence Olivier.

Statesmen and men of science—Disraeli, Newton, Charles Darwin—are also interred in the abbey or honored by monuments. Near the west door is the 1965 memorial to Sir Winston Churchill. In the vicinity of this memorial is the tomb of the **Unknown Warrior,** commemorating the British dead of World War I.

Although most of the Abbey's statuary commemorates notable figures of the past, 10 new statues were unveiled in July 1998. Placed in the Gothic niches above the West Front door, these statues honor 10 modern-day martyrs drawn from every continent and religious denomination. Designed by Tim Crawley and carved under his general direction from French Richemont limestone, the sculptures include Elizabeth of Russia, Janani Luwum, and Martin Luther King Jr., representatives of those who have sacrificed their lives for their beliefs.

Off the Cloisters, the **College Garden** is the oldest garden in England, under cultivation for more than 900 years. Established in the 11th century as the abbey's first infirmary garden, this was once a magnificent source of fruits, vegetables, and medicinal herbs. Five of the trees in the garden were planted in 1850 and they continue to thrive today. Surrounded by high walls, flowering trees dot the lawns, and park benches provide comfort where you can hardly hear the roar of passing traffic. The garden is open only Tuesday through Thursday April through September from 10am to 6pm, and October through March from 10am to 4pm.

Insider's Tip: Far removed from the pomp and glory is the **Abbey Treasure Museum,** which displays a real bag of oddities in the undercroft—or crypt—part of the monastic buildings erected between 1066 and 1100. You'll find royal effigies that were used instead of the real corpses for lying-in-state ceremonies because they smelled better. You'll see the almost lifelike effigy of Admiral Nelson (his mistress arranged his hair) and even that of Edward III, his lip warped by the cerebral hemorrhage that felled him. Other oddities include Henry V's funeral armor, a unique corset from Elizabeth I's effigy, and the Essex Ring that Elizabeth I gave to her favorite (Robert Devereux, the Earl of Essex) when she was feeling good about him.

On Sundays, the Abbey is not open to visitors; the rest of the church is open unless a service is being conducted. For times of services, phone the **Chapter Office** (© 020/ 7222-5152).

Broad Sanctuary, SW1. © 020/7654-4900. www.westminster-abbey.org. Admission £10 ($19) adults; £6 ($11) for students, seniors, and children 11–18; £22 ($42) family ticket; free for children under 11. Mon–Tues and Thurs–Fri 9:30am–3:45pm; Wed 9:30am–6pm, Sat 9:30am–2:45pm. Tube: Westminster or St. James's Park.

3 More Central London Attractions

See the "Sights & Attractions by Neighborhood" list on p. 206 for more information on which attraction is in which neighborhood.

CHURCHES & CATHEDRALS

Many of London's churches offer free lunchtime concerts; a full list is available from the London Tourist Board. It's customary to leave a small donation.

All Hallows Barking-by-the-Tower   This fascinating church, which houses a brass-rubbing center, is located next door to the Tower. It features a crypt museum, Roman remains, and traces of early London, including a Saxon arch predating the Tower. Samuel Pepys, the famed diarist, climbed the spire of the church to watch the raging fire of London in 1666. In 1644, William Penn was baptized here, and in 1797, John Quincy Adams was married here. Bombs destroyed the church in 1940, leaving only the tower and walls standing. The church was rebuilt from 1949 to 1958. See "'The City' Attractions" map (p. 227).

Byward St., EC3. © 020/7481-2928. www.allhallowsbythetower.org.uk. Free admission; crypt museum tour £2.50 ($4.75). Museum Mon–Fri 10am–5:30pm, Sat 10am–5pm, Sun 1–5pm; church Mon–Fri 9am–6pm, Sat–Sun 10am–5pm. Tube: Tower Hill.

St. Bride's ✦   Known as the "the church of the press," thanks to its location at the end of Fleet Street, St. Bride's is a remarkable landmark. The current church is the eighth one that has stood here. After it was bombed in 1940, an archaeologist excavated the crypts and was able to confirm much of the site's legendary history:

Finds Drake's Long Voyage

As you're strolling along the riverside, you come upon the old dock of St. Mary Overie, SE1. Here to your delight is an exact replica of the *Golden Hinde,* in which Sir Francis Drake circumnavigated the globe. It's amazingly tiny for such an around-the-world voyage. But this actual ship has sailed around the world some two dozen times, exploring both oceans and the American coast. Visits are daily from 10am to 6pm; entry costs £5.50 ($10) for adults, £5 ($9.50) for children, and £18 ($34) for a family ticket. For information, call © 0870/ 011-8700 or go to www.goldenhinde.org.

⌒ **Fun Fact   American Woman**

The parents of Virginia Dare, the first English child born in America (at Roanoke in 1587), were married in St. Bride's. An effigy of Virginia can be seen over the baptismal font.

A Roman house was discovered, and it was established that in the 6th century, St. Brigit of Ireland had founded the first Christian church that was built here. In addition, a crypt with evidence of six subsequent churches was discovered. Among the famous parishioners have been writers John Dryden, John Milton, Richard Lovelace, and John Evelyn. Diarist Samuel Pepys was baptized here, and novelist Samuel Richardson and his family are buried here. After the Great Fire destroyed it, Christopher Wren rebuilt the church with a spire that's been described as a "madrigal in stone." The crypt was a burial chamber and charnel house for centuries; today it's a museum. Evensong is every Sunday at 6:30pm, and choral concerts are sometimes staged—call for information or check the website below. See "'The City' Attractions" map.

Fleet St., EC4. ✆ 020/7427-0133. www.stbrides.com. Free admission. Mon–Fri 8am–6pm; Sat 11am–3pm; Sun 10am–1pm and 5–7:30pm. Choral concerts are Feb–July and Sept–Nov at 1:15pm Tues and Fri. Tube: Blackfriars.

St. Etheldreda's   The oldest Roman Catholic church in London, St. Etheldreda's stands on Ely Place, off Charterhouse Street, at Holborn Circus. Built in 1251, it was mentioned by the Bard in both *Richard II* and *Richard III*. A survivor of the Great Fire of 1666, the church and the area surrounding it were the property of the diocese of the city of Ely, in the days when many bishops had Episcopal houses in London, as well as in the cathedral cities in which they held their sees. The property still has a private road, with impressive iron gates and a lodge for the gatekeeper. Six elected commissioners manage the church and area.

St. Etheldreda, whose name is sometimes shortened to St. Audrey, was a 7th-century king's daughter who left her husband and established an abbey on the Isle of Ely. St. Etheldreda's has a distinguished musical tradition, with the 11am mass on Sunday sung in Latin. Other masses are on Sunday at 9am, Monday through Friday at 8am and 1pm, and Saturday at 9:30am. Lunch, with a varied choice of hot and cold dishes, is served Monday through Friday from noon to 2:30pm in the Crypt Café. See "'The City' Attractions" map.

14 Ely Place, Holborn Circus, EC1. ✆ 020/7405-1061. www.stetheldreda.com. Free admission. Daily 7:30am–6pm; Sat mass 9:30am; Sun masses 9 and 11am; weekday masses Mon–Fri 8am and 1pm. Tube: Farringdon or Chancery Lane.

St. Giles Cripplegate ✪   Named for the patron saint of cripples, St. Giles was founded in the 11th century. The church survived the Great Fire, but the Blitz left only the tower and walls standing. In 1620, English revolutionary Oliver Cromwell was betrothed to Elizabeth Bourchier here, and in 1674, John Milton, author of *Paradise Lost*, was buried here. More than a century later, someone opened the poet's grave, knocked out his teeth, stole a rib bone, and tore hair from his skull. Guided tours are available on most Tuesday afternoons. Call to confirm. See "'The City' Attractions" map.

At Fore and Wood sts., London Wall, EC2. ✆ 020/7638-1997. www.stgilescripplegate.com. Free admission. Mon–Fri 10am–4pm; Sat–Sun 8am–noon for services, 4pm for evensong. Tours most Tues afternoons 2–5pm. Tube: Moorgate, St. Paul's, or Barbican.

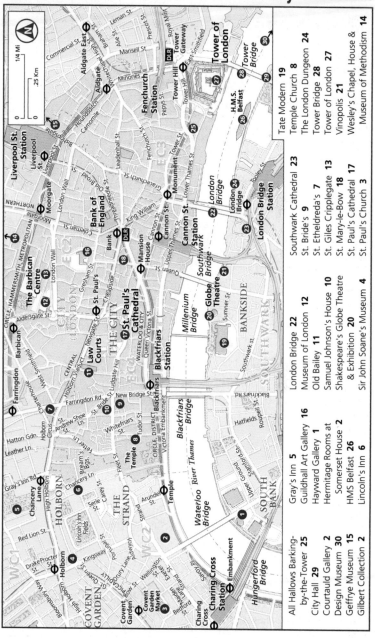

All Hallows Barking-
by-the-Tower **25**
City Hall **29**
Courtauld Gallery **2**
Design Museum **30**
Geffrye Museum **15**
Gilbert Collection **2**

Gray's Inn **5**
Guildhall Art Gallery **16**
Hayward Gallery **1**
Hermitage Rooms at
Somerset House **2**
HMS Belfast **26**
Lincoln's Inn **6**

London Bridge **22**
Museum of London **12**
Old Bailey **11**
Samuel Johnson's House **10**
Shakespeare's Globe Theatre
& Exhibition **20**
Sir John Soane's Museum **4**

Southwark Cathedral **23**
St. Bride's **9**
St. Etheldreda's **7**
St. Giles Cripplegate **13**
St. Mary-le-Bow **18**
St. Paul's Cathedral **17**
St. Paul's Church **3**

Tate Modern **19**
Temple Church **8**
The London Dungeon **24**
Tower Bridge **28**
Tower of London **27**
Vinopolis **21**
Wesley's Chapel, House &
Museum of Methodism **14**

West End Attractions

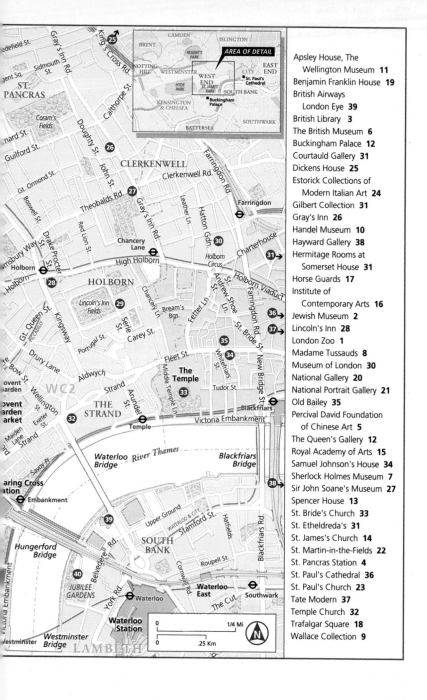

St. James's Church 🅐   When the aristocratic area known as St. James's was developed in the late 17th century, Sir Christopher Wren was commissioned to build its parish church. Diarist John Evelyn wrote of the interior, "There is no altar anywhere in England, nor has there been any abroad, more handsomely adorned." Wren's master carver Grinling Gibbons created the reredos (a screen decorated with religious icons and placed behind the altar), organ case, and font. As might be expected, this church has rich historical associations: The poet William Blake was baptized here, as was William Pitt, the first Earl of Chatham, who became England's youngest prime minister at age 24. Caricaturist James Gillray, auctioneer James Christie, and coffeehouse founder Francis White are all buried here. One of the more colorful marriages celebrated here was that of explorer Sir Samuel Baker and the woman he had bought at a slave auction in a Turkish bazaar. St. James's Church is a radical, inclusive Anglican church. It's also the Centre for Health and Healing and holds seminars on New Age and Creation Spirituality. There's a Bible Garden and a crafts market in the courtyard. The Wren Cafe is open daily, and lunchtime and evening concerts are presented. There is an antiques market at St. James's on Tuesday from 10am to 6pm, and a crafts market Wednesday to Saturday 10am to 6pm. (See map on p. 228.)

197 Piccadilly, W1. ℭ 020/7734-4511. www.st-james-piccadilly.org. Free admission. Lunchtime concerts are held on Mon, Wed, and Fri at 1:10pm. Suggested donation £3 ($5.70). Evening concerts are on an irregular schedule; check at the church for a poster listing the current slate of evening concerts. Tube: Piccadilly Circus or Green Park.

St. Martin-in-the-Fields 🅐   Designed by James Gibbs, a disciple of Christopher Wren, and completed in 1726, this classical church stands at the northeast corner of Trafalgar Square, opposite the National Gallery. Its spire, added in 1824, towers 56m (184 ft.) higher than Nelson's Column, which also rises on the square. The steeple became the model for many churches in colonial America. Since the first year of World War I (1914), the homeless have sought "soup and shelter" at St. Martin, a tradition that continues.

At one time, the crypt held the remains of Charles II (he's in Westminster Abbey now), who was christened here, giving St. Martin a claim as a royal parish church. His mistress, Nell Gwynne, and the highwayman Jack Sheppard are both interred here. The floors of the crypt are actually gravestones, and the walls date from the 1500s. The little restaurant, **Café in the Crypt,** is still called "Field's" by its devotees. Also in the crypt is **The London Brass Rubbing Centre** (ℭ **020/7930-9306**), with 88 exact copies of bronze portraits ready for use. Paper, rubbing materials, and instructions on how to begin are furnished, and there's classical music for you to enjoy as you proceed. Fees to make the rubbings range from £3 to £15 ($5.70–$29) the latter price for the largest—a life-size Crusader knight. There's also a gift shop with brass-rubbing kits for children, budget-priced ready-made rubbings, Celtic jewelry, miniature brasses, and model knights. The center is open Monday to Wednesday from 10am to 7pm, Thursday to Saturday 10am to 10pm, and Sunday noon to 7pm. See the "'West End Attractions" map.

Insider's Tip: In the back of the church is a crafts market. Also, lunchtime and evening concerts are staged Monday, Tuesday, and Friday at 1:05pm, and Tuesday, and Thursday to Saturday at 7:30pm. Lunch concerts are free, but evening tickets cost £6 to £22 ($11–$42).

Trafalgar Sq., WC2. ℭ 020/7766-1100. www.stmartin-in-the-fields.org. Mon–Fri 9am–6pm; Sat–Sun 8:45am–7:30pm as long as no service is taking place. Concerts Mon, Tues, and Fri 1:05pm; Tues and Thurs–Sat 7:30pm. Tube: Charing Cross.

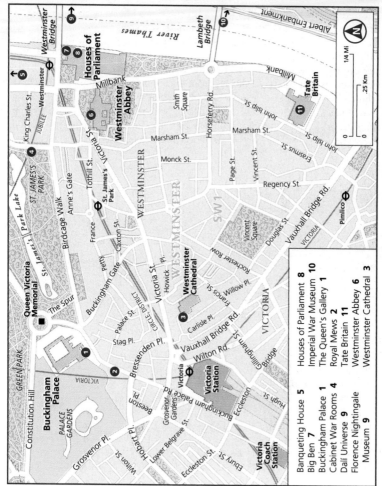

Banqueting House **5**	Houses of Parliament **8**
Big Ben **7**	Imperial War Museum **10**
Buckingham Palace **1**	The Queen's Gallery **1**
Cabinet War Rooms **4**	Royal Mews **2**
Dalí Universe **9**	Tate Britain **11**
Florence Nightingale	Westminster Abbey **6**
Museum **9**	Westminster Cathedral **3**

St. Mary-le-Bow ✦✦   It's said that a true Cockney must be born within the sound of this church's famous Bow bells. The church has a sometimes-gruesome history. In 1091, its roof was ripped off in a storm; in 1271, the church tower collapsed and 20 people were killed; in 1331, Queen Philippa and her ladies-in-waiting fell to the ground when a balcony collapsed during a joust celebrating the birth of the Black Prince. Wren rebuilt the church after the Great Fire of 1666 engulfed it. The original "Cockney" Bow bells were destroyed in the Blitz but have been replaced. The church was rededicated in 1964 after extensive restoration work. See "'The City' Attractions" map.

Cheapside, EC2. ℭ **020/7248-5139**. www.stmarylebow.co.uk. Free admission. Mon–Fri 6:30am–6pm. Tube: St. Paul's or Bank.

St. Paul's Church (the Actors' Church) ✦   With the Drury Lane Theatre, the Royal Opera House, and many other theaters within its parish, St. Paul's has long been

Knightsbridge to Kensington Attractions

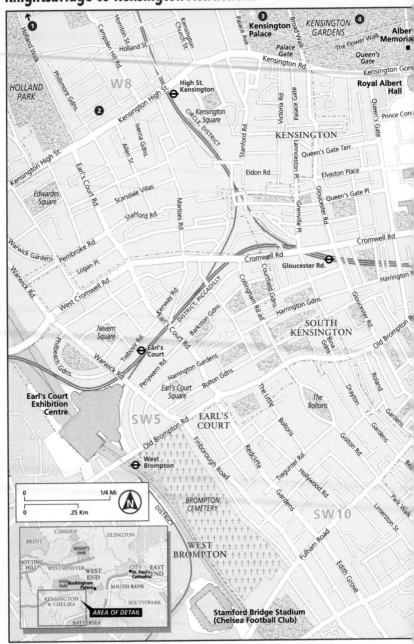

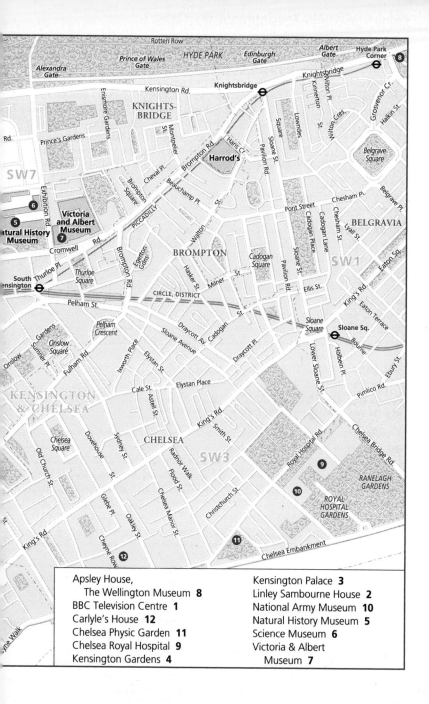

Apsley House,
   The Wellington Museum **8**
BBC Television Centre **1**
Carlyle's House **12**
Chelsea Physic Garden **11**
Chelsea Royal Hospital **9**
Kensington Gardens **4**

Kensington Palace **3**
Linley Sambourne House **2**
National Army Museum **10**
Natural History Museum **5**
Science Museum **6**
Victoria & Albert
   Museum **7**

associated with the theatrical arts. Inside you'll find scores of memorial plaques dedicated to such luminaries as Vivien Leigh, Boris Karloff, Margaret Rutherford, and Noel Coward, to name only a few. Designed by Inigo Jones in 1631, this church has been substantially altered over the years, but has retained a quiet garden-piazza in the rear. Among the famous people buried here are woodcarver Grinling Gibbons, writer Samuel Butler, and actress Ellen Terry. Landscape painter J. M. W. Turner and librettist W. S. Gilbert were both baptized here. The church often opens on Saturday at some point, but hours vary. There are free lunchtime piano recitals, most often scheduled on Thursday or Friday at 1pm—check before heading here if you want to attend one. The church still draws members of the entertainment world. See "'The City' Attractions" map.

Bedford St., Covent Garden, WC2. © 020/7836-5221. www.actorschurch.org. Free admission. Mon–Fri 8:30am–5:30pm; Sun service 11am. Tube: Covent Garden.

Southwark Cathedral 𝒦𝒦   There's been a church on this site, in the heart of London's first theater district, for more than a thousand years. The present one dates from the 15th century and was partly rebuilt in 1890. The previous one was the first Gothic church to be constructed in London (in 1106). A wooden effigy of a knight dates from 1275. Shakespeare and Chaucer worshipped here; a Shakespeare birthday service is held annually, and inside is a memorial to the playwright. In 1424, James I of Scotland married Mary Beaufort here. During the reign of Mary Tudor, Stephen Gardiner, the Bishop of Winchester, held a consistory court in the retro choir that condemned seven Protestants—the Marian martyrs—to death. Later, from 1540 to 1671, the same retro choir was rented to a baker and used to house pigs. Organ concerts are presented on Monday 1:10 to 1:50pm, and classical music concerts on Tuesday 3:15 to 4pm. Both are free. See "'The City' Attractions" map.

Montague Close, London Bridge, SE1. © 020/7367-6700. www.southwark.anglican.org/cathedral. Free admission; suggested donation £4 ($7.60). Mon–Fri 7:30am–6pm; Sat–Sun 8:30am–6pm. Tube: London Bridge.

Temple Church 𝒦𝒦   One of three Norman "round churches" left in England, this one was first completed in the 12th century. Not surprisingly, it has been restored. Look for the knightly effigies and the Norman door, and take note of the circle of grotesque portrait heads, including a goat in a mortarboard. Free organ recitals are presented Wednesday 1:15 to 1:35pm. On Inner Temple Lane, about where the Strand becomes Fleet Street going east, you'll see the memorial pillar called **Temple Bar,** which marks the boundary of the City of London. See "'The City' Attractions" map.

The Temple (within the Inner Temple), King's Bench Walk, EC4. © 020/7353-3470. www.templechurch.com. Free admission. Mon–Tues and Fri 11am–12:30am and 1–4pm; Wed 2–4pm; Thurs 11am–12:30pm and 2–3:30pm; Sat 11am–12:30pm and 1–3pm; Sun 1–3:30pm. Tube: Temple.

Wesley's Chapel, House & Museum of Methodism   John Wesley, the founder of Methodism, established this church in 1778 as his London base. Wesley, who rode on horseback throughout the English countryside and preached in the open air, lived at no. 47, next door to the chapel. He's buried in a grave behind the chapel. The house contains many of Wesley's belongings, including his "electrical machine" (a contraption that he claimed was successful in treating melancholy) and his study chair. While it survived the Blitz, the church later fell into disrepair; major restoration was completed in the 1970s. In the crypt, a museum traces the history of Methodism to present times.

Across the road in Bunhill Fields is the **Dissenters Graveyard,** where Daniel Defoe, William Blake, and John Bunyan are buried. See "'The City' Attractions" map.

49 City Rd., EC1. ✆ 020/7253-2262. www.wesleyschapel.org.uk. Chapel free. House and museum are also free, but donation of £2 ($3.80) per person is expected. House and museum Mon–Sat 10am–4pm, Sun noon–1:45pm. Tube: Old St. or Moorgate.

Westminster Cathedral ⚐ This spectacular brick-and-stone church (1903) is the headquarters of the Roman Catholic Church in Britain. Adorned in early-Byzantine style, it's massive: 108m (354 ft.) long and 47m (154 ft.) wide. One hundred different marbles compose the richly decorated interior, and eight marble columns support the nave. Eight yellow-marble columns hold up the huge canopy over the high altar. Mosaics emblazon the chapels and the vaulting of the sanctuary. If you take the elevator to the top of the 82m (269 ft.) campanile, you'll be rewarded with sweeping views that take in Buckingham Palace, Westminster Abbey, and St. Paul's Cathedral. There is a cafe serving light snacks and soft drinks from 9am to 5pm and a gift shop open Monday to Saturday from 9:30am to 5:15pm, Sunday from 10am to 4:45pm.

Ashley Place, SW1. ✆ 020/7798-9055. www.westminstercathedral.org.uk. Cathedral free. Audio tours £2.50 ($4.75). Tower £3 ($5.70). Cathedral services Mon–Sat 7am–7pm; Sun 8am–8pm. Tower daily 9:30am–12:30pm and 1–5pm. Tube: Victoria.

HISTORIC BUILDINGS

Banqueting House ⚐⚐ The feasting chamber in Whitehall Palace is probably the most sumptuous dining hall on earth. (Unfortunately, you can't dine here unless you're a visiting head of state.) Designed by Inigo Jones and decorated with, among other things, original ceiling paintings by Rubens, the hall is dazzling enough to make you forget food altogether. Among the historic events that took place here were the beheading of King Charles I, who stepped to his execution through a window onto the scaffold outside, and the restoration ceremony of Charles II, marking the return of monarchy after Cromwell's brief Puritan Commonwealth. The house often closes on short notice for official events, so it's best to call in advance if you want to see it. See "Westminster & Victoria Attractions" map.

Whitehall Palace, Horse Guards Ave., SW1. ✆ 0870/751-5178. www.hrp.org.uk. Admission £4.50 ($8.55) adults, £3.50 ($6.65) seniors and students, £3 ($5.70) children under 16. Mon–Sat 10am–5pm (last admission 4:30pm). Tube: Westminster or Embankment.

Benjamin Franklin House ⚐ The only surviving home of Benjamin Franklin in London opened as a museum in 2006. Off Trafalgar Square, the modest four-story brick building was Franklin's residence from 1757 to 1775, when he was a diplomat on behalf of American colonists. Curators call the house "the first de facto U.S. Embassy." The building was also the site of many of Franklin's scientific experiments. It was here that he invented bifocal glasses and created the ethereal-sounding musical instrument, the glass harmonica. Mozart, Bach, and Beethoven later created music for the harmonica. Franklin lived here in "serene comfort and affection," often having a full household of friends or relatives. Among other attractions, visitors can view the parlor where Franklin—a great fan of fresh air—sat "air bathing" naked by the open windows. The museum stages a "Historical Experience" every 45 minutes throughout the day. Visitors are taken through the various rooms by actors presenting a re-creation of Franklin's last night in London. (See map on p. 228.)

36 Craven St., WC2. ✆ 020/7839-2006. www.benjaminfranklinhouse.org. Admission £8 ($15) adults; £5 ($9.50) children, seniors, and students. Wed–Sun 10am–5pm; also Mon June–Sept 10am–5pm. Tube: Trafalgar Sq.

Cabinet War Rooms ✦ Visitors today can see the **Cabinet War Rooms,** the bombproof bunker suite of rooms, just as they were when abandoned by Winston Churchill and the British government at the end of World War II. You can see the Map Room with its huge wall maps; the Atlantic map is a mass of pinholes (each hole represents at least one convoy). Next door is Churchill's bedroom-cum-office, which has a bed and a desk with two BBC microphones on it—he used these to broadcast the now-famous speeches that stirred the nation. In 2003, nine more underground Cabinet War Rooms were restored and opened to the public, including the Chiefs of Staff map room, Churchill's kitchen and dining room, Sir Winston's private detectives' room, and Mrs. Churchill's bedroom. There's everything here from a pencil cartoon of Hitler to a mousetrap in the kitchen, to the original chamber pots under the beds (they had no flush toilets).

The **Transatlantic Telephone Room,** its full title, is little more than a broom closet, but it housed the Bell Telephone Company's special scrambler phone, called *Sigsaly,* and it was where Churchill conferred with Roosevelt. Visitors are provided with a step-by-step personal sound guide, providing a detailed account of each room's function and history.

Also in the war rooms is the **Churchill Museum,** the world's first major museum dedicated to the life of Sir Winston Churchill. Opened in February 2005, it explores in various exhibits and photographs the saga of Britain's wartime prime minister. The opening marked the 40th anniversary of the prime minister's death. The museum, through its memorabilia, introduces visitors to the private man but also traces his development as a world leader. (See map on p. 231.)

Clive Steps, at end of King Charles St. (off Whitehall near Big Ben), SW1. ✆ 020/7930-6961. www.iwm.org.uk/ cabinet. Admission £11 ($21) adults, £9 ($17) seniors and students, free for children 15 and under. Daily 9:30am–6pm (last admission at 5pm). Tube: Westminster or St. James's.

Chelsea Royal Hospital ✦✦ This dignified institution, founded by Charles II in 1682 as a home for veterans, was designed and completed by Sir Christopher Wren in 1692. It consists of a main block containing the hall and the chapel, flanked by east and west wings. There's been little change to Wren's design, except for minor work

---

Finds A City of Wine

At **Vinopolis,** 1 Bank End, Park St., SE1 (✆ **0870/241-4040;** www.vinopolis.co. uk), you can partake of London's largest selection of wine sold by the glass. On the South Bank, this "city of wine" lies under cavernous railway arches created in Victoria's era. The bacchanalian attraction was created in a multimedia format, at the cost of £23 million ($44 million). You can journey virtually through some of the earth's most prestigious wine regions, driving a Vespa through the Tuscan countryside or taking a "flight" over the vineyards of Australia. The price of entrance includes free tastings of five premium wines, and an on-site shop sells almost any item related to the grape. The site also boasts a good restaurant (see "Cantina Vinopolis," p. 155). Depending on the ticket and package purchased, admission ranges from £16 to £26 ($30–$49). Hours are Monday, Thursday, Friday, and Saturday noon to 9pm, Wednesday and Sunday noon to 6pm. Closed Tuesday.

done by Robert Adam in the 18th century and the addition of stables by Sir John Soane in 1814. The Duke of Wellington lay in state here from November 10 to 17, 1852. So many people thronged to see him that two were crushed to death. Today, the hospital is home to bachelor pensioners who fought in World War II or other conflicts. See "Knightsbridge to Kensington Attractions" map (p. 232).

Royal Hospital Rd., SW3. (©) 020/7881-5463. www.chelsea-pensioners.org.uk. Free admission. Mon–Sat 10am–noon and 2–4pm; Sun 2–4pm. Museum and shop closed Sun Oct–Mar. Tube: Sloane Sq.

City Hall   On the South Bank of the Thames, adjacent to Tower Bridge, the mayor of London and the London Assembly got a new home in 2002. A gleaming, 10-story egg-shaped steel-and-glass structure, it was dedicated by Her Majesty. The new home for city government has become London's latest—some say, most controversial—landmark. Half of City Hall is open to the public and the views from its rooftop gallery are worth the trek over to the South Bank. An exhibition space highlights changing cultural exhibits, and there is also a cafe on-site. (See map on p. 227.)

The Queen's Walk, SE1. (©) 020/7983-4100. www.london.gov.uk. Free admission. Visitors information desk Mon–Fri 9am–5pm; cafe Mon–Fri 8am–8pm. Tube: London Bridge.

Gray's Inn   Gray's Inn is one of four ancient Inns of Court still in operation. As you enter, you'll see a late-Georgian terrace lined with buildings that serve as both residences and offices. Gray's was restored after suffering heavy damage in World War II. It contains a rebuilt Tudor Hall, but its greatest attraction is the tree-shaded lawn and handsome gardens. A 17th-century atmosphere exists today in the square. Scientist-philosopher Francis Bacon (1561–1626) was the inn's most eminent tenant. See "'The City' Attractions" map.

Gray's Inn Rd. (north of High Holborn; entrance on Theobald's Rd.), 8 South Sq., WC1. (©) 020/7458-7800. www. graysinn.org.uk. Free admission to squares and gardens. Gardens Mon–Fri noon–2:30pm; squares Mon–Fri 6:30am–midnight. Tube: Chancery Lane, Holborn, or Farrington.

Horse Guards   North of Downing Street, on the west side of Whitehall, is the Horse Guards building, which is the headquarters of the British Army. The building was designed by William Kent, chief architect to George II. The real draw here is the Horse Guards themselves: the Household Cavalry Mounted Regiment, a combination of the oldest and most senior regiments in the British Army—the Life Guards and the Blues and Royals. In theory, their duty is to protect the sovereign. Life Guards wear red tunics and white plumes, and Blues and Royals are attired in blue tunics with red plumes. Two much-photographed mounted members of the Household Cavalry keep watch daily from 10am to 4pm. The mounted sentries change duty every hour as a benefit to the horses. Foot sentries change every 2 hours. The chief guard rather grandly inspects the troops here daily at 4pm. The guard, with flair and fanfare, dismounts at 5pm.

We prefer the **changing of the guards** here to the more famous ceremony at Buckingham Palace. Beginning around 11am Monday through Saturday and 10am on Sunday, a new guard leaves the Hyde Park Barracks on horseback, rides down Pall Mall, and arrives at the Horse Guards building, all in about 30 minutes. The old guard then returns to the barracks.

If you pass through the arch at Horse Guards, you'll find yourself at the **Horse Guards Parade,** which opens onto St. James's Park. This spacious court provides the best view of the various architectural styles that make up Whitehall. Regrettably, the parade ground itself is now a parking lot.

The military pageant—the most famous in Britain—known as **Trooping the Colour,** celebrating the Queen's birthday, takes place in June at the Horse Guards Parade (see "London Calendar of Events," in chapter 3). The "Colour" refers to the flag of the regiment. For devotees of pomp and circumstance, "Beating the Retreat" is staged here 2 successive evenings in June. It's only a dress rehearsal, though, for Trooping the Colour.

Whitehall, SW1. © 020/7414-2479. www.army.mod.uk. Free admission. Tube: Charing Cross, Westminster, or Embankment.

Lincoln's Inn ★★   Lincoln's Inn is the oldest of the four Inns of Court (see the box "Legal London" on p. 239). Between the City and the West End, Lincoln's Inn comprises 4.4 hectares (11 acres), including lawns, squares, gardens, a 17th-century chapel (open Mon–Fri noon–2pm), a library, and two halls. One of these, Old Hall, dates from 1490 and has remained almost unaltered, with its linenfold paneling, stained glass, and wooden screen by Inigo Jones. It was once the home of Sir Thomas More, and it was where barristers met, ate, and debated 150 years before the *Mayflower* sailed on its epic voyage. Old Hall is the scene for the opening chapter of Charles Dickens's *Bleak House.* The other hall, Great Hall, remains one of the finest Tudor Revival buildings in London and was opened by Queen Victoria in 1843. It's now the center of the inn and is used for the formal ceremony of calling students to the bar. See "'The City' Attractions" map.

Lincoln's Inn Fields, WC2. © 020/7405-1393. www.lincolnsinn.org.uk. Free admission to grounds. Mon–Fri 10am–4pm. Tube: Holborn or Chancery Lane.

Old Bailey   This courthouse replaced the infamous Newgate Prison, once the scene of hangings and other forms of "public entertainment." It's affectionately known as "Old Bailey" after a street that runs nearby. It's fascinating to watch the bewigged barristers presenting their cases to the high-court judges. Entry is strictly on a first-arrival basis, and guests line up outside; security will then direct you to one of the rooms where cases are being tried. It's impossible to predict how long a line you might face. If there's a London equivalent of the O. J. Simpson trial, forget about it—you'll never get in. On a day with trials attracting little attention, you can often enter after only 15 minutes or so. You never know until you show up. The best time to line up is 10am. You enter courts 1 to 4, 17, and 18 from Newgate Street, and the others from Old Bailey Street. See "'The City' Attractions" map.

Newgate St., EC4. To get here from the Temple, travel east on Fleet St., which becomes Ludgate Hill; cross Ludgate Circus and turn left at the Old Bailey, a domed structure with the figure of *Justice* atop it. © 020/7248-3277. Free admission. Court in session Mon–Fri 10am–1pm and 2–5pm. Children under 14 not admitted; those 14–16 must be accompanied by a responsible adult. No cameras, video equipment, large bags, food, tape recorders, or cellphones (and there are no coat-checking facilities). Tube: St. Paul's.

St. Pancras Station   The London terminus for the Eurostar trains, St. Pancras Station (built from 1863–67) is a masterpiece of Victorian engineering. Designed by W. H. Barlow, the 207m-long (679-ft.) glass-and-iron train station spans 72m (236 ft.) in width and rises to a peak of 30m (98 ft.) above the rails. The platforms were raised 6m (20 ft.) above the ground because the tracks ran over the Regent's Canal before entering the station. The pièce de résistance, though, is Sir George Gilbert Scott's fanciful St. Pancras Chambers. Done in high Gothic style, it's graced with pinnacles, towers, and gables; it now functions as office space. The facade runs 170m (558 ft.) and is flanked by a clock tower and a west tower. See "West End Attractions" map.

Euston Rd., NW1. Tube: King's Cross/St. Pancras.

Legal London

The smallest borough in London, bustling **Holborn** (*Ho*-burn) is often referred to as "Legal London." It's home to the majority of the city's barristers, solicitors, and law clerks, as well as the ancient **Inns of Court** (Tube: Holborn or Chancery Lane), the beautiful complexes where barristers have their chambers and law students perform their apprenticeships. All barristers (litigators) must belong to one of these institutions: **Gray's Inn, Lincoln's Inn** (the best preserved), the **Middle Temple,** or the **Inner Temple** (both just over the line inside the City). Many barristers also work from one of these dignified ancient buildings. The area was severely damaged during World War II, and some razed buildings were replaced with modern offices, but the borough still retains pockets of architecture of former days. See "'The City' Attractions" map.

Spencer House ✿✿   This is one of the city's most beautiful buildings. It was constructed in 1766 for the first Earl Spencer, who intended it as a shrine to Georgiana Poyntz, his childhood sweetheart whom he had secretly married the year before. It hasn't been a private residence since 1927, and it had something of a checkered history until it was restored and opened as a museum in 1990. Rooms are filled with period furniture and art, some even loaned by the Queen herself. The most spectacular salon is the Palm Room, all in white, gold, and green. See the "West End Attractions" map.

27 St. James's Place, SW1. ☎ 020/7499-8620. www.spencerhouse.co.uk. Admission £9 ($17) adults, £7 ($13) students, seniors and children 10–16; children under 10 not allowed. Garden admission one price, £3.50 ($6.65). Open only on Sun 10:30am–5:45pm (last admission 4:45pm). Closed Jan and Aug. Tube: Green Park.

LITERARY & MUSICAL LANDMARKS

Besides the homes of the authors and composers listed below, you can visit the abodes of other celebrated Londoners (detailed in other sections of this chapter), including Apsley House, the former mansion of the Duke of Wellington (p. 241). The homes of John Keats and Sigmund Freud are also open to the public; both are north of London in Hampstead (p. 259). Finally, the fascinating home of legendary architect Sir John Soane (p. 253) is open to the public and houses a museum about Soane.

Carlyle's House   From 1834 to 1881, Thomas Carlyle, author of *The French Revolution,* and Jane Baillie Welsh Carlyle, his noted letter-writing wife, resided in this modest 1708 terraced house. Furnished essentially as it was in Carlyle's day, the house is located about half a block from the Thames, near the Chelsea Embankment, along King's Road. It was described by his wife as being "of most antique physiognomy, quite to our humour; all wainscoted, carved, and queer-looking, roomy, substantial, commodious, with closets to satisfy any Bluebeard." The second floor contains Mrs. Carlyle's drawing room, but the most interesting chamber is the not-so-soundproof "soundproof" study in the skylit attic. Filled with Carlyle memorabilia—his books, a letter from Disraeli, personal effects, a writing chair, even his death mask—this is where the author did his work. See the "Knightsbridge to Kensington Attractions" map.

24 Cheyne Row, SW3. ☎ 020/7352-7087. Admission £4.20 ($8) adults, £2.10 ($4) children 5–16, free for children 5 and under. Mar 14–Oct Wed–Fri 2–5pm; Sat–Sun and bank holidays 2–5pm. Closed Nov–Mar 13. Tube: Sloane Sq. or South Kensington.

A Neighborhood of One's Own: The Homes of Virginia Woolf

Born in London in 1882, author and essayist Virginia Woolf used the city as the setting for many of her novels, including *Jacob's Room* (1922). The daughter of Sir Leslie Stephen and his wife, Julia Duckworth, Virginia spent her formative years at **22 Hyde Park Gate**, off Kensington Road, west of Royal Albert Hall. Her mother died in 1895 and her father in 1904.

After the death of their father, Virginia and her sister Vanessa left Kensington for Bloomsbury, settling near the British Museum. It was an interesting move, as Bloomsbury was a neighborhood that upper-class Victorians didn't view as "respectable." But Virginia was to make it her own, and in the process, make the district world-famous as the hub of literary London. From 1905, the Stephens lived at **46 Gordon Sq.**, east of Gower Street and University College. It was here that the celebrated literary and artistic circle known as the "Bloomsbury Group" came into being. In time, the group would embrace art critic Clive Bell and author Leonard Woolf, future husbands of Vanessa and Virginia, respectively. Later, Virginia went to live at **29 Fitzroy Sq.**, west of Tottenham Court Road, in a house once occupied by George Bernard Shaw.

During the next 2 decades, Virginia resided at several more Bloomsbury addresses, including **Brunswick Square, Tavistock Square,** and **Mecklenburg Square.** These homes have disappeared or been altered beyond recognition. During this time, the Bloomsbury Group reached out to include the artists Roger Fry and Duncan Grant, and Virginia became a friend of economist John Maynard Keynes and author E. M. Forster *(A Passage to India)*. At Tavistock Square (1924–39) and at Mecklenburg Square (1939–40), she operated the Hogarth Press with Leonard. She published her own early work here, as well as T. S. Eliot's *The Waste Land.*

Dickens House   Here in Bloomsbury stands the simple abode in which Charles Dickens wrote *Oliver Twist* and finished *The Pickwick Papers* (his American readers actually waited at the dock for the ship that brought in each new installment). The place is almost a shrine: Its reconstructed interiors contain his study, manuscripts, and personal relics. During Christmas week (including Christmas Day), the museum is decorated in the style of Dickens's first Christmas there. During Christmas, the raised admission prices of £10 ($19) for adults and £5 ($9.50) for children include hot mince pies and a few glasses of "Smoking Bishop," Dickens's favorite hot punch, as well as a copy of the museum's guidebooks. See the "West End Attractions" map.

48 Doughty St., WC1. © 020/7405-2127. www.dickensmuseum.com. Admission £5 ($9.50) adults, £4 ($7.60) students and seniors, £3 ($5.70) children, £14 ($27) family ticket. Mon–Sat 10am–5pm; Sun 11am–5pm. Tube: Russell Sq., Chancery Lane, or Holborn.

Handel Museum   This is the first composer museum to open in London. George Frederic Handel lived in this town house until his death in 1759, and it was here that he composed *Messiah*. Most of his organ concerts were written here, as well as "Israel in Egypt" and "Coronation Anthems." Handel settled in London in 1710 but didn't move to this Georgian house until 1723. The house has been restored to its original 18th-century styling, with furniture and fabrics accurate (though not original) to the time Handel lived here. The museum is hung with portraits and prints of Handel, his colleagues, and his patrons.

On display are two harpsichords, which are played frequently by professionals and harpsichord students when the museum is open. Precious objects include Mozart's handwritten arrangement of a Handel fugue, and furnishings such as a canopied bedroom from 1720 on loan from the Victoria and Albert Museum. Visit is by guided tour only. There are recitals every Thursday evening between 6:30 and 7:30pm and on occasional other days as well. Concerts cost £9 ($17) for adults or £7.50 ($14) for students and seniors. See the "West End Attractions" map.

25 Brook St., W1. ⓒ 020/7495-1685. www.handelhouse.org. Admission £5 ($9.50) adults, £4.50 ($8.55) students and seniors, £2 ($3.80) children 5–15. Free for children on Saturday. Tues–Sat 10am–6pm (until 8pm Thurs); Sun noon–6pm. Tube: Bond St.

Samuel Johnson's House ⚑⚑   Dr. Johnson and his copyists compiled his famous dictionary in this Queen Anne house, where the lexicographer, poet, essayist, and fiction writer lived from 1748 to 1759. Although Johnson also lived at Staple Inn in Holborn and at a number of other places, the Gough Square house is the only one of his residences remaining in modern London. The 17th-century building has been painstakingly restored, and it's well worth a visit.

After you're done touring the house, you might want to stop in at **Ye Olde Cheshire Cheese,** Wine Office Court, 145 Fleet St. (ⓒ **020/7353-6170**), Johnson's favorite locale. He must have had some lean nights at the pub because by the time he had compiled his dictionary, he'd already spent his advance of 1,500 guineas. G. K. Chesterton, author of *What's Wrong with the World* (1910) and *The Superstition of Divorce* (1920), was also a familiar patron at the pub. See "'The City' Attractions" map.

17 Gough Sq., EC4. ⓒ 020/7353-3745. www.drjohnsonshouse.org. Admission £4.50 ($8.55) adults, £3.50 ($6.65) students and seniors, £1.50 ($2.85) children, £10 ($19) family ticket, free for children 10 and under. Oct–Apr Mon–Sat 11am–5pm; May–Sept Mon–Sat 11am–5:30pm. Tube: Blackfriars, Chancery Lane, Temple, or Holborn. Walk up New Bridge St. and turn left onto Fleet St.; Gough Sq. is tiny and hidden, north of Fleet St.

MUSEUMS & GALLERIES

Apsley House, The Wellington Museum ⚑   This was the mansion of the Duke of Wellington, the "Iron Duke," one of Britain's greatest generals, who defeated Napoleon at Waterloo. Later, for a short period while he was prime minister, the duke had to have iron shutters fitted to his windows to protect him from a mob outraged by his autocratic opposition to reform. (His unpopularity soon passed, however.)

The house is crammed with art treasures, including three original Velázquez paintings, and military mementos that include the duke's medals and battlefield orders. Apsley House also holds some of the finest silver and porcelain pieces in Europe, displayed in the Plate and China Room. European monarchs grateful to Wellington for saving their thrones showered him with treasures. The collection includes a Sèvres Egyptian service originally intended as a divorce present from Napoleon to Josephine (she refused it); Louis XVIII eventually presented it to Wellington. Another treasure, the Portuguese Silver Service, created between 1812 and 1816, has been hailed as the single greatest artifact of Portuguese neoclassical silver. See the "West End Attractions" map.

149 Piccadilly, Hyde Park Corner, W1. ⓒ 020/7499-5676. Admission £5.10 ($9.70) adults, £3.80 ($7.20) seniors, £2.60 ($4.95) children under 16. Apr–Oct Tues–Sun 10am–5pm; Nov–Mar Tues–Sun 10am–4pm. Tube: Hyde Park Corner.

Value A Money-Saving Pass

The **London Pass** provides admission to more than 50 attractions in and around London, "timed" admission at some attractions (bypassing the queues), plus free travel on public transport (buses, Tubes, and trains) and a pocket guidebook. It costs £39 ($74) for 1 day, £73 ($139) for 3 days, and £112 ($213) for 6 days (children pay £22 ($42), £42 ($80), or £70 ($133), and includes admission to St. Paul's Cathedral, HMS *Belfast*, the Jewish Museum, and the Thames Barrier Visitor Centre—and many other attractions. This rather pricey pass is useful to persons who try to cram two days' worth of sightseeing into a single day. But if you're a slow-moving visitor, who likes to stop and smell the roses, you may not get your money's worth. Decide how much transportation and sightseeing you hope to get done, and, using this guide, calculate what the costs will be. It's a bit of paper work, but it will help you decide whether the London Pass is a good deal for you. You can also purchase the pass without the transportation package. Visit the website at **www. londonpass.com**.

BBC Television Centre   Have you ever wanted to go backstage to take a look at one of the most famous television studios in the world? The behind-the-scenes tours of this news center include visits to the weather center, the prop storehouse, and the production galleries. Because this is a working studio, no tours are exactly the same. Those looking for souvenirs, books, or videos will find an on-site shop. There is also a lunch cafe. You must book in advance, and visitors must be 10 years of age or over. *Tip:* Because this is such a popular attraction, make reservations 2 to 3 days in advance.

Television Centre, Wood Lane, W12. © 0870/603-0304. www.bbc.co.uk/tours. Admission £8.95 ($17) adults, £7.95 ($15) seniors, £6.50 ($12) students and children (over 9 years old), £25 ($48) family ticket. Mon–Sat tours are at 10am, 10:20am, 10:40am, 1:15pm, 1:30pm, 1:45pm, 3:30pm, 3:45pm, and 4pm. Tube: White City.

British Library 👶👶   In 1996, one of the world's great libraries began moving its collection of some 12 million books, manuscripts, and other items from the British Museum to its very own home in St. Pancras. In the new building, you get modernistic beauty rather than the fading glamour and the ghosts of Karl Marx, William Thackeray, and Virginia Woolf of the old library at the British Museum. You are also likely to get the book you want within an hour instead of 3 days. Academics, students, writers, and bookworms from all over the world come here. On a recent visit, we sat next to a student researching the history of pubs.

The bright, roomy interior is far more inviting than the rather dull red-brick exterior suggests (the writer Alain de Botton likened the exterior to a supermarket). Still, Colin St. John Wilson, the architect, says he has been delighted by the positive response to his building. The most spectacular room is the Humanities Reading Room, constructed on three levels with daylight filtered through the ceiling.

The fascinating collection includes such items of historic and literary interest as two of the four surviving copies of the *Magna Carta* (1215), a Gutenberg Bible, Nelson's last letter to Lady Hamilton, and the journals of Captain Cook. Almost every major author—Dickens, Jane Austen, Charlotte Brontë, Keats, and hundreds of others—is represented in the section devoted to English literature. Beneath Roubiliac's 1758 statue of Shakespeare stands a case of documents relating to the Bard, including a mortgage bearing his signature and a copy of the First Folio of 1623. There's also an unrivaled collection of stamps and stamp-related items.

Visitors can view the *Diamond Sutra,* dating from 868 and said to be the oldest surviving printed book. Using headphones set around the room, you can hear thrilling audio snippets such as James Joyce reading a passage from *Finnegans Wake.* Curiosities include the earliest known tape of a birdcall, dating from 1889. Particularly intriguing is an exhibition called "Turning the Pages," where you can, for example, electronically read a complete Leonardo da Vinci notebook by putting your hands on a special computer screen that flips from one page to another. There is a copy of *The Canterbury Tales* from 1410, and even manuscripts from *Beowulf* (ca. 1000). Illuminated texts from some of the oldest known biblical displays include the *Codex Sinaitticus* and *Codex Alexandrius,* 3rd-century Greek gospels. In the Historical Documents section are letters by everybody from Henry VIII to Napoleon, from Elizabeth I to Churchill. In the music displays, you can seek out original sheet music by Beethoven, Handel, Stravinsky, and Lennon and McCartney. An entire day spent here will only scratch the surface.

Walking tours of the library cost £6 ($11) for adults and £4.50 ($8.55) for seniors, students, and children. They are conducted Monday, Wednesday, and Friday at 3pm, and Saturday at 10:30am and 3pm. Library tours that include a visit to one of the reading rooms take place on Sundays and bank holidays at 11:30am and 3pm; £7 ($13) adults, £5.50 ($10) for seniors and students. Reservations can be made up to 2 weeks in advance. (See map on p. 228.)

96 Euston Rd., NW1. ℂ 020/7412-7332. www.bl.uk. Free admission. Mon, Wed–Fri 9:30am–6pm; Tues 9:30am–8pm, Sat 9:30am–5pm, Sun 11am–5pm. Tube: King's Cross/St. Pancras, or Euston Sq.

Courtauld Gallery

The nucleus of this collection was acquired by Samuel Courtauld, who upon his death in 1947, left it to the University of London. Today it houses the biggest collection of Impressionist and post-Impressionist paintings in Britain, with masterpieces by Monet, Manet, Degas, Renoir, Cézanne, van Gogh, and Gauguin. The gallery also has a superb collection of old-master paintings and drawings, including works by Rubens and Michelangelo; early-Italian paintings, ivories, and majolica; the Lee collection of old masters; and early-20th-century English, French, and British paintings.

The new galleries on the second floor display some 100 paintings and sculptures from the late 19th and 20th centuries, including an outstanding grouping of Fauve works (including a remarkable series of paintings and drawings by Kandinsky), and art by everybody from Matisse to Dufy. We come here at least once every season to revisit one work in particular: Manet's exquisite *A Bar at the Folies-Bergère* ⭐. Many of the paintings are displayed without glass, giving the gallery a more intimate feeling than most. This is but one of three major attractions at Somerset House. For information about the other attractions, such as the Gilbert Collection and the Hermitage Rooms, see below.

Somerset House, the Strand, WC2. ℂ 020/7848-2777. www.courtauld.ac.uk. Admission £5 ($9.50) adults, £4 ($7.60) seniors and students, free for children under 18. Daily 10am–6pm; last admission 5:15pm. Tube: Temple, Covent Garden, Charing Cross, or Holborn.

Dalí Universe ⭐ *(Finds)*

Next to the "London Eye," this exhibition is devoted to the remarkable Spanish artist Salvador Dalí (1904–89) and is one of London's newest attractions. Featuring more than 500 works of art, including the Mae West Lips sofa, the exhibitions are divided into a trio of themed areas: Sensuality and Femininity, Religion and Mythology, and Dreams and Fantasy. Showcased are important Dalí sculptures, rare graphics, watercolors, and even furnishings and jewelry. You can feast on such surreal works as Dalí's monumental oil painting for the Hitchcock movie *Spellbound,* or view a series of original watercolors and collages, including the mystical *Tarot Cards.* You can also see the world's largest collection of rare Dalí graphics, illustrating themes from literature. See the "Westminster & Victoria Attractions" map.

County Hall, Riverside Bldg., South Bank, SE1. ℭ 0870/744-7485. www.daliuniverse.com. May–Sept £12 ($23) adults, £8 ($15) children 8–16, family ticket £30 ($57). Oct–Apr £11 ($21) adults, £7 ($13) children 8–16, £28 ($53) family ticket. Year-round £10 ($19) seniors and students, £6 ($11) ages 4–7. Free 3 and under. Daily 10am–6:30pm. Tube: Waterloo or Westminster.

Design Museum   The Design Museum is a showcase of modern design—kind of like Pottery Barn without the price tags. It's the only museum in Europe that explains why and how mass-produced objects work and look the way they do and how design contributes to the quality of our lives. The collection of objects includes cars, furniture, domestic appliances, graphics, and ceramics, as well as changing displays of new products and prototypes from around the world. The cafe offers panoramic views of Tower Bridge and the Thames. See "'The City' Attractions" map.

28 Shad Thames, SE1. ℭ 0870/833-9955. www.designmuseum.org. Admission £7 ($13) adults, £4 ($7.60) students and seniors, free for children under 12. Daily 10am–5:45pm. Tube: Tower Bridge or London Bridge.

Dulwich Picture Gallery ★ *Finds*   Just 12 minutes by train from Victoria Station, this rarely visited museum houses one of the world's most significant collections of European old masters from the 17th and 18th centuries. In a purpose-built gallery designed by Sir John Soane in 1811, the collection is one of the oldest in Britain, having been assembled in the 1790s. Many of the paintings were collected by Stanislaus Augustus of Poland for shipment to his homeland. Before that happened, his kingdom was partitioned out of existence, and the paintings remained in London. You can view works by such old masters as Rembrandt, Rubens, Canaletto, Gainsborough, Watteau, Pousin, and others. The *Sunday Telegraph* has hailed Dulwich as "the most beautiful small art gallery in the world."

Gallery Road, Dulwich Village, SE21. ℭ 020/8693-5254. www.dulwichpicturegallery.org.uk. Admission £4 ($7.60) adults, £3 ($5.70) seniors, free for students and children. Tues–Fri 10am–5pm; Sat–Sun 11am–5pm. Tube: West Dulwich Station.

Estorick Collection of Modern Italian Art   Long dismissed as "unfashionable," early-20th-century Italian art is given a showcase in London. Eric Estorick (1913–93) was an American political scientist and writer who was a passionate collector. The year he died, he established a foundation to display his collection and to stage temporary-loan exhibitions. His collection has been hailed as one of the finest early-20th-century Italian art collections anywhere in the world. Estorick had a remarkable eye and prophetic judgment in art when he began his collection, although his treasure trove was dismissed by the art snobs of his day. Powerful images by the main protagonists of the early-20th-century Italian avant-garde Futurist movement, including Balla, Boccioni, Carrá, Serverini, and Russolo, are on permanent view. The collection includes works by figurative artists like Modigliani, Sironi, and Campigli, plus works by the metaphysical painter de Chirico. See the "West End Attractions" map.

39A Canonbury Sq., N1. ℭ 020/7704-9522. www.estorickcollection.com. Admission £3.50 ($6.65) adults, £2.50 ($4.75) seniors and children. Wed–Sat 11am–6pm; Sun noon–5pm. Tube: Victoria Line to Highbury and Islington.

Florence Nightingale Museum   The life and work of one of England's most influential women of the 1800s is celebrated here. You'll learn that her most famous accomplishment—nursing soldiers during the Crimean War—was only part of a career spanning half a century. Nightingale did everything from raising the image of the British soldier (from a brawling lowlife to a heroic working man) to making nursing a respectable profession. Before the "Lady with the Lamp," nursing was seen as a job fit only for prostitutes.

In 1896, Nightingale "retired to her bed" but didn't slow down. She continued to write on public health. Much of her advice is still valid today. By the time she died in 1910 at the age of 90, she had become so reclusive that the general public assumed she was already dead. The collection at this museum includes many objects owned or used by Nightingale, including 63 letters written by her. There are also exhibits relating to the Crimean War. See the "Westminster & Victoria" map.

St. Thomas' Hospital, 2 Lambeth Palace Rd., SE1. (C) 020/7620-0374. www.florence-nightingale.co.uk. Admission £5.80 ($11) adults; £4.80 ($9.10) seniors, students, children, and persons with disabilities; £16 ($30) family ticket. Mon–Fri 10am–5pm; Sat–Sun 10am–4:30pm. Last admission 1 hr. before closing. Tube: Westminster or Waterloo.

Geffrye Museum ✦   If you'd like an overview of British interiors and lifestyles of the past 4 centuries, head to this museum, housed in a series of restored 18th-century almshouses that escaped Hitler's Blitz. Period rooms are arranged chronologically, allowing you to follow changing tastes in the days of the Empire. You'll see the development of furnishings and *objets d'art* in English middle-class homes. The collection is rich in Jacobean and Georgian interiors and strongest in the Victorian period. In the 20th-century rooms, you'll see the richness of the Art Deco style and the bleakness of the utilitarian designs that followed in the aftermath of World War II. Newer galleries showcase the decor of the later 20th century.

Originally, in 1715, these almshouses belonged to the Ironmongers' Company. Their architecture alone is worth a visit. Gardens in front attract much attention, especially the herb garden. There is a design center, which showcases changing exhibitions of the latest works from contemporary British designers. There is also a cafe/restaurant. See "'The City' Attractions" map.

136 Kingsland Rd., E2. (C) 020/7739-9893. www.geffrye-museum.org.uk. Free admission. Tues–Sat 10am–5pm; Sun and bank holidays noon–5pm. Closed Good Friday, Dec 24–26, New Year's Day. Gardens open Apr–Oct. Tube: Liverpool St., then bus 149 or 242, or Old St. Tube, then bus 243.

Gilbert Collection ✦✦✦ *Finds*   In 2000, Somerset House became the permanent home for the Gilbert Collection of decorative arts, one of the most important bequests ever made to England. Sir Arthur Gilbert made his gift of gold, silver, mosaics, and gold snuffboxes to the nation in 1996, at which time the value was estimated at £75 million ($135 million). The collection of some 800 objects in three fields (gold and silver, mosaics, and gold snuffboxes) is among the most distinguished in the world. The array of mosaics is among the most comprehensive ever gathered, with Roman and Florentine examples dating from the 16th to the 19th centuries. The gold and silver collection has exceptional breadth, ranging from the 15th to the 19th centuries, spanning India to South America. The silver collection here is arguably better than the one at the V&A—it's strong in masterpieces of great 18th-century silversmiths, such as Paul de Lamerie. Such exhibits as the Maharajah pieces, the "Gold Crown," and Catherine the Great's Royal Gates are fabulous. The gallery also displays one of the most representative collections of gold snuffboxes in the world, with some 200 examples, including snuffboxes owned by Louis XV, Frederick the Great, and Napoleon. The Gilbert Collection is only one of three major museums and galleries at Somerset House. For recommendations of the other two, see Courtauld Gallery (above) or the Hermitage Rooms (below). (See map on p. 228.)

Somerset House, the Strand, WC2. © 020/7240-9400. www.gilbert-collection.org.uk. Admission £5 ($9.50) adults, £4 ($7.60) seniors, free for ages 17 and under. Daily 10am–6pm. Tube: Temple, Covent Garden, Charing Cross, or Embankment.

Guildhall Art Gallery ✦ In 1999, Queen Elizabeth opened a new £70-million ($130-million) gallery in the City, a continuation of an original gallery that was launched in 1886 but burned down in a severe air raid in May 1941. Many famous and much-loved pictures, which for years were known only through temporary exhibitions and reproductions, are again available for the public to see in a permanent setting. The new gallery can display only 250 of the 4,000 treasures it owns. The art ranges from classical to modern. A curiosity is the huge double-height wall built to accommodate Britain's largest independent oil painting, John Singleton Copley's *The Defeat of the Floating Batteries at Gibraltar, September 1782*. The Corporation of London in the City owns these works and has been collecting them since the 17th century. The most popular art is in the Victorian collection, including such well-known favorites as Millais's *My First Sermon* and *My Second Sermon*, and Landseer's *The First Leap*. There is also a landscape of Salisbury Cathedral by John Constable. Since World War II, all paintings acquired by the gallery concentrate on London subjects. See "'The City' Attractions" map.

Guildhall Yard, EC2. © 020/7332-3700. www.guildhall-art-gallery.org.uk. Admission £2.50 ($4.75) adults, £1 ($1.90) seniors and students, free for children under 16. Free Fri and after 3:30pm on all other days. Mon–Sat 10am–5pm; Sun noon–4pm. Tube: Bank, St. Paul's, Mansion House, or Moorgate.

Hayward Gallery Opened by Elizabeth II in 1968, this gallery presents a changing program of major contemporary and historical exhibits. It's managed by the South Bank Board, which also includes Royal Festival Hall, Queen Elizabeth Hall, and the Purcell Room. Every exhibition is accompanied by a variety of educational activities, including tours, workshops, lectures, and publications. The gallery closes between exhibitions, so call before crossing the Thames.

Belvedere Rd., South Bank, SE1. © 020/7960-5226. www.hayward.org.uk. Admission varies but usually £7.50 ($14) adults, £6 ($11) students and seniors, free for children under 12. Tickets half-price Mon. Hours subject to change, depending on the exhibit: Thurs, Sat, Sun, Mon 10am–6pm; Fri 10am–9pm; Tues–Wed 11am–8pm. Tube: Waterloo or Embankment.

Hermitage Rooms at Somerset House ✦✦✦ This is a virtual branch of St. Petersburg's State Hermitage Museum, which owns a great deal of the treasure trove left over from the Czars, including possessions of art-collecting Catherine the Great. Now you don't have to go to Russia to see some of Europe's great treasures.

The rotating exhibitions change, but you'll get to see such Czarist treasures as medals, jewelry, portraits, porcelain, clocks, and furniture. A rotating "visiting masterpiece" overshadows all the other collections. Some items that amused us on our first visit (and you are likely to see similar novelties) were a wig made entirely out of silver thread for Catherine the Great, a Wedgwood "Green Frog" table service, and two very rare Chinese silver filigree toilet sets. The rooms themselves have been designed in the style of the Winter Palace at St. Petersburg. *Note:* Because this exhibit attracts so much interest, tickets should be purchased in advance. Tickets are available from Ticketmaster at

© 020/7413-3398 (24 hr.). You can book online at **www.ticketmaster.co.uk**. The other two museums at Somerset House, the Courtauld Gallery and the Gilbert Collection, were previewed above.

Somerset House, the Strand, WC2. © 020/7845-4630. www.hermitagerooms.com. Admission £5 ($9.50) adults, £4 ($7.60) seniors, free for students and children under 18. Daily 10am–6pm. Tube: Temple, Covent Garden, Charing Cross, or Holborn.

Imperial War Museum ⍟   One of the few major sights south of the Thames, this museum occupies 1 city block the size of an army barracks, greeting you with 38cm (15-in.) guns from the battleships *Resolution* and *Ramillies*. The large domed building, constructed in 1815, was the former Bethlehem Royal Hospital for the insane, known as "Bedlam."

A wide range of weapons and equipment is on display, along with models, decorations, uniforms, posters, photographs, and paintings. You can see a Mark V tank, a Battle of Britain Spitfire, and a German one-man submarine, as well as a rifle carried by Lawrence of Arabia. In the Documents Room, you can view the self-styled "political testament" that Hitler dictated in the chancellery bunker in the closing days of World War II, witnessed by henchmen Joseph Goebbels and Martin Bormann, as well as the famous "peace in our time" agreement that Neville Chamberlain brought back from Munich in 1938. (Of his signing the agreement, Hitler later said, "[Chamberlain] was a nice old man, so I decided to give him my autograph.") It's a world of espionage and clandestine warfare in the major permanent exhibit known as the "Secret War Exhibition," where you can discover the truth behind the image of James Bond—and find out why the real secret war is even stranger and more fascinating than fiction. Displays include many items never before seen in public: coded messages, forged documents, secret wirelesses, and equipment used by spies from World War I to the present day.

Public film shows take place on weekends at 4pm and on certain weekdays during school holidays and on public holidays.

Supported by a £12.6-million ($23-million) grant from the Heritage Lottery Fund, a permanent Holocaust exhibition now occupies two floors. Through original artifacts, documents, film, and photographs, some lent to the museum by former concentration camps in Germany and Poland, the display poignantly relates the story of Nazi Germany and the persecution of the Jews. In addition, the exhibit brings attention to the persecution of other groups under Hitler's regime, including Poles, Soviet prisoners of war, people with disabilities, and homosexuals. Among the items on display are a funeral cart used in the Warsaw Ghetto, a section of railcar from Belgium, a sign from the extermination camp at Belzec, and the letters of an 8-year-old French Jewish boy who hid in an orphanage before being sent to Auschwitz.

Another exhibition, called "Crimes Against Humanity," explores the theme of genocide. See the "Westminster & Victoria" map.

Lambeth Rd., SE1. © 020/7416-5321 or 020/7416-5320 (info line). www.iwm.org.uk. Free admission. Daily 10am–6pm. Closed Dec 24–26. Tube: Baker Line to Lambeth North, Elephant and Castle, or Southwark.

Institute of Contemporary Arts   London's liveliest cultural program takes place in this temple to the avant-garde, launched in 1947. It keeps Londoners and others up-to-date on the latest in the worlds of cinema, theater, photography, painting, sculpture, and other visual and performing arts. Foreign and experimental movies are shown, and special tributes—perhaps a retrospective of the films of Rainer Werner Fassbinder—are often the order of the day. Classics and cult favorites are frequently dusted off here. On Saturday and Sunday at 3pm, the cinema offers screenings for kids. Sometimes well-known writers and artists speak here, which makes the low cost of membership even more enticing. Experimental plays are also presented. Sun Microsystems, the American Internet pioneer, donated money to build a state-of-the-art New Media Centre in 1998. The photo galleries, showing the latest from British and foreign photographers, probably wouldn't win the approval of the people who set up "decency" panels for the arts. There is a popular cafe/bar at ICA, and it often hosts club nights and musical performances in the evening. It's open until 11pm Monday, 1am Tuesday to Saturday, and 10:30pm Sunday. It opens daily when the museum does. See the "West End Attractions" map.

The Mall, SW1. ✆ 020/7930-3647. www.ica.org.uk. Admission £2 ($3.80) adults, £1.50 ($2.85) seniors, students, and children Mon–Fri, £3 ($5.70) Sat–Sun. Galleries daily noon–7pm; bookstore daily noon–9pm. Film screenings daily. Tube: Piccadilly Circus or Charing Cross.

Jewish Museum   This museum tells the story of Jewish life in Britain. Arriving at the time of the Norman Conquest, Jews survived in England until King Edward I forced them out in 1290. From that time, no Jews (or at least, no known Jews) lived in Britain until a small community returned in 1656 during the reign of Elizabeth I. The museum has recently been awarded designated status by the Museums and Galleries Commission for its outstanding collection of Jewish ceremonial art. On display are silver Torah bells made in London, and two loving cups presented by the Spanish and Portuguese Synagogue to the lord mayor in the 18th century. The museum's Ceremonial Art Gallery contains a beautiful 16th-century Venetian ark, one of the oldest preserved in the world. An old English lord bought it from a furniture dealer without knowing what it was, and for years his maid used it as a wardrobe until someone discovered its true identity. The museum also sponsors **walking tours of Jewish London.**

The Jewish Museum has another location in Finchley, which focuses on Jewish immigration and settlement in London. On display are reconstructions of East End tailoring and furniture workshops. Holocaust education is also a fundamental feature of this museum. The Finchley branch is open Monday through Thursday 10:30am to 5pm, and Sunday from 10:30am to 4:30pm. Admission is £2 ($3.80) adults, seniors, and students; children under 12 are admitted free. For further information, call ✆ **020/ 8349-1143.** See the "West End Attractions" map.

129–131 Albert St., NW1. ✆ 020/7284-1997. www.jewishmuseum.org.uk. Main branch admission £3.50 ($6.65) adults, £2.50 ($4.75) seniors, £1.50 ($2.85) students and children, £8 ($15) family. Main branch: Sun 10am–5pm; Mon–Thurs 10am–4pm. Closed Fri, Sat, bank holidays, and Jewish festivals. Tube: Camden Town or Finchley Central.

Linley Sambourne House ⊛ *Finds*   You'll step back into the days of Queen Victoria when you visit this house, which has remained unchanged for more than a century. Part of a terrace built in the late 1860s, this five-story Suffolk brick structure was the home of Linley Sambourne, a legendary cartoonist for *Punch.* In the entrance hall, you'll see the mixture of styles and clutter that typifies Victorian decor, with a plush portière, a fireplace valance, stained glass, and a large set of antlers vying for attention. The drawing room alone contains an incredible number of Victorian items. An actor in period costume leads tours. You should budget about 1½ hours for your visit. *Insider's Tip:* It's best to prebook your tour by phone. See the "Knightsbridge to Kensington" map.

18 Stafford Terrace, W8. ✆ 020/7602-3316. www.rbkc.gov.uk/linleysambournehouse. Admission £6 ($11) adults, £4 ($7.60) seniors and students, £1 ($1.90) children 17 and under. Sat–Sun 11am–3:30pm; Sat and Sun guided tours only (11:15am, 1pm, 2:15pm, and 3:30pm). Closed mid-Mar to mid-June. Tube: High St. Kensington.

Madame Tussaud's *(Overrated (Kids*   Madame Tussaud's is not so much a wax museum as an enclosed amusement park. A weird, moving, sometimes terrifying (to children) collage of exhibitions, panoramas, and stage settings, it manages to be most things to most people, most of the time.

Madame Tussaud attended the court of Versailles and learned her craft in France. She personally took the death masks from the guillotined heads of Louis XVI and Marie Antoinette (which you'll find among the exhibits). She moved her original museum from Paris to England in 1802. Her exhibition has been imitated in every part of the world, but never with the realism and imagination on hand here. Madame herself molded the features of Benjamin Franklin, whom she met in Paris. All the rest—from George Washington to John F. Kennedy, Mary Queen of Scots to Sylvester Stallone—have been subjects for the same painstaking (and often breathtaking) replication.

In the well-known Chamber of Horrors—a kind of underground dungeon—are all kinds of instruments of death, along with figures of their victims. The shadowy presence of Jack the Ripper lurks in the gloom as you walk through a Victorian London street. Present-day criminals are portrayed within the confines of prison. The latest attraction to open here is "The Spirit of London," a musical ride that depicts 400 years of London's history, using special effects that include audio-animatronic figures that move and speak. Visitors take "time-taxis" that allow them to see and hear "Shakespeare" as he writes and speaks lines, be received by "Queen Elizabeth I," and feel and smell the Great Fire of 1666 that destroyed London.

We've seen these changing exhibitions so many times over the years that we feel they're a bit cheesy, but we still remember the first time we were taken here as a kid. We thought it fascinating back then.

Insider's Tip: To avoid the long lines—sometimes more than an hour in summer— call the waxworks in advance and reserve a ticket for fast pickup at the entrance. If you don't want to bother with that, be aggressive and form a group of nine people waiting in the queue. A group of nine or more can go in almost at once through the "group door." Otherwise, go when the gallery first opens or late in the afternoon when crowds have thinned. (See map on p. 228.)

Marylebone Rd., NW1. ℂ **0870/999-0046**. www.madame-tussauds.com. Admission £23 ($44) adults, £20 ($38) seniors, £19 ($36) children under 16. **Note:** Admission prices can go higher at certain peak periods during the year. Mon–Fri 9:30am–5:30pm; Sat–Sun 9am–6pm. Tube: Baker St.

Museum of London *(★★*   In London's Barbican district, near St. Paul's Cathedral and overlooking the city's Roman and medieval walls, this museum traces the history of London from prehistoric times to the 20th century through archaeological finds; paintings and prints; social, industrial, and historic artifacts; and costumes, maps, and models. Exhibits are arranged so that you can begin and end your chronological stroll through 250,000 years at the main entrance to the museum. The museum's pièce de résistance is the Lord Mayor's Coach, a gilt-and-scarlet fairy-tale coach built in 1757 and weighing in at 3 tons. You can also see the Great Fire of London in living color and sound thanks to an audiovisual presentation; the death mask of Oliver Cromwell; cell doors from Newgate Prison, made famous by Charles Dickens; and most amazing of all, a shop counter showing pre–World War II prices. Early in 2002, the museum unveiled its latest permanent gallery, occupying an entire floor. Called the World City Gallery, the exhibit examines life in London between 1789 and 1914, the beginning of World War I. Some 2,000 objects are on view. See the "West End Attractions" map.

150 London Wall, EC2. ℂ 087/0444-3852. www.museumoflondon.org.uk. Free admission. Mon–Sat 10am–5:50pm; Sun 11:30am–5:50pm. Tube: St. Paul's or Barbican.

National Army Museum ⟨ Kids   The National Army Museum occupies a building adjoining the Royal Hospital, a home for retired soldiers. Whereas the Imperial War Museum is concerned with wars of the 20th century, the National Army Museum tells the colorful story of British armies from 1485 on. Here you'll find uniforms worn by British soldiers in every corner of the world, plus weapons and other gear, flags, and medals. Even the skeleton of Napoleon's favorite charger is here. Also on display are Florence Nightingale's jewelry, the telephone switchboard from Hitler's headquarters (captured in 1945), and Orders and Medals of HRH the Duke of Windsor. A more recent gallery, "The Rise of the Redcoats," contains exhibitions detailing the life of the British soldier from 1485 to 1793. Included in the exhibit are displays on the English Civil War and the American War of Independence. See the "Knightsbridge to Kensington Attractions" map.

Royal Hospital Rd., SW3. ℂ 020/7730-0717. www.national-army-museum.ac.uk. Free admission. Daily 10am–5:30pm. Closed Good Friday, 1st Mon in May, and Dec 24–26. Tube: Sloane Sq.

Natural History Museum ⟨⟨ Kids   This is the home of the national collections of living and fossil plants, animals, and minerals, with many magnificent specimens on display. The zoological displays are quite wonderful—not up to the level of the Smithsonian in Washington, D.C., but still definitely worthwhile. Exciting exhibits designed to encourage people of all ages to learn about natural history include "Human Biology—An Exhibition of Ourselves," "Our Place in Evolution," "Origin of the Species," "Creepy Crawlies," and "Discovering Mammals." The Mineral Gallery displays marvelous examples of crystals and gemstones. Visit the Meteorite Pavilion, which exhibits fragments of rocks that have crashed into the earth, some from the farthest reaches of the galaxy. The dinosaur exhibit attracts the most attention, displaying 14 complete skeletons. The center of the show depicts a trio of full-size robotic Deinonychus enjoying a freshly killed Tenontosaurus. "Earth Galleries" is an exhibition outlining humankind's relationship with planet Earth. Here, in the section "Earth Today and Tomorrow," visitors are invited to explore the planet's dramatic history from the big bang to its inevitable death. The latest development here is the new Darwin Centre. Dedicated to the great naturalist Charles Darwin, the center reveals the museum's scientific research and outreach facilities and activities. You're given an insider look at the storage facilities—including 22 million preserved specimens—and the laboratories of the museum. Fourteen behind-the-scenes free tours (ages 10 and up only) are given daily; you should book immediately upon entering the museum if you're interested. See the "Knightsbridge to Kensington Attractions" map.

Cromwell Rd., SW7. ℂ 020/7942-5000. www.nhm.ac.uk. Free admission. Mon–Sat 10am–5:50pm; Sun 11am–5:50pm. Tube: S. Kensington.

Percival David Foundation of Chinese Art ⟨   This foundation displays the greatest collection of Chinese ceramics outside China. Approximately 1,700 ceramic objects reflect Chinese court tastes from the 10th to 18th centuries and include many pieces of exceptional beauty. An extraordinary collection of stoneware from the Song (960–1279) and Yuan (1279–1368) dynasties includes examples of rare Ru and Guan wares. Among the justifiably famous blue-and-white porcelains are two unique temple vases, dated by inscription to A.D. 1351. A wide variety of polychrome wares is also represented; they include examples of the delicate doucai wares from the Chenghua period (1465–87), as well as a remarkable group of 18th-century porcelains.

53 Gordon Sq., WC1. © 020/7387-3909. www.pdfmuseum.org.uk. Free admission; donations encouraged. £4 ($7.60) per person for a guided tour of 10–20 people. Admission to the library must be arranged with the curator ahead of time. Mon–Fri 10am–12:30pm and 1:30–5pm. Library hours Tues 10:30am–12:30pm and Thurs 2–4pm. Tube: Russell Sq. or Euston Sq.

The Queen's Gallery ★★

The refurbished gallery on the grounds of Buckingham Palace reopened to the public in 2002 in time for the Golden Jubilee celebration of Queen Elizabeth II. Visitors going through the Doric portico entrance will find three times as much space as before. The 1831 building by John Nash was converted to a chapel for Queen Victoria in 1843 and later destroyed in an air raid in 1940. Today, the gallery is dedicated to changing exhibitions of the wide-ranging treasure trove that forms the Royal Collection. You'll find special showings of paintings, prints, drawings, watercolors, furniture, porcelain, miniatures, enamels, jewelry, and other works of art. At any given time, you may see such artistic peaks as Van Dyck's equestrian portrait of Charles I; the world-famous *Lady at the Virginal,* by Vermeer; a dazzling array of gold snuffboxes; paintings by Monet from the collection of the late Queen Mother; personal jewelry; studies by Leonardo da Vinci; and even the recent and very controversial portrait of the current queen by Lucian Freud.

Buckingham Palace, Buckingham Palace Rd., SW1. © 020/7766-7301. www.royalcollection.org.uk. Admission £7.50 ($14) adults, £6.50 ($12) students and seniors, £4 ($7.60) children 5–16, free for children 4 and under. Daily 10am–5:30pm. Tube: Hyde Park Corner, Green Park, or Victoria.

Royal Academy of Arts

Established in 1768, this organization counted Sir Joshua Reynolds, Thomas Gainsborough, and Benjamin West among its founding members. Since its beginning, each member has had to donate a work of art, and so, over the years, the academy has built up a sizable collection. The outstanding treasure is Michelangelo's beautiful relief of *Madonna and Child.* The annual Summer Exhibition has been held for more than 200 years; see the "London Calendar of Events" in chapter 3 for details. The main focus of the gallery, however, is on temporary exhibitions which are not related to the Royal Academicians. See the "West End Attractions" map.

Burlington House, Piccadilly, W1. © 020/7300-8000. www.royalacademy.org.uk. Admission varies, depending on the exhibition. Sat–Thurs 10am–6pm (last admission 5:30pm); Fri 10am–10pm (last admission 9:30pm). Tube: Piccadilly Circus or Green Park.

Royal Mews ★★

This is where you can get a close look at Her Majesty's State Coach, built in 1761 to the designs of Sir William Chambers and decorated with paintings by Cipriani. Traditionally drawn by eight gray horses, it was used by sovereigns when they traveled to open Parliament and on other state occasions; Queen Elizabeth traveled in it to her 1953 coronation and in 1977 for her Silver Jubilee Procession. There are other state coaches to see here as well, and you can also pay a visit to the Queen's carriage horses, which are housed here. See the "Westminster & Victoria Attractions" map.

Buckingham Palace, Buckingham Palace Rd., SW1. © 020/7766-7302. www.royalcollection.org.uk. Admission £7 ($13) adults, £6 ($11) seniors and students; £4.50 ($8.55) children 5–17; £19 ($35) family; free for children under 5. Mar 25–July 26 and Sept 26–Oct 31 Mon–Thurs and Sat–Sun 11am–4pm, July 27–Sept 25 daily 10am–5pm. Tube: Green Park or Victoria.

Science Museum ★★★ (Kids)

This museum traces the development of science and industry and their influence on everyday life. These scientific collections are among the largest, most comprehensive, and most significant anywhere. On display is Stephenson's original rocket and the tiny prototype railroad engine; you can also see Whittle's original jet engine and the *Apollo 10* space module. The King George III Collection of scientific instruments is the highlight of a gallery on 18th-century science. Health Matters is a permanent gallery on modern medicine. The museum has two hands-on galleries, as well as working models and video displays.

The museum also presents a behind-the-scenes look at the science and technology that went into making the film trilogy *The Lord of the Rings*. Exhibitions showcase the artifacts and animatronics, costumes, and characters from the fable. The exhibition also offers a number of interactive displays—for example, you are given the chance to be shrunk to the size of a hobbit.

Insider's Tip: A large addition to this museum explores such topics as genetics, digital technology, and artificial intelligence. Four floors of a new Welcome Wing shelter half a dozen exhibition areas and a 450-seat IMAX theater. One exhibition explores everything from drug use in sports to how engineers observe sea life with robotic submarines. On an upper floor, visitors can learn how DNA was used to identify living relatives of the Bleadon Man, a 2,000-year-old Iron Age man. On the third floor is the computer that Tim Berners-Lee used to design the World Wide Web outside Geneva, writing the first software for it in 1990.

Note also the marvelous interactive consoles placed strategically in locations throughout the museum. These display special itineraries, including directions for getting to the various galleries for families, teens, adults, and those with special interests.

Exhibition Rd., SW7. ✆ 087/0870-4868. www.sciencemuseum.org.uk. Free admission. Daily 10am–6pm. Closed Dec 24–26. Tube: S. Kensington.

Shakespeare's Globe Theatre & Exhibition ✪

This is a recent re-creation of what was probably the most important public theater ever built, Shakespeare's Globe, on the exact site where many of Shakespeare's plays opened. The late American filmmaker Sam Wanamaker worked for some 20 years to raise funds to re-create the theater as it existed in Elizabethan times, thatched roof and all. A fascinating exhibit tells the story of the Globe's construction, using the material (including goat hair in the plaster), techniques, and craftsmanship of 400 years ago. The new Globe isn't an exact replica: It seats 1,500 patrons, not the 3,000 who regularly squeezed in during the early 1600s, and this thatched roof has been specially treated with a fire retardant. Guided tours of the facility are offered throughout the day. See "'The City' Attractions" map.

See "The Play's the Thing: London's Theater Scene" on p. 295 for details on attending a play here.

21 New Globe Walk, SE1. ✆ 020/7902-1400. www.shakespeares-globe.org. Admission £9–£31 ($17–$59) adults, £7.50 ($14) seniors and students, £6.50 ($12) children 15 and under. Oct–Apr daily 10am–7:30pm; May–Sept daily 9am–noon and 12:30–5pm. Tube: Mansion House or London Bridge.

Sherlock Holmes Museum *(Overrated*

Where but on Baker Street would there be a museum displaying mementos of this famed fictional detective? Museum officials call it "the world's most famous address" (although 10 Downing St. is a rival for the title). Mystery writer Sir Arthur Conan Doyle created a fictional residence on Baker Street for Sherlock Holmes and his faithful Dr. Watson, and the famous sleuths "lived" here from 1881 to 1904. In Victorian rooms, you can examine a range of exhibits, including published Holmes adventures and letters written to Holmes. This is a very commercial and artificial museum, and strikes us as a tourist trap. Holmes fans might be better off just visiting the gift shop downstairs and buying a postcard or a deerstalker.

Some of the merchandise is interesting, though no Persian slippers—for shame. See the "West End Attractions" map.

221B Baker St., NW1. ℂ 020/7935-8866. www.sherlock-holmes.co.uk. Admission £6 ($11) adults, £4 ($7.60) children 16 and under. Daily 9:30am–6pm. Tube: Baker St.

Sir John Soane's Museum ℛ   This is the former home of Sir John Soane (1753–1837), an architect who rebuilt the Bank of England (although not the present structure). With his multiple levels, fool-the-eye mirrors, flying arches, and domes, Soane was a master of perspective and a genius of interior space (his picture gallery, for example, is filled with three times the number of paintings that a room of similar dimensions would normally hold). One prize of the collection is William Hogarth's satirical series *The Rake's Progress,* which includes his much-reproduced *Orgy and The Election,* a satire on mid-18th-century politics. Soane also filled his house with classical sculpture: The sarcophagus of Pharaoh Seti I, found in a burial chamber in the Valley of the Kings, is here. Also on display are architectural drawings from Soane's collection of 30,000. See the "West End Attractions" map.

13 Lincoln's Inn Fields, WC2. ℂ 020/7405-2107. www.soane.org. Free admission (donations invited). Tues–Sat 10am–5pm; 1st Tues of each month 6–9pm. Tours given Sat at 2:30pm; £3 ($5.70) tickets distributed at 2pm, first-come, first-served (group tours by appointment only). Tube: Holborn.

Wallace Collection ℛℛ *Finds*   Located in a palatial setting (the modestly described "town house" of the late Lady Wallace), this collection is a contrasting array of art and armaments. The collection is evocative of the Frick Museum in New York and the Musée d'Jacque André in Paris. The art collection (mostly French) includes works by Watteau, Boucher, Fragonard, and Greuze, as well as such classics as Frans Hals's *Laughing Cavalier* and Rembrandt's portrait of his son Titus. The paintings of the Dutch, English, Spanish, and Italian schools are outstanding. The collection also contains important 18th-century French decorative art, including furniture from a number of royal palaces, Sèvres porcelain, and gold boxes. The European and Asian armaments, on the ground floor, are works of art in their own right: superb inlaid suits of armor, some obviously for parade rather than battle, with more businesslike swords, halberds, and magnificent Persian scimitars. (See map on p. 228.)

Manchester Sq., W1. ℂ 020/7563-9500. www.the-wallace-collection.org.uk. Free admission (some exhibits require admission). Daily 10am–5pm. Tube: Bond St. or Baker St.

PARKS & GARDENS

London's parks are the most advanced system of "green lungs" in any large city on the globe. Although not as rigidly maintained as those of Paris (Britons traditionally prefer a more natural look), they're cared for with a loving and lavishly artistic hand that puts their American counterparts to shame.

The largest of the central London parks is **Hyde Park** ℛℛ (Tube: Marble Arch, Hyde Park Corner, or Lancaster Gate), once a favorite deer-hunting ground of Henry VIII. With the adjoining Kensington Gardens (see below), it covers 246 hectares (608 acres) of central London with velvety lawns interspersed with ponds, flowerbeds, and trees. Running through its width is a 17-hectare (41-acre) lake known as the **Serpentine,** where you can row, sail model boats, or swim (provided you don't mind sub-Florida water temperatures). **Rotten Row,** a 2.5km (1½-mile) sand riding track, attracts some skilled equestrians on Sunday. You can rent a paddleboat or a rowboat from the boathouse (open Mar–Oct) on the north side of **Hyde Park's Serpentine** (ℂ 020/7262-1330).

At the northeastern tip of Hyde Park, near Marble Arch, is **Speakers Corner** (www.speakerscorner.net). Since 1855 (before the legal right to assembly was guaranteed), people have been getting on their soapboxes about any and every subject under the sun. In the past you might have heard Karl Marx, Frederick Engels, or Lenin, and almost certainly William Morris and George Orwell. The corpse of Oliver Cromwell was hung here in a cage for the public to gape at or throw rotten eggs at. The king wanted to warn others against what might happen to them if they wished to abolish the monarchy. Hecklers, often aggressive, are part of the fun. Anyone can speak; just don't blaspheme, use obscene language, or start a riot.

Blending with Hyde Park and bordering the grounds of Kensington Palace, well-manicured **Kensington Gardens** (Tube: High St. Kensington or Queensway) contains the famous statue of Peter Pan, with bronze rabbits that toddlers are always trying to kidnap. The park is also home to that Victorian extravaganza, the Albert Memorial. The Orangery is an ideal place to take afternoon tea (p. 204).

East of Hyde Park, across Piccadilly, stretch **Green Park** 𝓡 (Tube: Green Park) and **St. James's Park** 𝓡 (Tube: St. James's Park), forming an almost unbroken chain of landscaped beauty. These parks are ideal for picnics; you'll find it hard to believe that this was once a swamp near a leper hospital. There's a romantic lake stocked with ducks and some surprising pelicans, descendants of the pair the Russian ambassador presented to Charles II in 1662.

Regent's Park 𝓡𝓡𝓡 (Tube: Regent's Park or Baker St.) covers most of the district of that name, north of Baker Street and Marylebone Road. Designed by the 18th-century genius John Nash to surround a palace for the prince regent (the palace never materialized), this is the most classically beautiful of London's parks. Its core is a rose garden planted around a small lake alive with waterfowl and spanned by Japanese bridges; in early summer, the rose perfume in the air is as heady as wine. The park is home to the **Open-Air Theatre** (p. 297) and the **London Zoo** (see "Especially for Kids" on p. 265). As at all the local parks, hundreds of chairs are scattered around the lawns, waiting for sunbathers. The deck-chair attendants, who rent the chairs for a

---

Memorial to Princess Diana

The life of the Princess of Wales was troubled, and so is the **Diana Princess of Wales Memorial Fountain** in the center of Hyde Park. The £3.6-million ($6.8-million) ring-shape water sculpture weighs 700 tons, and water flows from the highest point down both sides, through a 210m (715-ft.) trough, and into a basin called the Tranquil Pool. The fountain was originally opened by Queen Elizabeth in 2004 but had to be shut down after several people were injured swimming in it. After repairs, it was later reopened. You're not allowed to swim, but you can put your hands and feet into the fountain.

Before her death, Diana's mother, the late Frances Shand Kydd, criticized the memorial for its "lack of grandeur," and other critics have branded it a "storm drain." Culture Secretary Tessa Jowell said that the public has thrown garbage, including diapers, into the water and has also allowed dogs to paddle in the flow.

Not all criticism has been harsh. Jonathan Glancey, of *The Guardian,* likened the memorial to "the cycle of a princess's life, with all its ups and downs, and their ultimate draining away."

Tips Where to In-Line Skate

London's parks are great places to skate. Rental skates are available at **Slick Willies,** 12 Gloucester Rd., SW7 (© **020/7225-0004;** www.slickwillies.co.uk; Tube: Gloucester Rd.), costing £10 ($19) per day for skates and wrist guards, with a £100 ($190) credit card deposit required. Hours are Monday to Saturday 10am to 6:30pm, Sunday noon to 5pm.

---

small fee, are mostly college students on break. Rowboats and sailing dinghies are available in **Regent's Park** (© **020/7724-4069**). Sailing and canoeing cost between £6.50 ($12) per adult and £4.25 ($8.10) per child for 1 hour.

Chelsea Physic Garden, 66 Royal Hospital Rd., SW3 (© **020/7352-5646;** www.chelseaphysicgarden.co.uk; Tube: Sloane Sq.), founded in 1673 by the Worshipful Society of Apothecaries, is the second-oldest surviving botanical garden in England. Sir Hans Sloane, doctor to George II, required the apothecaries of the Empire to develop 50 plant species a year for presentation to the Royal Society. The objective was to grow plants for medicinal study. Plant specimens and even trees arrived at the gardens by barge, many to grow in English soil for the first time. Cottonseed from this garden launched an industry in the new colony of Georgia. Some 7,000 plants still grow here, everything from the pomegranate to the willow pattern tree; there's even exotic cork oak, as well as England's earliest rock garden. The garden is open April to October Wednesday noon to dusk, Thursday and Friday noon to 5pm, and Sunday noon to 6pm. Admission is £7 ($13) for adults and seniors, £4 ($7.60) for children 5 to 15 and students. The garden is a perfect setting for a well-recommended afternoon tea—you can carry your cuppa on promenades through the garden (p. 204).

Battersea Park, SW11 (© **020/8871-7530;** www.batterseapark.org; Tube: Sloane Sq.), is a vast patch of woodland, lakes, and lawns on the south bank of the Thames, opposite Chelsea Embankment, between Albert Bridge and Chelsea Bridge. Formerly known as Battersea Fields, the park was laid out between 1852 and 1858 on an old dueling ground. (The most famous duel was between Lord Winchelsea and the Duke of Wellington in 1829.) There's a lake for boating, a deer field with fenced-in deer and wild birds, and tennis and soccer areas. There's also a children's zoo, open from Easter to October 1 daily from 10am to 5pm, and weekends only in winter from 1 to 3pm. The park's architectural highlight is the Peace Pagoda, built by Japanese craftspeople in cooperation with British architects. The stone-and-wood pagoda was dedicated in 1986 to the now-defunct Council of Greater London by an order of Japanese monks. The park is open from dawn to dusk. From the Sloane Square Tube stop, it's a brisk 15-minute walk to the park, or you can pick up bus no. 137 (get off at the first stop after the bus crosses the Thames).

The hub of England's—and perhaps the world's—horticulture is in Surrey, at the **Royal Botanic Gardens at Kew** (also known as Kew Gardens). See "Attractions on the Outskirts," below.

4 Exploring London by Boat

All of London's history and development is linked with the River Thames: This winding ribbon of water connects the city with the sea, from which London first drew its wealth and power. The Thames was London's chief commercial thoroughfare and royal highway. Every royal procession was undertaken on gorgeously painted and gilded barges (which you can still see at the National Maritime Museum in Greenwich). Important state prisoners were delivered to the Tower of London by water, eliminating the chance of an ambush in one of the narrow, crooked alleys surrounding the fortress. Much commercial traffic on the water disappeared when London's streets were widened enough for horse-drawn coaches to maintain a decent pace.

RIVER CRUISES ALONG THE THAMES

A trip up or down the river will give you an entirely different view of London than the one you get from land. You'll see how the city grew along and around the Thames and how many of its landmarks turn their faces toward the water. Several companies operate motor launches from the Westminster piers (Tube: Westminster), offering panoramic views of one of Europe's most historic waterways.

Thames River Services, Westminster Pier, Victoria Embankment, SW1 (© 020/ 7930-4097; www.westminsterpier.co.uk), concerns itself only with downriver traffic from Westminster Pier to such destinations as Greenwich. The most popular excursion departs for Greenwich (a 50-min. ride) at half-hour intervals between 10am and 4pm in April, May, September, and October, and between 10am and 5pm from June to August; from November to March, boats depart from Westminster Pier at 40-minute intervals daily from 10:40am to 3:20pm. One-way fares are £7 ($13) for adults, £5.80 ($11) for seniors, £3.50 ($6.65) for children under 16. Round-trip fares are £9 ($17) for adults, £7.50 ($14) for seniors, £4.30 ($8.15) for children. A family ticket for two adults and up to three children under 15 costs £20 ($38) one-way, £25 ($48) round-trip.

Westminster Passenger Association (Upriver) Ltd., Westminster Pier, Victoria Embankment, SW1 (© 020/7930-2062 or 020/7930-4721; www.wpsa.co.uk), offers the only riverboat service upstream from Westminster Bridge to Kew, Richmond, and Hampton Court, with regular daily sailings from the Monday before Easter until the end of October on traditional riverboats, all with licensed bars. Trip time, one-way, can be as little as 1½ hours to Kew and between 2½ to 4 hours to Hampton Court, depending on the tide. Cruises from Westminster Pier to Hampton Court via Kew Gardens leave daily at 10:30, 11:15am, and noon. Round-trip tickets are £20 ($38) for adults, £13 ($25) for seniors, £9.75 ($19) for children ages 4 to 14, £49 ($94) for a family ticket; one child under 4 accompanied by an adult goes free.

THAMES-SIDE SIGHTS
THE BRIDGES

Some of the Thames bridges are household names. **London Bridge,** contrary to the nursery rhyme, never fell down, but it has been replaced a number of times and is vastly different from the original London Bridge, which was lined with houses and shops. The one that you see now is the ugliest of the versions; the previous incarnation was dismantled and shipped to Lake Havasu, Arizona, in the 1960s.

Also on the Thames, you can visit London's newest park, **Thames Barrier Park,** SE1, which is the city's first new riverside park in years. It lies on the north bank of the Thames alongside the Thames Barrier, a steel-and-concrete movable flood barrier inaugurated in 1982. The park is spread across 8.8 hectares (22 acres), and has fountains that flow into a channel in the 390m (1,279-ft.) sunken landscaped garden. There's also a riverside promenade and a children's playground here. The park is open daily from sunrise to sunset (reached via the no. 474 bus from the Canning Town

Bird's-"Eye" View of London

The world's largest observation wheel, the **British Airways London Eye** ⍟, Millennium Jubilee Gardens (✆ **0870/5000-600;** www.ba-londoneye.com), opened in 2000. It is the fourth-tallest structure in London, offering panoramic views that extend for some 40km (25 miles) if the weather's clear. Passengers are carried in 32 "pods" that make a complete revolution every half-hour. Along the way you'll see some of London's most famous landmarks from a bird's-eye view.

Built out of steel by a European consortium, it was conceived and designed by London architects Julia Barfield and David Marks, who claim inspiration from the Statue of Liberty in New York and the Eiffel Tower in Paris. Some 2 million visitors are expected to ride the Eye every year.

The Eye lies close to Westminster Bridge (you can hardly miss it). Tickets are £14 ($27) for adults, £10 ($19) for seniors and students, £6.50 ($12) for children 5 to 15. October to May daily 10am to 8pm; June to September daily 10am to 9pm. Tube: Westminster or Waterloo.

Tube station). It's also possible to take the DLR from Canning Town to Pontoon Dock, a 5-minute walk from the park—travel time is about 15 minutes shorter than the bus.

HMS *BELFAST*

An 11,500-ton cruiser, the **HMS *Belfast,*** Morgan's Lane, Tooley Street, SE1 (✆ **020/ 7940-6300;** www.hmsbelfast.iwm.org.uk; Tube: Tower Hill or London Bridge), is a World War II ship preserved as a floating museum. It's moored opposite the Tower of London, between Tower Bridge and London Bridge. During the Russian convoy period and on D-day, the *Belfast* saw distinguished service, and in the Korean War it was known as "that straight-shootin' ship." You can explore all its decks, right down to the engine room; exhibits above and below show how sailors lived and fought over the past 50 years. It's open daily from 10am, with last boarding at 5:15pm in summer, 4:15pm in winter. Admission is £9.95 ($19) adults, seniors and students £6.15 ($12), children under 16 free.

DOCKLANDS ⍟

What was a dilapidated wasteland surrounded by water—some 89km (55 miles) of waterfront acreage within a sailor's cry of London's major attractions—has been reclaimed, restored, and rejuvenated. **London Docklands** is coming into its own as a leisure, residential, and commercial lure.

Next to the Tower of London, **St. Katharine's Dock** was the first of the docks to be given an entirely new role. Originally built from 1827 to 1828, this was for many years a leading dock, with the advantage of being closest to the City. Today, as a residential center and yacht marina, St. Katharine's again profits from its proximity to the City. The modern World Trade Centre looks down on the brick-brown sails of barges and gleaming hulls of moored luxury yachts. Blocks of fashionable Manhattan-style loft apartments sit between the docks and the river.

Canary Wharf, on the Isle of Dogs, is the heart of Docklands. This huge site is dominated by a 240m (787-ft.) tower, the tallest building in the United Kingdom, designed by César Pelli. The **Piazza** is lined with shops and restaurants. A visit to the **Exhibition Centre** gives you an overview of the Docklands—past, present, and future. Already the area has provided welcome space for the overflow from the City of London's square mile, and its development is more than promising.

On the south side of the river at Surrey Docks, the Victorian warehouses of **Butler's Wharf** have been converted into offices, houses, shops, and restaurants; this area is home to the **Design Museum** (p. 244).

Docklands can be reached via the **Docklands Light Railway,** which links the Isle of Dogs to two London Underground stations. If you're coming from the Tower of London, you can pick up the DLR at the Tower Hill station. To see the whole complex, take the railway at Tower Gateway near Tower Bridge for a short journey through Wapping and the Isle of Dogs. You can get off at Island Gardens and then cross through the 100-year-old Greenwich Tunnel under the Thames to see the attractions at Greenwich (see "Attractions on the Outskirts," below).

The other DLR terminal in central London is Bank, which has even better tube connections than Tower Hill. (It has links to five lines rather than two.) Also, to visit Canary Wharf/Greenwich, it is better to go from Bank as it offers direct trains. From Tower Gateway, it is necessary to change trains at Westferry.

EXPLORING LONDON'S CANALS BY BOAT

Boat trips on London's canals, especially Regent's Canal in London's canal-laced "Little Venice," are an increasingly popular way to seeing the city. Bus no. 6 takes you to Little Venice, where you can board one of several boats for a tour along the canals. You can return either by boat or by Tube at the end of a one-way trip—Warwick Avenue on the Bakerloo line is only a couple of minutes walk from where the canal boats dock.

Since the Festival of Britain in 1951, some of the traditional painted canal boats have been resurrected for Venetian-style trips through the waterways. One of them is **Jason,** which takes you on a 90-minute round-trip ride from Bloomfield Road in Little Venice through the long Maida Hill tunnel under Edgeware Road, through Regent's Park, past the Mosque, the London Zoo, Lord Snowdon's Aviary, and the Pirate's Castle, to Camden Lock, and finally back to Little Venice. Passengers who opt to make the 45-minute one-way journey disembark at Camden Lock.

The season runs from April through October, with daily trips at 12:30 and 2:30pm. A canalside seafood specialty restaurant/cafe at *Jason*'s mooring offers lunches, dinners, and teas, all freshly made. The round-trip fare is £7.50 ($14) for adults, £6.50 ($12) for seniors, £6 ($11) for children (14 and under). One-way fares are £6.50 ($12) for adults, £5.50 ($10) for seniors, £5 ($9.50) for children (14 and under). Family tickets cost £20 to £22 ($38–$42). For reservations, contact **Jason's,** Jason's Wharf, opposite 60 Bloomfield Rd., Little Venice, London W9 (© **020/7286-3428;** www.jasons. co.uk; Tube: Warwick Ave.).

5 Attractions on the Outskirts

These sights are perfect for a morning or afternoon jaunt and are easily accessible by Tube, train, boat, or bus.

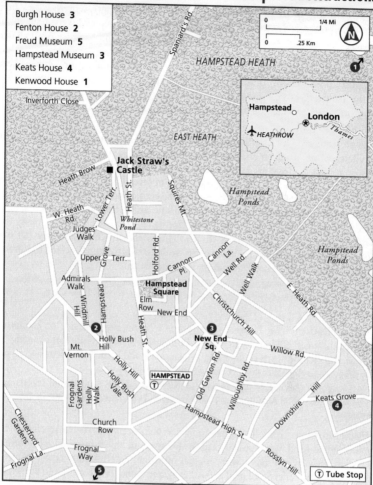

Burgh House **3**
Fenton House **2**
Freud Museum **5**
Hampstead Museum **3**
Keats House **4**
Kenwood House **1**

HAMPSTEAD ⊛

About 6.5km (4 miles) north of the center of London lies the lovely village of Hampstead (Tube: Northern Line to Hampstead) and scenic Hampstead Heath.

The 320-hectare (790-acre) expanse of high heath known as **Hampstead Heath** is a chain of formal parkland, woodland, heath, meadowland, and ponds. On a clear day, you can see St. Paul's Cathedral and even the hills of Kent. Londoners would certainly mount the barricades if Hampstead Heath were imperiled; for years, they've come here to sun-worship, fly kites, fish the ponds, swim, picnic, and jog. In good weather, it's also the site of big 1-day fairs. At the shore of Kenwood Lake, in the northern section, is a concert platform devoted to symphony performances on summer evenings. In the northeast corner, in Waterlow Park, ballets, operas, and comedies are staged at the Grass Theatre in June and July.

Once the Underground reached **Hampstead Village** in 1907, writers, artists, architects, musicians, and scientists were among those who decamped for the leafy village. Keats, D. H. Lawrence, Shelley, Robert Louis Stevenson, and Kingsley Amis all once lived here, and John Le Carré still does.

The Regency and Georgian houses of the village and the rolling greens of the heath are just 20 minutes by Tube from Piccadilly Circus. The village has a quirky mix of historic pubs, toy shops, and chic boutiques along **Flask Walk,** a pedestrian mall. The original village, on the side of a hill, still has old alleys, steps, courts, and groves ideal for strolling.

Burgh House   This Queen Anne home (1703), in the center of the village, was the residence of the daughter and son-in-law of Rudyard Kipling, who often visited here. It's now used for local art exhibits, concerts, recitals, talks, and public meetings on many subjects. The house is the headquarters of several local societies, including the Hampstead Music Club and the Hampstead Scientific Society. **Hampstead Museum,** in Burgh House, illustrates the local history of the area. It has a room devoted to reproductions of works by the great artist John Constable, who lived nearby for many years and is buried in the local parish church. There's also a licensed **buttery** (© **020/ 7431-2516**) that's popular for lunch or tea, with lunches for just £3 to £8 ($5.70–$15) during the week. In pricey Hampstead, it's a real bargain.

New End Sq., NW3. © 020/7431-0144 or 020/7431-2516 for buttery reservations. www.burghhouse.org.uk. Free admission. House and museum Wed–Sun noon–5pm, Sat by appt.; buttery Wed–Sun 11am–5:15pm. Tube: Northern Line to Hampstead.

Fenton House   This National Trust property is on the west side of Hampstead Grove, just north of Hampstead Village. Built in 1693, its paneled rooms contain furniture and pictures; 18th-century English, German, and French porcelain; and an outstanding collection of early keyboard musical instruments.

Windmill Hill, NW3. © 020/7435-3471. Admission £4.90 ($9.30) adults, £2.45 ($4.65) children, £12 ($23) family ticket. Mar Sat–Sun 2–5pm; Apr–Oct Sat–Sun 11am–5pm, Wed–Fri 2–5pm. Closed Nov–Feb. Tube: Northern Line to Hampstead.

Freud Museum   After he and his family left Nazi-occupied Vienna as refugees, Sigmund Freud lived, worked, and died in this spacious three-story house in northern London. In view are rooms with original furniture, letters, photographs, paintings, and the personal effects of Freud and his daughter, Anna. In the study and library, you can see the famous couch and Freud's large collection of Egyptian, Roman, and Asian antiquities.

20 Maresfield Gardens, NW3. © 020/7435-2002. www.freud.org.uk. Admission £5 ($9.50) adults, £3 ($5.70) full-time students and seniors, free for children under 12. Wed–Sun noon–5pm. Tube: Jubilee Line to Finchley Rd.

Keats House 𝒜𝒜   The poet lived here for only 2 years, but that was approximately two-fifths of his creative life; he died of tuberculosis in Rome at the age of 25 (in 1821). In Hampstead, Keats wrote some of his most celebrated odes, including "Ode on a Grecian Urn" and "Ode to a Nightingale." His Regency house possesses the manuscripts of his last sonnet ("Bright star, would I were steadfast as thou art") and a portrait of him on his deathbed in a house on the Spanish Steps in Rome.

Keats Grove, NW3. © 020/7435-2062. www.cityoflondon.gov.uk/keats. Admission £3.50 ($6.65) adults, £1.75 ($3.35) students and seniors, free for children under 16. Tues–Sun 1–5pm. Tube: Northern Line to Hampstead or Belsize Park.

Kenwood House ★★ Kenwood House was built as a gentleman's country home and was later enlarged and decorated by the famous Scottish architect Robert Adam, starting in 1764. The house contains period furniture and paintings by Turner, Frans Hals, Gainsborough, Reynolds, and more.

Hampstead Lane, NW3. © 020/8348-1286. www.English-heritage.org.uk. Free admission. Apr–Oct daily 11am–5pm; Nov–Mar daily 11am–4pm. Tube: Northern Line to Golders Green, then bus no. 210.

IN NEARBY HIGHGATE

Highgate Cemetery A stone's throw east of Hampstead Heath, Highgate Village has a number of 16th- and 17th-century mansions and small cottages, lining three sides of the now-pondless Pond Square. Its most outstanding feature, however, is this beautiful cemetery, laid out around a huge 300-year-old cedar tree and laced with serpentine pathways. The cemetery was so popular and fashionable in the Victorian era that it was extended on the other side of Swain's Lane in 1857. The most famous grave is that of Karl Marx, who died in Hampstead in 1883; his grave, marked by a gargantuan bust, is in the eastern cemetery. In the old western cemetery—accessible only by guided tour, given hourly in summer—are scientist Michael Faraday and poet Christina Rossetti.

Swain's Lane, N6. © 020/8340-1834. http://highgate-cemetery.org. Western Cemetery guided tour £5 ($9.50). Eastern Cemetery admission £2 ($3.80), £1 ($1.90) camera pass charge (no video cameras; hand-held still cameras only). Western Cemetery, Mar–Oct guided tours only Mon–Fri at 2pm, Sat–Sun hourly 11am–4pm; Nov–Feb, tours Sat–Sun hourly 11am–3pm. Eastern Cemetery, Apr–Oct Mon–Fri 10am–4:30pm, Sat–Sun 11am–4:30pm; Nov–Mar Mon–Fri 10am–3:30pm, Sat–Sun 11am–3:30pm. Both cemeteries closed at Christmas and during funerals. Tube: Northern Line to Archway, then walk or take bus no. 143, 210, or 271.

GREENWICH ★★★

When London overwhelms you and you'd like to escape for a beautiful, sunny afternoon on the city's outskirts, make Greenwich your destination.

Greenwich Mean Time is the basis of standard time throughout most of the world, and Greenwich has been the zero point used in the reckoning of terrestrial longitudes since 1884. But this lovely village—the center of British seafaring when Britain ruled the seas—is also the home of the Royal Naval College, the National Maritime Museum, and the Old Royal Observatory. Greenwich also has some wonderful shopping, including a famous weekend market (see the "GST: Greenwich Shopping Time" box on p. 274).

Greenwich was the site of Britain's Millennium Dome, a multimedia extravaganza mixing education and entertainment. Most of the project's cost, estimated at more than £1.3 billion ($2.45 billion), came from a national lottery. Then the much-heralded Dome bombed with audiences and the project became a national joke. Prince Charles ridiculing it as a monstrous *blanc mange,* that unattractive milky gelatin dessert, didn't help matters, and it finally closed. But the much-maligned Millennium Dome reopened in the summer of July 2007 as **"The 02,"** featuring an 11-screen cinema, a live music venue, exhibition spaces, theaters, bars, and restaurants. It will also host sports evenings during the 2012 Olympics. See the "Greater London Area" map on p. 74 to see Greenwich's location in relation to central London.

ESSENTIALS

GETTING THERE The fastest way to get to Greenwich is to take the Tube in Central London to Waterloo Station, where you can take a fast train to Greenwich Station.

The Tube is for speed (it takes only 15 min.), but if you'd like to travel the 6.5km (4 miles) to Greenwich the way Henry VIII did, you still can. In fact, getting to

Greenwich is half the fun. The most appealing way involves boarding any of the frequent ferryboats that cruise along the Thames at intervals that vary from every half-hour (in summer) to every 45 minutes (in winter). Boats that leave from Charing Cross Pier (Tube: Embankment) and Tower Pier (Tube: Tower Hill) are run by **Catamaran Cruises, Ltd.** (*© 020/7987-1185*). Depending on the tides and the carrier you select, travel time varies from 50 to 75 minutes each way. Passage is £5.60 to £6.80 ($11–$13) one-way.

VISITOR INFORMATION The **Greenwich Tourist Information Centre** is at 2 Cutty Sark Gardens (*© 020/8858-6376*); open daily from 10am to 5pm. The Tourist Information Centre conducts **walking tours** of Greenwich's major sights. Tours cost £5 ($9.50) for adults and £4 ($7.60) for students, seniors, and children; depart daily at 12:15 and 2:15pm; and last 1¼ to 1½ hours. Advance reservations aren't required, but you may want to phone in advance to find out any last-minute schedule changes.

SEEING THE SIGHTS

The **National Maritime Museum, Old Royal Observatory,** and **Queen's House** stand together in a beautiful royal park, high on a hill overlooking the Thames. All three attractions are free and open daily from 10am to 5pm (until 6pm in summer). For more information, call *© 020/8858-4422* or visit **www.nmm.ac.uk**.

From the days of early seafarers to 20th-century sea power, the **National Maritime Museum** *ⓡⓡ* illustrates the glory that was Britain at sea. The cannon, relics, ship models, and paintings tell the story of a thousand naval battles and a thousand victories, as well as the price of those battles. Look for some oddities here—everything from the dreaded cat-o'-nine-tails used to flog sailors until 1879 to Nelson's Trafalgar coat, with the fatal bullet hole in the left shoulder clearly visible. In time for the millennium, the museum spent £20 million ($38 million) in a massive expansion that added 16 new galleries devoted to British maritime history and improved visitor facilities.

Old Royal Observatory *ⓡ* is the original home of Greenwich Mean Time. It has the largest refracting telescope in the United Kingdom and a collection of historic timekeepers and astronomical instruments. You can stand astride the meridian and set your watch precisely by the falling time-ball. Sir Christopher Wren designed the Octagon Room. Here the first royal astronomer, Flamsteed, made the 30,000 observations that formed the basis of his *Historia Coelestis Britannica*. Edmond Halley, he of the eponymous Halley's Comet, succeeded him. In 1833, the ball on the tower was hung to enable shipmasters to set their chronometers accurately.

Designed by Inigo Jones, **Queen's House** *ⓡⓡ* (1616) is a fine example of this architect's innovative style. It's most famous for the cantilevered tulip staircase, the first of its kind. Carefully restored, the house contains a collection of royal and marine paintings and other objets d'art.

The Wernher Collection at Ranger's House *ⓡⓡ*, Chesterfield Walk (*© 020/8853-0035;* www.English-heritage.org.uk), is a real find and one of the finest and most unusual 19th-century mixed-art collections in the world. Acquired by a German diamond dealer, Sir Julius Wernher, the collection contains some 650 exhibits, some dating as far back as 3 B.C. It's an eclectic mix of everything, including jewelry, bronzes, ivory, antiques, tapestries, porcelain pieces, and classic paintings. Hanging on the walls of the gallery are rare works by such old masters as Hans Memling and Filippino Lippi, along with portraits by such English painters as Reynolds and Romney. One salon is devoted to the biggest collection of Renaissance jewelry in Britain. Look also for the carved medieval, Byzantine, and Renaissance ivories, along with Limoges enamels and Sèvres porcelain. The most unusual items are enameled skulls and a miniature coffin complete with 3-D skeleton. Don't expect everything to be beautiful—Wernher's taste was often bizarre. Admission is £5.50 ($10) adults, £4.10 ($7.80) seniors and students, £2.80 ($5.30) children, free for children under 5. The attraction is open only for part of the year: April 1 to September 30 Sunday to Wednesday 10am to 5pm. It is closed otherwise.

Nearby is the **Royal Naval College** ⚶⭐, King William Walk, off Romney Road (© **020/8269-4747**; www.greenwichfoundation.org.uk). Designed by Sir Christopher Wren in 1696, it occupies 4 blocks named after King Charles, Queen Anne, King William, and Queen Mary. Formerly, Greenwich Palace stood here from 1422 to 1640. It's worth stopping in to see the magnificent Painted Hall by Thornhill, where the body of Nelson lay in state in 1805, and the Georgian chapel of St. Peter and St. Paul. Open daily from 10am to 5pm; admission is free.

KEW ⚶⭐⭐

About 15km (9½ miles) southwest of central London, Kew is home to one of the best-known botanical gardens in Europe. It's also the site of **Kew Palace** ⚶⭐ (© **0870/751-5179**), former residence of George III and Queen Charlotte. A dark, red-brick structure, it is characterized by its Dutch gables. The house was constructed in 1631, and at its rear is the Queen's Garden in a very formal design and filled with plants thought to have grown here in the 17th century. The interior is very much an elegant country house of the time, fit for a king, but not as regal as Buckingham Palace. You get the feeling that someone could have actually lived here as you wander through the dining room and the breakfast room, and go upstairs to the queen's drawing room, where musical evenings were staged. The rooms are wallpapered with designs actually used at the time. Perhaps the most intriguing exhibits are little possessions once owned by royal occupants here—everything from snuffboxes to Prince Frederick's gambling debts. Open May to September daily 9:30am to 4pm, costing £5 ($9.50) for admission. The most convenient way to get to Kew is to take the **District Line** Tube to the Kew Gardens stop, on the south bank of the Thames. Allow about 30 minutes.

Royal Botanic Gardens, Kew ⚶⭐⭐ These world-famous gardens offer thousands of varieties of plants. But Kew Gardens, as it's known, is no mere pleasure garden—it's essentially a vast scientific research center that happens to be beautiful. The gardens, on a 120-hectare (296-acre) site, encompass lakes, greenhouses, walks, pavilions, and museums, along with examples of the architecture of Sir William Chambers. Among the 50,000 plants are notable collections of ferns, orchids, aquatic plants, cacti, mountain plants, palms, and tropical water lilies.

No matter what season you visit, Kew always has something to see, from the first spring flowers through to winter. Gigantic hothouses grow species of shrubs, blooms, and trees from every part of the globe, from the Arctic Circle to tropical rainforests. Attractions include a newly restored Japanese gateway in traditional landscaping, as well as exhibitions that vary by season. The newest greenhouse, the Princess of Wales Conservatory (beyond the rock garden), encompasses 10 climatic zones, from arid to tropical; it has London's most thrilling collection of miniature orchids. The Marianne North Gallery (1882) is an absolute gem, paneled with 246 different types of wood that the intrepid Victorian artist collected on her world journeys; she also collected 832 paintings of exotic and tropical flora, all displayed on the walls. The Visitor Centre at Victoria Gate houses an exhibit telling the story of Kew, as well as a bookshop.

Kew. ℂ 020/8332-5655. www.rbgkew.org.uk. Admission £12 ($23) adults, £10 ($19) students and seniors, free for children 16 and under. Open Apr–Aug Mon–Fri 9:30am–6pm, Sat–Sun 9:30am–7pm; Sept–Oct daily 9:30am–5:30pm, Nov–Jan daily 9:30am–3:45pm, Feb–Mar daily 9:30am–5pm. Tube: District Line to Kew Gardens.

KEW FOR TEA

Visitors are flocking to the historic **Orangery** at Kew Gardens. The Orangery, built for Princess Augusta by Sir William Chambers in 1761, serves top-quality refreshments, morning coffees, lunches, and afternoon snacks. For us, the highlight is the very traditional English tea offered here on the new outdoor terrace constructed of York and Portland stone, opening onto panoramic views of some of the world's most beautiful gardens.

Across the street from the Royal Botanic Gardens is one of the finest tearooms in the area, the **Original Maids of Honour Tearooms,** 288 Kew Rd. (ℂ **020/8940-2752;** www.theoriginalmaidsofhonour.co.uk). Oak paneling and old leaded-glass windows give the place a cozy warmth. The homemade cakes are delectable, as are the delightfully light scones. The Maids of Honour (flavored with jam, cottage cheese, golden raisins, almond extract, and almonds) is their pastry specialty, originally baked for Henry VIII, who liked it so much that its secret recipe has been passed along through the centuries. Afternoon tea is £6.55 ($12). The tearoom is open Monday from 9:30am to 1pm and Tuesday through Saturday from 9:30am to 6pm, and tea is served from 2:30 to 5:30pm.

HAMPTON COURT

Hampton Court, on the north side of the Thames, 21km (13 miles) west of London in East Molesey, Surrey, is easily accessible and is one of the great palaces of England. But if you have very limited time, we'd save it for a future visit. If you're going to be in London for perhaps a week, then we'd recommend a stop, but only after you've spent a day at Windsor. Frequent **trains** (ℂ 08457/484950 in the U.K. or 01603/764776) run from Waterloo Station (Network Southeast) to Hampton Court Station. **London Transport** (ℂ 020/7730-3466) bus nos. 111, 131, 216, 267, and 461 make the trip from Victoria Coach Station on Buckingham Palace Road (just southwest of Victoria Station). Boat service is offered to and from Kingston, Richmond, and Westminster (see "River Cruises along the Thames," on p. 256). If you're **driving** from London, take A308 to the junction with A309 on the north side of Kingston Bridge over the Thames. See the "Side Trips from London" map on p. 319 to find Hampton Court in relation to London.

Hampton Court Palace 🄰🄰🄰   The 16th-century palace of Cardinal Wolsey can teach us a lesson: Don't try to outdo your boss, particularly if he happens to be Henry VIII. The rich cardinal did just that, and he eventually lost his fortune, power, and prestige, and ended up giving his lavish palace to the Tudor monarch. Henry took over, even outdoing the Wolsey embellishments. The Tudor additions included the Anne Boleyn gateway, with its 16th-century astronomical clock that even tells the time of high tide at London Bridge. From Clock Court, you can see one of Henry's major contributions, the aptly named Great Hall, with its hammer-beam ceiling. Also added by Henry were the tiltyard (where jousting competitions were held), a tennis court, and a kitchen.

Although the palace enjoyed prestige and pomp in Elizabethan days, it owes much of its present look to William and Mary—or rather to Sir Christopher Wren, who designed and had built the Northern or Lion Gates, intended to be the main entrance to the new parts of the palace. The fine wrought-iron screen at the south end of the south gardens was made by Jean Tijou around 1694 for William and Mary. You can parade through the apartments today, filled as they were with porcelain, furniture, paintings, and tapestries. The King's Dressing Room is graced with some of the best art, mainly paintings by old masters on loan from Queen Elizabeth II. Finally, be sure to inspect the royal chapel (Wolsey wouldn't recognize it). To confound yourself totally, you may want to get lost in the serpentine shrubbery maze in the garden, also the work of Wren. More and more attention is now focused on improving and upgrading the famous gardens here—the formal gardens are among the last surviving examples of garden methods and designs from several important periods of history.

The 24-hectare (60-acre) gardens—including the Great Vine, King's Privy Garden, Great Fountain Gardens, Tudor and Elizabethan Knot Gardens, Board Walk, Tiltyard, and Wilderness—are open daily year-round from 7am until dusk (but not later than 9pm) and, except for the Privy Garden, can be visited free. A garden cafe and restaurant are located in the Tiltyard Gardens.

Hampton Court, on the north side of the Thames and 21km (13 miles) west of London, is easily accessible. Frequent trains run from Waterloo Station (Network Southeast) to **Hampton Court Station** (© **0845/748-4950**). Once at the station, buses will take you the rest of the way to the palace. If you're driving from London, take the A308 to the junction with the A309 on the north side of Kingston Bridge over the Thames.

East Molesey, Surrey. © **0870/752-7777.** www.hrp.org.uk. Admission £12 ($23) adults, £10 ($19) students and seniors, £8 ($15) children 5–15, free for children under 5, family ticket £36 ($69). Gardens open year-round daily 7am–dusk (no later than 9pm); free admission to all except south and east formal gardens (admission £4/$7.60 adults, £2.50/$4.75 children) without palace ticket during summer months. Cloisters, courtyards, state apartments, great kitchen, cellars, and Hampton Court exhibition Mar–Oct daily 10am–6pm; Nov–Feb daily 10am–4:30pm.

6 Especially for Kids

London has fun places for kids of all ages. In addition to the attractions listed below, kids love to explore **Buckingham Palace, Kensington Palace, Madame Tussaud's,** the **National Army Museum,** the **National Maritime Museum** (in Greenwich), the **Natural History Museum,** the **Science Museum,** and the **Tower of London,** all discussed above.

Bethnal Green Museum of Childhood (Kids)

This branch of the Victoria and Albert specializes in toys. The variety of dolls alone is staggering; some have such elaborate period costumes that you don't even want to think of the price tags they would carry today. With the dolls come dollhouses, from simple cottages to miniature mansions, complete with fireplaces, grand pianos, kitchen utensils, and carriages. You'll also find optical toys, marionettes, puppets, a considerable exhibit of soldiers and war toys from both World War eras, trains and aircraft, and a display of clothing and furniture relating to the social history of childhood.

Cambridge Heath Rd., E2. © **020/8983-5200.** www.museumofchildhood.org.uk. Free admission. Daily 10am–5:45pm. Tube: Central Line to Bethnal Green.

Horniman Museum (Kids)

This century-old museum set in 6.4 hectares (16 acres) of landscaped gardens is quirky, funky, and fun. The collection was accumulated by Frederick Horniman, a Victorian tea trader. A full range of events and activities takes place here, including storytelling and arts-and-crafts sessions for kids, along with

Especially for Kids

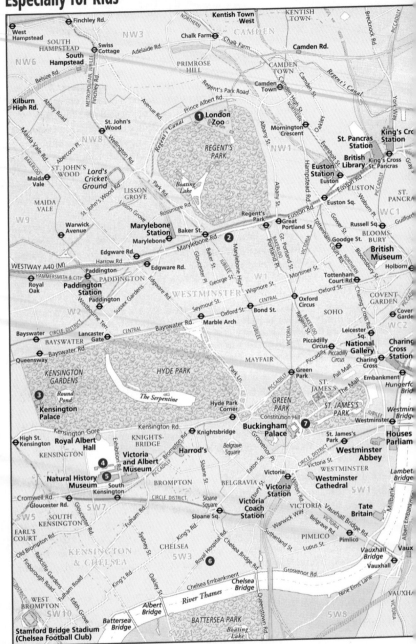

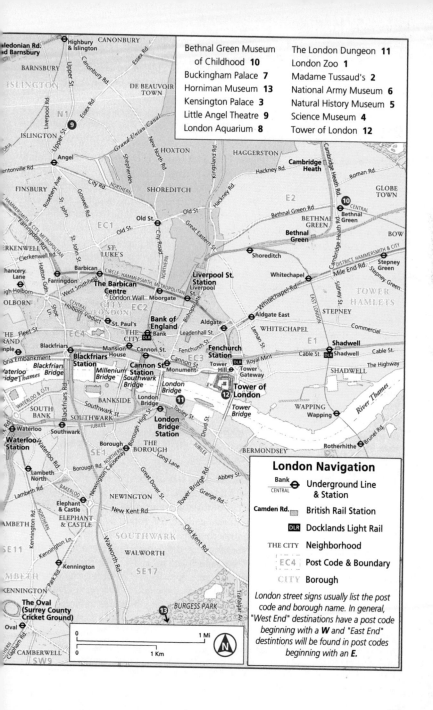

Bethnal Green Museum of Childhood **10**	The London Dungeon **11**
Buckingham Palace **7**	London Zoo **1**
Horniman Museum **13**	Madame Tussaud's **2**
Kensington Palace **3**	National Army Museum **6**
Little Angel Theatre **9**	Natural History Museum **5**
London Aquarium **8**	Science Museum **4**
	Tower of London **12**

London Navigation

Bank ⊖ CENTRAL	Underground Line & Station
Camden Rd. ▭	British Rail Station
DLR	Docklands Light Rail
THE CITY	Neighborhood
EC4	Post Code & Boundary
CITY	Borough

*London street signs usually list the post code and borough name. In general, "West End" destinations have a post code beginning with a **W** and "East End" destinations will be found in post codes beginning with an **E**.*

0 ——————— 1 Mi
0 ——————— 1 Km

workshops for adults. The museum owns some 350,000 objects ranging from a gigantic, overstuffed walrus to such oddities as oversize model insects. There are also displays of live insects and a small aquarium constructed in waterfall-like tiers. The torture chair thought to have been an original used during the Spanish Inquisition was proven to be a fake, although the instruments are genuine.

100 London Rd., SE23. ℂ 020/8699-1872. www.horniman.ac.uk. Free admission except for temporary exhibitions. Museum daily 10:30am–5:30pm. Library Tues–Sat 10:30am–5:30pm; Sun 2–5:30pm. Gardens Mon–Sat 7:15am– dusk; Sun 8am–dusk. Tube: London Bridge.

Little Angel Theatre *(Kids)*   Puppetry in all its forms is presented at this charming small theater in Islington, north of the city. There are homegrown shows that tour nationally and internationally, as well as performances by a variety of visiting companies. The range of puppetry is wide, from marionettes (string puppets) to rod-and-glove puppets. Most of the work is targeted at children; age limits are stated for every show presented (for example, "no under-3s allowed"); grown-ups will enjoy them, too. There's a coffee bar and an adjacent workshop where the puppets, sets, and costumes are made. Call for information. The theater is accessible to people with disabilities.

14 Dagmar Passage, N1. ℂ 020/7226-1787. www.littleangeltheatre.com. Admission £8–£20 ($15–$38) adults, £6–£9 ($11–$17) children. Show times Wed–Sun 11am and 2pm (sometimes 4:30pm Fri). Tube: Northern Line to Angel or Victoria Line to Highbury and Islington.

London Aquarium *(★) (Kids)*   One of the largest aquariums in Europe, this South Bank attraction boasts 350 species of fish—everything from British freshwater species to sharks that once patrolled the Pacific. Observe the bountiful riches of the coral reefs of the Indian Ocean, and what lurks in the murky depths of the Atlantic and Pacific oceans, including an array of eels, piranhas, rays, jellyfish, and other denizens of the deep. You ford a freshwater stream into a mangrove swamp to reach a tropical rainforest. The seawater, incidentally, is just normal Thames water mixed with 8 tons of salt at a time.

County Hall, Westminster Bridge Rd., SE1. ℂ 020/7967-8000. www.londonaquarium.co.uk. Admission £13 ($25) adults, £11 ($21) students and seniors, £9.75 ($19) ages 3–14, £44 ($84) family ticket. Sept–July daily 10am–6pm; Aug daily 10am–7pm. Closed Christmas Day. Tube: Waterloo.

The London Dungeon   This ghoulish place was designed to chill the blood while reproducing the conditions of the Middle Ages. Set under the arches of London Bridge Station, the dungeon is a series of tableaux more grisly than those at Madame Tussaud's. The rumble of trains overhead adds to the atmosphere, and tolling bells bring a constant note of melancholy; dripping water and caged rats make for even more atmosphere. Naturally, it offers a burning at the stake, as well as a torture chamber with racking, branding, and fingernail extraction, and a spine-chilling "Jack the Ripper Experience." The special effects were originally conceived for major film and TV productions. They've recently added a new show called "Judgment Day." You're sentenced to death (by actors, of course) and taken on a boat ride to meet your fate. If you survive, a Pizza Hut is on-site, and a souvenir shop sells certificates that testify you made it through the works.

28–34 Tooley St., SE1. ℂ 020/7403-7221. www.thedungeons.com. Admission £17 ($33) adults, £14 ($28) students and seniors, £12 ($24) children under 15, children under 5 free. Admission includes Judgment Day boat ride. Nov 1–Mar 18 daily 10:30am–5pm; Mar 19–Apr 3 daily 9:30am–5:30pm; Apr 4–May 27 daily 10am–5pm; May 28–Oct daily 10am–7:30pm. Tube: London Bridge.

London Zoo *Kids*   One of the greatest zoos in the world, the London Zoo is more than 1½ centuries old. This 14-hectare (35-acre) garden houses about 8,000 animals, including some of the rarest species on earth. There's an insect house (incredible bird-eating spiders), a reptile house (huge, dragonlike monitor lizards), and others, such as the Sobell Pavilion for Apes and Monkeys and the Lion Terraces. In the Moonlight World, special lighting simulates night for the nocturnal beasties while rendering them visible to onlookers, so you can see all the night rovers in action.

The Millennium Conservation Centre combines animals, visuals, and displays to demonstrate the nature of life on this planet. Many families budget almost an entire day here, watching the penguins being fed, enjoying an animal ride in summer, and meeting elephants on their walks around the zoo.

Regent's Park, NW1. ℂ 020/7722-3333. www.londonzoo.co.uk. Admission £12 ($23) adults, £11 ($21) students and seniors, £9.50 ($18) children 3–15, £39 ($74) family ticket (2 adults and 2 children or 1 adult and 3 children). Mar 5–Oct daily 10am–5:30pm; Nov–Feb 10 daily 10am–4pm; Feb 11–Mar 4 10am–4:30pm. Tube: Regent's Park or Camden Town. Bus: C2 or 274.

7 Organized Tours

BUS TOURS

For the first-timer, the quickest and most economical way to bring the big city into focus is to take a bus tour. One of the most popular is the **Original London Sight-seeing Tour,** which passes by all the major sights in just about 1½ hours. The tour—which uses a traditional double-decker bus with live commentary by a guide—costs £18 ($34) for adults, £12 ($23) for children under 16, free for those under 5. The tour allows you to hop on or off the bus at any point in the tour at no extra charge.

Departures are from convenient points within the city; you can choose your departure point when you buy your ticket. Tickets can be purchased on the bus or at a discount from any London Transport or London Tourist Board Information Centre. Most hotel concierges also sell tickets. For information or phone purchases, call ℂ **020/8877-1722.** It's also possible to book online at **www.theoriginaltour.com**.

Big Bus Company Ltd., Waterside Way, London SW17 (ℂ **020/7233-9533;** www.bigbus.co.uk), operates a 2-hour tour in summer, departing frequently between 8:30am and 4:30pm daily from Marble Arch by Speakers Corner, Green Park by the Ritz Hotel, and Victoria Station (Buckingham Palace Rd. by the Royal Westminster Hotel). Tours cover the highlights—18 in all—ranging from the Houses of Parliament and Westminster Abbey to the Tower of London and Buckingham Palace (exterior looks only), accompanied by live commentary. The cost is £20 ($38) for adults, £10 ($19) for children. A 1-hour tour follows the same route but covers only 13 sights. Tickets are valid all day; you can hop on and off the bus as you wish.

WALKING TOURS

The Original London Walks, 87 Messina Ave., P.O. Box 1708, London NW6 4LW (ℂ **020/7624-3978;** www.walks.com), the oldest established walking-tour company in London, is run by an Anglo-American journalist/actor couple, David and Mary Tucker. Their hallmarks are variety, reliability, reasonably sized groups, and—above all—superb guides. The renowned crime historian Donald Rumbelow, the leading authority on Jack the Ripper and author of the classic guidebook *London Walks,* is a regular guide, as are several prominent actors (including classical actor Edward Petherbridge). Walks are regularly scheduled daily and cost £6 ($11) for adults, £5 ($9.50) for students and seniors; children under 15 go free. Call for a schedule; no reservations needed.

8 Spectator Sports

CRICKET   In summer, attention turns to cricket, played either at **Lord's,** St. John's Wood Road, NW8 (© **020/432-1000;** www.lords.org; Tube: Jubilee Line to St. John's Wood), in north London, or at the somewhat less prestigious **Oval Cricket Ground,** The Oval, Kensington, London SE11 (© **020/7582-6660;** Tube: Northern Line to The Oval or Vauxhall), in south London. During the international test matches between Britain and Australia, the West Indies, India, or New Zealand (as important as the World Series in the United States), Britons go into a collective trance, with everyone glued to the nearest radio or TV.

FOOTBALL (SOCCER)   The season runs from August to April and attracts fiercely loyal fans. Games usually start at 3pm and are great to watch, but the stands can get very rowdy, so think about reserving seats. Centrally located premier division football clubs include **Arsenal,** Emirates Stadium, Ashburton Grove, N7 (© **020/7704-4000,** box office 020/7704-4040; www.arsenal.com; Tube: Piccadilly Line to Arsenal); **Tottenham Hotspur,** 748 High Rd., N17 (© **020/8365-5000,** box office 0870/420-5000; www.tottenhamhotspur.com; Tube: Victoria Line to Seven Sisters); and **Chelsea,** Stamford Bridge, Fulham Road, SW6 (© **020/7915-2951,** box office 0870/300-2322; www.chelseafc.com; Tube: Distri ct Line to Fulham Broadway). Tickets cost £20 to £110 ($38–$209).

HORSE RACING   Within reach of central London are horse-racing tracks at Kempton Park, Sandown Park, and the most famous, Epsom, where the Derby is the main event of early June. Contact **United Racecourses Ltd.** (© **01372/470047**) for information on the next race at one of these tracks.

TENNIS   Fans from around the world focus on **Wimbledon** (Tube: District Line to Wimbledon). At Wimbledon's All England Lawn Tennis & Croquet Club, you'll see some of the world's best tennis players. The famous annual championship spans roughly the last week in June to the first week in July, with matches lasting from about 2pm until dark. (The gates open at 10:30am.) Tickets usually range in price from £20 to £85 ($38–$162). Coveted center-court seats are sold by lottery. A limited number of tickets for the outside courts are available at the gate. For recorded ticket information, call © **020/8946-2244,** go to www.wimbledon.org, or send a self-addressed stamped envelope to the **All England Lawn Tennis & Croquet Club,** P.O. Box 98, London, SW19 5AE.

9

Shopping

When Prussian Field Marshal Blücher, Wellington's stout ally at Waterloo, first laid eyes on London, he allegedly slapped his thigh and exclaimed, "Herr Gott, what a city to plunder!" He was gazing at what, for the early 19th century, was a phenomenal mass of shops and stores. Since those days, other cities may have equaled London as a shopping mecca, but none has surpassed it.

1 Shopping London

Although London is one of the world's best shopping cities, it often seems made solely for wealthy visitors. To find real values, do what most Londoners do: Wait for sales or search out discount stores.

American-style shopping has taken Britain by storm, in concept—warehouse stores and outlet malls—and in actual name: One block from Hamleys, you'll find the Disney Store. Gap is everywhere, and Tiffany sells more wedding gifts than Asprey these days. Your best bet is to concentrate on British goods. You can also do well with French products; values are almost as good as in Paris.

TAXES & SHIPPING Value-added tax (VAT) is the British version of sales tax. VAT is a whopping 17.5% on most goods, but it's included in the price, so the number you see on the price tag is exactly what you'll pay at the register. Non-E.U. residents can get back much of the tax by applying for a VAT refund (see "How to Get Your VAT Refund," above).

In Britain, the minimum expenditure needed to qualify for a refund on value-added tax is £30 ($57). Not every single store honors this minimum, but it's far easier to qualify for a tax refund in Britain than almost any other country in the European Union.

Vendors at flea markets may not be equipped to provide the paperwork for a refund, so if you're contemplating a major purchase and are counting on a refund, ask before you buy. Be suspicious of any dealer who tells you there's no VAT on antiques. This was once true, but things have changed—the European Union has made the British add VAT to antiques, and pricing should reflect this. So ask if it's included—before you bargain. Get to a price you're comfortable with first, then ask for the VAT refund.

VAT is not charged on goods shipped out of the country, whether you spend £30 ($57) or not. Many London shops will help you beat the VAT by shipping for you. But watch out: Shipping may be even more expensive than the VAT, and you might also have to pay U.S. duties when the goods get to you at home.

You can ship your purchases on your flight home by paying for excess baggage (rates vary by airline) or have your packages shipped independently, which is generally less expensive than shipping it through the airlines. To ship independently, try **Burns**

Tips   How to Get Your VAT Refund

You *must* get your VAT refund form from the retailer. Several readers have reported that merchants have told them they can get refund forms at the airport as they leave the country. *This is not true.* Don't leave the store without a form—it must be completed by the retailer on the spot. After you have asked if the store does VAT refunds and determined their minimum, request the paperwork.

Global Refund (www.globalrefund.com) is your best bet for getting VAT refunds at the airport. Shop where you see the Global Refund Tax-Free Shopping sign, and ask for a Global Refund Tax-Free check when you purchase your items.

Fill out your form and then present it—with the goods, receipts, and passports—at the Customs office in the airport. Allow an hour to stand in line. *Remember:* You're required to show the goods, so put them in your carry-on.

Once the paperwork has been stamped, you have two choices: You can mail the papers (remember to bring a stamp) and receive your refund as a British check (no!) or a credit card refund (yes!), or go to the Cash VAT Refund desk at the airport and get your refund in cash. Know that if you accept cash other than British pounds, you will lose money on the conversion.

Many stores charge a fee for processing your refund, so £3 to £5 ($5.70–$9.50) may be deducted from the total you receive. But since the VAT in Britain is 17.5%, it's worth the trouble to get the money back.

Note: If you're heading to other countries in the European Union, you should file all of your VAT refunds at once at your final E.U. destination.

International Facilities, at Heathrow Airport Terminal 1 (© **020/8745-5301**). You can avoid the VAT upfront *only* if you have the store ship directly for you. If you ship via excess baggage or an independent shipping company, you still have to pay the VAT upfront and apply for a refund.

HOURS   London keeps fairly uniform store hours, mostly shorter than American equivalents. The norm is a 10am opening and 6pm closing Monday to Saturday, with a late Thursday night until 7pm. Most stores on Oxford Street and in Covent Garden don't close until 7pm every day. However, more upmarket stores on Bond Street usually shut earlier—around 6pm.

Sunday shopping is now legal. Stores are allowed to be open for 6 hours; usually they choose 11am to 5pm. Stores in designated tourist areas and flea markets are exempt from this law and may stay open all day on Sunday. Therefore, Covent Garden, Greenwich, and Hampstead are big Sunday destinations for shoppers.

SALES   Traditionally, stores in Britain held only two sale periods: January and July. Now, whenever they need cash they have a sale, although January and July sales are still prevalent. July sales begin in June—or earlier—and promotions are commonplace. The January sale is still the big event of the year. Boxing Day in England (Dec 26), following the Christmas shopping spree, marks the beginning of year-end clearance sales, which often run through January. On Boxing Day itself, many merchants take an additional 10% off merchandise that has already been marked down. Though some stores start their after-Christmas sales on December 26, most start after the first week in January, when round-trip airfares are in the low range, and savings on sale items might earn your travel money back if you find enough bargains.

Discounts can range from 25% to 50% at leading department stores. Depending on their inventories and their sense of timing, Harrods produces some very visible sales events, spending large amounts on promotions and publicity. Depending on the sale, extra discounts might apply to souvenirs with Harrods logos, furniture and gift items, English china (seconds are trucked in from factories in Stoke-on-Trent), and English designer brands like Jaeger. But while the Harrods sale is the most famous in London, it's not the only game in town. Just about every other store—except Boots—also has big sales in January and June. Beware, though: There's a huge difference in the quality of the finds at genuine sales, when stores are actually clearing the shelves, and the goods bought at "produced" sales, when special merchandise has been hauled in just for the sale.

DUTY-FREE AIRPORT SHOPPING   Shopping at airports is big business. Terminal 4 at Heathrow is a virtual shopping mall, and each of the other terminals at Heathrow has a wide range of shopping outlets, with not a lot of crossover between brands. Prices at the airport for items like souvenirs and candy bars are, of course, higher than on the streets of London, but duty-free prices on luxury goods are usually fair. There are often promotions and coupons that allow for pounds off at the time of purchase. Most of the sales at these airport shops are made for passengers passing through Heathrow en route to other destinations, usually home. Most passengers, by the end of their stay in London, have at least some grasp of what items are available in London shops and at what prices, and therefore have some basis of comparison to prices of equivalent goods outside the airports.

2 Central London Shopping

Thankfully for those pressed for time, several key streets offer some (or even all) of London's best retail stores, compactly located in a niche or neighborhood so you can just stroll and shop.

THE WEST END   As a neighborhood, the West End includes Mayfair and is home to the core of London's big-name shopping. Most of the department stores, designer shops, and multiples (chain stores) have their flagships in this area.

The key streets are **Oxford Street** (in either direction) for affordable shopping (start at Marble Arch Tube station if you're ambitious, or Bond St. station if you care to see only some of it), and **Regent Street,** which intersects Oxford Street at Oxford Circus (Tube: Oxford Circus). The Oxford Street flagship (at Marble Arch) of the private-label department store Marks & Spencer ("Marks & Sparks" in the local parlance) is worth visiting for quality goods. Regent Street, which leads all the way to Piccadilly, has more upscale department stores (including the famed Liberty of London), chains (Laura Ashley), and specialty dealers.

Parallel to Regent Street, **Bond Street** (Tube: Bond St.) connects Piccadilly with Oxford Street and is synonymous with the luxury trade. Divided into New and Old, it has experienced a recent revival and is the hot address for international designers—Donna

Tips   GST: Greenwich Shopping Time

Though many London shops are now open on Sundays, the best Sunday shopping is in the stalls of the flea and craft markets in the royal city of Greenwich.

The ideal way to enjoy the trip is to float downstream on a boat from Charing Cross or Westminster Pier (service begins at 10:30am on Sun; see "River Cruises along the Thames," under "Exploring London by Boat," p. 255). The trip takes about a half-hour, and you'll get a knowledgeable commentary on the Docklands development and the history of the river. You'll also be able to view the Tower and much of London from the water along the way.

The boat leaves you in the heart of Greenwich, minutes from the craft market held on Saturday and Sunday. Follow the signs—or the crowd. After you're done, follow the crowd again to Greenwich's several antiques markets which fall under the general category of the **Greenwich Market** (© 020/8923-3110; www.greenwichmarket.neet), open Thursday 7:30am to 5:30pm and Friday and Sunday 9:30am to 5:30pm. First is **Canopy Market**, which isn't under a canopy at all, but sprawls through several parking lots where junk and old books abound, and then onto **High Street**, where the fancier flea market is held. It's possible that there will be yet another antiques market at **Town Hall**, across the street, but these shows usually charge an admission fee.

You're only a half-block from the Greenwich rail station now, which is on Greenwich High Road, and there's a train back to London every half-hour until about 11:30pm.

Karan has two shops here. A slew of international hotshots, from Chanel to Ferragamo, to Versace, have digs nearby.

Burlington Arcade (Tube: Piccadilly Circus), the famous glass-roofed, Regency-style passage leading off Piccadilly, looks like a period exhibition and is lined with intriguing shops and boutiques. Lit by wrought-iron lamps and decorated with clusters of ferns and flowers, its small, smart stores specialize in fashion, jewelry, Irish linen, cashmere, and more. If you linger there until 5:30pm, you can watch the beadles (the last London representatives of Britain's oldest police force), in their black-and-yellow livery and top hats, ceremoniously place the iron grills that block off the arcade until 9am, at which time they just as ceremoniously remove them to start a new business day. (There are only three beadles remaining.) Also at 5:30pm, a hand bell called the Burlington Bell is sounded, signaling the end of trading.

For a total contrast, check out **Jermyn Street** (Tube: Piccadilly Circus), on the far side of Piccadilly, a tiny 2-block-long street devoted to high-end men's haberdashers and toiletries shops; many have been doing business for centuries. Several hold royal warrants, including Turnbull & Asser, where HRH Prince Charles has his pj's made. A bit to the northwest, Savile Row (between Regent St. and New Bond St.) is synonymous with the finest in men's tailoring.

The West End theater district borders two more shopping areas: the still-not-ready-for-prime-time **Soho** (Tube: Tottenham Court Rd.), where the sex shops are slowly converting into cutting-edge designer boutiques, and **Covent Garden** (Tube: Covent Garden), a shopping masterpiece full of fashion, food, books, and everything else. The original Covent Garden marketplace has overflowed its boundaries and eaten up the surrounding neighborhood; it's fun to wander the narrow streets and shop. Covent Garden is mobbed on Sundays.

Just a stone's throw from Covent Garden, **Monmouth Street** is somewhat of a London shopping secret: Londoners know they can find a wide array of stores in a space of only 2 blocks. Many shops here are outlets for British designers and some along this street sell both used and new clothing. In addition, stores specialize in everything from musical instruments from the Far East to palm and crystal-ball readings.

KNIGHTSBRIDGE & CHELSEA Knightsbridge (Tube: Knightsbridge), the home of Harrods, is the second-most-famous London retail district. (Oxford St. edges it out.) Nearby Sloane Street is chock-a-block with designer shops.

Walk southwest on **Brompton Road** (toward the Victoria and Albert Museum) and you'll find **Cheval Place,** lined with designer resale shops, and Beauchamp (*Bee*-cham) Place. It's only a block long, but it's very "Sloane Ranger" or "Sloanie" (as the Brits would say), featuring the kinds of shops where young British aristocrats buy their clothing for the "season."

If you walk farther along Brompton Road, you'll connect to **Brompton Cross,** another hip area for designer shops made popular when Michelin House was rehabbed by Sir Terence Conran, becoming the Conran Shop. Seek out **Walton Street,** a tiny snake of a street running from Brompton Cross back toward the museums. Most of the shops here specialize in nonessential luxury products, the kind a severe and judgmental Victorian moralist might dismiss as vanities and fripperies. This is where you'll find aromatherapy from Jo Malone, needlepoint, and costume jewelry. **King's Road** (Tube: Sloane Sq.), the main street of Chelsea, will forever remain a symbol of the Swinging '60s. It's still popular with the young crowd, but there are fewer mohawk haircuts, Bovver boots, and Edwardian ball gowns than before. More and more, King's Road is a lineup of markets and "multistores," conglomerations of indoor stands, stalls, and booths within one building or enclosure. About a third of King's Road is devoted to "multistore" antiques markets, another third houses design-trade showrooms and stores of household wares, and the remaining third is faithful to the area's teenybopper roots.

Finally, don't forget all those museums in nearby **South Kensington**—they all have great gift shops.

KENSINGTON, NOTTING HILL & BAYSWATER Kensington High Street (Tube: High St. Kensington) is the hangout of the classier breed of teen, the one who has graduated from Carnaby Street and is ready for street chic. While there are a few staples of basic British fashion here, most of the stores feature items that stretch and are very, very short, very, very tight, and very, very black.

From Kensington High Street, you can walk up **Kensington Church Street,** which, like Portobello Road, is one of the city's main shopping avenues for antiques, selling everything from antique furniture to Impressionist paintings.

Kensington Church Street dead-ends at the Notting Hill Gate Tube station, jumping-off point for Portobello Road, whose antiques dealers and weekend market are 2 blocks beyond.

Not far from Notting Hill Gate is **Whiteleys of Bayswater,** 151 Queensway, W2 (© **020/7229-8844;** www.whiteleys.com; Tube: Bayswater or Queensway), an

Edwardian mall whose chief tenant is Marks & Spencer. Whiteleys also contains 75 to 85 other shops, mostly specialty outlets, plus restaurants, cafes, bars, and an eight-screen movie theater.

3 The Department Stores

Contrary to popular belief, Harrods is not the only department store in London. The British invented the department store, and they have lots of them, mostly in Mayfair, and each has its own customer profile.

DAKS   Opened in 1936 as the home of DAKS clothing, DAKS has been going strong ever since. It's known for menswear—its basement-level men's shoe department is a model of the way quality shoes should be fitted and sold—as well as women's fashions, perfume, jewelry, and lingerie. Many of the clothes are lighthearted, carefully made, and casually elegant. Solid and dependable, this is a well-established store whose core market is male and female clients ages 30 to 50. Clothes aren't particularly cutting edge (and indeed, many of the regular clients here aren't looking for that), except for the recently inaugurated youth line, Daks E1. 10 Old Bond St., W1. © 020/7409-4040. Tube: Green Park.

Fenwick of Bond Street   Fenwick (the *w* is silent), dating from 1891, is a stylish store that offers an excellent collection of designer womenswear, ranging from moderately priced ready-to-wear items to more expensive designer fashions. An extensive selection of lingerie in all price ranges is also sold. 63 New Bond St., W1. © 020/7629-9161. www.fenwick.com. Tube: Bond St.

Fortnum & Mason 🏵🏵🏵   Catering to well-heeled clients as a full-service department store since 1707, Fortnum & Mason recently spent £14 million ($26 million) on an overhaul of its premises and inventories. Offerings include one of the most comprehensive delicatessens and food markets in London, as well as stationery, gift items, porcelain and crystal, and lots and lots of clothing for men, women, and children. 181 Piccadilly, W1. © 020/7734-8040. www.fortnumandmason.com. Tube: Piccadilly Circus.

Harrods   Harrods remains an institution, but in the last decade or so, it has grown increasingly dowdy and is not nearly as cutting edge as it used to be. For the latest trends, shop elsewhere. However, we always stop here during our visits to London. As entrenched in English life as Buckingham Palace and the Ascot Races, it's still an elaborate emporium. Goods are spread across 300 departments, and the range, variety, and quality will still dazzle the visiting out-of-towner.

The whole fifth floor is devoted to sports and leisure, with a wide range of equipment and attire. Toy Kingdom is on the fourth floor, along with children's wear. The Egyptian Hall, on the ground floor, sells crystal from Lalique and Baccarat, plus porcelain.

There's also a barber, a jewelry department, and a fashion department for younger customers. You'll have a choice of 18 restaurants and bars. Best of all are the **Food Halls,** with a huge variety of foods and several cafes. Harrods began as a grocer in 1849, and food and drinks are still at the heart of the business. The motto remains "If you can eat or drink it, you'll find it at Harrods." 87–135 Brompton Rd., SW1. © 020/7730-1234. www.harrods.com. Tube: Knightsbridge.

Harvey Nichols   Locals call it "Harvey Nicks." Once a favorite of the late Princess Di, this store is large, but it doesn't compete directly with Harrods because it has a more upmarket, fashionable image. Harvey Nicks has its own gourmet food hall and fancy restaurant, **The Fifth Floor,** and is crammed with the best in designer home furnishings, gifts, and fashions for all, although women's clothing is the largest segment of its business. The store carries many American designer brands; avoid them, as they're more expensive in London than they are in the U.S. 109–125 Knightsbridge, SW1. ℂ 020/7235-5000. www.harveysnichols.com. Tube: Knightsbridge.

John Lewis   This department store remains one of the most tried-and-true outlets in London. Their motto is that they are never knowingly undersold, and they mean it. We've always found great bargains here, most recently in a clearance sale of fine earthenware by Royal Stafford. Whatever you're looking for, ranging from Egyptian towels to clothing and jewelry, it's likely to be for sale here. 278–306 Oxford St., W1. ℂ 020/ 7629-7711. www.johnlewis.com. Tube: Oxford St.

Liberty 𝘈𝘈   This department store is celebrated for its Liberty Prints: top-echelon fabrics, often in floral patterns, prized by decorators for the way they add a sense of English tradition to a room. The front part of the Regent Street store isn't particularly distinctive, but don't be fooled: Other parts of the place have been restored to Tudor-style splendor that includes half-timbering and interior paneling. There are six floors of fashion, china, and home furnishings, including the famous Liberty Print fashion fabrics, upholstery fabrics, scarves, ties, luggage, gifts, and more. 210–220 Regent St., W1. ℂ 020/7734-1234. www.liberty.co.uk. Tube: Oxford Circus.

Peter Jones   Founded in 1877 and rebuilt in 1936, Peter Jones is known for household goods, household fabrics and trims, china, glass, upholstered furniture, and linens. The linen department is one of the best in London. Sloane Sq., SW1. ℂ 020/7730-3434. www.peterjones.co.uk. Tube: Sloane Sq.

4 Goods A to Z

ANTIQUES

Also check out the description of **Portobello Market** on p. 293.

Alfie's Antique Market   This is the biggest (and one of the best-stocked) conglomerates of antiques dealers in London, crammed into the premises of a 19th-century store. It has more than 370 stalls, showrooms, and workshops in over 3,252 sq. m (35,000 sq. ft.) of floor space. You'll find the biggest Susie Cooper (a well-known designer of tableware and ceramics for Wedgwood) collection in Europe here. A whole antiques district has grown up around Alfie's along Church Street. 13–25 Church St., NW8. ℂ 020/7723-6066. Fax 020/7724-0999. www.alfiesantiques.com. Tube: Marylebone or Edgware Rd.

Antiquarius   The recently redecorated Antiquarius echoes the artistic diversity of King's Road. More than 120 dealers offer specialized merchandise, usually of the small, domestic variety, such as antique and period jewelry, porcelain, silver, first-edition books, boxes, clocks, prints, and paintings, with an occasional piece of antique furniture and many items from the 1950s. 131–141 King's Rd., SW3. ℂ 020/7351-5353. Tube: Sloane Sq. or S. Kensington.

Bond Street Antiques Centre 𝘈𝘈   This place, in the heart of London's finest shopping district, enjoys a reputation for being London's preeminent center for antique jewelry, silver, watches, porcelain, glass, and Asian antiques and paintings. 124 New Bond St., W1. ℂ 020/7351-5353 or 020/7493-1854. Tube: Bond St. or Green Park.

Grays Antiques and Grays Mews   These markets have been converted into walk-in stands with independent dealers. Here, the term *antiques* covers items from oil paintings to, say, the 1894 edition of the *Encyclopedia Britannica*. Also sold are antique jewelry; silver; gold; maps and prints; bronzes and ivories; arms and armor; Victorian and Edwardian toys; furniture; Art Nouveau and Art Deco items; antique lace; scientific instruments; craft tools; and Asian, Persian, and Islamic pottery, porcelain, miniatures, and antiquities. There's a cafe in each building. Check out the 1950s-style **Victory Cafe** on Davies Street for their homemade cakes. 58 Davies St. and 1–7 Davies Mews, W1. © 020/7629-7034. www.graysantiques.com. Tube: Bond St.

The Mall at Camden Passage   The Mall contains one of Britain's greatest concentrations of antiques dealers. In individual shops, you'll find some 35 dealers offering fine furniture, porcelain, and silver. The area expands into a street market on Wednesday and Saturday. Islington, N1. © 020/7354-2839. Tube: Northern Line to Angel.

ARCHITECTURAL SALVAGE

LASSCO (London Architectural Salvage & Supply Co.) 𝒻   Established in 1978, this company controls the largest inventories of architectural remnants in the U.K., with warehouses chock-full of mantelpieces, stained-glass windows, antique doors, statuary, ecclesiastical accessories (including, among others, assorted pews from Victorian-era churches), and garden ornaments. Each piece was rescued during the renovation or demolition of buildings throughout Greater London. Many of them originated within unheralded private homes; others come from public buildings that have included the Palace of Westminster and the Royal Opera House. The company's headquarters and most impressive showroom occupy a deconsecrated Victorian church.

A particularly interesting annex of this outfit (same phone, same Tube stop) lies within a 5-minute walk at Britannia Walk, N1. It specializes in antique doors, a resource that building contractors and architects usually find fascinating. Small, easy-to-transport antique items are also available, including some charming 19th-century woodworking tools. All of the large objects available here can be crated and shipped. Headquarters at St. Michael and All Angels, on Mark St., off Paul St., EC2. © 020/7749-9944. www.lassco.co.uk. Tube: Old St.

ART & CRAFTS

ACAVA *(Finds)*   This London-based visual-arts organization provides studios and other services for professional artists, and represents about 250 artists working in spaces around London. Call for individual open-studio schedules, as well as dates for the annual Open Studios weekend. 54 Blechynden St., W1. © 020/8960-5015. www.acava.org.

Camden Arts Centre 𝒻   Hailed by *The Times of London* as "the best place to see contemporary art in north London," the Camden Arts Centre has a cafe, bookstore, and studios in addition to its exhibition galleries, where the displays are frequently changed. Arkwright Rd., NW3. © 020/7472-5500. www.camdenartscentre.org. Tube: Finchley Rd.

Cecilia Colman Gallery   One of London's most established crafts galleries, Cecilia Colman features decorative ceramics, studio glass, jewelry, and metalwork. Among the offerings are glass sculptures by Lucien Simon, jewelry by Caroline Taylor, and pottery by Simon Rich. Exhibitions of contemporary original works are featured. There's also a large selection of mirrors and original-design perfume bottles. 67 St. John's Wood High St., NW8. © 020/7722-0686. www.ceciliacolmangallery.com. Tube: Jubilee Line to St. John's Wood.

(Finds) Go East, Art Lover

The East End neighborhood of Hoxton was a tawdry backwater until very recently, when artists starting flocking here and opening studios, cleaning up the discarded mattresses, and rejuvenating abandoned buildings.

Success was ensured with the opening of **White Cube**, 48 Hoxton Sq., N1 (© **020/7930-5373**; www.whitecube.com), owned by Jay Jopling, the leading dealer in modern English art, whose artists include Britain's most contentious, Damien Hirst. The other hot gallery is **Victoria Miro Gallery**, 16 Wharf Rd., N1 (© **020/7336-8109**; www.victoria-miro.com). Some of London's most controversial art appears here. Miro represents Chris Ofili, whose "Madonna and Dung" painting enraged former New York mayor and art critic Rudolph Giuliani.

These art dealers and the artists themselves (that is, those who've sold a painting recently) can be found dining at **Cantaloupe**, 35–42 Charlotte Rd., EC2 (© **020/7729-5566**), which serves Mediterranean cuisine and great tapas. This informal bar/restaurant, with its wooden tables and industrial fittings, prepares such superb dishes as chargrilled Aberdeen Angus steak with rosemary butter, and fried *halloumi* (a white cheese from Cyprus) with olive salsa. Open Monday through Friday from noon to 3pm and 6 to 11pm, and Saturday from 7 to 11pm. Main courses cost from £9.50 to £20 ($18–$38).

Take the Tube to Old Street to arrive near the doorsteps of all of these establishments.

Contemporary Applied Arts ⭐ This association encourages traditional and progressive contemporary artwork. Many of Britain's best-established craftspeople, as well as promising talents, are represented within this contemporary-looking space. The gallery houses a diverse display of glass, ceramics, textiles, wood, furniture, jewelry, and metalwork—all by contemporary artisans. A program of special exhibitions, including solo and small-group shows, focuses on innovations in craftwork. There are new exhibitions every six weeks. 2 Percy St., W1. © **020/7436-2344**. www.caa.org.uk. Tube: Tottenham Court Rd.

England & Co. Under the guidance of Jane England, this gallery specializes in Outsider Art and Art in Boxes (that is, art that incorporates a box structure into the composition or frame of a three-dimensional work). The gallery focuses attention on neglected postwar British artists such as Tony Stubbings and Ralph Romney. One-person and group shows are mounted frequently, and many young artists get early exposure here. 216 Westbourne Grove, W11. © **020/7221-0417**. www.englandgallery.com. Tube: Notting Hill Gate.

Gabriel's Wharf This South Bank complex of shops, restaurants, and bars is open Tuesday to Sunday 11am to 6pm (dining and drinking establishments are open later). Lying 2 minutes by foot from Oxo Tower Wharf, it is filled with some of London's most skilled craftspeople, turning out original pieces of sculpture, jewelry, ceramics, art, and fashion. Food, fashion, art, and crafts await you here, making this place a lot of fun to poke around. 56 Upper Ground, SE1. ℂ 020/7401-2255. www.gabrielswharf.co.uk. Tube: Blackfriars, Southwark, Waterloo, or Embankment.

Gong   One of the best selections of furniture and offbeat crafts and jewelry in England awaits you here. The merchandise is the work of both Asian and other international artisans. 142 Portobello Rd., W11 ℂ 020/7565-4162. www.gong.co.uk. Tube: Notting Hill Gate.

Grosvenor Prints   London's largest stock of antique prints, ranging from the 17th up to the 20th centuries, is on sale here. Obviously, views of London are the biggest-selling items. Some prints depict significant moments in the city's history, including the Great Fire. Of course, the British are great animal lovers, so expect plenty of prints of dogs and horses. 28 Shelton St., WC2. ℂ 020/7836-1979. www.grosvenorprints.com. Tube: Covent Garden.

Kelly Hoppen   The British press has labeled interior designer Kelly Hoppen as its own minimalist Martha Stewart (prescandal, of course). Hoppen's designer emporium on Fulham Road opened to great fanfare, and even Hoppen herself has been pleased with the "stock just flying out." Expect a little bit of everything here, including her own charming medley of ceramics (some designed for Wedgwood), furniture, and original accessories such as giant horn buttons or pony-skin bags from Argentina. 177 Fulham Rd., SW3. ℂ 020/7351-1910. www.kellyhoppen.com. Tube: S. Kensington.

BATH & BODY

The Body Shop   There's a branch of The Body Shop in every shopping area and tourist zone in London. Some are bigger than others, but all are filled with politically and environmentally friendly beauty, bath, and aromatherapy products. Prices are much lower in the U.K. than they are in the U.S. There's an entire children's line, a men's line, and lots of travel sizes and travel products. 374 Oxford St., W1. ℂ 020/7409-7868. www.bodyshop.com. Tube: Bond St. Other locations throughout London.

Boots the Chemist   This store has branches all over Britain. The house brands of beauty products are usually the best, including the original Boots line (try the cucumber facial mask), Boots's versions of The Body Shop (two lines, Global and Naturalistic), and Boots's versions of Chanel makeup (called No. 7). They also sell film, pantyhose (called tights), sandwiches, and all of life's other little necessities. 490 Oxford St., W1G. ℂ 020/7491-8546. www.boots.com. Tube: Marble Arch. Other locations throughout London.

Culpeper the Herbalist 𝕲   You'll have to put up with a cramped space to check out all the food, bath, and aromatherapy products, but it's worth it. Stock up on essential oils, or go for the dream pillows, candles and sachets. The Market, Covent Garden, WC2. ℂ 020/7379-6698. www.culpeper.co.uk. Tube: Covent Garden.

Floris 𝕲𝕲   A variety of toilet articles and fragrances fill Floris's floor-to-ceiling mahogany cabinets, which are architectural curiosities in their own right. They were installed relatively late in the establishment's history—that is, 1851—long after the shop had received its royal warrants as suppliers of toilet articles to the king and queen. 89 Jermyn St., SW1. ℂ 0845/702-3239. www.florislondon.com. Tube: Piccadilly Circus.

Lush   In our view, the handmade soaps and cosmetics sold here are the most intriguing in London. The store is always launching something new, and their products include Rock Star Soap, which is very pink and smells like candy. Among the extensive selection is Tam O'Santa, an allspice, sandalwood, and frankincense bubble bath, and Banana Moon, a creamy banana soap. The products are made with fresh fruit and vegetables, the finest essential oils, and safe synthetics—no animal ingredients. 11 The

Shopping in "Banglatown"

Some of London's most fashionable and trendsetting shoppers are trekking over to the famous old Brick Lane in the East End of the city. Brick Lane is the main drag along "Banglatown," known for its low-cost curry restaurants and sari stores, catering to London's burgeoning Indian population. Almost overnight, funky little boutiques and home furnishing stores started moving in, no doubt attracted by the low rents. Today you can seek out such shopping delights as **Beyond Retro**, 110–112 Cheshire St. (✆ **020/7613-3636**; www.beyond retro.com), where the managers keep the displays interesting by adding 300 new vintage pieces daily; **Mar Mar Co.,** 16 Cheshire St. (✆ **020/7729-1494**; www.marmarco.com), where you'll find Scandinavian ceramics and china boxes glazed with retro wallpaper designs, along with dozens of other delights; and **At Work Gallery,** 156 Brick Lane (✆ **020/7377-0597**; www.atworkgallery.co.uk), with its collection of quirky jewelry. Dozens of other shops await your discovery.

West Piazza, Covent Garden. ✆ **020/7240-4570.** www.lush.co.uk. Tube: Covent Garden. Other locations throughout London.

Neal's Yard Remedies   Noted the world over for their cobalt-blue bottles, these chic bath, beauty, and aromatherapy products are must-haves for those who pooh-pooh The Body Shop as too common. Prices are higher in the United States, so stock up here. 15 Neal's Yard, WC2. ✆ **020/7379-7222.** www.nealsyardremedies.com. Tube: Covent Garden.

Penhaligon's 𝕏𝕏𝕏   This Victorian perfumery, established in 1870, holds royal warrants to HRH Duke of Edinburgh and HRH Prince of Wales. All items sold are exclusive to Penhaligon's. The store offers a large selection of perfume, aftershave, soap, and bath oils for women and men. Gifts include antique-silver scent bottles, grooming accessories, and leather traveling goods. Penhaligon's is now in more than 20 Saks Fifth Avenue stores across the United States. 41 Wellington St., WC2. ✆ **020/7836-2150.** www.penhaligons.co.uk. Tube: Covent Garden.

BOOKS, MAPS & ENGRAVINGS

In addition to the bookstores below, **Waterstone's** 𝕏𝕏𝕏, 203–206 Piccadilly, SW1 (✆ **020/7851-2400;** www.waterstones.com), is the largest bookstore in Europe—and it even has a bar.

Children's Book Centre   With thousands of titles, this is the best place to go for children's books. Fiction is arranged according to age, up to 16. There are also videos and toys for kids. 237 Kensington High St., W8. ✆ **020/7937-7497.** Tube: Kensington.

Foyle's Bookshop   Claiming to be the world's largest bookstore, Foyle's has an impressive array of hardcovers and paperbacks, as well as travel maps, new records, CDs, videotapes, and sheet music. The store also has a cafe and "jazz shop," which sometimes hosts live performances. Foyles also has a tradition of rehousing local independent bookstores forced to close because of high rents—for example, it now carries the stock of Silver Moon, once the best-known women's bookstore in London. 113–119 Charing Cross Rd., WC2. ✆ **020/7437-5660.** Tube: Tottenham Court Rd. or Leicester Sq.

Gay's the Word   Britain's leading gay and lesbian bookstore offers a large selection of books, as well as magazines, cards, and guides. There's also a used-books section. 66 Marchmont St., WC1. ✆ **020/7278-7654.** Tube: Russell Sq.

Hatchards On the south side of Piccadilly, Hatchards offers a wide range of books on all subjects and is particularly renowned in the areas of fiction, biography, travel, cookery, gardening, art, history, and finance. In addition, Hatchards is second to none in its range of books on royalty. 187 Piccadilly, W1. ✆ 020/7439-9921. Tube: Piccadilly Circus or Green Park.

The Map House of London An ideal place to find an offbeat souvenir. The Map House sells antique maps and engravings, plus a vast selection of old prints of London and England, both original and reproduction. The cost of a century-old original engraving begins at £22 ($40). 54 Beauchamp Place, SW3. ✆ 020/7589-4325. Tube: Knightsbridge.

Murder One *(Finds)* Maxim Jakubowski's bookshop is dedicated to the genres of crime, romance, science fiction, and horror. Crime and science fiction magazines, some of them obscure, are also available. 71–73 Charing Cross Rd., WC2. ✆ 020/7734-3483. www.murderone.co.uk. Tube: Leicester Sq.

Stanfords Established in 1852, Stanfords is the world's largest map shop. Many maps, including worldwide touring and survey maps, are unavailable elsewhere. It's also London's best travel bookstore (with a complete selection of Frommer's guides!). 12–14 Long Acre, WC2. ✆ 020/7836-1321. www.stanfords.co.uk. Tube: Covent Garden.

CASHMERE & WOOLENS

Belinda Robertson Some of the most beautiful and most chic cashmeres, in lovely colors, are sold at this centrally located outlet at Knightsbridge. Bold colors are a hallmark of Ms. Robertson's designs, ranging from carnival red to canary yellow. She designs for women, men, and children. 4 West Halkin St., SW1. ✆ 020/7235-0519. Tube: Knightsbridge.

Berk This store boasts one of the largest collections of cashmere sweaters in London—at least the top brands. The outlet also carries capes, stoles, scarves, and camelhair sweaters. 46 Burlington Arcade, W1. ✆ 020/7493-0028. Tube: Piccadilly Circus or Green Park.

CHINA, GLASS & SILVER

London Silver Vaults *(Finds)* Don't let the out-of-the-way location or the facade's lack of charm slow you down. Downstairs you'll enter vaults—40 in all—filled with tons of silver and silverplate, plus collections of jewelry. It's a staggering selection of old and new, with excellent prices and friendly dealers. Chancery House, 53–64 Chancery Lane, WC2. ✆ 020/7242-3844. Tube: Chancery Lane.

Reject China Shop *(Value)* Don't expect too many rejects or too many bargains, despite the name. This shop sells seconds (sometimes) along with first-quality pieces of china from such names as Royal Doulton, Spode, and Wedgwood. You can also find a variety of crystal, glassware, and flatware. If you'd like to have your purchases shipped home for you, the shop can do it for a fee. 183 Brompton Rd., SW3. ✆ 020/7581-0739. Tube: Knightsbridge. Other locations throughout London.

Royal Doulton Founded in the 1930s, this company has one of the largest inventories of china in Britain. A wide range of English bone china, as well as crystal and giftware, is sold. The firm (www.royaldoulton.com) no longer operates its own outlet in London. But its products are sold in many upmarket stores, notably **Selfridges** at 400 Oxford St., W1 (✆ 020/7318-3098; Tube: Bond St.), and **John Lewis**, Oxford St. (✆ 020/7629-7711; Tube: Bond St.).

Thomas Goode This is one of the most famous emporiums in Britain; it's worth visiting for its architectural interest and nostalgic allure alone. Originally built in 1876, Goode's has 14 rooms loaded with porcelain, gifts, candles, silver, tableware, and even a private museum. There's also a tearoom-cum-restaurant tucked into the corner. 19 S. Audley St., W1. © 020/7499-2823. www.thomasgoode.co.uk. Tube: Bond St., Green Park, Marble Arch, or Hyde Park.

CHOCOLATES

Godiva Chocolates ⚜ This world-famous chocolate maker has invaded Covent Garden with the tastiest sweets in town. The store offers London's finest selection of chocolates, with some seasonal products. In addition to handcrafted chocolates, the salespeople here hawk the chocolate jam. 17 The Piazza, WC2. © 020/7836-5706. Tube: Covent Garden.

FASHION

We have divided this category into "Classic," "Cutting Edge," and "Vintage & Second-hand," below.

CLASSIC

While every internationally known designer worth his or her weight in Shantung silk has a boutique in London, the best buys are on the sturdy English styles that last forever. See also the separate sections on "Cashmere & Woolens," "Handbags," "Jewelry," and "Shoes."

Austin Reed Austin Reed has long stood for superior-quality clothing and excellent tailoring. Chester Barrie's off-the-rack suits, for example, are said to fit like tailor-made. The polite employees are unusually honest about telling you what looks good. The store always has a wide variety of top-notch jackets and suits, and men can outfit themselves from dressing gowns to overcoats. For women, there are carefully selected suits, separates, coats, shirts, knitwear, and accessories. 103–113 Regent St., W1. © 020/7534-7777. www.austinreed.co.uk. Tube: Piccadilly Circus.

Beau Monde This outlet earns its fame selling chic "nouvelle couture" for women—fitted and adjusted to your body. All designs are by the locally famous London designer Sylvia Young. Her design philosophy is that a busy woman should be conscious of fashion, but not a victim of its whims, and clothes should work for her—not against her. Her women's wear is comfortable and fashionable, but not stuffy. 20 Kingly St., W1. © 020/7734-6563. www.beaumonde.uk.com. Tube: Piccadilly Circus.

Burberry ⚜⚜⚜ The name has been synonymous with raincoats ever since Edward VII ordered his valet to "bring my Burberry" when the skies threatened. An impeccably trained staff sells the famous raincoats, plus excellent men's shirts, sportswear, knitwear, and accessories. Raincoats are available in women's sizes and styles as well. Prices are high, but you get quality and prestige. 18–22 Haymarket, SW1. © 020/7839-5222. www.burberry.com. Tube: Piccadilly Circus.

Designer Sale UK (Value) Amazingly, you can sometimes get 90% off designer clothing for both men and women at this outlet. Of course, you've got to sift through 140 rails of clothing and accessories, much of which had a good reason for not selling in the first place. The shop claims it caters to both the discerning label lover and the devoted bargain hunter. Yes, those rails carry Stella McCartney, Vivienne Westwood, Alexander McQueen, and a lot of the lesser lights in designer fashion. A £2 ($3.80) admission is charged to attend the sale. Studio 95, Old Truman Brewery, 95A Brick Lane, E1. © 020/7247-8595 or 01273/470880 in Lewes. Tube: Aldgate E. or Liverpool St.

Emmett ⍟ Some of the finest men's shirts in London are sold at this Chelsea outlet. Shirt styles are sold in limited editions of about two dozen each, so chances are, you'll never run into another man wearing the same garb as you. Complementary patterns line collars and cuffs, and the look is very British, very Prince Charles sophisticated. Beautiful woven silk ties are also featured. 380 King's Rd., SW3. ℂ 020/7351-7529. www.emmettlondon.com. Tube: Sloane Sq.

Gieves & Hawkes This men's clothing store has a prestigious address and a list of clients that includes the Prince of Wales, yet its prices aren't as lethal as others on this street. They're high, but you get good quality. Cotton shirts, silk ties, Shetland sweaters, and exceptional ready-to-wear and tailor-made ("bespoke") suits are sold. 1 Savile Row, W1. ℂ 020/7434-2001. www.gievesandhawkes.com. Tube: Piccadilly Circus or Green Park.

Hilditch & Key The finest name in men's shirts, Hilditch & Key has been in business since 1899. The two shops on this street both offer men's clothing (including a custom-made shirt service) and women's ready-made shirts. There's also an outstanding tie collection. Shirts go for half-price during the twice-yearly sales (in Jan and June); men fly in from all over the world for them. 37 and 73 Jermyn St., SW1. ℂ 020/7734-4707. www.hilditchandkey.co.uk. Tube: Piccadilly Circus or Green Park.

Jigsaw Branches of this fashion chain are numerous, but the Long Acre branch features trendy, middle-market womenswear. 21 Long Acre, WC2. ℂ 020/7240-3855. www.jigsaw-online.com. Tube: Covent Garden.

Laura Ashley This is the flagship store of the company whose design ethos embodies the flowery English country look. The store carries a wide choice of women's clothing, plus home furnishings. Prices are lower than in the United States. 256–258 Regent St., W1. ℂ 0871/223-1425. www.lauraashley.com. Tube: Oxford Circus. Other locations around London.

Next This chain of "affordable fashion" stores saw its heyday in the 1980s, when it was celebrated for its success in marketing avant-garde fashion ideas to a wide spectrum of the British public. No longer at its peak, it still merits a stop. The look remains very contemporary, with a Continental flair, and there are clothes for men, women, and kids. 15–17 Long Acre, WC2. ℂ 0870/386-5325. Tube: Covent Garden. Other locations throughout London.

Reiss In a city where men's clothing often sells at exorbitant prices, Reiss is a haven of reasonable sporty and casual wear. Take your pick from everything from pullovers to rugged cargo pants. Reis also stocks womenswear and has become quite a sophisticated and trendy label, with more than 15 stores in London. 114 King's Rd., SW3. ℂ 020/7225-4910. Tube: Sloane Sq.

Thomas Pink This Jermyn Street shirt-maker, named after an 18th-century Mayfair tailor, gave the world the phrase "in the pink." It has a prestigious reputation for well-made cotton shirts for both men and women. The shirts are created from the finest two-fold Egyptian and Sea Island pure-cotton poplin. Some patterns are classic, others new and unusual. All are generously cut with long tails and finished with a choice of double cuffs or single-button cuffs. A small pink square in the tail tells all. 85 Jermyn St., SW1. ℂ 020/7930-6364. www.thomaspink.co.uk. Tube: Green Park or Piccadilly Circus.

Turnbull & Asser Over the years, everyone from David Bowie to Ronald Reagan has been seen in custom-made shirts from Turnbull & Asser. Excellent craftsmanship and simple lines—plus bold colors—distinguish these shirts. The outlet also sells shirts and blouses to women, a clientele that has ranged from Jacqueline Bisset to Candice

The Comeback of Carnaby Street

What happened to Carnaby Street? Is it just a faded echo left over from the Swinging '60s? That was true for a long time. But Carnaby is rising again. A new influx of talented designers and offbeat shops are popping up not only on Carnaby, but along its offshoot streets—Newburgh; Foubert's Place; Kingly Street; Marlborough Court; and Lowndes Court. Innovative boutiques seem to open each week behind small Georgian shop fronts.

Among the zillions of shops are such favorites as **Lambretta Clothing,** 29 Carnaby St., W1 (© 020/7437-7078; www.lambrettaclothing.co.uk), which retains the mod lifestyle philosophy and has launched a range of casual wear for men and footwear for men and women. The line has a retro feel but uses the latest fibers and fabric finishes of today. **Stella McCartney,** 30 Bruton St., W1 (© 020/7518-3100; www.stellamccartney.com; Tube: Bond St.) is a showcase for the clothing designs of Paul McCartney's daughter. Vegetarians and animal lovers adore her "no leather, no suede, and no fur policy," while *fashionistas* seek out the chic look of her designs. Both male and female clients are shown to a drawing room on the second floor of this glamorous Mayfair townhouse where they are presented with some 50 illustrations for trousers, jackets, skirts, and overcoats—all of which are very expensive. Another hot store is **Office,** 20 Carnaby St. (© 020/7434-2530; www.office.co.uk), selling chic and well-designed footwear for both men and women.

To reach the stores above, take the Tube to Oxford Circus.

Bergen. Note that T&A shirts come in only one sleeve length and are then altered to fit, a ritual that takes only a few days and costs £8 ($15). If you want custom shirts created from scratch, the made-to-measure service takes 10 to 12 weeks, and you must order at least a half-dozen. Of course, the monograms are included. 71–72 Jermyn St., SW1. © 020/7808-3000. Tube: Green Park.

CUTTING EDGE

Currently, the most cutting-edge shopping area in London is **Conduit Street,** W1, in Mayfair (Tube: Oxford Circus or Green Park). Once known for its dowdy airline offices, it is now London's smartest fashion street. Trendy shops are opening between Regent Street and the "blue-chip" boutiques of New Bond Street. Current stars include **Vivienne Westwood,** 44 Conduit St., W1 (© 020/7434-1109; www.vivienne westwood.com), who has left her punk origins behind and is now the grande dame of English fashion. See below for her flagship store. **Krizia,** 24–25 Conduit St., W1 (© 020/7491-4987; www.krizia.net), the fashion rage of Rome since the 1950s, displays not only Krizia's clothing lines, but her luxury home goods as well.

For muted fashion elegance, **Yohji Yamamoto,** 14–15 Conduit St., W1 (© 020/ 7491-4129), is hard to beat, and **Issey Miyake,** 52 Conduit St., W1 (© 020/7851-4620; www.isseymiyake.com), is the Japanese master of minimalism.

Accessorize *(Value)*   This aptly named store is often packed with women who have an eye for bargains but want top-notch style. The store stays abreast of the latest fads and trends, especially in evening bags, which range from antique to high fashion. All sorts of treasures are stocked here, everything from hologram-flecked nail polish to silk scarves. 123A Kensington High St., W8. ℂ 020/7937-1433. Tube: High St. Kensington.

Anya Hindmarch   Although her fashionable bags are sold at Harvey Nichols, Liberty, Harrods, and throughout the U.S. and Europe, this is the only place to see the complete range of Anya Hindmarch's handbags, wallets, purses, and key holders. Smaller items start at £40 ($76), whereas handbag prices start at £145 ($276), with alligator being the most expensive. The outlet is famous for its "Be a Bag" merchandise. You supply them with a photo which they print onto a bag of your choice. It takes 6 weeks to deliver, but they will ship overseas. The shop will also print personal inscriptions onto bags. 15–17 Pont St., SW3. ℂ 020/7838-9177. www.anyahindmarch.com. Tube: Sloane Sq. or Knightsbridge.

Browns *★★*   This is the only place in London to find the designs of Alexander McQueen, head of the House of Givenchy in Paris and one of the fashion industry's stars. Producing his own cottons, silks, and plastics, McQueen creates revealing, feminine women's couture and ready-to-wear, and has started a menswear line. McQueen made his reputation creating shock-value apparel that was more photographed than worn. But recently, fashion critics have called his new outfits "consumer friendly." Browns has introduced "Browns Living," an eclectic array of lifestyle products. Browns stocks a range of designers, including Marc Jacobs and Dolce & Gabbana. Across the street, **Browns Focus,** 38–39 S. Molton St. (ℂ 020/7514-0063), stocks younger, more daring designs. Just down the street, Browns Labels for Less, 50 S. Molton St. (ℂ 020/7514-0052), is a discount outlet designer store. 23–27 S. Molton St., W1. ℂ 020/7491-7833. www.brownsfashion.com. Tube: Bond St.

Egg   This shop is hot, hot, hot with fashionistas. It features imaginatively designed, contemporary clothing by Indian textile designer Asha Sarabhai and knitwear by Eskandar. Designs, created from handmade textiles at a workshop in India, range from everyday dresses to hand-embroidered silk coats. Crafts and ceramics are also available. Closed Sunday and Monday. 36 Kinnerton St., SW1. ℂ 020/7235-9315. Tube: Hyde Park Corner or Knightsbridge.

H&M Hennes   Here are copies of hot-off-the-catwalk fashions at affordable prices. While the quality isn't anything to brag about, the prices are. For disposable cutting-edge fashion, you can't beat it. 271 Regent St., W1. ℂ 020/7493-4004. www.hm.com. Tube: Oxford Circus.

Joseph   Joseph Ettedgui, a fashion retailer born in Casablanca, is a maverick in the fashion world. He's known for his daring designs and his ability to attract some of the most talented designers in the business to work with him. The stretch jeans with flair ankles are the label's best-selling items.

The most complete collection of Joseph Ettedgui clothing anywhere, with clothes for both men and women (including suits, knitwear, suede, and leather clothing), is available within the two largest branches of his empire. Both carry signs that simply say JOSEPH on the front.

Three smaller branches of Joseph (www.joseph.com) lie clustered close to one another, each of them within a very short walk of the South Kensington Tube stop. They're at 315 Brompton Rd., SW3 (ℂ 020/7225-3335), and 77 Fulham Rd., SW4

(📞 020/7823-9500). Close by, and focusing only on menswear, is a Joseph boutique at 74 Sloane Ave., SW3 (📞 020/7591-0808). Newest of all is a branch in Notting Hill selling clothes for men and women at 236 Westbourne Grove, W11 (📞 020/7243-9920; Tube: Notting Hill Gate). 23 Old Bond St., W1. 📞 020/7629-3713. Tube: Green Park. Also at 16 Sloane St., SW1X. 📞 020/7235-1991. Tube: Knightsbridge.

The Library   Despite its name, this is a showcase for some of the best young designers for men. It's cutting edge without dipping into the extremes of male fashion. The Library is famous for having introduced Helmut Lang to London and now features such designers as Fabrizio del Carlo, Kostas Murkudis, and even Alexander McQueen. 268 Brompton Rd., SW3. 📞 020/7589-6569. Tube: S. Kensington.

Miss Selfridge   This is a hip young women's clothing and accessories store that sells its own cosmetic brand, Kiss & Make-Up. For pajama parties, there is a wide selection of sexy cotton pajamas. There is also a large array of products you can't live without, like two-toned nail polish and shimmery hair mascara. 36–38 Great Castle St., W1. 📞 020/7927-0214. Tube: Oxford Circus or Tottenham Court Rd.

Paul Smith's Westbourne House   This shop was converted from a stately three-story Edwardian town house into a showcase for the clothing of Paul Smith, whose well-made ready-to-wear men's (and, to a lesser extent, women's and children's) clothing defies the preconceptions of Savile Row tailors who believe that only custom-made garments will fit well. Preferred colors, with occasional exceptions, include grays, browns, and blacks, though there is a medley of velvet prints inspired by Carnaby Street in the 1960s. Look for women's clothes and accessories on the building's street level, men's clothes and accessories on the two floors above street level. 122 Kensington Park Rd., W11. 📞 020/7727-3553. www.paulsmith.co.uk. Tube: Notting Hill Gate or Kensington Park Rd.

Topshop 🏵🏵   This is the largest fashion store in the world. It is similar to Miss Selfridge but with better design and quality, although Topshop remains quite affordable. Its versatile and ever-changing merchandise is aimed at younger shoppers, but that doesn't stop many women in their 30s and 40s from shopping here. The outlet was the first to release a range of designs from Kate Moss. The shop, though aimed mainly at women, also has a men's floor. Women's shoes, vintage clothing, and other designer labels are sold in the basement. 216 Oxford St., W1. 📞 020/7636-7700. www.topshop.co.uk. Tube: Bond St.

Vivienne Westwood 🏵🏵   No one in British fashion is hotter than the unstoppable Vivienne Westwood. While it's possible to purchase some Westwood pieces around the world, her U.K. shops are the best places to find her full range of designs. The flagship location (on Conduit St.) concentrates on her couture line, known as the Gold Label. One of the U.K.'s most watched designers, Westwood creates clothes that manage to be elegant, alluring, and stylish all at the same time. Many of the fabrics and accessories for her garments are made in Britain, and at least some of them are crafted and tailored there as well. Westwood's Anglomania line of clothing focuses on casual designs for youthful bodies, including T-shirts, jeans, and sportswear. The outlet also carries a line of clothing for men. 44 Conduit St., W1. 📞 020/7439-1109. Tube: Oxford Circus. Also at 430 King's Rd., SW3. 📞 020/7352-6551. www.viviennewestwood.com. Tube: Sloane Sq.

VINTAGE & SECONDHAND

Note that there's no VAT refund on used clothing.

Annie's Vintage Clothes *(Finds* This shop concentrates on carefully preserved dresses from the 1920s and 1930s but also has a range of clothing and textiles from the 1880s through the 1960s. A 1920s fully beaded dress will run you about £300 ($570), but there are scarves for £15 ($29), camisoles for £30 ($57), and a range of exceptional pieces priced between £50–£70 ($95–$133). Clothing is located on the main floor; textiles, including old lace, bed linens, and tapestries, are upstairs. 12 Camden Passage, N1. © 020/7359-0796. Tube: Northern Line to Angel.

Pandora *(Value* A London institution since the 1940s, Pandora stands in fashionable Knightsbridge, a stone's throw from Harrods. Several times a week, chauffeurs drive up with bundles packed anonymously by England's gentry. One woman voted best-dressed at the Ascot Horse Races several years ago was wearing a secondhand dress acquired here. Prices are generally one-third to half the retail value. Chanel and Anne Klein are among the designers represented. Outfits are usually no more than two seasons old. 16–22 Cheval Place, SW7. © 020/7589-5289. Tube: Knightsbridge.

Pop Boutique For the best in original streetwear from the 1950s, 1960s, and 1970s, this clothing store is tops. Right next to the chic Covent Garden Hotel, it sells fabulous vintage wear at affordable prices: Leather jackets that would run in the hundreds in the vintage shops of downtown New York go for as little as £45 ($81) here. 6 Monmouth St., WC2. © 020/7497-5262. www.pop-boutique.com. Tube: Covent Garden.

Steinberg & Tolkien London's leading dealer in vintage costume jewelry and clothing also offers some used designer clothing that's not old enough to be vintage but is prime for collectors; other pieces are merely secondhand designer thrills. 193 King's Rd., SW3. © 020/7376-3660. Tube: Sloane Sq.

FILOFAX

All major department stores sell Filofax supplies, but for the full range (and a shopping experience), check out a Filofax store. They also have good sales; calendars for the next year go on sale very early the previous year (about 10 months in advance), so you can stock up and save.

The Filofax Centre Go to the Conduit Street shop if you can; it stocks the entire range of inserts and books at prices that will floor you—half what you pay in the U.S. 21 Conduit St., W1. © 020/7499-0457. www.filofax.co.uk. Tube: Oxford Circus. Also at 69 Neal St., WC2. © 020/7836-1977. Tube: Covent Garden.

FOOD

English food has come a long way, and it's worth enjoying and bringing home. Don't miss the Food Halls in Harrods. Consider the Fifth Floor at Harvey Nicks if Harrods is too crowded—it isn't the same, but it'll do. Also check out the internationally famous Fortnum & Mason food emporium. See "The Department Stores," earlier for descriptions, plus other options.

Charbonnel et Walker *(* Charbonnel et Walker is famous for its hot chocolate in winter (buy it by the tin) and its chocolate-covered strawberries, available whenever strawberries are available or in season. The company will send messages of thanks or love spelled out on the chocolates themselves. Ready-made presentation boxes are also available. 1 The Royal Arcade, 28 Old Bond St., W1. © 020/7491-0939. www.charbonnel.co.uk. Tube: Green Park.

Neal's Yard Dairy   Specializing in British and Irish cheeses, this shop occupies the very photogenic premises of what was originally built as a warehouse for the food stalls at Covent Garden. Today you'll see a staggering selection of artisanal cheeses, including cloth-bound cheddars and a wide selection of mild farmer's cheeses, set in big display windows behind an antique, dark-blue Victorian facade. There are also olive oils, breads, fresh produce, and a lot of the fixings of a picnic. 17 Shorts Gardens, WC2. ℂ 020/ 7240-5700. www.nealsyarddairy.co.uk. Tube: Covent Garden.

GIFTS & SOUVENIRS

Asprey & Garrard   This is as well-known and well-respected a name in luxury gift giving as anything you're likely to find in all of Britain, with a clientele that includes the likes of the Sultan of Brunei and Queen Elizabeth. Scattered over four floors of a dignified Victorian building, it's filled with antiques, porcelain, leather goods, crystal, clocks, and enough unusual objects of dignified elegance to stock an entire English country house. 167 New Bond St., W1. ℂ 020/7493-6767. www.asprey.com. Tube: Green Park.

Muji   An emporium for Japanese wares, this store is known for its bargain offerings. Among its merchandise, the frugal shopper will find everything from "simple and functional chic" clothing to flatware, most of it in avant-garde, minimalist styles completely devoid of any traditional or baroque influences of Olde England. The bath soaps are a delight, coming in such unusual scents as grapefruit and mandarin orange. Funky umbrellas and a host of other ever-changing wares tempt shoppers. 157 Kensington High St., W8. ℂ 020/376-2484. www.muji.co.uk. Tube: High St. Kensington.

HANDBAGS

Bill Amberg's   Most famous for his logo-free classic handbags, Amberg has opened his own shop and expanded his line to include luggage, picture frames, and furniture. Fans of Amberg's designs include Donna Karan, Romeo Gigli, Jerry Hall, and Christy Turlington. Given those celebrity clients, fashion-conscious shoppers may consider the £45 to £450 ($86–$855) price range of most items a steal. 21-22 Chepstow Corner, W2. ℂ 020/7727-3560. www.billamberg.com. Tube: Notting Hill Gate or Westbourne Park.

Lulu Guinness   This self-taught British handbag designer, who launched her business in 1989, is known as the finest such designer in London. Many of the world's greatest retail outlets, such as Neiman Marcus, sell her handbags. Her signature handbags, such as the "Florist Basket" and the "House Bag," are immortalized in the fashion collection at the Victoria and Albert Museum. Seen about London carrying Lulu Guinness handbags are such celebrities as Madonna and Elizabeth Hurley. 3 Ellis St., SW1. ℂ 020/7823-4828. www.luluguinness.com. Tube: Sloane Sq.

HOME DESIGN, FURNISHINGS & HOUSEWARES

Also see "Jewelry" and "Art & Crafts."

The Conran Shop   You'll find Sir Terence Conran's high style at reasonable prices at this outlet. The fashion press cites Conran as "the director" of British middle-class taste since the 1960s. This place is great for gifts, home furnishings, and tabletop ware—or just for gawking. Michelin House, 81 Fulham Rd., SW3. ℂ 020/7589-7401. www.conranshop. co.uk. Tube: S. Kensington.

The Couverture Shop   This is an emporium of the unexpected, with original products for both adults and children as well as the home. It's strongest on what they call "bedroom must-haves," embracing bed linen, throws, cushions, and the like. Vintage finds along with designer pieces—often handmade—are also sold. 310 King's Rd., SW3. © 020/7795-1200. www.couverture.co.uk. Tube: Sloane Sq.

David Linley Furniture ✹✹✹ This is a showcase for the remarkable furniture of Viscount Linley, son of the late Princess Margaret. His designs are complex. For example, his Apsley House Desk is done in French walnut with ebony and nickel-plated detailing, contains secret drawers, and is rimmed with a miniature of the neoclassical Apsley House. Linley's clients include Elton John, Mick Jagger, and Nina Campbell. The director at the Victoria and Albert Museum predicts that Linley's furnishings and accessories will become "the antiques of the future." 60 Pimlico Rd., SW1. © 020/7730-7300. www.davidlinley.com. Tube: Sloane Sq.

Designers Guild After more than three decades in business, creative director Tricia Guild and her young designers still lead the pack in all that's bright and whimsical. They are often copied but never outdone. There's an exclusive line of handmade furniture and accessories at the no. 267–271 location, and wallpaper and more than 2,000 fabrics at the neighboring no. 275–277 shop. The colors remain vivid forever, and the designs are always irreverent. Also available are children's accessories, toys, crockery, and cutlery. 267–271 and 275–277 King's Rd., SW3. © 020/7351-5775. www.designerguild.com. Tube: Sloane Sq.

Summerill & Bishop Some of London's most sophisticated kitchenware is sold here—items that may not be available in your hometown store. The range is from Edward S. Wohl's charming bird's-eye maple breadboards to John Julian Sainsbury's black granite mortar with a stainless-steel-handled pestle. Some of the top designers in Britain created the unusual wares at this outlet. 100 Portland Rd., W11. © 020/7221-4566. www.summerillandbishop.com. Tube: Holland Park.

JEWELRY

Asprey & Garrard Previously known as Garrard & Co., this recently merged jeweler specializes in both antique and modern jewelry, and silverware. The in-house designers also produce pieces to order and do repairs. You can have a pair of pearl earrings or silver cufflinks for a £60 ($114)—but the prices go nowhere but up from there. 167 New Bond St., W1. © 020/7493-6767. Tube: Green Park.

Lesley Craze Gallery/Textiles This complex has developed a reputation as a showcase of the best contemporary British jewelry and textile design. The gallery shop focuses on precious metals and includes pieces by such renowned designers as Wendy Ramshaw. Prices start at £60 ($114). The gallery also features costume jewelry in materials ranging from bronze to paper, with prices starting at £15 ($29). Textiles feature contemporary designs, including wall hangings, scarves, and ties by artists such as Jo Barker, Dawn DuPree, and Victoria Richards. 33–35A Clerkenwell Green, EC1. © 020/7608-0393 (jewelry), 020/7251-9200 (textiles). www.lesleycrazegallery.co.uk. Tube: Farringdon.

Rigby & Peller ✹✹ Established in 1939, this upmarket outlet even has a Royal Warrant. Queen Elizabeth II herself purchases her lingerie here and has done so for many years. 2 Hans Rd., W3. © 0845/076-5545. www.rigbyandpeller.co.uk. Tube: Knightsbridge.

Sanford Brothers Ltd. In business since 1923, this family firm sells all styles of jewelry (Victorian through modern), silver, and a fine selection of clocks and watches. Old Elizabeth Houses, 3 Holborn Bars, EC1. © 020/7405-2352. www.sanfords.co.uk. Tube: Chancery Lane.

LUGGAGE

Mulberry Company   This flagship store offers a complete line of the town's most cutting-edge designer luggage. Their signature grosgrain luggage begins at £195 ($371). Mulberry is also earning a name in fashion for its English country–style ready-to-wear clothes for men and women. Plus, it carries fashionable furnishings and accessories for the home, including throws and cushions in chenille and damask. 11–12 Gees Court, W1. ℭ 020/7493-2546. www.mulberry.com. Tube: Bond St.

MUSEUM SHOPS

Victoria and Albert Museum Gift Shop 🐾🐾   This is the best museum shop in London—indeed, one of the best in the world. It sells cards, a fabulous selection of art books, and the usual items, along with reproductions from the design museum archives. Cromwell Rd., SW7. ℭ 020/7942-2696. www.vandashop.com. Tube: S. Kensington.

MUSIC

Collectors should browse **Notting Hill** because there are a handful of good shops near the Notting Hill Gate Tube stop. Also browse **Soho** in the Wardour Street area, near the Tottenham Court Road Tube stop. Sometimes dealers show up at Covent Garden on the weekends.

Virgin Megastore   If a record has just been released—and if it's worth hearing in the first place—chances are, this store carries it. It's like a giant musical grocery store. You get to hear many of the new releases on headphones at listening stations before making a purchase. Even rock stars come here to pick up new releases. A large selection of classical and jazz recordings is sold, as are computer software and video games. In between selecting your favorites, you can enjoy a coffee at the cafe or purchase an airline ticket from the Virgin Atlantic office. 14 Oxford St., W1. ℭ 020/7631-1234. www.virginmega.co.uk. Tube: Tottenham Court Rd. Also at King's Walk Shopping Centre, King's Rd., SW3. ℭ 020/7591-0957. Tube: Sloane Sq. or South Kensington.

SHOES

Also see **DAKS** in "The Department Stores," earlier.

Koko   This sprawling, trendy, style-conscious shop sells footwear, and only footwear, from three different vendors, the most famous and visible being Dr. Marten's. Dr. Marten's shoes have unisex punk-rock associations, and you can expect lots of British rocker types trying on shoes around you. This store has the largest inventory of Doc Marten's in London. 1–2 Carnaby St., W1. ℭ 020/7734-8890. Tube: Oxford Circus or Piccadilly Circus.

Natural Shoe Store   A range of shoes for men and women is stocked in this shop, which also does repairs. The selection includes all comfort and quality footwear, from Birkenstock to the British classics. 21 Neal St., WC2. ℭ 020/7836-5254. www.thenaturalshoestore.com. Tube: Covent Garden.

Office   In spite of its dull name, this is an excellent store for style-setters on a budget. Its imitations of some of the world's leading shoe designers have earned it the reputation of being the "Madame Tussaud's of footwear." All the fashionable shoe designers, from Kenneth Cole to Patrick Cox, get ripped off here. 107 Queensway, W2. ℭ 020/7792-4000. www.office.co.uk. Tube: Queensway or Bayswater.

Shelly's   Shelly's flagship on Oxford Circus is the largest shoe store in London, selling footwear to fashionable young things and style-conscious individuals at affordable prices. 266–270 Regent St., W1. © 020/7287-0939. Tube: Oxford Circus or King's Rd. Other locations throughout London.

SPORTING GOODS

Harrods (see "The Department Stores," earlier) has a surprising collection of sporting goods, including everything you'll need for a polo match.

Lillywhites Ltd. ★★★   Europe's biggest and most famous sports store has floor after floor of sports clothing, equipment, and footwear. It also offers collections of fashionable leisurewear for men and women. 24–36 Lower Regent St., SW1. © 020/7915-4000. Tube: Piccadilly Circus.

STATIONERY & PAPER GOODS

Paperchase   This flagship store has three floors of paper products, including handmade paper, wrapping paper, ribbons, picture frames, and a huge selection of greeting cards. It's the best of its kind in London. 213–215 Tottenham Court Rd., W1. © 020/7467-6200. www.paperchase.co.uk. Tube: Goodge St. or Tottenham Court Rd. Other locations throughout London.

TEA

Of course, don't forget to visit **Fortnum & Mason** for tea as well (see "The Department Stores," earlier).

The Tea House   This shop sells everything associated with tea, tea drinking, and teatime. It boasts more than 70 quality teas and tisanes, including whole-fruit blends, the best tea of China (Gunpowder, and jasmine with flowers), India (Assam leaf, and choice Darjeeling), Japan (Genmaicha green), and Sri Lanka (pure Ceylon), plus such longtime-favorite English blended teas as Earl Grey. The shop also offers novelty teapots and mugs. 15A Neal St., WC2. © 020/7240-7539. Tube: Covent Garden.

TOYS

Hamleys   This flagship is the finest toy shop in the world—more than 35,000 toys and games on seven floors of fun and magic. The huge selection includes soft, cuddly stuffed animals as well as dolls, radio-controlled cars, train sets, model kits, board games, outdoor toys, computer games, and more. 188–196 Regent St., W1. © 0870/333-2455. www.hamleys.com. Tube: Oxford Circus or Piccadilly Circus. Also at Covent Garden and Heathrow Airport.

5 Street & Flea Markets

If Mayfair stores are not your cup of tea, don't worry; you'll have more fun, and find a better bargain, at any of the city's street and flea markets.

THE WEST END   Covent Garden Market ★ (© 020/7836-9136; www.covent gardenmarket.com; Tube: Covent Garden), the most famous market in all of England, offers several markets Monday to Saturday from 10am to 6pm (we think it's most fun to come on Sun 11am–6pm). It can be a little confusing until you dive in and explore. **Apple Market** is the bustling market in the courtyard, where traders sell—well, everything. Many of the items are what the English call collectible nostalgia: a wide array of glassware and ceramics, leather goods, toys, clothes, hats, and jewelry. Some of the merchandise is truly unusual. Many items are handmade, with some of the craftspeople selling their own wares—except on Monday, when antiques dealers take over. Some goods are new, some are very old. Out back is **Jubilee Market** (© 020/7836-2139), also an antiques market on Monday. Tuesday to Sunday, it's sort of a fancy hippie market with cheap clothes and books. Out front there are a few tents of cheap stuff, except on Monday.

The indoor market section of Covent Garden Market (in a superbly restored hall) is one of the best shopping venues in London. Specialty shops sell fashions and herbs, gifts and toys, books and dollhouses, cigars, and much more. There are bookshops and branches of famous stores (Hamleys, The Body Shop), and prices are kept moderate.

St. Martin–in-the-Fields Market (Tube: Charing Cross) is good for teens and hipsters who don't want to trek all the way to Camden Market (see "North London," below) and are interested in imports from India and South America, crafts, and local football (soccer) souvenirs. It's located near Trafalgar Square and Covent Garden; hours are Monday through Saturday from 11am to 5pm and Sunday from noon to 5pm.

Berwick Street Market (Tube: Oxford Circus or Tottenham Court Rd.) may be the only street market in the world that's flanked by rows of strip clubs, porno stores, and adult-movie dens. Don't let that put you off. Humming 6 days a week in the scarlet heart of Soho, this array of stalls and booths sells the best and cheapest fruit and vegetables in town. It also hawks ancient records, tapes, books, and old magazines, any of which may turn out to be a collector's item one day. It's open Monday to Saturday 9am to 6pm.

On Sunday mornings artists hang their work on the railings along a 1.5 km (1 mile) stretch of **Bayswater Road,** along the edge of Hyde Park and Kensington Gardens. If the weather's right, start at Marble Arch and walk. You'll see the same thing on the railings of Green Park along Piccadilly on Saturday afternoons.

NOTTING HILL   Portobello Market (Tube: Notting Hill Gate) is a magnet for collectors of virtually everything. It's mainly a Saturday happening, from 6am to 5pm. You needn't be here at the crack of dawn; 9am is fine. Once known mainly for fruit and vegetables (still sold here throughout the week), in the past 4 decades Portobello has become synonymous with antiques. But don't take the stallholder's word for it that the fiddle he's holding is a genuine Stradivarius left to him by his Italian great-uncle; it might just as well have been "nicked" from an East End pawnshop.

The market is divided into three major sections. The most crowded is the antiques section, running between Colville Road and Chepstow Villas to the south. (*Warning:* There's a great concentration of pickpockets in this area.) The second section (and the oldest part) is the "fruit and veg" market, lying between Westway and Colville Road. In the third and final section is a flea market, where Londoners sell bric-a-brac and lots of secondhand goods they didn't really want in the first place. But looking around still makes for interesting fun.

Note: Some 90 antiques and art shops along Portobello Road are open during the week when the street market is closed. This is actually a better time for the serious collector to shop because you'll get more attention from dealers, and you won't be distracted by the organ grinder.

SOUTH BANK   Open on Fridays only, **New Caledonian Market** is commonly known as the **Bermondsey Market** because of its location on the corner of Long Lane and Bermondsey Street (Tube: London Bridge, then bus no. 78 or walk down Bermondsey St.). The market is at the extreme east end, beginning at Tower Bridge Road. It's one of Europe's outstanding street markets for the number and quality of the antiques and other goods. The stalls are well known, and many dealers come into

London from the country. Prices are generally lower here than at Portobello and the other markets. It gets under way at 5am—with the bargains gone by 9am—and closes at noon. Bring a "torch" (flashlight) if you go in the wee hours.

NORTH LONDON   If it's Wednesday or Saturday, it's time for **Camden Passage** (© 020/7359-0190; Tube: Northern Line to Angel) in Islington, where there's a very upscale antiques market. It starts in Camden Passage and sprawls into the streets behind. The market is held on Wednesday from 7am to 4pm, Thursday 7am to 4pm, and Saturday 8am to 4pm.

Don't confuse Camden Passage with Camden Market (very downtown). **Camden Market** (Tube: Camden Town) is for teens and others into body piercings, blue hair, and vintage clothing. Serious collectors of vintage may want to explore during the week, when the teen scene isn't quite so overwhelming. Market hours are from 9:30am to 5:30pm daily, with some parts opening at 10am. Of course, Saturday and Sunday are by far the busiest days.

10

London After Dark

London's pulsating nightlife scene is the most vibrant in Europe. Although pubs still close at 11pm, the city is staying up later, and more and more clubs have extended partying into the wee hours.

London is on a real high right now, especially in terms of music and dance—much of the currently popular techno and electronica originated in London clubs. Youth culture prevails here, as downtown denizens flock to the clubs where pop-culture superstars are routinely spotted.

London nightlife is always in a state of flux. What's hot today probably just opened, and many clubs have the lifespan of fruit flies. At the time of this writing, **Groucho,** at 45 Dean St., W1 (© **020/ 7439-4685**), is still the *in* club, although it is members only. A few perennials, like Ronnie Scott's, are still favorites.

But London nightlife is not just about music and dance clubs. The city abounds with the world's best theater (sorry, New York!), loads of classical music, pubs oozing historic charm, and tons of other options for a night out.

1 The Play's the Thing: London's Theater Scene

Even more than New York, London is the theater capital of the world. Few things here are as entertaining and rewarding as the theater. The number and variety of productions, and the standards of acting and directing, are unrivaled. The London stage accommodates both the traditional and the avant-garde and is, for the most part, accessible and reasonably affordable. The Globe Theatre is an exciting addition to the theater scene. Because the Globe is a sightseeing attraction as well, it's also listed in chapter 8 on p. 252. You'll find most of the theaters listed in this section on the "Central London Theaters" color map at the beginning of this book. To find out what's on stage before you leave home, check www.officiallondontheatre.co.uk.

GETTING TICKETS

To see specific shows, especially hits, purchase your tickets in advance. The best method is to buy your tickets from the theater's box office, which you can do over the phone using a credit card. You'll pay the theater price and pick up the tickets the day of the show. You can also go to a ticket agent, especially for discount tickets.

For tickets and information before you go, try **Keith Prowse,** 234 W. 44th St., Suite 1000, New York, NY 10036 (© **800/669-8687** or 212/398-1468; www.keith prowse.com). Their London office (which operates under the name of both Global Tickets and First Call Tickets) is at the British Visitors Center, 1 Regent St., SW1 Y4XT (© **0870/840-1111**). They'll mail your tickets, fax a confirmation, or leave your tickets at the appropriate production's box office. Instant confirmations are available for most shows. A booking and handling fee of up to 20% is added to the price of all tickets.

(*Value* Ticket Bargains

The **Society of London Theatre** (② 020/7557-6700; www.officiallondontheatre.
co.uk) operates the **tkts** booth in Leicester Square, where same-day tickets for
many shows are available at half-price or 25% off, plus a £2.50 ($4.75) service
charge. tkts also sells full-price same-day tickets for shows that are not offering
half-price or 25%-off tickets. In addition, the booth often offers a limited number of seats for shows that are usually sold out. Tickets are available for any of
55 theaters. All major credit and debit cards are accepted. Tickets (limited to
four per person) are sold only on the day of performance. No refunds. Hours
are Monday to Saturday 10am to 7pm; Sunday noon to 3pm. We prefer this
ticket agency to the others that populate Leicester Square, which don't always
offer reliable discounts.

Applause Theatre and Entertainment Service, 311 W. 43rd St., Suite 601, New
York, NY 10036 (② **800/451-9930** or 212/307-7050; fax 212/397-3729; www.
applause-tickets.com), can sometimes get you tickets when Prowse can't. In business
for some 2 decades, they are a reliable and efficient company.

Another option is **Theatre Direct International** (**TDI**; ② **800/BROADWAY** or
212/541-8457 in U.S. only; www.broadway.com). TDI specializes in providing London fringe theater tickets but also has tickets to major productions, including those at
the Royal National Theatre and the Barbican. The service allows you to arrive in London with your tickets already in hand or have them held for you at the box office.

If you're staying at a first class or deluxe hotel with a concierge, you can also ask
them to help arrange tickets before you arrive, putting them on a credit card.

London theater tickets are priced quite reasonably when compared with the United
States. Prices vary greatly depending on the seat—from £20 to £80 ($38–$152).
Sometimes gallery seats (the cheapest) are sold only on the day of the performance, so
you'll have to head to the box office early in the day and then return an hour before
the performance to queue up because the seats are not reserved.

Many of the major theaters offer reduced-price tickets to students on a stand-by
basis, but not to the general public. When available, these tickets are sold 30 minutes
prior to curtain. Line up early for popular shows, as standby tickets go fast and furi-
ous. Of course, you must have a valid student ID.

Warning: Beware of scalpers who hang out in front of theaters with hit shows.
Many report that scalpers sell forged tickets, and their prices are outrageous.

MAJOR THEATERS & COMPANIES

We have listed some of the most popular theaters and companies below. To find out
what's on currently in all of the major and fringe theaters, pick up *Time Out London,
Where,* a London daily newspaper, or "The Official London Theatre Guide" pamphlet
(online at www.officiallondontheatre.co.uk), available at ticket brokers and all West
End theaters. For locations, see "Central London Theaters" color map at the beginning of this book.

One of the world's finest theater companies, the **Royal Shakespeare Company** ✿✿✿,
performs at various theaters throughout London. Check its website at www.rsc.org.uk
for current shows and venues or call ② **0870/609-1110** Monday to Saturday 9am to

8pm. The theater troupe performs in London during the winter months, naturally specializing in the plays of the Bard. In summer, it tours England and abroad.

Cadogan Hall   Nestled in the heart of Chelsea, this decommissioned church, the first Christian Science church in the world, founded in 1893, has been turned into a concert hall for the Royal Philharmonic Orchestra. Completely restored and massively altered, the building now boasts a 900-seat auditorium and all the acoustics of the 21st century. The box office is open Monday to Saturday from 10am to 7pm, and Sunday from 10am to 7pm performance days only. 5 Sloane Terrace, Sloane Sq., SW1. ☎ 020/7730-4500. www.cadoganhall.com. Tickets vary according to the event. Tube: Sloane Sq.

Open-Air Theatre   This outdoor theater is in Regent's Park; the setting is idyllic, and both seating and acoustics are excellent. Presentations are mainly of Shakespeare, usually in period costume. Its theater bar, the longest in London, serves both drink and food. In the case of a rained-out performance, tickets are offered for another date. The season runs from June to mid-September, Monday to Saturday at 8pm, plus Wednesday, Thursday, and Saturday matinees at 2:30pm. Inner Circle, Regent's Park, NW1. ☎ 08700/601811. www.openairtheatre.org. Tickets £10–£33 ($19–$63). Tube: Baker St.

Royal Court Theatre   This theater has always been a leader in producing provocative, cutting-edge, new drama. In the 1950s, it staged the plays of the angry young men, notably John Osborne's then-sensational *Look Back in Anger;* earlier it debuted the plays of George Bernard Shaw. A recent work was *The Beauty Queen of Leenane,* which went on to win a Tony on Broadway. The theater is home to the English Stage Company, formed to promote serious writing for the stage. Box office hours are daily from 10am to 6pm. Sloane Sq., SW1. ☎ 020/7565-5000. www.royalcourttheatre.com. Tickets £10–£25 ($19–$48); call for the latest information. Tube: Sloane Sq.

Royal National Theatre   Home to one of the world's greatest stage companies, the Royal National Theatre is not one but three theaters—the Olivier, reminiscent of a Greek amphitheater with its open stage; the more traditional Lyttelton; and the Cottesloe, with its flexible stage and seating. The National presents the finest in world theater, from classic drama to award-winning new plays, including comedies, musicals, and shows for young people. A choice of at least six plays is offered at any one time.

New Venues for London Opera Lovers

Frank Matcham, famed designer of the Coliseum, built **Hackney Empire,** Mare St., E8 (☎ 020/8985-2424; www.hackneyempire.co.uk), an Italian-style rococo opera house that opened in 1901. The music building was restored, to the tune of £16.5 million ($31 million). Today its cultural offerings range from opera to the Bard.

The Savoy Theater, the Strand, WC2 (☎ 0870/164-8787), also presents operas and other musicals such as a revival of *Porgy and Bess.* This was the famous opera theater built in 1880 by Richard D'Oyly Carte that specialized in Gilbert & Sullivan musicals. Today, the 1,100-seat theater has been completely refurbished and is one of the few West End theaters with an orchestra pit; this one holds the Royal Philharmonic Opera Orchestra.

(Tips Curtain Going Up!

Matinees, performed Tuesday through Saturday, are cheaper than evening performances. Evening performances begin between 7:30 and 8:30pm, midweek matinees at 2:30 or 3pm, and Saturday matinees at 5:45pm. West End theaters are closed Sunday.

Many theaters accept telephone bookings at regular prices with a credit card. They'll hold your tickets for you at the box office, where you pick them up at show time—just remember to bring your credit card.

It's also a full-time theater center, with an amazing selection of bars, cafes, restaurants, free foyer music and exhibitions, short early-evening performances, bookshops, backstage tours, riverside walks, and terraces. You can have a three-course meal in Mezzanine, the National's restaurant; enjoy a light meal in the brasserie-style Terrace cafe; or have a snack in one of the coffee bars. South Bank, SE1. ℂ 020/7452-3000. www. nt-online.org. Tickets £10–£38 ($19–$72); midweek matinees, Sat matinees, and previews cost less. Tube: Waterloo, Embankment, or Charing Cross.

Shakespeare's Globe Theatre In May 1997, the new Globe Theatre—a replica of the Elizabethan original, thatched roof and all—staged its first slate of plays (*Henry V* and *A Winter's Tale*) yards away from the site of the 16th-century theater where the Bard originally staged his work.

Productions vary in style and setting; not all are performed in Elizabethan costume. In keeping with the historic setting, there is no theatrical lighting, but floodlights are used during evening performances to replicate daylight in the theater—Elizabethan performances took place in the afternoon. Theatergoers sit on wooden benches of yore but these days you can rent a cushion to make yourself more comfortable. About 500 "groundlings" can stand in the uncovered yard around the stage, just as they did when the Bard was here.

From May to September, the company intends to hold performances Tuesday to Saturday at 2 and 7pm. There will be a limited winter schedule. In any season, the schedule may be affected by weather because this is an outdoor theater. Performances last 2½ to 4 hours, depending on the play.

For details on the exhibition that tells the story of the painstaking re-creation of the Globe, as well as guided tours of the theater, see p. 252. New Globe Walk, SE1. ℂ 020/7401-9919 for box office. www.shakespeares-globe.org. Tickets £5 ($9.50) for groundlings, £15–£31 ($29–$59) for gallery seats. Exhibition tickets £9 ($17) adults, £7.50 ($14) seniors and students, £6.50 ($12) ages 5–15, £25 ($48) family ticket. Tube: Mansion House or Blackfriars.

Theatre Royal Drury Lane Drury Lane is one of London's oldest and most prestigious theaters, crammed with tradition—and not all of it respectable. This, the fourth theater on this site, dates from 1812; the first was built in 1663. Nell Gwynne, the rough-tongued Cockney lass who became Charles II's mistress, used to sell oranges under the long colonnade in front. Nearly every star of London theater has taken the stage here at some time. It has a wide-open repertoire but leans toward musicals, especially long-running hits. Guided tours of the backstage area and the front of the house are given most days at 10:15am, noon, 2:15, and 4:45pm. Call ℂ **020/7494-5091** for more information. The box office is open Monday to Saturday from 10am to 8pm.

Evening performances are Monday to Saturday at 7:30pm; matinees are Wednesday and Saturday at 2:30pm. Catherine St., WC2. ℰ **020/7494-5000.** Tickets £10–£49 ($19–$93). Tube: Covent Garden.

FRINGE THEATER

Some of the best theater in London is performed on the "fringe"—at the dozens of theaters devoted to alternative plays, revivals, contemporary dramas, and musicals. These shows are usually more adventurous than established West End productions, and they're cheaper. Expect to pay from £6 to £30 ($11–$57). Most offer discounted seats to students and seniors. Fringe theaters are scattered around London; so check listings in *Time Out* and www.officiallondontheatre.co.uk and www.londontheatre.co.uk.

Almeida Theatre   The Almeida is known for its adventurous stagings of new and classic plays. The theater's legendary status is validated by consistently good productions at lower-than-average prices. Performances are usually held Monday to Saturday. The Almeida is also home to the Festival of Contemporary Music (also called the Almeida Opera) from mid-June to mid-July, featuring everything from atonal jazz to 12-tone chamber orchestra pieces. Box office is open Monday through Saturday 10am to 6pm. Almeida St., N1. ℰ **020/7359-4404.** www.almeida.co.uk. Tickets £6–£30 ($11–$57). Tube: Northern Line to Angel or Victoria Line to Highbury & Islington.

The Gate   This tiny room above a Notting Hill pub is one of the best alternative stages in London. Popular with local cognoscenti, the Gate specializes in translated works by foreign playwrights. Performances are held Monday through Saturday at 7:30pm. Call for shows and times. Box office is open Monday through Friday 10am to 6pm. 12 Pembridge Rd., W11. ℰ **020/7229-5387.** www.gatetheatre.co.uk. Tickets £10–£15 ($19–$29). Tube: Notting Hill Gate.

The King's Head   London's most famous fringe locale, the King's Head is also the city's oldest pub-theater. Despite its tiny stage, the theater is heavy on musicals; several have gone on to become successful West End productions. Matinees are held on Saturday and Sunday at 3:30pm. Evening performances are held Tuesday through Saturday at 8pm. Box office is open daily from 10am to 8pm. 115 Upper St., N1. ℰ **020/7226-1916.** www.kingsheadtheatre.org. Tickets £15–£20 ($29–$38). Tube: Northern Line to Angel.

Young Vic   Long known for presenting both classical and modern plays, the famous theater company is back at its home base following a 2-year restoration that ended in 2006. The acoustics, the seating, and the stage equipment are better than ever. The Young Vic nurtures younger talent than its sister theater, **The Old Vic** (www.old victheatre.com), across the road which puts on productions by more established artists. Productions at the Young Vic could be almost anything and are priced depending on the show. Prices are usually £7.50 and £25 ($14 and $48), and note that discounted tickets are available for students and others 26 and under. The box office is open Monday to Saturday 10am to 8pm. 66 The Cut, SE1 ℰ **020/7922-2922.** www.young vic.org. Tube: Oval.

2 Classical Music, Dance & Opera

Currently, London supports four major orchestras—the **London Symphony,** the **Royal Philharmonic,** the **Philharmonia Orchestra,** and the **BBC Symphony**—several choirs, and many smaller chamber groups and historic instrument ensembles. Look for the **London Sinfonietta,** the **English Chamber Orchestra,** and of course, the **Academy of St. Martin-in-the-Fields.** Performances are in the South Banks Arts Centre and the Barbican. Smaller recitals are at Wigmore Hall and St. John's Smith Square.

Barbican Centre (home of the London Symphony Orchestra & more)   The largest art and exhibition center in Western Europe, the roomy and comfortable Barbican complex is the perfect setting for enjoying music and theater. Barbican Hall is the permanent home address of the London Symphony Orchestra, as well as host to visiting orchestras and performers of all styles, from classical to jazz, folk, and world music.

In addition to its hall and two theaters, Barbican Centre encompasses the Barbican Art Gallery, the Curve Gallery, and foyer exhibition spaces; Cinemas One and Two, which show recently released mainstream films and film series; the Barbican Library, a general lending library with a strong emphasis on the arts; the Conservatory, one of London's largest greenhouses; and restaurants, cafes, and bars. The box office is open daily from 9am to 8pm. Silk St., EC2. (°) 020/7638-8891. www.barbican.org.uk. Tickets depend on the event. Tube: Barbican or Moorgate.

Kenwood Lakeside Concerts   These band and orchestral concerts on the north side of Hampstead Heath have been a British tradition for more than half a century. In recent years, laser shows and fireworks have been added to a repertoire that includes everything from rousing versions of the *1812 Overture* to jazz to operas such as *Carmen.* The final concert of the season always features some of the "Pomp and Circumstance" marches of Sir Edward Elgar. Music drifts across the lake to serenade wine-and-cheese parties on the grass. Concerts take place from June to early September Saturday at 7:30pm. The box office is open Monday to Saturday from 9:30am to 6:30pm. Kenwood, Hampstead Lane, NW3 7JR. (°) 0870/890-0146. www.picnicconcerts.com. Tickets cost £15–£17 ($29–$32) for seats on the grass lawn, £21–£25 ($40–$48) for reserved deck chairs. Reductions of 12.5% for students and persons over 60. Tube: Northern Line to Golders Green or Archway, then bus no. 210, a 30- to 45-minute jaunt to the north of London.

London Coliseum (home of the English National Opera)   Built in 1904 as a variety theater and converted into an opera house in 1968, the London Coliseum is the city's largest theater. For its 100th birthday, the renowned opera house received a $75-million (U.S.) restoration fit for a diva. Today not only is the Edwardian splendor restored, but there are roomier foyers, plus a two-story lobby and bar with views of Trafalgar Square. The 2,358-seat Coliseum still remains the largest proscenium theater in England. One of two national opera companies, the English National Opera, performs a range of works here, from classics to Gilbert & Sullivan to new experimental works. All performances are in English. The Opera presents a repertory of 18 to 20 productions 5 or 6 nights a week for 10 months of the year (the theater is dark mid-July to mid-Sept). The theater also hosts touring companies. Although balcony seats are cheaper, many visitors seem to prefer the upper circle or dress circle. The box office is open Monday to Saturday from 10am to 8pm. London Coliseum, St. Martin's Lane, WC2. (°) 0870/145-0200. www.eno.org. Tickets from £10 ($19) balcony, £26–£81 ($49–$154) upper or dress circle or stalls; about 100 discount balcony tickets sold on the day of performance from 10am. Tube: Charing Cross or Leicester Sq.

Royal Albert Hall   Opened in 1871 and dedicated to the memory of Victoria's consort, Prince Albert, this circular building holds one of the world's most famous auditoriums.

With a seating capacity of 5,200, it's a popular place to hear music by stars. Occasional sporting events (especially boxing) figure strongly here, too.

Since 1941, the hall has hosted the BBC Henry Wood Promenade Concerts, known as "The Proms," an annual series that lasts for 8 weeks between mid-July and mid-September. The Proms, incorporating a medley of rousing, mostly British orchestral music, have been a British tradition since 1895. Although most of the audience occupies reserved seats, true aficionados usually opt for standing room in the orchestra pit, with close-up views of the musicians on stage. Newly commissioned works are often premiered here. The final evening is the most traditional; the rousing favorites "Jerusalem" and "Land of Hope and Glory" echo through the hall. After its 8-year restoration, the Albert Hall now allows tours for the first time, every 45 minutes, starting at 10am Friday to Tuesday and ending at 3:30pm, at a cost of £7.50 ($14). Limited to only 15 participants, tours take in such sights as the Queen's Box and the Royal Retiring Room used by royals during intermission. Those on tour are also shown the Royal Albert Hall organ with it 9,999 pipes. The box office is open daily from 9am to 9pm. Kensington Gore, SW7 2AP. © 020/7589-8212. www.royalalberthall.com. Tickets £5–£150 ($9.50–$285), depending on the event. Tube: S. Kensington.

Royal Festival Hall   Three of the most acoustically perfect concert halls in the world were erected in this complex between 1951 and 1964: the Royal Festival Hall, the Queen Elizabeth Hall, and the Purcell Room. Together, the halls present more than 1,200 performances a year, including classical music, ballet, jazz, popular music, and contemporary dance. Also here is the internationally renowned Hayward Gallery (p. 246).

Royal Festival Hall, which usually opens daily at 10am, offers an extensive array of things to see and do, including free exhibitions in the foyers and occasional free lunchtime music at 12:30pm. On Fridays, there is a free Commuter Jazz performance in the foyer from 5:15 to 6:45pm. The Poetry Library is open Tuesday to Sunday 11am to 8pm, and shops display a selection of books, records, and crafts. Food and drink are also served at various venues. The box office is open daily from 9am to 8pm. On the South Bank, SE1. Box office © 08703/800-400. www.rfh.org.uk. Tickets £8–£60 ($15–$114). Tube: Waterloo or Embankment.

The Royal Opera House (home of the Royal Ballet & the Royal Opera)   The Royal Ballet and the Royal Opera are at home again in this magnificently restored theater. Opera and ballet aficionados hardly recognize the renovated place, with its spectacular public spaces, including the Floral Hall (a chamber-music venue), a rooftop restaurant, and bars and shops. The entire northeast corner of one of London's most famous public squares has been transformed, finally realizing Inigo Jones's original vision for this colonnaded plaza.

Performances at the Royal Opera are usually sung in the opera's original language, but supertitles are projected above the stage. The Royal Ballet, which ranks with top companies such as the Kirov and the Paris Opera Ballet, performs a repertory with a tilt toward the classics, including works by its earlier choreographer-directors Sir Frederick Ashton and Sir Kenneth MacMillan. The box office is open Monday to Saturday from 10am to 8pm. Bow St., WC2. © 020/7304-4000. www.royalopera.org. Tickets £6–£185 ($11–$352). Tube: Covent Garden.

Sadler's Wells Theatre   This is a premier venue for dance and opera. It occupies the site of a series of theaters, the first built in 1683. In the early 1990s, the turn-of-the-century theater was mostly demolished, and construction began on an innovative new design completed at the end of 1998. The turn-of-the-century facade has been retained, but the interior has been completely revamped with a stylish, cutting-edge design. The new theater offers classical ballet, modern dance of all degrees of "avant-garde-ness," and children's theatrical productions, including a Christmas ballet. Performances are usually at 7:30pm. The box office is open Monday to Saturday from 9am to 8:30pm. Rosebery Ave., EC1. © 0870/737-7737. www.sadlers-wells.com. Tickets £10–£50 ($19–$95). Tube: Northern Line to Angel.

Wigmore Hall   An intimate auditorium, Wigmore Hall offers an excellent series of voice recitals, piano and chamber music, early and baroque music, and jazz. A cafe-bar and restaurant are on the premises; a cold supper can be preordered if you are attending a concert. Performances are held nightly in addition to the Sunday Morning Coffee Concerts and Sunday concerts at 11:30am or 4pm. The box office is open Monday to Saturday from 10am to 8:30pm and Sunday from 10:30am to 5pm. 36 Wigmore St., W1. © 020/7935-2141. www.wigmore-hall.org.uk. Tickets £10–£35 ($19–$67). Tube: Bond St. or Oxford Circus.

3 The Club & Music Scene

BLUES

Ain't Nothin' But Blues Bar   This club, which bills itself as the only true blues venue in town, features local acts and, occasionally, touring American bands. On weekends, prepare to wait in line for a while. Open Monday to Wednesday 6pm to 1am, Thursday 6pm to 2am, Friday 6pm to 3am, Saturday 2pm to 3am, and Sunday 3pm to midnight. 20 Kingly St., W1. © 020/7287-0514. www.aintnothinbut.co.uk. Cover £5 ($9.50). Free Sun–Wed, free Thurs before 9:30pm, free Fri–Sat before 8:30pm. Tube: Oxford Circus or Piccadilly Circus. From the Oxford Circus Tube stop, walk south on Regent St., turn left on Great Marlborough St., and then make a quick right on Kingly St.

COMEDY

The Comedy Store   This is London's showcase for both established and rising comic talent. Inspired by comedy clubs in the U.S., the club has given many comics their start, and today a number of them are established TV personalities. Even if their names are unfamiliar, you'll enjoy the spontaneity of live comedy before a British audience. Visitors must be 18 and older; dress is casual. Reserve through **Ticketmaster** (© 0870/060-2340); the club opens 1½ hours before each show. *Insider's Tip:* Go on Tuesday when the humor is more cutting-edge. Tuesday to Sunday, doors open at 6:30pm and the show starts at 8pm; on Friday and Saturday, an extra show starts at midnight (doors open at 11pm). 1A Oxendon St., off Piccadilly Circus, SW1. © 020/7344-0234. www.thecomedystore.co.uk. Cover £16 ($30). Tube: Leicester Sq. or Piccadilly Circus.

JAZZ & FOLK

Bull's Head   This club has showcased live modern jazz every night of the week for more than 40 years. One of the oldest hostelries in the area, it was a 19th-century staging post where travelers on their way to Hampton Court could rest while coach horses were changed. Today the bar features jazz by musicians from all over the world. Since it's way off the tourist trail, it attracts mainly locals in a wide age group, all of whom appreciate good music. Live jazz plays on Sunday from 1 to 3pm and 8:30 to 10:30pm; Monday to Saturday, from 8:30 to 11pm. You can order lunch in the Pub or dinner in Nuay's Thai Bistro. The club is open Monday to Saturday from noon to midnight, and Sunday from noon to 10:30pm. 373 Lonsdale Rd., Barnes, SW13. © 020/8876-5241. www.thebullshead.com. Cover £6–£15 ($11–$29). Tube: Hammersmith, then bus no. 209 to Barnes Bridge, then retrace the path of the bus for some 91m (298 ft.) on foot; or take Weybridge train from Waterloo Station and get off at Barnes Bridge Station, then walk 5 min. to the club.

Cecil Sharpe House   CSH was the focal point of the folk revival in the 1960s, and it continues to treasure and nurture folk music and dance. You'll find a whole range of traditional music and dance here, with evenings devoted to, among others, Irish set dances, English barn dances (similar to American square dances), dances from Louisiana's Cajun country, and even the re-enactment of 18th-century quadrilles. Although many of the regular patrons of this bar and dance club know these arcane dances by heart, they're usually charitable towards quick-learning and agile newcomers who can pick up the steps and the beat quickly. Call to see what's happening on the nights you're in town. The box office is open Monday to Friday from 9:30am to 5:30pm. 2 Regent's Park Rd., NW1. © 020/7485-2206. Tickets £3–£10 ($5.70–$19). Tube: Northern Line to Camden Town.

100 Club   Although less plush and expensive than some jazz clubs, 100 Club is a serious contender on the music front, with presentations of some remarkably good jazz. Its cavalcade of bands includes the best British jazz musicians and some of their Yankee brethren. Rock, R&B, and blues are also on tap. Serious devotees of jazz from ages 20 to 45 show up here. Open Monday to Thursday and Sunday 7:30 to 11:30pm, Friday from noon to 3pm and 8:30pm to 2am, and Saturday from 7:30pm to 1am. *Note:* These hours are subject to change. 100 Oxford St., W1. © 020/7636-0933. www.the 100club.co.uk. Cover £18–£20 ($34–$38). Club members get a £1 ($1.90) discount on Sat nights. Tube: Tottenham Court Rd. or Oxford Circus.

Pizza Express   Don't let the name fool you: This restaurant/bar serves up some of the best jazz in London by mainstream artists, along with thin-crust Italian pizza. You'll find both local bands and visiting groups, often from the United States. The place draws an equal mix of Londoners and visitors in the 20s-to-40s age bracket. Although the club has been enlarged, it's still important to reserve ahead of time. The restaurant is open daily from 11:30am to midnight; jazz plays from 7:30pm to midnight. 10 Dean St., W1. © 020/7734-3220. www.pizzaexpresslive.com. Cover £15–£20 ($29–$38). Tube: Tottenham Court Rd.

Ronnie Scott's Jazz Club   Inquire about jazz in London, and people immediately think of Ronnie Scott's, the European vanguard for modern jazz. Only the best English and American combos, often fronted by top-notch vocalists, are booked here. The programs make for an entire evening of cool jazz. In the heart of Soho, Ronnie Scott's is a 10-minute walk from Piccadilly Circus along Shaftesbury Avenue. In the Main Room, you can watch the show from the bar or sit at a table, at which you can order dinner, while the Downstairs Bar is more intimate. This place is so well known that, along with the die-hard music fans, some of the world's most famous musicians show up here when they're in town. The club is open Monday to Saturday 6pm to 3am, and Sunday 6pm to midnight. Reservations are recommended. 47 Frith St., W1. © 020/7439-0747. www.ronniescotts.co.uk. Cover nonmembers £20–£26 ($38–$49), members £20 ($38). Tube: Leicester Sq. or Piccadilly Circus.

606 Club   Located in a discreet basement in Chelsea, this jazz supper club in the boondocks of Fulham presents live music nightly. Predominantly a venue for modern jazz, styles range from traditional to contemporary. Local musicians and some very big names play here, whether at planned gigs or informal jam sessions after they finish shows elsewhere in town. Because of license requirements, patrons can order alcohol only with food. Locals show up here along with a trendy crowd from more posh neighborhoods in London. Open Monday to Wednesday 7:30pm to 1am; Thursday to Saturday 8pm to 1:30am; selected Sundays noon to 4pm and 8pm. 90 Lots Rd., SW10. ℂ 020/7352-5953. www.606club.co.uk. Cover Mon–Thurs £8 ($15), Fri–Sat £10 ($19), Sun £9 ($17). Bus: 11, 19, 22, 31, 39, C1, or C3. Tube: Earl's Court.

ROCK & POP

The Bull & Gate   Outside central London, and smaller, cheaper, and often more animated and less touristy than many of its competitors, The Bull & Gate is the unofficial headquarters of London's pub rock scene. Indie and relatively unknown rock bands are served up in back-to-back handfuls at this somewhat battered Victorian pub. The place attracts a young crowd mainly in their 20s. If you like spilled beer, this is off-the-beaten-track London at its most authentic. Bands that have played here and later ascended to fame on Europe's club scene have included Madness, Blur, and Pulp. There's music nightly from 8pm to midnight. 389 Kentish Town Rd., NW5. ℂ 0201/8826-5000. www.bullandgate.co.uk. Cover from £5 ($9.50). Tube: Northern Line to Kentish Town.

Shepherd's Bush Empire   Located in an old BBC television theater with great acoustics, this is a major venue for big-name pop and rock stars. Announcements appear in the local press. There's a seating capacity of 2,000. The spot mostly attracts fans in their 20s. The box office is open Monday to Friday from noon to 4pm, but you can book through **Ticketweb** at ℂ **0870/771-2000** 24 hours. Shepherd's Bush Green, W12. ℂ 020/8354-3300. www.shepherds-bush-empire-co.uk. Ticket prices vary according to show. Tube: Hammersmith & City Line to Shepherd's Bush or Goldhawk Rd.

Sound   In the heart of London, this club is a three-story music venue, restaurant, and bar. The music venue books big acts, while the restaurant and bar have limited live music and a DJ until 11pm; after 11pm, the mood changes, the menu is simplified to include only bar snacks, and the site focuses much more heavily on live music and dancing. The music program is forever changing; call to see what's on at the time of your visit and to reserve tickets. Crowds and age levels can vary here depending on what act is featured. Reservations are recommended for dinner, but reservations after 11pm are not accepted. The box office is open Monday to Saturday 10am to 8pm. 1 Leicester Sq., W1. ℂ 020/7287-1010. Tickets £5–£15 ($9.50–$29). Tube: Leicester Sq.

4 Dance, Disco & Eclectic

Bar Rumba   Despite its location on Shaftesbury Avenue, this Latin bar and music club could be featured in a book of "Underground London." A hush-hush address, it leans toward radical jazz-fusion on some nights and phat funk on others. It boasts two full bars and a different musical theme every night. All the music here is live. On weeknights you have to be 18 or older; on Saturday and Sunday, nobody under 21 is allowed in. 36 Shaftesbury Ave., W1. ℂ 020/7287-6933. www.barrumba.co.uk. Cover £5–£10 ($9.50–$19). Free Sat before 10pm. Tube: Piccadilly Circus.

Cargo   This watering hole in ultra-trendy Hoxton draws a smart urban crowd from their expensive West End flats. Its habitués assure us it's the place to go for a "wicked time" and great live bands. If there are no bands on a particular night, then great DJs dominate the club. Music and dancing start at 6pm and the joint is jumping by 9:30

nightly. It's fun and funky, with two big arched rooms, fantastic acoustics, and a parade of videos. As for the patrons, the bartender characterized it just right: "We get the freaks and the normal people." Drinks are reasonably priced, as is the self-styled "street food." Open Monday to Thursday noon to 1am, Friday noon to 3am, Saturday 6pm to 3am, and Sunday 1pm to midnight. Kingsland Viaduct, 83 Rivington St., EC2. ℂ 020/7739-3440. www.cargo-london.com. Cover £5–£10 ($9.50–$19) after 10pm. Tube: Liverpool St.

The Cross   In the backwaters of King's Cross, this club has been hot since 1993. Hipsters come here for private parties thrown by Rough Trade Records or Red Or Dead, or to dance in the space's industrial-looking brick-lined vaults. Music runs the gamut from acid rock to Caribbean/African fusion to Jamaican soca. This place is shadowy, sweaty, raunchy, and sometimes down and dirty. Call to find out who's performing. Open Friday and Saturday from 10pm to 6am. The Arches, King's Cross Goods Yard, York Way, N1. ℂ 020/7837-0828. www.thecross.co.uk. Cover £8–£15 ($15–$29). Tube: King's Cross.

Cuba   This Spanish/Cuban bar-restaurant, which has a music club downstairs, features live acts from Spain, Cuba, Brazil, and the rest of Latin America. The crowd is equal parts restaurant diners, after-work drinkers, and dancers. Salsa classes are offered daily from 7:30 to 9:30pm from free to £9 ($17). Happy hour is daily 5:30 to 7:30pm. Open Monday to Saturday noon to 2am, and Sunday 5pm to midnight. 11–13 Kensington High St., W8. ℂ 020/7938-4137. www.fiestahavana.com/fiesta/cuba. Cover £5–£8 ($9.50–$15). Tube: High St. Kensington.

The End   This club is better than ever after its recent enlargement. Now you'll find a trio of large dance floors, along with four bars and a chill-out area. Speaker walls will blast you into orbit. The End is the best club in town for live house and garage music. It draws both straight and gay Londoners. "We can't tell the difference anymore," the club owner confessed, "and who cares anyway?" From its drinking fountain to its swanky toilets, the club is alluring. Dress to be seen—go glam. Some big names in London appear on the weekends to entertain. Open Monday and Wednesday 9pm to 3am, Tuesday 6pm to 3am, Thursday 8pm to 3am, Friday 6pm to 3:30am, Saturday 9pm to 3:30am, and Sunday 9pm to 1:30pm. 16A W. Central St., WC1. ℂ 020/7419-9199. www.endclub.com. Cover £4–£20 ($7.60–$38). Tube: Tottenham Court Rd.

Fabric   While other competitors have come and gone, Fabric has continued to draw crowds since opening in 1999. This is one of the most famous clubs in the increasingly trendy East London sector, and its main allure is that it has a license for 24-hour music and dancing from Thursday to Sunday night. It's said that when the owners power up the underfoot subwoofer, lights dim in London's East End. On some crazed nights, at least 2,500 young Londoners and international visitors crowd into this mammoth place. It has a trio of dance floors, bars wherever you look, unisex toilets, chill-out beds, and even a roof terrace. Live acts are presented every Friday, with DJs reigning on weekends. You'll hear house, garage, soca, reggae, and whatever else is on the cutting edge of London's underground music scene at the time. Open Thursday and Friday 9:30pm to 5am, and Saturday 10pm to 7am. 77A Charterhouse St., EC1. ℂ 020/7336-8898. www.fabriclondon.com. Cover £12–£15 ($23–$29). Tube: Farringdon.

Ministry of Sound   Removed from the city center, this club-of-the-hour remains hot, hot, hot. With a large bar and huge sound system, it blasts garage and house music for the energetic crowds that pack the two dance floors. If the music and lights in the rest of the club have gone to your head, you can chill in the lounge. *Note:* The cover charge is stiff, and bouncers decide who is cool enough to enter, so slip into your most glamorous club gear. Open Friday 10:30pm to 5am and Saturday 11pm to 7am. Student night is Tuesday 10pm to 4am. 103 Gaunt St., SE1. © 020/7740-8600. www.ministry ofsound.com. Cover £10–£25 ($19–$48). Tube: Northern Line to Elephant & Castle.

Notting Hill Arts Club   This is one of the hippest nighttime venues in London, with the action taking place in a no-frills basement in increasingly fashionable Notting Hill Gate. One habitué called it "the coolest night club on earth." To justify the name of the club, art exhibitions are sometimes staged here. Most of the clients are under 35, and they come from a wide range of backgrounds—from Madonna to Bob Marley wannabes. The music is eclectic, varying from night to night—jazz, salsa, hip-hop, indie, and so on. Open Monday to Friday from 6pm to 2am, Saturday 4pm to 2am, and Sunday 4pm to 1am. Bands perform Monday to Thursday, Saturday, and Sunday. 21 Notting Hill Gate, W11. © 020/7460-4459. www.nottinghillartsclub.com. Cover £5–£11 ($9.50–$21). Tube: Notting Hill Gate.

The Roxy   This is an eclectic club featuring more traditional recorded pop, rock, soul, and disco. Ambience wins out over decor. During the week, a social lounge atmosphere pervades; on the weekends, this place is pure dance club. Open Monday to Thursday from 5pm to 3am, Friday 5pm to 3:30am, and Saturday 9:30pm to 3:30am. 3 Rathbone Place, W1. © 020/7636-1598. Cover £3–£9 ($5.70–$17). Tube: Tottenham Court Rd.

Salsa   This lively bar/restaurant/club for Latin music aficionados mostly features bands from Central and South America. Dance lessons are available nightly between 7 and 7:15pm; live music starts at 9:30pm. Some of the best dancers in London strut their stuff here. Open Monday to Saturday from 5:30pm to 2am, and Sunday 6pm to 1am. 96 Charing Cross Rd., WC2. © 020/7379-3277. www.barsalsa.info. Cover Mon–Thurs £4 ($7.60) after 9pm; Fri–Sat £2–£10 ($3.80–$19); Sun £3–£4 ($5.70–$7.60). Tube: Leicester Sq. or Tottenham Court Rd.

Scala   This area of London is risky at night—so much so that the security staff at the club is happy to escort you to a taxi when you leave. But despite its sketchy surroundings, this is a hot, happening venue for young London. It's a converted former movie theater where DJs spin the latest music, and ramped balconies offer dancing on different tiers. The gigantic screen will blow your mind with scintillating visuals. There is often some form of live entertainment, including theme nights. One of these events is the Friday bash called Popstarz, at which extroverted performers wear campy outfits inspired by the rock stars of the 1980s. Music runs the range from garage to R&B to salsa. Wear anything except on Saturday night, when caps and sportswear are forbidden. Open Sunday to Thursday 8pm to 2am (although hours can vary), Friday 10pm to 4am, and Saturday 10pm to 6am. 275 Pentonville Rd., N1. © 020/7833-2022. www.scala-london.co.uk. Cover £9–£20 ($17–$38). Tube: King's Cross.

Smollensky's on the Strand   This is an American eatery and bar where you can dance from Thursday to Saturday nights. Sunday night features a special live jazz session. Meals average £30 ($57). Open Sunday to Thursday noon to 11:30pm and Friday and Saturday noon to 12:30am. 105 the Strand, WC2. © 020/7497-2101. www.smollenskys.com. Cover £5 ($9.50) on Sun, when they present big jazz bands. Tube: Charing Cross or Embankment.

Vibe Bar   As more and more of hip London heads east, bypassing even Clerkenwell for Hoxton, Vibe has been put on the map. The *Evening Standard* named it among the top five DJ bars in London. The paper compared it to an "expensively distressed pair of designer jeans." It's a nightspot operated by Truman Brewery. In summer the action overflows onto a courtyard. Patrons check their e-mail, lounge on comfortable couches, and listen to diverse music such as reggae, Latin, jazz, R&B, Northern Soul, African, or hip-hop. Hours are Sunday to Thursday 1:30 to 11:30pm and Friday and Saturday 5pm to 1am. 91 Brick Lane, E1. © 020/7426-0491. www.vibe-bar.co.uk. Cover £2–£5 ($3.80–$9.50) sometimes assessed after 6pm. Tube: Liverpool St.

Zoo Bar   The owners spent millions outfitting this club in the slickest, flashiest, and most psychedelic decor in London. If you're looking for a true Euro nightlife experience replete with gorgeous *au pairs* and trendy Europeans, this is it. Zoo Bar upstairs is a menagerie of mosaic animals beneath a glassed-in ceiling dome. Downstairs, the music is intrusive enough to make conversation futile. Clients range from 18 to 35; androgyny is the look of choice. Hours are Monday to Friday 4pm to 3am, Saturday 1pm to 3am, and Sunday 1pm to midnight. 13–18 Bear St., WC2. © 020/7839-4188. www.zoobar.co.uk. Cover £5–£10 ($9–$18) after 10pm. Tube: Leicester Sq.

THE GAY & LESBIAN SCENE

Time Out also carries listings on gay and lesbian clubs. Another good place for finding out what's hot and hip is **Prowler Soho,** 3–7 Brewer St., W1. (© 020/7734-4031; Tube: Piccadilly Circus), the largest gay lifestyle store in London. (You can also buy everything from jewelry to CDs and books, fashion, and sex toys.) It's open until 10pm Monday to Saturday. On the Web (www.gingerbeer.co.uk) is the best lesbian-centric site for what's going on in London; the magazine *G3* (www.g3magazine.co.uk) is also popular among lesbians.

Admiral Duncan   Gay men and their friends go here to drink, to have a good time, and to make a political statement. It was the site of a horrific 1999 bombing in which three people were killed. Within 6 weeks, the pub reopened its doors. We're happy to report that the bar is better than ever and now also attracts nongays showing their support. 54 Old Compton St., W1. © 020/7437-5300. No cover. Tube: Piccadilly Circus or Leicester Sq.

Bar Code   This is a very relaxed and friendly bar. Hosting everyone from skinheads to "pint-of-lager" types, it has much of a "local pub" atmosphere. On Tuesday the club presents "Comedy Camp," stand-up comedy night. The bar is fairly male dominated but does not object to women entering. Open Monday to Saturday from 4pm to 1am and Sunday 4 to 11pm. 3–4 Archer St., W1. © 020/7734-3342. www.bar-code.co.uk. £4 ($7.60) Fri–Sat after 10pm. Tube: Piccadilly Circus.

The Box   Adjacent to one of Covent Garden's best-known junctions, Seven Dials, this sophisticated Mediterranean-style bar attracts all kinds of men. In the afternoon, it is primarily a restaurant, serving meal-size salads, club sandwiches, and soups. Food service ends abruptly at 5:30pm, after which the place reveals its core: a cheerful, popular rendezvous for London's gay and counter-culture crowds. The Box considers itself a "summer bar," throwing open doors and windows to a cluster of outdoor tables at the slightest hint of sunshine. The bar is open Monday to Saturday 11am to 11pm and Sunday noon to 10:30pm. The cafe is open Monday to Saturday 11am to 5:30pm and Sunday noon to 6pm. 32–34 Monmouth St. (at Seven Dials), WC2. © 020/7240-5828. No cover. Tube: Leicester Sq.

Candy Bar   This is the most popular lesbian bar in London at the moment. It has an extremely mixed clientele, ranging from butch to femme and from young to old. There are a bar and a club downstairs. Design is simple, with bright colors and lots of mirrors upstairs and darker, more flirtatious decor downstairs. Men are welcome as long as a woman escorts them. Open Monday to Thursday 5 to 11:30pm, Friday and Saturday 5pm to 2am, and Sunday 5 to 11pm. 4 Carlisle St., W1. © 020/7494-4041. www.thecandybar.co.uk. Cover Fri £5 ($9.50), Sat £6 ($11). Tube: Tottenham Court Rd.

The Chocolate Lounge   This is a private members' club for women and men. It offers one of the most activity-filled agendas in London, everything from poetry nights to drag cabaret, even a singles night and a chocolate fountain. A day's membership costs £2 ($3.80). Open Tuesday to Thursday 5pm to midnight, Friday 7pm to 2am, and Saturday 7pm to 4am. 146–148 Newington Butts, SE11. © 020/7735-5306. www.thechocolateloungelondon.com. Tube: Kensington.

The Edge   Few bars in London can rival the tolerance, humor, and sexual sophistication found here. The first two floors are done up with decorations that, like an English garden, change with the seasons. Dance music can be found on the crowded, high-energy lower floors. Three menus are featured: a funky daytime menu, a cafe menu, and a late-night menu. Dancers hit the floors starting around 7:30pm. Clientele ranges from flamboyantly gay to hetero pub-crawlers. One downside: A reader claims the bartenders water the drinks. Open Monday to Saturday noon to 1am and Sunday 2 to 11:30pm. 11 Soho Sq., W1. © 020/7439-1313. No cover. Tube: Tottenham Court Rd.

First Out Café Bar   First Out prides itself on being London's first (est. 1986) all-gay coffee shop. Set in a 19th-century building whose wood panels have been painted the colors of the gay-liberation rainbow, the bar and cafe are not particularly cruisy. Cappuccino and whiskey are the preferred libations, and an exclusively vegetarian menu includes curry dishes, potted pies in filo pastries, and salads. Don't expect a raucous atmosphere—some clients come here with their grandmothers. Look for the bulletin board with leaflets and business cards of gay and gay-friendly entrepreneurs. Open Monday to Saturday 10am to 11pm and Sunday 11am to 10:30pm. 52 St. Giles High St., W1. © 020/7240-8042. No cover. Tube: Tottenham Court Rd.

Friendly Society   This is a Soho hot spot that bustles with young gay life, and there's even a rumor that Mrs. Guy Ritchie (Madonna) made a secret appearance here heavily disguised. "As what?" we asked, but no one knew. The action takes place in the basement of the building, which one patron called a "space-age lair." Perhaps the white-leather pod seating creates that aura. Come here for the drinks and the company—it's very cruisy. *Time Out London* describes the spot as a "gay, women-friendly venue with an alternative underground feel." Open Monday to Friday 4 to 11pm, Saturday 2 to 11pm, and Sunday 2 to 10:30pm. In the basement of 79 Wardour St. (entrance is via a side street named Tisbury Court), W1. © 020/7434-3805. No cover. Tube: Piccadilly Circus.

G.A.Y.   Name notwithstanding, the clientele here is mixed, and on a Saturday night this could be the most rollicking club in London. You may not find love here, but you could discover a partner for the evening. Patrons have been known to strip down to their briefs or shorts. A mammoth place, this club draws a young crowd to dance beneath its mirrored disco balls. Open Monday, Thursday, Friday 11pm to 4am and Saturday 10:30pm to 5am. London Astoria, 157 Charing Cross Rd., WC2. www.g-a-y.co.uk. Cover £10–£13 ($19–$25). Tube: Tottenham Court Rd.

Glass Bar   This is a classy, friendly lesbian bar near Euston Station, run by a tall Afro-Caribbean woman named Elaine. You'll find good drinks with women of all types, plus live music, comedy, reading groups, films, and even a singles night. Technically, this is a private club, but women visitors are granted membership for £1

($1.90) daily. Open only Monday to Friday from 5pm to 11:30pm, when a £1 ($1.90) cover is imposed. West Lodge, Euston Gardens, 190 Euston Rd., NW1. ℂ 020/7387-6184. www.glassbar.ndo.co.uk. Tube: Euston Station.

Heaven   This club, housed in the vaulted cellars of Charing Cross Railway Station, is a London landmark. Heaven is one of the biggest and best-established gay venues in Britain. Painted black and reminiscent of an air-raid shelter, the club is divided into at least four areas, connected by a labyrinth of catwalk stairs and hallways. Each room offers a different type of music, from hip-hop to rock. Heaven also has theme nights, which are frequented, at different times, by gays, lesbians, or a mostly heterosexual crowd. Thursday in particular seems open to anything, but on Saturday it's gays only. Call before you go. Open Monday 10pm to 6:30am, Wednesday 10:30pm to 3am, Friday 11pm to 6am, and Saturday 10:30pm to 5am. The Arches, Villiers, and Craven sts., WC2. ℂ 020/7930-2020. www.heaven-london.com. Cover £5–£15 ($9.50–$29). Tube: Charing Cross or Embankment.

Ku Bar   The Happy Hour here lasts from noon to 9pm, and the bartenders assure us that their watering hole attracts "the tastiest men in London." Those bartenders serve up some of the tastiest drinks, including peach, melon, apple, lemon, and butterscotch schnapps. On Sunday the staff hosts a gay tea dance. Come here for a fab time, to throw a bash, and to cruise. 30 Lisle St., WC2. ℂ 020/7437-4303. www.ku-bar.co.uk. No cover. Tube: Leicester Sq.

Shadow Lounge   This is the current hot spot for gay men in Soho. "Our male patrons are fresh and sexy," a seasoned bartender told us. Shadow Lounge is in the vanguard of gay life in London, which, as the millennium deepens, is showing a tendency to shift from gargantuan dance palaces like Heaven to more intimate rendezvous points. Young men, who look like the cast of the British version of "Queer as Folk," meet here at 9pm for drinks. Some return after dinner to dance to raucous house music. Open Monday and Wednesday 10pm to 3am; Tuesday, Thursday and Saturday 9pm to 3am; and Friday 9pm to 4am. 5 Brewer St., W1. ℂ 020/7287-7988. www. theshadowlounge.co.uk. Cover £3–£10 ($5.70–$19). Tube: Piccadilly Circus.

5 The Best of London's Pubs: The World's Greatest Pub Crawl

Dropping into the local pub for a pint of real ale or bitter is the best way to soak up the character of the different villages that make up London. You'll hear local accents and slang, and see firsthand how far removed upper-crust Kensington is from blue-collar Wapping. Catch the local gossip or football talk—and, of course, enjoy some of the finest ales, stouts, ciders, and malt whiskies in the world.

Anchor   You can follow in the footsteps of Shakespeare and Dickens by quenching your thirst at this pub. If literary heroes are not your bag, then perhaps you'll enjoy knowing that Tom Cruise had a pint or two here during the filming of *Mission Impossible*. Rebuilt in the mid–18th century to replace an earlier pub that managed to withstand the Great Fire of 1666, the rooms are worn and comfortable. You can choose from Scottish and Newcastle brews on tap. 34 Park St., SE1. ℂ 020/7407-1577. Tube: Jubilee Line to London Bridge.

Black Friar   The Black Friar will transport you to the Edwardian era. The wedge-shape pub is swimming in marble and bronze Art Nouveau, featuring bas-reliefs of monks, a low-vaulted mosaic ceiling, and seating recesses carved out of gold marble.

World's Greatest Pub Crawl

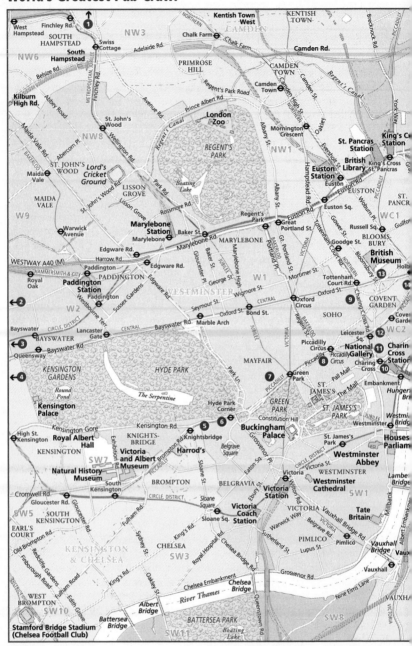

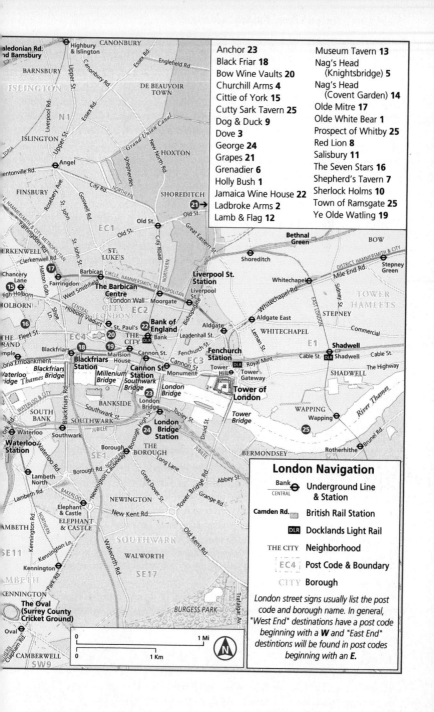

Anchor **23**
Black Friar **18**
Bow Wine Vaults **20**
Churchill Arms **4**
Cittie of York **15**
Cutty Sark Tavern **25**
Dog & Duck **9**
Dove **3**
George **24**
Grapes **21**
Grenadier **6**
Holly Bush **1**
Jamaica Wine House **22**
Lamb & Flag **12**

Museum Tavern **13**
Nag's Head
(Knightsbridge) **5**
Nag's Head
(Covent Garden) **14**
Olde Mitre **17**
Olde White Bear **1**
Prospect of Whitby **25**
Red Lion **8**
Salisbury **11**
The Seven Stars **16**
Shepherd's Tavern **7**
Sherlock Holms **10**
Town of Ramsgate **25**
Ye Olde Watling **19**

London Navigation

Bank **Underground Line & Station**
CENTRAL

Camden Rd. **British Rail Station**

DLR **Docklands Light Rail**

THE CITY **Neighborhood**

EC4 **Post Code & Boundary**

CITY **Borough**

*London street signs usually list the post code and borough name. In general, "West End" destinations have a post code beginning with a **W** and "East End" destinations will be found in post codes beginning with an **E**.*

0 _____ 1 Mi
0 _____ 1 Km

N

It's popular with the City's after-work crowd, and it features Adams, London Pride, and Speckled Hen on tap. 174 Queen Victoria St., EC4. ℭ 020/7236-5474. Tube: Blackfriars.

Bow Wine Vaults   Bow Wine Vaults has existed since long before the wine-bar craze began in the 1970s. One of the most famous in London, the bar attracts cost-conscious diners and drinkers to its vaulted cellars for such traditional fare as deep-fried Camembert, lobster ravioli, and a mixed grill, along with fish. The cocktail bar is popular with City employees after work (open weekdays 11:30am–11pm). More elegant meals, served in the street-level dining room, include Thai green mussels in curry sauce, escalope of veal Milanese garnished with pasta, and haddock Monte Carlo. Wines from around the world are available; the last time we were there, the wine of the day was a Chilean chardonnay. 10 Bow Churchyard, EC4. ℭ 020/7248-1121. Tube: Mansion House, Bank, or St. Paul's.

Churchill Arms   Stop here for a nod to the Empire's end. Loaded with Churchill memorabilia, the pub hosts a week of celebration leading up to Churchill's birthday on November 30. Show up at the right time and you may be recruited to help decorate the place—visitors are often welcomed like regulars. Decorations and festivities are featured for Halloween, Christmas, and St. Paddy's Day, as well as for Churchill's birthday, helping to create the homiest village pub atmosphere you're likely to find in London. 119 Kensington Church St., W8. ℭ 020/7727-4242. Tube: Notting Hill Gate or High St. Kensington.

Cittie of Yorke   This pub boasts the longest bar in all of Britain, rafters ascending to the heavens, and a long row of immense wine vats, all of which give it the air of a great medieval hall—appropriate because a pub has existed at this location since 1430. Samuel Smith's is on tap. 22 High Holborn, WC1. ℭ 020/7242-7670. Tube: Holborn or Chancery Lane.

Cutty Sark Tavern   Retreat here for great antiquarian ambience inside a 16th-century dwelling with flagstones, barrel tables, open fires, and rough-hewn brick walls. The pub has such an Old London feel that you may find yourself seeing Dickensian riffraff after a few pints of Timothy Taylor or Shepherd Neame. Ballast Quay, off Lassell St., SE10. ℭ 020/8858-3146. Train: Docklands Light Railway to Cutty Sark.

Dog & Duck   This snug little joint, a Soho landmark, is the most intimate pub in London. A former patron was the author George Orwell, who came here to celebrate his sales of *Animal Farm* in the United States. A wide mix of ages and persuasions flock here, usually chatting amiably. Publicans here stock an interesting assortment of English beers, including Tetleys, Fuller London, and Timothy Taylor Landlord. In autumn, customers will ask for Addlestone's Cider. A lot of patrons head to Ronnie Scott's Jazz Club, which is close by, after having a few pints here. The cozy upstairs bar is also open. 18 Bateman St. (corner of Frith St.), W1. ℭ 020/7494-0697. Tube: Tottenham Court Rd. or Leicester Sq.

The Dove   You can relax by the Thames at the place where James Thomson composed "Rule Britannia" and part of his lesser-known "The Seasons." To toast Britannia, you can hoist a Fullers London Pride or ESB. 19 Upper Mall, W6. ℭ 020/8748-9474. Tube: District Line to Ravenscourt Park.

George   The existing structure was built in 1877 to replace the original pub, which was destroyed in the Great Fire of 1666. That pub's accolades date to 1598, when it was reviewed as a "faire inn for the receipt of travelers." The present pub was built in the typical "traditional Victorian" style, with stripped oak floors, paneled walls, a curved bar counter, brass ceiling lights, and windows with etched and cut glass. Three huge mirrors decorate the walls. It's still a great place to enjoy Flowers Original, Boddingtons, and London Pride Abbot on tap. 77 Borough High St., SE1. © 020/7407-2056. Tube: Northern Line to London Bridge or Borough.

Grapes This rustic 16th-century pub served as Dickens's inspiration for "Six Jolly Fellowship Porters" in *Our Mutual Friend*. Whistler came here, too, inspired by the view of the river. Taps include Friary Meux, Pedigree, and Tetleys; there are several single-malt whiskies to choose from as well. 76 Narrow St., E14. © 020/7987-4396. Tube: Docks Light Railway, West Ferry.

Grenadier Tucked away in a mews, the Grenadier is one of London's reputedly haunted pubs, the ghost here being an 18th-century British soldier. Aside from the poltergeist, the basement houses the original bar and skittles alley used by the Duke of Wellington's officers. The scarlet front door of the one-time officers' mess is guarded by a scarlet sentry box and shaded by a vine. The bar is nearly always crowded. Lunch and dinner are offered daily—even on Sunday, when it's a tradition to drink Bloody Marys (made from a well-guarded recipe) here. In the stalls along the side, you can order good-tasting fare based on seasonal ingredients. Well-prepared dishes include pork Grenadier, Beef Wellington, and a chicken-and-Stilton roulade. Snacks like fish and chips are available at the bar. 18 Wilton Row, SW1. © 020/7235-3074. Tube: Hyde Park Corner.

Holly Bush The Holly Bush is the real thing: authentic Edwardian gas lamps, open fires, private booths, and a tap selection of Fuller's London Pride, Adnams, and Harveys. 22 Holly Mount, NW3. © 020/7435-2892. www.hollybushpub.com. Tube: Northern Line to Hampstead.

Jamaica Wine House This was one of the first coffeehouses in England and, reputedly, the Western world. For years, merchants and sea captains came here to transact deals over rum and coffee. Nowadays, the two-level house dispenses coffee, beer, ale, lager, and fine wines, among them a variety of ports. The oak-paneled bar is on the street level and attracts crowds of investment bankers. You can order standard but filling dishes such as a ploughman's lunch and toasted sandwiches. 12 St. Michael's Alley, off Cornhill, EC3. © 020/7929-6972. Tube: Bank.

Ladbroke Arms Previously honored as London's "Dining Pub of the Year," Ladbroke Arms is that rare pub known for its food. A changing menu includes roast cod filet with lentils and salsa verde, and aged bone-in rib steak with mustard, peppercorn, and herb and garlic butter. With background jazz and rotating art prints, the place strays from the traditional pub environment. This place makes for a pleasant stop and a good meal. The excellent Eldridge Pope Royal is on tap, as well as John Smiths, Courage Directors, and several malt whiskies. 54 Ladbroke Rd., W11. © 020/7727-6648. Tube: Notting Hill Gate.

Lamb & Flag Dickens once frequented this pub, and the room has changed little from the days when he prowled the neighborhood. The pub has an amazing and scandalous history. Poet and author Dryden was almost killed by a band of thugs outside its doors in December 1679, and the pub gained the nickname the "Bucket of Blood" during the Regency era (1811–20) because of the bare-knuckled prizefights here. Tap beers include Courage Best and Directors, Old Speckled Hen, John Smiths, and Wadworths 6X. 33 Rose St., off Garrick St., WC2. © 020/7497-9504. Tube: Leicester Sq.

Museum Tavern Across the street from the British Museum, this pub (ca. 1703) retains most of its antique trappings: velvet, oak paneling, and cut glass. It lies right in the center of the University of London area and is popular with writers, publishers, and researchers from the museum. Supposedly, Karl Marx wrote while dining here. Traditional English food is served: shepherd's pie, sausages cooked in English cider, turkey-and-ham pie, ploughman's lunch, and salads. Several English ales, cold lagers, cider, Guinness, wines, and spirits are available. Food and coffee are served all day. The pub gets crowded at lunchtime. 49 Great Russell St., WC1. © 020/7242-8987. Tube: Holborn or Tottenham Court Rd.

Nag's Head This Nag's Head (not to be confused with the more renowned one at 10 James St.; see below) is on a back street a short walk from the Berkeley Hotel. Said to be the smallest pub in London, it was previously a jail dating from 1780—it was sold for £12 and 6p in 1921. Have a drink up front or wander to the tiny bar in the rear. For food, you might enjoy "real ale sausage" (made with pork and ale), shepherd's pie, or the quiche of the day, all served by the welcoming staff. A cosmopolitan clientele—newspaper people, musicians, and travelers—patronizes this warm, cozy pub. It touts itself as an "independent," or able to serve any "real ale" they choose because of their lack of affiliation. 53 Kinnerton St., SW1. © 020/7235-1135. Tube: Hyde Park.

Nag's Head This Nag's Head is one of London's most famous Edwardian pubs. In days of yore, patrons had to make their way through a fruit-and-flower market to drink here. Today, the pub is popular with young people. The draft Guinness is very good. Lunch (served noon–4pm) is typical pub grub: sandwiches, salads, pork cooked in cider, and garlic prawns. Snacks are available all afternoon. 10 James St., WC2. © 020/ 7836-4678. Tube: Covent Garden.

Olde Mitre Olde Mitre is the name of a working-class inn built here in 1547, when the Bishops of Ely controlled the district. It's a small pub with an odd assortment of customers. Adnams and Tetley are on tap. Ely Court, EC1. © 020/7405-4751. Tube: Chancery Lane.

Olde White Bear This is a friendly place, hosting many regulars, that's decorated with Victorian prints, cartoons, and furnishings. Tap offerings include Adnams and Youngs Bitter. Well Rd., NW31. © 020/7435-3758. Tube: Hampstead.

Prospect of Whitby One of London's most historic pubs, Prospect was founded in the days of the Tudors, taking its name from a coal barge that made trips between Yorkshire and London. Come here for a tot, a noggin, or whatever it is you drink, and soak up the atmosphere. The pub has got quite a pedigree. Dickens and diarist Samuel Pepys used to drop in, and Turner spent weeks at a time here studying views of the Thames. In the 17th century, the notorious Hanging Judge Jeffreys used to get drunk here while overseeing hangings at the adjoining Execution Dock. Tables in the courtyard look out over river views. You can order a Morlands Old Speckled Hen from a hand-pump or a malt whisky. 57 Wapping Wall, E1. © 020/7481-1095. Tube: Wapping.

Red Lion This Victorian pub, with its early-1900s decorations and 150-year-old mirrors, has been compared to Manet's painting *A Bar at the Folies-Bergère* (on display at the Courtauld Gallery). You can order premade sandwiches, and on Saturday, homemade fish and chips are served. Wash down your meal with Ind Coope's fine ales or the house's special beer, Burton's, a brew made of spring water from the Midlands town of Burton-on-Trent. 2 Duke of York St. (off Jermyn St.), SW1. © 020/7321-0782. Tube: Piccadilly Circus.

Salisbury   An original gin palace, Salisbury's cut-glass mirrors reflect the faces of English stage stars (and hopefuls) sitting around the curved buffet-style bar. A less prominent place to dine is the old-fashioned wall banquette with its copper-topped tables and Art Nouveau decor. The pub's specialties—home-cooked pies set out in a buffet cabinet with salads, and fish and chips—are quite good and inexpensive. 90 St. Martin's Lane, WC2. ✆ 020/7836-5863. Tube: Leicester Sq.

The Seven Stars   This tranquil little pub facing the back of the Royal Courts of Justice dates back to 1602 and is now run by Roxy Beaujolais, author of the pub cookbook *Home From the Inn Contented,* whose former pub was voted the Soho Society's Pub of the Year. Within the ancient charm of two narrow rooms that are listed landmarks, drinking in Queer Street (as Carey St. was once called because of the bankruptcy courts) is pleasant. One can linger over pub food and real ales behind Irish-linen lace curtains with litigants, barristers, reporters, and pit musicians from West End shows. Then try to navigate to the lavatories up some comically narrow Elizabethan stairs. In mild weather, the law courts' stone balustrade under the trees provides customers with a long bar and beer garden. 53 Carey St., WC2. ✆ 020/7242-8521. Tube: Chancery Lane or Temple.

Shepherd's Tavern   One of the focal points of the all-pedestrian shopping zone of Shepherd's Market, this pub occupies an 18th-century town house amid a warren of narrow, cobble-covered streets behind Park Lane. The street-level bar is cramped but congenial. Many of the regulars recall this tavern's popularity with the pilots of the Battle of Britain. Bar snacks include simple plates of shepherd's pie, and fish and chips. More formal dining is available upstairs in the cozy, cedar-lined Georgian-style restaurant. The classic British menu probably hasn't changed much since the 1950s, and you can always get honey roasted ham or roast beef with Yorkshire pudding. 50 Hertford St., W1. ✆ 020/7499-3017. Tube: Green Park.

Sherlock Holmes   The Sherlock Holmes was the gathering spot for the Baker Street Irregulars, a once-mighty clan of mystery lovers who met to honor the genius of Sir Arthur Conan Doyle's famous fictional character. Upstairs, you'll find a re-creation of the living room at 221B Baker St. and such "Holmesiana" as the serpent from *The Speckled Band* and a faux beast's head from *The Hound of the Baskervilles.* In the upstairs dining room, you can order complete meals with wine. Try "Copper Beeches" (grilled chicken breasts with lemon and herbs), and then select dessert from the trolley. Downstairs is mainly for drinking, but there's also a good snack bar with cold meats, salads, cheeses, and wine and ales sold by the glass. 10 Northumberland St., WC1. ✆ 020/7930-2644. www.sherlockholmespub.com. Tube: Charing Cross or Embankment.

Town of Ramsgate   At this old-world pub, overlooking King Edward's Stairs and the Thames, you can enjoy Youngs Billing and Fullers London Pride on tap. 62 Wapping High St., E1. ✆ 020/7481-8000. Tube: East London Line to Wapping.

Ye Olde Watling   Ye Olde Watling was rebuilt after the Great Fire of 1666. On the ground level is a mellow pub. Upstairs is an intimate restaurant where, sitting at trestle tables under oak beams, you can dine on simple English main dishes for lunch. The menu varies daily, with such reliable standbys as fish and chips, lasagna, fish cakes, and usually a vegetarian dish. All are served with two vegetables or salad, plus rice or potatoes. 29 Watling St., EC4. ✆ 020/7653-9971. Tube: Mansion House.

6 Bars & Cocktail Lounges

American Bar   The bartender in this sophisticated gathering place, drawing a hot crowd, is known for his special concoctions, including "Savoy Spirit" and "Racing Lady," as well as what is reputedly the best martini in town. Monday to Thursday evenings, jazz piano is featured from 7pm to midnight, and on Friday and Saturday from 7pm to 1am. It's also open on Sunday 10am to 10:30pm. Located near many West End theaters, this spot is ideal for a pre- or post-theater drink. Dress is smart casual: no jeans, sneakers, or T-shirts. In the Savoy, the Strand, WC2. © 020/7836-4343. Tube: Charing Cross, Covent Garden, or Embankment.

Annex 3   On the fringe of Soho and in spite of its kitschy decor, this is one of the hottest bars in London. Its decor has been compared to a psychedelic Christmas show, but its cocktail menu is among the finest in town. Some of the concoctions are based on recipes served in the West Indies in the 1800s. Fortunately, "Millionaire Cocktail," one of the bartender's specialties, doesn't cost that. 6 Little Portland St., W1. © 020/7631-0700. Tube: Oxford Circus.

Beach Blanket Babylon   Go here if you're looking for a hot singles bar that attracts a crowd in their 20s and 30s. This Portobello joint is very cruisy. The decor is a bit wacky, no doubt designed by an aspiring Salvador Dalí who decided to make it a fairy-tale grotto (or was he going for a medieval dungeon look?). It's close to the Portobello Market. Friday and Saturday nights are the hot, crowded times for bacchanalian revelry. 45 Ledbury Rd., W11. © 020/7229-2907. Tube: Notting Hill Gate.

Cantaloupe   This bustling pub and restaurant is hailed as the bar that jump-started the increasingly fashionable Shoreditch scene. Businesspeople commuting from their jobs in the City mix with East End trendoids in the early evening at what has been called a "gastro pub/pre-club bar." Wooden tables and benches are found up front, although the Red Lounge is more comfortable, as patrons of various ages lounge on Chesterfield chairs. The urban beat is courtesy of the house DJ. The restaurant and *tapas* menus are first rate. 35–42 Charlotte Rd., EC2. © 020/7613-4411. Tube: Old St.

Claridge's Macanudo Fumoir   The most stylish and luxurious venue for cigar aficionados is sheltered at London's poshest address, Claridge's Hotel in Mayfair. Both sumptuous and moody, this eggplant-colored, leather-clad bar seats only 17. It features the largest selection of Macanudo cigars in the country, plus more than 20 different Cuban cigars. Along with your smoke, you can enjoy London's most revered selection of cognacs, armagnacs, tequilas, and ports. At Brook St., W1. © 020/7629-8860. Tube: Bond St.

The Library   One of London's poshest drinking retreats, this deluxe bar boasts high ceilings, leather Chesterfields, respectable oil paintings, and grand windows. Its collection of ancient cognacs and rare cigars is unparalleled in London. In the Lanesborough Hotel, 1 Lanesborough Place, SW1. © 020/7259-5599. Tube: Hyde Park Corner.

The Lobby Bar & The Axis Bar   These bars are found in one of London's best deluxe hotels. We advise that you check out the dramatic visuals of both bars before selecting your preferred nesting place. The Lobby Bar occupies what was built in 1907 as the grand, high-ceilinged reception area for one of London's premier newspapers. If the Lobby Bar setting doesn't appeal, take a look at the travertine, hardwood, and leather-sheathed bar in the Axis restaurant. Many fashionistas under 40 frequent this spot. The Lobby Bar is open Monday to Saturday 8am to midnight, Sunday 9am to 10:30pm; the Axis bar is open Monday through Saturday from 5:45 to 11pm. In the Hotel One Aldwych, 1 Aldwych, WC2. ℂ 020/7300-1000. Tube: Covent Garden.

The Mandarin Bar   No other bar in London showcases the art of the cocktail as beautifully as this one, attracting a 40-plus crowd. Created by design-industry super-star Adam Tihany around a geometric theme of artfully backlit glass, it provides the kind of cool, hip, confidently prosperous venue where men look attractive, women look fantastic, and cocktails are sublime. Drinks are prepared without fuss behind frosted-glass panels, in a style akin to a holy rite at a pagan temple, and are then pre-sented with charm. There's live music daily 9pm until closing and a leather-uphol-stered area off to the side, with a state-of-the-art air-filtration system, for cigar smokers and their friends. In the Mandarin Oriental Hyde Park Hotel, 66 Knightsbridge, SW1. Cover £5 ($9.50) after 10:30pm. ℂ 020/7235-2000. Tube: Knightsbridge.

Match EC1   This epicenter for the fashionable 20s-to-30s set in London has put the *P* in partying in the once-staid Clerkenwell district. Drinkers sit on elegant sofas or retreat to one of the cozy booths for a late snack. The bar claims to be the home of the Cosmopolitan cocktail, which swept across the drinking establishments of New York. The bartenders make some of the best drinks in London but warn you "there is no such thing as a chocolate martini." 45–47 Clerkenwell Rd., EC1. ℂ 020/7250-4002. Tube: Farringdon.

The Met Bar   Very much the place to be seen, this has become one of the hottest bars in London. Mix with the elite of the fashion, TV, and music worlds. A lot of American celebrities, from Demi Moore to Courtney Cox, have been seen here sip-ping on a martini. Despite the caliber of the clientele, the bar has managed to main-tain a relaxed and unpretentious atmosphere. In the Metropolitan Hotel, 19 Old Park Lane, W1. ℂ 020/7447-1000. Members and hotel guests only. Tube: Hyde Park Corner.

The Phoenix Artist Club   What's something so old it's new again? This is where Laurence Olivier made his stage debut in 1930, although he couldn't stop giggling even though the play was a drama. Live music is featured, but it's the hearty welcome, the good beer, and the friendly patrons from 20 to 50 who make this rediscovered theater bar worth a detour. It's open to the general public from 5 to 8pm only—it's members only after 8pm. 1 Phoenix St., WC2. ℂ 020/7836-1077. Tube: Tottenham Court Rd.

11

Side Trips from London

You could spend the best part of a year—or a lifetime—exploring London, without risking boredom or repetition. But there's much more to England than just London. We advise you to tear yourself away from Big Ben for at least a day or two to explore some of the easily accessible and wonderfully memorable spots that surround the city.

1 Windsor & Eton ⟨★⟩

34km (21 miles) W of London

Windsor—the site of England's best-known and greatest castle and its most famous boys' school, Eton—would be a captivating Thames-side town to visit even if it were not associated with the royal Windsors.

Though a disastrous fire raged through the building in 1992, things are on the mend at Windsor Castle. But not without controversy—some of the new designs being unveiled have been called "Gothic shockers" and "ghastly." If you visit, you can decide for yourself. In summer it's overrun with tourists, which tends to obscure its charm, so plan your visit for spring or fall, if possible.

ESSENTIALS

GETTING THERE More than a dozen trains per day make the 30-minute trip from Waterloo or Paddington Station in London (you'll have to transfer at Slough to the Slough–Windsor shuttle train). The cost is £7.70 ($14) round-trip. Call ℂ **0845/ 748-4950** or visit www.networkrail.co.uk for more information.

Green Line coaches (ℂ **0870/608-7261;** www.greenline.co.uk) nos. 700 and 702 from Hyde Park Corner in London take about 1½ hours, depending on the day of the week. A same-day round-trip costs between £8.20 and £10 ($15–$18) depending on the time of the day and week. The bus drops you near the parish church, across the street from the castle. Buses also depart from Victoria station, Colonnades, stop 1.

If you're driving from London, take the M4 west.

VISITOR INFORMATION A **Tourist Information Centre** is located across from Windsor Castle at 24 High St. (ℂ **01753/743900;** www.windsor.gov.uk). It is open Monday to Friday 10am to 4pm, Saturday 10am to 5pm, and Sunday 11am to 4pm. It also books walking tours for the Oxford guild of guides.

CASTLE HILL SIGHTS

Jubilee Gardens To celebrate Queen Elizabeth's Jubilee, the .8-hectare (2-acre) Jubilee Gardens were created inside the castle's main entrance. Filled with trees, roses, and flowering shrubs, they were designed by Tom Stuart-Smith, a Chelsea Flower

Side Trips from London

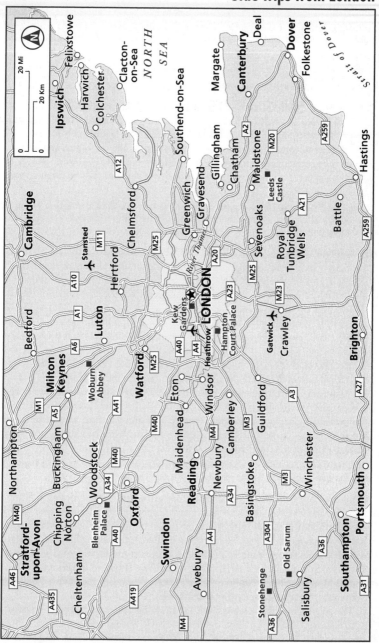

show gold medalist. The gardens are the first to have been established at Windsor Castle since the days of George IV in the 1820s. They extend from the main gates of Windsor to St. George's Gate on Castle Hill. Color is provided by broad swaths of woodland perennials. White rambling roses clothing the old stone walls are particularly romantic.

Same hours and admission as for castle; www.jubileewalkway.com.

Queen Mary's Dolls' House
A palace in perfect miniature, the Dolls' House was given to Queen Mary in 1923 as a gift by members of the royal family, including the king. The house, designed by Sir Edwin Lutyens, was created on a scale of 1:12. It took 3 years to complete and involved the work of 1,500 tradesmen and artists. It is a miniature masterpiece; each room is exquisitely furnished and every item is made exactly to scale. Working elevators stop on every floor, and there is running water in all five bathrooms.

Castle Hill. ℂ 01753/831118 for recorded information. Admission is included in entrance to Windsor Castle. Mar–Oct daily 9:45am–4pm; Nov–Feb daily 9:45am–4:15pm. As with Windsor Castle, it's best to call ahead to confirm opening times.

St. George's Chapel ✹✹✹
A gem of the Perpendicular style, this chapel shares the distinction with Westminster Abbey of being a pantheon of English monarchs (Victoria is a notable exception). The present St. George's was founded in the late 15th century by Edward IV on the site of the original Chapel of the Order of the Garter (Edward III, 1348). You first enter the nave, which contains the tomb of George V and Queen Mary, designed by Sir William Reid Dick. Off the nave in the Urswick Chapel, the Princess Charlotte memorial provides an ironic touch; if she had survived childbirth in 1817, she, and not her cousin Victoria, would have ruled the British Empire. In the aisle are tombs of George VI and Edward IV. The latest royal burial in this chapel was an urn containing the ashes of the late Princess Margaret. The Edward IV "Quire," with its imaginatively carved 15th-century choir stalls, evokes the pomp and pageantry of medieval days. In the center is a flat tomb, containing the vault of the beheaded Charles I, along with Henry VIII and his third wife, Jane Seymour. Finally, you may want to inspect the Prince Albert Memorial Chapel, reflecting the opulent tastes of the Victorian era.

Castle Hill. ℂ 01753/848888. www.stgeorges-windsor.org. Admission is included in entrance to Windsor Castle. Mon–Sat 10am–4:15pm, last admission 4pm. Closed Sun and for a few days in June and Dec.

Windsor Castle ✹✹✹
William the Conqueror first ordered a castle built on this location, and since his day it has been a fateful spot for English sovereigns: King John cooled his heels at Windsor while waiting to put his signature on the Magna Carta at nearby Runnymede; Charles I was imprisoned here before losing his head; Queen Bess did some renovations; Victoria mourned her beloved Albert, who died at the castle in 1861; the royal family rode out much of World War II behind its sheltering walls; and when Queen Elizabeth II is in residence, the royal standard flies. With 1,000 rooms, Windsor is the world's largest inhabited castle.

The apartments display many works of art, armor, three Verrio ceilings, and several 17th-century Gibbons carvings. Several works by Rubens adorn the King's Drawing Room and the relatively small King's Dressing Room contains a Dürer, along with Rembrandt's portrait of his mother and Van Dyck's triple portrait of Charles I. Of the apartments, the grand reception room, with its Gobelin tapestries, is the most spectacular.

George IV's elegant **Semi-State Chambers** 𝒢𝒢 are open only from the end of September until the end of March. They were created by the king in the 1820s as part of a series of Royal Apartments designed for his personal use. Seriously damaged in 1992, they have been returned to their former glory, with lovely antiques, paintings, and decorative objects. The Crimson Drawing room is evocative of the king's flamboyant taste with gilt, crimson silk damask hangings, and sumptuous artworks.

It is recommended that you take a free guided tour of the castle grounds, including the Jubilee Gardens. Guides are very well informed and capture the rich historical background of the castle.

In our opinion, the Windsor **changing of the guard** 𝒢 is a more exciting experience than the London exercise. The guard marches through the town whether the court is in residence or not, stopping traffic as it wheels into the castle to the tunes of a full regimental band; when the queen is not here, a drum-and-pipe band is mustered. From April to July, the ceremony takes place Monday to Saturday at 11:30am. In winter, the guard is changed every 48 hours Monday to Saturday. It's best to call ℂ **020/7766-7304** for a schedule.

Castle Hill. ℂ **01753/83118**. www.royalcollection.org.uk. Admission £14 ($27) adults, £13 ($25) students and seniors, £8 ($15) children 16 and under, £37 ($70) family of 4 (2 adults and 3 children under 17). Mar–Oct daily 9:45am–5:15pm; Nov–Feb daily 9:45am–4:15pm. Last admission 1 hr. before closing. Closed for periods in Apr, June, and Dec when the royal family is in residence.

Windsor Farm Shop 𝒢 *Finds*   Had any of the queen's jars of jam lately, or maybe her homemade pork pie or a bottle of her special brew? If not, head for this outlet, which sells items from her estates outside Windsor, including pheasants and partridges bagged at royal shoots, produce bearing the seal of the Royal Farms, and cream, yogurt, and milk from the two Royal Dairy farms. This shop is located in converted Victorian potting sheds on the edge of the royal estate. This latest make-a-pound scheme is the brainchild of Prince Philip. The meat counter is especially awesome, with its cooked hams and massive beef ribs. The steak-and-ale pies are very tasty. You can stock up on the queen's vittles and head for a picnic in the area. You can also purchase 15-year-old whisky from Balmoral Castle in Scotland.

Datchet Rd., Old Windsor. ℂ **01753/623800**. www.windsorfarmshop.co.uk. Free admission. Mon–Sat 9am–5pm, Sun 10am–5pm.

EXPLORING THE TOWN

Windsor is a largely Victorian town of brick buildings, with a few remnants of Georgian architecture. Antiques shops, silversmiths, and pubs line cobblestone Church and Market streets near the castle. Charles II's mistress, Nell Gwynne, supposedly lived on Church Street, which allowed her to be within shouting distance of her beau's chambers. After lunch or tea, you may want to stroll the 4.8km (3 miles) along the aptly named Long Walk.

On Sunday, in Windsor Great Park and at Ham Common, you may see Prince Charles playing polo and Prince Philip serving as umpire while the Queen watches. The park is also the site of Her Majesty's occasional equestrian jaunts. On Sunday she attends a little church near the Royal Lodge. Traditionally, she prefers to drive herself there, later returning to the castle for Sunday lunch.

EXPLORING ETON COLLEGE

From Windsor, Eton is an easy stroll across the Thames Bridge. Follow Eton High Street to the college.

Eton College (© 01753/671000; www.etoncollege.com) was founded by 18-year-old Henry VI in 1440. Some of England's greatest men, notably the duke of Wellington, have played on these fields. Twenty prime ministers were educated here, along with such literary figures as George Orwell, Aldous Huxley, Ian Fleming, and Percy Bysshe Shelley, who, during his years at Eton (1804–10), was called "Mad Shelley" or "Shelley the Atheist" by his fellow pupils. Prince William, second in line to the throne, is also a graduate. If it's open, take a look at the Perpendicular chapel, with its 15th-century paintings and reconstructed fan vaulting.

The history of Eton College since its inception in 1440 is depicted in the **Museum of Eton Life,** Eton College (© 01753/671000), located in vaulted wine cellars under College Hall, which were originally used as a storehouse by the college's masters. The displays, ranging from formal to extremely informal, include a turn-of-the-20th-century boy's room, schoolbooks, and canes used by senior boys to apply punishment they felt needful to their juniors.

Admission to the school and museum is £4 ($7.60) for adults and £3.20 ($6.10) for seniors and children under 15. You can also take guided tours for £5 ($9.50) adults or £4.20 ($8) seniors and children. Eton College is open from March 25 to April 20 and July 2 to September 5, daily 10:30am to 4:30pm; and April 21 to July 1 and September 6 to October 1, daily from 2 to 4:30pm. It's best to call in advance; Eton closes for special occasions. These dates vary every year depending on term and holiday dates.

ORGANIZED TOURS OF WINDSOR & ETON

BOAT TOURS   Tours depart from The Promenade, Barry Avenue, for a 35-minute round-trip ride to Boveney Lock. There's also a 35-minute round-trip tour from Runnymede on the *Lucy Fisher,* a replica of a Victorian paddle steamer. The boat passes Magna Carta Island (commemorating the signing of the document), among other places. Both tours cost £4.80 ($9.10) for adults and £2.40 ($4.55) for children. A 2-hour tour through the Boveney Lock and up past stately private riverside homes, the Bray Film Studios, Queens Eyot (a beautifully landscaped private island), and Monkey Island is £7.60 ($14) for adults or half-price for children. Longer tours are offered between Maidenhead and Hampton Court. The boats serve refreshments and have a well-stocked bar, and the decks are covered in case of an unexpected shower. Contact **French Brothers, Ltd.,** Clewer Boathouse, Clewer Court Road, Windsor (© 01753/851900; fax 01753/832303; www.boat-trips.co.uk).

HORSE-DRAWN CARRIAGE RIDES   You can take a horse-drawn carriage for a half-hour promenade up the sycamore-lined length of Windsor Castle's Long Walk. Carriages and drivers should be lined up beside the castle waiting for fares, which run from £29 ($55) for up to four passengers for a 30-minute ride, or £38 ($72) for a 1-hour ride. Call South Gates, © 01784/435983, or go to www.orchardpoyle.co.uk for more information.

WHERE TO DINE
WINDSOR & ETON

Antico *(Value* ITALIAN   Eton's finest Italian restaurant, Antico serves Mediterranean food in a formal setting. People have been dining here for 200 years, though not always from an Italian menu. On your way to the tiny bar, you pass a cold table, displaying hors d'oeuvres and cold meats. With many fish dishes, such as grilled fresh salmon, Dover sole, or sea bass, and a wide selection of pastas, the food is substantial and filling—a good value, though rarely exciting.

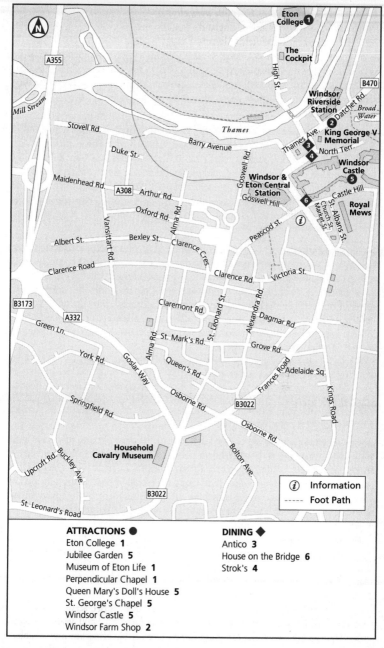

ATTRACTIONS ●
Eton College **1**
Jubilee Garden **5**
Museum of Eton Life **1**
Perpendicular Chapel **1**
Queen Mary's Doll's House **5**
St. George's Chapel **5**
Windsor Castle **5**
Windsor Farm Shop **2**

DINING ◆
Antico **3**
House on the Bridge **6**
Strok's **4**

42 High St., Eton. ℰ **01753/863977.** Reservations strongly recommended. Main courses £11–£20 ($20–$36); 3-course fixed-price lunch menu £13 ($23). AE, MC, V. Mon–Fri 12:30–2:30pm; Mon–Sat 7–10:30pm. Closed bank holidays.

House on the Bridge ENGLISH/INTERNATIONAL   This charming restaurant is housed in a lovely red-brick and terra-cotta Victorian building adjacent to the bridge at the edge of Eton. Near the handful of outdoor tables is a steep garden whose plants range down to the Thames. For what the British call a "good tuck-in," begin with the chicken liver and Cointreau pâté or a sauté of wild mushrooms with truffle oil and Parmesan shavings. Among the more delightful main dishes are grilled salmon in a champagne sauce with asparagus tips, and a confit of duck with a honey and apple sauce. A specialty is filet of beef in pepper sauce flavored with a port and Stilton cheese sauce. Some specialties, such as roast rack of herb-flavored lamb, are served only for two. Although traditionally based, the preparations have many modern touches, and the chefs always use good, fresh ingredients. Desserts include flambés and crepes suzette.

Windsor Bridge. ℰ **01753/860914.** www.house-on-the-bridge.co.uk. Reservations recommended. Main courses £17–£26 ($32–$49) fixed-price lunch £20 ($38); dinner £35 ($67); Sun lunch £25 ($48). AE, DC, MC, V. Mon–Sat noon–2:30pm, Sun noon–3:30pm, and daily 6–11pm.

Strok's MODERN BRITISH/CONTINENTAL   This restaurant, located near the castle, is Windsor's most elegant and charming, possessing garden terraces, a conservatory, and a dining room designed a bit like a greenhouse. Chef Philip Wild selects an individual garnish to complement each well-prepared dish. For starters, try the tower of smoked salmon and asparagus. For a main course, enjoy the rosettes of spring lamb with beans, artichokes, and an herb Yorkshire pudding, or a seafood platter of lobster, king prawns, crab, mussels, and shrimps. A variety of vegetarian dishes is also offered. At dinner, a pianist entertains.

In Sir Christopher Wren's House Hotel, Thames St., Windsor. ℰ **01753/861354.** Main courses £15–£20 ($27–$36). AE, DC, MC, V. Daily 12:30–2:30pm and 6:30–10pm.

2 Oxford: The City of Dreaming Spires ★★

87km (54 miles) NW of London; 87km (54 miles) SE of Coventry

A walk down the long sweep of The High, one of the most striking streets in England; a mug of cider in one of the old student pubs; the sound of May Day dawn when choristers sing in Latin from Magdalen Tower; students in traditional gowns whizzing past on rickety bikes; towers and spires rising majestically; nude swimming at Parson's Pleasure; the roar of a cannon launching the bumping races; a tiny, dusty bookstall where you can pick up a valuable first edition—all that is Oxford, home of one of the greatest universities in the world.

Romantic Oxford is still here, but to get to it, you have to experience the bustling and crowded city that is also Oxford. You may be surprised by the never-ending stream of polluting buses and fast-flowing pedestrian traffic—the city core feels more like London than once-sleepy Oxford. Surrounding the university are suburbs that keep growing, and not in a particularly attractive manner.

At any time of the year, you can enjoy a tour of the colleges, many of which represent a peak in England's architectural history, as well as a valley of Victorian contributions. The Oxford Tourist Information Centre (see below) offers guided walking tours daily throughout the year. Just don't mention the other place (Cambridge), and you shouldn't have any trouble. Comparisons between the two universities are inevitable: Oxford is better known for the arts, Cambridge more for the sciences.

Oxford

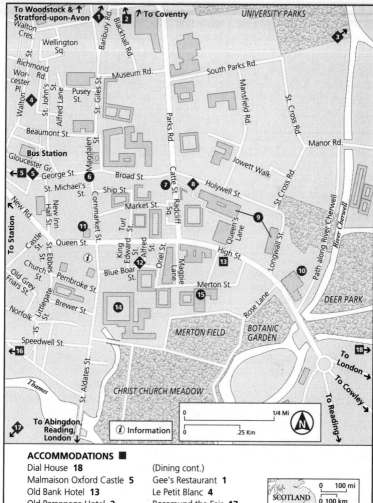

The city predates the university—in fact, it was a Saxon town in the early part of the 10th century. By the 12th century, Oxford was growing in reputation as a seat of learning, at the expense of Paris, and the first colleges were founded in the 13th century. The story of Oxford is filled with conflicts too complex and detailed to elaborate upon here. Suffice it to say, the relationship between town and gown wasn't always as peaceful as it is today. Riots often flared, and both sides were guilty of abuses. Nowadays, the young people of Oxford take out their aggressions in sporting competitions.

Ultimately, the test of a great university lies in the caliber of the people it turns out. Oxford can name-drop a mouthful: Roger Bacon, Sir Walter Raleigh, John Donne, Sir Christopher Wren, Samuel Johnson, William Penn, John Wesley, William Pitt, Matthew Arnold, Lewis Carroll, Harold Macmillan, Graham Greene, A. E. Housman, T. E. Lawrence, and many others. Women were not allowed until 1920, but since then many have graduated from Oxford and gone on to fame—Indira Gandhi and Margaret Thatcher both graduated from Somerville College.

ESSENTIALS

GETTING THERE   Trains from Paddington Station reach Oxford in 1½ hours. Five trains run every hour. A cheap, same-day round-trip ticket costs £18 ($34); a regular round-trip ticket, valid for a month, is £20 ($38). For more information, call © 0845/748-4950 or visit www.networkrail.co.uk.

The National Express provides coach service from London's Victoria Station (© 0870/580-8080; www.nationalexpress.com) to the Oxford Bus Station (bus no. X90). Coaches usually depart about every 20 minutes during the day; the trip takes approximately 1¾ hours. A same-day round-trip ticket costs £15 ($29) for adults, £7.50 ($14) for children 3 to 15.

If you're driving, take the M40 west from London and just follow the signs. Traffic and parking are a disaster in Oxford, and not just during rush hours. However, there are four large park-and-ride parking lots on the north, south, east, and west of the city's ring road, all well marked. Parking is 60p ($1.15) per car. From 9:30am on and all day Saturday, you pay £2 ($3.80) for a round-trip ticket for a bus ride into the city, which drops you off at St. Aldate's Cornmarket or Queen Street to see the city center. The buses run every 8 to 10 minutes in each direction. There is no service on Sunday. The parking lots are on the Woodstock road near the Peartree traffic circle, on the Botley road toward Farringdon, on the Abingdon road in the southeast, and on the A40 toward London.

VISITOR INFORMATION   The **Oxford Tourist Information Centre** is at 15–16 Broad St. (© 01865/726871; www.oxfordcity.co.uk/info/visitors.html). The center sells a comprehensive range of maps, brochures, and souvenir items, as well as the famous Oxford University T-shirt. It provides hotel-booking services for £5 ($9.50). Guided walking tours leave from the center daily (see later in this chapter). Open Monday to Saturday 9:30am to 5pm and Sunday and bank holidays in summer 10am to 1pm and 1:30 to 3:30pm.

EXPLORING OXFORD UNIVERSITY

Many visitors arriving at Oxford ask, "Where's the campus?" If a local chortles when answering, it's because Oxford University is made up of 35 widely dispersed colleges. To tour all of these would be a formidable task—it's best to focus on a handful of the better-known colleges.

The Oxford Story, 6 Broad St. (© **01865/728822;** www.oxfordstory.co.uk), is a concise and entertaining audiovisual ride through the university. It explains the structure of the colleges and highlights architectural and historical features. Visitors are also filled in on the general background of the colleges and the antics of some of the famous people who have passed through the University's portals. In July and August, the audiovisual presentation is daily 9:30am to 5pm. From September to June, it runs Monday to Saturday 10am to 4:30pm, Sunday 11am to 4:30pm. Admission is £7.25 ($14) for adults, £5.95 ($11) for seniors and students, and £5.25 ($10) for children 12 and under.

GUIDED TOURS

The **Tourist Information Centre,** 15–16 Broad St. (© **01865/726871**), offers a ghost tour, which explores Oxford's ghoulish and gory past. The office also has a number of walking tours, with the ghost tour available Friday and Saturday evenings June to October from 7:45pm, covering the dark alleyways around the ancient schools. The cost is £5 ($9.50) for adults and £3 ($5.70) for children; tickets are available at the office during the day. Day tours begin at 10am daily, including Christmas, even for one person.

For a good orientation, hour-long, open-top bus tours around Oxford are available from **Guide Friday** (© **01865/790522;** www.guidefriday.com), whose office is at the railway station (tours also start from the railway station; other pick-up points are Sheldonian Theatre, Gloucester Green Bus Station, and Pembroke College). Buses leave every 20 minutes daily; in summer, buses leave every 5 to 10 minutes. Tickets are good for the day. Tours run daily from 9:30am to 3:40pm November to February, daily from 9:30am to 4:40pm in March, and daily 9:30am to 6:30pm April to October. The cost is £9.50 ($18) for adults, £8.50 ($16) for students and seniors, £4.50 ($8.55) for children 5 to 14 years old; a family ticket for two adults and three children is £24 ($46). Children under 5 get to ride free. Tickets can be purchased from the driver.

THE COLLEGES

CHRIST CHURCH ✻✻   Begun by Cardinal Wolsey as Cardinal College in 1525, Christ Church (© **01865/276150;** www.chch.ox.ac.uk), known as the House, was founded by Henry VIII in 1546. Facing St. Aldate's Street, Christ Church has the largest quadrangle of any college in Oxford. Tom Tower houses Great Tom, an 18,000-pound bell. It rings at 9:05pm nightly, signaling the closing of the college gates. The 101 times it peals originally signified the number of students in residence at the time the college was founded. Although the student body has grown significantly, Oxford traditions live forever. There are some interesting portraits in the 16th-century Great Hall, including works by Gainsborough and Reynolds. There's also a separate portrait gallery.

The college chapel was constructed over a period of centuries, beginning in the 12th century. (Incidentally, it's not only the college chapel but also the cathedral of the diocese of Oxford.) The cathedral's most distinguishing features are its Norman pillars and the vaulting of the choir, dating from the 15th century. In the center of the great quadrangle is a statue of Mercury mounted in the center of a fishpond. You can visit the college and cathedral between 9am and 5:30pm, though times vary (1 to 5:30pm on Sunday). It's best to call before you visit. The entrance fee is £4.70 ($8.95) for adults and £3.70 ($7.05) for children.

MAGDALEN COLLEGE   Pronounced *Maud*-lin, Magdalen College, High Street (© 01865/276000; www.magd.ox.ac.uk), was founded in 1458 by William of Wayn-flete, bishop of Winchester and later chancellor of England. Its alumni range from Wolsey to Wilde. Opposite the botanic garden, the oldest in England, is the bell tower, where choristers sing in Latin at dawn on May Day. Charles I, his days numbered, watched the oncoming Roundheads from this tower. Visit the 15th-century chapel, in spite of many of its latter-day trappings. Ask when the hall and other places of special interest are open. The grounds of Magdalen are the most extensive of any Oxford college; there's even a deer park. You can visit all year round between 1 and 6pm daily. Admission is £3 ($5.70) adults, £2 ($3.80) seniors, students, and children.

MERTON COLLEGE ✸✸   Founded in 1264, Merton College, Merton Street (© 01865/276310; www.merton.ox.ac.uk), is among the three oldest colleges at the university. It stands near Corpus Christi College on Merton Street, the sole survivor of Oxford's medieval cobbled streets. Merton College is noted for its library, which was built between 1371 and 1379 and is said to be the oldest college library in England. Though a tradition once kept some of its most valuable books chained, now only one book is secured in that manner to illustrate that historical custom. One of the library's treasures is an astrolabe (an astronomical instrument used for measuring the altitude of the sun and stars) thought to have belonged to Chaucer. You pay £1 ($1.90) to visit the ancient library as well as the Max Beerbohm Room (the satirical English caricaturist who died in 1956). Call ahead for information. The library and college are open Monday to Friday 2 to 4pm, and Saturday and Sunday 10am to 4pm. It's closed for 1 week at Easter and Christmas and on weekends during the winter.

NEW COLLEGE   New College, Holywell Street (© 01865/279555; www.new.ox.ac.uk), was founded in 1379 by William of Wykeham, bishop of Winchester and later lord chancellor of England. The quadrangle, dating from before the end of the 14th century, was the first quadrangle to be built in Oxford and formed the architectural design for the other colleges. In the antechapel is Sir Jacob Epstein's remarkable modern sculpture of Lazarus and a fine El Greco painting of St. James. One of the treasures of the college is a crosier (a bishop's pastoral staff) belonging to the founding father. Don't miss the beautiful garden outside the college, where you can stroll among the remains of the old city wall and the mound. It's an evocative, romantic site. The college (entered at New College Lane) can be visited from Easter to October, daily between 11am and 5pm; and in the off season daily between 2 and 4pm. Admission is £2 ($3.80) from Easter to October and free off season.

THE OLD BODLEIAN LIBRARY ✸✸   This famed library on Catte Street (© 01865/277224; www.bodley.ox.ac.uk) was launched in 1602, initially funded by Sir Thomas Bodley. It is home to some 50,000 manuscripts and more than five million books. Over the years the library has expanded from the Old Library complex to other buildings, including the Radcliffe Camera next door. The easiest way to visit the library is by taking a guided tour, leaving from the Divinity School across the street from the main entrance. In summer there are four tours Monday to Friday and two on Saturday; in winter, two tours leave per day. Call for specific times.

WHERE TO STAY

Oxford Tourist Information Centre, Gloucester Green, opposite the bus station (© 01865/726871; fax 01865/240261; www.visitoxford.org), operates a year-round room-booking service for a fee of £5 ($9.50), plus a refundable deposit. If you'd like to seek lodgings on your own, the center has a list of accommodations, plus maps and guidebooks.

EXPENSIVE

Malmaison Oxford Castle 🎭🎭 *Finds*   In a recent poll of the top 10 quirkiest hotels in the world, the Malmaison in Oxford made the list. It formerly housed inmates detained at Her Majesty's Pleasure, and many aspects of prison life, including barred windows, have been retained. In a converted Victorian building, rooms are installed in cells that flank two sides of a large central atrium, a space that rises three stories and is criss-crossed by narrow walkways like in one of those George Raft prison movies of the '30s. The former inmates never had it so good—great beds, mood lighting, power showers, CD players and libraries, satellite TV, serious wines, and "naughty nibbles." The bathrooms are among the best in town, with under-floor heating, toasty towel racks, and free-standing tubs. In spite of its former origins, this is a stylish and comfortable place at which to stay.

3 Oxford Castle, Oxford OXI 1AY. (€) **01865/248432.** Fax 01845/3654247. www.malmaison.com. 94 units. £150 ($285) double, £195 ($371) suite. AE, DC, MC, V. **Amenities:** 2 restaurants; bar; room service; laundry service/dry cleaning; nonsmoking rooms. *In room:* TV, Wi-Fi, minibar, beverage maker.

Old Bank Hotel 🎭🎭   The first hotel created in the center of Oxford in 135 years, the Old Bank opened late in 1999 and immediately surpassed the traditional favorite, the Randolph, in style and amenities. Located on Oxford's main street and surrounded by some of its oldest colleges and sights, the building dates back to the 18th century and was indeed once a bank. The hotel currently features a collection of 20th-century British art handpicked by the owners. Bedrooms are comfortably and elegantly appointed, often opening onto views. A combination of velvet and shantung silk-trimmed linen bedcovers give the accommodations added style. Each unit includes a well-kept bathroom with terra-cotta or marble tiles.

92–94 High St., Oxford OX1 4BN. (€) **01865/799599.** Fax 01865/799598. www.oxford-hotels-restaurants.co.uk. 42 units. £175–£210 ($333–$399) double; £325 ($618) suite. AE, DC, MC, V. Bus: 7. **Amenities:** Restaurant; bar; room service; babysitting; laundry service; dry cleaning; all nonsmoking rooms; rooms for those w/limited mobility. *In room:* A/C, TV, beverage maker, hair dryer, safe.

Old Parsonage Hotel 🎭🎭   This extensively renovated hotel, near St. Giles Church and Keble College, is so old it looks like an extension of one of the ancient colleges. Originally a 13th-century hospital, it was restored in the early 17th century. In the 20th century, a modern wing was added, and in 1991 it was completely renovated and made into a first-rate hotel. This intimate old place is filled with hidden charms such as tiny gardens in its courtyard and on its roof terrace. In this tranquil area of Oxford, you feel like you're living at one of the colleges yourself. The rooms are all nonsmoking and individually designed but not large; all the units have marble bathrooms with tub/shower combinations and each of them opens onto the private gardens; 10 of them are on the ground floor. Every Friday jazz is played in the bar from 8 to 10pm.

1 Banbury Rd., Oxford OX2 6NN. (€) **01865/310210.** Fax 01865/311262. www.oldparsonage-hotel.co.uk. 30 units. £160–£200 ($304–$380) double; £225 ($428) suite. AE, DC, MC, V. Bus: 7. **Amenities:** Restaurant; bar; car and limo service for hire; room service; laundry service; dry-cleaning. *In room:* A/C, TV, hair dryer, trouser press.

MODERATE

Dial House *Value*   Three kilometers (2 miles) east of the heart of Oxford, beside the main highway leading to London, is this country-style house originally built between

1924 and 1927. Graced with mock Tudor half-timbering and a prominent blue-faced sundial (from which it derives its name), it has cozy and recently renovated rooms. Bathrooms are small and most have showers only, but a few offer a combination tub and shower. The owners, the Morris family, serve only breakfast in their bright dining room. The entire property is nonsmoking.

25 London Rd., Headington, Oxford, Oxfordshire OX3 7RE. © 01865/425100. Fax 01865/427388. www.oxfordcity. co.uk/accom/dialhouse. 8 units. £60–£75 ($114–$143) double; £75–£95 ($143–$181) family room. AE, MC, V. Bus: 2, 7, 7A, 7B, or 22. **Amenities:** All nonsmoking rooms. *In room:* TV, beverage maker, hair dryer, safe, no phone.

River Hotel This hotel lies a quarter-mile west of Oxford's commercial core and charges less than many of its more central competitors. It was built around 1900 by a local craftsman whose casement windows and flower boxes are still in place. About a quarter of the accommodations are across the street in a stone-sided annex. Bedrooms have cozy furnishings, including comfortable beds, and are continually renewed. Bathrooms are small and come with showers.

17 Botley Rd., Oxford, Oxfordshire OX2 0AA. © 01865/243475. Fax 01865/724306. www.riverhotel.co.uk. 20 units. £80–£90 ($152–$171) double; £100 ($190) family room. Rates include English breakfast. MC, V. Bus: 2 or 4. **Amenities:** Breakfast room; bar. *In room:* TV, dataport, coffeemaker, hair dryer.

Tilbury Lodge Private Hotel *(Value)* This small hotel lies on a quiet country lane 3km (1¾ miles) west of the center of Oxford, less than a mile from the railway station. Guests are housed in well-furnished and comfortable bedrooms; each room is immaculately kept and furnished in traditional English style with wood furnishings, excellent beds (the most expensive room has a four-poster bed), rugs, and wall art to give each accommodation a homelike touch. Like similar accommodations at Dial House, Tilbury Lodge offers a tranquil location on a country lane right outside the bustle of town. Many use it as a base for exploring not only Oxford, but the Cotswolds, Blenheim Palace, Stratford-upon-Avon, and even Bath. Because of the ample street parking, you can leave your car here and go by bus into the city center. Rooms vary in size; most have adequate space, and each comes with a tiny, well-kept bathroom with a shower.

5 Tilbury Lane, Eynsham Rd., Botley, Oxford, Oxfordshire OX2 9NB. © 01865/862138. www.tilburylodge.com. £70–£85 ($133–$162) double. Rates include English breakfast. MC, V. Bus: 4C or 100. **Amenities:** Breakfast room. *In room:* TV, Wi-Fi, coffeemaker, hair dryer.

WHERE TO DINE
EXPENSIVE

Cherwell Boathouse Restaurant *(★)* FRENCH/MODERN ENGLISH An Oxford landmark on the River Cherwell, this restaurant is owned by Anthony Verdin, assisted by a young crew. With an intriguing fixed-price menu, the cooks change the fare every 2 weeks to take advantage of the availability of fresh vegetables, fish, and meat. There is a very reasonable, even exciting, wine list. The kitchen is often cited for its "sensible combinations" of ingredients. The success of the main dishes is founded on savory treats such as grilled quail with a garlic and oregano dressing, pan-fried medallions of beef with a shallot and truffle sauce, and chargrilled loin of pork with a chorizo-laced butter. A special treat is the grilled gray mullet with ratatouille accompanied by a basil and chile sauce. For dessert, indulge in the lemon and almond roulade. The style is sophisticated yet understated, with a heavy reliance on quality ingredients that are cooked in such a way that natural flavors are always preserved.

Bardwell Rd. ℃ **01865/552746**. www.cherwellboathouse.co.uk. Reservations recommended. Main courses £13–£18 ($25–$34). Fixed-price dinner from £25 ($48); Mon–Fri set lunch £22 ($42); express lunch £13–£16 ($25–$30). AE, MC, V. Mon–Fri noon–2pm, Sat–Sun noon–2:30pm, and daily 7–9pm. Closed Dec 24–30. Bus: Banbury Rd.

Rosamund the Fair ⓚ *Finds* CONTINENTAL/BRITISH   This establishment accurately bills itself as Oxfordshire's cruising restaurant. A purpose-built narrow-boat restaurant, this floating dining room cruises along the Oxford Canal in and around Banbury; say hello to the swans as you dine. The chefs might get by on the novelty of it all, but they also serve a sublime cuisine. The boat seats 20 people who for 2½ hours enjoy the dinner and the cruise. Between courses you can go on deck and admire the view. A recent menu delighted us with such starters as mango, avocado, and papaya salad with a lime and yogurt dressing, followed by sea bream with deep-fried leeks and a lime butter sauce. Our dining partner selected ravioli with a salmon and chervil mousse with champagne sauce—a wonderful choice—followed by a perfectly pre-pared best end of lamb with a mustard hollandaise glaze and rosemary *jus*. The dessert specialty is "swan profiteroles" with a rich chocolate sauce.

Tooley's, Banbury Museum, Spiceball Park Rd., Banbury. ℃ **01295/278690**. www.rosamundthefair.co.uk. Reservations required. Fixed-price menu £52 ($99) per person lunch or dinner. MC, V. Lunch and dinner cruises Tues–Sun at noon and 7pm. Closed Jan.

MODERATE

Gee's Restaurant ⓚ MEDITERRANEAN/INTERNATIONAL   This restaurant, in a spacious Victorian glass conservatory, was converted from what for 80 years was the leading florist of Oxford. Its original features were retained by the owners, who also own the Old Parsonage Hotel (see above), and who have turned it into one of the most nostalgic and delightful places to dine in the city. Open since 1983, it has come more into fashion under its talented chefs. From students to professors, clients are mixed, but all enjoy a well-chosen list of offerings. Based on fine ingredients and a skilled preparation, you are likely to enjoy such main courses as pan-fried venison with carrot and beet root puree, whole roasted partridge with red wine *jus*, or homemade semolina gnocchi with baby spinach, goat's cheese, and pine nuts. A good dessert would be the lemon tart with blackberries.

61 Banbury Rd. ℃ **01865/553540**. Reservations recommended. Main courses £14–£22 ($27–$42); 2-course fixed-price menu £20 ($38), 3-course fixed-price menu £24 ($46). Set lunch and pre-theater menu £15–£19 ($29–$36). AE, MC, V. Mon–Fri noon–2:30pm and 6–10:30pm, Sat–Sun 11am–10:30pm.

Le Petit Blanc ⓚ FRENCH/MEDITERRANEAN   The biggest culinary news in Oxford is the return of Raymond Blanc with another Le Petit Blanc (a previous one proved disappointing). Monsieur Blanc is a wiser restaurateur now, and this buzzing brasserie is doing just fine. A former piano shop has been converted into a stylish place offering a menu that promises something for every palate. Here you can get a taste of the famous chef's creations without the high prices of his famed Le Manoir aux Quat' Saisons. The menu is more straightforward here, with a large emphasis on fresh ingredients.

The food is wholesome and delicious, based on authentic provincial French cuisine and complemented by Mediterranean and Asian accents. You'll be enticed by appetiz-ers such as a Roquefort soufflé with a pear and walnut salad, followed by Loch Duart salmon and fish cakes. For other main courses, the braised rabbit with sweet onion *tarte tatin* and flap mushrooms, and the Oxford sausage with parsley mash, Madeira, and sweet onion sauce are superb. The desserts are first-rate, especially the raspberry soufflé.

71–72 Walton St. ⓒ 01865/510999. Reservations recommended. Main courses £11–£18 ($21–$34); 2-course fixed-price lunch £12 ($23). AE, MC, V. Mon–Fri noon–2:45pm and 5:30–10:30pm, Sat noon–11pm, Sun noon–10pm.

INEXPENSIVE

Al-Salam *(R) (Value* LEBANESE   Some Oxford students think this place offers the best food value in the city. You'll dine within one of three sand-colored dining rooms, each separated from the other with antique (and very solid) wooden doors. Ironically, the newest of the three rooms, added only in 2002, looks the oldest, thanks to stone-built arches and a commitment to the kinds of raw materials (wood and masonry) that would have been available in Lebanon a century ago. The menu depends on what's available in the marketplace, and the chef's skill is reflected in such dishes as king prawns sautéed with a garlic and tomato sauce, or spicy lamb with a chile-and-onion sauce. Long lines can form at the door, especially on Friday and Saturday. The location is 2 minutes from both the bus and train stations.

6 Park End St. ⓒ 01865/245710. Reservations recommended. Main courses £7.50–£12 ($14–$23). MC, V. Daily noon–midnight.

Browns *(Value* ENGLISH/CONTINENTAL   Oxford's busiest and most bustling English brasserie suits all groups, from babies to undergraduates to grandmas. A 10-minute walk north of the town center, it occupies the premises of five Victorian shops whose walls were removed to create one large, echoing, and very popular space. A thriving bar trade (where almost everyone seems to order Pimms) makes the place an evening destination in its own right.

A young and enthusiastic staff serves traditional English cuisine. Your meal may include meat pies, hot salads, burgers, pastas, steaks, or poultry. Afternoon tea here is a justly celebrated Oxford institution. Reservations are not accepted, so if you want to avoid a delay, arrive here during off-peak dining hours.

5–11 Woodstock Rd. ⓒ 01865/511995. Main courses £8.50–£16 ($16–$30). AE, MC, V. Mon–Sat 11am–11pm; Sun 11am–10:30pm. Bus: 2 or 7.

PUBS

The Bear Inn   A short block from The High Street, overlooking the north side of Christ Church College, this village pub is an Oxford tradition. Its swinging sign depicts a bear and a ragged staff, the old insignia of the Earls of Warwick, who were among its early patrons. Many famous Oxford students and residents have caroused within the pub's walls since the 13th century, earning it a well-worn place in English literature. Some past owners developed the prankish habit of clipping their guests' neckties. Around the lounge bar you'll see the remains of thousands of ties, all labeled with their owners' names.

6 Alfred St. ⓒ 01865/728164. Snacks and bar meals £3–£9 ($5.70–$17). MC, V. Mon–Sat 11am–11pm; Sun noon–10:30pm. Bus: 2A or 2B.

The Turf Tavern   This 13th-century tavern, the oldest in Oxford, stands on a very narrow passageway near the Bodleian Library. Thomas Hardy used it as a setting in *Jude the Obscure.* Today's patrons include a healthy sampling of the university's students and faculty. During warm weather you can choose a table in one of the three separate gardens that radiate outward from the pub's core. For wintertime warmth, braziers are lit in the courtyard and in the gardens. A separate food counter, set behind a glass case, displays the day's fare. The pub is reached via St. Helen's Passage, which stretches between Holywell Street and New College Lane.

7 Bath Place (off Holywell St.). © **01865/243235.** Main courses £5.50–£9 ($10–$17). MC, V. Mon–Sat 11am–11pm; Sun noon–10:30pm, last meal served at 7:30pm. Bus: 52.

3 The Pursuit of Science: Cambridge ⋆⋆⋆

89km (55 miles) N of London, 129km (80 miles) NE of Oxford

The university town of Cambridge is a collage of images: the Bridge of Sighs; spires and turrets; willows; dusty secondhand bookshops; the lilt of Elizabethan madrigals; lanes where Darwin, Newton, and Cromwell walked; the grassy Backs of the colleges, sweeping down to the banks of the Cam; punters; and the tattered robes of hurried upperclassmen flying in the wind.

Along with Oxford, Cambridge is one of Britain's ancient seats of knowledge. In many ways their stories are similar. However, beyond its campus, Cambridge has a thriving, high-tech industry. And while Oxford concentrates on the arts, Cambridge has embraced the sciences. Both Isaac Newton and Stephen Hawking are graduates, joined by luminaries in every field.

There is much to explore in Cambridge, so give yourself time to wander.

ESSENTIALS

GETTING THERE Trains depart frequently from London's Liverpool Street and King's Cross stations, arriving an hour later. For inquiries, call © **0845/748-4950.** A one-way ticket costs £19 to £32 ($36–$61).

National Express buses leave hourly from London's Victoria Coach Station for the 2-hour trip to Drummer Street Station in Cambridge. A one-way ticket costs £10 ($19). For schedules and information, call © **0870/580-8080.**

If you're driving from London, head north on the M11.

GETTING AROUND The center of Cambridge is made for pedestrians, so park your car at one of the car parks (they increase in price as you approach the city center) and stroll the widely dispersed colleges. Follow the courtyards through to the Backs (the college lawns) and walk through to Trinity (where Prince Charles studied) and St. John's colleges, where you'll find the Bridge of Sighs.

Another popular way of getting around is bicycling. **Station Cycles** (© **01223/307125;** www.stationcycles.co.uk) has bicycles for rent for £6 ($11) per half-day, £8 ($15) per day, or £16 ($30) per week. A deposit of £50 ($95) is required. Call their number to reserve a bike. At that time you'll be told the address at which to pick up the cycle. Open Monday to Friday 7am to 8pm, Saturday 9am to 5pm, and Sunday 10am to 4pm.

Stagecoach Cambus, 100 Cowley Rd. (© **01223/423-578**), services the Cambridge area with a network of buses, with fares ranging in price from 65p to £3 ($1.25–$5.70) for a day pass. The local tourist office has bus schedules.

VISITOR INFORMATION In back of the guildhall, the **Cambridge Tourist Information Centre,** Wheeler Street (© **01223/464732;** www.visitcambridge.org), has a wide range of information, including data on public transportation and sightseeing attractions. From October to March, hours are Monday to Friday 10am to 5:30pm and Saturday 10am to 5pm. April to September, the office is open daily 10am to 5:30pm, Saturday 10am to 5pm, and Sunday 11am to 4pm.

City Sightseeing at Cambridge Railway Station (© **01223/457574**) operates a tourist reception center for Cambridge and Cambridgeshire. The center, on the concourse of the railway station, sells brochures and maps. Also available is a full range of tourist services, including accommodations booking. Open in summer daily from 8:45am to 7pm (closes at 5pm off season). Guided tours of Cambridge leave the center daily.

SPECIAL EVENTS Cambridge's artistic bent peaks at the end of July during the **Cambridge Folk Festival** (www.cambridgefolkfestival.co.uk). Event tickets are generally from £8 to £14 ($15–$27).

EXPLORING THE UNIVERSITY

Oxford University predates Cambridge, but by the early 13th-century scholars began gathering here. Eventually, Cambridge won partial recognition and received funds from Henry III. After Henry III's reign, approval and funding rose and fell depending on the monarch. Cambridge consists of 31 colleges for both men and women. Colleges are closed to the public during exams from mid-April until the end of June.

The following listing is only a sample of some of the more interesting colleges. If you're planning to be in Cambridge awhile, you might also want to visit **Magdalene College,** on Magdalene Street, founded in 1542; **Pembroke College,** on Trumpington Street, founded in 1347; **Christ's College,** on St. Andrew's Street, founded in 1505; and **Corpus Christi College,** on King's Parade, which dates from 1352.

EMMANUEL COLLEGE On St. Andrew's Street, Emmanuel (© **01223/334200**; www.emma.cam.ac.uk) was founded in 1584 by Sir Walter Mildmay, a chancellor of the exchequer to Elizabeth I. John Harvard, of the university that bears his name in another city called Cambridge, studied here. You can stroll around Emmanuel's attractive gardens and visit the chapel designed by Sir Christopher Wren, consecrated in 1677. Both the chapel and college are open daily during sunlight hours.

Insider's Tip: Harvard men and women, and those who love them, can look for a memorial window in Wren's chapel dedicated to John Harvard, an alumnus of Emmanuel who lent his name to that other university.

KING'S COLLEGE 𝒜𝒜 The adolescent Henry VI founded King's College on King's Parade (© **01223/331100**; www.kings.cam.ac.uk) in 1441. Most of its buildings today date from the 19th century, but the construction of its crowning glory, the **Perpendicular King's College Chapel** 𝒜𝒜𝒜, began in the Middle Ages. Owing to the whims of royalty, the chapel wasn't completed until the early 16th century.

Henry James called King's College Chapel "the most beautiful in England." Its most striking features are its magnificent fan vaulting, all in stone, and its great windows, most of which were fashioned by Flemish artisans between 1517 and 1531 (the west window dates from the late Victorian period). The chapel also boasts Rubens's *Adoration of the Magi* and an ornamental screen from the early 16th century. The chapel is famous for its choir and musical concerts. You can call the college (phone number above) for concert dates and times.

Insider's Tip: For a classic view of the chapel, go around to the rear of the architectural complex. E. M. Forster came here to contemplate scenes for his novel *Maurice.* It also happens to be an ideal picnic spot along the river. To acquire the makings of a picnic, head for the vendors who peddle inexpensive food, including fresh fruit, at **Market Square,** open daily Monday to Saturday 9:30am to 4:30pm. You can also

Cambridge

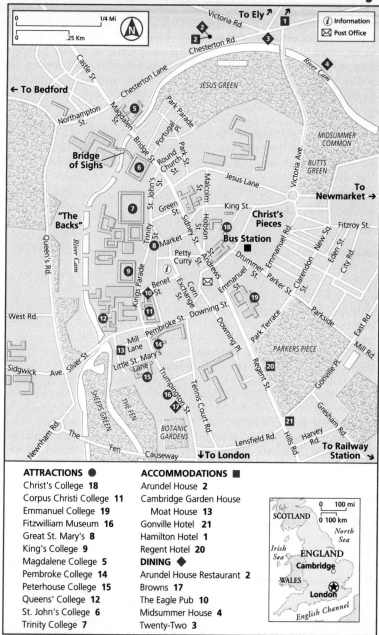

To Ely
Victoria Rd.
Chesterton Rd.
Castle St.
Chesterton Lane
JESUS GREEN
← To Bedford
Northampton St.
Magdalen St.
Park Parade
Portugal Pl.
Bridge St.
Bridge of Sighs
Round Church St.
Park St.
Jesus Lane
St. John's St.
Green St.
Malcolm St.
MIDSUMMER COMMON
Victoria Ave.
BUTTS GREEN
To Newmarket →
"The Backs"
Trinity St.
Sidney St.
Hobson St.
King St.
Christ's Pieces
Fitzroy St.
New Sq.
River Cam
Queen's Rd.
Market
Petty Curry
St. Andrews St.
Bus Station
Emmanuel Rd.
Drummer St.
Parker St.
Clarendon St.
Eden St.
City Rd.
Benet St.
Corn Exchange St.
Downing St.
Emmanuel St.
Park Terrace
Parkside
East Rd.
West Rd.
Kings Parade
Pembroke St.
Downing St.
Downing Pl.
PARKERS PIECE
Mill Rd.
Sidgwick Ave.
Silver St.
Mill Lane
Little St. Mary's Lane
Trumpington St.
Tennis Court Rd.
Regent St.
Gonville Pl.
Gresham Rd.
SHEEPS GREEN
THE FEN
BOTANIC GARDENS
Newnham Rd.
The Fen
Causeway
Lensfield Rd.
Hills Rd.
Harvey Rd.
↓To London
To Railway Station ↘
River Cam

ⓘ Information
✉ Post Office

ATTRACTIONS ●
Christ's College **18**
Corpus Christi College **11**
Emmanuel College **19**
Fitzwilliam Museum **16**
Great St. Mary's **8**
King's College **9**
Magdalene College **5**
Pembroke College **14**
Peterhouse College **15**
Queens' College **12**
St. John's College **6**
Trinity College **7**

ACCOMMODATIONS ■
Arundel House **2**
Cambridge Garden House
  Moat House **13**
Gonville Hotel **21**
Hamilton Hotel **1**
Regent Hotel **20**

DINING ◆
Arundel House Restaurant **2**
Browns **17**
The Eagle Pub **10**
Midsummer House **4**
Twenty-Two **3**

SCOTLAND
North Sea
Irish Sea
ENGLAND
Cambridge
WALES
London
English Channel
0   100 mi
0   100 km

get the makings of a picnic at a major grocery store, **Sainsbury's,** 44 Sidney St. (© **01223/366891**), open Monday to Saturday 8am to 10pm and Sunday 11am to 5pm.

The chapel is open during college term, Monday to Friday 9:30am to 3:30pm, Saturday 9:30am to 3:15pm, and Sunday 1:15 to 2:15pm and 5 to 5:30pm. During the term, the public is welcome to attend choral services Monday to Saturday at 5:30pm and on Sunday at 10:30am and 3:30pm. During school vacations, the chapel is open to visitors Monday to Saturday 9:30am to 4:30pm and on Sunday 10am to 5pm; it is closed from December 23 to January 1. It may be closed at other times for recording sessions, broadcasts, and concerts.

An exhibition in the seven northern side chapels shows why and how the chapel was built. Admission to the college and chapel, including the exhibition, is £4.50 ($8.55) for adults; £3 ($5.70) for students and seniors. The attraction is free for children 11 and under.

PETERHOUSE COLLEGE On Trumpington Street, Peterhouse College (© **01223/ 338200;** www.pet.cam.ac.uk) attracts visitors because it's the oldest Cambridge college, founded in 1284 by Hugh de Balsham, the bishop of Ely. Of the original buildings, only the hall remains. It was restored in the 19th century and has stained-glass windows by William Morris. The chapel, called Old Court, dates from 1632 and was renovated in 1754. Ask to enter at the porter's lodge.

Insider's Tip: Now almost sadly neglected, the Little Church of St. Mary's next door was the college chapel until 1632. Pay it the honor of a visit.

QUEENS' COLLEGE ★★ On Silver Street, Queens' College (© **01223/335511;** www.quns.cam.ac.uk) is the loveliest of Cambridge's colleges. Dating back to 1448, it was founded by two English queens, Margaret of Anjou, the wife of Henry VI, and Elizabeth Woodville, the wife of Edward IV. Its second cloister is the most intriguing, flanked by the early 16th-century half-timbered President's Lodge.

Admission is £1.50 ($2.85) for adults, free for children under 12 accompanied by parents. A printed guide is issued. From October until March 16, hours are daily from 1:45 to 4:30pm; from March 17 to April 5, Monday to Friday from 11am to 3pm, Saturday and Sunday 10am to 4pm; April 6 to April 9, hours are daily 10am to 4:30pm; April 10 to May 20, hours are Monday to Friday 11am to 3pm, Saturday and Sunday 10am to 4:30pm; closed from May 21 to June 23. From June 24 to September 30, hours are daily 10am to 4:30pm; October 1 to October 28, hours are Monday to Friday from 1:45 to 4:30pm, Saturday and Sunday 10am to 4:30pm. Entry and exit is by the old porter's lodge in Queens' Lane only. The old hall and chapel are usually open to the public when not in use.

Insider's Tip: Queens' College's wide lawns lead down to the "Backs" (the backs of the colleges), where you can stroll, sit, or go punting. Take in Mathematical Bridge, best viewed from the Silver Street bridge, dating from 1902.

ST. JOHN'S COLLEGE ★★ Located on St. John's Street, this college (© **01223/ 338600;** www.joh.cam.ac.uk) was founded in 1511 by Lady Margaret Beaufort, mother of Henry VII, who himself had launched Christ's College a few years earlier. The impressive gateway bears the Tudor coat of arms, and the Second Court is a fine example of late Tudor brickwork. The college's best-known feature is the Bridge of Sighs crossing the Cam. Built in the 19th century, it was patterned after the covered bridge in Venice. It connects the older part of the college with New Court, a Gothic revival on the opposite bank, where there is an outstanding view of the famous

"Backs" (the backs of the colleges). The Bridge of Sighs is closed to visitors but can be seen from neighboring Kitchen Bridge. Wordsworth was an alumnus of this college, which is open March to October daily 9:30am to 5:30pm (on weekends only from Nov–Feb). Admission is £2.50 ($4.75) for adults, £1.50 ($2.85) for seniors and children, £5 ($9.50) for family admission. Visitors are welcome to attend choral services in the chapel.

Insider's Tip: The Bridge of Sighs links the old college with an architectural "folly" of the 19th century, the elaborate New Court, which is a crenellated neo-Gothic fantasy. It's adorned with a riot of pinnacles and a main cupola. Students call it "the wedding cake."

TRINITY COLLEGE 🏛🏛 On Trinity Street, Trinity College (not to be confused with Trinity Hall; ✆ **01223/338400;** www.trin.cam.ac.uk) is the largest college in Cambridge. It was founded in 1546 by Henry VIII, who consolidated a number of smaller colleges that had existed on the site. The courtyard is the most spacious in Cambridge, built when Thomas Neville was master. Sir Christopher Wren designed the library.

Insider's Tip: It's fun to contemplate what went on here before you arrived. Pause at Neville's Court where Isaac Newton first calculated the speed of sound. Take in the delicate fountain of the Great Court where Lord Byron used to bathe naked with his pet bear. Why a bear? The university forbade students from having dogs, but there was no proviso for bears. Years later, Vladimir Nabokov walked through that same courtyard dreaming of the young lady he would later immortalize as *Lolita.* For admission to the college, apply at the porter's lodge. There's a charge of £2.20 ($4.20) adults, £1.30 ($2.45) seniors and children, and £4.40 ($8.35) for families, from March to November.

MORE CAMBRIDGE ATTRACTIONS

Fitzwilliam Museum 🏛🏛 This is one of Britain's finest museums, founded by the bequest of the seventh viscount Fitzwilliam of Merrion to the University of Cambridge in 1816. The permanent collections contain remarkable antiquities from ancient Egypt, Greece, and Rome. Galleries display Roman and Romano-Egyptian art along with Western-Asiatic exhibits. The Fitzwilliam's Applied Arts section showcases English and European pottery and glass, as well as furniture, clocks, armor, fans, rugs and samplers, Chinese jades, and ceramics from Japan and Korea. The museum also has married a rare ancient and medieval coin collection with a host of medals created from the Renaissance onward. The Fitzwilliam is best loved for its collection of paintings, which includes masterpieces by Simone Martini, Titian, Veronese, Rubens, Van Dyck, Canaletto, Hogarth, Gainsborough, Constable, Monet, Degas, Renoir, Cézanne, and Picasso. There is also a fine collection of other 20th-century art, miniatures, drawings, watercolors, and prints. The Fitzwilliam stages occasional musical events, including evening concerts, in Gallery III. Throughout the year, it plays host to some of the best lectures in England.

Trumpington St., near Peterhouse. ✆ **01223/332900.** www.fitzmuseum.cam.ac.uk. Free admission; donations appreciated. Tues–Sat 10am–5pm; Sun noon–5pm. Guided tours £6 ($11) per person Sun 2:45pm. Closed Jan 1, Good Friday, May Day, and Dec 24–31.

Great St. Mary's Closely associated with events of the Reformation because the leaders of the movement (Erasmus, Cranmer, Latimer, and Ridley) preached here, this university church was built mostly in 1478 on the site of an 11th-century church. The cloth that covered the hearse of King Henry VII is on display in the church. There is a fine view of Cambridge from the top of the tower.

King's Parade. ☎ 01223/741716. Admission to tower £2 ($3.80) adults, £1 ($1.90) children. Tower summer Mon–Sat 9:30am–5pm, Sun 12:30–5pm; church daily 9am–6pm.

WHERE TO STAY
EXPENSIVE
Cambridge Garden House Moat House ⭐⭐ This modern hotel sits between the riverbank and a cobblestone street in the oldest part of town, a short stroll from the principal colleges. (Because of its riverside location, we prefer it over its nearest competitor, the University Arms, which is in the center of town.) It offers ample parking. You can rent punts at a boatyard next door. Visitors can relax on comfortable sofas and chairs in the bars and lounge. The soundproof bedrooms have wooden nightstands, adequate desk space, and private balconies. The expensive units (premium rooms) are very spacious, with large sitting areas with face-to-face sofas. The river-view rooms are the most desirable. Bathrooms are large with tub/shower combinations.

Overlooking the river and gardens, the hotel's restaurant, Riverside Brasserie, offers fixed-price and a la carte menus, including vegetarian meals. The Terrace Bar and Lounge provides light meals, accompanied in the evening by piano music. The hotel has a series of outdoor terraces where drinks and afternoon tea are served in nice weather.

Granta Place, Mill Lane, Cambridge, Cambridgeshire CB2 1RT. ☎ 01223/259988. Fax 01223/316605. www.moat househotels.com. 121 units. £149–£209 ($283–$397) double. AE, DC, MC, V. **Amenities:** Restaurant; bar; indoor heated pool; health club; Jacuzzi; sauna; business center; room service; laundry service; dry cleaning; beauty salon; all nonsmoking rooms; rooms for those w/limited mobility. *In room:* TV, Wi-Fi, minibar, coffeemaker, hair dryer, iron, safe.

MODERATE
Arundel House Occupying one of the most desirable sites in Cambridge, this hotel consists of six interconnected identical Victorian row houses—all fronted with dark-yellow local bricks. In 1994, after two additional houses were purchased, the hotel was enlarged, upgraded, and expanded into the well-maintained hostelry you'll see today. It competes successfully with the Gonville and has the better cuisine of the two. Rooms overlooking the River Cam and Jesus Green cost more, as do those on lower floors (there's no elevator). All rooms are clean, simple, and comfortable, with upholstered chairs, carpeting, and small but efficient and tidily kept shower-only bathrooms.

53 Chesterton Rd., Cambridge, Cambridgeshire CB4 3AN. ☎ 01223/367701. Fax 01223/367721. www.arundel househotels.co.uk. 103 units. £95–£120 ($181–$228) double; £120–£135 ($228–$257) family bedroom. Rates include continental breakfast. AE, DC, MC, V. Bus: 1 or 3. **Amenities:** Restaurant; bar; laundry facility; all nonsmoking rooms. *In room:* A/C, TV, coffeemaker, hair dryer.

Gonville Hotel This hotel and its grounds are opposite Parker's Piece Park, only a 5-minute walk from the center of town. The Gonville has been much improved in recent years and is better than ever. It's like an ivy-covered country house, with shade trees and a formal car entry. The recently refurbished rooms are comfortable and modern in style. Bedrooms have small but well-kept bathrooms with showers.

Gonville Place, Cambridge, Cambridgeshire CB1 1LY. ☎ 800/780-7234 in the U.S. and Canada, or 01223/366611. Fax 01223/315470. www.gonvillehotel.co.uk. 73 units. £125–£149 ($238–$283) double. AE, DC, MC, V. **Amenities:** Restaurant; bar; room service; laundry service; dry cleaning; nonsmoking rooms. *In room:* TV, coffeemaker, hair dryer, iron, safe.

Regent Hotel   This is one of the most desirable of Cambridge's reasonably priced small hotels. Right in the city center, overlooking Parker's Piece Park, the house was built in the 1840s as the original site of Newnham College. It became a hotel when the college outgrew its quarters. Bedrooms are on the small side but are redecorated frequently in traditional Georgian style. Bathrooms are small but have adequate shelf space and tubs with shower attachments.

41 Regent St., Cambridge, Cambridgeshire CB2 1AB. ℂ 01223/351470. Fax 01223/464937. www.regenthotel. co.uk. 22 units. £99–£130 ($188–$247) double. Rates include continental breakfast. AE, DC, MC, V. Bus: 1. Closed Dec 22–Jan 2. **Amenities:** Bar; all nonsmoking rooms. *In room:* TV, coffeemaker, hair dryer, trouser press.

INEXPENSIVE
Hamilton Hotel *Value*   One of the better and more reasonably priced of Cambridge's small hotels, this red-brick establishment lies about a mile northeast of the city center, close to the River Cam. Well run and modestly accessorized, the hotel stands on a busy highway, but there's a parking area out back. The well-furnished bedrooms contain reasonably comfortable twin or double beds. Bathrooms are compact with shower stalls. The hotel has a small, traditionally styled licensed bar, offering standard pub food and snacks.

156 Chesterton Rd., Cambridge, Cambridgeshire CB4 1DA. ℂ 01223/365664. Fax 01223/314866. www.hamilton hotelcambridge.co.uk. 25 units. £65–£75 ($124–$143) double. Rates include English breakfast. AE, DC, MC, V. Bus: 3 or 3A. **Amenities:** Bar. *In room:* TV, coffeemaker, hair dryer.

WHERE TO DINE
EXPENSIVE
Midsummer House *★★ Finds* MEDITERRANEAN   Located in an Edwardian-era cottage near the River Cam, the Midsummer House is a real find. We prefer to dine in the elegant conservatory, but you can also find a smartly laid table upstairs. The fixed-price menus are wisely limited, and quality control and high standards are much in evidence here. Daniel Clifford is the master chef, and he has created such specialties as filet of beef Rossini with braised winter vegetables and sauce Perigourdine and roast squab pigeon, *pomme* Anna, *tarte tatin* of onions, caramelized endives, and *jus* of morels.

Midsummer Common. ℂ 01223/369299. Reservations required. 3-course fixed-price menu £55 ($105). AE, MC, V. Tues–Sat noon–2pm and 7–10pm.

MODERATE
Arundel House Restaurant *★* BRITISH/FRENCH/VEGETARIAN   One of the best and most acclaimed restaurants in Cambridge is in a hotel overlooking the River Cam and Jesus Green, a short walk from the city center. Winner of many awards, it's noted not only for its excellence and use of fresh produce, but also for its good value. The decor is warmly inviting with Sanderson curtains, Louis XV–upholstered chairs, and spacious tables. The menu changes frequently, and you can dine both a la carte or from the set menu. Perhaps you'll begin with a homemade golden-pea-and-ham soup or a white-rum-and-passion-fruit cocktail. Fish choices include plaice and salmon; try the pork-and-pigeon casserole or the Japanese-style braised lamb.

53 Chesterton Rd. ℂ 01223/367701. Reservations required. Main courses £10–£19 ($19–$36); 2-course fixed-price menu £17 ($32); 3-course fixed-price menu £21 ($40). AE, DC, MC, V. Daily 7:30–10am, 12:15–1:45pm and 6:30–9:30pm. Bus: 3 or 5.

Browns ⊛ *(Value* CONTINENTAL/ENGLISH   After wowing them at Oxford, Browns now lures Cambridge students in equal numbers. The building lies opposite the Fitzwilliam Museum and was constructed in 1914 as the outpatient department of a hospital dedicated to Edward VII; that era's grandeur is apparent in the building's neoclassical colonnade. Today, it's the most lighthearted place for dining in the city, with wicker chairs, high ceilings, pre–World War I woodwork, and a long bar covered with bottles of wine. The extensive bill of fare includes pastas, scores of fresh salads, several selections of meat and fish (from charcoal-grilled leg of lamb with rosemary to fresh fish in season), hot sandwiches, and the chef's daily specials. If you drop by in the afternoon, you can also order thick milkshakes or natural fruit juices. In fair weather, outdoor seats are prized possessions.

23 Trumpington St. (5 min. from King's College and opposite the Fitzwilliam Museum). ⓒ 01223/461655. Reservations not accepted on weekends. Main courses £9–£16 ($17–$30). AE, MC, V. Mon–Sat 10am–11pm; Sun 11:30–10:30pm. Bus: 2.

The Volunteer ⊛ BRITISH/CONTINENTAL   It looks like a pub from the outside, which it used to be in a former life. Today it's been turned into a smart restaurant with white linen-set tables and upholstered chairs. Dried flowers, carpeting, and landscape pictures evoke a country living room. Local and regional materials figure into the menus, which are strong on sauces and combined flavors, as evoked by the foie gras and chicken parfait or the grilled asparagus and quail's egg salad. Our rack of lamb was a sublime treat and roasted to perfection. Another member of our party took delight in the organic salmon served on a bed of fresh spinach. The hot chocolate fondant with pistachio ice cream is an excellent dessert. You might also opt for the poached pears in red wine.

60 Trumpington Rd. ⓒ 01223/841675. Reservations recommended. Main courses £15–£21 ($29–$39). MC, V. Daily noon–2:30pm; Mon–Sat 7–9:30pm.

Twenty Two ⊛ CONTINENTAL/ENGLISH   One of the best in Cambridge, this restaurant is located in a quiet district near Jesus Green and is a secret jealously guarded by the locals. The homey but elegant Victorian dining room offers an ever-changing fixed-price menu based on fresh market produce. Owner David Carter uses time-tested recipes along with his own inspirations, offering creations such as white onion soup with toasted goat's cheese, and sautéed breast of chicken on braised celery with thyme *jus*.

22 Chesterton Rd. ⓒ 01223/351880. Reservations required. Fixed-price menu £26 ($49). AE, MC, V. Tues–Sat 7–9:30pm.

INEXPENSIVE

The Eagle Pub   This pub dates back to the 1500s and was the favorite Cambridge watering hole for American and British pilots during World War II. It's still going strong, and you don't have to visit it just in the evening, as it also serves pub lunches. A former coaching inn, it offers several separate bars and a cobblestone courtyard for summer-overflow beer drinking. It is famous as the place where Nobel laureates Watson and Crick first announced their discovery of the DNA double helix. Real ales include Icebreaker and Greene King's Abbot. Place your order and raise a pint to the wonders of modern science.

Benet St. off King's Parade. ⓒ 01223/505020. Main courses £6–£8 ($11–$15). DC, MC, V. Mon–Sat 11am–11pm; Sun noon–10:30pm.

CAMBRIDGE AFTER DARK

You can take in a production at the spot where Emma Thompson and other well-known thespians got their start, **The Amateur Dramatic Club,** Park Street near Jesus Lane (© **01223/359547** or 01223/300085 for box office; www.cuadc.org). It presents two student productions nightly, Tuesday through Saturday, with the main show tending toward classic and modern drama or opera, and the late show being of a comic or experimental nature. The theater is open nearly year-round, closing in September, and tickets run from £3.50 to £8 ($6.65–$15).

The most popular Cantabridgian activity is the **pub crawl** (www.cambridge-pubs.co.uk). With too many pubs in the city to list, you may as well start at Cambridge's oldest pub, the **Pickerel,** on Magdalene Street (© **01223/355068**), dating from 1432. English pubs don't get more traditional than this. If the ceiling beams or floorboards groan occasionally—well, they've certainly earned the right over the years. Real ales on tap include Bulmer's Traditional Cider, Old Speckled Hen, Theakston's 6X, Old Peculiar, and Best Bitter. **The Maypole,** Portugal Place at Park Street (© **01223/352999**), is the local hangout for actors from the nearby ADC Theatre. Known for cocktails and not ales, you can still get a Tetley's 6X or Castle Eden.

The Eagle, Benet Street off King's Parade (© **01223/505020**), will be forever famous as the place where Nobel Laureates Watson and Crick first announced their discovery of the DNA double helix. Real ales include Icebreaker and local brewery Greene King's Abbott, so make your order and raise a pint to the wonders of modern science.

To meet up with current Cambridge students, join the locals at the **Anchor,** Silver Street (© **01223/353554**), or **Tap and Spiel (The Mill),** 14 Mill Lane, off Silver Street Bridge (© **01223/357026**), for a pint of Greene King's IPA or Abbott. The crowd at the Anchor spills out onto the bridge in fair weather, whereas the Tap and Spiel's clientele lay claim to the entire riverside park.

For musical entertainment, you can find out who's playing by checking out fliers posted around town or by reading the *Varsity.* **The Corn Exchange,** Wheeler Street and Corn Exchange (© **01223/357851**), hosts everything from classical concerts to bigger-name rock shows. **The Graduate,** 16 Chesterton Rd. (© **01223/301416**), a pub located in a former movie theater, is open from noon to 11pm with no cover charge.

Entertainment in some form can be found nightly at **The Junction,** Clifton Road, near the train station (© **01223/511511**), where an eclectic mix of acts takes to the stage weeknights to perform all genres of music, comedy, and theater, and DJs take over on the weekend. Cover charges vary from £8 to £15 ($15–$29), depending on the event.

Ballare, Lion Yard (© **01223/364222**), a second-story club, has a huge dance floor and plays everything from house to the latest pop hits, Monday to Saturday 9pm until 2am. Sometimes they even DJ the old-fashioned way, by taking requests. The cover charge ranges from £3 to £8 ($5.70–$15), depending on what night you're here.

4 Shakespeare's Stratford-upon-Avon ★ ★

147km (91 miles) NW of London, 65km (40 miles) NW of Oxford

Crowds of visitors overrun this market town on the River Avon during the summer months. In fact, Stratford so aggressively hustles its Shakespeare connection that it seems at times that everybody here is trying to make a buck off the Bard. If he could return today, Shakespeare would be inundated with T-shirts bearing his likeness and china models of Anne Hathaway's cottage. He might look for a less trampled town in which to pen his masterpieces.

One visitor magnet is the Royal Shakespeare Theatre, where Britain's foremost actors perform (though note that construction in 2007 will divert the action to a secondary stage). Other than the theater, Stratford is nearly devoid of cultural life, and you may want to rush back to London after you've done the literary pilgrimage and seen a show. If you can, visit in winter, when the throngs dwindle.

ESSENTIALS

GETTING THERE   The journey from London to Stratford-upon-Avon takes about 2¼ hours, and a round-trip ticket costs £28 to £69 ($53–$131) depending on the train. For schedules and information, call © **0845/748-4950,** or go to www. nationalrail.co.uk. The train station at Stratford is on Alcester Road.

Four **National Express** buses a day leave from London's Victoria Station, with a trip time of 3¼ hours. A single-day round-trip ticket costs £17 ($31). For schedules and information, call © **0870/580-8080;** www.nationalexpress.co.uk.

If you're driving from London, take the M40 toward Oxford and continue to Stratford-upon-Avon on the A34.

VISITOR INFORMATION   The **Tourist Information Centre,** Bridgefoot, Stratford-upon-Avon, Warwickshire, CV37 6GW (© **0870/160-7930;** www.shakespeare-country.co.uk), provides any details you may wish to know about the Shakespeare houses and properties and will assist in booking rooms (see "Where to Stay," below). Call and ask for a copy of their free *Shakespeare Country Holiday* guide. They also operate a Thomas Cook currency-exchange office (© **01789/269750**). It's open from April to October, Monday to Saturday 9am to 5:30pm and Sunday from 10:30am to 4:30pm; from November to March, Monday to Saturday 9:30am to 5pm and Sunday from 10am to 4pm.

To contact **Shakespeare Birthplace Trust,** which administers many of the attractions, call the Shakespeare Centre (© **01789/204016;** www.shakespeare.org.uk).

VISITING THE SHRINES

Besides the attractions on the periphery of Stratford, many Elizabethan and Jacobean buildings are in town, a number of them administrated by the **Shakespeare Birthplace Trust** (© **01789/204016;** www.shakespeare.org.uk). One ticket—costing £14 ($27) adults, £12 ($23) for seniors and students, and £6.50 ($12) for children—lets you visit the five most important sights. You can also buy a family ticket to all five sights (good for two adults and three children) for £29 ($55)—a good deal. Pick up the ticket if you're planning to do much sightseeing (obtainable at your first stopover at any one of the Trust properties).

Guided tours of Stratford-upon-Avon are conducted by **City Sightseeing,** Civic Hall, Rother Street. In summer, open-top double-decker buses depart every 15 minutes daily from 9am to 6pm. You can take a 1-hour ride without stops, or you can get off at any or all of the town's five Shakespeare properties. Though the bus stops are clearly marked along the historic route, the most logical starting point is the sidewalk in front of the Pen & Parchment Pub, at the bottom of Bridge Street. Tour tickets are valid all day, so you can hop on and off the buses as many times as you want. The

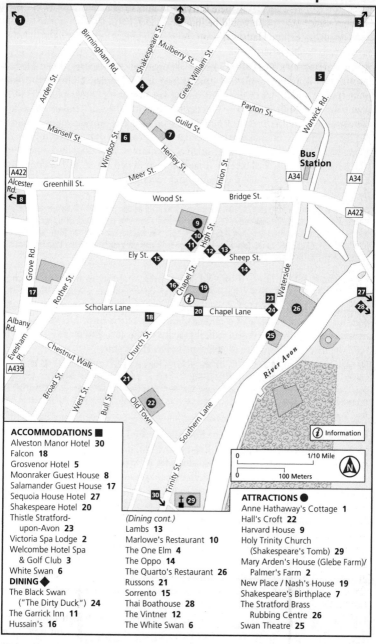

ACCOMMODATIONS ■
Alveston Manor Hotel **30**
Falcon **18**
Grosvenor Hotel **5**
Moonraker Guest House **8**
Salamander Guest House **17**
Sequoia House Hotel **27**
Shakespeare Hotel **20**
Thistle Stratford-
upon-Avon **23**
Victoria Spa Lodge **2**
Welcombe Hotel Spa
& Golf Club **3**
White Swan **6**
DINING ◆
The Black Swan
("The Dirty Duck") **24**
The Garrick Inn **11**
Hussain's **16**

(Dining cont.)
Lambs **13**
Marlowe's Restaurant **10**
The One Elm **4**
The Oppo **14**
The Quarto's Restaurant **26**
Russons **21**
Sorrento **15**
Thai Boathouse **28**
The Vintner **12**
The White Swan **6**

(i) Information

0   1/10 Mile
0   100 Meters

N

ATTRACTIONS ●
Anne Hathaway's Cottage **1**
Hall's Croft **22**
Harvard House **9**
Holy Trinity Church
(Shakespeare's Tomb) **29**
Mary Arden's House (Glebe Farm)/
Palmer's Farm **2**
New Place / Nash's House **19**
Shakespeare's Birthplace **7**
The Stratford Brass
Rubbing Centre **26**
Swan Theatre **25**

tours cost £9 ($17) for adults, £7 ($13) for seniors or students, and £4 ($7.60) for children under 16. A family ticket sells for £22 ($42) and children under 5 are free. Tour frequency depends on the time of the year; call for information. The first departures are at 9:30am.

Anne Hathaway's Cottage   Before she married Shakespeare, Anne Hathaway lived in this thatched, wattle-and-daub cottage in the hamlet of Shottery, 1.6km (1 mile) from Stratford. It's the most interesting and the most photographed of the Trust properties. The Hathaways were yeoman farmers, and their descendants lived in the cottage until 1892. As a result, it was never renovated and provides a rare insight into the life of a family in Shakespearean times. The Bard was only 18 when he married Anne, who was much older. Many original furnishings, including the courting settle (the bench on which Shakespeare is said to have wooed Anne) and various kitchen utensils, are preserved inside the house. After visiting the house, take time to linger in the garden and orchard.

Cottage Lane, Shottery. Ⓒ **01789/292100.** Admission £5.50 ($10) adults, £4.50 ($8.55) seniors and students, £2 ($3.80) children, £13 ($25) family ticket (2 adults, 3 children). Nov–Mar daily 10am–4pm; Apr–May Mon–Sat 9:30am–5pm, Sun 10am–5pm; June–Aug Mon–Sat 9am–5pm, Sun 9:30am–5pm; Sept–Oct Mon–Sat 9:30am–5pm, Sun 10am–5pm. Closed Dec 23–26. Take a bus from Bridge St. or walk via a marked pathway from Evesham Place in Stratford across the meadow to Shottery.

Hall's Croft   This house is on Old Town Street, not far from the parish church, Holy Trinity. It was here that Shakespeare's daughter Susanna probably lived with her husband, Dr. John Hall. Hall's Croft is an outstanding Tudor house with a walled garden, furnished in the style of a middle-class home of the time. Dr. Hall was widely respected and built up a large medical practice in the area. Fascinating exhibits illustrate the theory and practice of medicine in Dr. Hall's time.

Old Town St. (near Holy Trinity Church). Ⓒ **01789/292107.** Admission £3.75 ($7.15) adults, £3 ($5.70) seniors and students, £1.75 ($3.35) children, £10 ($19) family ticket (2 adults, 3 children). Nov–Mar daily 11am–4pm; Apr–May daily 11am–5pm; June–Aug Mon–Sat 9:30am–5pm, Sun 10am–5pm; Sept–Oct daily 11am–5pm. Closed Dec 23–28. To reach Hall's Croft, walk west from High St., which becomes Chapel St. and Church St. At the intersection with Old Town St., go left.

Harvard House   The most ornate home in Stratford, Harvard House is a fine example of an Elizabethan town house. Rebuilt in 1596, it was once the home of Katherine Rogers, mother of John Harvard, founder of Harvard University. In 1909, the house was purchased by a Chicago millionaire, Edward Morris, who presented it as a gift to the famous American university. Today, following a restoration, it has reopened a Museum of British Pewter. The museum displays trace the use of pewter from the Roman era until modern times. Pewter, as you learn, used to be the most common choice for household items. Even kiddie toys were made from pewter. Highlights include a tankard engraved with the images of William and Mary, a teapot inspired by the Portland Vase, and a rare bell-based Elizabethan candlestick. Two "hands-on" activities allow children to examine original items.

High St. Ⓒ **01789/201806.** £2.75 ($5.25) adults. Free for children. May–June and Sept–Oct Fri–Sun noon–5pm; July–Aug Wed–Sun noon–5pm. Closed Nov–Apr.

Holy Trinity Church (Shakespeare's Tomb)   In an attractive setting near the River Avon is the parish church where Shakespeare is buried ("and curst be he who moves my bones"). The Parish Register records his baptism in 1564 and burial in 1616 (copies of the original documents are on display). The church is one of the most beautiful parish churches in England.

Shakespeare's tomb lies in the chancel, a privilege bestowed upon him when he became a lay rector in 1605. Alongside his grave are those of his widow, Anne, and other members of his family. You can also see the graves of Susanna, his daughter, and those of Thomas Nash and Dr. John Hall. Nearby on the north wall is a bust of Shakespeare that was erected approximately 7 years after his death—within the lifetime of his widow and many of his friends.

Old Town St. © 01789/266316. Church, free admission; Shakespeare's tomb, admission £1.50 ($2.85) adults, 50p (95¢) students. Apr–Sept Mon–Sat 8:30am–6pm, Sun 12:30–5pm; Mar and Oct Mon–Sat 9am–5pm, Sun 12:30–5pm; Nov–Feb Mon–Sat 9am–4pm, Sun 12:30–5pm. Walk 4 min. past the Royal Shakespeare Theatre with the river on your left.

Mary Arden's House (Glebe Farm)/Palmer's Farm

So what if millions of visitors have been tricked into thinking this timber-framed farmhouse with its old stone dovecote and various outbuildings was the girlhood home of Shakespeare's mother, Mary Arden? It's still one of the most intriguing sights outside Stratford, even if local historian, Dr. Nat Alcock, discovered in 2000 that the actual childhood home of Arden was the dull-looking brick-built farmhouse, Glebe Farm, next door. Glebe's Farm has now been properly renamed Mary Arden's House. It was all the trick of an 18th-century tour guide, John Jordan, who decided Glebe Farm was too unimpressive to be the home of the Bard's mother, and told tourists it was this farmstead instead. What was known for years as "Mary Arden's House" has been renamed Palmer's Farm. Actually, this farm wasn't constructed until the late 16th century, a little late to be Mary Arden's actual home. After the name confusion, local authorities have converted Palmer's Farm into a working farm. Visitors can tour the property seeing first hand how a farming household functioned in the 1570s—yes, cows to be milked, bread to be baked, and vegetables cultivated in an authentic 16th-century manner. In the barns, stable, cowshed, and farmyard is an extensive collection of farming implements illustrating life and work in the local countryside from Shakespeare's time to the present.

Wilmcote. © 01789/204016. Admission £6 ($11) adults, £5 ($9.50) students and seniors, £2.50 ($4.75) children, £15 ($29) family ticket, children under 5 free. Nov–Mar daily 10am–4pm; Apr–May daily 10am–5pm; June–Aug daily 9:30am–5pm; Sept–Oct daily 10am–5pm. Closed Dec 23–26. Take A3400 (Birmingham) for 5.5km (3½ miles).

New Place/Nash's House

Shakespeare retired to New Place in 1610 (a prosperous man by the standards of his day) and died here 6 years later. Regrettably, the house was torn down, so only the garden remains. A mulberry tree planted by the Bard was so popular with latter-day visitors to Stratford that the garden's owner chopped it down. The mulberry tree that grows here today is said to have been planted from a cutting of the original. You enter the gardens through Nash's House (Thomas Nash married Elizabeth Hall, a granddaughter of the poet). Nash's House has 16th-century period rooms and an exhibition illustrating the history of Stratford. The popular Knott Garden adjoins the site and represents the style of a fashionable Elizabethan garden.

Chapel St. © 01789/204016. Admission £3.75 ($7.15) adults, £3 ($5.70) seniors and students, £1.75 ($3.35) children, £10 ($19) family ticket (2 adults, 3 children). Nov–Mar daily 11am–4pm; Apr–May daily 11am–5pm; June–Aug Mon–Sat 9:30am–5pm, Sun 10am–5pm; Sept–Oct daily 11am–5pm. Closed Dec 23–26. Walk west down High St.; Chapel St. is a continuation of High St.

Shakespeare's Birthplace

The son of a glover and whittawer (leather worker), the Bard was born on St. George's Day, April 23, 1564, and died on the same date 52 (copies of the original documents are on display). The church is one of the most beautiful parish churches in England.

Shakespeare's tomb lies in the chancel, a privilege bestowed upon him when he became a lay rector in 1605. Alongside his grave are those of his widow, Anne, and other members of his family. You can also see the graves of Susanna, his daughter, and those of Thomas Nash and Dr. John Hall. Nearby on the north wall is a bust of Shakespeare that was erected approximately 7 years after his death—within the lifetime of his widow and many of his friends.

Old Town St. ℂ 01789/266316. Church, free admission; Shakespeare's tomb, admission £1.50 ($2.85) adults, 50p (95¢) students. Apr–Sept Mon–Sat 8:30am–6pm, Sun 12:30–5pm; Mar and Oct Mon–Sat 9am–5pm, Sun 12:30–5pm; Nov–Feb Mon–Sat 9am–4pm, Sun 12:30–5pm. Walk 4 min. past the Royal Shakespeare Theatre with the river on your left.

Mary Arden's House (Glebe Farm)/Palmer's Farm ✿ So what if millions of visitors have been tricked into thinking this timber-framed farmhouse with its old stone dovecote and various outbuildings was the girlhood home of Shakespeare's mother, Mary Arden? It's still one of the most intriguing sights outside Stratford, even if local historian, Dr. Nat Alcock, discovered in 2000 that the actual childhood home of Arden was the dull-looking brick-built farmhouse, Glebe Farm, next door. Glebe's Farm has now been properly renamed Mary Arden's House. It was all the trick of an 18th-century tour guide, John Jordan, who decided Glebe Farm was too unimpressive to be the home of the Bard's mother, and told tourists it was this farmstead instead. What was known for years as "Mary Arden's House" has been renamed Palmer's Farm. Actually, this farm wasn't constructed until the late 16th century, a little late to be Mary Arden's actual home. After the name confusion, local authorities have converted Palmer's Farm into a working farm. Visitors can tour the property seeing first hand how a farming household functioned in the 1570s—yes, cows to be milked, bread to be baked, and vegetables cultivated in an authentic 16th-century manner. In the barns, stable, cowshed, and farmyard is an extensive collection of farming implements illustrating life and work in the local countryside from Shakespeare's time to the present.

Wilmcote. ℂ 01789/204016. Admission £6 ($11) adults, £5 ($9.50) students and seniors, £2.50 ($4.75) children, £15 ($29) family ticket, children under 5 free. Nov–Mar daily 10am–4pm; Apr–May daily 10am–5pm; June–Aug daily 9:30am–5pm; Sept–Oct daily 10am–5pm. Closed Dec 23–26. Take A3400 (Birmingham) for 5.5km (3½ miles).

New Place/Nash's House Shakespeare retired to New Place in 1610 (a prosperous man by the standards of his day) and died here 6 years later. Regrettably, the house was torn down, so only the garden remains. A mulberry tree planted by the Bard was so popular with latter-day visitors to Stratford that the garden's owner chopped it down. The mulberry tree that grows here today is said to have been planted from a cutting of the original. You enter the gardens through Nash's House (Thomas Nash married Elizabeth Hall, a granddaughter of the poet). Nash's House has 16th-century period rooms and an exhibition illustrating the history of Stratford. The popular Knott Garden adjoins the site and represents the style of a fashionable Elizabethan garden.

Chapel St. ℂ 01789/204016. Admission £3.75 ($7.15) adults, £3 ($5.70) seniors and students, £1.75 ($3.35) children, £10 ($19) family ticket (2 adults, 3 children). Nov–Mar daily 11am–4pm; Apr–May daily 11am–5pm; June–Aug Mon–Sat 9:30am–5pm, Sun 10am–5pm; Sept–Oct daily 11am–5pm. Closed Dec 23–26. Walk west down High St.; Chapel St. is a continuation of High St.

Shakespeare's Birthplace ✿ The son of a glover and whittawer (leather worker), the Bard was born on St. George's Day, April 23, 1564, and died on the same date 52 years later. Filled with Shakespeare memorabilia, including a portrait and furnishings

of the writer's time, the Trust property is a half-timbered structure, dating from the early 16th century. The house was bought by public donors in 1847 and preserved as a national shrine. You can visit the living room, the bedroom where Shakespeare was probably born, a fully equipped kitchen of the period (look for the "babyminder"), and a Shakespeare Museum, illustrating his life and times. Later, you can walk through the garden. You won't be alone: It's estimated that some 660,000 visitors pass through the house annually.

Built next door to commemorate the 400th anniversary of the Bard's birth, the modern **Shakespeare Centre** serves both as the administrative headquarters of the Birthplace Trust and as a library and study center. An extension houses a visitor center, which acts as a reception area for those coming to the birthplace.

Henley St. (in the town center near the post office, close to Union St.). (℃) **01789/204016.** Admission £7 ($13) adults, £6 ($11) students and seniors, £2.75 ($5.25) children; £17 ($32) family ticket (2 adults, 3 children). Nov–Mar Mon–Sat 10am–4pm, Sun 10:30am–4pm; Apr–May daily 10am–5pm; June–Aug Mon–Sat 9am–5pm, Sun 9:30am–5pm; Sept–Oct daily 10am–5pm. Closed Dec 23–26.

The Stratford Brass Rubbing Centre This is a brass-rubbing center, where medieval and Tudor brasses illustrate the knights and ladies, scholars, merchants, and priests of a bygone era. The Stratford collection includes a large assortment of exact replicas of brasses. Entrance is free, but visitors are charged depending on which brass they choose to rub. According to size, the cost ranges from £1 ($1.90) to make a rubbing of a small brass, to a maximum of £15 ($29) for a rubbing of the largest.

The Royal Shakespeare Theatre Summer House, Avon Bank Gardens. (℃) **01789/297671.** www.stratfordbrassrubbing. co.uk Free admission. Mar–Oct daily 10am–6pm; Nov–Feb daily 11am–4pm.

GOING TO THE PLAYS

On the banks of the Avon, the **Royal Shakespeare Theatre,** Waterside, Stratford-upon-Avon CV37 6BB (℃ **01789/403444;** www.rsc.org.uk), is a major showcase for the Royal Shakespeare Company and seats 1,500 patrons. The theater's season runs from November to September and typically features five Shakespearean plays. The company has some of the finest actors on the British stage. *Warning:* The theater is currently undergoing restoration—its Art Deco exterior will remain but a new thrust stage is being built inside. Due to construction delays, the theater is not set to reopen until 2010. During the work, the company will perform at a new theater, **The Courtyard,** being constructed as an extension to The Other Place studio theater near the RST.

You usually need **ticket reservations,** with two successive booking periods, each one opening about 2 months in advance. You can pick these up from a North American or English travel agent. A small number of tickets are always held for sale on the day of a performance, but it may be too late to get a good seat if you wait until you arrive in Stratford. Tickets can be booked through **Keith Prowse** (℃ **800/223-6108** in North America or 0870/840-1111 in England; www.keithprowse.com).

You can also call the **theater box office** directly (℃ **0870/609-1110**) and charge your tickets. The box office is open Monday to Saturday 9am to 8pm, although it closes at 6pm on days when there are no performances. Seat prices range from £5 to £45 ($9.50–$86). You can make a credit card reservation and pick up your tickets on the performance day, but you must cancel at least 1 full week in advance to get a refund.

The **Swan Theatre,** which opened in 1986, is architecturally connected to the back of the RST and shares the same box office, address, and phone number. It seats 425 on three sides of the stage, as in an Elizabethan playhouse. The Swan presents a repertoire of about five plays each season, with tickets ranging from £5 to £30 ($9.50–$57). The Swan is a smaller and more intimate space than the RST and stages plays by other distinguished playwrights, not just the Bard. Its plays, however, are just as professional as those staged at the bigger theater—in fact, many of England's most talented actors appear on the boards at the Swan.

Within the Swan Theatre is a **painting gallery,** which has a basic collection of portraits of famous actors and scenes from Shakespeare's plays by 18th- and 19th-century artists. It also operates as a base for **guided tours,** with lively running commentary through the world-famous theaters. Guided tours are conducted Monday to Saturday at 1:30 and 5:30pm, and four times every Sunday afternoon, production schedules permitting. On Saturday there is always a tour at 11:30am, but on matinee days tours begin at 11:30am—not 1:30pm. Tours cost £5 ($9.50) for adults and £4 ($7.60) for students, seniors, or children. Call ahead for tour scheduling, which is subject to change.

WHERE TO STAY

During the theater season, it's best to reserve in advance. The Tourist Information Centre (part of the national "Book-a-Bed-Ahead" service, which enables visitors to make reservations in advance) will help find accommodations in all ranges. The fee for any room reservations the service makes is 10% of the first night's stay (bed-and-breakfast rate only), deductible from the visitor's final bill.

VERY EXPENSIVE

Welcombe Hotel Spa & Golf Club 𝒦𝒦𝒦   For a formal, historic hotel in Stratford, there's nothing better than the Welcombe. One of England's great Jacobean country houses, this hotel is a 10-minute ride from the heart of Stratford-upon-Avon. Its key feature is an 18-hole golf course. It's surrounded by 63 hectares (156 acres) of grounds and has a formal entrance on Warwick Road, a winding driveway leading to the main hall. Bedrooms are luxuriously furnished in traditional Jacobean style, with fine antiques and elegant fabrics. Most bedrooms are seemingly big enough for tennis matches, but those in the garden wing, although comfortable, are small. Some of the bedrooms are sumptuously furnished with elegant four-posters, and all of them have deluxe linens and well-kept bathrooms with tub/shower combinations.

Warwick Rd., Stratford-upon-Avon, Warwickshire CV37 0NR. ℭ **01789/295252.** Fax 01789/414666. www.welcombe.co.uk. 78 units. £195–£245 ($371–$466) double; £245–£470 ($466–$893) suite. Rates include English breakfast. AE, DC, MC, V. Take A439 2km (1¼ miles) northeast of the town center. **Amenities:** 2 restaurants; bar; golf course; business center; indoor pool; spa; gym; aerobics studio; tennis court; room service; laundry service; dry cleaning; rooms for those w/limited mobility. *In room:* TV, hair dryer, iron.

EXPENSIVE

Alveston Manor Hotel 𝒦𝒦   This Tudor manor is perfect for theatergoers—it's just a 5-minute walk from the theaters. The hotel has a wealth of chimneys and gables, and everything from an Elizabethan gazebo to Queen Anne windows. Mentioned in the *Domesday Book,* the building predates the arrival of William the Conqueror. The rooms in the manor will appeal to those who appreciate the old-world charm of slanted floors, overhead beams, and antique furnishings. Some triples or quads are available in the modern section, connected by a covered walk through the rear garden. Most rooms here are original and have built-in walnut furniture and a color-coordinated decor; 15 are set aside for nonsmokers. All come equipped with well-maintained bathrooms with tub/shower combinations. Your opinion of this hotel will depend on your room assignment. You can live in luxury in the original rooms or be assigned a rather routine standard twin that, though comfortable, lacks romance. Ask for an original.

Clopton Bridge (off B4066), Stratford-upon-Avon, Warwickshire CV37 7HP. © 800/225-5843 in the U.S. and Canada, or 0870/400-8181. Fax 01789/414095. www.macdonaldhotels.co.uk. 114 units. £140–£210 ($266–$399) double; £220–£250 ($418–$475) suite. Rates include breakfast. AE, DC, MC, V. **Amenities:** Restaurant; bar; indoor pool; gym; sauna; spa; sauna; room service; babysitting; laundry service; dry cleaning. *In room:* TV, coffeemaker, hair dryer, iron.

Shakespeare Hotel ✩✩ Filled with historical associations, the original core of this hotel, dating from the 1400s, has seen many additions in its long life. Quieter and more plush than the Falcon (see below), it is equaled in the central core of Stratford only by Alveston Manor. Residents relax in the post-and-timber-studded public rooms, within sight of fireplaces and playbills from 19th-century productions of Shakespeare's plays. Bedrooms are named in honor of noteworthy actors, Shakespeare's plays, or Shakespearean characters. The oldest are capped with hewn timbers, and all have modern comforts. Even the newer accommodations are at least 40 to 50 years old and have rose-and-thistle patterns carved into many of their exposed timbers. Bathrooms range in size, but each is adequate and well appointed with a tub and shower. Since this is a sister hotel of Alveston Manor, guests can use its spa and leisure facilities (see above).

Chapel St., Stratford-upon-Avon, Warwickshire CV37 6ER. © 888/892-0038 in the U.S. or 0870/400-8182. Fax 01789/415411. www.macdonaldhotels.co.uk. 74 units. £137–£167 ($260–$317) double; from £177 ($336) suite. Rates include buffet breakfast. Children up to 13 stay free in parent's room. AE, DC, MC, V. **Amenities:** 2 restaurants; bar; room service; laundry service; dry cleaning; nonsmoking rooms; rooms for those w/limited mobility. *In room:* A/C, TV, coffeemaker, minibar (in some), hair dryer, iron.

MODERATE

Falcon This inn blends the very old and the very new. The black-and-white timbered inn was licensed a quarter of a century after Shakespeare's death; connected to its rear by a glass passageway is a more sterile bedroom extension added in 1970. In the heart of Stratford, the inn faces the Guild Chapel and the New Place Gardens. The recently upgraded rooms in the older section have oak beams, diamond leaded-glass windows, antiques, and good reproductions. Bathrooms aren't special; some have brown linoleum floors and plastic tub/shower enclosures.

In the inn's intimate Merlin Lounge, you'll find an open copper-hooded fireplace where fires are stoked under beams salvaged from old ships. The Oak Bar is a forest of weathered beams, and on either side of the stone fireplace is paneling removed from the Bard's last home, New Place.

Chapel St., Stratford-upon-Avon, Warwickshire CV37 6HA. © 0870/832-9905. Fax 0870/832-9906. www.legacy-hotels.co.uk. 84 units. £67–£134 ($127–$255) double; from £164 ($312) suite. AE, DC, MC, V. **Amenities:** 2 restaurants; 2 bars; room service; rooms for those w/limited mobility. *In room:* TV, coffeemaker, hair dryer, trouser press.

Grosvenor Hotel A pair of Georgian town houses, built in 1832 and 1843, join together to form this hotel, which is one of the second-tier choices in Stratford, on equal footing with the Thistle Stratford-upon-Avon (below). In the center of town, with lawns and gardens to the rear, it is a short stroll from the intersection of Bridge Street and Waterside, allowing easy access to the Avon River, Bancroft Gardens, and the Royal Shakespeare Theatre. There is a rambling ground floor that has tremendous character—it reminds us of an elegant English country house, with small intimate lounges and open fires. The Garden Restaurant, with its hand-painted mural, serves a

Continental and British menu. Bedrooms are midsize to spacious, each personally designed with a high standard of tasteful modern furnishings. Rooms are not overly adorned or stylish, but they're snug and cozy. All bedrooms have small bathrooms with well-maintained showers.

12–14 Warwick Rd., Stratford-upon-Avon, Warwickshire CV37 6YT. © **01789/269213.** Fax 01789/266087. www. bwgh.co.uk. 73 units. £100–£175 ($190–$333) double; £165 ($314) suite. AE, MC, V. **Amenities:** Restaurant; bar; free pass to nearby recreation center; room service; babysitting; laundry service; nonsmoking rooms; rooms for those w/limited mobility. *In room:* TV, coffeemaker, hair dryer, iron, safe (in some), trouser press.

Thistle Stratford-upon-Avon ✹
Theatergoers flock to this Georgian-town-house-style hotel, located across the street from the entrance to the Royal Shakespeare and Swan theaters. The hotel's redbrick main section dates from the Regency period, although over the years a handful of adjacent buildings were included in the hotel and an uninspired modern extension was added. Today, the interior has a well-upholstered lounge and bar, a covered garden terrace, and comfortable but narrow bedrooms. Though small, rooms have a sitting area with a couple of armchairs and round side tables, plus twin beds (for the most part). Sometimes a room is graced with a four-poster bed. The bathrooms are small but efficient, with a tub/shower combination.

44 Waterside, Stratford-upon-Avon, Warwickshire CV37 6BA. © **0870/333-9146.** Fax 0870/333-9246. www.stratford thistle.co.uk. 63 units. £70–£225 ($133–$428) double. AE, DC, MC, V. **Amenities:** Restaurant; bar; room service; laundry service; dry cleaning. *In room:* TV, coffeemaker, hair dryer, trouser press.

White Swan
This cozy, intimate hotel, housed in Stratford's oldest building, is one of the most atmospheric in Stratford. In business for more than a century before Shakespeare appeared on the scene, it competes successfully with the Falcon (above) in offering an ancient atmosphere. The gabled medieval front would present the Bard with no surprises, but the modern comforts inside would surely astonish him. Many of the rooms have been well preserved despite the addition of modern conveniences. Paintings dating from 1550 hang on the lounge walls. All bedrooms are well appointed; bathrooms are small but have tub/shower combinations.

Rother St., Stratford-upon-Avon, Warwickshire CV37 6NH. © **01789/297022.** Fax 01789/268773. 41 units. £80 ($152) double. Rates include English breakfast. AE, DC, MC, V. **Amenities:** Restaurant; bar; room service. *In room:* TV, coffeemaker, hair dryer, trouser press.

INEXPENSIVE

Moonraker Guest House ✹ *Finds*
Privately owned and personally managed by Ruth and Morris Masaaki, this is a delightful choice and a discovery, lying midway between Anne Hathaway's House Cottage and Shakespeare's birthplace. Each non-smoking bedroom is comfortably and attractively furnished, six with showers and the others with combination tub/shower. A luxury suite is available with a bedroom, lounge, and kitchenette, as are two more suites, each with two rooms. Among the amenities are four-poster beds, a nonsmoking lounge area, and garden patios. A hearty English breakfast is followed by toast and homemade marmalade and jams, all served and prepared by the Leonards.

40 Alcester Rd., Stratford-upon-Avon, Warwickshire CV37 9DB. ©/fax **01789/268774.** www.moonrakerhouse.com. 7 units. £70–£85 ($133–$162) double. Rates include English breakfast. MC, V. 2 min. by car from the heart of town on A422. **Amenities:** Breakfast room; nonsmoking lounge; garden patio; all nonsmoking rooms; rooms for those w/limited mobility. *In room:* TV, coffeemaker, hair dryer.

Salamander Guest House   This 1906 Edwardian house is a 5-minute walk from the town center just off B439 (Evesham Rd.). One of the better guesthouses in the area, the homey Salamander fronts a woodsy park. The owners rent comfortable, attractive rooms, including one for families. Each unit comes with a shower.

40 Grove Rd., Stratford-upon-Avon, Warwickshire CV37. £36–£60 ($68–$114) double. Rates include English breakfast. MC, V. Bus: X16. **Amenities:** Breakfast room; babysitting; all nonsmoking rooms. *In room:* TV, coffeemaker, hair dryer (on request), no phone.

Sequoia House Hotel *Value*   This privately run hotel stands in its own beautiful garden across the Avon opposite the Royal Shakespeare Theatre, conveniently located for visiting the major Shakespeare sites. Renovations in 2007 have vastly improved the house, which was created from two late-Victorian buildings. Bedrooms retain some Victorian features and come in various shapes and sizes. They have fine beds and are warmly decorated and color-coordinated. Bathrooms are small, seven with a tub/shower combination, the others with a stall shower only.

51–53 Shipston Rd., Stratford-upon-Avon, Warwickshire CV37 7LN. © **01789/268852.** Fax 01789/414559. www.sequoiahotel.co.uk. 23 units. £75–£100 ($143–$190) double. Rates include English breakfast. AE, DC, MC, V. **Amenities:** Bar; nonsmoking rooms. *In room:* TV, coffeemaker, hair dryer.

Victoria Spa Lodge   This B&B is old fashioned and atmospheric. Opened in 1837, the year Queen Victoria ascended the throne, this was the first establishment to be given her name, and it is still going strong. This lodge was originally a spa frequented by the queen's eldest daughter, Princess Vicky. The accommodating hosts offer tastefully decorated, comfortable bedrooms. The small bathrooms are neatly organized with a shower stall. No smoking.

Bishopton Lane (2.5km/1½ miles north of the town center where A3400 intersects A46), Stratford-upon-Avon, Warwickshire CV37 9QY. © **01789/267985.** Fax 01789/204728. www.victoriaspa.co.uk. 7 units. £70 ($133) double. Rates include English breakfast. MC, V. **Amenities:** Breakfast room. *In room:* TV, coffeemaker, hair dryer.

WHERE TO DINE

After visiting the birthplace of Shakespeare, pop across the street for tea at **Brasserie,** Henley Street (© **01789/262189**). This airy tearoom is tremendously popular, but the very attentive staff more than compensates for the throngs of patrons. Choose from an array of tea blends, cream teas, and various cakes, pastries, and tea cakes—all freshly baked in their own kitchen.

EXPENSIVE TO MODERATE

Lambs *☞* CONTINENTAL/ENGLISH   A stone's throw from the Royal Shakespeare Theatre, this cafe-bistro is housed in a building dating back to 1547 (and with connections to Lewis Carroll). For a quick light meal or pre-theater dinner, it's ideal. The menu changes monthly. Begin with such starters as smoked salmon with a potato cake and a chive crème fraîche. Our party enjoyed the roast breast of Gressingham duck with croquette potatoes and Savoy cabbage in a cassis sauce, finishing off with Italian chocolate cake with white chocolate ice cream. Look to the blackboard for daily specials. The chef takes chances (no doubt inspired by trips to the Continent), and it's a nice departure from the bland tearoom food served for decades in Stratford.

12 Sheep St. © **01789/292554.** www.lambsrestaurant.co.uk. Reservations required Fri and Sat night. Main courses £11–£19 ($21–$36); fixed-price menu £15 ($29) for 2 courses, £20 ($38) for 3. DC, MC, V. Daily noon–2pm; Mon–Sat 5–10pm; Sun 6–9:30pm.

Marlowe's Restaurant ENGLISH   Many famous actors appearing in Shakespeare plays have made their way here for dinner, including Paul Schofield, Vanessa Redgrave, Sir Ralph Richardson, and Sir John Gielgud. You can dine formally in the Elizabethan Room or more casually in The Bistro. In winter, a large bar has a fireplace blazing with logs, and it opens into a splendid oak-paneled room. In summer there is a spacious courtyard for al fresco dining. Starters are a harmonious blend of flavors, including terrine of guinea fowl and oyster mushrooms with sherry and a red onion marmalade. Among the fish dishes, grilled sea bass emerges from the kitchen with roasted fennel and a tomato fondue, or else you can opt for one of the charcoal-grilled dishes such as a filet steak with pan-fried mushrooms and grilled tomatoes. Drunken duck has been a longtime specialty here. It's marinated in gin, red wine, and juniper berries before it's roasted in the oven. Old-fashioned English desserts such as a treacle sponge with custard is served, though you can also opt for the apple-and-cinnamon pudding with crème fraîche.

18 High St. © 01789/204999. Reservations recommended. Main courses £7.95–£12 ($15–$22). AE, MC, V. Elizabethan Room daily Mon–Sat 5:30–10:30pm, Sun 7–9pm; The Bistro daily noon–2:15pm and 5:30–11pm.

The One Elm BRITISH   As you're rushing around to all the Shakespeare properties, this is a convenient stopover because of its long hours of food service. Guess can enjoy its pub, its separate ground-floor restaurant, or its courtyard dining and drinking. The cooks pride themselves on serving dishes concoted from local or organic produce from regional suppliers.

A special feature is the Elm's "Deli Board," featuring all sorts of antipasti and charcuterie, such as a hot chorizo and butter bean salad. Starters range from a truly excellent double baked cheese soufflé, with a pear and walnut salad, to the soup of the day with fresh baked crusty bread. Several selections are prepared on the charcoal grill, and other enticing main dishes include smoked haddock and salmon fish cakes with creamed leeks or else chicken breast with Brie and garlic. The restaurant also serves a special menu, including sandwiches, from noon to 6:30pm Monday to Saturday. "Puds" feature an apple-and-date turnover custard or sticky toffee pudding with a caramel sauce.

1 Guild St. © 01789/404919. Reservations not needed. Main courses £11–£13 ($21–$25). MC, V. Mon–Sat 11am–10pm, Sun noon–3pm and 6:30–9:30pm.

The Quarto's Restaurant ✿ FRENCH/ITALIAN/TRADITIONAL ENGLISH This restaurant enjoys the best location in town—it's in the Royal Shakespeare Theatre itself—with glass walls providing an unobstructed view of the swans on the Avon. You can partake of an intermission snack of smoked salmon and champagne or dine by flickering candlelight after the performance. Many dishes are definitely old English, but others reflect a Continental touch. You can revel in such appetizers as Stilton cheese with a cucumber and red pepper salad, enhanced with a walnut dressing, or sample the ham terrine with parsley dressing and an apple and onion marmalade. The chef has learned his craft well, as reflected by such main dishes as seared tuna with fresh thyme and baby spinach with a mango and lime chutney. You might also try the local corn-fed chicken with smoked bacon and apricots, served with Savoy cabbage and a tarragon cream sauce. There are duck, steak, and vegetarian options on the menu.

In the Royal Shakespeare Theatre, Waterside. © 01789/403415. Reservations recommended. Main courses £11–£17 ($21–$32). AE, MC, V. Thurs and Sat 11:30am–2:30pm; Mon–Sat 5:30pm–11pm. Closed when theater is shut down.

Sorrento ☆ ITALIAN   For a taste of Italy, visit this family-run restaurant, where Jackie and Tony de Angelis welcome you at a location just a 4-minute walk from the Shakespeare Theatre. Guests seated on leather furniture can enjoy a pre-dinner apéritif in the lounge before heading into the stylish yet informal restaurant itself. Everything is cooked to order, using market-fresh ingredients, so you need to allow time for each dish to be prepared. In summer those dishes can be enjoyed al fresco on the patio.

A selection of well-chosen Italian wines complements the meal, which might begin with such starters as the chef's homemade chicken liver pâté or else a roast pepper and artichoke salad dressed with olive oil, basil, and capers. The pastas are among the best in town. You can ask about the pasta of the day or select such classics as penne lightly tossed in broccoli and prawns and cooked in a white wine sauce and served with mascarpone cheese. For a main course, a fish of the day is regularly featured, although meat eaters might opt for the filet steam flambéed in brandy with a sauce laced with green peppercorns. Finish with the chef's ever-changing selection of homemade desserts.

8 Ely St. ℰ **01789/297999.** Reservations recommended. Main courses £13–£17 ($25–$33). Set lunch £8.90 ($17) for 2 courses, £13 ($25) for 3 courses. MC, V. Mon–Sat 5–10:30pm.

Thai Boathouse ☆ THAI   The only restaurant set on the Avon, this charming choice is reached by crossing Clopton Bridge toward Oxford and Banbury. The second-floor dining room opens onto vistas of the river. This restaurant, originally established 4 decades ago in Bangkok, has brought spice and zest to Stratford's lazy restaurant scene. The decor comes from Thailand itself, with elephants, woodcarvings, and Buddhas adorning the restaurant. Seasonal specialties such as wild duck and pheasant are a special feature of the menu. Fresh produce, great skill in the kitchen, and exquisite presentations are the hallmarks of this restaurant. Sample a selection of authentic Thai appetizers before going on to the delectable main courses, which include a stir-fried mixed seafood with fresh chili and sweet Thai basil or else chicken stir fried with sweet peppers, pineapple, and onion in a sweet-and-sour sauce.

Swan's Nest Lane. ℰ **01789/297733.** Reservations recommended. Main courses £6–£12 ($11–$23); fixed-price menus £18–£26 ($34–$49). MC, V. Sun-Fri noon–2:30pm, daily 5:30–10:30pm.

INEXPENSIVE

Hussain's INDIAN   This restaurant has many admirers—it's one of the brighter spots on the bleak culinary landscape hereabouts. The owner has chosen a well-trained and alert staff that welcomes guests and advises them about special dishes. You can select from an array of northern Indian dishes, many from the tandoor, plus various curries with lamb or prawn. Offering a 10% discount on pre- and post-theater dinners, Hussain's is across from the Shakespeare Hotel and historic New Place.

6A Chapel St. ℰ **01789/267506.** Reservations recommended. Main courses £6–£15 ($11–$29). AE, MC, V. Fri–Sun 12:30–2:30pm; daily 5pm–midnight.

The Oppo INTERNATIONAL   Located in the heart of Stratford within a 16th-century building, this refreshingly unpretentious restaurant serves up good bistro cooking at reasonable prices. Menu choices include breast of chicken with banana roasted in lime butter, basmati rice with a mild curry sauce, or salmon fish cakes served on a bed of spinach.

13 Sheep St. ℰ **01789/269980.** Reservations recommended. www.theoppo.co.uk. Main courses £10–£18 ($19–$34). DC, MC, V. Daily noon–2pm; Mon-Sat 5–10pm; Sun 6–9:30pm.

Index

See also Accommodations, Restaurant, and Tearoom indexes, below.

Shop at the new London's Transport Museum store

Unit 26, Covent Garden Market

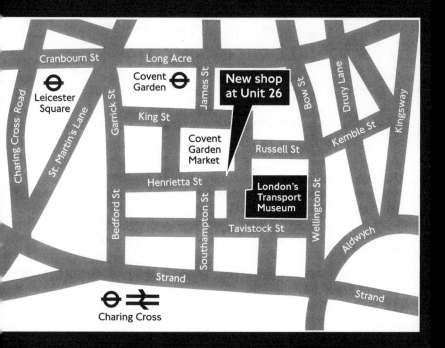

Shop online at **www.ltmuseum.co.uk**

Store open daily: **10.00 - 18.00** (Closed 25 and 26 December)

London's Transport Museum is closed for refurbishment until 2007

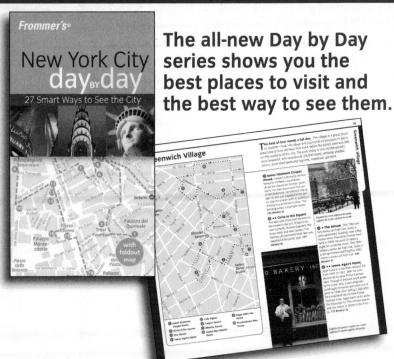

A Guide for Every Type of Traveler

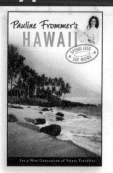

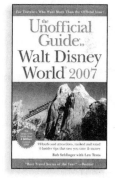
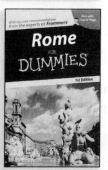

FROMMER'S® COMPLETE TRAVEL GUIDES

Alaska
Amalfi Coast
American Southwest
Amsterdam
Argentina & Chile
Arizona
Atlanta
Australia
Austria
Bahamas
Barcelona
Beijing
Belgium, Holland & Luxembourg
Belize
Bermuda
Boston
Brazil
British Columbia & the Canadian
 Rockies
Brussels & Bruges
Budapest & the Best of Hungary
Buenos Aires
Calgary
California
Canada
Cancún, Cozumel & the Yucatán
Cape Cod, Nantucket & Martha's
 Vineyard
Caribbean
Caribbean Ports of Call
Carolinas & Georgia
Chicago
China
Colorado
Costa Rica
Croatia
Cuba
Denmark
Denver, Boulder & Colorado Springs
Edinburgh & Glasgow
England
Europe
Europe by Rail
Florence, Tuscany & Umbria

Florida
France
Germany
Greece
Greek Islands
Hawaii
Hong Kong
Honolulu, Waikiki & Oahu
India
Ireland
Israel
Italy
Jamaica
Japan
Kauai
Las Vegas
London
Los Angeles
Los Cabos & Baja
Madrid
Maine Coast
Maryland & Delaware
Maui
Mexico
Montana & Wyoming
Montréal & Québec City
Moscow & St. Petersburg
Munich & the Bavarian Alps
Nashville & Memphis
New England
Newfoundland & Labrador
New Mexico
New Orleans
New York City
New York State
New Zealand
Northern Italy
Norway
Nova Scotia, New Brunswick &
 Prince Edward Island
Oregon
Paris
Peru
Philadelphia & the Amish Country

Portugal
Prague & the Best of the Czech
 Republic
Provence & the Riviera
Puerto Rico
Rome
San Antonio & Austin
San Diego
San Francisco
Santa Fe, Taos & Albuquerque
Scandinavia
Scotland
Seattle
Seville, Granada & the Best of
 Andalusia
Shanghai
Sicily
Singapore & Malaysia
South Africa
South America
South Florida
South Pacific
Southeast Asia
Spain
Sweden
Switzerland
Tahiti & French Polynesia
Texas
Thailand
Tokyo
Toronto
Turkey
USA
Utah
Vancouver & Victoria
Vermont, New Hampshire & Maine
Vienna & the Danube Valley
Vietnam
Virgin Islands
Virginia
Walt Disney World® & Orlando
Washington, D.C.
Washington State

FROMMER'S® DAY BY DAY GUIDES

Amsterdam
Chicago
Florence & Tuscany

London
New York City
Paris

Rome
San Francisco
Venice

PAULINE FROMMER'S GUIDES! SEE MORE. SPEND LESS.

Hawaii

Italy

New York City

FROMMER'S® PORTABLE GUIDES

Acapulco, Ixtapa & Zihuatanejo
Amsterdam
Aruba
Australia's Great Barrier Reef
Bahamas
Big Island of Hawaii
Boston
California Wine Country
Cancún
Cayman Islands
Charleston
Chicago
Dominican Republic

Dublin
Florence
Las Vegas
Las Vegas for Non-Gamblers
London
Maui
Nantucket & Martha's Vineyard
New Orleans
New York City
Paris
Portland
Puerto Rico
Puerto Vallarta, Manzanillo &
 Guadalajara

Rio de Janeiro
San Diego
San Francisco
Savannah
St. Martin, Sint Maarten, Anguila &
 St. Bart's
Turks & Caicos
Vancouver
Venice
Virgin Islands
Washington, D.C.
Whistler

FROMMER'S® CRUISE GUIDES

Alaska Cruises & Ports of Call

Cruises & Ports of Call

European Cruises & Ports of Call

FROMMER'S® NATIONAL PARK GUIDES

Algonquin Provincial Park
Banff & Jasper
Grand Canyon

National Parks of the American West
Rocky Mountain
Yellowstone & Grand Teton

Yosemite and Sequoia & Kings
 Canyon
Zion & Bryce Canyon

FROMMER'S® MEMORABLE WALKS

London
New York

Paris
Rome

San Francisco

FROMMER'S® WITH KIDS GUIDES

Chicago
Hawaii
Las Vegas
London

National Parks
New York City
San Francisco

Toronto
Walt Disney World® & Orlando
Washington, D.C.

SUZY GERSHMAN'S BORN TO SHOP GUIDES

France
Hong Kong, Shanghai & Beijing
Italy

London
New York

Paris
San Francisco

FROMMER'S® IRREVERENT GUIDES

Amsterdam
Boston
Chicago
Las Vegas

London
Los Angeles
Manhattan
Paris

Rome
San Francisco
Walt Disney World®
Washington, D.C.

FROMMER'S® BEST-LOVED DRIVING TOURS

Austria
Britain
California
France

Germany
Ireland
Italy
New England

Northern Italy
Scotland
Spain
Tuscany & Umbria

THE UNOFFICIAL GUIDES®

Adventure Travel in Alaska
Beyond Disney
California with Kids
Central Italy
Chicago
Cruises
Disneyland®
England
Florida
Florida with Kids

Hawaii
Ireland
Las Vegas
London
Maui
Mexico's Best Beach Resorts
Mini Mickey
New Orleans
New York City

Paris
San Francisco
South Florida including Miami &
 the Keys
Walt Disney World®
Walt Disney World® for
 Grown-ups
Walt Disney World® with Kids
Washington, D.C.

SPECIAL-INTEREST TITLES

Athens Past & Present
Best Places to Raise Your Family
Cities Ranked & Rated
500 Places to Take Your Kids Before They Grow Up
Frommer's Best Day Trips from London
Frommer's Best RV & Tent Campgrounds
 in the U.S.A.

Frommer's Exploring America by RV
Frommer's NYC Free & Dirt Cheap
Frommer's Road Atlas Europe
Frommer's Road Atlas Ireland
Great Escapes From NYC Without Wheels
Retirement Places Rated

FROMMER'S® PHRASEFINDER DICTIONARY GUIDES

French

Italian

Spanish

CLOSED
due to
accidental demolition

WEGEN BISSIGEN
EICHHÖRNCHEN GESCHLOSSEN

CERRADO

CABRAS

Κλειστό
Μετεωρίτες

プール
も

POOL CLOSED

ELECTRIC EELS

閉
鎖
中

Hotel
closed for
facelifting

FERMÉ POUR
RAISON
DE GRÈVE
DES BONNES

FECHADO!
POR CAUSA DE
ATAQUES DOS CROCODILOS

— I don't speak
sign language.

A hotel can close for all kinds of reasons.
Our Guarantee ensures that if your hotel's undergoing construction, we'll
let you know in advance. In fact, we cover your entire travel experience.
See www.travelocity.com/guarantee for details.

travelocity
You'll never roam alone.

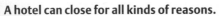

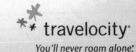